The Joan Palevsky  Imprint in Classical Literature

In honor of beloved Virgil—

"O degli altri poeti onore e lume . . ."

—Dante, *Inferno*

The publisher gratefully acknowledges the generous support
of the Classical Literature Endowment Fund of the University
of California Press Foundation, which was established by
a major gift from Joan Palevsky.

Doctrine and Power

TRANSFORMATION OF THE CLASSICAL HERITAGE
Peter Brown, General Editor

I. *Art and Ceremony in Late Antiquity,* by Sabine G. MacCormack

II. *Synesius of Cyrene: Philosopher-Bishop,* by Jay Alan Bregman

III. *Theodosian Empresses: Women and Imperial Dominion in Late Antiquity,* by Kenneth G. Holum

IV. *John Chrysostom and the Jews: Rhetoric and Reality in the Late Fourth Century,* by Robert L. Wilken

V. *Biography in Late Antiquity: The Quest for the Holy Man,* by Patricia Cox

VI. *Pachomius: The Making of a Community in Fourth-Century Egypt,* by Philip Rousseau

VII. *Change in Byzantine Culture in the Eleventh and Twelfth Centuries,* by A. P. Kazhdan and Ann Wharton Epstein

VIII. *Leadership and Community in Late Antique Gaul,* by Raymond Van Dam

IX. *Homer the Theologian: Neoplatonist Allegorical Reading and the Growth of the Epic Tradition,* by Robert Lamberton

X. *Procopius and the Sixth Century,* by Averil Cameron

XI. *Guardians of Language: The Grammarian and Society in Late Antiquity,* by Robert A. Kaster

XII. *Civic Coins and Civic Politics in the Roman East, A.D. 180–275,* by Kenneth Harl

XIII. *Holy Women of the Syrian Orient,* introduced and translated by Sebastian P. Brock and Susan Ashbrook Harvey

XIV. *Gregory the Great: Perfection in Imperfection,* by Carole Straw

XV. *"Apex Omnium": Religion in the "Res gestae" of Ammianus,* by R. L. Rike

XVI. *Dioscorus of Aphrodito: His Work and His World,* by Leslie S. B. MacCoull

XVII. *On Roman Time: The Codex-Calendar of 354 and the Rhythms of Urban Life in Late Antiquity,* by Michele Renee Salzman

XVIII. *Asceticism and Society in Crisis: John of Ephesus and "The Lives of the Eastern Saints,"* by Susan Ashbrook Harvey

XIX. *Barbarians and Politics at the Court of Arcadius,* by Alan Cameron and Jacqueline Long, with a contribution by Lee Sherry

XX. *Basil of Caesarea,* by Philip Rousseau

XXI. *In Praise of Later Roman Emperors: The Panegyrici Latini,* introduction, translation, and historical commentary by C. E. V. Nixon and Barbara Saylor Rodgers

XXII. *Ambrose of Milan: Church and Court in a Christian Capital,* by Neil B. McLynn

XXIII. *Public Disputation, Power, and Social Order in Late Antiquity,* by Richard Lim

XXIV. *The Making of a Heretic: Gender, Authority, and the Priscillianist Controversy,* by Virginia Burrus

XXV. *Symeon the Holy Fool: Leontius's "Life" and the Late Antique City,* by Derek Krueger

XXVI. *The Shadows of Poetry: Vergil in the Mind of Augustine*, by Sabine MacCormack
XXVII. *Paulinus of Nola: Life, Letters, and Poems*, by Dennis E. Trout
XXVIII. *The Barbarian Plain: Saint Sergius between Rome and Iran*, by Elizabeth Key Fowden
XXIX. *The Private Orations of Themistius*, translated, annotated, and introduced by Robert J. Penella
XXX. *The Memory of the Eyes: Pilgrims to Living Saints in Christian Late Antiquity*, by Georgia Frank
XXXI. *Greek Biography and Panegyric in Late Antiquity*, edited by Tomas Hägg and Philip Rousseau
XXXII. *Subtle Bodies: Representing Angels in Byzantium*, by Glenn Peers
XXXIII. *Wandering, Begging Monks: Spiritual Authority and the Promotion of Monasticism in Late Antiquity*, by Daniel Caner
XXXIV. *Failure of Empire: Valens and the Roman State in the Fourth Century A.D.*, by Noel Lenski
XXXV. *Merovingian Mortuary Archaeology and the Making of the Early Middle Ages*, by Bonnie Effros
XXXVI. *Quṣayr 'Amra: Art and the Umayyad Elite in Late Antique Syria*, by Garth Fowden
XXXVII. *Holy Bishops in Late Antiquity: The Nature of Christian Leadership in an Age of Transition*, by Claudia Rapp
XXXVIII. *Encountering the Sacred: The Debate on Christian Pilgrimage in Late Antiquity*, by Brouria Bitton-Ashkelony
XXXIX. *There Is No Crime for Those Who Have Christ: Religious Violence in the Christian Roman Empire*, by Michael Gaddis
XL. *The Legend of Mar Qardagh: Narrative and Christian Heroism in Late Antique Iraq*, by Joel Thomas Walker
XLI. *City and School in Late Antique Athens and Alexandria*, by Edward J. Watts
XLII. *Scenting Salvation: Ancient Christianity and the Olfactory Imagination*, by Susan Ashbrook Harvey
XLIII. *Man and the Word: The Orations of Himerius*, edited by Robert J. Penella
XLIV. *The Matter of the Gods*, by Clifford Ando
XLV. *The Two Eyes of the Earth: Art and Ritual of Kingship between Rome and Sasanian Iran*, by Matthew P. Canepa
XLVI. *Riot in Alexandria: Tradition and Group Dynamics in Late Antique Pagan and Christian Communities*, by Edward J. Watts
XLVII. *Peasant and Empire in Christian North Africa*, by Leslie Dossey
XLVIII. *Theodoret's People: Social Networks and Religious Conflict in Late Roman Syria*, by Adam M. Schor
XLIX. *Sons of Hellenism, Fathers of the Church: Emperor Julian, Gregory of Nazianzus, and the Vision of Rome*, by Susanna Elm

XLX. *Shenoute of Atripe and the Uses Of Poverty: Rural Patronage, Religious Conflict and Monasticism in Late Antique Egypt,* by Ariel G. López

LI. *Doctrine and Power: Theological Controversy and Christian Leadership in the Later Roman Empire,* by Carlos R. Galvão-Sobrinho

LII. *Crisis of Empire: Doctrine and Dissent at the End of Late Antiquity,* by Philip Booth

Doctrine and Power

Theological Controversy and Christian Leadership in the Later Roman Empire

Carlos R. Galvão-Sobrinho

UNIVERSITY OF CALIFORNIA PRESS

University of California Press, one of the most distinguished university presses in the United States, enriches lives around the world by advancing scholarship in the humanities, social sciences, and natural sciences. Its activities are supported by the UC Press Foundation and by philanthropic contributions from individuals and institutions. For more information, visit www.ucpress.edu.

University of California Press
Oakland, California

© 2013 by The Regents of the University of California

First Paperback Printing 2021

Library of Congress Cataloging-in-Publication Data

Galvão-Sobrinho, Carlos R. (Carlos Roberto)
  Doctrine and power : theological controversy and Christian leadership in the later roman empire / Carlos R. Galvao-Sobrinho.
    p. cm. — (Transformation of the classical heritage ; 51)
  Includes bibliographical references and index.
  ISBN 978-0-520-25739-9 (cloth, alk. paper); 978-0-520-38316-6 (pbk. : alk. paper); 978-0-520-95466-3 (ebook)
  1. Church history—Primitive and early church, ca. 30–600. 2. Th eology,

Doctrinal—History—Early church, ca. 30–600. 3. Christian leadership—History—Early church, ca. 30–600. 4. Arianism. I. Title.
  BR205.G35 2013
  270.2—dc23   2012038608

CONTENTS

Acknowledgments ix

Introduction 1

PART ONE. POINTS OF DEPARTURE: THEOLOGY AND CHRISTIAN LEADERSHIP IN THE THIRD-CENTURY CHURCH 11

1. Christian Leadership and the Challenge of Theology 15
2. "Not in the Spirit of Controversy": Truth, Leadership, and Solidarity 23

PART TWO. GOD IN DISPUTE: DEVOTION AND TRUTH, A.D. 318–325 31

3. Precision, Devotion, and Controversy in Alexandria 35
4. Making the People a Partner to the Dispute 47
5. "For the Sake of the Logos": Spreading the Controversy 66
6. "To Please the Overseer of All": The Emperor's Involvement and the Politicization of Theology 78

PART THREE. DEFINING GOD: TRUTH AND POWER, A.D. 325–361 95

7. Claiming Truth, Projecting Power, A.D. 325–337 99
8. The Challenge of Theology and Power in Action: Bishops, Cities, and Empire, A.D. 337–361 125

Conclusion 153

Appendix 161
  Bishops Investigated or Deposed for Doctrinal Reasons before the
    Arian Controversy 161
  Compromise and Solidarity in Doctrinal Controversy in the Early Church 163
  The Workshops of Alexandria 163
  Kolluthus's Schism and the Arians 164
  The Recall of Arius and the Bithynian Bishops 165
  The Arian Community of Alexandria after Nicaea 171
  Athanasius and Arsenius of Hypsele 172
  Events Involving Athanasius from Spring 330 to Winter 332 173
  From Athanasius's Flight to the Councils of Rome and Antioch, 339–341 174

List of Abbreviations 183
Notes 187
Bibliography 273
Index 289

ACKNOWLEDGMENTS

This book goes back to a doctoral dissertation completed in the late 1990s. It took me more than ten years to transform it into a book, and at several points along the way I thought of giving it up. That I did not is due in no small measure to the encouragement and help I received from mentors, friends, colleagues, and family members, beginning with Ramsay MacMullen, my dissertation adviser, whose erudition and scholarship have been a constant source of inspiration and intellectual stimulation. I am deeply thankful for his support, advice, friendship, and boundless patience. I also owe a huge debt of gratitude to Peter Brown, who commented on more than one version of the manuscript. His belief in the value of this project is one of the reasons this book is being published. I will never be able to thank him enough for his generosity and encouragement.

Much gratitude goes to John Matthews, who commented generously on my dissertation, and to Debra Hamel, Susan Mattern, Zlatko Plese, Vasily Rudich, and Antigone Samellas, who have in one way or another helped me get through graduate school. In Brazil, Maria Beatriz Florenzano, Francisco Marshall, and Francisco Murari Pires cheered me and kept me sane with their friendship and camaraderie. I thank them as well as the history faculty at the University of Campinas, particularly my friends in the Centro de Pesquisa em História Social da Cultura, for their support.

I am also grateful to my current and former colleagues at the University of Wisconsin-Milwaukee for their moral support and sage advice, especially Ellen Amster, Margo Anderson, Martha Carlin, Bruce Fetter, Anne Hanson, Aims McGuinness, Jeff Merrick, Amanda Seligman, Phil Shashko, Dan Sherman, and Merry Wiesner-Hanks. Jeff Merrick was a trusted mentor and a guiding light in trying times. A special thank-you to Yuri Kitov, who helped me locate the manuscript containing the image on the book cover, and to Christine Evans, for translating the image caption from Russian into English.

In Rome, I benefited from many enlightening conversations with Kim Bowes, Patrick Geary, Jacob Latham, Michael Maas, Júlio César Magalhães de Oliveira, and Michele Salzman. Júlio César Magalhães de Oliveira and Kim Bowes read portions of an earlier version of the manuscript. Their sharp comments and insightful criticism helped me revise and sharpen my argument.

I would also like to express my gratitude for the generosity of the institutions that provided me with financial support at different stages of this project. A scholarship from CAPES, Brazil, funded my graduate education. A Yale University dissertation fellowship gave generous support during the writing of the dissertation. I wrote the three first chapters of the book as a fellow at the Center for 21st Century Studies at the University of Wisconsin-Milwaukee in 2002–2003. The Institute for Research in the Humanities at the University of Wisconsin, Madison, and the American Academy in Rome honored me with fellowships in the fall of 2004 and in 2005–2006, respectively. Even though I was then working on a different project, I would be amiss not to acknowledge my debt to these institutions.

Likewise, I thank the library staff at Yale University, especially Carla Lucas at the Yale Classics Library; the Instituto de Filosofia e Ciências Humanas at the University of Campinas; the Mosteiro de São Bento (Vinhedo, Brazil); the American Academy in Rome; the Institutum Patristicum Augustinianum; and the University of Wisconsin-Milwaukee, especially the Interlibrary Loan Department, for their patience and efficiency.

The readers and editors at the University of California Press deserve special recognition for their outstanding work and warm encouragement. Hal Drake and an anonymous reader issued exceedingly detailed reports on earlier versions of the manuscript, raising provocative questions and making many invaluable suggestions. I thank Laura Cerruti and Rachel Lockman for their willingness to consider a partly revised manuscript. Mary Frances helped me rethink the structure of the book. I thank Stephanie Fay, Cindy Fulton, and above all, Marian Rogers, whose eye for detail is something of a marvel. Marian struggled with my "Portugueseisms" and the quirks of my nonnative English prose, patiently correcting mistakes and painstakingly copyediting the final manuscript; the book benefited immensely from her thoughtful suggestions. Eric Schmidt oversaw the final and crucial stages of publication; I thank him for his encouragement, patience, and advice. Errors and omissions that remain are due solely to my stubbornness.

Finally, I owe more than I can ever express in words to my family, whose love and support sustained me throughout and gave meaning to everything. I dedicate this book to them: my parents, João and Neide; my daughters, Carolina and Rachel; and Loren, my wife and partner in adventure.

Introduction

This study began as an attempt to understand a baffling chapter in the religious history of the fourth century, the so-called Arian controversy. My interest in the subject began many years ago when I first read the ecclesiastical histories of the fourth century for a graduate seminar on late antiquity. Like the emperor Constantine, when he came to learn of the dispute, I, too, was struck by the magnitude and severity of the conflict over a seemingly trivial matter.[1] In its duration, acrimony, and divisiveness, the Arian controversy surpassed all other, earlier or contemporary, Christian disputes. Far from being a limited or regional ecclesiastical affair like the Paulist or Donatist schism, it divided Christian communities in the empire's Eastern half into theological camps, making them rivals and hostile to one another. For two or three generations without interruption, the controversy engaged church leaders in a vicious struggle concerning the definition of the truth about God and for the leadership of Christian congregations. Especially intriguing to me was the vast number of people involved, of high and low station, inside and outside the church, from the woman in the street to the emperor himself, as the dispute spread from a "little spark into a large fire throughout ... provinces and cities."[2]

Why was the Arian controversy so extensive and so incendiary? And why did it last so long?[3] Contemporaries could answer these questions with stunning clarity. The dispute was the work of the devil, who could not bear the sight of a triumphant church and the happy state of Christian affairs.[4] Only sheer evil could sow hatred and division in this manner and wish to bring ruin to the church. This explanation should not be dismissed too readily, nor should we take it too metaphorically, not least because getting rid of that evil often meant getting rid of its supposed earthly agents, human beings of flesh and blood whose opinions and actions were at one time or another considered dangerous.

But historians, of course, are not convinced. The social and political implications of the dispute and the methods of those who were engaged in it have been most puzzling: intrigue and blackmail, exile and murder, street riots and violence, divided provinces, and even the threat of a civil war.[5] These developments were puzzling for at least two reasons. First, because at various points in the controversy some very real opportunities for mutual understanding and tolerance arose that were either ignored or not seriously taken to heart.[6] Secondly, the methods employed and the general attitude of churchmen engaged in the controversy contrasted sharply with behavior that had generally characterized the approach of prelates to similar conflicts in an earlier age. Why the change?

It was easier to explain theological disagreement. Disputes over interpretation of scripture were part and parcel of the history of Christianity, going back to its very beginnings, and had not always been peacefully or easily solved. Disagreement about theology, however, was not what made the Arian controversy different from earlier disputes, but the manner in which theology came to divide Christians, the upheaval it generated, and the frequent recourse to coercion and violence. Contemporaries of the dispute, pagan and Christian, noticed these differences and commented on them.[7]

When I first raised these questions, no published work had tried, at least not in a systematic fashion, to explain why the Arian dispute became so divisive. Despite the large and ever-growing scholarship devoted to the subject, most studies of the dispute had concentrated on its theological aspects—that is, on its intellectual dimension, rather than on its impact on the life of church and city.[8] Similarly, the general historical accounts of the later empire tended to treat the dispute as a chapter in the history of the church or Christian doctrine, to be approached as a history of ideas in isolation from society.[9] In these works, the turmoil caused by the dispute was generally taken for granted as a consequence of the new historical circumstances in which the church found itself after Constantine.

On the one hand, the Roman state played an important role in the dispute. After Constantine, emperors increasingly demanded from the church a measure of institutional unity and uniformity of faith that, without secular pressure, would perhaps never have been attempted.[10] Ancient wisdom had always taught that the prosperity of humankind was inextricably linked to the correct worship of divinity.[11] Failure to appease or worship the gods might put that prosperity at risk.[12] In the later empire, the need for church unity and uniformity of faith became more urgent as dissent came to be seen as a threat to the stability and integrity of the imperial order.[13] Thus, Christian emperors insisted that church leaders agree on a definition of God, and were ready to punish those who refused to conform—hence the troubles and violence.

On the other hand, churchmen's own insistence on uniformity of faith also helped fuel the dispute. While the ideal of unity in the faith was certainly not new in the church, after Constantine it had become possible for bishops to realize that ideal by appealing to the emperor.[14] But because rival bishops courted the emperor to support their views, the incentives to compromise with their peers were removed, perpetuating the conflict.[15]

Although there is much truth in these explanations, it seems nonetheless odd that imperial intervention should have resulted in more rather than less contention. At least since Nicaea, church leaders had been made acutely aware that theological speculation and disagreement might pose serious risks to their positions and, sometimes, even to their lives. In theory, this should have discouraged doctrinal innovation and disputation, especially when the principals of the controversy, who were also the main beneficiaries of imperial patronage, had an interest in preserving consensus to secure their careers and enjoy the privileges that flowed from them.[16] Yet, instead of more conformity, there was more dissent; instead of compromise and solidarity, intrigue and strife. The Arian dispute took shape in the wake of growing *resistance,* and sometimes entrenched opposition, to imperial pressure— that is, in open defiance of imperial power.[17] Why were churchmen willing to risk their positions and even renounce their benefits and privileges on account of their views on God?

Surely, imperial intervention was part of the reason for the persistent turmoil, but the emperors' involvement in the conflict explained neither the motivation of bishops who often acted, so to speak, in the face of imperial power, nor the upheaval that originated in their local struggles. Indeed, many years ago, in an influential article on the role of the Christian bishop, Peter Brown questioned the extent to which imperial support of the church affected the conduct of its leadership. Citing Pierre Nautin, Brown justly observed that the "Church styles of life and action that shock our modern aspirations" were the product "of the internal logic of the church's institutions," and, as such, they went "back before the fourth century."[18] The turbulent events in the history of the church were due to tensions inherent in its internal structures. Bishops always struggled to contain "potentially explosive elements" in the heart of church communities, and they could be just as arrogant, insensitive, and domineering as some of their fourth-century counterparts.[19] In the fourth century no less than in the third, personal ambitions, rivalries, and factions played a role in the life of the church. Yet, in their frequency, magnitude, and impact, the scenes of "priests in iron chains," "crowds with cudgels," burnt churches, torture, beatings, and street riots had no equivalent in the doctrinal controversies of the third century.[20] In my view, what was new in the fourth century was not Christian feuding, but the confrontational posture that churchmen adopted in their dealings with one another as they pursued theological uniformity, the violent methods they employed, and the murderous intolerance that dissenting views generated. What was at stake?

I began this study to attempt to understand why the Arian dispute in the fourth century generated so much conflict and violence—why, despite the sincere efforts of many to put an end to the tumult, the controversy nonetheless escalated and spread, unabated and passionate, spawning intolerance and unrest for nearly a century within Christian communities.

From the start, I was concerned neither with the specific theological content nor with the historical theology of the Arian controversy. Many fine and detailed narratives of the Arian dispute have addressed the main theological developments, situating them in the larger flow of the history of the church—councils, creeds, who-did-what-to-whom, and so on. Theology was of course crucial, but the study of creeds and theological formulations or the sources and permutations of theological concepts helped me understand neither the intensity of churchmen's sentiments about an idea of God nor the acts that issued from those sentiments. I also wanted to avoid an approach centered on the careers of the main protagonists of the dispute, not only because many excellent biographies have already been written, but also because biography, however much it might illuminate ecclesiastical politics, did not help me understand why theology had become such a contentious field.[21]

Instead, I turned more generally to the impact of the controversy on episcopal authority, because, at the heart of the dispute, was a struggle not only to define God, but also to determine the legitimacy of ecclesiastical leaders whose authority derived from a claim to possess God's spirit and knowledge of divine truth. The Arian dispute revolved around the quest to find and fix the truth about the deity, but precisely because that truth was constantly being disputed, the legitimacy of church leaders and their claims to authority could be, and were, openly and frequently contested. Such challenges were obviously unwelcome, because loss of legitimacy threatened authority, and, by extension, churchmen's control over congregations and their resources, which were significant political and economic assets. The persistence and viciousness of the dispute seemed to owe a great deal to the struggles of the protagonists to hold onto that control as they sought simultaneously to prove the orthodoxy of their views and the legitimacy of their leadership. In other words, fueling the dispute were crucial questions about the relationship between authority and orthodoxy, theology and power.[22]

As I began to examine the evidence more carefully, however, it struck me that the Arian controversy was not only about churchmen's struggle to *enforce* their authority, but also about "creating" power. Already in the early years of the dispute, before Constantine's conquest of the East, and then of course throughout the fourth century, the dispute opened to prelates a vast and exciting field of opportunities. In order to make their theological views prevail, clerics proceeded to expand their social networks, to mobilize the support of the faithful, to strengthen the ecclesiastical hierarchy, and to move efficiently in the slippery world of the imperial court. In other words, as bishops strove to advance their views and discredit their rivals, they also engaged in behavior that created new forms of power.

It was plausible, therefore, to postulate a connection between engagement in doctrinal controversy and the growing assertion of episcopal leaders in late Roman communities. That the theological controversies of the fourth century had a lasting impact on the development of ecclesiastical institutions and hierarchy was undeniable, but their effects on the style of church leadership were less clear, at a time when holding certain views on the truth might endanger church leaders' careers and lives.[23] And here my work changed focus. I became less interested in explaining the conduct of church leaders engaged in the dispute than in the wider implications of that engagement for the construction of episcopal authority. What impact did their attempts to promote and defend a theological position have on the ecclesiastical leadership? How did the challenges posed by the dispute shape the actions of church leaders? And how did engagement in controversy affect their position in church and society? Ultimately, of course, these questions cannot be separated from others I raised earlier, but the focus of my study shifted from an attempt to explain the confrontational behavior of bishops to an inquiry into the impact of that behavior on patterns of episcopal authority.

The central argument of this study, then, is that the Arian controversy played an important role in the establishment of a new style of church leadership, which emerged from the concrete actions prelates took to confront one another as they engaged in the dispute. The argument can be summarized as follows. As the Arian controversy escalated, first in Alexandria, then elsewhere, at stake was not only the orthodox definition of God, but also the authority of churchmen, whose legitimacy rested on their willingness to embrace and validate that definition. Since neither the definition of God nor the willingness of churchmen to embrace it could be effectively secured, prelates' claims to leadership of the church were frequently challenged. In order to meet this challenge, they embarked on quests to prove their orthodoxy and legitimacy—a task that called for organized, sustained, and effective action, and that required prelates to be constantly mobilized and permanently performing—or, as a group of bishops put it, that they be "continuously engaged in [machinations and] designs."[24] These actions partly accounted for the turmoil associated with the controversy, but more importantly, they resulted in the projection of episcopal authority into the public arena, in the strengthening of bishops' grip on church communities, and in the adoption of a more forceful, assertive, and aggressive style of leadership.

My premise here is that church leaders set out more forcefully to affirm themselves in church and society,*in response to* the challenges posed by theological dispute and dissent. The new style of church leadership grew out of prelates' struggles to secure legitimacy in a politically charged atmosphere in which consensus on the definition of God could not be obtained. I suggest that the persistent challenge of theological uncertainty produced new modes of behavior—dispositions and tendencies to act in particular ways—that continuously channeled powers and produced new patterns of church authority.[25] While these changes were largely the work of fourth-century bishops, especially prelates in the first half of the fourth century, the style of command they inaugurated was incorporated into a dynamic model of ecclesiastical leadership that came to define the episcopal office in late antiquity. In other words, engagement in doctrinal controversy contributed not only to the assertion of episcopal power in late Roman communities, but also to the formation of Christian expectations about the leadership of the church.

These developments gained momentum and visibility after Constantine, but, I contend, they owed little to imperial patronage of the church. Rather, what energized church leaders and triggered an engaged response was a shift from an ethos of "theological imprecision," dominant in the third century, to one of precision, first in Alexandria, and then, as the controversy spread, also elsewhere.[26] Not only did the disputants in Alexandria advance precise, albeit incompatible, ideas about the Son of God, but more significantly, they brought these ideas into the public arena, where, with unprecedented zeal and passion, they set out to convince other Christians that their views represented the truth about God and the orthodox teaching of the church. This shift to greater precision in theological thinking made compromise much more difficult to achieve—precise definitions of the deity not only encouraged greater personal investment in an idea of God but also left little room for negotiation. What I am suggesting here is that the onset of the Arian dispute marked an important rupture in the history of the church: it was not the dispute itself, over how to conceive and represent God, that was significant, but the manner in which church leaders reacted to the challenges the dispute posed to their authority.

This book is divided into eight chapters. Chapter 1 offers a general discussion of the challenges that theological disagreement and dissent posed to church leaders, beginning in the third century, when their authority had come to rest increasingly on their claims to possess God's spirit. In these circumstances, whenever bishops were believed to have strayed from the truth—as often happened in theological disputes—those claims were questioned, and the bishops' legitimacy was challenged.

Chapter 2 examines how bishops reacted to these challenges, showing how, in the third century, bishops adhered to a pattern of conduct rooted in a tradition of solidarity and cooperation with one's peers. When confronted with doctrinal dissent, bishops strove to end disagreement and settle disputes by seeking compromise through negotiation and debate. The absence of precise criteria for orthodoxy and the benign ambiguity of the "rule of faith" discouraged sustained confrontation even as disagreements over doctrine became more common.

By contrast, in the early years of the Arian controversy, there was a subtle but fundamental change in the nature of the bishops' response to theological disagreement. Persistent confrontation, combined with a determination to undermine fellow prelates, replaced the former striving for consensus. This change was first evident in Alexandria, where it resulted from the need to achieve greater precision and clarity in defining the truth about God's Son. These developments form the subject of chapter 3, which also looks at how the new definitions of God altered church leaders' relationship with their belief, generating a deep sense of devotion to rival notions of God that hindered efforts to reach any compromise. Challenged by their rivals and driven by a new certainty that they possessed the truth, church leaders embarked on a disruptive quest to prove their orthodoxy and to discredit their opponents.

Chapter 4 examines in detail the consequences of these actions by following closely the efforts of rival churchmen in Alexandria to make ordinary Christians their partners in the dispute. It is here, as churchmen interacted with one another and with their congregations, that we begin to see the rise of a new type of church leader—brash, enterprising, and combative.

Chapter 5 looks at similar developments elsewhere in the East as the dispute migrated outside Egypt. Chapter 6 picks up the controversy from the time of Constantine's conquest of the East. It considers the impact on the dispute of Constantine's intervention and the "criminalization" of doctrinal dissent that followed the proclamation of Nicene orthodoxy. Thereafter, theological positions became politically charged, and dissent from orthodoxy, however that was defined, brought with it the ugly specter of dishonor and the danger of deposition and exile.

Chapter 7 considers the implications of continued theological disagreement in the politically charged climate from the time of Nicaea until the death of Constantine. Nicaea failed to produce theological consensus, and the dispute rekindled soon after the council. In a treacherous political atmosphere, theological disagreement became even more threatening to church leaders, who understood that their leadership—and thus their control of congregations, wealth, and people—had come to depend on their ability to convince as many people as possible of the orthodoxy of their views and the legitimacy of their positions. Chapter 7 tries to show how prelates reacted to this sense of insecurity not by seeking consensus and compromise, but by mobilizing the church's ever-growing resources to assert their authority and undertake campaigns to suppress opposition, eliminate dissent, and promote their views on a much wider field. One consequence of these actions was the consolidation of the new style of church leadership that had emerged in the early years of the Arian controversy.

Chapter 8 carries these developments forward into the middle decades of the fourth century, from the death of Constantine into the early 360s, as the façade of Nicene unity finally crumbled, and rival groups of bishops brought the dispute out into the open, scrambling to impose their own definition of faith. The chapter looks into how bishops devised new strategies of power that enabled them to assert their authority, sometimes in complete opposition to the emperor. One of the most dramatic signs of this assertion was the emergence of a discourse that questioned the legitimacy of a Christian emperor, something unthinkable before.[27] That a critique of imperial power could be so openly made and justified on theological grounds was a sign of how the dispute helped generate the conditions for a redefinition of the church leadership in late Roman society.

This study centers on the provinces of the Roman East, where the Arian controversy dragged on for most of the fourth century. During this time, in contrast to the Latin half of the empire, the Greek-speaking East maintained a certain social, economic, cultural, and political uniformity that allows us to treat it as a unit. Despite the mosaic of local cultures, languages, and traditions, the region was more or less united under a firm political system and the universal appeal of Hellenic culture.[28] The dynamism of its cities, especially in the Near East, and the continued long-distance exchange of goods and people helped to keep that cultural appeal alive. In contrast to the Western provinces of the empire, the focal point of the Eastern provinces was Constantinople, its senate, and the imperial court. The result was the creation of a common political culture shared by secular magnates and ecclesiastical leaders alike, which, when combined with the economic and social effects of a dynamic urban civilization, gave to the empire's Eastern half a measure of coherence unmatched in the West.[29]

The East also lacked a politically active, respected, and powerful pagan aristocracy, as was embodied in the senate at Rome.[30] As A. H. M. Jones noted, pagan opposition in the East was largely academic, not political. The history of the church in the East, therefore, must differ from that of the West. Damasus of Rome, for instance, had to worry about the continued appeal of a city steeped in pagan tradition, and his struggles were of a different nature from those of Athanasius and George in Alexandria or, say, Hypsius and Ecdicius, rival bishops of Parnassus, a backwater in Cappadocia.[31]

Moreover, in the West, with the exception of North Africa, where the Donatist schism provides interesting parallels with developments in the East, in Gaul and Spain, the circumstances of life in the church were also different, concerns of quite another sort occupied prelates, and other models of church leadership emerged in a different political and historical context.[32] In short, the persistence of a greater degree of political cohesion and cultural uniformity in the East allows us to make generalized inferences about developments there that are difficult to make for the West.

Finally, a word on the chronological limits of this inquiry. Although this study begins with the third century, in general it coincides roughly with the Constantinian empire, covering the period beginning shortly before Constantine's conquest of the East and ending with Constantius's death. It was during this time, especially in the middle decades of the fourth century, that the Arian dispute intensified and that a new model of church leadership clearly began to spread. While the early 360s may strike the reader as odd as an upper chronological limit, there are two important reasons for setting this terminus. First and most important, the changes discussed in this book took place before that time. Indeed, by 360, Christians and non-Christians had come to recognize bishops not only as spiritual or community leaders, but also as political players, men endowed with *auctoritas*, and expected them to behave accordingly.[33] Extending this study to the fifth century or to the Theodosian age would not have substantially added to this argument, important though the evidence from, say, Cappadocia or Constantinople in the 370s might be. The other compelling reason for setting this chronological limit is that had I extended this inquiry into the later fourth century, I probably would never have finished this book.

PART ONE

Points of Departure

Theology and Christian Leadership in the Third-Century Church

> *Apelles, in his conversations with me, was proven to have said many wrong things. Wherefore he said that one must not at all argue about theology, but each one hold fast to what he believed, because, he declared, all who have hope in the crucified would be saved if only they persisted in good deeds.*
> EUSEBIUS, HE 5.13.5

SOMETIME IN THE MID-240S a Christian priest set out from Palestine on a journey eastward across the Judaean desert to Arabia. The priest, a native of Alexandria now living in Palestinian Caesarea, was also a well-known scholar whose reputation for wisdom and piety had spread widely in the eastern Mediterranean among educated circles, Christian and non-Christian alike. His erudition had often taken him places—twice before to Arabia, once at the invitation of the Roman governor, who wished to learn about Christian philosophy. The empress herself was reported to have once summoned him to court to lecture about God. But this time, he had been invited by fellow Christians, who had asked him to help them settle a controversy over the teachings of a bishop suspected of heresy.[1]

It was not the first time that Origen had been asked to travel abroad to deal with dissent in the church. A few years before this journey, he had come to Bostra to debate the controversial teachings of the bishop Beryllus.[2] Earlier still he had visited Athens to refute the views of a heretic. That trip cost him his teaching job in the church of Alexandria,[3] for on his way to Greece, Origen was ordained priest in Caesarea, to the dismay of Demetrius, the Alexandrian bishop, who declared the ordination invalid and began an unsuccessful campaign to destroy Origen's reputation.[4]

We do not know exactly where in Arabia Origen went this time, but we do know that the community he visited had previously been rocked by disputes about doctrine.[5] In this case the issue was the views of Heracleides, a local bishop, on a sensitive and difficult subject: the nature of the relationship between God the Father and God the Son.

The details of the "affair of Heracleides" are murky.[6] Our only source is a partial transcript of Origen's debate with the bishop, in which Origen himself provides most of the background information. According to this report, the dispute began when the faithful disagreed about the proper way to honor God in their prayers. Should they pray to the Father? To the Son? To both at the same time?[7] Origen tells us that, to many local Christians, Heracleides' opinion on the matter appeared tainted with "Monarchianism," a doctrine long condemned in the church.[8] As a result, the community had split into different camps, some siding with the bishop, others rejecting his views. To judge from Origen's comments, the faithful became restless and circulated petitions demanding that the clergy sign written statements about their views on God. Bishops of neighboring communities were also drawn into the controversy but failed to end it.[9]

At the root of the dispute, Origen claimed, was the lack of a precise definition of God.[10] Neither the faithful nor local church leaders could offer a definition of the deity that satisfied all parties. Indeed, Origen noted that no one in the community was certain what the correct—that is, orthodox—view on the matter should be.[11] His visit, therefore, was intended to address this thorny issue and to restore peace to the community.

Origen first met with Heracleides behind closed doors for a preliminary discussion. A public debate before the people then followed, as was customary in the early church.[12] The occasion must have been fraught with tension, and the outcome of the debate unpredictable, but the exchanges between the two men proceeded in a remarkably amicable tone. Despite the tense climate, the event was friendly, and the participants at ease with one another, striving to arrive at a consensus.

> *Origen.* Is the Father God?
> *Heracleides.* Yes.
> O. Is the Son distinct from the Father?
> H. How could He be simultaneously Son and Father?
> O. Is the Son, who is distinct from the Father, also God?
> H. He too is God.
> O. Thus, do the two gods make one?
> H. Yes.
> O. It follows then that we affirm that there are two gods?
> H. Yes, but the power is one.[13]

The proposition "two gods, one power" ruffled the audience. But their unease subsided as Origen proceeded to explain the meaning of the phrase.[14] Then, turning to the clergy and faithful, he said: "If you agree on these points, we shall consider them codified and fixed, with the people as witnesses." The discussion moved on to other topics, but for all we know this was the end of the dispute, and the bishop was reconciled with his congregation.[15]

Two decades later, another itinerant Alexandrian, the deacon Eusebius, set out on a journey to Syria.[16] The reason for his trip was the upheaval in the Antiochene church caused by the teachings of Paul of Samosata, the bishop of Antioch.[17] The controversy over Paul's teachings was far more turbulent than that over Heracleides'.[18] It had mobilized a great number of prelates and clerics from neighboring cities and provinces, dragged on for several years, led to three large church councils, and, in the end, could be settled only by imperial fiat.[19]

Like Heracleides, Paul had come under suspicion of heresy not long after his ordination, in the early 260s.[20] The precise nature of his teachings is unknown; almost all the surviving evidence concerning his theology is fragmentary, secondhand from later, hostile sources, and generally unreliable.[21] The most important source for the affair, the letter of the church council that excommunicated him in 268, called the bishop a "disciple of Artemas" and accused him of being an "adoptionist"—that is, of holding the opinion that Christ was a "lesser" god.[22]

When Eusebius arrived in Antioch, he would have found a deeply divided Christian community. Attempts to overcome the division seemed to have been exhausted. Two synods had taken place. The letter of 268 implies that at least twice before the bishop had agreed to change his mind.[23] But the third council failed to reach an agreement, and Paul stood fast by his views—why should they be any less true than those of others?[24]

Our Eusebius may have witnessed one of the last debates between Paul and Malchion, a local priest and professor of rhetoric who "succeeded in exposing the crafty dissembler."[25] After these debates, Paul's refusal to abandon his teachings led the council to depose him and replace him with a new bishop.[26]

Paul's deposition fractured the Antiochene church. Many Christians disagreed with the council's decision and continued to acknowledge Paul as the legitimate bishop.[27] Together with his supporters, Paul refused to leave the church building, depriving the newly appointed bishop of a meeting place.[28] For two years Paul held his own until an imperial decree forced him to relinquish the building to his rival.[29] But Paul continued to lead his own church community, which was to last for at least two generations, well into the fourth century.[30]

The affairs of Heracleides and Paul of Samosata introduce us to the main themes of part 1 of this study—what challenge did theological dissent pose to early leaders of the church? And how did these leaders respond? By *challenge,* I mean the threat that theological disputes presented to bishops as leaders of church communities, and by *response,* the manner in which churchmen dealt with that threat as they struggled to define theological concepts, remove dissent, and keep the church united.

Although this study focuses on the fourth century, it begins with the third century, in order to establish a basis for contrast with the responses of church leaders at a later time, in the wake of the Arian controversy. The third century is also a useful starting point because, by that time, many church communities around the Mediterranean were being reconfigured under the leadership of monarchical bishops, and the essential ecclesiastical institutions that would characterize them for centuries were coming into being. Likewise, as R. A. Markus reminds us, in the third century, doctrine had come to play an increasingly important role in defining the boundaries of the "great church."[31]

First, we will consider how theological speculation and dissent challenged the authority of bishops by compelling them to make statements about the truth that might be contested and rejected as false, as in the examples of Heracleides and Paul of Samosata. At a time when bishops legitimated their claims to leadership of Christian communities by claiming to possess God's spirit, doubts about their capacity to enunciate the truth could seriously undermine their authority. A bishop suspected of heresy was believed to have lost the Spirit, and with it the ability to discharge his priestly functions. Indeed, in the third century, as bishops asserted themselves, the spiritual component of their authority—possession of the Spirit—came to underpin all others.[32]

Next, taking the affairs of Heracleides and Paul of Samosata as examples of how third-century church leaders responded to these challenges, and examining other examples as necessary, we will consider how leaders in the third-century church approached theological dissent in a markedly cautious, tolerant, and more or less predictable manner, striving to achieve consensus and compromise. Despite a growing desire to achieve doctrinal uniformity during this period, churchmen expressed solidarity and extended friendship to their peers and hesitated to attack them. This approach gave prelates considerable latitude in settling doctrinal differences, but, as we shall see, it was a workable strategy only while churchmen were willing to tolerate a great deal of theological imprecision. This generally cautious response to theological disputes has been described before,[33] but it is underscored here to make the changes that came with the fourth century stand out more clearly.

The goal of characterizing churchmen's reactions to doctrinal controversy is not comprehensiveness. Rather, a typology of social action is sketched out for comparison with a pattern of conduct that emerged later with the controversy over Arius's teachings.

1

Christian Leadership and the Challenge of Theology

"Your church must not differ from the other churches in opinion," stated Origen at the opening of the debate with Heracleides, "because you are not the false church."¹ The bewildering diversity in Christian thought and practice presented a constant dilemma to theorists and intellectuals in early Christian communities.² There was only one true, orthodox church. On this, most third-century Christians could agree, and there were plenty of reasons for doing so. Uniformity of faith was at the center of Christian teaching going back to Paul: "For just as in a single human body there are many limbs and organs, all with different functions, so all of us, united in Christ, form one body."³ But Christians would not always agree on how to attain unity or achieve uniformity and to what degree.⁴ Most Christians did not wish to part from the "true" church or be labeled heretic, a term to which the Christian tradition attached a negative connotation.⁵ Heresy, like anger, envy, and passion, was a product of the flesh.⁶ Yet who was to decide what was true and false, right and wrong? What was to count as orthodoxy?⁷

In the second century, Christians facing these questions, who subscribed to a tradition later claimed by (and thus closely identified with) Catholic Christianity, developed a set of propositions known as the "rule of faith" (*regula fidei* or κάνον), which functioned as a common denominator, a set of commonly shared ideas about God, the Christian community, and the proper relation between God and humanity.⁸ One of the main purposes of the rule was to provide a measure of doctrinal or ideological coherence to a network of church communities in the Mediterranean world that contemporaries called the "great church." Tied to one another by their acceptance of a common body of divine knowledge and sacred texts, these communities, in the third century, rapidly crystallized around a hierarchy of bishops, priests, and deacons keen on preserving church unity and doctrinal uniformity.[9] The rule also served as the "yardstick" of orthodoxy—a standard of truth that enabled the ecclesiastical hierarchy to decide which forms of belief and worship were acceptable and which compromised too much with the world. Christian leaders in the second century had insisted that it was unacceptable to depart from the rule, but the rule itself could still accommodate a remarkable range of incongruent views, contradictory ideas, and divergent interpretations of scripture.[10]

Yet in the increasingly sophisticated, diverse, and intellectually demanding environment of the third-century church, it was clear that the rule could no longer function as the sole standard of orthodoxy, even though a large number of Christians upheld and accepted it.[11] Origen was not the only one to acknowledge this limitation, but he was explicit about it: "Since so many of those who profess faith in Christ disagree with one another not only on little and minimal things but truly also on many great and important ones . . . it is necessary first to define that which is certain and the rule of faith, [and] *only then to inquire about other things.*"[12] Origen was speaking not only of those Christians outside the Catholic tradition, but also of churchmen such as Heracleides and his opponents, who accepted the rule of faith but disagreed about the "great and important" things. Indeed, although the rule continued to be the repository of Christian truth and the starting point for determining the validity of any theological proposition, the ideas it comprised had themselves become the subject of philosophical speculation, interpretation, and disagreement.[13] As H. Lietzmann aptly put it, "The rule [of faith] demanded commentary and instruction . . . and the demands of instruction caused the introduction of new terms and concepts"; these, in turn, introduced new sources of disagreement.[14]

Since at least the mid-second century, Christian intellectuals had been interested in understanding the ontological realities underlying these "concepts," but in the third century, the concepts themselves attracted enormous attention.[15] Theologians like Tertullian or Hippolytus focused on the idea of God, and as E. Troeltsch long ago noted, "The need to make this idea quite clear . . . became the main concern of the Church."[16] As scholars have pointed out, this new interest was fueled both by Christianity's need to achieve "intellectual respectability" as it parted ways with Judaism and confronted pagan philosophy and by a perceptible change in the social and intellectual makeup of early Christian communities, which were growing more socially diverse and attracting better-educated believers.[17]

By the mid-third century, therefore, Christians representing a wide variety of traditions, some of which would later be condemned as heterodox, might profess the same rule of faith, the truth of whose propositions they might agree on while understanding and explaining them in radically different ways, as in the controversies sparked by the teachings of Heracleides and Paul of Samosata and numerous others.[18] In other words, without further qualification, the rule alone could not continue to serve as the sole criterion of Christian truth.[19]

Origen himself, having often been asked to help with difficult theological questions, expressed serious doubts about the possibility of defining the truth: "I must openly confess that my spirit has often been troubled by something a wise and pious man once told me: about God, it is dangerous to speak even the truth. Not only falsehood is dangerous, but so is the truth, when inappropriately said."[20] The deficiencies of the human intellect troubled Christian thinkers like Origen, who recognized that perception was necessarily impaired by the condition of being human: divine truth would always be partly distorted by the prism of human interpretation, and so could never be fully grasped.[21] "[The apostle] said not that God's judgment can be understood only with difficulty, but that one cannot understand it at all; he said not that his ways can be investigated with effort, but that they cannot be investigated."[22] Origen recognized that scripture, the source of all truth, could be interpreted in a number of ways, right and wrong.[23]

Christian leaders and theologians, then, faced a conundrum. On the one hand, scripture, to have any meaning at all in the lives of Christians, must be deciphered and interpreted.[24] On the other, the potential for idiosyncrasy and disagreement in interpreting the word of God was always high. Indeed, exegesis was marked by constant tension between a received tradition and the need to reinvent it.[25] As each succeeding generation of Christians sought to make sense of scripture, disputes over its meaning—what was acceptable and what must be excluded—became inevitable.[26]

Again, Origen understood this best. He knew well that the truth about God and the "great things" was never easily or wholly revealed, and he realized that the meaning of scripture could not be fixed, let alone imposed on fellow Christians.[27] He openly admitted that uniformity of thought on matters of theology was, regrettably (to him!), impossible. Divine truth could not be reduced to simple formulas. Statements of orthodoxy, such as the one he had presented to settle the controversy in Arabia, could only be provisional until a new understanding (or new revelation) was achieved or new questions posed that compelled one to discard, revise, or reinstate old propositions.[28] "If something profound occurs to someone in a disputation," he wrote, "this must be expressed, but not with *absolute certainty*. To do so is for the *imprudent*, those who have lost the sense of human weakness.... Of the great things, those things that are high above us, we do not forget our own ignorance."[29] Such an opinion was at once enlightened and mystical. One arrived at the truth through reasoning and argumentation, but only the truly inspired grasped its meaning, and then never fully, so that, in practice, orthodoxy could not exist out there *an sich*;[30] rather, it must evolve in continuous debates about the meaning of God's word. The truth was meant to be rationally demonstrated and to convince by reasoned persuasion.[31] Many other Christians shared these views, including some of Origen's fiercest critics.[32]

The impossibility of defining orthodoxy, then, was part of the challenge theology posed to Christian leaders. The notion of orthodoxy rested on a paradox. On the one hand, it referred to a set of ideas and symbols that were believed to represent or embody absolute, eternal, immutable truths about God, humanity, and the universe. On the other, these ideas and symbols were always provisionally true, their meaning malleable and constantly changing, or, as the believer would have understood it, never revealed in their entirety.[33] As a body of knowledge, orthodoxy was perpetually in flux, its meaning deriving from the continuous collective effort of many people to elucidate scripture. The truth could be revealed only through sustained inquiry and debate, and, thus, it was alive and moving in the community.[34] As A. Martin put it, "L'orthodoxie ne cesse de sculpter sa propre statue. Elle n'est pas, en effet, un objet fixe, rigide."[35] For this very reason, orthodoxy could not be defined and controlled by any theologian, bishop, or single individual. At its core, there always remained a large fluid area where much was left ambiguous and indeterminate, open to speculation, innovation, and dispute.

Yet, as is well known, since the second century, Christian leaders had actively tried to control the interpretation of the word of God, adding precision to slippery concepts, setting parameters for scriptural exegesis, and fixing the limits of acceptable religious experience.[36] Since bishops had first appeared in the historical record, they had been claiming superior knowledge on all matters concerning scripture and Spirit—this was true not only in high-brow theological debates among Christian intellectuals, but also in local conflicts among the ordinary faithful, who were believed to command special forms of divine knowledge and to possess the gifts of the Spirit.[37] These claims to supremacy in theological and spiritual matters belonged to a larger process of concentration of all forms of church authority in the hands of the episcopate, which had begun in the second century and continued during the third as the bishop's standing in the Christian community steadily increased.

Although the historical development of the monarchical episcopate lies outside the scope of this book, the bishops' claim to superior spiritual power concerns us because challenges to it had the potential to undermine their authority.[38] In the third century, when bishops emerged as more forceful leaders, they became sensitive to charisma and grew wary of spiritually gifted Christians. The church hierarchy grew suspicious of prophets, wonderworkers, inspired teachers, and other charismatic lay Christians, even confessors.[39] Spiritual gifts were a vital source of power in the Christian community, but that power remained diffuse only while authority in the church was diffuse.[40] As the demands on the bishops' patronage and protection expanded, and bishops themselves were recognized as de facto community leaders, they also claimed greater authority in spiritual and doctrinal matters—authority they declared they had received directly from God.[41]

These developments were reflected in narratives of the apostolic origins of the episcopate that began to circulate at the end of the second century, with Irenaeus and Hegesippus, and in the third-century liturgical-canonical writings associated with Hippolytus, the *Didascalia,* and later Cyprian.[42] They were also dramatized in the ceremony of ordination that was being elaborated in the early third century. A treatise attributed to Hippolytus describes the ritual:

> The people will gather ... with the council of elders and the bishops.... With the assent of all, the ... bishops [or everyone?] will *place their hands upon him.*... Everyone will keep silent, praying in their hearts for the descent of the Spirit. Then, one of the bishops ... shall *lay his hand* upon him who is being ordained bishop and pray: "God and Father of our Lord Jesus Christ ... *now pour out upon him the power of the commanding Spirit which comes from you,* which through your beloved Son Jesus Christ, you gave to your holy apostles, who founded the Church in every place ... for the glory and endless praise of your name."[43]

This text is fraught with problems of authorship, dating, and redaction, which I cannot address here, but two elements of the ceremony are generally accepted:[44] the laying on of hands and the participation of the faithful.[45] By placing his hand on the candidate and calling on God to pour forth his Spirit, the officiating bishop channeled heavenly power onto the ordained bishop before the eyes of an audience that, through earnest prayer, contributed to make the glorious descent of the Spirit possible. Such compelling scenes were meant to mute any doubts about the divine origins of episcopal authority. Cyprian was not playing with words when he remarked that it was "God who made ... a bishop."[46] By the mid-third century, prelates were openly fashioning themselves as living embodiments of God's spirit, and the possession of the Spirit validated their exalted position.[47]

At the time of Origen and Heracleides, however, these developments still had the flavor of innovation. For many Christians, spiritual authority was neither the prerogative of priests nor a function of the episcopal office.[48] The interpretation of the word of God must be a matter of inspiration, not of standing, and as such it transcended the episcopate and its claims to greater wisdom and higher power.[49] Tertullian, for instance, envisioned "a church of the Spirit through spiritual individuals," insisting that "a collection of bishops does not make the church."[50] Origen considered the church's "deep" knowledge to be immanent in the body of the church—that is, to be located equally in its leadership *and* the community of rank and file.[51] He spoke of the handing of collective knowledge from one generation to the next since the time of the apostles, through the *praedicatio ecclesiastica,* not the bishop's agency alone. Apostolic teaching was the source of all truth, but that teaching was not a monopoly of bishops.[52] As H. von Campenhausen observed, even though Origen acknowledged and fully supported bishops as leaders of the great church, he could not bring himself to agree that because of their rank and liturgical functions, they possessed any more wisdom than their fellow Christians, clerical or lay like himself.[53] "It is one thing to discharge the duties of the priest, quite another to be learned and *perfect.*"[54] Origen's critique of the monarchical episcopate was informed by the notion of a church that could, within the limits defined by the apostolic tradition (which he supported), accommodate alternative sources of authority as well as, we must suppose, variety in religious experience.[55]

Origen believed that scripture must be interpreted and explained rationally. Knowledge of the truth resulted from responsible inquiry and careful reflection and could not be arbitrarily imposed.[56] Origen's views on this matter may have been conditioned by his acceptance of free will as a fundamental principle that shaped human nature (and not vice versa).[57] His insistence that humans were free to govern their own lives made him wary of unfounded interpretations of God's word and impatient with rash, imperious judgments. "God created things this way so that each spirit or soul might not be coerced to act against its own will, but might follow its own free judgment."[58] This must be most true of life in the church. In theory, Christians could find out for themselves the meaning of the divine word, and for what he or she found, each individual alone was responsible to God.[59] In the search for the truth, then, bishops may well be dispensable; their duty was to gather and guide God's people, to cleanse people of sin and to prepare them to receive and celebrate, with a clear and unhindered mind, the mystery of God.[60] Prepare, not impose; guide, not coerce.

No other Christian theorist of the early church wrote of human liberty with such clarity and daring. In so many ways Origen stands alone, a towering figure in the intellectual landscape of the third-century church. His views on the priesthood, however, were in no way unusual. Outside the learned world of the Alexandrian *didaskaleion* and other erudite circles, many pious, ordinary Christians, clerical and lay, would have shared his views, taking liberty of judgment for granted and refusing to subscribe blindly to the bishops' pronouncements or to accept their teachings on God and other matters passively and uncritically.[61] Many Christians, albeit willing, like Origen, to embrace prelates as community leaders or patrons, realized the insufficiency of bishops' claims to be the only bearers of the Spirit and the source of all divine truth.[62]

We have seen how the ordinary faithful in Arabia and Antioch did not hesitate to question the orthodoxy of Heracleides and Paul of Samosata. But at every turn in the history of the early church, we find pious Christians seeking for themselves more intimate and meaningful forms of religiosity and direct, personal communion with divine power. Origen described them as "inquisitive souls who lacked the nourishment that saves"; devout Christians who were "constantly seeking";[63] visionaries, prophets, martyrs, "heretics," ordinary men and women, who, nonchalant, did not hesitate to dismiss prelates' claims to be sole arbiters of the truth. They came from all corners of the empire.[64] These pious Christians, whether in Asia Minor, North Africa, Rome, or Alexandria, understood spiritual power as a numinous, harrowing presence, diffused throughout the Christian community, not the exclusive possession of any member or of any bishop.

It is not surprising, then, that bishops tried zealously to check the enthusiasm of these inspired Christians, chastising and rebuking those who refused to be disciplined, condemning and labeling them schismatics, heretics, or rebels as the occasion demanded, and excluding them from the church.[65] And if it was impossible to ban all the operations of the Spirit in the community, bishops sought jealously to limit them, to channel divine power to their own advantage, and to control the interpretation of scripture.[66] As bishops assumed greater powers of direction, possession of God's spirit served to justify their claims to supreme authority in church communities.[67] Paradoxically, however, this development also created areas of vulnerability. By tying their authority more directly to their command of spiritual power, bishops also exposed themselves to new challenges, because, in theory, every time a prelate's claim to possess the Spirit was contested, the very foundations of his authority were also called into question.

The greatest threat came from scriptural exegesis and theological speculation, unpredictable and treacherous fields in which bishops were expected to be able to make or to sanction pronouncements on the truth—to state, for instance, "what God is." Here everyone agreed that only those who possessed the gift of the Spirit could discern and enunciate the truth.[68] But since the truth could not be fixed and interpretation of scripture could never entirely be under the control of a single bishop, prelates could not avoid being exposed to doubt, speculation, and dissent—that is, the bishop's capacity to pronounce the truth attracted constant scrutiny, and because that capacity had become a sign of the inner workings of the Spirit, doubts about the bishop's orthodoxy suggested to the outside world that the inner light of the Spirit had been dimmed. "The Spirit," Hippolytus wrote, "[confers] perfect grace on those who have the *correct faith*," which was another way of saying that the spirit of God abandoned those who strayed from the truth.[69]

Here, then, is the other part of the challenge that theology posed. A hint of heresy or spurious teaching signaled the depletion of the gift of the Spirit. In the eyes of the faithful this was a problem because the Spirit invested prelates with the powers of redemption and salvation, the "power of the keys"[70]—regenerative and transformative power that regulated admission to and membership in church communities, and that, invoked in the rituals of baptism, excommunication, penitence, and ordination, controlled the boundaries of the church community. "If one could baptize, he could also give the Holy Spirit," remarked Cyprian, "but if he cannot give the Holy Spirit . . . he cannot baptize . . . since baptism is one and the Holy Spirit is one."[71] So also the bishop of tiny Rusicada: "A man who is a heretic . . . cannot give what he has not; much more a schismatic, who has lost what he once had."[72] Loss of the Spirit invalidated a bishop's ministrations, his capacity to define the boundaries of the community, and his qualifications to lead the church.[73] And so it was for Heracleides and Paul of Samosata. Under suspicion of heresy, these two prelates saw their standing slip in the eyes of many among the faithful, who questioned not only the truth of their teachings, but also the legitimacy of their leadership.[74]

Episcopal authority, then, as it expanded in the third century, was intertwined with orthodoxy—a relation that helps explain why theological disagreement remained a source of tension and conflict in church communities. When controversy arose, not simply theological concepts were at stake, but also always prelates' control of the Spirit and the legitimacy of their claims to leadership. This vulnerability was inherent in the episcopal office as it took shape in the third century. In theory, neither the bishop's claims to possess God's spirit nor his prestige and his control of the resources of the community could entirely remove it. Indeed, considering the success of the monarchical episcopate, it may seem surprising that a matter of great importance, the legitimacy of the bishop's authority, had come to rest on such shaky foundations—concepts believed to embody divine and immutable truths, whose meaning was constantly shifting. This was possible, I suggest, only because even as theological dissent divided church communities and challenged priestly authority, churchmen, in practice, developed mechanisms to manage and minimize that challenge. Indeed, in contrast to priests, prophets, teachers, deacons, and others, who were often excommunicated and expelled from the community, we hardly ever hear of bishops being deposed or removed from office for doctrinal reasons.

In chapter 2 we will examine the impact of doctrinal challenges on the church leadership, in particular how prelates *responded* to these challenges. Their response was such that they were almost always able to diffuse the threat theological disputes posed to their leadership. Whenever disagreements emerged, bishops demonstrated remarkable flexibility and a willingness to reach consensus through debate and compromise. If prelates remained vulnerable to the challenges of theology, in the third century their reaction to those challenges considerably attenuated that vulnerability.

2

"Not in the Spirit of Controversy"

Truth, Leadership, and Solidarity

When accused of heresy, church leaders reacted by defending their views, even if that defense led to further conflict and division in the community.[1] Heracleides did so, as did Paul of Samosata, who stubbornly stood by his teachings, taking many of the faithful with him. Church leaders often had to defend themselves, as Celsus and others noted.[2] If disputes concerned not only the truth, but also qualification for leadership, bishops could not afford to vacillate. "Urge them and argue with them," Paul recommended. "And speak with authority: let no one slight you."[3] Cyprian of Carthage, perhaps the greatest theorist of the monarchical episcopate, recommended preemption against those who challenged the bishop's authority: "For if we fear the boldness of the most wicked . . . the strength of the episcopate and the divine and sublime power to govern the church are done for."[4] Paul of Samosata, who kept his priests "under his thumb," would have wholeheartedly agreed.[5] Defending the bishop's position of supremacy in the Christian community, Cyprian declared that the root of dissent was always rebellion against the authority of the priesthood: "From nowhere else have heresies sprung and schisms been born than from the lack of obedience to God's priest . . . who is at one time the priest and at another the judge in the place of Christ."[6] Such rhetoric illustrates the bishops' view that dissent and opposition undermined episcopal authority. It also reveals their readiness to discipline dissenters to preserve church unity under their leadership.

In practice, however, despite the growing theological ferment of the third century, bishops learned to minimize the challenge of doctrinal disputes to their leadership. Bishops rarely lost standing in the community for doctrinal reasons, and only a few were excommunicated and deposed for heresy in the manner of Paul of

Samosata.⁷ Cyprian's harsh declaration notwithstanding, churchmen tried to resolve disputes through thoughtful discussion and debate and were prepared to live with a great deal of dissonance and disagreement.

The main reason for such toleration, I argue, lay in the "imprecision" of orthodoxy. Indeed, if divine truth was difficult to define, so was falsehood. Although prelates were vulnerable to charges of heresy, it was not always easy to prove them in the wrong, precisely because orthodoxy could not be reduced to a set of criteria against which their—or anyone's—views could be verified. Despite the rule of faith, orthodoxy was being constantly shaped and reshaped in exegesis and debate. Given these circumstances, it could be difficult to convince Christian believers, clerical or lay, that a prelate's teachings were unorthodox, especially if that prelate was a popular and esteemed bishop.⁸ Moreover, the complexity and ambiguity of theological concepts and churchmen's awareness of their own vulnerability to doctrinal challenges generally discouraged their attachment to inflexible theological positions that might be difficult to defend or invite questions about their orthodoxy and, by extension, their qualifications to lead the Christian community.

For these reasons, even as theological dissent became increasingly common, bishops facing doctrinal disputes were inclined to debate their differences, often in congenial fashion, respectful of each other's opinions, rather than engage in open confrontation. The rhetoric against heresy and dissent may have been poisonous in early Christian writings, but prelates forced to deal with a suspicion of heresy generally strove to achieve consensus and compromise.⁹ In the controversy over the teachings of Heracleides, local clerics and believers, divided over the "soundness" of his doctrine, invited neighboring bishops to debate it, and, when that was not enough, reached out to one of the best minds of the time to help them sort out the main points of disagreement.¹⁰ In the affair of Paul of Samosata, too, Paul's peers generously offered to come to terms with the prelate at least twice, when he seemed willing to change his mind.¹¹ They took action against him only after he clung to his views even after years of prolonged discussion, two large international synods, and many local disputations. In another case from the first half of the third century, Privatus, bishop of Lambaesis, was similarly removed from office for heresy only after a large council of bishops found him guilty of "many and serious offenses."¹²

In yet another contentious third-century affair, the so-called Sabellian controversy, we find an example of how prelates themselves could easily be harmed when they condemned their peers and advanced their own views on controversial points of doctrine. This dispute apparently began with the teachings of a certain Sabellius, who was known in the East as a native of Libya. Hippolytus refers to him as a teacher of Monarchian doctrine whom Bishop Callistus of Rome denounced as a heretic in the early third century.¹³ Despite Callistus's condemnation, many Christians embraced Sabellius's views, which spread widely, leading to controversy and causing division, especially in the churches of the Libyan Pentapolis.[14] As the controversy grew, some Libyan Christians referred the matter to Dionysius, bishop of Alexandria, who condemned Sabellius's teachings as impious and blasphemous and tried to put an end to the controversy in Libya.[15] "Approaching the matter in a most didactic fashion," Dionysius wrote letters to the Libyan clergy, explaining his views on God, and sent envoys to local congregations to persuade the faithful of the truth, not impose it on them.[16] Many Libyans, however, and apparently not only Sabellian Christians, rejected Dionysius's views. They dispatched their own envoys to the bishop of Rome, also named Dionysius, accusing the Alexandrian Dionysius of heresy. The Roman prelate, in response, assembled a synod and demanded that his Alexandrian namesake demonstrate the orthodoxy of his own teachings.[17] Dionysius promptly complied, writing an apology "not in the spirit of controversy, but to defend his views on the issues that had brought him under suspicion."[18]

The predicament of Dionysius of Alexandria shows how a prelate could find himself in hot water for having condemned a peer and expressing his opinions on controversial issues. The Libyans not only rebuffed Dionysius's teachings but also questioned their orthodoxy, and, thus, Dionysius' qualifications to serve as bishop. At the same time, however, the Sabellian affair attests to the efforts of church leaders to settle disputes and reconcile disputants by reaching out to peers in far-flung places (Libya, Alexandria, and Rome), consulting colleagues in synods, sending embassies, exchanging letters, and showing a willingness to negotiate with those expressing contrary opinions even when disagreements had hardened into a schism.[19]

We find a similar determination to arrive at compromise solutions, sometimes engaging the entire "great church," in the Christian leaders' efforts to reintegrate into the church those who had lapsed during persecution.[20] Cyprian insisted that any solution for the *lapsi* be arrived at through discussion and collective deliberation: "An assembly for counsel being gathered together ... with bishops, presbyters, deacons, and confessors, as well as with the laity, ... we should deal with the case of the lapsed."[21] And again: "When the persecution was quieted ... a large number of bishops ... met together ... [and] balanced the decision with wholesome moderation."[22] In that case, Cyprian was willing to include in the deliberations even his greatest rivals and detractors, such as Felicissimus and his followers. Although he had expelled Felicissimus from the church for rashly communicating with lapsed Christians, Cyprian was prepared to meet with him and his party to discuss the matter, "because," he wrote, "the church is neither closed here to anyone, nor is the bishop denied to anyone. Our patience ... and humanity are ready for those who come. I entreat all to return into the Church."[23]

This generally tolerant and conciliatory attitude was rooted in the practices of the pre-Constantinian church.[24] Paul provided the model: "Have nothing to do with ... speculations.... They breed quarrels, and the servant of the Lord must not be quarrelsome, but kindly towards all. He should be a good teacher, tolerant, and gentle when discipline is needed for the refractory. The Lord may grant them a change of heart and show them the truth."[25] Where heresy was already established, the minister should be firm and resolute, but never intolerant: "A heretic should be warned once, and once again; after that, have done with him, recognizing that a man of that sort has a distorted mind and stands self-condemned in his sin."[26] By and large, bishops seem to have followed Paul's advice. When nothing else could be done to end schism, Cyprian urged his peers to "let [heretics and schismatics] perish alone for themselves who have wished to perish; let them remain outside the Church alone who have departed from the Church."[27] Only when reconciliation seemed impossible or a schism inevitable would Christian leaders proceed more openly and stridently to condemn dissent, calling it heresy, branding dissenters "rebels" and their leaders "pseudobishops," another term dear to Cyprian.[28] In these cases, prelates would not hesitate to excommunicate and expel from the community whoever refused to submit, repent, and reconcile. But when these decisions were taken collectively, in consultation with one's peers and with their consent, the threat posed to prelates' authority by doctrinal dissent was greatly reduced. In the third century, then, prelates typically reacted to theological disagreement "not in the spirit of controversy" (οὐ ... ὡς φιλονεικῶν), but with the time-honored mechanisms of dispute resolution that emphasized collective deliberation and compromise. Largely because such mechanisms existed, the network of church communities that contemporaries called the "great church" was able successfully to spread despite the enormous diversity of Christian thought and the many differences in belief and practice between church communities.

Other, more pragmatic considerations, however, also contributed to the generally conciliatory approach to doctrinal disputes. First was the growth of a corporate feeling among prelates. The rise of the clergy in the Christian community and their gradual distancing from the laity encouraged bishops to see themselves as belonging to an exalted class of Christians—a "college of priests," as Cyprian liked to put it.[29] This identification with a special group—an *ordo*, "the clergy"—evolved in the third century with the rise of the episcopate, generating feelings of fellowship, solidarity, and mutual respect among prelates, who found little to be gained by confronting their peers. As Gibbon once remarked, "Bishops obtained by their alliance a much larger share of executive and arbitrary power; and as soon as they were connected by a sense of their common interest, they were enabled to attack, with united vigour, the original rights of their clergy and people."[30] By questioning the orthodoxy and spiritual authority of their episcopal colleagues—all of whom claimed to have received God's spirit from other bishops—they might only draw attention to the fragility of their own claims to spiritual power and greater authority over other Christians. For these reasons, prelates, despite disagreements, rivalries, and personal animosities, in practice usually found it to their advantage to cultivate collegiality, equality, and respect for the autonomy of their peers.[31] By adopting cautious postures and pursuing collegial relations, they raised the status of the episcopal office and shaped the reaction to controversy within their ranks.[32] As Dionysius of Alexandria observed, "I would not think of changing the decisions [of our brothers] and of firing them to strife and contention. 'For you shall not change your neighbor's boundaries, which have been fixed by your ancestors.'"[33]

A second contributing factor was that, unlike the condemnation and excommunication of ordinary Christians, the deposition of a bishop entailed a real possibility of weakening a church already beset by dispersal, impoverishment, disengagement, and intermittent persecution. These vulnerabilities were noted again and again, in a range of regional settings: Rome, North Africa, Egypt, Pontus, and so on.[34] As already mentioned, before Constantine, it was very hard to unseat a renegade bishop. A prelate who enjoyed the support of his congregation might suffer little practical effect from a sentence of deposition for heresy, which would then result only in the weakening of the church. Deposed bishops might be tempted to form parallel communities, about which not much could be done should the faithful chose to join them, as had happened, for instance, at Antioch after Paul of Samosata's deposition.[35] An awareness of this possibility would have informed prelates' approach to their peers whenever disputes erupted.

In practice, therefore, church leaders facing dissent in their own communities or called to examine charges of heterodoxy against their colleagues stepped gingerly into the matter and worked to find consensual solutions. They consulted one another, read each other's works, sought reassurance for their own views, and met to debate, many at a time, in synods.[36] Often they invited and welcomed the opinions of learned men like Origen or Dionysius, whose erudition might throw light on difficult points.[37] The salient image in our sources of angry and frustrated bishops heaping abuse on one another in the midst of crises needs to be placed against the less exciting, larger background of consultations, negotiations, and compromise that preceded confrontation, often preventing depositions and schisms and creating conditions for the growth and expansion of the church as an empire-wide institution.[38] Although we know little about those activities, we should not underestimate their effectiveness in settling most church disputes. Furthermore, secular assemblies of all sorts provided a well-known and acceptable model for conduct. In them the most commended leaders, to whose level bishops might aspire or already belong, settled their differences not by breaking into factions, but by finding unanimity.[39]

Synods, whether local or regional, small or large, were especially important formal arenas for theological debates, providing the proper context for collective deliberation on matters of doctrine. In these gatherings disagreement could be openly voiced, doubts candidly expressed, and questions posed in a process that continuously shaped orthodoxy.[40] Although synods could be turbulent affairs, in the end, they eased tensions, creating conditions for bishops to discuss thorny theological issues and offering churchmen the opportunity to arrive at face-saving solutions. Although the views of any single individual or faction might prevail, pressure to negotiate and compromise would make a synodical decision look like a collective and "official" product, as in the affairs of Heracleides and Paul of Samosata.

In contrast to the great number of preachers, prophets, teachers, and common folk who ended up being condemned as heretics and expelled from the church, few bishops seem ever to have been investigated for heresy *by their peers* in the early church, and among those who were, even fewer suffered condemnation and deposition.[41] Only in exceptional circumstances did opposition to a bishop on doctrinal grounds result in deposition as in the example of Paul of Samosata, and even in his case, removal from office came only after several attempts to negotiate a solution. In a representative reading of the evidence I have found only ten instances before the fourth century of dissenting *bishops* who were suspected of heresy and whose views were scrutinized *by their peers*. In one case, a bishop was charged posthumously, and in five others, the accusation may not in fact have been doctrinal. Of these ten bishops, only two were condemned and deposed for their teachings: Paul of Samosata and Privatus of Lambaesis. This does not mean that there were no other cases, but the absolute number of cases matters less here than their relative infrequency, a pattern that contrasts with later times. It is probably safe to say that in the third century, despite the challenges theology posed to the authority of the church leadership, only rarely did theological dissent lead a bishop to fall from office.

To conclude, let us consider an example that further illustrates conciliatory behavior on the part of prelates in matters of doctrinal controversy. In this case, Dionysius of Alexandria addressed the controversy over the teachings of Nepos, "bishop of those in Egypt," who, in the 250s and 260s, taught that Christ's kingdom would be realized on earth.[42] Many Egyptian Christians had embraced Nepos's teachings as pious and orthodox, but many opposed them. In the Fayum, where the controversy became particularly heated, the Christian community had split, and many believers, including clerics, had seceded and formed separate congregations.[43]

We do not know how or when Dionysius intervened in the affair, only that, when he did, Nepos's ideas had already spread and divided many Egyptian churches. Notified of these events, Dionysius decided to hold a synod at Arsinoë, inviting priests, teachers, and laymen to participate and "urging them to thrash out the matter in public."[44] The synod proceeded in a most congenial atmosphere, like that of the debate between Origen and Heracleides. Acknowledging the uncertainties of the subject matter under investigation, the bishop recognized that he had held wrong, "unorthodox" (μὴ ... ὀρθῶς), views on some points, and later even admitted to having been defeated on others. Likewise, the Arsinoïtes reacted mildly and respectfully to the bishop's interference. Here is Dionysius's report:

> I tried thoroughly to criticize [Nepos's] writings. As I did so, I marveled at the soundness of argument, honesty, logical grasp, and wisdom of the brethren, as we methodically and good-temperedly went over the questions, objections, and points of agreement. And if our previous opinions seemed to have been wrong, in every way we refused to cling to them in a contentious manner. We did not shy away from difficulties. Rather, taking issue with the problems set before us as best as we could, we tried to master them. Nor, if we lost an argument, were we ashamed to admit defeat and to be won over; but conscientiously, with no dissimulation, and with our hearts turned to God, we accepted the conclusions that were drawn from the demonstrations and teachings of Holy Scripture.[45]

I can think of no better example of solidarity and effort toward consensus among clerics engaged in a doctrinal disputation. Even if Dionysius sugarcoated his report in order to emphasize harmony and consensus, there is no reason to doubt the good feelings on both sides. It is true that the case was atypical: Nepos was condemned posthumously, and the bishop of Alexandria debated the matter with local priests rather than bishops, but this makes the conciliatory attitude no less revealing.[46] Dionysius and the Arsinoïtes, despite their differences, seem to have made a notable effort to ease tension, remove controversy, and arrive at a compromise together.[47] How many times would a bishop in the fourth century—not least the bishop of Alexandria—voluntarily admit to having been "not orthodox"? Furthermore, the controversy over Nepos's teachings is also relevant because, excluding those bishops excommunicated in the early Arian controversy, Nepos is the *only* other pre-Constantinian prelate, besides Paul of Samosata, to have been condemned for his *doctrinal* views.[48]

As noted in the introduction, my goal in this discussion is not to describe individual bishops' responses to theological controversy, but to characterize a pattern of response in the actions and behavior of prelates dealing with disputes over difficult points of doctrine. To summarize, the imprecision of orthodoxy left bishops, as authorities and leaders of church communities, vulnerable to the challenges of theological speculation and dissent. By the third century, these challenges had become particularly dangerous because the rising episcopal leadership had come increasingly to base their legitimacy on claims to possess God's spirit—which claims, as we have seen, could easily be contested when bishops were believed to have strayed from the truth.

Yet in practice those challenges hardly ever posed a serious threat. As bishops emerged as leaders of Christian communities, they not only were willing to tolerate a measure of doctrinal dissonance but also developed formal and informal mechanisms to deal with disputes, minimize tension, and generate consensus through collective deliberation. When disagreements arose, as they often did, prelates tried to stay above the fray, "managing" disputes, investing heavily in debate and compromise, seeking to restore harmony, maintain unity, or mend division. And when disputes broke out in their ranks, they tended to approach them in a collegial and conciliatory manner. Paradoxically, the imprecision of orthodoxy encouraged this conciliatory approach; for imprecision could accommodate variety in interpretation, allowing bishops ample room to negotiate doctrinal differences and letting them take positions from which they could, if necessary, retreat without losing their standing. Thus, this pattern of behavior sheltered bishops from the challenges doctrinal dissent posed to their authority, so that they were rarely excommunicated or deposed by their peers for their doctrinal views.

With these preliminaries, we leave the third century. Chapter 3 examines the dispute over Arius's teachings, and the dramatic changes that followed in its wake, as church leaders broke with the prevailing pattern of tolerance and solidarity and were drawn into ever-deepening conflict. Now, challenges that prelates had once managed posed a serious threat, which they met with new strategies that reasserted their authority and created, in the process, a new style of church leadership.

PART TWO

God in Dispute

Devotion and Truth, A.D. 318–325

> *There was a time when our affairs were flourishing and brilliant, when such excesses as the wanton speaking of theology and punditry were barred from the godly halls; for it resembled playing with dice, which deceive by the quickness of their change, or entertaining an audience with all kinds of lascivious dances. And to speak of and hear about God was a novel and a fascinating thing. Piety was thought to lie in the simple and well-born speech. This present madness began with Arius.*
> GREGORY NAZIANZENUS, OR. 21 (PG 35.1093–96)

CONSTANTINE HAD JUST DEFEATED LICINIUS and begun a tour of the Eastern provinces when he received news that Christians in the East had been drawn into a bitter dispute over the teachings of Arius, a priest in the church of Alexandria.[1] The dispute had begun a few years earlier as a quarrel among Alexandrian clerics on the subject of God, but it had since spread far and wide, dividing the Christian community of Alexandria and other cities throughout the East.[2] By the time Constantine set foot in Asia, every attempt to settle the dispute had failed, unity had been broken, and the church stood on the verge of a schism.

At the heart of the Arian controversy was the recurrent problem of how to represent the relationship between God the Father and God the Son.[3] Most Christians agreed that there was only one God, who was at once Father and Son, but there had always been much debate about how to conceive and represent the relationship between them. How were Christians to believe that Father and Son were one and two at the same time? How were they to distinguish the two while maintaining that they were one?

This debate had long been informed and complicated by sophisticated arguments and concepts borrowed from Greek philosophy, especially from later Platonism. Steeped in Hellenic thought, many Christian thinkers conceived the Father as a Platonic God—an entirely spiritual being, without beginning and end, self-sufficient, perfect, immutable, impassible, and fully removed from the corrupting and always-changing world of matter.[4] They spoke of the Father as first principle and origin of all things, and of the Son or the Logos as a cosmic intermediary between perfect God and imperfect creation. The Father had created the universe through the Son, who could be compared to a Platonic demiurge. As a generated being, however, the Son was dependent on the Father for his existence, but how could a *begotten* being, dependent on another, be the *same* as an *unbegotten* one? What manner of begetting simultaneously produced identity and difference?

The Arian controversy revolved around precisely these questions. Stressing the majesty and transcendence of the Father, Arius envisioned the Son as a subordinate being, generated by the Father not out of his own being, because the Father, like the Platonic God, was "indivisible . . . unchangeable . . . incorporeal" and incapable of "suffering the experiences proper to a body," but as a "perfect creature."[5] Since the Son was begotten, Arius, taking cues from Proverbs 8:22–23, had also proposed a dimension of existence in which the Son "was not"—that is, he postulated that the Father must have preexisted the Son in eternity, before time was created.[6] Alexander, the bishop of Alexandria, utterly rejected these propositions, arguing instead that the Son had always coexisted with the Father in eternity, eternally generated "out of the Father's being," begotten from the Father in a way unfathomable to human beings.[7]

Convinced that their views represented the orthodoxy of the Catholic Church, bishop and priest and their supporters could not arrive at a compromise. This was not unusual in disputes about God, as we have seen in the examples of Heracleides and Paul of Samosata. What was new about this dispute, however, was its fierceness. In the third century, churchmen might strongly disagree with one another, but as we have seen, they tried to settle their differences in a cautious and conciliatory manner. When disputes erupted, they generally avoided confrontation and were eager to reach consensus solutions by openly debating the points of controversy.

Indeed, this was also the case at the beginning of the Arian dispute. Presented with conflicting ideas about God, churchmen in Alexandria and elsewhere at first struggled to find a solution even as they disagreed with one another. As in the past, they engaged in debates, met in synods, and consulted with their peers, seeking expert advice. Yet, at the same time that they sought a solution, they found themselves sliding more deeply into conflict, embracing with ever-greater zeal theological positions of ever-greater depth, complexity, and detail, making reconciliation ever more difficult to achieve. As the dispute escalated, persistent and widespread confrontation and conflict replaced the conciliatory approach that had been the norm in past disputes. Why and how did this happen?

Part 2 of this study will suggest that persistent theological confrontation resulted from a groundswell of devotion to the new ideas about God formulated in Alexandria[8]—devotion that, for reasons discussed below, compelled churchmen to define and represent God with much greater precision and forcefulness than before, and that swept up churchmen and ordinary believers alike in Alexandria and elsewhere. While in earlier doctrinal controversies, church leaders were willing to tolerate a measure of theological ambiguity and dissonance for the sake of unity, in Alexandria, the pursuit of precision not only made compromise much harder to achieve but also encouraged even greater attachment to a particular view of the truth.

Yet the main point of the chapters in part 2 is to discuss how this engagement in theological confrontation gave birth to a new style of church leadership. Chapters 3–6 attempt to show how churchmen, claiming to possess the truth of God, but repeatedly challenged by their opponents, sought to prove their orthodoxy—and thus their legitimacy as spiritual and community leaders—asserting themselves in the community, redefining their relationship with their congregations, and projecting their authority in a new and aggressive manner. In suggesting a direct, even causal, relationship between engagement in theological dispute and the emergence of a new type of church leader, part 2 proposes that the early years of the Arian controversy marked a significant rupture in the history of the church as church leaders engaged in the dispute abandoned a pattern of conduct observed in previous centuries, and produced new forms of authority in Christian communities.[9]

3

Precision, Devotion, and Controversy in Alexandria

The sequence of events leading up to the turmoil in the Alexandrian church in the wake of Arius's teachings is likely to be forever a subject of controversy.[1] Contemporary sources are few and partisan.[2] Ecclesiastical historians, writing in the late fourth and fifth centuries, drew heavily on Nicene sources or on equally biased non-Nicene authors—sources that tell little about the Alexandrian church before Constantine.[3] Documents, letters, and decrees pertaining to the early phase of the dispute must also be interpreted with caution, because most of them have come down to us embedded in the sectarian narratives they were used to support.[4] They give us a discontinuous and fragmented view of the dispute in its early stages. Although scholars have devoted much energy and time to sorting out documents and reconstructing events, they have come to no agreement on the chronological sequence of either.[5]

Later Byzantine, Syrian, and Latin chronicles are no more enlightening than the church historians. Although they draw on the same sources, they diverge on many points and often contradict one another.[6] Their authors, whose aims and methods differed from those of modern scholars, may not have found these sources in any way inconsistent.[7] The accounts of modern scholars are no less at odds with one another on chronological details and other points, with theologians and church historians emphasizing the doctrinal content of documents as the main evidence for reconstituting events and historians looking to context and narrative. Thus, any attempt to reconstruct the chronological order of events must be tentative, imprecise, and subject to revision as scholars of different backgrounds, training, and confessional affiliation privilege one or another element, source, or version of the dispute.[8]

According to one Nicene historiographical tradition, which drew on the accounts of Sozomen and Epiphanius, the dispute began with the preaching of Arius.[9] Imbued with religious zeal, "seized by an evil spirit," swollen with "Satanic pride," Arius proposed new and outlandish things, "foreign to the faith"—for example, that "before the Son was begotten, He was not," that "the Father existed before the Son in a timeless dimension," and that the Son was a "perfect creature of God."[10] Arius claimed that his faith was the faith "received from the forefathers," and that the bishop of Alexandria had always taught the same in the church.[11] In truth, it is difficult to know exactly what Arius preached; his views were often misquoted or distorted, and they evolved over time.[12]

According to another historiographical tradition, Arius formulated his views in response to Alexander's own teachings in the church, which Arius thought came dangerously close to the doctrine of Sabellius.[13] This tradition is best represented by Socrates.[14] The account of Ignatius of Selymbria, who, like Socrates and Sozomen, may have used the lost work of Gelasius of Caesarea, blends these two traditions and other Nicene material.[15] The source closest in time to the events in Alexandria, Eusebius of Caesarea, or rather, Constantine *apud* Eusebius, blames the bishop, who kept prodding local priests to express their opinions about a certain passage in scripture.[16]

Regardless of how the dispute started, almost all our sources agree that clerics tried to reconcile the disputants and suppress disagreement, and that they had enormous difficulty doing so. In looking more closely at the unfolding of this dispute, I draw on Sozomen and Epiphanius, both of whom followed sources closer in time to the events they describe; their accounts, as H.-G. Optiz noted, also converge on many points.[17]

Arius would have taught and preached his views on God first to his parishioners at the church in Baukalis, which was located, if Nicetas Choniates' information can be trusted, near the city's gymnasium, not far from Alexandria's civic and administrative center.[18] The Alexandrian church of that time had inherited a peculiar organizational structure. The city's large Christian congregation was divided into parishes assigned to priests who enjoyed a great deal of autonomy vis-à-vis the bishop.[19] In each parish, priests based in different parts of the city convened assemblies to preach and teach scripture.[20] Proud and prickly, they vied with one another, like the orators and sophists of the time, for the applause of the faithful and for prominence in the Christian community. Epiphanius implies that they often attended each other's performances, paying careful attention to what was being taught and preached.[21]

In this competitive environment, Arius's teachings would surely have been noted. Indeed, his views on God seem to have attracted suspicion as soon as they began to spread among local Christians, dividing the clergy and the faithful.[22] Both Epiphanius and Sozomen tell us that Arius's fellow priests brought his teachings to the attention of the bishop, accusing Arius of "having fallen outside of the truth" and of proposing "innovations inconsistent with the teaching of the church."[23] Alexander himself wrote that the priest Kolluthus, who led his own large congregation, had charged Arius with corrupting the faith.[24] It is impossible to prove the veracity of these accounts, but it is reasonable to suppose that Alexander would have heard of Arius's teachings from the beginning and may even have attended the priest's lectures.[25]

Sozomen writes, however, that after Arius's views became known, the bishop took a long time to react to them;[26] some authors later interpreted the delay as a sign of Alexander's favoritism toward Arius.[27] The bishop may well have admired Arius for his talents as exegete and orator, and he may even have nurtured warm feelings toward him. In Nicephorus's account, Arius, before being excommunicated, appears as one of "the leading priests in the interpretation of Scripture," and in a letter sent to fellow bishops later in the controversy, Alexander acknowledged that he had taken too long to respond properly to Arius's teachings and doings, having "come to know about [Arius's teachings] only belatedly."[28] It is more likely, however, that he did not know what to do.[29] He wrote that he first intended "to deliver the matter to silence"—that is, he had hoped that the quarrel among his priests would go away like so many other disputes in the church.[30] The subject of God had been debated many times in the church, and Alexander knew that agreement on the matter was difficult to obtain.

Alexander also had other, more pressing problems to address. The Melitian schism had continued to expand. The Melitian Christians had set up a separate church in Alexandria and were gaining ground in Egypt.[31] A certain Hieracas of Leontopolis, whose teachings had been declared heretical, continued to spread his views among Christians from the Delta to the city, and particularly among ascetics.[32] Any rash decision on his part might only have led to further controversy, which was the last thing the bishop wanted at that time.

But, according to Sozomen, the accusers of Arius kept demanding action against him and found fault with the bishop for not disciplining the priest.[33] Alexander would have known the danger of doing nothing: in ignoring Arius, he risked being accused of sharing or condoning Arius's views. Such charges might have brought Alexander himself under the scrutiny of his peers; indeed, the "heresy" of Paul of Samosata had been exposed by one of his own priests. The affair posed a challenge to the prelate; the proud and independent priests of his diocese may have shared Origen's opinion that bishops did not necessarily command greater spiritual and theological authority.[34] Alexander would have been reminded of how rivals had questioned the authority of more than one bishop of Alexandria during the persecutions of the recent past.[35]

Thus, as pressure mounted, Alexander called for a debate, summoning "the priests and other bishops who happened to be there" to discuss the points of controversy. Alexander may have intended this debate as a means to end the dispute quickly and to showcase his authority as a mediator or, as Sozomen put it, "as a judge," performing a role most appropriate to a bishop, as Cyprian had long emphasized.[36] Alexander approached the dispute as prelates typically did in their church communities: moving cautiously, appeasing fractious elements, standing above the fray, and mediating quarrels. As long as the core principles of the faith had not been blatantly contradicted, bishops waited to support fully one or another theological proposition until broad consensus had been reached. Arius may have welcomed the bishop's summons, for he seems to have come to the debates convinced that Alexander either shared his views or at least did not oppose them.[37] He may have interpreted the bishop's initial delay as a sign of sympathy for his teachings and, confident of success, may have sharpened his arguments and elaborated his ideas in preparation for the debates.

Sozomen tells us that the first debate had no winner.[38] Other debates followed, likewise inconclusive, with the "bishop first praising one side, then the other."[39] In the course of subsequent meetings, however, Arius's ideas seem to have become much clearer to Alexander, or, rather, the bishop assimilated them more fully, and as he did, he no longer wavered between sides but concluded that the priest was wrong, and moved abruptly to the anti-Arius camp.

In his own writings, Alexander gives the impression that he began to realize Arius's mistake only gradually, but full realization, when it came, struck him like a lightning bolt. As much as he may have esteemed the priest, he condemned his views, harshly rebuked him, and called off the debates.[40] Thereafter, Arius and his supporters seem to have been denied any further opportunity to explain their views to their opponents or defend themselves against the suspicion of heresy that hovered over them. The bishop's decision frustrated the Arians greatly, especially now that Arius's ideas, sharpened by the recent debates, had become more elaborate and consistent, and his belief that they represented the truth about God, ever stronger.[41] After Arius refused to accept the bishop's condemnation, the controversy expanded, and the church of Alexandria began to unravel.

Before turning to what followed, I want to consider why Alexander rejected Arius's views on God so adamantly, and what he proposed as the correct way to describe the Son's relationship to the Father. Indeed, when Alexander condemned Arius's propositions, he found that he also had to explain his own views on God. Our sources, written from a Nicene perspective, naturally claimed that Alexander could only choose the side of the truth, but in the early fourth century, the truth on the matter of God was far from clear. Although some local priests opposed Arius's teachings, not all clerics, let alone the faithful, had formed a firm opinion on the matter;[42] hitherto, there had been no need to.

In condemning Arius, Alexander may have considered several factors. The theological inclinations of the majority of local clergy, made apparent over the course of several debates, may have played a role in his decision.[43] Alexander may have thought that if he had to choose one side, Arius would more easily have been persuaded to change his mind than his accusers.[44] But to judge from his own comments, what seems to have troubled Alexander the most was the content of Arius's teachings, specifically his ideas on the Son's mutability, which carried enormous implications for the way in which Christians conceived human nature, salvation, and authority in the church community.[45]

The notion of a changeable Christ, as it emerged in the debates in Alexandria, became one of the most disputed points of the controversy. In a synodical letter composed before Nicaea, Alexander wrote: "Someone asked them [the Arians] whether the Word of God could change as the Devil changed, and they had the audacity to say that, yes, it was possible."[46] And in another letter he wrote of the Arians: "They say that He is by nature liable to change, capable of good and evil. They argue that he was made out of that which was nonexistent, completely ignoring Divine Scripture, which says that He always is, and declares the immutability of the Word and the divinity of the Word's wisdom."[47] Taken out of context, Alexander's quotations of Arius's words probably do not accurately represent the whole of Arius's thought, but what matters here is the bishop's understanding of Arius's theology rather than its authenticity.[48] And when we turn to the bishop's writings, we cannot fail to notice his deep revulsion at the idea of a changeable Son. With horror, Alexander again quoted the Arians: "'We are also able,' proclaim these wretches, 'to become sons of God, just like Him.'"[49] And a little further on, he declared an "impious assertion . . . [that His] Sonship . . . has nothing in common with the sonship of others. . . . Partaking in His paternal Divinity, His Sonship differs, in its indescribable dignity, from those who have been adopted as sons by His will [i.e., ordinary Christians]."[50]

Alexander seems to have been particularly disturbed that Arius's views on Christ made it possible for Christians to imagine that they, too, like the Son, could attain divine wisdom and perfection through moral and spiritual progress.[51] In other words, Alexander seems to have seen in Arius's propositions the implication that ordinary believers might bridge the cosmic gulf separating humans from God, reaching God's spirit *on their own*, "thinking themselves superior," as Peter, Alexander's predecessor, had once scornfully said of devout believers "[who imitated] the holy martyrs" in their quest for eternal life.[52] As we have seen, that personal and powerful contact with the spirit of God experienced through martyrdom, *askesis*, or revelation continued to have great appeal for the faithful, especially ascetically minded Christians, many of whom would have attended the heated exchanges between Arius and his opponents.[53] To the bishop (and no doubt to many Christians in the audience of these debates), Arius's idea of a "humanized" Christ had to be condemned because it seemed to open the door to a view of the church that denied prelates their monopoly of spiritual power. "For the Son," Alexander insisted, "is of an unchangeable nature, perfect ... [while] humans are subject to change and need His help"[54]—help that must come from prelates, who, filled with God's spirit, were alone capable of interpreting the word of God and saving souls.[55]

From the moment Alexander grasped more fully the implications of Arius's teachings, he was convinced that Arius was wrong. The thought of a close kinship between humans and the Son of God horrified the bishop. The image of the "Arian" Son that Alexander formed in his mind—Christ stripped of full divine attributes and the highest dignity—was unacceptable. "They forget," he wrote, "the passages [of scripture] that proclaim His glory and honor."[56] This sense of outrage at the likeness of human beings to God's Son pervades all the bishop's writings following the debates with the Arians, in sharp contrast to his cautious and hesitant initial approach to the dispute.[57]

Arius, however, may never have proposed that Christ was changeable—at least not in the manner the bishop reported—and he may even have proposed something different or many different things. In a later letter to Eusebius of Nicomedia, he stressed that the Son was "immutable" (ἀναλλοίωτος), and, more emphatically, in a statement of faith, that he was "unchangeable and immutable" (ἄτρεπτον καὶ ἀναλλοίωτον).[58] Scholars attempting to reconcile Alexander's depiction of the priest's views on the Son with Arius's own testimony have suggested that Arius intended to distinguish subtly between the Son's essential and de facto mutability.[59] Because he was a created being, the Son could not be immutable in his essence, but he was de facto immutable. Alexander and, later, Athanasius may have blurred this distinction in order to make Arius's views (in *Or. contra Arianos* 1.5) appear contradictory,[60] but it is unlikely that Alexander would fabricate his representation of Arius's theology, given that the "unchangeability" of the Son became the linchpin of anti-Arian doctrine for a long time to come.[61]

Thus, after condemning the priest, Alexander set out to underscore the vast and unbridgeable gulf that separated imperfect humanity from the Son's divinity. "The Sonship of the only begotten Son of the Father," he insisted, "is *incapable* of falling, but the ... creatures that are not God's sons by nature, but only on account of strength of character and through a gift of God, *may* fall."[62] By contrasting the perfect nature of the Son and the sinfulness of human beings, Alexander reminded Christians that they could not hope to obtain salvation on their own, and for that reason needed priests. If Arius's theology seemed to assign prelates a minor role in the salvation of humankind, Alexander sought to reassert the bishops' central place in that drama.

Alexander's reaction to Arian Christology has sometimes been interpreted as an attack on an "academic" model of the church, in which divinely inspired teachers like Arius could still claim wisdom and spiritual authority for themselves.[63] It was certainly that, but it was also, and more significantly, an attempt to control a stubborn undercurrent of personal religiosity that insisted on raising its head. The bishop's view of the Son as fully divine with the Father validated a hierarchical vision of the church led by bishops who, since the third century, had grown increasingly jealous of competing lay and clerical claims to spiritual authority. In attacking Arius's theology, Alexander not only drew a line separating bishops and teachers, but also emphasized the gulf dividing the members of the priesthood from everyone else.

Thus, to the bishop, Arius's theology would have appeared particularly dangerous, even subversive, because it seemed to call into question the central role of the priesthood in the salvation of humankind. As in any other doctrinal controversy, the dispute in Alexandria tested the orthodoxy of churchmen by compelling them to take a stand on a set of theological propositions. But Arius's theology seemed to invite Christians to consider an alternative model of church community to that under the leadership of priests alone. It is not surprising, therefore, that Alexander reacted so negatively to the priest's teachings.[64]

What happened after Alexander closed the debates? The bishop ordered Arius to renounce his views and most likely forbade him to preach, but he did not expel Arius from the church.[65] In an effort to preserve unity, Alexander first tried to persuade Arius and his followers "with exhortations and counsels."[66] He gave them time to recant, a concession that angered Kolluthus and other clerics, who demanded decisive action.[67] Even though the bishop had repudiated Arius's views, he may have been torn between the need to suppress a pernicious doctrine and the desire to keep the church united. Fearful of causing even greater controversy and disruption, he must have struggled to restrain the impulse to impose (as Cyprian had urged) the bishop's "divine and sublime power to govern the church."[68] This attitude was in keeping with a code of conduct that had governed relations between churchmen in the early church.

As Kolluthus observed, however, it was a puzzling way to end the affair. Alexander had accomplished little. On the one hand, despite condemning Arius's doctrine, he kept the priest in the fold of the church, drawing much criticism from the anti-Arian camp. On the other, by closing the debate, he left pressing questions unresolved, and the Arians baffled and unpersuaded. To Arius's opponents, condemnation of the priest may have appeared halfhearted; to the Arians, however, it looked like an arbitrary act of power.

The bishop should have known how hard it is to silence ideas and beliefs. The Arians, once condemned, refused to keep their views to themselves. They continued to preach and claim orthodoxy, putting increasing pressure on the bishop to explain his decision theologically—that is, to present his own views.[69] If Arius's teachings on God were wrong, what was right? What was the truth about the Son? It may have been then, as Alexander tried to answer these questions and articulate his own views, that the dispute deepened and the possibility of reconciliation receded even further. In order to counter Arius's propositions, the bishop assigned to the Son attributes that the Arians could not possibly accept, introducing, as a result, what amounted to a new Logos theology.[70] Socrates tells us that "with all the priests and the rest of the clerics present," the bishop took upon himself "enthusiastically to teach about the Holy Trinity, that the monad of the philosophers was in the Triad," and that the Son always coexisted with the Father, perfect, unchangeable, and immutable, only begotten, generated in a unique and indescribable way, less than the Father only in that he had been generated.[71] Sozomen says that the bishop taught that the Son was *homoousios* with the Father, but this is probably a later addition.[72]

Although Alexander crafted these ideas about God in response to Arius's challenge, his propositions were nonetheless invested with the full weight of his authority and presented as the final, orthodox word on the matter, the new point of departure for any further discussion. R. P. C. Hanson rightly called Alexander's teachings a "Rule of Faith."[73] With them, Alexander set a clear boundary between orthodoxy and heresy with respect to a subject that had proved intractable to some of the best minds in the church, one that earlier had been treated collectively, in synods, councils, and disputations, as we have seen in the affairs of Heracleides and Paul of Samosata. Perhaps Alexander took such a drastic step to convey his firm control of spiritual and doctrinal matters in Alexandria. But by offering his own detailed view of the relationship between Father and Son *and* by presenting this view as normative, the bishop not only invited controversy but also left little room for negotiation and compromise with his opponents.

Controversy over the bishop's views on the matter would have been of little consequence had Alexander not insisted that they represented the orthodox teachings of the Catholic Church. The bishop's claim on the truth in effect made his position as the head of the Alexandrian Christian community dependent on others accepting his views as valid. In other words, criticism of his theology was tantamount to a direct attack on his claim to orthodoxy and, by extension, on the legitimacy of his authority as the spiritual leader and bishop of the church of Alexandria.

And sure enough, doubts about the orthodoxy of his views soon arose within the local community and outside Alexandria and Egypt.[74] The Arians challenged the bishop, because they disagreed with what he had proposed and were dissatisfied with what his theology omitted. How, after all, was the Son generated? That was the question Arius had originally asked. Alexander, in his writings, did not answer it.[75] Instead, he contended that humans could not truly grasp the nature of so awesome a phenomenon.[76] The Son's generation was beyond human understanding—"beyond," he wrote, "the keenest apprehension of the evangelists and perhaps even of the angels." "[Only] a person in a melancholic state of mind," he noted, "would waste time describing the *hypostasis* of the Word of God."[77] To Arius, however, Alexander seemed to suggest the pointlessness and futility of pursuing knowledge about God—an astonishing, if not impious, idea not only to the Arians, but to many devout Christians who longed for knowledge of the divine and for spiritual plenitude.

Indeed, Christians must be prepared to recognize the limitations imposed by the human intellect in pursuing knowledge about God. As Origen had observed, human understanding of God was flawed and incomplete.[78] But to deny believers the possibility of asking about God or, worse, to dismiss their efforts to attain a knowledge of God, a most pious task, as a waste of time was nothing short of capricious. One implication of Alexander's reasoning was that certain topics must be forever confined to darkness, removed from the sphere of human comprehension and discourse. Many Christians would have found perfectly justifiable the bishop's attempt to draw the line between what could and could not be preached, between orthodoxy and heresy, so long as that boundary had resulted from common agreement.[79] But dictating what could and could not be known and what should and should not be investigated was new and arbitrary and difficult not only for Arians, but also for many other Christians, to accept.

The bishop's position caused further problems. To Arius, Alexander's own attempts to characterize the Son seemed clumsy and confused. "Our bishop," Arius complained, "asserts publicly that there was always the Father and there was always the Son; that the Son was always with the Father; and that the Son always existed with God ingeneratedly, eternally generate, ingeneratedly generated."[80] How could the Son be son if he was always with the Father? How could he be simultaneously generated and exist ingeneratedly?[81] Hanson and R. Williams have contended that in the war of words between the two sides, Arius deployed the same rhetorical weapons that Alexander had used against him, so as to render the bishop's doctrine contradictory.[82] In his own writings, however, Alexander, at least at first, seems to have been unable to articulate a convincing alternative to Arius's views.[83] How could his insufficient propositions represent the truth about the pure faith—the orthodox teachings of the apostolic church?

So the Arians, in their turn, rejected the bishop's views as impious, if not outright heretical.[84] Arius complained that *homoousios*—a term that may have been floated by Arius's opponents during the early debates to describe the Son's relationship to the Father—was a Manichaean, materialistic concept, "[as if] the Father were a compounded, divisible, and changeable being, possessed of a body, . . . the incorporeal God suffering the experiences proper to a body."[85] Further, to the Arians, many of Alexander's propositions appeared tinged with the heresy of Sabellius.[86] To rank the Son with the Father was to diminish the infinite majesty and unceasing glory of God or, worse, to imply the existence of two "Unbegotten" beings—a blasphemy.[87] These considerations must have filled Arius with alarm and, when the bishop declared his views the orthodoxy of the Catholic Church, Arius was left with no choice but to denounce them for their falsehood. The possibility that the bishop of Alexandria had fallen away from the truth, dragging others with him and compromising the salvation of thousands of souls, deeply troubled the priest. How could the bishop be so mistaken?

Rejecting Alexander's views, Arius, too, settled on a more decisive course of action. Alexander's condemnation of his teachings seemed to him ill advised and unjustified, but it was clear that the bishop would not back down. Alexander may initially have entreated the Arians to abandon their views, but he certainly did not intend to reopen the debate with them.[88] Arius must have realized that if he did not give up his views, he would be excommunicated and deposed.[89] We can imagine how that message was delivered: cold stares in church meetings, ugly gestures in the streets, and in the churches themselves provocative preaching of views that the priest later asserted he could not bear to hear.[90]

Arius, faced with the prospect of excommunication, circulated a statement of faith—a "manifesto" addressed to the bishop but intended more broadly to publicize his views and reaffirm his belief in them.[91] The pamphlet would help clarify his view on the mutability of the Son, which the bishop had so strongly opposed. But to give more weight to his statement, Arius looked for help outside Alexandria. Two Libyan bishops, Secundus of Ptolemais and Theonas of Marmarica, who may already have been in contact with Arius, agreed to declare their support for the priest openly and publicly and to add their names to the manifesto.[92] Their subscription would show to the bishop that Arius was indeed committed to his views and had no intention of retreating, in case doubt about that commitment was what kept the prelate from reopening debate and seeing the truth. It would also reveal to Christians in Alexandria and elsewhere that Arius counted on the support of other bishops who, like him, questioned the soundness of Alexander's views.[93] The bishop, Arius may have reasoned, would have to think twice before excommunicating all who subscribed to the pamphlet—seven priests, six deacons, and two men of episcopal rank—because to expel them all from the church would no doubt precipitate a crisis.

So I place the Arians' statement of faith here, before Arius's deposition, a last-ditch attempt on the part of the beleaguered priest to compel the bishop to reopen discussion before an impending excommunication.[94] The document is remarkable for its mixture of deference and self-confidence, signaling simultaneously the Arians' desire to work toward reconciliation and the certainty that they possessed the truth. Arius wrote:

> Our faith, the faith of our forefathers, holy papa, which we have learned *from you,* is this: we acknowledge one God, the only Unbegotten, the only eternal, the only without beginning, the only true God . . . of all things judge, ruler, governor, immutable and unchangeable, just and noble, God of the law and the prophets and the New

Testament, begetter of his only-begotten Son before all times, through whom He made all ages and all matter, begetting him not in appearance but in truth, giving him existence out of His own will, an immutable and unchangeable Son, a perfect creature of God, but not like one among the creatures, a begotten being, not like one of the things generated . . . nor as something existing beforehand and later begotten or recreated as a Son, as you yourself, *holy papa,* have many times censured those who have proposed such things. . . . Rather, we affirm that the Son was created before all time and before all ages and he received life and existence from the Father. . . . So we say that there are three realities (*hypostaseis*). But the Father, who is the cause of all things, is without beginning and exists by himself (*monotatos*), while the Son, begotten outside of time by the Father, created and established before all ages, did not exist before he was begotten, but was timelessly begotten before all things, alone he received existence from the Father. For he is neither eternal nor co-eternal with the Father. He does not have existence together with the Father, as some say of his relation with Him, proposing two Unbegotten principles. But as monad and beginning of all, God alone exists before all things. Thus, He exists before the Son, *as we have learned from you, papa,* preaching in the middle of the church.[95]

Note the deferential tone of Arius's address and the appeal to common ground: "holy papa," "we have learned from you," and so forth. The courteous language of this manifesto nonetheless suggests that the Arians had little hope of achieving reconciliation.[96] As a whole, the statement reads like a lecture and betrays a growing sense of confidence on the part of the Arians that they possessed the truth. As Williams has observed, Arius argued "clearly and pertinaciously for a distinctive and controversial interpretation of the faith received."[97] While the priest respectfully reminded Alexander of their fellowship in the faith, his words convey the sense that the time for debate had passed.[98] By reaffirming their beliefs in the manifesto in this manner, the Arians staked out a theological position, making clear that their views on God were not negotiable. Cornered by the bishop, they, too, had hardened their views and were prepared to stand their ground.

After the publication of the manifesto, if Alexander still harbored doubts about excommunicating the priest, those doubts dissipated. He could not afford to repeat the mistake of Paul of Samosata and allow a new Malchion to rise against him. He assembled a synod of Egyptian and Libyan bishops, not to discuss the matter and examine Arius's teachings anew, but, more pointedly, to depose the priest, excommunicate his supporters, and crush their "cabal."[99] The Arians seem to have been excluded from the synod's deliberations, because their views were to be the subject not of a debate, but of an inquest and a trial.[100]

Once the manifesto had been published, Alexander must also have realized that excommunicating Arius would not end the affair. He would have been aware that the Arians enjoyed the support of many Alexandrians and maintained close ties with influential churchmen outside Egypt and Libya. Yet the bishop may have reasoned that the excommunication would give him the upper hand in the controversy. By throwing the "unrepentant" Arians out of the church, Alexander would again show that he controlled the "power of the keys"—the power to decide who was in and who was out of the Christian community. And if the two Libyan bishops were excommunicated along with the priest, that would be the decision of a synod of nearly a hundred Egyptian and Libyan prelates. Alexander clearly raised the stakes of the controversy and, like the Arians, prepared himself for battle.

And indeed Arius's deposition and excommunication widened the controversy. In the grip of zeal even greater than that of Alexander, Arius, to reverse his excommunication and deposition, set out to persuade the clergy and the people of Alexandria of his orthodoxy. Unlike so many clerics who had acquiesced after their secession or expulsion from the church, the priest and his followers refused to accept that fate. The Arians always saw themselves as orthodox Christians who believed that they could find salvation only in the bosom of the great church. Alexander, in turn, worked to keep them out, to advance his own views, and to strengthen his position as head of the local church.

As the likelihood of compromise faded, the conviction of rightness on both sides of the dispute and their determination to fight for their beliefs had important consequences. Neither that conviction nor determination was new to the church. The novelty was that both sides turned conviction into action, shattering the pattern of civility and tolerance that had dominated the approach to similar disputes in a previous age. As reconciliation became impossible to achieve, both parties mobilized to engage the remainder of the clergy and to win the support of the faithful—efforts that led only to more division and ensured that the controversy would persist. As they worked to achieve their goals, the disputants discovered that they could find strength in division and conflict.

Chapter 4 leaves behind the lofty theological debates and steps into the mundane and vibrant world of ordinary Christians and popular preaching. Here, in congregations, public assemblies, private churches, and the mean streets of Alexandria, we find the souls the disputants wanted so badly to save. Ultimately, it was because of these souls that the subject of God truly mattered. And in the disputants' interaction with these faithful, we begin to see a new style of church leadership emerge.

4

Making the People a Partner to the Dispute

The progressive theological polarization in Alexandria dramatically increased the involvement and participation of the faithful in the controversy. Virtually all our sources emphasize the people's engagement in the dispute and the impact of their engagement on its course. Given the traditional lack of interest in the affairs of the people on the part of the literate classes, Christian and pagan, it is impressive how well represented ordinary Christians are in the evidence. No other doctrinal dispute of the pre-Constantinian era can provide us with such a wealth of information about popular action and its role in shaping a controversy; no other Christian dispute had so divided the faithful and generated so much unrest.[1]

To a certain extent, popular involvement in the dispute was inevitable and would have begun early on. Church assemblies were by nature "popular"—if not always well attended.[2] In these assemblies, scripture was read, interpreted, and taught to the people, though it was still necessary for preachers to make such meetings attractive and interesting. Since the third century, priests had been trying to do just that, working hard on their oratory and exegetical skills. Eusebius tells us that enthusiastic crowds flocked to hear a certain Paul of Antioch, a popular Christian preacher in Alexandria who was a heretic and the adoptive son of a Christian matron in whose house Origen had spent his years as an adolescent orphan.[3] Paul of Samosata, too, learned to endear himself to his audiences with his oratory. At his performances, the "faithful shouted, leaped, and waved their kerchiefs in the manner of a theater crowd."[4]

Thus from the very start of the Arian controversy, ordinary Christians would have been taught about God, each side preaching its own views. Alexander, we have seen, "enthusiastically" explained the Trinity in public meetings.[5] According to

Ignatius, "Alexander ... standing up ... preached to the people for a long time about the eternity of the Word of God, and of his generation without beginning and before the aeons."[6] In one of his sermons, preserved only in Latin, Alexander himself preached that, "on the third day after His death, the Lord rose from the dead, leading humans to knowledge of the Trinity."[7] Arius, too, lectured about God. At first, perhaps—as Anastasius, the ninth-century papal librarian, suggests—to select audiences, possibly in those Wednesday and Friday meetings devoted to exegesis and hermeneutics that Socrates and H.-I. Marrou have told us about. These were the days of fasting in the Alexandrian church, which made them auspicious for inspired exegesis.[8] On these occasions, Alexander himself used to tell his priests what to lecture on.[9] Arius would of course have also preached to his own congregation in Baukalis—but not overtly, openly, and publicly or with the intensity and dedication or intention to inflame and excite the public that our sources suggest became a feature of Christian preaching in Alexandria as the conflict deepened.

Our sources, conveying the impression that there was a moment when the controversy went truly "public," and popular participation particularly intensified, associate that intense participation with the expansion of popular preaching and gatherings outside churches, beyond the boundaries of preachers' congregations.[10] These popular gatherings were cause for much consternation in the imperial court. Constantine complained bitterly that Arius had "taught things which should ... not have readily been taken to *popular assemblies* or recklessly trusted to the *ears of the people.*"[11] Theodoret also tells us that Arius "taught perseveringly, not only in the church, but *in gatherings and assemblies outside of it.*"[12] Later writers were even more explicit in connecting the escalation of public preaching and popular participation in the dispute. In the epilogue of a Latin *Passio* of Saint Peter, Anastasius, drawing on Alexandrian sources now lost to us, reported that "Arius ... began to expose to the people the dogmas of scripture. He called for meetings in the church ... so that they hear the word of God. Thereafter, the false teaching began to grow not only in shadowy sermons but in the *mouth of the people.* He preached *persistently* not only in the church but in *conventicles and meetings outside.*"[13] And Ignatius wrote: "[Arius] spoke these things, and tried to attack the Logos ... through sophistical displays and in syllogisms and paralogisms. *Falling into the ears of the people,* this raised a great disturbance."[14] "Arius brought everything into the open and trumpeted [his doctrine] in the halls, *carrying many* into his impiety."[15] Syriac chroniclers embroidered this tradition, noting: "Arius was allowed to preach in a festival: he climbed on a chair and began a sermon.... The next day, he preached again the same thing."[16] There could not perhaps have been a better way to call attention to the public dimension of Arius's preaching than to say that he had begun to do so at a festival.

What motivated disputants to expand their preaching? And how did this expanded preaching affect the church leadership?

FACIENS CONGREGATIONEM: TEACHING GOD, PUBLIC GATHERINGS, AND POPULAR PREACHING

At first, the expansion of popular preaching was motivated by the need to teach the people not only about God, but also how properly to worship Father and Son.[17] The right manner of worship had often been debated in the third century as Christians struggled to define how to honor each individual person of the Divine Triad. In his treatise on prayer, Origen explained:

> Prayer *to* the Son and not *to* the Father is most out of place and in defiance of the truth.... So ... let us pray *to* God *through* Him, all with one accord and without division.... For are we not indeed divided if we pray some to the Father, others to the Son—those who pray to the Son, whether with the Father or without the Father, committing a foolish sin in all their simplicity due to lack of critical thinking and discernment?[18]

The concern to teach Christians how to pray correctly, therefore, was not new, but in Alexandria, as the idea of God came into sharp focus, the language of worship had to reflect more accurately the status of the Son in the divine hierarchy. How should I properly honor God? Should I pray equally to Father and Son? In Alexandria, the answer to these questions depended on how one conceived the relationship between the two. "To the Unbegotten Father," Alexander explained, "must be reserved his own ... glory, to the Son the proper honor that befits him.... We must worship [the Son] ... not rejecting his divinity, but ascribing him a perfect likeness ... to His Father."[19] The Arians, in turn, insisted that "He [the Father] has none of like glory.... We sing praises due to Him as without a beginning through the one who has a beginning.... There is a Triad, not in equal glories. Their subsistences do not mix with one another; one [is] more magnificent than the other."[20]

As the two sides grew increasingly aware of their different views on God, they set out actively to teach believers how to praise Son and Father in a way that reflected their notions of the deity. Teaching the people was especially important in the context of the Eucharistic celebration, when the faithful were expected to join the officiating priest with silent but "great and wondrous prayers," in order to make God's spirit descend from heaven into the bread and into their midst.[21] Here it was crucial that these prayers properly glorify Father and Son according to their attributes and rank, because only when believers praised God in the right manner could they expect to benefit from the life-giving gifts of the Spirit at communion.[22]

It was a wondrous moment when the bread became the body of Christ, but following communion, the mystical joining of Christ's flesh with the flesh of the believer was even more spectacular, because the bread, the "body of the Word," gave life to the faithful—it healed, canceled sins, and transformed and hallowed the believer.[23] "To eat God," as Caroline Bynum put it, "was a kind of deification."[24]

Theodoret of Mopsuestia explained: "The Holy Spirit flows unto us and feeds us into an immortal and incorruptible existence in anticipation of the future benefits ... when [we] shall become completely immortal, incorruptible and unchangeable."[25] Yet none of these things would happen if the prayers sent up to heaven were uttered incorrectly, the ritual performed imperfectly, or Father and Son honored improperly.[26] As Constantine himself noted, the use of improper language brought the Christian people dangerously close to blasphemy;[27] and Alexander said woefully of the Arians: "We grieve over the perdition of these men's souls"[28]—the Arians would likewise have lamented the damnation of their opponents.

Thus preachers, driven by the need to secure the salvation of fellow Christians, sought to gather the faithful with a new sense of urgency, calling frequent meetings to teach the truth about God, bringing them closer to the church and to themselves. Arius "preached on one day. . . . On the second day he preached the same."[29] Alexander "preached most enthusiastically"; Arius did so "perseveringly"—*faciens ... congregationem,* noted Anastasius, "making congregations"—lecturing to the faithful on the right way to praise Son and Father.[30] The Arians gathered in meetings "night and day" so that ordinary people could attend their assemblies before or after work—"people [who were] eager to know [Arius's] opinion."[31] The frequency and intensity of these meetings and the passion and zeal with which disputants set out to preach disrupted the pace of life in the church of Alexandria. It also affected the manner in which disputants presented themselves to make their meetings more attractive and their message more effective.

So, Arius. His personal skills and charisma had always been among his greatest assets. His style of preaching was engaging. All our sources speak of his rhetorical ability and virtuoso oratory. "Charming and well spoken," noted Constantine, "gracious with words."[32] A devilish man, whose sweetness of speech, ascetic manners, and affected habits seduced the "unpolluted hearts" of the faithful, remarked Epiphanius.[33] Arius had cultivated an ascetic "look," which he could now turn to his advantage. "He dressed in the garb of a monk, with a short-sleeved tunic, and went about with bare arms."[34] As R. Williams noted, this costume "would have identified him easily as a teacher of the way of salvation—a guru, we might almost say."[35] Indeed, to a Christian audience primed to spot signs of saintliness in their midst, such an appearance revealed purity of heart and spiritual power. As Claudia Rapp has observed, "The practice of asceticism prepares the individual for the reception of the gifts of the spirit, and thus of spiritual authority, from God."[36] Arius's public image would have inspired trust and projected authority, requirements for the priest who needed to convince his audiences that his views were orthodox.

Alexander also refashioned his image. Shedding his initial hesitation, as the controversy deepened, he portrayed himself as the stalwart guardian of a truth besieged by the "Christ-fighters." He wrote (and preached?): "These things we teach, these things we preach, these are the apostolic dogmas of the church, for which *we are prepared to die.*"[37] Such militant rhetoric (note the anaphora) was thoroughly at home in the church, but "readiness to die," like a martyr, on behalf of an idea of God, signaled a degree of commitment to a doctrinal cause rarely if ever seen in previous theological disputes. This spectacular display of devotion would not have been lost on the faithful: it was likewise calculated to convey assuredness, elicit respect, and restore confidence in the bishop.

It is not difficult to see how these novelties—the increase of rival preaching, the cultivation of charisma, and the show of piety and devotion—involved the people in the controversy. The faithful, attending frequent meetings and sermons, must have become not only more self-conscious about their own belief and the need to honor Father and Son in the right way, but also progressively more divided on what the right manner of worship must be.

In short, as the dispute worsened, preaching expanded in response to the need to teach fellow Christians how to praise God, "lest we become," Alexander remarked, "partners in sin."[38] But a consequence of this expansion of preaching more directly relevant to my own purpose was the emergence of an assertive church leadership whose vigorous sermonizing at once energized the faithful and raised their profile in the Christian community. If instructing the people about God and how to honor God continued to be a central element of preaching, as the rift between the disputants grew wider, other, more practical considerations must have convinced both sides that if they wished their views to prevail, they needed to cast a wider net, that is, to draw the ordinary faithful even more fully into the dispute and to engage them more firmly in support of their ideas. As they proceeded to do so, priest and bishop learned to mobilize the people and to channel popular power to their advantage. Here we find prelates and priests acting like true popular leaders, wielding new forms of authority, trying to settle the controversy not by debate and discussion, but by a direct appeal to the people and popular action.

ENGINEERING SUPPORT: PUBLIC PERFORMANCE AND POPULAR POWER

As the possibility of compromise receded, bishop and priest continued to assemble the faithful to teach them how to worship God, but as the competition between them became more aggressive and focused, the two sides sought not only to teach believers, but to strengthen their ties with them in order to create a broad base of support. This shift in strategy may have been inevitable, for Alexander and Arius would have realized that by winning the hearts and souls of the faithful, they could effectively challenge the validity of each other's ideas.[39] Arius was especially concerned to prove that he possessed the truth by bringing ordinary Christians and public opinion over to his side. If he succeeded, the bishop might be convinced to reopen the debate. It is important to remember that Arius and his followers hoped for a solution to the crisis that would lead to their readmission to the church.

Arius's excommunication must have been a turning point because, as the possibility of negotiation receded, winning the support of the people became ever more urgent. Cut off from the church, the priest might hope for reconciliation if he could raise widespread doubt among the clergy and people about the fairness of the bishop's decision. He had to show not only that the truth about God was on his side, but also that Alexander had abandoned it, and ordinary Christians, with their large numbers, might help him do precisely that.

Alexander, in turn, alarmed by the boldness of the "lawless" Arians and weakened by the division in the church, yet unwilling to give in to the priest, had no choice but to canvass support himself among the people to shore up his position or, as he put it, "to win back . . . the faithful deceived by those men."[40] The bishop reached out to ordinary Christians from his vantage as head of the Alexandrian see. He worked through the hierarchical structures of the church, rallying the clergy of Alexandria and the Mareotic district, seeking their support and endorsement, and demanding their loyalty and that of their congregations.[41] He deposed clerics who refused to subscribe to his views—a move that certainly provoked more controversy but must also have convinced many undecided churchmen to align themselves more firmly behind the episcopal throne.[42] He warned Christian virgins, those beacons of virtue in the Christian community, to be on their guard against the Arians, who were also actively courting their support.[43] Alexander wanted to have this highly regarded group of women on his side; many of them came from wealthy, respectable Christian families and were assiduous donors to the church.[44] As competition with the priest became more heated, their support may have become even more valuable.[45] We return to this below.

To boost his credibility in the community and to reassert his legitimacy in the eyes of the people, Alexander also sought to show that he counted on the support of bishops elsewhere. Thus, sometime following Arius's excommunication, Alexander wrote several letters to his own clergy and to churchmen in other provinces, recounting his view of events in Alexandria and declaring the Arians heretic.[46] He also circulated a *Tomos,* a petition containing a summary of his views on God, to which he asked his peers to subscribe.[47] The *Tomos* was intended partly to unite foreign bishops in a broad ecclesiastical front against the Arians,[48] and partly to give evidence to the faithful and clergy in the city that Alexander and his peers were at one in thought and sentiment. This, Alexander claimed, was "the best medicine" to restore "the people . . . deceived [by the Arians]."[49] We wish we knew how Alexander used such a document to win over the local people, but we can perhaps make some inferences.

Socrates tells us that the bishop (like Arius) "assembled a dossier of favorable missives," which he passed on to his priests, who, in turn, shared them with fellow

Christians in congregations throughout the city.[50] The dossier may also have been circulated among the faithful, either in pamphlets quoting excerpts of supporting letters (such as were used later in conciliar proceedings) or in lists containing the names of prelates declaring their support in the *Tomos*—"roughly 200," drawn from twenty-six provinces all over the East from Greece to Libya.[51] I suspect these written testimonies were read aloud to the faithful in church assemblies and lecture halls. They became, to use E. Schwartz's term, *Kampfinstrumente* that both sides used to their advantage.[52] The names of friendly bishops may also have been recited in the liturgy when a large number of Christians gathered together.[53] As they have been transmitted to us, the subscriptions to the *Tomos* do look as if they were meant to be read and reenacted in the church for greater effect, as in the following fragment:

> I, Philogonius, bishop of the Catholic Church of Antioch, praise to the highest degree the faith contained in the *Tomos* of my lord Alexander, with whom I share the same views; I assent to the faith and to the opinions of those in the holy order who are of the same mind; and I subscribe to . . . everything that has been written above.[54]

Public readings of such statements of praise for Alexander's doctrine, signed by distinguished bishops like Philogonius, "a lawyer who exchanged the courts for the pulpit," a man famous for "his science, virtue, and fear of God," would have legitimated Alexander's claims to orthodoxy and supreme authority in the Christian community.[55]

Alexander's dossier may also have found its way into the hands of Arius's followers, whom he tried to bring back to his side. The bishop's supporters may have infiltrated or heckled Arian assemblies, shouting the names of prelates who favored the bishop in an attempt to disrupt Arian meetings and undermine support for the priest. We know that Arius reacted angrily at the mere mention of the names of bishops who subscribed to the *Tomos*, whom he called "heretics and uninstructed in divine matters."[56] Such tactics to communicate unity and concord among factions and groups (and to expose Christians who had been cast out of the community) were not new in the church.[57] What *was* new was their persistent use to persuade the people of one's orthodoxy and to secure their loyalty and support. Such use bespeaks the bishop's perception that his authority in the community had eroded.

The bishop also had no qualms about resorting to intimidation and violence to recover lost ground. Alexander's relentless attacks against the Arians, portraying them as dangerous heretics, "Christ-fighters, . . . teachers of apostasy, . . . harbingers of the Antichrist," were meant to whip up zeal and passion among his followers and to rally them around him.[58] Arius complained that the bishop "spared no effort to throw us out of the city . . . because we do not agree with him."[59] Yet, to shape public perception of the dispute in his favor, Alexander actually distorted the controversy, describing it not as a disagreement over a difficult theological matter but as a struggle of the true church against the forces of darkness. He called fellow prelates and Christians to do battle against those "destroyers of souls."[60] He urged them to "unite ... against this daring madness" and insisted that "we are prepared to die."[61]

This rhetoric was dangerously inflammatory. Demonizing the Arians may have helped Alexander win support in the city, but it also deepened the division and worsened the confrontational and combative climate in the Christian community. By presenting the controversy in this manner, however, Alexander could avoid sensitive questions about the "correctness" of his own controversial views, which he expected everyone to accept as the truth.[62] The struggle against the forces of darkness justified the bishop's tightened control of and vigilance over his subordinates and their congregations, purchasing him an opportunity to project his authority more broadly and to reinforce the hierarchy of the local church.

Alexander's efforts to reassert his leadership must be seen vis-à-vis Arius's relentless campaign to recruit the greatest number of the faithful to his side. In Baukalis, he could count on the loyalty of many of his own parishioners, the more assiduous among them forming a core of supporters, the so-called "Areianoi," who may have been organized in a claque or faction.[63] Arius, however, was not satisfied with the loyalty of a few, and as the bishop continued to attack him, he tried to extend his sway over other parishes. Unlike Alexander, who could rely on loyal priests and deacons to reach out to Christians throughout the city, Arius and his followers approached the people directly, devising various strategies to establish a more personal relationship with local Christians and forge strong bonds with them.

One novel strategy was the use of music to teach about God. Scholars have often underscored the role of music in instructing believers during doctrinal disputes in late antiquity.[64] Arius may not have been the first Christian leader to make music a pedagogical tool, but his music marks a departure in early Christian hymnology because his compositions were meant, ingeniously, both to argue a point and to engage his followers. Scholarship on Arius's music has generally focused on its doctrinal content. Theologians have dissected his compositions many times, trying to discover in them the essence of the priest's theology. Few, however, have asked how these songs might have been used in practice, and what impact they might have had on those who sang them. It is worth looking into these "mechanical" aspects of Arius's compositions because they not only reveal how the teaching of doctrine, in the context of the dispute, became an enterprising, dynamic, and organized affair but also tell us how Arius sought to strike deep roots in the Christian community and to involve the ordinary faithful actively in the diffusion of his views.

After his excommunication, if not before, Arius composed songs full of doctrinal slogans, among which the *Thalia* was the only one to survive, though only in fragments quoted by Athanasius.[65] By turning theology into music, Arius could condense complex theological formulations into a "bite-size" format that was easy for believers to memorize.[66] And as M. L. West has noted, Arius tried to make these songs more appealing by casting them in a popular "subliterary" meter traditionally associated with popular spectacle and entertainment.[67] This conscious appeal to a "plebeian" cultural form made it easier for Arius both to teach his views to ordinary Christians and to involve them in spreading them

The *Thalia* was an effective vehicle for propagating Arius's views among the people because it invested in them the authority to teach doctrine. The song was intended not for the faithful to sing the praises of the deity, as was customary in early Christian hymnology, but for them to address one another.[68] When they sang the poem, believers spoke not to God, but to *one another* about God.[69] Arius conceived the poem not only to teach ordinary Christians, but also to make *them* do the teaching, as can be inferred from the following fragments:

> These are the things *I have learned* from the partakers of wisdom,
> Sharp-minded men, taught by God, and wise in all things
> ...
> And learning under God, *I have gained* wisdom and knowledge
> ...
> *I shall proclaim* clearly how by the Son the Invisible is seen
> ...
> *Understand* that the Monad was, but the Dyad was not before it came to be.
> It follows at once that the Father is God, when the Son is not
> ...
> *Understand* that He is conceived as Radiance and as Light
> Equal to the Son, the Powerful One is able to beget,
> But not one more excellent, mightier, or greater.[70]

Note the use of the first person and of the imperative, along with the argumentative tone. The piece reads in fact like a "minisermon," a cross between a statement of faith and a lecture.[71] When singing the *Thalia*, the faithful addressed themselves to fellow Christians, speaking to them about Arius's faith, which they had also now fully embraced—"I shall proclaim ... how by the Son the Invisible is seen," sang, say, a craftswoman, one of the "simple-minded" followers of Arius, whom Alexander insisted in calling "unlearned ... ignorant, and untrained,"[72] but who dared defiantly to teach about God and thus to violate the preserve of bishops and theologians. In singing the poem, ordinary Christians joined Arius in proclaiming the truth, and in that new, dignified role, they came to embody the idea of a church in which believers, once properly taught ("I have learned from the partakers of Wisdom"), were to be regarded as a source of divine knowledge[73]—an idea that we have seen Alexander could not tolerate.

Furthermore, the poem's suggestion that the faithful, guided by teachers (who clearly need not be clerics), could arrive at the truth by themselves appealed to popular piety and devotion, again reflecting a model of church community in which any Christian could seemingly attain divine knowledge on his or her own. The *Thalia* seemed to propose that the path to the truth lay in individual learning and understanding, not in conformity to the injunctions of bishops and priests—Arius exalted the human intellect, not blind obedience to authority.

Modern scholars have seen in the poem's references to learning and teaching evidence that Arius celebrated an "academic," throwback model of the church community under the leadership of bishops *and* teachers.[74] We have encountered this model before, in the third century, and we have seen how it might pose a challenge to the monarchical claims of bishops.[75] Yet in admitting the possibility (or at least in creating the illusion) that believers (in theory, according to the poem, any believer, not only inspired teachers) could "gain divine wisdom" and transmit that wisdom to others, the *Thalia* subverted the very notion of "academic," as it encouraged *all* believers to take an active role in learning and teaching the truth. Even more remarkable, this expanded model of the church was not created as a theoretical construct for learned churchmen alone, but it was meant to be enacted when believers sang the poem to one another in parish services, church assemblies, and popular gatherings.

All this was new. At the same time that the *Thalia* communicated ideas about the deity, it also taught believers to replicate in life the very vision of the church that it proclaimed, enticing them, like thousands of "Ariuses," to propagate the truth, fanning out through the city, each of them boldly reciting the hymn, dancing to its beat at center stage. This was a most unusual way to connect with the faithful—not only by recourse to a popular medium, but by integrating their experience into the content of the message. No wonder Athanasius later lashed out against the poem, saying: "Dancing away to such verses, these worthless men teach [about God], and they compare God [i.e., Christ] to human beings."[76]

We wish we knew more about the *Thalia*, how the faithful received it, how they performed it, and in what settings—in church assemblies, to be sure, but church choirs, however inspiring and uplifting, could have only a limited effect. To reach out to larger audiences in a vast and diverse metropolis like Alexandria, it was more effective to take music outside the church and to places where ordinary Christians lived and worked. Churchmen were well aware that music was integral to the everyday life of laborers, including slaves, who spent their days doing repetitive chores in houses, workshops, the fields, and elsewhere. Singing helped pace workers' tasks and pass the time.[77] In the teeming tenements and crowded workshops of Alexandria, Arius's views could perhaps spread more rapidly and more effectively among Christians (and non-Christians), who, living under the same roof or working for the same master, sang as they threaded warp on the looms, sifted flour or kneaded bread, or shared tools.[78]

The *Thalia* may well have been sung in these work settings, but as Arius sought to recruit more Christians to his side, he used music in other innovative ways, composing songs for specific groups of Christians according to their occupation. Philostorgius gives us a more precise idea of whom the priest targeted: "After being expelled from the church, Arius wrote ballads for sailors, millers, travelers, and others . . . , and through the sweetness of the melody he stole into the minds of the unlearned, bringing them to his impiety."[79] Drawing on Philostorgius, an anonymous author of a *Life of Constantine* adds further detail, noting that "[Arius] resorted to composing psalms . . . and ballads for sailors and millers as well as songs of the kind that the donkey drivers are accustomed to sing on their journeys."[80] Why target these occupations? The answer suggests how widely Arius cast his net.

In a city where shipping constituted the most important economic activity, sailors, longshoremen, dockers, skippers, and harbor workers in general certainly formed a large part of the population. Together, they perhaps comprised the largest fraction of free male workers, active not only in the maritime ports, but also in the harbors of Lake Mareotis and on the barges linking Alexandria to the Nile.[81] Many of them would have been part-time or seasonal laborers.[82] Others belonged to a mobile crowd of migrants or liturgists—sailors, stevedores, and unskilled workers (*ergatai*)—drawn out, every year, from the towns and villages of Egypt to assist with the transport of imperial grain during high season.[83] By late November, these men were out of a job.[84] Some would gladly have returned home, to their villages in the countryside.[85] Others, however, perhaps the majority, would have stayed behind, adding to the city's bustle, swelling the ranks of "those in the agora."[86]

It is not difficult, then, to see the advantages of reaching out to sailors, whose occupation placed them at the center of the city's social networks, through which ideas traveled and information flowed.[87] Sailors not only connected Alexandria to the *chora* and the world but were also in close contact with stevedores and harbor workers and, through seasonal labor, with other categories of laborers in the city.[88]

To embattled clerics, the mobility and the connections of these groups were more than sufficient reason to have them on one's side. In the low season, they would have swelled church assemblies and listened to fiery sermons just as they used to gather to hear the harangues of ubiquitous Cynic beggars in the "street corners, alleyways, and temple gates."[89] And as life in Alexandria moved southward from the docks to the Dromos, sailors mingled with the mass of humanity on the boulevards that led to lofty temples and Christian churches.[90] They hung out in the hippodrome, theaters, and steamy taverns, where many a monk would lose his soul.[91] In places of sociability—the docks, baths, theaters, taverns, shops, streets, and so on—the city's public mood was shaped, and as the dispute evolved, it became important to win the sympathies of the crowd, whose Christian elements had shown before how they might vigorously and loyally lend their support to a cause they thought worth defending.[92]

Furthermore, when the shipping season opened, "the dance of the ships" began on the Nile, and "[the sailors'] chanting," mixed with the "applause of the passengers," filled the air.[93] We can imagine these scenes of singing and clapping, the melody rising above the din of the docks or drifting from the decks of vessels plying the city's frenetic waterways.[94]—in the summer, every twelve seconds barges loaded with grain entered the canal linking the Nile to the city![95] Singing crews would have formed veritable floating choirs under the open sky. What better way to disseminate the truth about God and to unite its supporters? Could it be that Christian sailors sang "Arian" tunes to one another, to harbor workers, travelers, and onlookers—songs akin to popular nautical melodies such as the *Hymn to the Rhodian Winds* or *Sailors of the Deep Waters*, composed in the same metrical scheme as Arius's *Thalia*?[96]

Then, the millers. Like the sailors, they were integral to the social fabric of a city that thrived on the grain business. The millers of Alexandria, as in other Roman urban centers, would have been concentrated in bakeries, where milling was often combined with baking.[97] Alexandria must have had dozens, perhaps hundreds, of such establishments, several of them maintained by the state.[98] In the latter, millers and bakers would have worked in more or less coherent groups under close supervision.[99] In these places, millers could easily be reached out to *en bloc*, and, as they went about their chores and around the mills, they sang. Milling was one of those repetitive activities often accompanied by chanting. There could hardly have been a better way to teach them about God than through singing.

And, like the sailors, the millers interacted with a large number of people. They were in touch with suppliers, retailers, shopkeepers, pastry makers, and domestic servants and slaves from aristocratic households, to whom they might teach their songs and their faith. In Mediterranean cities, people often picked up the latest news in bakeries. Basil commented on the appetite for gossip of mischievous "girls at the mill," who spread slander, rumor, ideas, and perhaps also ballads, which, once learned, could be brought home, where customarily women working would "sing at the mill."[100] Did they sing "Arian" milling tunes?

Finally, the muleteers and donkey drivers, whose trade would have enabled them to carry Arius's message farther afield, also played a crucial role. In Egypt's export-driven economy, the first stages of the grain-shipping operation took place on the backs of donkeys transporting grain from farms and villages in the *chora* to the banks of the Nile.[101] But these gentle beasts were no less important in the city, where they also helped to haul grain from the fluvial ports and canals to the imperial granaries in the Neapolis and on to the sea harbors.[102] A late fourth-century papyrus refers to the "donkeys of Alexandria," and in such an enterprising city, these animals must have been ubiquitous and numerous. Their drivers would have traveled everywhere in town and in the *chora,* often in caravans, singing as they went the "travelers' ballads" and "mule drivers' songs."[103] Moreover, some of the drivers were formally organized in colleges, such as the public *onelatai* attached to the imperial post. They were also found in the service of military commanders and officers like the prefect of the annona of Alexandria.[104] The advantages of reaching out to organized groups of workers who might lend their support en bloc are clear. And teaching these workers to sing about God enabled Arius to touch a large number of ordinary Christians (and non-Christians) in the city and beyond.[105]

Arius's creative methods of winning over the people—through singing and dancing, integrating marginal groups in the proclamation of his message, enhancing the self-worth of the faithful, focusing strategically on occupational groups—had no precedent in the church. His efforts to build widespread support among ordinary Christians changed the way church leaders interacted with their congregations, making it possible for them to claim legitimacy for their views and themselves through a direct appeal to the people.[106]

But music represented only one aspect, and perhaps not even the most important one, of a larger strategy to engineer public support. We have seen how, since the beginning of the controversy, the Arians had frequently sought to gather the faithful. Alexander had vehemently condemned those meetings, calling them "workshops to fight Christ," "caves of robbers," and worse.[107] Like the bishop and his followers, Arius also read letters from bishops supportive of his views, "in order to confirm," Alexander complained, "those deceived by them ... in their impiety, as they see that the bishops ... agree with them."[108] But a novel feature of these assemblies deserves further comment: the Arians' choice of topics for scriptural exegesis and preaching. Alexander noted with surprise and indignation that, in their meetings, the Arians picked for discussion passages that stressed Christ's suffering, poverty, and humiliation, "denying the divinity of Our Savior, declaring that He was on an equal level with humans," and exalting the "works of [His] humanity."[109]

The theme of Christ's humanity suited well the Arians' claim that the Son was God's creation. But beyond that, the emphasis on the suffering and poverty of Christ would have resonated with their audiences, reminding them of the unfairness of their excommunication by a seemingly unorthodox bishop. The Arians' emphasis on the suffering of Christ would also have led to a comparison with the daily hardship of poor folk who attended their church assemblies.[110] It is worth noting here how unusual it was, in the pre-Constantinian church, for preachers to dwell on the themes of poverty and suffering in their sermons.[111] Before the fourth century, preaching about poverty centered on almsgiving and its benefits to the donor, not on the poverty of Christ or the plight of the destitute. Only later in the fourth century did the focus shift to the bodily and emotional suffering of the poor.[112] Indeed, Arius may have helped make these themes legitimate subjects of public discourse in the church.

One can only speculate about the impact of these teachings on the faithful, but the hostility they attracted from Arius's opponents suggests they had a powerful effect. The subject of poverty and humility appealed to the common experiences that ordinary believers shared with one another and with the Son of God. P. Bourdieu has called attention to how dissenting discourses derive their power less from their explicit content than from their capacity to make "unformulated experiences" public by expressing them.[113] By dwelling on the humility, suffering, and poverty of Jesus, Arian exegesis underscored the intimate bond that united the ordinary faithful and the Son of God.[114] Arian assemblies, poignant and dramatic, would have fostered feelings of fellowship and solidarity among Arius's supporters—feelings that were reinforced by preaching, singing, and the settings and circumstances in which those meetings took place.

We do not know whether the Arians continued to occupy their churches after excommunication, but if they did, they also assembled in improvised venues to celebrate the liturgy and to preach to the people—perhaps in warehouses, bakeries, or even in the city's *ergasteria*, where they could always find an audience, or in the communal courtyards of the tenements where the poor lived.[115] Instead of waiting for the people to come to church, Arius may have tried to take the cult directly to the people.

As Theodoret noted, the Arians sought the people "not only in churches, but in open meetings, assemblies, and *going from house to house*," visiting the faithful, linking up with them, and presumably also making arrangements to tend to the needy and the ill, according to a long-established custom in the church that had special significance in times of persecution, "lest the people, absent the pastor, be weakened before the faithlessness of so many."[116] The expulsion of the Arians from the church and the bishop's hostility toward them would have justified these efforts, even though, as the bishop noted, they lived in a "time of peace." By reaching out to the people, the Arians sought to establish a new, closer, and more personal relationship with the faithful as the dispute continued to escalate.

The warm atmosphere of house meetings would have further strengthened ties of fellowship among Arius's followers. Christians had often gathered in private homes, the property or the gift of wealthy patrons, in Alexandria as elsewhere.[117] H. Maier has shown how persecuted Christians, before and after Constantine, were often forced to retreat into private, domestic space, where they could safely meet, worship, and teach their faith.[118] In the early fourth century, some of the private houses frequented by the Arians may also have functioned as safe and well-known gathering points—clandestine "shelters" that could be "reactivated" in times of persecution.[119] In these settings, in the flickering light of candles and lamps, amid singing and dancing, devout Christians could bond with one another and learn about God from Arian sermons.

Yet, except perhaps during the brief period of Licinius's ban on Christian meetings, the Arians did not intend to hide or shut themselves off from public view as so many (Nicene and non-Nicene) Christians would later do when chased out of church buildings.[120] Nor did they seek to found an exclusive "Church of Martyrs" on the model of the Melitians. On the contrary, they saw themselves as the true church and aimed to be visible and present to all Christians.[121] We find them active all over the city, recruiting supporters and haranguing the crowd, teaching their doctrine in public spaces, approaching the people in a way rarely seen before, committed to their mission of bringing Christian souls to the truth.

Thus they went to the agora, where, "falling in with young men," wrote Athanasius, "they asked them about God," a practice that continued well into Athanasius's day (μέχρι δὲ νῦν).[122] "Then, turning to the lowly women, they addressed them with this womanish talk: 'Did you have a son before you gave birth? Just as you did not, so too the Son of God did not exist before he was begotten.'"[123] Fascinating! Like the bishop, but more insistently, they also tried to convince Christian virgins to embrace their views, "coming to [them] . . . desiring to destroy [their hearts] . . . lying and saying that 'The Word of God is created.'"[124] And when Alexander complained that "Arian preachers hunted for the applause of pagans and Jews," it is possible that they had indeed set out to evangelize aggressively among the large pagan and Jewish populations of the city.[125] Perhaps that was what "their young women" were doing when the bishop noted with disgust that they "walked about *all over town,* unseemingly."[126] We can picture delicate and devout ladies—young virgins, widows, and matrons—inspired by Arius's teachings and imbued with his missionary zeal, coming down from their secluded quarters on the city heights to venture into the sketchier areas around the harbor and the Rhakotis, and then on through the dark and rough alleys of the *laures,* on the south side, toward Lake Mareotis, in the area of present-day Moharrem Bey, where a habitation quarter filled with the rubble of haphazardly built houses has also been found.[127] There, in cramped dwellings, lived the underclass that both sides wished to bring over to their views.[128] We can imagine the wealthiest of those women moving about with a train of attendants, and with spectacular litanies, handing out alms to impress and convince bystanders of the truth of Arius's doctrine.[129]

These spatial practices—moving about town, shuttling from house to house, gathering the faithful, seeking them out in marketplaces, turning from streets to alleyways, linking churches to neighborhoods, people to churches, and preachers to people—required enormous energy and continuous performance, which, in turn, affirmed the authority of Arian leaders and inscribed "their" church in the public sphere of the city. Because the dispute required permanent performance, it helped to shape a new Christian leadership that derived its strength from a personal and unmediated relationship with the faithful, the appeal of a holy cause, and the ability to mobilize large numbers of people. Did these efforts create a base of support? Our sources speak only generally and not very informatively, but the strident complaints of contemporaries about Arius's activities suggest that the Arians were at least able to earn the confidence, loyalty, and support of many local Christians.

After Arius was excommunicated, no fewer than seven hundred virgins left the church with him—an exaggerated figure, no doubt, but one that, as S. Elm notes, "suggests large numbers."[130] We have seen how the Arians tried to persuade Christian virgins of the orthodoxy of their views. At that time in Alexandria, as D. Brakke has shown, most of these women were only loosely attached to the episcopal church, and Arius's theology, with its emphasis on individual progress in virtue, must have attracted them.[131] So it is not surprising that, inspired by Arius's teachings, many ascetic women sided with him.[132] What *is* surprising is that so many women cared so little about being excommunicated by the bishop— a sign of how strongly they felt about Arius's ideas, and of how deeply the Arians had undercut the bishop's authority. Indeed, it is possible, albeit speculative, that Arius, with his ascetic "credentials," was the first to tie a group of female ascetics in Alexandria more closely to a set of teachers and ideas, formally and systematically, in an experiment that foreshadowed Athanasius's later efforts to do the same.[133]

Some Melitians may have also sided with Arius. From the beginning of the Melitian schism until Nicaea, relations between Arius and Melitius have been controversial. As many scholars have shown, the alleged connection between Arius and Melitius in Sozomen's pre-Nicene narrative seems to have been forged at a later time.[134] For my purposes, however, the reaction of the Melitian rank and file matters more than the relations between the two clerics. Socrates writes believably about a split among the Melitians, some siding with Alexander, others offering solidarity to the Arians.[135]

Many clerics in Alexandria had supported Arius from the start, but soon after Arius's excommunication there were further defections from Alexander's camp: "Pistus and Chares, priests, and Sarapion, Parammon, Zosimos, and Eirenaios, deacons, followed the Arians and were happy to be deposed with them."[136] This second wave of depositions bespeaks the continued gains of the Arians among the local clergy. And as priests left Alexander, they may have taken with them part of their congregations, which would have further undermined the bishop's position.

Epiphanius also noted that a "great mob" moved to Arius's camp:[137] "Some because they thought he was right about God; others, as often happens with the crowd, because they took pity on men thrown out of the church, as they claimed, unjustly."[138] Again, there is no reason to doubt Epiphanius's remarks. Constantine would later note with dismay that "the *crowd* cheerfully applauded Arius," and the onset of riots and the outbreaks of violence as the dispute deepened not only suggest that both sides were able to win many followers, but also signal the depth of commitment of those followers, who were ready to harm their opponents with force if necessary.[139]

Mobilizing the faithful to commit violence ultimately became a way to show strength and intimidate one's rivals. Collective violence became increasingly common as the two sides vied to gain the allegiance of the faithful, to occupy cultic spaces, and to frequent the holy places that defined the true church. "The Arians," Alexander wrote, "raised persecutions and seditions every day."[140] And Arius complained, "The bishop oppresses us badly and persecutes us."[141] Alexander's attacks may have prompted Arius to turn to the city authorities for help.[142]

Indeed, as more people became involved, the dispute moved from the confined and controllable setting of church assemblies and house meetings into a more public, popular, unpredictable, and volatile arena.[143] As tension rose, confrontation became inevitable: "people rising against people cutting down one another";[144] "the holiest flock divided in support of either side . . . divided in the spirit of contention."[145] Nicephorus reports an incident in which a "mob . . . massed in the agora, taking sides, some lending their support to one party and others to another. [They] took arms against one another, using their tongues for spears, biting into each other."[146] Some of these clashes would have been orchestrated, but church leaders might not always have been responsible for them.[147] In fact, one wonders how much Arius and Alexander were able to control the actions of their followers, who may have felt empowered by their numbers in their holy duty to defend the truth. Conflict would have flared up spontaneously as rival Christians faced each other on public occasions, during religious festivals, and in the streets, markets, martyrs' shrines, and churches.[148] Convinced that the bishop was wrong, the Arians believed they were entitled to frequent Christian holy sites as they always had done, or if they had not, as they now believed necessary. It is unlikely that Alexander's followers would have allowed them unimpeded access to those places, whose control had enormous symbolic value, as we shall see below. In time, as the clashes between the two groups intensified, the people showed a remarkable capacity to act independently.[149] The attack against the statues of Constantine, an act of treason no church leader would have directed or condoned, is but one example of how far ordinary Christians might be willing to go on their own.[150] Arius himself may have decided to leave Alexandria when emotions in the city reached too feverish a pitch.[151]

Rarely, if ever, in the history of the church had a theological question so passionately engaged the people. Our awareness of the intensity of this engagement is not simply a function of the survival of a more detailed historical record of these troubles than of previous controversies. As Gregory Nazianzenus and church historians observed, the Arian dispute marked a rupture in the history of the church, and certainly the intense popular involvement had something to do with this. There had been schisms in the church before. For over a decade, the Alexandrian church had been divided over the Melitian question. Countless Christian preachers had seceded from the great church. As we have also seen, moreover, the involvement of the faithful in ecclesiastical controversy was nothing new, but the Arian controversy was far more serious. Arius not only insisted on being readmitted to the church but also galvanized the faithful as few churchmen had ever done before. Therein lay his strength and also a reason that the bishop could not ignore him as he had other dissidents.

Arius's success in winning a large following cast a shadow of doubt on the bishop's orthodoxy, challenging his authority and his qualifications to lead the church community. While the Arians remained active and strong, and while they demanded that the bishop reverse the sentence of excommunication, Alexander could not feel secure. In turn, unwilling to give in, the bishop scrambled to respond in the same currency, strengthening his grip on his subordinates, securing the loyalty of his followers, and launching his own campaign to make the people his partners in the dispute.

The showdown between bishop and priest demanded enormous personal investment and strategies of action that, if not entirely new to the church, acquired a new public dimension and evolved into sustained practices—frequent assemblies, public preaching, popular meetings, outreach to organized groups, contact with the faithful in their houses and workplaces, displays of strength, and, if necessary, violence, "every day"! What may (or may not) surprise the reader was the seemingly ethereal nature of the prize of the struggle: admission to heaven and eternal life, which could be had only with the triumph of the truth. But what a powerful force that was!

By the time Constantine learned of the conflict in Alexandria, the attempts of Alexander and Arius to recruit popular support were transforming the relationship between churchmen and their congregations. Eager to propagate his faith, Arius had not only taken pains to teach his views on God to ordinary Christians but had also built an energized, devout, and combative network of followers loyal to, and closely identified with, his views on God. Challenged by the Arians and eager to recover lost ground, Alexander had also proceeded to assert himself more forcefully. Through these efforts, both sides brought into being new forms of popular power in the public realm of church and city that would prove a source of both communal tension and personal strength.[152] This outcome did not go unnoticed by contemporaries and the next generation of church leaders, who, in the decades that followed, under Christian emperors, used popular power to consolidate their own positions as the dispute showed no signs of abating.

But before we turn to those developments, we need to follow the controversy as it moved out of Alexandria, dividing Christians in other sees. We also need to consider Constantine's intervention in the dispute. The emperor's interference may not have changed the response of churchmen to the controversy, but it dramatically raised the stakes of the dispute. As we will see in chapters 5 and 6, before Constantine embraced the church, the controversy was as much about theology as local power; after he did so, the controversy migrated to a much larger, imperial stage.

5

"For the Sake of the Logos"

Spreading the Controversy

Inevitably the controversy spilled over into other sees, engaging bishops outside Egypt. The issue was no longer simply the fate of a rebellious and heretic priest, as Alexander had insisted, but the orthodoxy of the bishop of Alexandria. Did the great See of St. Mark have a heretic at its helm? Was Alexander of Alexandria a new Paul of Samosata? Although these questions were never posed so bluntly, they could be read between the lines of Arius's correspondence with bishops overseas, which, according to Sozomen, began after Arius was expelled from the church.[1] Sozomen reported that after his excommunication, Arius wrote to the bishops "to muster their goodwill," but in fact Arius seems to have established contact with prelates in other cities at the beginning of the controversy, just as he had been in touch with bishops in neighboring Libya.[2]

Modern reconstructions of the controversy, drawing on Epiphanius, place Arius's overseas contacts in the context of his travels in Palestine (on which, see below).[3] But Epiphanius and others suggest that the priest was still in Alexandria when he first reached out to other bishops.[4] Sozomen again noted that "the situation in Alexandria having deteriorated, the Arians ... sent embassies to [the bishops of every city]."[5] Indeed, Arius may have tried to inform other prelates of events in Alexandria when he heard that Alexander had summoned the Egyptian bishops to a synod to excommunicate him. In those circumstances, outside help would have been invaluable. As we have seen, Arius had welcomed the backing of the two Libyan bishops, but the favor and support of such "venerable and formidable" prelates as Eusebius (bishop of Caesarea, scholar, and author of a magisterial history of the church who was widely known for his erudition), Paulinus ("thrice-holy" bishop of Tyre and well-to-do lawyer and municipal notable), and

Theodotus (bishop of Laodicea and "skilled physician" who, after the end of the persecutions, had, like Paulinus, used his personal fortune to restore the local church to prosperity) would have given Arius a much needed boost.[6] It is worth remembering that Arius hoped to persuade Alexander to take him back into the church. Even if Alexander had ignored the opinion of the two Libyan bishops, he surely would not dismiss the entreaties of the distinguished prelates and learned men whose support Arius now solicited.

Thus, envoys carried Arius's letters to prelates in "every city." We do not know the content of those letters, but the priest certainly provided churchmen with a précis of his theology, attaching copies of the statement of faith he had composed for Alexander.[7] He approached these prelates cautiously and carefully, to avoid giving the impression of superficiality or arrogance. He invited them to comment on his propositions, asking them to tell him "whether it was orthodox to think as he did about God," and if they disagreed with what he proposed, to teach him how to conceive the deity and then inform Alexander that he was not angry with him.[8] It was a polite request for Alexander's peers to intercede with the bishop on his behalf, but of course such a request called for those he addressed to look carefully into the disputed matter and to express their opinion about it.

Arius's request would have put many bishops in an awkward and uncomfortable position. The nature of the relationship between the Son and the Father was a frequent subject of discussion and controversy, but no churchman had been asked to pass judgment on these questions or decide for himself what was right and wrong about the Son of God, especially under such delicate circumstances—in the midst of a crisis involving the bishop of one of the largest Christian sees in the Roman Empire. Arius had asked the bishops either to confirm or to reject his teachings and, in doing so, to issue an opinion on Alexander's proceedings. The standoff in Alexandria, according to ecclesiastical custom, called for expanded debate, that is, for a synod like those that had many times assembled in Antioch to discuss the teachings of Paul of Samosata. The debate Arius wished for was not to happen—at least not until Constantine became emperor of the East. Instead, the controversy migrated to other churches and divided Christians elsewhere as no other theological dispute had done before. How did that happen and why?

Many of the prelates, compelled to reply to Arius, approached his request in the spirit of an intellectual exercise[9]—γυμναστικῶς—as Origen had many times suggested. Most would have hesitated to commit themselves to either side, as often happened in doctrinal disputes, unsure whether to embrace or to reject Arius's teachings. And indeed there may have been no need to decide either way at that stage in the controversy. But in this matter many prelates *did* take sides and expressed strong opinions. Several bishops wrote to Alexander urging him "not to admit the Arians to the church unless they repudiated their faith. Others entreated him to let them in."[10] Many prelates also communicated their views directly to the priest.[11]

Both the greatest support and the greatest opposition to the Arians came from churches in Palestine, Phoenicia, Syria, and Cilicia. Bishops Eusebius of Caesarea, Paulinus of Tyre, Theodotus of Laodicea, Athanasius of Anazarbus, Gregory of Berytus, and Aetius of Lydda endorsed Arius's teachings as orthodox, whereas the bishops of Antioch, Jerusalem, Beroea, and Tripoli strongly rejected them.[12] These prelates not only wrote back to disputants but also offered their own views on the status of the Son and his mode of generation:[13] "emission," "emanation," "co-unbegotten," "image of the true God," "a second god . . . a more human-like god," and so forth.[14] Many churchmen also wrote to other bishops, communicating their views and articulating arguments for or against Arius's teachings.[15] For instance, Eusebius of Caesarea explained to Euphration of Balanea: "We do not say that the Son coexisted with the Father, but that the Father preexisted the Son. For if they coexisted, how could the Father be father and the Son son? One first and the other second? And how could one be unbegotten and the other begotten?"[16] Likewise, albeit *contra* Arius, Eustathius, bishop of Beroea, composed and published a treatise in eight books (!) attacking the priest's theology.[17]

Some prelates overseas, challenged by Arius's teachings, sought to refine the priest's ideas, while others set out to devise alternative views on God to justify their rejection of Arius's theology. And as Christian leaders applied themselves to these tasks, the controversy not only moved out of Egypt but also gained new impulse. The effects of this expansion were felt immediately in Alexandria, where the contributions of overseas prelates to the questions Arius raised added fuel to the fire, setting in motion a chain of events that would escalate and broaden the controversy to bring the entire church into the dispute.

As we have seen, the support of overseas bishops, broadcasted prominently in Alexandria, boosted Arius's prestige in that city and encouraged him to harden his stance vis-à-vis Alexander. That so many distinguished bishops had embraced his teachings legitimated his propositions, helping him to convince many among the Alexandrian clergy and faithful that he indeed possessed the truth. That embrace also gave Arius, by now excommunicated and deposed, strength to resist the bishop's attempts to silence him and the confidence to demand that he be reintegrated into the church as an orthodox Christian.

But Alexander also reacted strongly to overseas support of the priest, hardening his resolve to keep Arius out of the church and taking drastic measures to prevent that support from having an impact on Christian public opinion in Alexandria. Arius tells us that when the bishop learned of the many foreign prelates who shared Arius's views on the Son, he declared God's curse on Eusebius of Caesarea, Paulinus of Tyre, Theodotus of Laodicea, Athanasius of Anazarbus, Gregory of Berytus, Aetius of Lydda, and all those around the East who affirmed that "God without beginning preexisted the Son."[18] To declare God's curse on a Christian was a severe measure normally used against unrepentant heretics to mark their expulsion from the church. That Alexander used the device against several respectable colleagues shows, again, how he felt threatened by the growing acceptance of Arius's theology and his increasing popularity among the Christians of Alexandria.

In anathematizing his peers, Alexander wished not only to strip the priest of the legitimacy that foreign support had given him, but also to warn potential supporters that Arius's teachings were heresy. Those who thought like Arius, regardless of rank and position, committed blasphemy and should be cut out from the church. The anathema of fellow bishops also signaled that Alexander, despite the opinions of his peers, would not reopen debate or back down from his sentence of excommunication. Here we have definitely moved away from the world of the early church, where prelates facing similar difficulties usually worked together to settle their differences, consulting one another and taking important decisions collectively.

Alexander, by condemning his peers and cursing them without debating them, selfishly claimed for himself the authority to define the orthodox position on the matter *for the entire church*. As we have seen, such behavior might be commendable with regard to subordinates but was unacceptable with one's peers and insufferable with clerics of equal rank and authority. To show contempt for fellow colleagues, to pass judgment on them, and to consider one's views more truthful than theirs was haughty, arbitrary, and contrary to the tradition of the church. It comes as no surprise, then, that Alexander's anathema deepened the crisis by offending his peers, who could not but see in the gesture more reason to believe that Arius was right. As a result, many prelates outside Egypt warmed to Arius's views, while in Alexandria the priest, increasingly frustrated by Alexander's intransigence and frightened by the growing hostility of the bishop's supporters, decided to appeal for more robust help.

Arius turned to another Eusebius, the bishop of Nicomedia, an old acquaintance, a man "honored in the [imperial] palace," and, like the priest, a former disciple of the martyr Lucian.[19] In a letter to Eusebius, Arius spoke in dark tones about the deteriorating situation in Alexandria. He explained to Eusebius his views on the Son, informed him of Alexander's anathema of his peers, and bitterly protested the bishop's persecution:[20]

> To the most longingly missed Eusebius, my lord, a believer in God, and a man of the orthodox faith, from Arius, the one unfairly persecuted by Pope Alexander on account of the truth that conquers all, on behalf of which, you, too, have exerted yourself. Greetings in the name of the Lord.[21]

The letter was meant to arouse Eusebius's indignation by reminding him of points of doctrine to which both of them supposedly subscribed.[22] Eusebius took a deep interest in Arius's predicament. He replied to the priest that "[his] ideas were noble" and orthodox.[23] Like many others, Eusebius saw the dispute in Alexandria as a struggle for the truth about the Son—no trivial matter, because the salvation of humankind hinged on the teaching of that truth.[24] Alarmed by the escalation of the controversy, however, Eusebius first tried to mediate between the disputants. More than once, he wrote to Alexander, urging moderation, pleading with the bishop to end the inquiries into the matter and to take back the Arians.[25] But his requests went unheard and unanswered. Unable to persuade the bishop, Eusebius launched a campaign in support of Arius. He prodded his peers to write to the bishop to make him change his mind, canvassing their support "on behalf of the true Logos," for "it is not right," he declared, "to be silent about the truth."[26]

Once Eusebius intervened, the controversy expanded even further, engaging even more Christians in the East; again, that engagement reverberated widely in Alexandria. Arius, as we have seen, was forced to leave the city, partly because of the threat of violence and partly to bid for the support of more prelates and their congregations.[27] The priest may have wanted to call attention to his plight and to gather enough backers to force the bishops to call for a council to debate his differences with Alexander. Together with his closest followers, Arius went first to Palestine, and then north, traveling through Asia Minor to Nicomedia.[28] As the group traveled, they visited local congregations, communicated with churchmen through envoys and couriers, and preached their views on God to Christian audiences.[29] The trip earned the Arians more supporters but also some fierce opponents.

In Palestine, Patrophilus, bishop of the important city of Scythopolis, became an influential and steadfast ally.[30] In Phoenicia, Arius may now (if not before) have won over Amphion of Sidon.[31] In Syria, Agapius mentions an unknown bishop of Hierapolis.[32] At Antioch, Philogonius would have rebuffed the priest, but many local Christians welcomed him, including a large section of the Antiochene priesthood. Leontius, another of Lucian's disciples and friend of Athanasius of Anazarbus, became a staunch supporter.[33] Likewise, George of Alexandria and the priests Stephen, Eudoxius, and Eustathius of Sebaste—men who would later be promoted to the episcopate—embraced Arius's views.[34] Further, at Antioch, the Cappadocian sophist Asterius, a layman and brilliant orator, became a zealous defender of Arius's theology. His writings and homilies would themselves become the focus of much controversy, attracting both widespread praise and condemnation.[35]

Further north, in Cilicia, Athanasius of Anazarbus, who had already expressed his support, may have helped Arius to connect with bishops Narcissus of Neronias, Amphion of Epiphaneia, and Tarcondimantos of Aegeai.[36] Together with Eusebius of Caesarea, Narcissus would boldly defend Arius's propositions in the Council of Antioch in early 325, when he chose excommunication rather than signing the anti-Arian manifesto promulgated by that council. The later theological allegiances of the Cilicians Theodorus and Macedonius, bishops, respectively, of Tarsus and Mopsuestia, suggest that they too may have lent Arius their support.[37]

To the north of the Taurus, many church leaders threw their sympathies with the priest. Philostorgius names Leontius of Caesarea, Longinus of Neocaesarea, Eulalius of Sebaste, Basil of Amasea, and Melitius of Sebastopolis.[38] Indeed, in Cappadocia and Armenia, Arius's theology seems to have found a large following. The Armenian Eustathius, who would later become bishop of Sebaste, became an enthusiastic supporter and "was counted as one of Arius's most trustworthy disciples."[39] He had apparently studied with Arius in Alexandria and may have brought Arius's views with him to Armenia.[40] In Asia and Bithynia, Eusebius of Nicomedia may have facilitated contact with other bishops, such as Menophantus of Ephesus, Theognis of Nicaea, and Maris of Chalcedon, all of whom had been Lucian's disciples.[41] With Eusebius of Nicomedia, Theognis and Maris would form the core of a party that carried on the struggle on behalf of the priest and subordinationist theology well after Nicaea.[42] But in some communities in Asia Minor, as in Antioch, the Arians also met with hostility. For instance, Marcellus, the bishop of Ancyra, who became one of their most vocal opponents, may have first expressed his dislike for Arius's doctrine as the priest traveled and taught in the region.[43]

In the meantime, Alexander, who by now was asserting in Alexandria that he was "ready to die" for the truth, realized that his silence was hurting his cause and undermining his reputation. He had to act to stop Arius's progress in other provinces. Moved by Eusebius of Nicomedia's campaign and the increasing manifestation of support for Arius from prelates overseas, he decided to address his fellow bishops formally about the crisis in Alexandria.[44] Above all, he had to neutralize Eusebius of Nicomedia, whose position as bishop in the imperial capital of the East and possible ties with the imperial family made him a powerful foe.[45] In other words, the dispute forced Alexander to explain his decisions to the rest of the church and to strengthen his position on the international stage.

Thus, the controversy, which had already reached a critical point, became truly explosive when Alexander responded to Eusebius of Nicomedia's campaign on Arius's behalf. Epiphanius, Socrates, and Sozomen all agree that this was a turning point in the dispute.[46] Alexander admitted that Eusebius's patronage of the Arians had pushed him to break his silence and move more forcefully against the Arians. Appealing to his peers, Alexander sent out an encyclical, thought to have been written by Athanasius, his loyal deacon, exhorting the bishops to unity and pleading with them not to receive the Arians into communion.[47] The letter portrayed Arius as the forerunner of the Antichrist, but its main target was Eusebius of Nicomedia. Alexander reminded the bishops that the church was "one body"; he blamed the Arians for tearing that body apart and accused Eusebius of Nicomedia of becoming a "patron of . . . apostates . . . who sought to drag the unawares into this most shameful and Christ-fighting heresy."[48] The bishop's strategy seems to have been to sow mistrust in Eusebius by playing on prelates' fears of outside interference in their dioceses by "a man who now thought the affairs of the church lay under him." He urged the bishops to disregard Eusebius's letters, to stand fast against his suasive "writings or those of the Arian faction," and to reject the Arians "lest we become partners in their sins."[49]

Although church leaders often reviled heretic and schismatic subordinates, rarely did they attack fellow bishops before many of them had consented to condemn and depose their colleagues. Here, however, in one cavalier stroke, Alexander assailed a noted bishop who also happened to be a pious and learned man, admired throughout the East. For the second time, in dealing with his equals, Alexander adopted a combative tone and a confrontational posture. True, he may have intended to signal that Arius's views on God were neither acceptable nor negotiable, and his letter may indeed have hampered Arius's progress and reversed some of his gains (see below), but his assault on Eusebius was callous and enormously divisive. It produced sufficient ill feeling to polarize the entire Eastern church. "From that moment," Sozomen wrote, "the zeal for controversy burned more fiercely on both sides, and the strife turned for the worse."[50]

Eusebius, although furious that "Alexander had spoken so ill of him in his letter," continued, with studied tact, to plead with the bishop, asking him to relent and receive the Arians, and urging "the bishops in every city not to concur with Alexander."[51] Epiphanius writes that a frantic exchange of letters followed Alexander's encyclical. Many churchmen wrote back to the bishop apologizing, though not always in good faith, for having received the Arians; others pleaded with him to soften his stance and end the dispute.[52] An exasperated Eusebius of Caesarea claimed that the bishop had accused Arius of saying things that he had not said:[53] "With what great agony and anxiety do I come to this letter," he wrote in his reply to the encyclical. "You censure them [the Arians] for saying that 'the one who is' begot 'the one who was not.' I wonder if anyone can say otherwise."[54] Athanasius of Anazarbus, Theognis of Nicaea, and the priest George of Alexandria wrote in the same vein, expressing similar feelings, mustering arguments from scripture and the writings of earlier Christian authors, trying at once to strengthen the Arian position and to persuade Alexander to change his mind.[55]

These entreaties produced no effect. Subsequently, Eusebius of Nicomedia and other bishops, "thinking themselves insulted" (ὡς ὑβρισμένοι), assembled a synod in Bithynia, attended, according to Nicetas Choniates, by 250 prelates, who pronounced Arius's teachings orthodox.[56] The synod issued a letter inviting all Christians to enter into communion with Arius and his followers and to exert themselves to convince Alexander to do the same.[57] According to Socrates, they also insisted that Alexander's sentence of excommunication be lifted, though they prudently avoided condemning the bishop, whose own views on the Son of God were still poorly known at the time.⁵⁸ This was a triumph of sorts for the priest, albeit not exactly what he and his followers had hoped for—Alexander's recognition of their orthodoxy and readmission into communion with the church of Alexandria. Alexander gave short shrift to the decisions of the bishops in Bithynia, and to many contemporary Christians, the church would have seemed headed toward a schism.

With his teachings proclaimed orthodox in Bithynia, Arius decided to return to Alexandria, even if that meant confronting the bishop—if his views were orthodox, there was no longer reason to stay away from the city. Prudently, however, he clothed himself with legitimacy by eliciting assurances from his supporters in Palestine that it was proper for him assemble the faithful and return to preaching. A hastily assembled synod, led by Eusebius of Caesarea, Paulinus of Tyre, and Patrophilus of Scythopolis, granted him the endorsement he needed. The bishops confirmed Arius's claim to orthodoxy, already asserted in Bithynia, and restored him to his pastoral functions.⁵⁹ In a show of defiance to Alexander, Arius reentered the city and took over his church. Carrying with him the authority of conciliar decrees and a bundle of letters from distinguished bishops, he made it much harder, in theory at least, for Alexander to assail him. At this point, any harm done him would have elevated him to the status of a martyr.

Alexander recognized the danger that Arius's return posed to his authority. The priest's reinstatement by two episcopal synods cast doubt on the wisdom of Alexander's judgment and, more important, on the orthodoxy of his teachings.⁶⁰ The Alexandrian priest Kolluthus, who may have first denounced Arius to the bishop, possibly decided to break with the prelate when Arius returned, perhaps accusing Alexander of being too soft on the priest and using the priest's reinstatement as a pretext to appoint himself "bishop" of yet another schismatic community.⁶¹ The church of Alexandria continued to unravel.

Unable or unwilling to reinstate Arius, Alexander stepped up his campaign against the priest with another attempt to undo the support he had received overseas. Encouraged by the (modest) success of his first encyclical, Alexander may have realized that to discredit the priest, it was not enough to condemn his teachings as heresy and portray him as the Antichrist. The dispute with the Arians was a war of ideas—ideas that informed religious behavior, views of salvation, and Christian identity, but ideas nonetheless. To win this war, Alexander needed to present his own views on the Logos to his peers; he had to offer churchmen who remained either noncommittal or suspicious of the priest a convincing alternative to Arius's theology to unite them in a coherent anti-Arian theological front.

Alexander began by circulating a *Tomos,* containing a statement of his belief and a petition for subscriptions, following it with another encyclical that explained in great detail his own controversial views on the Son.⁶² Alexander wrote the letter to heighten the bishops' fear of challenges from subordinates, hoping to convince them that they could not afford to support the Arians, whom he again demonized, and suggesting that the Arian vision of a human-like Christ encouraged the faithful to pursue virtue and salvation on their own, dispensing with bishops. Alexander's letter dwelled at length on Arius's seditious activities in the city, painting the priest as a deceitful, power-hungry rabble-rouser who, driven by maddening ambition, had "left" the church to lead splinter communities in which believers were taught they could become like Christ. The bishop's portrait of the Arians' mobilization of fanatical crowds; their praises of Christ's poverty and suffering; their loose women, walking about the streets of the city; and the continuous cabals against the bishop offered his peers a nightmarish vision of the church that an "Arian" theology might lead to. The encyclical seems to have resonated with many overseas prelates, especially at a time when the dispute had moved beyond the higher church leadership and was mobilizing the faithful in large urban congregations and traditional small-town church communities (on which see below). To many prelates, the specter of popular unrest dividing their churches was truly frightening. Many bishops signed Alexander's *Tomos,* declaring their support for Alexander and his views, including not only undecided prelates, but also a few who had previously embraced Arius's teachings and now changed their minds.[63]

With Alexander's second encyclical, the dispute reached an impasse. Church leaders throughout the East had now positioned themselves either with those who professed the co-eternity of the Son with the Father or with those who did not. Neither side would give up its views. The dispute had sown mistrust, enmity, and acrimony among the bishops, souring relationships and adding a personal dimension to the controversy that became an obstacle to negotiation. The only hope of breaking such an impasse lay in assembling a synod in which the opposing camps could discuss their differences, but because the emperor Licinius had banned Christian assemblies—an attempt, some scholars have suggested, to contain the growing popular agitation in increasingly divided Christian congregations—a synod could not be convened.[64]

The involvement of the faithful played an important role in escalating the dispute not only in Egypt but also overseas. The views of disputants on both sides inevitably reached people in many Christian communities outside Egypt. As in Alexandria, disagreement among clerics engaged the faithful, and several communities experienced a great deal of popular unrest.[65] In Theodoret's words, "Disputes and contentions arose in every city, and in every village, concerning theological dogmas."[66] The church of Antioch was particularly affected and may have been the first see in which the succession of a bishop became deeply embroiled in the dispute.[67] In the wake of Philogonius's death, probably in late 323, and the appointment of the pro-Arian Paulinus of Tyre as his successor (if R. W. Burgess is right, in January 324), local Arian sympathizers and anti-Arians fought for the control of the church and the loyalty of the faithful.⁶⁸ Indeed, the pro-Arian priests of Antioch and like-minded bishops may have collaborated to have Paulinus transferred from Tyre. Paulinus, in his brief tenure, however (he died later that same year), may have been plagued by opposition from Philogonius's supporters, who, following Paulinus's death secured the transfer of the anti-Arian Eustathius of Beroea to replace him.⁶⁹

This quick succession of pro- and anti-Arian bishops suggests that the See of Antioch was the locus of a hard-fought battle between the two theological factions, foreshadowing the struggles that would become so common in the post-Nicene period. In a panegyric to Eustathius, delivered later in the fourth century, John Chrysostom wrote approvingly that in the years before Nicaea (but then also after) "the holy [Eustathius] fought on behalf of our church and overpowered the disease that had come like a deadly plague from the land of Egypt."⁷⁰ Eustathius, upon his transfer, campaigned to suppress and silence Arian supporters and preachers, perhaps employing the heavy-handed tactics Alexander had used in Alexandria and Philogonius had already tried in Antioch. John also praised Eustathius for sending "his men everywhere to teach, to urge, to dispute, and to block the way of the enemy."⁷¹ Arian priests and preachers were certainly doing the same, defying Eustathius by preaching to public gatherings, vying and clashing with the bishop's men to bring the Christian faithful over to their side.⁷²

As in Alexandria, Christian unrest may have become a more or less permanent state of affairs in the Syrian capital. Ossius of Corduba, who presided over a synod assembled in the city in the winter of 325, described the scene he encountered: "When I arrived in Antioch [in late 324], I found the church firmly in the grip of a great disturbance due to the teaching of certain men and the strife it had caused."⁷³ One of these preachers on the Arian side may have been the sophist Asterius, who was active not only in Antioch, but also in many churches in Syria and elsewhere. Athanasius tells us that "Asterius went around the churches of Syria and other places.... Wretched in every way, this man even sat in the place of clerics and read his little book publicly ... so that he did not cease to lead astray the uncontaminated souls."⁷⁴ Note the emphasis on public preaching, winning over the faithful, and the same sense of mission we have already encountered in Alexandria. Asterius crafted his sermons with an audience of ordinary Christians in mind: he explained in simple terms difficult points of doctrine, using analogies from everyday life, dwelling at length, as the Arians had also done in Alexandria, on the themes of poverty and the suffering of Christ.⁷⁵ Through the efforts of such preachers the dispute spread widely among the faithful, dividing Christian congregations throughout the East.⁷⁶

What fueled the controversy in Antioch and elsewhere beyond Egypt? The subject of the dispute was certainly not new. As we have seen, prelates in an earlier age had often debated the subject of God, though with less intensity and urgency than when the controversy migrated out of Alexandria. In Alexandria, I have argued, the new ideas about God that took shape in the early debates between Arius and other priests had made it much harder, however, for churchmen to find common ground for compromise. Those ideas reflected incompatible notions of church community and authority, but more important, the precision with which the disputants defined the Son of God encouraged Christians to invest themselves fully in an idea of the deity. Convinced that they possessed the truth, bishop and priest refused to compromise their beliefs, struggling to teach the faithful their ideas about the Son of God, taking those ideas into the public arena as the orthodoxy of the church. And here, as they mobilized the faithful in novel ways, both sides discovered that the support of the people helped them validate their claims of orthodoxy, which made the escalation of the conflict inevitable, both in the church and in the streets.

The same processes are evident in the expansion of the conflict outside Egypt. As prelates received and assimilated the ideas about God coming out of Alexandria, it became crucial to determine who was right and whose conception of the deity represented orthodoxy, because by upholding and teaching falsehood, prelates might endanger the salvation of their congregations. Thus, as the controversy spread to other churches, Sozomen remarked that "the same zeal to examine the issue took over the bishops everywhere."[77] The dispute first challenged prelates to take a stand, to scrutinize their own views, and to bring those views into line with one of the two Logos theologies. Forced to justify, to themselves and their flocks, the choices they made, prelates also broadened the controversy by elaborating arguments in support of either side and campaigning among their peers "for the sake of the true Logos." Then, as they brought their views to the faithful, enthusiastically teaching them the right way to honor and praise God, they also involved their congregations in the dispute, dividing ordinary Christians and encouraging them to become active participants in the conflict.

We should note, however, that, even as the controversy worsened, many bishops spared no effort to contain and confine it, to avoid confrontation, and to reopen debate. As we have seen, Arius's supporters outside of Alexandria repeatedly tried to convince Alexander to return to the debate and to consider a compromise, even after he had anathematized the Palestinian bishops and vilified Eusebius of Nicomedia. Indeed, the Palestinian bishops recommended that Arius return to Alexandria and submit himself to the bishop's authority![78] Here again we note how devotion to an idea of the truth clashed with and, ultimately, eroded the traditional method of handling disputes in the church. At the same time that prelates struggled to preserve an older way of doing things, seeking reconciliation through an appeal to fellowship and tolerance, their conviction that they possessed the truth about God and their need to teach that truth to save Christian souls made the resolution of differences increasingly irrelevant.

The outcome of the controversy might have been different. Had it not been for Licinius's temporary ban on synods, prelates might have eventually met to end the dispute and restore unity to the church, as had often happened in the past. But maybe not. We shall never know. Events beyond the control of churchmen—namely, Constantine's conquest of the East and intervention in the dispute—had a profound impact on the controversy, as we shall discover in chapter 6.

6

"To Please the Overseer of All"

The Emperor's Involvement and the Politicization of Theology

Nicetas Choniates tells us that Constantine came to know of the Arian controversy through the bishops, but it is more likely that he was first informed by secular officers, as had been the case with the Donatist affair in North Africa.¹ Local authorities in Alexandria would have been aware of the dispute from the popular unrest in the churches.² Alexander tells us that the Arians had taken the matter before the secular courts, complaining perhaps of persecution at the hands of the bishop.³ Constantine would have had informants, in Alexandria, Antioch, and other cities, reporting to him on church affairs, especially because he was planning a tour of the East, where he hoped the bishops would help him put an end to the schism in Africa.⁴ Once the emperor was informed of the dispute, however, he also sought to learn more about it from the churchmen themselves, who would have been the only sources able to outline for him the theological details of the controversy.⁵

Constantine soon discovered that the situation was worse than that in Africa.⁶ The dispute had divided church leaders and the faithful: unity had been broken, unrest had rattled the churches, and public order had been disturbed. From the perspective of a devout ruler who saw himself as "chosen by God to be the agent of His divine will," turmoil in the church was dangerous: it displeased God and threatened to bring down God's wrath on the emperor and the empire. "Strife in the church," Constantine warned in a speech at the opening of the Council of Nicaea, "is more dangerous than any war."⁷ It posed a threat to the security of the state and to public affairs.⁸ *Plurimum impediat!*⁹

Even more disturbing to the emperor were the reasons for the dispute, which, as we have already seen, baffled him. How had a "foolish and petty disagreement about words" provoked such great upheaval?[10] The disagreement seemed neither to compromise the truth nor to constitute an impediment to salvation.[11] "No new heresy," Constantine wrote in a letter addressed to Alexander and Arius, "has arisen [among you]; you have but one and the same reasoning, so that it is possible for you to come together in communion."[12] Christian quarrels hampered Constantine's plans to build a glorious future for a new, united empire. After his conquest of the East, the emperor hoped to create a new commonwealth in which all his subjects would live in peace and harmony—including pagans, who would surely give up their error and voluntarily come over to the truth.[13] Constantine expected church leaders to work closely with him to realize his vision, but their squabbles threatened to ruin his project. Indeed, how could the bishops lead God's people—the "just ones"—when they were so badly divided among themselves?[14] How could pagans find "tranquility and peace" in a church plagued by strife?[15] Disheartened by the news he received from various churches, Constantine determined to put an immediate end to the division the controversy had caused.[16] His intervention, as we shall see, politicized theology and transformed theological disputes—indeed, theological speculation in general—into highly charged affairs, full of intrigue and danger, for dissenting churchmen.

Constantine's demand for church unity led bishops to formulate an "official" definition of God, the creed of Nicaea, which the emperor received as a "gift from God," and to which he accorded a quasi-legal status. But a consequence of making belief "official" was that churchmen could subsequently achieve positions of leadership in the church only if they accepted that creed as the standard of orthodoxy. Prelates who rejected or dissented from the Nicene creed risked being challenged by Christians who had supported it, and being punished by an emperor who saw himself acting as God's agent on earth.

These developments made doctrinal disputes treacherous affairs, because, despite Constantine, doubts remained about the orthodoxy of the formula ratified at Nicaea. The Nicene creed sought to accomplish the impossible: to reconcile notions of the Son that could not be reconciled. It was hailed as the product of universal agreement, but many bishops accepted it only grudgingly, only because the emperor himself had promoted it and pressured all into an agreement. Caught between the emperor's call for unity and their own convictions, bishops who disagreed with the formula struggled to interpret creedal statements according to their own views on God, but many would eventually reject the creed or try to change it, so that orthodoxy, despite the emperor's efforts, remained in flux, and the controversy continued to churn.[17] In a world where the imperial power insisted on adherence to a standard of truth, and dissent was interpreted as defiance of God's will, the renewal of the dispute posed unprecedented challenges for church leaders.

"WAR AGAINST THE INVISIBLE ENEMY": FROM ALEXANDRIA TO ANTIOCH TO NICAEA

Constantine at first exhorted Alexander and Arius to reconciliation. In the fall of 324, he dispatched the *notarius* Marianos to Alexandria, together with Ossius, the bishop of Corduba, carrying an impartial but impatient letter to Alexander urging him and Arius to come to their senses and restore concord and harmony.[18] Differences in judgment concerning God and other points of theology were understandable, even expected, but schism and disorder would not be tolerated.[19] As Constantine saw it, the dispute did not justify a schism or the breakdown of public order.[20]

Once in Alexandria, under circumstances that remain unclear, Ossius and Alexander assembled a synod, which managed to settle the Kolluthian schism but failed utterly when it came to the Arians and Melitians.[21] Although Arius had always insisted that he be readmitted to the church, Alexander must have demanded that he repudiate his views, which Arius had no intention of doing. In fact, because he had been excommunicated, Arius may not even have been invited to the synod. But whether he attended it or not, he resisted the bishop's demands, and the synodal proceedings may have been disrupted repeatedly by popular unrest.[22] Consorting with the bishop and readmitting the anti-Arian Kolluthus to communion, Ossius may have seemed to many local Christians to side with Alexander. In the tense climate of the Alexandrian church, that perception would have sparked protests and demonstrations. Eusebius tells us that in the wake of Ossius's frustrated efforts at reconciliation, angry Christians clashed with one another and hurled insults at the images of Constantine, whose authority Ossius represented in Alexandria.[23]

Unable to negotiate a compromise in Egypt, Ossius conveyed that news to Constantine.[24] Did he blame the Arians in his report for his own failure to end the dispute? Possibly, for subsequent events reveal the Spaniard firmly aligned with Alexander. During his stay in the Egyptian capital, Ossius may have seen a copy of Alexander's *Tomos* with its two hundred or so subscriptions, evidence of the substantial support the bishop had garnered among prelates all over the East. That alone may have been enough to convince Ossius to declare himself for Alexander. The Spaniard may have reasoned that, to bring unity to the Eastern churches the emperor so desired, having the majority of bishops on one's side mattered more than achieving reconciliation with a subordinate priest. Arius may have won over the hearts and minds of many influential churchmen and a large portion of the faithful in Alexandria, but Alexander offered persuasive testimony that his own teachings appealed to a much larger constituency across the Eastern provinces. Furthermore, the Arian idea of a Son as capable of change, making progress in virtue and wisdom, may also have disturbed Ossius. That view harked back to a model of the church in which ordinary believers could still claim spiritual authority. It is unlikely that such a vision of the Christian community would have appealed to a conservative westerner like Ossius, accustomed to seeing the world through the lens of patronage and hierarchy. The idea that the ordinary faithful might become spiritually enlightened by imitating Christ was hardly in keeping with the creation of an imperial church with bishops firmly at the helm. So Ossius threw his sympathies with Alexander from the very start.[25]

Informed of the debacle in Alexandria, the emperor called a church council to deal with the matter.[26] "He made up his mind," Eusebius writes, "and announced that he must win this war against the invisible enemy that was overturning the church."[27] In late fall of 324, Constantine summoned the bishops to what was to be the largest council the church had ever seen. It was scheduled to coincide with the celebration of Constantine's *vicennalia* in late spring or early summer of 325.[28] The emperor expected to mark the dawn of a new age in a united empire by restoring peace and communion in the church.[29] The bishops were originally told to assemble at Ancyra, but the meeting was later changed to Nicaea, the city of victory, a more fitting place to commemorate a triumph over visible and invisible enemies.[30] Between the time of Ossius's mission in Alexandria and the opening session of the Council of Nicaea, however, a series of events set the stage for the council and convinced Constantine to intervene more decisively in the controversy to ensure that the council produced consensus and that the bishops put the dispute behind them.

In early 325, nearly sixty prelates attended a synod, which met in the city of Antioch under the presidency of Ossius and Eustathius.[31] The main reason for this synod seems to have been the ongoing upheaval in the Antiochene church.[32] In the synodical letter, Ossius tells us that, when he arrived in the Syrian capital, he found the local church rattled by "a great disorder" (πολλὴν ἀταξίαν), which he attributed partly to the "teaching of some individuals"[33]—a reference to the rivalry between anti- and pro-Arian preachers—and partly to a disregard of ecclesiastical canons. The letter tells us that theology—"the faith of the church," "the most pressing and most urgent issue for our brethren," was the focus of discussion.[34]

Why did this synod assemble when its agenda matched that of Nicaea? And who called the meeting? The need to elect a new bishop for the church of Antioch or to confirm an episcopal election has often been adduced as an explanation, but Eustathius seems to have already been in charge of the local church for several months with the support of most Syrian prelates.[35] Likewise, it is unlikely that Eustathius would have called a synod to confirm his own ordination when many of the synod's participants were pro-Arians from outside Syria.[36] Nor did the meeting benefit local pro-Arian priests, who would have known that many Syrian bishops supported Eustathius. The synodical issued by the council, moreover, makes no mention of an episcopal election. Rather, the bishops debated "Alexander's proceedings against Arius," and Ossius vigorously interrogated the pro-Arian Narcissus of Neronias and, most likely, Eusebius of Caesarea.[37]

I would suggest that Ossius (together with Eustathius?) called the synod of Antioch. Acting as an imperial envoy with a mission to negotiate peace among Christians in the East—the same mission that had brought him to Alexandria in the fall of 324—Ossius would have come to Antioch in the capacity of mediator, with a mandate to do everything possible to reconcile the disputants and restore peace to the church.[38] True, by the time the bishops assembled in Antioch, Constantine had already called a general council at Ancyra, but when that summons went out, it may have been too late or too inconvenient to cancel the meeting at Antioch, where many Eastern bishops would eagerly have awaited the bishop sent from the imperial court.

The synod of Antioch is important for two reasons. First, it foreshadowed many of the novelties introduced at Nicaea, one of which was the promulgation of a statement of faith that the bishops used as a criterion of orthodoxy to exclude from the church those who disagreed with it.[39] Nothing like this had ever been tried before in the church. Baptismal creeds and professions of faith had been formulated and adopted in early Christian communities. Both Arius and Alexander had also composed statements of faith, but there had never been an attempt to define God in a single formula, to turn that formula into a normative document, and to make its acceptance a test of orthodoxy for all Christians.[40] Following heated debates, the majority of prelates subscribed to Alexander's teachings as the "apostolic and saving doctrine" of the church.[41] They then put forward an anti-Arian statement of faith, to which they added anathemas against Arius's teachings—"the first known anathemas against doctrinal deviations in any Church Council."[42] Those prelates who refused to sign the statement were provisionally excommunicated until the Council of Ancyra/Nicaea.

Scholars have argued that Ossius manipulated the Council of Antioch "to close the ranks" of the anti-Arians in anticipation of Nicaea.[43] This is plausible, given the overwhelming support for Alexander's views and the outcome of the synod. But Ossius's successes must have owed a great deal to the authority he derived from his association with the emperor. His access to the imperial power would perhaps have helped to sway the undecided, and even some of Arius's earlier supporters, to reject Arius's theology and sign the anti-Arian statement of faith. It is worth noting here that, perhaps for the first time in a doctrinal dispute, prelates' personal convictions gave way to political considerations as the opinion of the emperor's emissary entered into their calculations.

To the Arians, the outcome of the synod of Antioch was ominous. The bishop closest to the emperor had turned decidedly against their views. Many Arian sympathizers, including Aetius of Lydda, Gregory of Berytus, Tarcondimantos of Aegeae, and perhaps Macedonius of Mopsuestia, threw in their lot with the majority.[44] The assembled bishops excommunicated three among Arius's most distinguished supporters—Eusebius of Caesarea, Narcissus of Neronias, and Theodotus of Laodicea—for refusing to subscribe to the statement of faith.[45] It was a bitter foretaste of things to come.

The synod of Antioch was also important because it unsettled Constantine. The emperor was surely informed of its outcome—how could he not be?[46] An imperial letter embedded in the *Historia universalis* of Agapius, the tenth-century bishop of Menbidj (ancient Hierapolis), makes an explicit reference to the council.[47] The letter is addressed to the Eastern bishops, summoning them to Nicaea: "With the first synod," the emperor writes, "having met in the *city of Antioch* in a contentious manner, we have decided to convoke another meeting in the city of Nicaea."[48] The wording of this letter, preserved in Arabic, mirrors that of another imperial missive, known only from a Syriac manuscript, communicating to the bishops the change in the council's venue from Ancyra to Nicaea.[49] When writing his history, Agapius seems to have had access (possibly in the archives of the church of Menbidj or Antakya) to a Syriac translation of a Greek source containing the emperor's letter. Some words or phrases seem to have dropped out of the text, so that parts of it seem garbled, but Constantine's reference to the synod of Antioch is unmistakable.

As far as I can determine, no one has ever discussed this document, which provides the only historical reference to the synod of Antioch other than the synodical letter extant in Syriac and first published by Edouard Schwartz with a Greek translation in 1905.[50] I suspect that this is because Alexandre Vasiliev, in his French translation of the Arabic text of Agapius's *Historia* for the *Patrologia orientalis*, substituted Ancyra for Antioch.[51] The document clearly deserves more attention than I can give here, but if authentic, it would confirm not only that the emperor was notified of the events at the council, but also how troubled he was by its outcome—the letter in Agapius refers specifically to the bickering at Antioch as one of the reasons for bringing the bishops to Nicaea, where the emperor could more closely monitor the proceedings.[52]

Constantine may have been particularly disturbed by the excommunication of three notable prelates, including the scholar Eusebius of Caesarea.[53] Despite the signs of an emerging consensus around Alexander's theology, a sizable portion of the Eastern episcopate continued to reject Alexander's views, including not only Eusebius of Caesarea but also Eusebius of Nicomedia, who repeatedly approached the emperor, "requesting some alliance . . . so that he might not be expelled from his honorable position."[54] The Arians of Alexandria may also have appealed directly to the emperor.[55]

In the wake of Ossius's failure in Alexandria, then, the outcome of Antioch did not bode well for the emperor's plans to unify Christians. By exposing deep fissures in the body of the church, the synod only confirmed the need for Constantine's personal involvement in order to show the bishops the way to a compromise. Constantine would have remembered how he had too readily dismissed the

Donatist Christians in the West. The troubled Council of Arles in 314 had alienated them, and his subsequent attempts to impose unity by force in the African church had been disastrous.[56] Now he wished to avoid those mistakes and find a truly lasting solution, which meant working together with all parties to remove, as he put it, "all points that furnished a pretext for ambiguity or dissension."[57]

As scholars have noted, the change of the great council's venue from Ancyra to Nicaea may have owed something to the emperor's desire to make some concessions to the Arian party[58]—the church of Nicaea was under the Arian Theognis, whereas Marcellus, bishop of Ancyra, had, like Eustathius of Antioch, sided with Alexander.[59] But Constantine had also made up his mind personally to attend the council, and Nicaea was closer to his capital.[60] As he later reminded the bishops, "I myself . . . as one of you, so to speak, . . . undertook to examine the truth."[61] Given the outcome of Antioch, the emperor was determined to leave nothing to chance, and at Nicaea, he decided to monitor the proceedings carefully to make sure that, this time, peace and order returned to the church.[62]

"WITH DIVINE AND MYSTERIOUS WORDS": THE "ESSENCE" OF GOD AND THE POLITICIZATION OF BELIEF

The Council of Nicaea opened in late May or early June of 325, but the proceedings of the meeting have not survived.[63] Our main sources for events at the council are the partial and partisan accounts of four participants: Eusebius of Caesarea, Eustathius of Antioch, Eusebius of Nicomedia, and the deacon Athanasius of Alexandria, who accompanied Alexander to Nicaea.[64] The ecclesiastical historians provide additional bits of information.

Drawing on these sources, we surmise that the council met for several weeks, and that the emperor joined the bishops only for the closing assembly (or assemblies?), when a solution to the controversy was expected. During the early sessions, prelates were allowed to meet on their own and, presumably, to debate freely.[65] Rufinus and Sozomen tell us that the bishops assembled "many times" to discuss Arius's propositions. "They summoned Arius to their meetings and investigated his theses with great care. . . . When the day arrived to put an end to all ambiguities, the bishops came to the palace because the emperor thought it best to join them in their deliberations."[66]

The point of debating was to reach some form of compromise between the conflicting parties. Readings of different statements of faith helped kick off the discussion.[67] Eustathius (*apud* Theodoret) reports that there was an uproar when Arius's supporters read theirs, but Rufinus and Philostorgius also note that many bishops defended the priest, including those who had subscribed to Antioch a few months earlier.[68] The pro-Alexander profession of faith of Antioch may also have been read and discussed, and, if so, it was evidently rejected by Arius, the two Eusebii, and their supporters.

The council's objective, following a precedent set at Antioch, was the formulation of a statement of faith agreeable to all parties. Since that synod, everyone had come to accept the necessity and, given the pressure for unity coming from the emperor, inevitability of producing a creed of faith that distilled the truth about God. Athanasius reports on the bishops' efforts to find the proper language to define the Son that would accommodate different opinions.[69] In practice, however, it was clear that neither side was prepared or willing to give in to the other. Alexander continuously sabotaged the bishops' efforts to reach a consensus, insisting on defining the Son in terms that the Arians, and particularly Arius himself, could not accept.[70] The bishop could not abide the thought of having the priest of Baukalis back in the city, preaching to enthusiastic followers, partaking of communion, all the while enjoying the support of Eusebius, the bishop of the imperial capital. Thus, according to Athanasius, every time the Arians and their supporters agreed to a set of attributes to describe the Son, Alexander's party was "compelled to restate and rewrite what they had said before"—that is, Alexander and his supporters repeatedly modified their own propositions until they finally introduced the term *homoousios* to define the Son as being of the same essence or substance as the Father.[71]

Alexander knew Arius could not accept this term—the priest had already criticized it as a Manichaean concept.[72] But there was more to Alexander's choice of wording than Arius's criticism of it. By imagining a Son who shared the divine essence of the Father, Alexander may have intended definitively to close the possibility of conceiving Christ as a changeable being. If the Son possessed the same essence as the Father, he must also be immutable, impassible, perfect, and eternal. The *homoousios* offered an effective antidote to Arius's blasphemy, a solution to what Alexander considered to be the most disturbing implication of the priest's theology. So Alexander became convinced that *homoousios* must be incorporated into the creed as an intrinsic attribute of Christ—the key to understanding his nature, and his relationship with the Father—and the cornerstone of Christian orthodoxy. How precisely the Son could be begotten of the *ousia* of the Father, Alexander did not bother to explain. In fact, he may have wished to shift the focus of the discussion from the specific question of the Son's generation to the related, but far more complex, subject of the nature of his very being.

Arius certainly reviled the term, and so did his supporters, arguing that "*consubstantial* is that which is from another either by partition, derivation or germination; by germination, as a shoot from the roots; by derivation, as children from their parents; by division, as two or three vessels of gold from a mass, and the Son is from the Father by none of these modes."[73] This was precisely what the unforgiving Alexander wanted, and it of course meant that the Nicene creed would never be the magical formula of consensus the emperor had envisioned. In truth, many bishops felt uneasy about the use of such a polemical term to conceive the Son's relationship to the Father.[74] The difficulty with *homoousios* resided not only in its materialistic connotation but also in its seeming introduction of an aporia—how could a *begotten* being possess the same essence as an *unbegotten* one? Alexander and Ossius did not answer that question. Nonetheless, their party seems to have yet again convinced many to join them in supporting the term. There may be a kernel of truth in Philostorgius's story of a compact between Alexander and Ossius to write *homoousios* into the creed and to send Arius into exile[75]—Philostorgius (or his source) may have incorporated into his narrative the memory of Alexander's backstage effort to elicit the assent of reluctant and exhausted bishops to include the polemical term in a creed of faith. In spirit, if not in every detail, Philostorgius's account essentially corroborates Athanasius's testimony.

Confident that the bishops would embrace the term, Alexander set out to draft a creed to present to the assembly in the final session of the council. At the same time, with Ossius, he sought disingenuously to reassure the emperor that even if no consensus had arisen on the generation of the Son, the bishops agreed on the use of *homoousios* to define the Son's relationship with the Father. Eusebius of Caesarea tells us that in the council's closing sessions, the emperor himself proposed the inclusion of the term in a statement of faith.[76] If this account is credible, and there is no compelling reason to doubt it, Alexander would have to have succeeded in persuading Constantine to accept his view on the Son, though the emperor also heeded the Arians' objections, because he addressed some of them in the final sessions of the council. Constantine's forceful intervention in the council with the suggestion that the bishops accept the term *homoousios* as defining the Son may have helped forge a temporary compromise. In the long run, however, such compromise was doomed to failure, because it was the view of one party that was being imposed.

Let us look more closely at Eusebius's account of the final moments of the council. The bishops assembled before the emperor in the reception hall of the imperial palace at Nicaea for the closing sessions.[77] Scholars have underscored the emperor's commanding effect—his spectacular *adventus,* the gold and the purple, the deference he showed to prelates, and the speech delivered in the "Roman tongue." The entire event was carefully staged to magnify the emperor's presence and instill awe in the participants. Constantine's opening speech made it clear yet again to the bishops his expectation of a solution to the crisis and the restoration of communion.[78] His burning of slanderous *libelli* that the bishops had submitted to him and his call for solidarity and forgiveness reinforced the expectation that the council would end all division:[79]

"The proper time for [mutual] accusations," Constantine declared, "will come on the Day of the Great Judgment, when the judge will come to try us all. It is not licit for me as a mere man to pay attention to these things when priests are accusers and accused—priests who, least of all, should be judged by anyone else. Come, then, let us imitate divine philanthropy and pardon one another. Let us remove all these charges and apply ourselves to matters of faith."[80]

So divided were the bishops that, despite the emperor's exhortation to solidarity, they descended into mutual recriminations as soon as the debate started.[81] In the *Vita Constantini*, Eusebius of Caesarea praised the emperor's role as an agent of consensus, reporting that he moderated the discussion patiently, listening to the arguments of each party: "He appeared mild and pleasant, persuading some, convincing others by his reasoning, praising those who spoke well, bringing all bishops into harmony, so that he left them of one mind and one judgment on every disputed question."[82] But in the detailed account Eusebius sent to his congregation, he tells how, despite this mild attitude, Constantine did not hesitate to use his authority to extract from the bishops the compromise he so much wanted.

According to Eusebius's letter, the crucial moment in the proceedings came when Eusebius himself was called to give testimony of his faith to the assembled bishops, probably, as scholars have argued, because he had been excommunicated at Antioch. Eusebius proceeded to read a carefully crafted but vague statement of faith describing the Son and the Father in simple, scriptural terms, avoiding the precise theological language that had sparked controversy.[83] Then, to the surprise of all present, the emperor declared that he approved Eusebius's creed and urged everyone to embrace it—with the epithet *homoousios*, inserted into the creed to describe how the Son related to the Father. Constantine defended the addition of the term, arguing that it did not contradict Eusebius's creed because "it did not indicate corporeal affections, nor division or some separation from the Father.... For the incorporeal nature cannot undergo corporeal affections. It is proper to conceive these things with divine and mysterious words."[84]

Given the emperor's surprising endorsement of Eusebius's creed and, by extension, of Eusebius himself as an orthodox Christian, it is unlikely that Constantine had joined an anti-Arian conspiracy out of some deep-seated conviction that Alexander alone possessed the truth. Instead, the emperor's approach suggests his continuing pragmatic effort—genuine if somewhat clumsy—to appease both sides, to reconcile them, and to find a lasting solution to the crisis. In the days leading up to the final sessions of the council, Constantine may have reckoned that the chances of the bishops settling the dispute on their own again looked grim. After weeks of continuous debate, disagreement persisted and may even have become more entrenched than at Antioch: on the one hand, Alexander insisted on a solution that excluded Arius (or forced the priest to condemn his own views); on the other, support for the *homoousios*, outside the inner circle of Alexander's allies, was lukewarm and among the Arians, nonexistent. If Alexander's views could not be dismissed because, except for the controversial *homoousios*, they seemingly enjoyed the support of the majority and thus represented the best hope to restore concord, Constantine knew he had to convince Alexander's opponents that *homoousios* best described the status of the Son vis-à-vis the Father.[85]

We should not think, however, that Constantine knew exactly how to proceeed or that the outcome of the council was in any way predetermined. The emperor may have pounced on the opportunity afforded by the assembly's generally favorable reaction to Eusebius's creed as an opening, a golden chance for a compromise in making concessions to both sides: to Alexander, by introducing the *homoousios*; to the Arians, by praising Eusebius, whom Constantine may have sincerely admired, openly declaring his views orthodox, glossing the *homoousios* to address the concerns of the Arians, and offering them a chance to save face.[86] The emperor may have hoped that, by proposing to include *homoousios*, he would more effectively deflect criticism of the term and persuade the bishops to accept it.

It must have been a jarring moment in the council: not only was the emperor making positive doctrinal statements, but he was also trying to reconcile the views of a man who had only recently been excommunicated (and whom, despite his "innocent" creed, many considered a heretic) with articles of faith proposed by his excommunicators! Alexander would have derived little pleasure from the emperor's friendly gesture toward Eusebius—a man who had, after all, once authorized the excommunicated Arius to preach in Alexandria—but the bishop could hardly complain, not when the emperor had embraced his view of God's Son, and then not after the emperor had already shamed and embarrassed everyone by burning the *libelli* and setting an example of "godlike philanthropy." It was not easy to discount the opinions of a ruler who had built a colossal image of himself, some thirty-five feet high, and had ordered icons of himself placed at the gates of the palaces of many cities.[87] Likewise, the Arians would have found it difficult to antagonize the emperor. Constantine's gloss on the *homoousios* and his praise of Eusebius's faith may have disarmed them. At that point, any attempt to oppose the creed would have been tantamount to, at best, defying the emperor and, at worst, calling him a heretic.

One can only imagine, once the emperor finished his speech, the silence that blanketed the assembly. It did not last long. According to Eusebius, "some bishops" (οἱ δὲ) quickly set out to draw up a creed, which, in its final version, bore only a faint resemblance to his own profession of faith that the emperor had so highly praised.[88] In truth, as we have noted, the draft of the Nicene formula may have been long in the making in the scriptoria of Alexander and Ossius.[89] Philostorgius stated cynically that these two prelates had "a book ready" for all to subscribe, which "they brought to the assembly and put to the vote."[90]

When the final version of the creed was presented to the bishops, the Arians, the two Eusebii, and others did put up some resistance, but, at that stage, their opposition was largely academic.[91] Writing to his congregation to justify his own subscription to the creed, a seemingly embarrassed Eusebius of Caesarea reported having signed the formula of Nicaea only after it had been thoroughly investigated and the meaning of each phrase—"out of the *ousia* of the Father," "*homoousios*," "begotten, not made," the anathemas, and so forth—had been contested and parsed minutely.[92] But once all the necessary qualifications had been made, although they were never written into the creed, the majority of the Arians succumbed. Eusebius of Caesarea subscribed to the Nicene formula, stressing that he did so "with a view to peace."[93] Eusebius of Nicomedia and Theognis of Nicaea likewise subscribed for the sake of "the security of the churches."[94] Other pro-Arians followed them. Eustathius later remarked that Arius's supporters acted "on the pretense of peace," lest they be thrown out of the church.[95]

Once the council ratified the creed, the bishops condemned and anathematized Arius's teachings.[96] According to the anonymous author of a *Life of Constantine*, the emperor proclaimed that "if any priest, . . . deacon . . . or . . . member of the clergy refused to concur in the common sentiment of the bishops . . . he would be punished with banishment."[97] Philomenos, master of offices, "brought the creed to Arius and his followers and ordered them to choose between . . . subscription . . . or exile. They chose the latter and were cast into the depths of perdition as they deserved."[98] The Libyan bishops Secundus and Theonas also refused to subscribe and were excommunicated as heretics and banished together with Arius.[99]

Despite the emperor's sympathetic treatment of Eusebius of Caesarea and his concern to appease the pro-Arians, the Nicene creed was undoubtedly a triumph for Alexander. The idea of a Son "of one essence with the Father" made it impossible to conceive Christ as a "human-like" God, whose progress in virtue taught Christians that they, too, could take charge of their own salvation. Here was a formula of faith that assumed a wide chasm between God and humanity. Its concept of God reflected a paternalistic and condescending view of Christian salvation history—one in which an all-powerful Logos, perfect, glorious, and sharing the essence of the Father, descended from the heights of heaven to intervene in history and save wicked and helpless human souls, who were incapable of finding divine wisdom on their own. It was a top-heavy theology for an increasingly top-heavy church, led by a hierarchy wary of rival sources of spiritual power that insisted on placing the salvation of ordinary Christians and the leadership of the church firmly in the hands of bishops.

Even before the council ended, Alexander was celebrating victory. The assembled bishops wrote a cheerful letter to the churches in Alexandria, Egypt, and

Libya, congratulating Alexander for his struggle against the impious Arius. The letter claimed that the priest's tenets had been examined, rejected, and "unanimously" anathematized, especially the proposition that the Son was "capable of virtue and vice." It praised Alexander for his role as a "leader of the synod and a participant in all the proceedings." And it also invited Christians to rejoice in the restoration of peace and the "extirpation of heresy," urging all churches to receive "with great honor and abundant love . . . the holy Alexander . . . who has undergone many toils to bring peace back to you."[100] Similar letters must have been written to other troubled congregations.

Constantine, too, could finally celebrate the reconstitution of church unity. All but two obstinate bishops and a few priests had agreed harmoniously to uphold the same views on the Son of God. Thanks to Constantine's mediation, the leaders of the Eastern churches had arrived at a compromise and restored communion. There was, no doubt, something uneasy about this compromise, in which prelates such as Eusebius and Alexander, who held incompatible views on God, were declared equally orthodox.[101] Constantine knew that many bishops disagreed about the *homoousios* despite their embrace of the creed. But that may have mattered less to the emperor than the achievement of unity that "the enemy" had shattered. Indeed, in private quarters, surrounded by friends, Constantine would admit that he believed "the mysteries of Christ to be greater than the power of words."[102] The emperor realized that a standard for orthodoxy was necessary to keep whole the body of the church, but he may have been aware that uniformity of belief could never truly be attained, because, as he also noted, there would always be different "levels of knowledge."[103] Nor, indeed, in his judgment, was such uniformity necessary as long as all were willing to share "one and the same reasoning."[104] The emperor's idea of truth was that of the philosophers, who, as he had once noted, "many times disagree with one another when they differ in their understanding, but come together again in the unity of their dogmas."[105] In his letter to Alexander and Arius in 324, the emperor had already expressed the view that "it is possible to save . . . your synod and preserve it intact . . . even when some disagreement about something minor remains . . . because not all of us are of the same mind on everything, nor is there one disposition or judgment common to all of us."[106] Although he upheld the new official symbol of faith as the truth about God, Constantine's thinking *about* the truth seems to have changed little at Nicaea, and his later actions suggest that it never changed at all.

When the council adjourned, Constantine communicated to all churches that "everything was minutely investigated until a sentence that pleased the overseer of all was brought to light so that nothing might be left to division and ambiguity in matters of belief."[107] But the emperor seems to have thought that the symbol of Nicaea admitted different levels of understanding. And later, as we shall see, once the crisis was seemingly over, in another show of "divine philanthropy," he accepted as orthodox the revised profession of faith of a "repentant" Arius that made no mention whatsoever of a *homoousios* Son.[108] If the Nicene creed had been inevitable, to Constantine, the truth about God was perhaps larger than the creed and transcended its formulaic statements.[109] Many churchmen who rejected Nicaea as the standard of truth would have shared the emperor's opinion, and these men would soon lead the effort to change or replace Nicaea with a symbol that more faithfully represented their views on God. The dispute was far from over.

"DEADLY POISONS OF DISCORD": CRIMINALIZING THEOLOGICAL DISSENT

Nicaea dealt a blow to Arius and his closest followers.[110] True to their beliefs, they refused to change their minds even as their teachings were exposed as abominations.[111] As the council drew to a close, the emperor himself also wrote letters with the force of the law to the churches everywhere, and to Alexandria especially:[112]

> Rejoice, dearest brothers. We have received from divine Providence the perfect grace, so that we now have been delivered from all error and acknowledge only one and the same faith. The devil no longer has power over us.... The splendor of truth at the command of God has put an end to dissent, schisms, and turmoil, ... deadly poisons of discord.... Arius alone, overcome by the devil's snares, was discovered to be the cause of the spread of this evil, first among you, and then with an impious mind also among others. Let us return to our beloved brethren from whom that irreverent servant of the devil has separated us. Let no one hesitate or delay, but let all return enthusiastically to the way of the truth.[113]

"Servant of the devil." Evil doctrine. Banishment. Constantine's interference in the conflict and the establishment of an "official" doctrine "criminalized" theological dissent.[114] The emperor would no longer admit disputes among Christians, because they displeased God, and to please God by uniting the church was, he believed, the emperor's duty.[115] In Constantine, the church had found not only a patron but a master.[116] After Nicaea, bishops had to learn to deal with a force that insisted on making their affairs the affairs of the state and a matter of public security—a force that made few concessions against its interests and, when it did, made very clear that it was still in charge.

In the aftermath of Nicaea, then, a suspicion of heresy no longer only posed a challenge to a bishop's claim to legitimate authority but also brought with it the frightening possibility of exile or worse. Contemporaries would not easily forget the banishment of Arius, Secundus, and Theonas—the first political exiles on account of theological dissent. A few months after the council, as we shall see, Eusebius of Nicomedia and Theognis of Nicaea also met that unpleasant fate. From the beginning of the Arian controversy to the end of 325, no fewer than seven or eight bishops and several priests and deacons were excommunicated or deposed (a record worth comparing with the evidence from the early church compiled in the appendix, "Bishops Investigated or Deposed for Doctrinal Reasons before the Arian Controversy").[117]

None of this would matter, nor would I be writing about it, had the Nicene creed produced genuine concord. But Nicaea was above all an imperial event, the culmination of the emperor's own efforts to rebuild communion in the church. In the short run, the emperor succeeded in uniting churchmen and suppressing the dispute, but the unity he achieved was fragile. As a formula of compromise, the Nicene creed put theology in a straitjacket. The term *homoousios* was too precise, too technical, and too rigid to represent different shades of opinion on the matter of God. If the creed allowed room for divergent interpretations, it did so only within a narrowly defined range of possibilities—and as we shall see, these interpretations constantly threatened to detract from its force.[118] Moreover, as a profession of faith, the formula left old questions unanswered (e.g., the manner of generation of the Son) and led to new questions that would prove equally challenging.[119]

In the months following the council and for several decades thereafter, the question of how to define God again came to the fore and continued, more than ever, to excite controversy. Despite the danger that dissent posed to the Christian leadership, churchmen would not shrink from teaching their beliefs even when they conflicted with Nicaea. Indeed, their congregations may have left them with no choice, because many ordinary Christians, less constrained to accept the Nicene formula than church leaders, clung to views of the Son deemed heretical after Nicaea. After Constantine, however, the controversy was fought in a high-voltage atmosphere in which theological positions had taken on a new political meaning. Moreover, the emperor's willingness sometimes to ignore theological differences for the sake of church unity made him an unpredictable force. Nicaea also revealed to prelates that it was not easy to steer the imperial power to support a particular doctrinal position. Despite the efforts of both sides to win over the throne, Constantine showed remarkable independence of mind, and his unpredictability added to uncertainty about the nature of orthodoxy.

Amid the feasting that marked the council's adjournment and the imperial triumph, the implications of these developments may not have been immediately appreciated.[120] The pomp and splendor of the festivities would have seduced the bishops' hearts, and the power being celebrated filled them with a sense of reverence and awe.[121] But once the dispute resumed, church leaders, to defend their views on God and to minimize the threat that controversy presented to their positions, sought to assert and build up their authority, engaging, with even greater zeal and daring, in a struggle to persuade a large number of people that they, not their rivals, possessed the truth. In practice, this meant that bishops competed fiercely and treacherously not only to bring the faithful over to their side, but also to convince the emperor that they were right and their rivals wrong. How they pursued these goals in a new environment, and the consequences of their efforts, are the focus of the next two chapters.

PART THREE

Defining God

Truth and Power, A.D. 325–361

O dearly beloved, the decisions of the Church are no longer according to the Gospel, but tend only to banishment and death.
JULIUS OF ROME, APUD ATHANASIUS, ACA 35

With the assistance of the imperial power, those infested with Arius's worms first contended with each single bishop individually to subvert the Catholic faith to make the Arian impiety prevail.... Those who resisted them, they assaulted with calumnies, either punishing them with exile or other sufferings or killing them.
EP. MARCELLINI ET FAUSTINI DE CONFESSIONE VERAE FIDEI 13
(CSEL 65, P. 10)

SOON AFTER THE CELEBRATIONS ENDED, it became clear that Nicaea had failed to unite the church. Although the majority of participants seemed to agree with Alexander and subscribed to the creed, several bishops had done so because of imperial pressure.[1] Many Christians also felt uneasy about using an unscriptural term to define Christ. Others found unsettling the attempt to turn a creed of faith into an official document and public decree to mark the boundaries of orthodoxy.[2]

To make matters worse, as they brought the new creed to their congregations, church leaders disagreed on how to interpret it. Some prelates, in trying to make the creed "fit" their own views about God, blurred the meaning of creedal statements. In addition, the introduction of *ousia* language to define the Son provoked new questions: How could a *begotten* being have the *same* essence as an *unbegotten* one? Wasn't this a "Sabellian" idea? Did the creed of Nicaea imply the coexistence of two first principles? Were Christians to worship two "equal" gods?[3]

The unfavorable reception of Nicaea in several Christian communities meant in practice that orthodoxy remained in dispute. It also meant that the controversy over the relationship between the Son and the Father was bound to flare up again. And flare up it did, amid an explosion of violence and unrest, as some church leaders dissatisfied with the outcome of the council sought to modify the creed and others reaffirmed it, refusing to consider alternatives. The dispute grew particularly fierce because both the truth about God and the power to set the boundaries of orthodox Christianity were at stake.[4] Because God could now be "officially" defined and the definition imposed on the church, creedal statements gained enormous political weight, which could be used as litmus tests of orthodoxy—that is, as instruments of power deployed to distinguish "true" Christians from "false" and to control ecclesiastical appointments and, by extension, access to the rapidly increasing wealth of the church.

As truth became politicized, the dispute to define and fix it posed an enormous challenge to church leaders committed to theological positions whose orthodoxy could not be guaranteed. The chapters that follow examine how prelates responded to the challenge in a manner that strengthened and expanded their authority in church and city and transformed the episcopate into a full-time political enterprise. As they engaged in the dispute and defended themselves and their views, prelates projected their authority into new areas of public life, asserting themselves with an effectiveness and viciousness unmatched in earlier times, solidifying that aggressive and performative style of church leadership that had emerged in the pre-Nicene years of the dispute.

Part 3 begins with the twelve years from Nicaea to the death of Constantine. This period is treated as a unit because while Constantine lived, in theory there could be no theological dispute or hope of changing the Nicene faith. To the emperor, the matter had been settled at Nicaea through the very agency of the Holy Spirit dwelling in the bishops' hearts.[5] Constantine may have seen the introduction of the *homoousios* as a strategic maneuver to appease Alexander's party and quickly settle the controversy, but the Nicene formula, once ratified by the council, took on the quality of divine truth. Yet the emperor's feelings about Nicaea did not prevent the rekindling of the dispute among church leaders even as they agreed to uphold Nicaea.

This struggle is traced on the local stage, where bishops worked systematically to impose their authority, take control of congregations, win over the faithful, and eliminate opposition and dissent. We will also consider how the conflict led prelates to engage imperial power brokers, members of the imperial family, and the emperor himself to boost their positions and undermine their enemies. The evidence for these developments comes primarily from Alexandria and Egypt, because the careers of Alexander and especially Athanasius are far better documented than those of other prelates, although the affirmation of episcopal power in response to theological controversy was also taking place elsewhere.

The discussion then turns to the decades following Constantine's death, an event that freed many churchmen in the East publicly to express their dislike of Nicaea and to embark on a quest to redefine God. Unable to reach consensus and determined that their views prevail, church leaders now moved the dispute to the center of social life in the cities, creating, in the process, new forms of power.[6] After Constantine, and especially under Constantius, dissenting bishops resisted the emperors' efforts to impose theological uniformity and, posing as arbiters of truth, came to inhabit a space from which, among other things, they could legitimately and effectively contest imperial power.

7

Claiming Truth, Projecting Power, A.D. 325–337

"ROUSING STRIFE AGAINST ONE ANOTHER": THE CONTROVERSY RESUMES

The dispute erupted again as soon as prelates returned to their sees following Nicaea. Dissatisfaction with Nicaea provoked disturbances in many places. As the faithful were asked to recite the creed in prayers, doxologies, and worship, church leaders found themselves having to justify their subscriptions to the Nicene formula to their congregations.[1] Even before returning home, Eusebius of Caesarea wrote to explain to his flock why and under what conditions he had agreed to the creed—not "sameness" of essence, but "similarity in all things," he glossed the *homoousios*, offering an interpretation of Nicaea that Alexander of Alexandria or Eustathius of Antioch would have repudiated.[2]

Back in Alexandria, epicenter of the affair, news of the council's outcome and its treatment of Arius rankled the priest's supporters. Arian preachers rejected the *homoousios* and continued to teach Arius's theology to the faithful, fanning the "flames of discord," Constantine complained.[3] In Antioch, too, tensions between local pro- and anti-Arians mounted as many Christians refused to accept Nicaea and, led by a faction of Arianizing priests, questioned Eustathius's orthodoxy. The latter replied by excommunicating those among the clergy and the faithful who rejected the creed.[4] As in Alexandria, however, clerics expelled from the church gathered their supporters and carried on teaching their views.

In Nicomedia, within sight of the imperial palace, Eusebius also went back to preaching openly to the "simple-minded multitude" that the "Son was not *homoousios* with the Father," denying, Constantine observed, that "the Son proceeded from the indivisible substance of the Father."[5] Theognis of Nicaea, Maris of Chalcedon (perhaps), and, in Syria, Theodotus of Laodicea seem to have taught the same, despite having subscribed to the creed.[6] In churches all over Asia Minor, where Arius's ideas on God had previously enjoyed support, the publication of the Nicene decrees may also have led to popular protests.[7]

These disturbances did not escape notice in the imperial court. The emperor seems to have expected criticism of the creed and sought at first to appease dissenters, who surely, given time, would come over to the side of the truth. Indeed, he often invited Eusebius and Theognis to court, hoping to convince them to embrace the *homoousios*. According to Sozomen, in one of these encounters, Eusebius boldly addressed the emperor, affirming that "if this cloak was cut in the middle under my eyes, I would never again say that each one is of the same essence."[8] The words are probably fictitious, but the theological debates with the emperor are credible. Constantine would later write that he had tolerated Eusebius and Theognis, despite their continued "support of a false teaching," because the council had preserved them for "recantation and penitence," and the exercise of clemency had always been a virtue of godly rulers.[9]

Yet as the protests against the *homoousios* gathered steam and again threatened to divide the church and disrupt public order, Constantine changed his approach. He had the Arian preachers in Alexandria arrested and brought to court; then, when Eusebius and Theognis imprudently communicated with these hapless men, he ordered the two bishops seized and sent into exile in Gaul, probably in late 325.[10] After this purge, Constantine warned Theodotus of Laodicea to adhere firmly to the Nicene faith if he wished to avoid the same fate.[11] Similar warnings must also have been sent out to other critics of Nicaea.

A few months after the council, then, the arrest and exile of Arian sympathizers reinforced the emperor's commitment to the Nicene creed as the cornerstone of Christian orthodoxy. Constantine's punitive actions also taught churchmen to exercise caution when speaking about God. It was wiser to conceal one's true opinion and publicly profess support for the creed even when one opposed its definition of God.[12] Yet fear of punishment did not necessarily keep church leaders from speculating about divinity and expressing their views to one another. The ecclesiastical historians tell us that, constrained to accept the *homoousios*, prelates continued to disagree on "the precise meaning of the term, rousing strife against one another," and Constantine's absence from the East for much of 326 may have emboldened many Christians to criticize the creed.[13] In letters and pamphlets, church leaders offered conflicting interpretations of it and accused each other of falling into heresy.[14] Socrates commented that "the affair was like a battle fought in the dark, as neither side appeared to know exactly on what grounds they blasphemed one another."[15]

Less than two years after the council, this battle had grown particularly bitter in Syria and Palestine, where it escalated into a full-blown confrontation that showed how support for Nicaea did not necessarily make prelates safe in their episcopal seats. After returning from the council, Eustathius of Antioch, facing growing opposition from his fractious clergy, launched an attack against his peers who had defended Arius at Nicaea. He wrote damaging pamphlets, treatises, and homilies intended for reading and delivery before his congregation and for circulation throughout the East.[16] In the *Commentary on Proverbs*, he openly accused Eusebius and his "gang" of supporters of lying at the council, labeling them "Ariomaniacs" long before Athanasius used the term:

> The Ariomaniacs, afraid they should be thrown out of the Church ... unanimously signed the dogma..... Thus, having retained possession of their episcopal seats through the most shameful deception ... they continue, sometimes secretly, and sometimes openly, to patronize the condemned doctrines, plotting with many different schemes. Intent on planting these weeds ... they wage war against the preachers of piety.[17]

Eustathius attacked all supporters of Arius, but his main targets were Eusebius of Caesarea and Patrophilus of Scythopolis, whose views on Nicaea resonated widely with many Antiochene Christians, including those clerics now peeling away from his church. Eusebius of Caesarea may have further infuriated Eustathius by traveling in Syria and preaching wherever he went his own views on the creed.[18] Eustathius, by accusing Eusebius and Patrophilus of "holding the same views as Arius" and conspiring to overturn Nicaea, may ultimately have tried to capture the emperor's attention in the hope that these men would suffer the same fate as Eusebius of Nicomedia and Theognis of Nicaea.[19]

Macarius of Jerusalem may have shared the same feelings. He accused Eusebius and Patrophilus of "sharing Arius's theology ... and trying to introduce new ideas."[20] Before Nicaea, the Christians of Jerusalem had also been divided over Arius's teachings, and according to Sozomen at least, Macarius feared that Eusebius and Patrophilus would appoint one of their own to succeed him in the church of Jerusalem—a highly prized possession, since the tomb of Christ had been revealed, and the emperor had opened the purse for the building of the famous Church of the Holy Sepulcher.[21]

Eusebius and Patrophilus, aware of the danger of Eustathius's accusations, did not remain silent. They publicly reaffirmed their commitment to Nicene orthodoxy but secretly conspired to get rid of their accusers.[22] Macarius was hard to touch, but Eustathius was particularly vulnerable. Not only did many Antiochene Christians oppose him, but in his eagerness to stress the unity and sameness of Father and Son, Eustathius had proposed an interpretation of the *homoousios* that made it possible to accuse him of failing to distinguish between the two; that is, his teachings on God left him open to the charge of Sabellianism.[23]

So, in the fall of 327, Eusebius and Patrophilus managed to assemble a synod at Antioch and convinced their peers to examine Eustathius's teachings.[24] The synod, which the pro-Arians clearly dominated, condemned the bishop and deposed him and several of his priests and deacons, ostensibly for heresy, but in truth, as Sozomen noted, because Eustathius "approved the faith of Nicaea and openly accused the followers of Eusebius [of Caesarea], Paulinus of Tyre, ... and Patrophilus of Scythopolis of sharing the views of Arius."[25] Eulalius, an Arian sympathizer, replaced Eustathius on the throne of Antioch, and when he died a few months later, after an unsuccessful attempt to transfer Eusebius from Caesarea to Antioch, another synod ordained Euphronius, a Cappadocian priest with deep Arian sympathies.[26]

None of these events unfolded peacefully, however. Like Paul of Samosata, Eustathius refused to give up his seat; his allies urged him to fight back, and so he did by calling on the faithful to resist Eulalius.[27] But the similarities with Paul of Samosata's affair end here. Eustathius's call led to massive riots. The bishop's supporters occupied the main church and collided with Eulalius's followers, who in the meantime had also worked up a large crowd of people to fight Eustathius's takeover of the building. Socrates tells us that a "military force was arrayed on each side as if to go to war."[28] Eusebius, who must have witnessed these events, noted that "the general population of the city including the magistrates and military personnel were stirred up to warlike attitudes," and that "the city was all but completely destroyed" in the riots that followed.[29] Agapius asserted that "the people of Antioch chased out Eustathius ... asked for Arius, and declared themselves in his favor"—an exaggeration, which nonetheless reflects the hostile feelings against Eustathius and his teachings among many local Christians.[30] So severe was the violence in Antioch that Constantine had to intervene with a military force "to inject fear in the people and quell the conflict before it led to more unrest and destruction."[31]

But Constantine's intervention did not end the troubles. After the riots, Eustathius was apparently brought to the imperial court, where the emperor blamed him for the violence, endorsed his deposition, and sent him with "a great number of priests and deacons into exile."[32] Eustathius's supporters, however—the "Eustathians," as they came to be called—refused to recognize Eulalius as a legitimate bishop, broke away from the church, and continued to assemble in a private house.[33] Then, a few months later, when Eulalius died, and his peers proposed transferring Eusebius from Caesarea to Antioch, the Eustathians again rose up demanding Eustathius's reinstatement while the pro-Arians agitated for Eusebius, campaigning among the people, requesting testimonials, praising Eusebius as "worthy of rank and placement," and circulating petitions to convince the emperor of his popularity.[34] We are once again in the world of Arius and Alexander in the early years of the controversy, with rival church leaders reaching out to the people—preaching, teaching, canvassing support, mobilizing them for action—to assert their claims to legitimacy and orthodoxy. Nicaea did nothing to end the dispute.

Just as significant, the debacle at Antioch taught churchmen that support for Nicaea was no guarantee of security. Eustathius's downfall was a delectable triumph for the pro-Arian faction. In an astonishing reversal of fortune, the pro-Arians who had just recently been humiliated at Nicaea succeeded in taking control of the church of Antioch, a patriarchal see with jurisdiction over all the churches of the diocese of Oriens.[35] This carried enormous advantages.

At Antioch, Eulalius immediately reinstated the priests Eustathius had deposed and appointed as clerics "men whom Eustathius," Athanasius later complained, "had refused to admit into the clergy on account of their impiety."[36] The synod that elected Euphronius in early 328 also issued a series of canons designed specifically to reinforce the authority of metropolitan prelates—that is, of bishops like Euphronius and Eusebius—and to discourage anyone from joining the Eustathians, who continued to meet in private assemblies.[37]

Then, Eusebius and Patrophilus mercilessly removed from their sees those prelates who had antagonized them and supported Eustathius. The prelates fell one after another, sometimes in wholesale depositions that significantly altered the theological makeup of the churches of Syria, Phoenicia, and Palestine,[38] making local congregations more receptive to Eusebius's views on Nicaea and, in the long run, as we shall see, more inclined to accept a revision of the creed. Hellanicus of Tripoli, Cymatius of Paltus, and Asclepas of Gaza were among the first to go, probably a few months after Eustathius's fall. In fact, the first two may have been deposed together with Eustathius. We do not know much about Cymatius, of tiny Paltus, but before Nicaea both Hellanicus and Asclepas had condemned Arius's theology and supported Alexander of Alexandria.[39] Cymatius and Hellanicus seem to have been replaced by Patricius and Theodosius, respectively, both critics of Nicaea.[40] Asclepas may have been deposed by the synod that ordained Euphronius a few months later, and, like Eusthatius, he was sent into exile.[41]

The shake-up in Syria and elsewhere in the East continued in the years that followed. At uncertain dates, but before the mid-330s and probably much earlier, Cyrus of Beroea fell, charged with Sabellianism. Cymatius of Gabala, Carterius of Antaradus, and Euphration of Balanea, another supporter of Alexander of Alexandria, were deposed on one charge or another.[42] In Thrace, Eutropius of Adrianople, a friend of Eustathius and bitter critic of Eusebius of Nicomedia, was expelled from his see and banned; and in Pannonia, Domnus of Sirmium, who "hated the heresy," was also deposed and replaced.[43]

As metropolitans of Syria and Palestine, Euphronius and Eusebius also secured the appointment of pro-Arian bishops to several sees. When Theodotus of Laodicea died, George of Alexandria took over his flock, ensuring that Laodicea remained in Arian-friendly hands. The priest Eudoxius became bishop of Germanicia.[44] In Asia Minor and Thrace, with the help of Eusebius of Nicomedia (after his return from exile below), the pro-Arian party also engineered the election of like-minded prelates. Sometime before 335, the Armenian Eustathius, a disciple of Arius, was ordained bishop of Sebaste in Lesser Armenia, where he founded a brand of rigorous asceticism that was perhaps inspired by Arian ideas of personal salvation. In Thrace, Theodorus, yet another Arian sympathizer and erudite writer, rose to the throne of the Heraclean church;[45] and in Cyzicus, Ascholius replaced Theonas.[46]

The changing fortunes of the pro-Arian faction owed a great deal to imperial patronage. The sentences of exile passed against so many bishops clearly necessitated the involvement of the imperial court and Constantine's assent. Athanasius later noted that many of the deposed bishops had been banned "by the authority of imperial letters."[47] The pro-Arian faction succeeded in winning the emperor's goodwill and the support of powerful courtiers, including the women of the imperial house.[48] Eutropius of Adrianople, for instance, was banished through the influence of Basilina, Julian's mother. We know that Constantia, Constantine's sister, exchanged letters with Eusebius of Caesarea, once asking him for an "image of Christ."[49] Given his connections in the imperial court, Eusebius of Nicomedia, may also have played a role in these events after his return from exile in mid-327, perhaps even in Eustathius's downfall.[50]

Growing in strength, the pro-Arian party also targeted Marcellus of Ancyra. After Nicaea, to Marcellus's chagrin, pro-Arian views had continued to find favor among the Christians of Galatia and Cappadocia. This was in part due to the work of the sophist Asterius, whose writings and lectures convinced many Christians to embrace his views, not least in Ancyra, where Marcellus was opposed by many in his own congregation.[51] When Asterius published a defense of Eusebius of Nicomedia, sometime between 325 and 328, Marcellus replied with his *Against Asterius,* a pamphlet that, as S. Parvis put it, sought to shred "to pieces" the theology of the pro-Arian alliance.[52] Marcellus took on broad targets, not only the sophist but also other pro-Arian churchmen and theologians—the two Eusebii, Paulinus of Tyre, and Narcissus of Neronias. The pro-Arians replied in kind. Asterius composed *Against Marcellus,* accusing the bishop of Ancyra of espousing, like Eustathius, the Sabellian heresy. Basil, a young physician who would later replace Marcellus as bishop, wrote his own *Against Marcellus,* and so, a few years later, did Eusebius of Caesarea.[53]

Marcellus managed nonetheless to retain his see for several years but became increasingly isolated and, as we shall see, was also eventually deposed and banned. By the late 320s and early 330s, this beleaguered bishop protested that many prelates were sending "letters everywhere for the overthrow of ... Nicaea."[54] While Constantine was alive, that could not happen, but it is clear that less than two years after that council, the dispute had resumed, and it was now fought in a treacherous atmosphere where stakes were much higher and the outcome uncertain.

And as the dispute reignited, it engaged bishops not only as theologians, but also as leaders of Christian congregations, compelling them more than ever before to entrench themselves in the community and to resist their rivals and, eventually, the emperor. In previous chapters we have seen how this led to the birth of a new, bold, and assertive church leadership. After 325, such entrenchment and resistance was incorporated into a pattern of behavior that helped consolidate episcopal authority and transformed bishops' position in society at large. Nowhere were these changes as well documented as in Alexandria and Egypt, especially during the episcopate of Athanasius, whose career, the stuff of legend in the church, best illustrates the rise of a new type of church leader.

THE CONTROVERSY DEEPENS: ALEXANDRIA AND EGYPT

Constantine recalled Arius and Euzoius from exile in late 326.[55] He seems always to have seen the priests' banishment as a temporary, "corrective" measure, to be undone at the right time.[56] As long as the exiles were willing to see the truth, the emperor never lost hope in the possibility of reconciling them with the church. Indeed, Constantine had remained in touch with them in exile, urging Arius to abandon his views, repent, and return to the fold of the church.[57] Arius and Euzoius at first declined these invitations, but in late fall 326 they agreed to come to the *comitatus*. Constantine received them somewhere in the Balkans on his way back to the East after spending almost a year in the West.[58] During their interview, they offered Constantine a new statement of faith, acknowledging that the Son had been generated by the Father before all ages. The statement made no mention of the *homoousios*, but also did not reject it.[59] To Constantine, that was enough to warrant their reinstatement, and after a local council of bishops confirmed the orthodoxy of their faith, he sent them back to Alexandria, probably in the spring of 327.[60]

Next, it was the Bithynians' turn. As soon as they learned about the return of Arius, they petitioned to be recalled from exile, and again Constantine was happy to indulge them as long as they agreed to embrace Nicaea.[61] Like Arius, Eusebius and Theognis never accepted the *homoousios*, but for the second time they found it expedient to uphold the creed. They would have pondered that openly resisting Nicaea was counterproductive; had they continued to reject the formula, they would have languished in exile, unable to fight for the true faith. Thus, after declaring their support for the creed, in 327 Eusebius and Theognis were also reinstated to their sees,[62] determined, however, to get rid of the *homoousios* and to rewrite orthodoxy—a theological and political project that could be realized only with the removal of Nicene supporters like Eustathius, Marcellus, and Alexander.

When Arius arrived in Egypt he found the local churches in turmoil. His followers had refused to accept Nicaea, and though his exile and the arrest of Arian preachers had deprived them of effective leaders, they had remained loyal to his teachings and united in opposition to Alexander.[63] In the weeks or months before his arrival, and perhaps in anticipation of his return, that opposition to the bishop had grown stronger as many Arian Christians became entangled in the Melitian schism.

The Council of Nicaea had also tried to settle that dispute, which had long divided Christians in the Egyptian *chora*. Nicaea had declared that the Melitian clergy were to retain their offices and continue to discharge their pastoral functions even in cities where Alexander had ordained rival Catholic bishops. However, the Melitians could not nominate candidates for bishoprics or appoint clerics without Alexander's approval, which effectively placed their congregations under Alexander's authority.[64] Since there were no doctrinal differences between Melitians and Catholics, the bishops expected that, in a generation or two, the Melitian churches would merge with the Catholic Church, ending the schism.[65]

Some Melitians, however, resented this arrangement, which deprived them of autonomy. The Catholics were no less pleased. Many had found it hard to compete with their rivals for the hearts and minds of the faithful, and in many communities with two bishops the Catholics tried to meddle in Melitian affairs.[66] Yet the two parties cooperated at least until Melitius's death, sometime before the spring of 327, when relations between them soured, reigniting the dispute.[67]

Melitian clerics, weary of continued Catholic intervention, pleaded with Alexander to make the Catholics respect their right to hold church assemblies in peace. Alexander not only ignored these requests but also, according to Epiphanius, "proceeded to *disrupt, contain,* and *constrain* in every way those who had been appointed by Melitius."[68] Alexander certainly wanted to see an end to the schism, but his decision suddenly to "oppress" the Melitians bespoke a change of tactics prompted by new, more urgent concerns, which, I suggest, had to do with the Arians' support of the Melitian cause.

It is possible that, in the months preceding Arius's return, the Alexandrian Arians saw in the deterioration of relations between Catholics and Melitians an opportunity to challenge the bishop. Sozomen noted that "when the Arians saw the Melitians innovating, they joined them in disrupting the churches."[69] The Melitians, in turn, despite their theological differences with the Arians, may have welcomed Arian support in Alexandria, where they had always been few in number.[70] Indeed, both Epiphanius and Sozomen suggest that Arians and Melitians discussed their doctrinal disagreement and reached some sort of compromise. Sozomen reports that they "debated their [theological] differences among themselves" and "because of their frequent debates ... the Melitians came to accept Arius's dogmas and to praise God in the same manner."[71] Epiphanius also speaks to that effect, adding that "the Melitians, who professed a pure and most correct faith, were mixed with Arius's disciples," so that, "thereafter," according to Sozomen, "Arius's teachings ... caused a storm ... dividing the clergy and the people."[72]

Arius and Euzoius would have arrived in Alexandria in the middle of this storm, expecting to be reintegrated into the Alexandrian church. Alexander, however, "with Athanasius urging him," refused to receive them. Restoring Arius was not an option to the bishop, not when Arius's hymns in praise of the suffering Jesus could still be heard, loud and defiant, in the harbors and mills of Alexandria, and now perhaps also in some Melitian assemblies. Arius remained an inspiring figure and a potential rival; the danger was that the popular priest, with his ascetic demeanor and proven powers of oratory, would again captivate the minds of local Christians, uniting his followers in Alexandria and the "rebellious" Melitians in Egypt to oppose Alexander's rule of the church. Thus Alexander "[turned Arius] away as a man stained by heresy," ignoring both the bishops who had declared his orthodoxy, and the emperor's wishes for reconciliation.[73] Alexander wrote apologetically to Constantine, explaining that "it was impossible to take back [into the church] those who had once broken with the faith and were declared anathema for it."[74]

The bishop's decision only provoked more turmoil and controversy. By refusing to communicate with Arius, Alexander further alienated the priest's followers and deepened the divide in the Alexandrian church. The rejection of Arius also put the bishop on a collision course with pro-Arian churchmen elsewhere, especially Arius's former supporters in Syria, Palestine, and Asia Minor, who would now work relentlessly to reinstate the priest and override the bishop's excommunication.

But more significant to our purposes here, Arius's return to the city once again brought Alexander's claims to orthodoxy and legitimacy into sharp focus and prompted the bishop more aggressively to assert his authority in the community. This became even more urgent after Eusebius of Nicomedia once again intervened on Arius's behalf and (some) Melitians agreed to receive Arius into communion. These developments led Alexander to tighten episcopal control of local churches, claim full sovereignty over church affairs, and adopt an engaged posture that kept the faithful in a constant state of mobilization.

Unable to convince Alexander to take him back, Arius wrote to Eusebius in Nicomedia, who, though only just returned from exile, readily took up the cause of the priest.[75] Eusebius clearly esteemed Arius, but he may also have hoped that the talented and charismatic priest would challenge Alexander and help convince the Christians of Alexandria and Egypt to support his project to redefine orthodoxy.[76]

Eusebius may first have pleaded with Alexander to take back the priest; then he persuaded the emperor to rebuke the bishop and his deacon Athanasius.[77] Constantine wrote a letter, asking Alexander to forgive the priest, "to conquer hate with concord," and to show mercy "to [Arius and Euzoius], men who came to me as suppliants."[78] When Constantine's letter also failed, Eusebius, convinced that conciliatory language would not be enough, enlisted the help of the disgruntled Melitians. If the latter, whose orthodoxy and ascetic rigor were widely admired in Egypt, agreed to receive Arius, whatever doubts remained about the priest's orthodoxy would perhaps dissipate, making Alexander's refusal to accept the priest seem motivated by vendetta or, worse, jealousy.[79] Moreover, Eusebius knew that throughout Egypt the Melitians had become a major force of opposition to Alexander, so the idea of assisting them would have appeared irresistible.

It might be said that the Melitians themselves came knocking on Eusebius's door. A few weeks or months before the latter's return from exile, the Melitians had sent an embassy to court to complain to the emperor about Alexander's oppressive conduct. The envoys failed to obtain an audience until Eusebius, "recently returned from exile," promised them he would arrange an interview if they agreed to communicate with Arius.[80] The Melitians accepted the offer,[81] and Constantine received them and confirmed their right to assemble the faithful in peace.[82] By mid-fall of 327, the envoys returned to Egypt, carrying imperial letters, ready to confront Alexander and communicate with Arius, "plunging the affairs of Egypt into turmoil."[83]

The Melitian gesture infuriated Alexander and he did nothing to stop his bishops from harassing the Melitians. Instead, he accused them of conspiring with Eusebius and the Arians to overthrow the Nicene faith.[84] Eusebius of Caesarea, commenting on the situation of the church in Egypt at that particular time, lamented that "when all were at peace . . . among the Egyptians alone the mutual bitterness remained undiluted."[85]

As tension mounted, Alexander proceeded to seize control of church buildings, calling the faithful to block their doors to Arius and probably to his closest followers, too.[86] As Eustathius had done in Antioch, Alexander urged his supporters to resist Arius's attempts to defile the houses of the Lord, but unlike Eustathius, he kept the faithful mobilized for weeks, perhaps longer, and charged them with keeping Arius out of the churches. Alexander's objective was to rob Arius of legitimacy by treating him as a heretic and a fraud, but his efforts to do so by laying claim to Christian sacred space in the city enabled him to tighten his grip on the local church.[87] The need to monitor and sustain the blockade for as long as the Arian "threat" persisted made it possible for Alexander to justify intervening in Alexandria's parishes in a more intrusive manner, eroding the traditional autonomy Alexandrian priests had enjoyed. The calls for the faithful to defend sacred buildings would also have weakened their attachment to local priests, redirecting their loyalties more effectively to the bishop leading the struggle against the fallen priest. If some of these developments were already under way before Nicaea, they now gained new impulse, leading to the concentration of a great deal of priestly power in the bishop's hands and the crystallization of the monarchical episcopate as a more palpable, perceptible, and intrusive presence in the Alexandrian Christian community.

The attempts to control sacred space more effectively also gave a face to Alexander's claim to orthodoxy. Not only were churches places where priests gathered the faithful, shaped their opinion, and channeled their devotions; they also served as venues for many community-building activities, such as distributing alms or holding banquets on festive days—events that the bishop could exploit to gain affection and popularity.[88] And after Constantine, church buildings, everywhere rebuilt, newly built, and richly decorated,[89] had come to embody the idea of an "official" orthodox church.[90]

The measures Alexander took in reaction to Arius's new challenge, then, not only enabled him to enhance his control of the Alexandrian church but also strengthened the episcopate as an institution. This strengthening would continue under his successor, Athanasius, who rose to the episcopal throne a year later likewise determined to prevent Arius's restoration and to unite all Christians in Egypt under his rule. As we shall see next, in his efforts to achieve these goals, Athanasius went far beyond his predecessor, taking the episcopate into new areas, expanding its scope of action, and using violence as part of a calculated strategy to impose his authority. Athanasius consolidated the assertive, brazen, and militant style of leading the church that had emerged in the early years of the dispute into a new and enduring model of church leadership. With his episcopate we complete the transition from the world of the early church, where Origen and Dionysius of Alexandria were willing to debate their disagreements over doctrine in a cordial and tolerant atmosphere, to one in which dialogue was replaced by intolerance, confrontation, and compulsion. I emphasize this shift in the ethics of the church leadership because recourse to force as a strategy of self-assertion looms large in the rise of bishops in the late Roman world. Athanasius was a product of that new world, but he also played a leading role in creating it as he confronted his opponents and struggled to impose the faith of Nicaea and his authority over all Egyptian Christians.

THE MAKING OF A NEW CHRISTIAN LEADERSHIP: ATHANASIUS IN ACTION

Athanasius rose to the episcopate as the theological rift in the Eastern churches deepened and the controversy over the fate of Arius had reached an impasse. Alexander, having shut down the churches of Alexandria to Arius, found himself increasingly at odds with many of his peers and the emperor. Given the bishop's adamant refusal to take back the priest, Constantine, still reeling from the showdown in Antioch, decided to call a new synod of bishops to settle all conflicts in Alexandria and Egypt. Shortly thereafter, sometime between late 327 and early 328, the prelates assembled before the emperor in Nicomedia.[91]

Unfortunately, we know next to nothing about this synod, because our sources seem to have deliberately omitted information about it. Eusebius of Caesarea states vaguely that Constantine "mediated between the same people"—presumably

Arius, Alexander, and the Melitians—but we do not know who attended the gathering.[92] Eusebius also writes that the synod issued a series of decrees, endorsed by the emperor, to guarantee a return to peace and order in Egypt.[93] We are also in the dark about the content of these decrees, though I suspect that the bishops and the emperor again, and in stronger terms, ordered Alexander to allow the Melitians to assemble in peace, which Alexander did,[94] and to readmit Arius, which he refused to do—hence the impasse.[95]

The sources are also silent on what happened to Arius after this council, but nothing suggests that he left Alexandria. He seems rather to have remained there, patiently waiting for Alexander, and when he died, shortly after the council, on April 17, 328, for his successor, to abide by the synod's decrees and take him back into the church.[96] If that was indeed the case, Arius was to be deeply disappointed. The deacon Athanasius, whom Alexander had apparently picked as his successor, had no intention of reintegrating the priest, for reasons of theology and politics. An ambitious young man, Athanasius not only coveted the episcopate but distrusted Arius's claim to have changed his mind about God. Athanasius shared Alexander's belief in a Son generated "out of the essence of the Father," partaking equally in the Father's glory, radiance, and wisdom, because only such a Son could truly have saved humanity. Like his predecessor, Athanasius abhorred the idea of a church community in which believers might attain salvation on their own, learning from Jesus's example, with priests playing a lesser role. If the Son was conceived as a mere "teacher," Athanasius would later write, "from whom we received instruction," then "sin has not lost its hold over the flesh, being inherent and not cast out of it."[97]

Athanasius would also have followed with alarm the depositions in the churches of Syria and Palestine and the rapid rise of Eusebius of Nicomedia in the imperial capital. Arius's old allies had just brought down the bishops of Antioch and other sees and were now busy appointing prelates hostile to the Nicene formula to key bishoprics in the East. Athanasius had no desire to see their influence extended to Alexandria, which would have been inevitable if their protégé were restored to the church and the priesthood. Thus, Athanasius strove to be elected bishop at any cost, lest other candidates, in a moment of weakness and a gesture of reconciliation, showed leniency to the priest.[98]

The details of the election are murky, and the sources disagree on how it happened, but all of them tell us that the process was marked by intimidation and coercion.[99] In employing such methods, Athanasius was following precedents set by Alexander, Arius, and others elsewhere. As we have seen, since the outbreak of the dispute, church leaders had occasionally used force as a strategy to display strength, show that they possessed the truth, and attack their rivals. Athanasius, however, in time turned force into a permanent feature of his episcopate, repeatedly using violence against Arian and Melitian Christians. Indeed, violence was not only used to suppress dissent and silence those who contested his authority, but it also became a way for Athanasius publicly to enact his claims to legitimacy and orthodoxy; its larger effect was to establish the bishop, and more generally, the episcopate, as shall see in the next chapter, as a spectacular public force.

Thus, driven by the need to assert himself in the face of growing opposition, Athanasius first dealt with Arius, who hoped to be readmitted into the church. Immediately after his election, Athanasius renewed Arius's excommunication, gathering the people in the church and announcing publicly that he would not take back the priest.[100] He also tightened the blockade of church buildings, perhaps extending the ban to all Arius's followers.[101] This decision seemingly brought the Arian faithful to the streets in protests and demonstrations, to which Athanasius at first responded by deploying his own supporters. Calling the Arians "godless men . . . who vomited forth [their doctrine] from their heart as from a seat of destruction," he incited the more militant elements in the Christian community and urged the faithful to hold fast to the holy churches.[102] The ecclesiastical historians speak generally of incessant "seditions and turmoil" as Arians and Athanasians clashed for access to the churches of Alexandria.[103] We return to these clashes below.

Athanasius also knew he needed to do something about the Melitians in the Mareotis and Egypt who had refused to recognize him as the head of the Egyptian church.[104] To make his authority more visible and present in the Mareotis,[105] Athanasius seems to have restructured the local parishes, reducing the number of clergy, placing a "priest in charge of each one of the [ten] largest villages," thereby facilitating the surveillance of subordinate clerics and creating a more effective chain of command.[106] He insisted on visiting the district often, moving about from parish to parish, accompanied by "all the priests and deacons . . . and a large number of laypeople."[107] These events, perhaps orchestrated to resemble the *adventus* ceremonies of late Roman magnates, broke the tedious routine of village life and enabled the bishop to connect directly with local Christians. Athanasius not only demanded the loyalty of the Mareotic clergy and faithful but insisted on repeated public performances of that loyalty. He had learned from Alexander and Arius that, in the competitive climate of the dispute, effective power in the Christian church depended as much on the control of ecclesiastical hierarchy as on how others perceived power. Athanasius turned his visitations to the Mareotis into displays of strength calculated to project his authority. Acts of provocation, which he tolerated and perhaps encouraged, would have had that same effect. Epiphanius reports that, during one of Athanasius's visits, "when the Melitians were assembling . . . a certain deacon in the Athanasian crowd rushed forth and, together with some laymen, broke one of the torches of the Melitians, and, so the story goes, a battle ensued."[108] A battle!

In a bid to take full control of sacred space, Athanasius also set out to shut down private Christian assemblies in the name of church unity.[109] Ision's house-church in the Mareotic village of Peace of Secontarurus was the most dramatic example, but there were probably others.[110] We know about Ision's church because of the famous incident involving Ischyras, which, as T. D. Barnes noted, would "haunt Athanasius for two decades."[111] Athanasius tells us that when he learned Ischyras was assembling the faithful in Ision's house, he dispatched the priest Macarius to warn Ischyras to stop preaching to the villagers and close the church.[112] According to Ischyras, however, Macarius and his men came to the village on a Sunday and, following Athanasius's orders, rushed into the building during the service, profaned the mysteries, overturned the holy table, demolished the priest's seat, and smashed the sacred chalice to pieces.[113] Macarius may also have seized the sacred books, burned them, and ordered the church razed to the ground.[114] Episodes like this would not have failed to impress the local faithful. They projected the image of a bold, vengeful and hard-biting Athanasius ready to use force to bring the Christian community under his thumb.

Then, the bishop turned his attention to the Melitians in the *chora*. In 329 and 330, he journeyed to Upper Egypt, going from town to town, "inspecting the churches of God" to secure their loyalty and to harass the Melitians.[115] His attacks against the latter were vicious, surpassing in ruthlessness anything Alexander had tried before. The Melitians later accused him and his bishops and henchmen of committing assault, murder, and arson.[116] Epiphanius, a pro-Athanasian writer, described Athanasius's persecution of the Melitians as follows: "Being a zealot about the faith and passionate about the church, when the Melitians were holding assemblies everywhere, . . . wishing to unify the church, he prosecuted, threatened, and admonished them," but beyond admonishments and threats, "[when] the Melitians would not listen . . . [he] oppressed them and used violence against them."[117]

One notorious victim of this violence was Arsenius, the Melitian bishop of Hypsele, who "disappeared" about the time Athanasius visited the Thebaid.[118] According to the Melitians, who later claimed they took Arsenius for dead, Athanasius asked Plousianos, the Catholic bishop of neighboring Lykopolis, to teach Arsenius a lesson, and Plousianos was merciless.[119] The Melitians reported that he "burned down [Arsenius's] house, tied him to a column, flogged and tortured him, and locked him up in a hut." Arsenius managed eventually to escape by climbing through a window, but "because [Plousianos and his henchmen] pursued him, he hid himself for a long time."[120] Other Melitians fell victim to similar atrocities, and some of them fled or went missing.[121]

Indeed, the fact that Athanasius and his bishops had savagely taken on the Melitians and suffered no consequences for it suggests that the civic authorities had been either complicit bystanders or passive collaborators, willing to "turn a blind eye" to the bishop's operations. Collusion between imperial officers and the powerful was not new in the Roman Empire, but it was still something of a novelty in the church and a phenomenon of great consequence inasmuch as such collaboration gave church leaders freedom to act with impunity by enlisting Roman officials to bring their opponents to their knees.[122] Imperial officers could apply terrifying pressure on ordinary citizens through either the use of force or their control of the courts and tax collection.[123] We shall see more of this below.

Let us now return to Alexandria, where after his tour of Egypt, and especially after 332, Athanasius launched a brutal campaign to dismantle Arian congregations. As we have seen, following Athanasius's election, the Arians clashed with the bishop's supporters in response to the church closings. As the unrest escalated, Arius's friends and allies outside of Egypt became involved and tried to persuade the emperor to unseat the bishop. Athanasius would then have realized that it was no longer enough that only some Christians in his see shared his beliefs and accepted his authority; he would never be able fully to assert his supremacy or hold on to the episcopal throne while the Arians continued to oppose him. The very existence of dissenting Christians in the city posed a threat to his episcopate. To eliminate this threat, Athanasius changed his approach to the Arians, setting out to break up their assemblies, impose theological uniformity, and subject all Christians to his authority.

But to understand how Athanasius tried to accomplish these goals, we need to consider developments in the imperial court, where the Melitians, encouraged by Eusebius of Nicomedia and his party, brought charges against Athanasius for the atrocities he committed in Egypt. It was perhaps the attempt, orchestrated by the Eusebians, to depose Athanasius and make the emperor punish him that ultimately convinced the bishop radically to change his approach to the Arians and Melitians. These events also allow us a glimpse of how the dispute drove Athanasius as well as other church leaders to compete for the support of high-ranking power brokers, which resulted in the creation of networks of influence that allowed churchmen to connect more intimately with the empire's political elite and use those connections to enhance their authority locally.

SUPPRESSING DISSENT, PROJECTING POWER

Arius appealed to Eusebius of Nicomedia for assistance probably in late 328 or early 329. In a replay of the events of the earlier confrontation with Alexander, Eusebius urged Athanasius to receive the Arians.[124] When the latter ignored the request, Eusebius waited for the emperor to return to the East in May 330 and persuaded him to write Athanasius ordering him to take Arius back into the church.[125] Constantine this time wrote sternly to the bishop, commanding him "to allow unimpeded access to all wishing to enter the church," and threatening to depose him and "to drive [him] away from those places" if he "hindered any who claimed to be of the church or . . . if he blocked their way."[126] But Athanasius did not obey the emperor. Instead, he replied to Constantine that he could not receive Arius because "the Christ-fighting heresy had no communion with the church"—that is, he accused Arius of clinging to heresy, contradicting Eusebius's claim that the priest shared the emperor's faith.[127] In narrating these events, Athanasius states that his letter persuaded the emperor to withdraw his order, but it is more plausible to think that Constantine postponed taking any action against the bishop until he had looked into the troublesome charge that Arius remained a heretic.[128]

Eusebius, however, could not wait. With Athanasius now openly accusing Arius of heresy and refusing to communicate with the priest, Eusebius understood that his plan to revise Nicaea would never be realized while Athanasius remained the bishop of Alexandria. And here again, Eusebius turned to the aggrieved Melitians.[129] The emperor's return to the East in the spring of 330 had brought them back to court—probably in the summer of that year. Led by John Arkaph, they accused Athanasius and his bishops of "murder, arrests, ... whippings, battery, assault, and burning down churches."[130]

Athanasius naturally claimed innocence and, in turn, accused the Melitians of "illegal ordinations, innovation with respect to the agreements of Nicaea, and corrupt faith." In the wake of the allegations that Arius remained a heretic, the bishop's claim that the Melitians, too, had tried to innovate the faith unsettled Constantine, who, as Sozomen noted, "no longer knew whom to believe."[131] Yet the arrival of more Melitians in court, between fall 330 and winter 331, bringing new charges against Athanasius, swayed the emperor and led him to summon Athanasius to court.[132]

And this time Athanasius had no choice but to come before the emperor, probably in late 331 or early 332.[133] When he arrived, the Melitians added yet more charges, including sacrilege and treason.[134] Both sides seem to have tried hard to influence the outcome of the trial by seeking the patronage of powerful imperial officers.[135] Whether or not Athanasius received help at court, the emperor acquitted him in the winter of 332, at Psamathia, a suburb of Nicomedia.[136] Persuaded that the bishop was innocent and worthy of the episcopate, Constantine sent him back to Alexandria, writing a letter to the Alexandrian church, praising Athanasius as a "man of God" and urging all Christians to embrace concord and peace.[137] Although Constantine did not punish the Melitians, in his letter to Alexandria he nonetheless scolded them for being moved by jealousy—jealousy that caused a man to "destroy, to consume, to be ill disposed, to recommend himself with false praises, ... to mess up the truth and corrupt the faith."[138]

A triumphant Athanasius made the most of these events, advertising widely the praises the emperor had lavished on him. From Nicomedia, he wrote a jubilant letter addressed to all Egyptian Christians, announcing his acquittal, revealing the names of his accusers, and parading his association with the praetorian prefect Ablabius, whose favor had made possible the delivery of his missive.[139] Having thus prepared the ground for his return, emboldened, he arrived in Alexandria just in time to celebrate Easter and poised to lash out against Arians and Melitians.[140]

Athanasius may have inveighed against his opponents as early as the Easter season of 332, immediately after his return from Nicomedia. The feast was an ideal time to unleash his campaign against dissenters, because a large number of ordinary Christians, among them many catechumens, would have congregated in Alexandria's churches.[141] What more fitting time to display his triumph over his enemies and to consolidate his control over the church in every sector of the city? The Eastern prelates assembled in Serdica in 343 reported:

> Even during the holiest days of Easter, [Athanasius] behaved savagely and atrociously, allying himself with the dukes and counts, who at his request threw people in jail, tyrannized others with blows and beatings, and used diverse torments to coerce yet others into sacrilegious communion with [him]. . . . Hoping that, in this way, his faction and his men would prevail, through the dukes, judges, and their dungeons, using blows and many-fold tortures, he forced those unwilling to communicate with him, compelled those who refused, and terrorized . . . those who fought back and resisted him.[142]

This report was naturally partisan, but the recourse to force, as we have seen, was not new or exclusive to Athanasius and should not discredit the bishops' testimony. On the contrary, one of the novelties here, the bishop's reliance on secular, "official" power to achieve his goals, lends credibility to the account. Indeed, the appeal to the public authorities—dukes, counts, and judges—to compel dissenters to communicate with him and to spread fear, "terrorizing tyrannically,"[143] signals a new approach to dissent—an approach that made coercion a central component of the dynamics of episcopal power, as we shall see further in the next chapter.

In the weeks and months that followed Athanasius's return to Alexandria, the crackdown against the Arians continued and grew more savage because Arius and his supporters fought back. Athanasius's acquittal at Psamathia and his assault against Arian Christians now convinced Arius to take action. Thinking himself a victim of injustice, the embittered priest decided that he had had enough.[144] For the first time since his return from exile, he set out openly to organize his followers and publicly to criticize Nicaea. Although he had never recognized the *homoousios* as the truth about the Son of God, he had hitherto agreed to uphold the Nicene creed for the sake of church unity.[145] But seven years after Nicaea, his attempt to make peace had taken him nowhere: Alexander and Athanasius had rejected him, Athanasius had branded him a heretic, both prelates had treated him as an outcast, and the emperor had again come to doubt his orthodoxy.[146] Throughout these years, Arius had kept a low profile, perhaps following Eusebius's advice, patiently waiting for Alexander to take him back and hoping for Athanasius's undoing, but Constantine's verdict exonerating the bishop shattered his hopes for reintegration.

If Athanasius refused to restore him, he was now left with no other alternative than to gather his followers and reestablish the true church, even if that meant defying the emperor himself.[147]

In the spring of 332, then, as Athanasius began his anti-Arian campaign, Arius reemerged as the head of the Arian Christians of Alexandria. He mobilized and assembled his followers, setting up, in Constantine's words, "a workshop of lawlessness," "constituting . . . a synod for himself . . . procuring and preserving by the law of adoption your Son, Christ, O Father, born from you and author of our salvation."[148] Defying Athanasius, he went back to teaching and preaching and composing sermons, speeches, and songs.[149] In clandestine meetings, unobserved by Athanasius's henchmen, he engaged in scriptural exegesis and joined his flock in holy choirs, singing "with a sweet voice" hymns about God that continued to enthrall the people—"pleasing" to the faithful, noted Constantine, who accused Arius of "singing evil things for the perdition of senseless persons," that is, for those Christians who saw "hope for a virtuous life in [Arius's] . . . words and music" and who "sought salvation for themselves" in his faith and speeches.[150]

Arius, returned to his old charismatic self, seems to have again electrified old and new supporters, injecting new vitality and a renewed sense of purpose into a battered and demoralized Arian community.[151] The Arian faithful seem to have rallied around him and cheered his decision to be forthcoming about his belief and stand up to Athanasius. His public rejection of the *homoousios* also lifted the theological fog created by an earlier reluctance to speak against Nicaea, allowing the doctrinal fault line that divided the Alexandrian Christian community to reveal itself more clearly.

The evidence for these events derives mostly from Arius's correspondence with Constantine in 332–333, which alludes to Arius's recent schismatic activities and the growing unrest in the Alexandrian church. Constantine complained that Arius was trying "to destroy the wretched, giving freely of his error to them."[152] Arius naturally saw the matter differently:

> Away! . . . I do not want a God who appears subject to the suffering of outrages and degradation. . . . God, when he made the newly begotten and newly created essence of Christ, prepared an assistant for Himself. . . . For if you subtract from Him [the Father], you make Him less. . . . Christ suffered because of us. . . . But it is imperative that we do not diminish Him [the Father] in any respect.[153]

We should always remember that this was a conflict over an idea of God. In the letters exchanged with Constantine, Arius appears liberated by his decision to break with Athanasius's church and relieved to speak his mind: "This is what . . . we believe," he boldly replied to the emperor. And if he knew that he was courting danger, as he must have, he derived pleasure from his newfound *parrhesia*—"I am full of joy and I leap and I jump with grace and I soar."[154]

Once again, many Alexandrian Christians, lay and cleric, flocked to Arius's assemblies.[155] Heedless of the danger they faced in supporting Arius, many Arian faithful were willing to suffer punishment with the priest, like true martyrs.[156] Their devotion in turn soothed and uplifted Arius, who declared to the emperor that the support of the crowd "lightens up my worries."[157] Challenged by the reemergent Arius, Athanasius quickly stepped up his attacks against his followers, "driving [the Arian Christians] away" by force.[158] Claiming that Arius's "real fight" was not "with us . . . but against the Godhead Itself," he ratcheted up his anti-Arian rhetoric and incited his supporters to assail the Arian assemblies.[159]

So fierce was Athanasius's reaction that Arius again had to leave Alexandria, this time for Libya, probably in the summer or fall of 332, taking with him many followers—"a multitude"—including several well-to-do Alexandrian citizens.[160] In Libya, Arius found much support among local Christians,[161] but Athanasius pursued him there, perhaps with a view to extending the ban on the priest to the local churches, apparently with little success.[162] Arius managed to evade the bishop and continued to preach his doctrine, according to Constantine, "[going] farther . . . leaving nothing unsaid . . . opening the treasury of madness."[163] In a letter to the emperor in late 332, Arius claimed that "all the people of Libya shared his views"—an overstatement, no doubt, but his ideas did gain widespread acceptance in the region, because a pro-Arian, anti-Nicene theology became dominant in many Libyan congregations throughout the fourth century, despite Athanasius's efforts to suppress it.[164]

Arius's departure, however, did not ease unrest in Alexandria. Athanasius would have carried on his persecution, forcing Arian Christians to communicate with him, beating, imprisoning, and threatening those who continued to resist him, until Constantine once again intervened, this time giving Athanasius the means to inflict a severe blow on the dissenters. In late 332 or early 333, Arius, already in Libya, but buoyed by the enthusiastic response of the faithful, asked Constantine to reinstate him to the priesthood and allow him to celebrate Mass.[165] The petition infuriated the emperor. Accusing Arius of "endeavoring to throw the whole world into confusion with [his] impieties" and lamenting these "wars of insanity," Constantine denied the request and published a series of decrees designed to disperse the Arian congregations, stop Arius's schismatic activities, and force not only Arian clerics, but also, and for the first time, ordinary Christians to revile Arius's doctrine and embrace Nicene orthodoxy.[166] Warning Arius "to have regard for himself and to condemn the present madness," Constantine threatened to make "the multitude . . . of those wandering with [Arius]" pay "ten additional capitation taxes . . . unless they ran as quickly as possible to the salvation-bringing church."[167] The fine would have been a hefty one, to judge from the capitation rates charged in Oxyrhynchus.[168] "Burdened by these taxes," the emperor declared, "each one [of your followers] will immediately break a sweat."[169] Arian clerics were also to be punished with suspension of immunity from public service and curial duty, "unless they flee as quickly as possible their association with you and embrace, in exchange, the uncorrupted faith."[170] Constantine also banned Arius's songs and made possession of his books a capital crime.[171]

These decrees delivered into Athanasius's hands new legal instruments of intimidation and persecution that enabled the bishop to rely on the imperial authorities to carry on his campaign against the Arians as if they were criminals. In the winter or spring of 333, a copy of the emperor's letter to Arius, verbally abusing the priest, was read publicly in the prefect's palace in Alexandria to the bishop's delighted satisfaction.[172] Constantine's diatribe against Arius contrasted starkly with his lavish praise of the bishop in the previous year and confirmed what Athanasius had been arguing all along about Arius's heterodoxy, making his crackdown now appear fully justified.

The emperor's decrees were quickly put into practice, no doubt at Athanasius's urging.[173] The bishop may have drafted lists with the names of Arius's followers and their families, inviting their denunciation to the prefect and the bureau of the *katholikos*, the office responsible for the collection of capitation taxes and the assignment of curial liturgies.[174]

It is reasonable to suppose that Athanasius's persecution disrupted the Arian community of Alexandria, forcing many Arians to move underground. From 332 to 335, they fade from our sources, but this silence should not be taken as a sign of weakness.[175] Arius's own fate after the publication of the decrees is uncertain, and he may have been banned, with his closest followers, from Egypt. Under the weight of heavy taxation and costly liturgies, many Arian supporters would have abandoned the priest, and some, constrained by the emperor, may in fact have joined Athanasius's church, even as they held him and the faith he preached in contempt. The charge brought by the Eastern bishops at Serdica that Athanasius compelled Christians to enter into communion with him may also have referred to Arians forced by the circumstances to "run to the salvation-bringing church," as the emperor had ordered them to do.[176]

But Athanasius's successes did not spell the end of the troubles in Egypt. The developments of 332 and 333 significantly strengthened the bishop's hand and bespoke the emergence of a pattern of behavior that was transforming the episcopate into a greater political force. Athanasius had been able to sway the imperial court, mobilize devoted supporters, and effectively co-opt secular power to terrorize his enemies, but the Eusebians, who followed these events from afar, did not give up their struggle. On the contrary, they only intensified their efforts to unseat the bishop, which encouraged Athanasius to assert himself even more aggressively, projecting his power all over Egypt, and widening the scope of his reach until his banishment into exile.

The Eusebian reaction started in late 333. Eusebius must have watched with horror Arius's debacle in the aftermath of Psamathia. How imprudent of the priest to speak out against Nicaea! Arius's open rejection of the Nicene formula would only have confirmed the charge of heresy directed against him and made it more difficult to defend his reintegration into the church. Instead of pleading for the priest's reinstatement, Eusebius now opted to concentrate his efforts on removing Athanasius.

Together with the Melitians, twice he plotted to depose the bishop. First, in late 333, when the Melitians accused Athanasius of the murder of Arsenius, the Melitian bishop of Hypsele and revived the charge of sacrilege.[177] Constantine ordered his half brother Dalmatius to investigate the charges and, for the third time, called the bishops to assemble a synod, in Palestinian Caesarea in late spring 334.[178] With the help of the duke (of the Thebaid?), however, Athanasius's deacons found that Arsenius was alive and in hiding in a Melitian monastery.[179] With Athanasius's men on his trail, Arsenius kept moving from place to place, but eventually left for Tyre, where John Arkaph, then based in Antioch, may have helped him find a place to hide.[180] By mid-May, as the Eastern bishops began to congregate in Caesarea, Athanasius's men caught up with Arsenius in Tyre.[181] Informed of these events, Constantine called off the trial, disbanded the synod, condemned the Melitians' prevarication, and wrote to Athanasius, again praising him and urging him to "restore the people of God to tranquility."[182] The Eusebians, however, "because they cared not for the Melitians ... [but] were concerned [with the Arians]," did not relent.[183]

In late 334, Eusebius again gained the emperor's ear and, using as a pretext the protests against Athanasius in Alexandria and Egypt (probably resulting from the implementation of the anti-Arian decrees), persuaded Constantine to give the bishops yet another opportunity to sort out their differences and bring peace to the church.[184] The timing of these developments worked in Eusebius's favor. As the date of Constantine's *tricennalia* approached, the emperor had become more sensitive to the troubles in the church and perhaps even remorseful about persecuting Arian Christians in Alexandria.[185] He had planned to combine the feast of the *tricennalia* with the consecration of the newly built Church of the Holy Sepulcher in Jerusalem, but the ongoing dispute in Egypt and the ugly crackdown against the Arian Christians threatened to tarnish the event.[186] Eusebius's suggestion of another synod would also have reminded Constantine that his many efforts to settle church quarrels had accomplished little: Arius had rejected Nicaea and established schismatic congregations, and Athanasius, the "man of God," whom he had so often supported, had repeatedly failed to unite the Christians of Egypt. Athanasius's episcopate in fact marched from one crisis to another. Even if his opponents had conspired against him, it was disturbing that the bishop seemed always more concerned to repress them and strengthen his position than to negotiate a compromise.[187] If Arius had tried to corrupt the faith, Athanasius too had stood in the way of harmony and concord in the church. Constantine complained bitterly of the "unhealthy rivalry" that plagued the church and brought "blasphemy" upon it.[188]

So the emperor heeded Eusebius's advice and called a new council for the summer of 335 in the city of Tyre to end all disputes and restore peace to the church so as to "lighten [his] worries."[189] The council was to revisit the charges against Athanasius and settle the matter, after which the bishops were to travel to Jerusalem to participate in the consecration of the Holy Sepulcher.[190] Constantine wrote personally to Eastern prelates, ordering them to attend the meeting, but Eusebius's hand in the drafting of the list of recipients is manifestly clear, as Athanasius's supporters in Egypt were not invited.[191] Athanasius received the summons while traveling in the Delta.[192] As in previous times, he sent the loyal Macarius to court to canvass support in an attempt to counteract the influence of Eusebius, but Constantine unexpectedly ordered Macarius arrested and brought to Tyre "in chains."[193] Athanasius reacted to news of the arrest by organizing an operation "to rescue Macarius," dispatching to Syria or Phoenicia a posse of thuggish priests.[194] John Arkaph, however, who by now had returned to Antioch, managed to intercept those men and secure their arrest, but the bishop's daring in undertaking this operation is striking.[195] In April of 335, Athanasius, "greatly distraught" because of the arrest of his priests and aware that he would face a hostile assembly in Tyre, decided to sabotage the meeting: on the one hand, he would disrupt the proceedings by taking with him his Egyptian supporters, cleric and lay, whom he began to mobilize in the spring of 335; on the other, he would use every means possible to prevent Arians and Melitians from coming to Tyre,[196] including intimidation and violence, again enlisting the support of the imperial authorities in Egypt.

A Melitian private letter, preserved in a well-known papyrus published by H. I. Bell in 1924, gives us, in tantalizing detail, an account of Athanasius's brutal treatment of the Melitians converging on Alexandria in mid-May 335 en route to the council.[197] On May 18 the *commentariensis* Heraclius—a ducal officer in charge of criminal trials and commander of a staff of torturers—arrested several Melitian clerics, deprived them of bread, and forced them to reveal the Melitians' plans.[198] A day or so later, "those carrying on the campaign of Athanasius," together with the duke's soldiers and, perhaps, a few thugs from the camp, tried to seize two Melitian prelates, who managed to escape only because other soldiers, no doubt sympathetic to the Melitians, hid them in the "cells."[199] Then, Athanasius's goons went on a rampage, seizing several other Melitians and beating them cruelly. They raided an inn in Alexandria, apprehended more Melitians and locked them up.[200]

The attacks continued for several days. The Athanasians beat a Melitian bishop and kept him under house arrest so that he could neither communicate with his companions nor leave for Tyre.[201] As more Melitians arrived in Alexandria, working with the duke and other officers, Athanasius locked up a bishop from the Delta in the city's meat market, threw clerics in jail, and caused several Melitian bishops to be banned from Egypt, probably with imperial letters bought from friends in high places in the imperial administration.[202] Yet, despite these attacks, Athanasius could not prevent the Melitians from attending the council, and he also had no choice but to come and face his accusers. He left Alexandria for Tyre on July 11, 335, with a large delegation comprising many priests and forty-nine Egyptian bishops—a wandering synod in and of itself.[203]

Not surprisingly, given Athanasius's plans to disrupt the proceedings and his enemies' determination to remove him from office, the Council of Tyre was a very turbulent affair. Athanasius arrived "with a mass of people and caused trouble and tumult, refusing to defend himself, insulting his peers, and ignoring the convocations to appear in court."[204] One of his supporters repeatedly offended Eusebius, who, losing his temper, is said to have replied: "If you come here to insult us, your accusers speak the truth. For if you behave like a tyrant here, you must do even worse in your homeland."[205] Count Dionysius, whom Constantine had sent to the council with a "military detachment" to prevent trouble from breaking out, was forced repeatedly to intervene ("the soldiers hurried us about") and compelled a recalcitrant Athanasius to appear in court, led by the "chief jailor."[206]

At Tyre things finally began to unravel for the bishop. Eusebius managed to prevent the Catholic Egyptian prelates, who were excluded from the council's deliberations, from giving depositions on behalf of Athanasius. Despite Athanasius's protests that he was being tried by his accusers, the council acquitted him from the old charges of murder (of Arsenius) and illegitimate election.[207] Athanasius failed, however, to convince the bishops of his innocence in the chalice incident in the Mareotis, so the synod and the count agreed to send a committee of bishops to the Mareotis to investigate the matter and report back to the council. Athanasius acquiesced but demanded that the "implicated or suspected parties not be sent."[208]

It is impossible to know what happened next because our sources are the biased testimonies of Athanasius and the Catholic Egyptian bishops. The Eusebians seem to have picked for the committee prelates loyal to their cause—Theognis of Nicaea, Maris of Chalcedon, Macedonius of Mopsuestia, and from Pannonia, Ursacius of Singidunum and Valens of Mursa.[209] Athanasius and his supporters did their best to disqualify the choice, protesting that the gathering was partisan and that the delegates supported the "Arian heresy"—all in vain as the committee left for Alexandria in late June or early August of 335.[210]

In Egypt, both sides called the people to action. The Melitians sent a party to Alexandria for the purpose of bringing "Melitian [Christians] out of Egypt into the Mareotis ... and Kolluthians and Ariomaniacs from other places and [having] them all testify against us [Athanasius's party]." When the committee arrived in Alexandria, Athanasius's supporters had also gathered a large number of ascetics, men and women, recruited from the cells, monasteries, and convents in and about the city to defend the bishop, threaten witnesses, and disrupt the inquiries.[211]

The disturbances in the Mareotis, however, did not prevent the delegates from completing the investigation. With the help of Philagrius, the new prefect of Egypt and Arian sympathizer, appointed during that summer, as Athanasius suggested, through the patronage of Eusebius, the committee collected damaging testimony against the bishop.[212] By late August the committee reported back to the council, and the bishops found Athanasius guilty of sacrilege for his involvement in the chalice incident and, more generally, of violence against his opponents. To the delight of the Eusebians, the council deposed him from office and banned him from Alexandria to spare the city an outbreak of rioting like the one that had rattled Antioch after Eustathius's deposition.[213]

After these events, the synod moved from Tyre to Jerusalem, to celebrate the consecration of the Holy Sepulcher, and there Arius reappeared at the invitation of Constantine.[214] Perhaps following Eusebius's advice, Arius and his closest associates submitted or signed another statement of faith to the emperor and the council, which declared him orthodox and admitted him into the church.[215] The council then wrote a letter to Alexandria and Egypt announcing the reinstatement of the priest whom "envy had . . . excluded from the church."[216] Eusebius of Caesarea later celebrated the Council of Jerusalem as the "greatest [synod] of those we know" after Nicaea.[217]

While in Jerusalem, the bishops may also have nominated as the new bishop of Alexandria Pistus, a priest under Alexander who had joined the Arians in the early stages of the controversy. Scholars have often dismissed Pistus as an ineffective leader, but that is unlikely, and, at that time, there may have been no better choice. Pistus would have been a familiar name, known to many Alexandrian Christians as a devout, principled pastor who had not hesitated to sacrifice his post as priest to be on the side of the truth.[218]

Athanasius, meanwhile, ignored his sentence of deposition. While the Council of Tyre was still in session, he withdrew stealthily, together with at least five Egyptian bishops, bound for Constantinople to appeal to the emperor.[219] On November 6, 335, he boldly accosted Constantine in the suburbs of the capital as the emperor was about to enter it.[220] Astonished at the sight of the bishop and at first unwilling to receive him, Constantine reluctantly granted him an audience. Athanasius complained that he had again been the victim of a plot and asked Constantine to assemble a new council to hear his defense. The emperor summoned the bishops from Tyre to Constantinople to disclose what happened at Tyre and prove that they had passed a just sentence.[221] The two Eusebii, Theognis, Patrophilus, Ursacius, and Valens, who must have already been in the capital (or about to arrive), came before the emperor the next day.[222] According to Sozomen, whose narrative here does not follow Athanasius, the bishops maneuvered to avoid a new inquiry.

Instead, they charged Athanasius with threatening to retain in Egypt the corn fleet of Constantinople and convinced Constantine that the bishop had committed sacrilege in the chalice affair.[223] In trying to defend himself, Athanasius used harsh words against Constantine, infuriating the emperor, who sent him into exile in Gaul, convinced that Athanasius was a source of division, violence, and disorder in the church.[224] This was a signal triumph for the Eusebians, whose maneuvering, skill, and influence with the emperor at last succeeded in creating an environment more favorable to a revision of Nicaea. Redefining God would now have seemed to be within their grasp.

In Alexandria, however, Athanasius's supporters rose up against the deposition and exile of their bishop. They rejected Arius and, according to Sozomen, protested continuously against the synod and the emperor.[225] Like the Arians in the wake of Nicaea, the Athanasian priests stirred up the faithful. The holy virgins organized public supplications to demand the reinstatement of the bishop.[226] The Athanasians wrote to the emperor expressing their outrage and pleading with him to drop the charges. The monk Antony more than once entreated Constantine to reinstate the bishop. This time, however, Constantine was inflexible. Incensed by the ongoing disturbances, when all the church was at peace, he wrote back to the Alexandrians, "accusing them of disorder and recklessness, warning the holy virgins and clerics to return to peace, and confirming that he would not recall Athanasius, because he was an agitator condemned by an ecclesiastical sentence."[227] To Antony, the emperor also replied: "I cannot overturn the vote of the council. If a few ... have cast their vote in hate or in return for some favor ... I cannot believe that [everyone] in such a great assembly of noble bishops ... shared those sentiments. Athanasius was arrogant, vain, and the cause of seditions and schisms."[228] The commotion, however, did not subside; it spread from Alexandria to Egypt, prompting Constantine to summon Arius back to court, probably in the spring of 336.[229] Arius was never to return to Egypt. That same spring, Marcellus of Ancyra submitted his *Contra Asterium* to the emperor, accusing the Eusebians of heresy and polytheism.[230] But his attempt to incriminate his enemies backfired: Constantine handed the book to Eusebius, who assembled a synod in Constantinople, condemned Marcellus, deposed him, and convinced Constantine to exile him.[231] Alexander, bishop of Constantinople, who had also refused to communicate with Arius, apparently tried to disrupt this synod, and the Eusebians threatened to unseat him if he did not receive Arius, but the priest apparently died in Constantinople soon after.[232]

In July 336 the bishops joined Constantine in Constantinople to celebrate his *tricennalia* and the restoration of peace and concord in the church, but the attack against Nicaea continued and gained impetus. Sozomen tells us that about this time Eusebius of Nicomedia and Theognis of Nicaea put forth an alternative formula of faith, announcing to the bishops throughout the East that they accepted the concepts in the Nicene creed only when subject to interpretation. "As a result of . . . these writings," he adds, "the old controversy erupted once again." And, as we shall see in chapter 8, it did so with even greater fierceness, especially after the death of Constantine, as church leaders again confronted each other in a struggle to define orthodoxy and take control of the church.[233]

8

The Challenge of Theology and Power in Action

Bishops, Cities, and Empire, A.D. 337–361

Constantine died in May 337 in Nicomedia on his way to the Eastern front to lead an invasion of Persia.¹ His death put the plans for war on hold, and the empire was subsequently divided among his heirs—his three sons, Constantine II, Constantius, and Constans, and nephew, Dalmatius. In the months that followed, however, Dalmatius and other members of his family were murdered, possibly on the orders of Constantius, heir of the East, and in September of that same year, Constantine's sons became the new masters of the Roman world.²

Church leaders did not take long to realize the implications of these developments for ecclesiastical affairs. To the Eusebian circle, Constantine's death removed the main obstacle to a revision of Nicaea and made it possible to reopen the great theological debate Arius had started twenty years earlier.³ At the other end of the empire, it was also clear to Athanasius, Marcellus, and other exiled clerics that the Eusebians would try to attack Nicaea. Constantine's firm commitment to the Nicene faith had made that impossible; now, however, that formula and the divine truth it embodied were threatened. Thus, as soon as news of Constantine's death became public, these clerics acted quickly to make the most of the circumstances of the imperial transition to advance themselves and their causes. The Eusebians, who had long enjoyed the benefit of proximity to and connections in the imperial court, worked to consolidate their influence with the new rulers. They ingratiated themselves with Constantius, by carefully watching over his interests even as Constantine lay dying in the suburbs of Nicomedia.⁴ Winning the new emperor's trust was crucial to their plans to redefine God and rewrite orthodoxy.

In the West, the exiles petitioned Constantine II to end their banishment. Athanasius, who had frequented Constantine II's court in Trier, convinced this emperor to send him back to Alexandria.[5] In a letter to the Alexandrian church, Constantine II claimed that his father had exiled the bishop only to protect him from his enemies, which is unlikely, though Constantine may have indeed intended to rehabilitate the bishop at a later time.[6] Athanasius seems in fact to have benefited from a grant of amnesty extended by the new emperors to *all* exiled bishops, including Marcellus of Ancyra, Asclepas of Gaza, and others, who were also allowed to regain their sees.[7]

In the next three decades or so, as the Nicene façade of unity collapsed, churchmen continued to engage in a colossal struggle for the definition of God and the control of the church. The motivation for the dispute remained theological: to ensure the salvation of humankind against the dangers of false teaching and blasphemous worship, but the stakes were much higher because one's theological views could compromise access to the church's expanding resources and the perquisites of ecclesiastical office precisely at a time when these were becoming indispensable for the legitimation of episcopal authority. Remarking on the viciousness of the controversy, Gregory Nazianzenus wrote: "The souls were the pretext [for the dispute], but the real thing was the love of power."[8] In truth, in the years following Constantine's death, the two could no longer be clearly separated—the struggle to save souls was also a struggle for power inside and outside the church. Suspended in an atmosphere of deepening uncertainty about the right faith, and repeatedly challenged to prove their orthodoxy and legitimacy, many prelates embarked on a turbulent quest to assert themselves in order to show they possessed both. Indeed, the more their claims to leadership were threatened with deposition or exile, the more they became dependent on their capacity to demonstrate legitimacy through action. Thus, in the years following Constantine's death, that militant, bold model of church leadership we saw with Athanasius spread more widely as church leaders acted in ways that dramatically expanded their capacities in local communities and on the imperial stage.

Recourse to violence continued to be one key element in this process, but the novelty in the 340s and 350s was, first, its scale and destructiveness, and second, its "routinization."[9] Episodes of collective violence in particular, whether spontaneous or orchestrated by ecclesiastical or secular leaders, became far more frequent, indeed, often the preferred means of conducting the dispute: beatings, rape, banishment, and loss of property and life became common features of life in many troubled Christian communities as church leaders attacked dissenters and compelled the faithful to embrace their views.

As we will see, the sustained theological conflict in the years after Constantine's death produced "modes of behavior" or ways of being and acting—a *habitus*, in P. Bourdieu's definition—that contributed to transforming the episcopate into a powerful social and political force, pushing church leaders into the center of public life, and reconfiguring relations between churchmen and traditional power holders, including the emperor. The demands on prelates constantly to prepare and organize for confrontation—that is, the need persistently to engineer popular support, build a climate of militancy, suppress dissent, and stage displays of strength—had the effect of giving church leaders effective power over large groups of people, foregrounding episcopal authority in the public sphere and altering the way in which bishops' power came to be perceived. The frequent mobilization of gangs and crowds, the repeated protests and demonstrations, and the spectacle of public violence created a space for social and political performance that enabled church leaders not only to criticize the imperial power from a position of strength, but also to challenge its authority and legitimacy—and this was one of the most significant developments of the late Roman world.

POPULOS DEI IN SUUM DOMINIUM CAPTIVARE: RIVALS, RIOTS, AND THE STRUGGLE FOR THE CHURCHES

As soon as the exiles set foot in the East, they faced fierce opposition from many of their peers and the faithful. None of them had been rehabilitated by a church council as Eusebius of Nicomedia, Theognis of Nicaea, and Arius once had been, when Constantine recalled them from banishment.[10] How could these men claim to be bishops when they had been deposed for such egregious crimes as sacrilege, sedition, and heresy? How could they be reinstated when their flocks had been entrusted to the care of true pastors? Ignoring these questions, the returning bishops proceeded boldly to take control of their sees and churches, triggering riots and protests everywhere. The evidence for the turmoil comes from different places in the East, but our main source, as usual, is Athanasius, and it is to his writings, fuller for events surrounding his return to Alexandria, that we turn first.

Athanasius left Trier in early summer 337, traveling over land through the Balkans, Asia Minor, and the Near East.[11] The choice of a land route had partly to do with the need to meet Constantius along the way and perhaps formally to receive the express authorization for his return.[12] But the bishop clearly saw the journey as an opportunity to muster support in communities where the Eusebians had appointed friendly bishops under Constantine. According to the report of the Eastern bishops assembled at Serdica in 343,

> [Athanasius] arrived at Alexandria from Gaul after a long time. Disregarding what happened in the past, this time he behaved even more ruthlessly. . . . For the crimes he had previously committed were trivial compared to the ones that followed. Throughout the course of his journey, he overturned churches, restored condemned bishops, gave others the hope of returning to the episcopate, and made bishops out of unbelievers through the blows and murder of the pagans. . . . He paid no respect to the law and threw everything into despair.[13]

Athanasius's tumultuous ordinations outside Egypt were meant to build a front of opposition to the Eusebians as he prepared to confront them and the Arians of Alexandria.[14]

The bishop's arrival in Alexandria on November 23, 337,[15] sparked protests and demonstrations. His allies claimed the faithful rejoiced at his return,[16] which was no doubt true of his supporters, but according to the Eusebians, the city filled with "riots, lamentations, and mourning."[17] The Eusebians complained that the Christians who refused to recognize Athanasius endured trials and tribulations; and they spoke of "murders and butcheries."[18] Athanasius himself never denied the turmoil but rather blamed the Arians for "exciting continuous seditions,"[19] calling their opposition an uprising—the "Ariomaniacs," as he now took to calling them, "rose up against the churches."[20]

Leading the Arians' opposition against Athanasius was Pistus, who refused to hand over the church to a rival reinstated without the sanction of a synod.[21] But Athanasius, who clearly understood the importance of controlling Christian sacred spaces, organized an assault on the churches to expel Pistus and the Arians. "Gathering a crowd of pagans . . . he seized the basilicas . . . by force, by murder, and by war. . . . Like a barbarian marauder and an abominable plague . . . he set God's temple on fire and smashed an altar."[22] Possibly with the cooperation of Theodorus, prefect of Egypt, Athanasius also managed to lay his hands on imperial subsidies of grain intended for the poor, widows, and clerics of Alexandria,[23] which, during his exile, must have been entrusted to Pistus. Athanasius's enemies accused him of selling the grain and embezzling the money, but it is possible that the bishop distributed the grain (or the proceeds from its sale) among the poor.[24] Charity, especially when it involved imperial funds, increasingly played a role in the assertion of episcopal power. As Peter Brown has shown, the control and dispensation of church wealth and charity brought the bishop's image as a leader into sharp focus.[25] Feeding the poor on a large scale would have enabled Athanasius to reward his followers, expand his clientage, encourage defections from the Arian camp, and strengthen himself.

Violent conflict also erupted in other Christian communities. At Ancyra, Basil refused to surrender the churches to Marcellus,[26] provoking a confrontation in which "houses were burned and there were all kinds of combats."[27] Many of the "combatants" would have been drawn from the ranks of the workers and urban poor who, in Ancyra, as in Alexandria and elsewhere, had a stake in who controlled the churches. In the riots, Marcellus had the upper hand, perhaps because he also counted on the help of the civic authorities,[28] but once the tumult subsided, he arrested Basil's virgins and rounded up his priests, tied "the consecrated body of the Lord . . . around [their] necks," and paraded them naked through the streets of Ancyra to the agora—the place associated with public justice and the law courts—as if they were criminals. It was "a terrifying and repulsive spectacle."[29]

The violence inflicted on virgins and clerics and the desecration of the holy bread taught the Ancyrene faithful that Basil's ordinations and sacrifices had been false, unclean, and invalid: the bread Basil had consecrated could confer no salvation, and the priests he ordained could not be true priests, because he lacked the power of the Spirit. Marcellus's treatment of Basil's virgins was particularly vicious. By removing their veils and stripping them of their clothes—a practice that would become widespread as the controversy escalated—he not only disregarded their claims to purity but also profaned their bodies.[30] Humiliating fellow Christians in this manner and turning it into a public spectacle was new; Christians had not experienced anything like this since the end of the tetrarchic persecutions, more than a generation ago.

In Gaza and Adrianople, too, the exiles Asclepas and Lucius used force to repossess their churches and expel their rivals. Asclepas's attempts to wrest the episcopal throne from Quintianus triggered riots in which an altar was shattered. Lucius, who had a devoted following in the city, especially among the workers in the imperial weapons factory, seized the church and commanded "that the sacrifice made by holy and virtuous priests be thrown to the dogs," making sure, no doubt, that, as in Ancyra, all the faithful watched it.[31]

In previous chapters we have seen churchmen mobilizing the faithful, inciting riots, co-opting secular officers, and using thuggery to assert themselves and neutralize their rivals. They continued to do so in the years after Constantine's death, but we now discern two new and disturbing trends: first, the dramatic, unapologetic, and blatant use of compulsion to break up dissent and secure control of the church; second, violence as a legitimate means to engage in dispute—not only outbursts of episodic collective violence, but, as we shall see, also a new, chronic "low-level" conflict that was insidious and persistent. These developments stemmed from the bishops' attempts to claim legitimacy, prove their orthodoxy, and entrench themselves in divided congregations where their leadership was repeatedly contested, but their combined effect was to elevate bishops as powerful forces in late Roman communities.

Take the example of Athanasius. Since becoming bishop, but especially after Psamathia, this prelate had resorted to coercion as part of a strategy to subject Arian and Melitian Christians to his authority, but after returning from exile in 337, violence became part of a systematic pattern of behavior, reenacted often, openly, every day, in the streets and churches of Alexandria. Moreover, Athanasius's targets were no longer obscure priests in the dusty villages of the Mareotis or impoverished Melitian clerics in the *chora*, but rather the man officially appointed to sit on the throne of St. Mark and his clergy, whom Athanasius, with the prefect's complicity, brutally and mercilessly assailed in the heart of the city amid scenes of fire, bloodshed, and destruction that had enormous visibility. To some Christians, such behavior would have been interpreted as a sign that Athanasius was indeed right, that he possessed the Spirit, the truth, and the power to save. To others—Christian and non-Christian alike—it reinforced the public image of the bishop as an aggressive, uncompromising, and fearless leader, who, for the sake of the true God and preeminence in the church, was ready to crush opponents while protecting and rewarding his followers—precisely the qualities that defined a "leader of the people" (προστάται τοῦ δήμου) in the later Roman Empire.[32]

The same was true of his fellow churchmen in Ancyra, Gaza, and elsewhere. Marcellus's ritualized humiliation of his opponents and public profanation of virgins and priests also marked a departure in the modus operandi of church leaders "striving for primacy in the church against the dictates of religion."[33] As the Eastern bishops declared at Serdica in 343, "[Athanasius, Marcellus, Asclepas, and their allies] tried to terrorize us.... They waged wars against the holy churches and brutally persecuted them and in a tyrannical fashion strove to place the people of God under their dominion."[34] We have already caught a glimpse of this behavior on the part of Athanasius in the early 330s, but these dramas were now acquiring a new public face and becoming more destructive, habitual, and widespread.

Before we expand on this subject, we need to bring a fuller picture of the controversy into view to better characterize the climate of growing competition and progressive theological polarization in which church leaders operated and which informed their actions. The confrontations in local communities were only battles in a much larger struggle to win over public opinion and to convince the emperors to take sides as the dispute grew more ferocious and the stakes became even higher.

Beginning in the summer of 337 and then continuously for two or three years, the Eusebians mounted a feverish campaign against the exiles in an effort again to depose them from office and replace them and their allies with like-minded clerics.[35] In fall 337, Eusebius of Nicomedia took control of the church of Constantinople—a huge prize. A contested episcopal election in the summer of 337 resulted in the consecration of Paul, the candidate of the Nicene faction, as bishop of Constantinople. However, his rival, the deacon Macedonius, and anti-Nicene Christians refused to accept Paul, leading to violent disturbances. Using the turmoil as a pretext, the Eusebians convinced Constantius to call a synod, which deposed Paul and appointed Eusebius bishop.[36] Eusebius quickly established himself in the Constantinopolitan church. He must have been no less forceful in imposing his authority than his peers in Alexandria or Antioch, but our sources speak only of his conciliatory efforts to organize the Christian community.[37]

With the Constantinopolitan see safely in their hands, the Eusebians moved more decisively against the exiles who were now regaining their sees. They wrote damaging letters to their peers and to the three emperors, complaining of the exiles' usurpations.[38] In early 338, soon after Athanasius's arrival in Alexandria, they accused him to the emperors, reviving old charges and adding new ones of murder, sedition, stealing the grain of the poor, and behaving like a magistrate.[39]

Athanasius's accusers prompted Constantius to rebuke the bishop and summon him to court.[40] In the meantime, the Eusebians convinced Constantius to replace Theodorus with Philagrius, who, as prefect of Egypt in 335, had collaborated with the Mareotic commission. Constantius was again easily persuaded: Philagrius was popular in Alexandria, and the local citizens had in fact recently petitioned the emperor for his reappointment. Thus, sometime in spring 338, to the delight of the Alexandrian people, Philagrius returned to Egypt.[41]

The Eusebians also worked hard to keep Pistus's episcopate afloat. They communicated with him and his flock, "sending deacons to the Arians, joining them in their assemblies, exchanging letters with them," ignoring Athanasius's claim to be the bishop of Alexandria.[42] The Athanasians complained that Eusebius's men "incited the Ariomaniacs against the church" and "divided the churches with their threats and terrors so that they would have assistants to their impiety everywhere."[43] In spring 338, they approached Julius of Rome, dispatching the priest Macarius and deacons Martyrius and Hesychius, to encourage him to communicate with Pistus.[44]

As the Eusebians intensified their campaign, Athanasius, Marcellus, and their allies attacked them, denouncing them for being in league with the "Ariomaniacs." Marcellus's supporters circulated letters, defending the bishop from the charge of heresy, reminding fellow churchmen how he had stood as a bulwark against Arius at Nicaea.[45] Athanasius also wrote to the emperors and sent embassies to them and to Julius of Rome.[46] In winter 338, he assailed Arian Christians in his paschal letter to the Egyptian bishops,[47] and, in the spring, in anticipation of his audience with Constantius, he summoned a council of Egyptian bishops in Alexandria to revisit the charges the Eusebians filed against him. Not surprisingly, this council pronounced him innocent and communicated its acquittal in a synodical probably written by Athanasius himself, calling old and new charges fabrications of the devilish Eusebians, who would have "murdered" Athanasius "if they had the chance," in order to "establish their impious doctrines and bring the Arians into the church."[48] Murdered!

Armed with this letter, Athanasius traveled to Cappadocian Caesarea to see the emperor in late spring or early summer 338. We know little about this encounter, but Constantius, now busy with the Persian conflict, seems to have either accepted the bishop's defense or (more likely, in my view) deferred the matter to an ecclesiastical panel scheduled to meet sometime in the near future.[49] More than ever in need of support, on his journey back to Alexandria, Athanasius once again struck alliances and founded new churches and bishoprics outside Egypt. By now, both sides were firmly engaged in a war to win the sympathy of all Christians and the votes of as many churchmen as possible.[50]

In spring 338, Athanasius's embassy reached Rome, where they debated the Eusebian envoys before Julius, "defeated" them, and persuaded Julius to withhold communion from Pistus.[51] The Eusebian envoys, however, urged Julius to call a synod to address the deepening crisis in the church, and Julius did so, writing, sometime between summer and fall 338, to the Eastern bishops, inviting them for a council "whenever [they] should desire."[52]

By the time Julius's invitations arrived in Eastern capitals, however, the ground had shifted. A synod at Antioch in winter 339 had declared the restoration of the exiled bishops in 337 uncanonical,[53] deposed them from office, and appointed or reappointed "true" bishops to replace them.[54] Basil and Quintianus were reinstated to Ancyra and Gaza, respectively, and, with Pistus probably dead, the Cappadocian Gregory was appointed bishop of Alexandria.[55] The synod also deposed prelates whom Athanasius (and presumably others?) had irregularly ordained or restored to office since his return from exile.[56] Constantius, occupied with an impending conflict with Persia,[57] and eager to quell the tumult in the church, endorsed this council's decrees and agreed to use force if necessary to evict recalcitrant bishops and install their replacements.[58] Thus, for the first time, we find high-profile bishops being escorted to their sees by military detachments sent from the imperial court to ensure their installation and the expulsion of their rivals.[59]

"RAPINE AND DEATH FILLED CHURCH AND CITY": THE ROUTINIZATION OF VIOLENCE

Let us return now to local communities to see how these developments drove church leaders to assert themselves even more aggressively. First, Alexandria. In late winter 339, in the wake of the synod at Antioch, Philagrius "published ... a decree," announcing that "Gregory ... was coming from the *comitatus*" to be the new bishop.[60] Gregory was no stranger to Alexandria and its Christian community. He had studied there earlier, when Athanasius himself had received him.[61] The bishops assembled at Antioch were careful to choose a prelate acquainted with the city, its clergy, and congregation.[62]

The Arian Christians cheered the news, especially the poor, widows, and virgins, whom Athanasius had deprived of grain after his return.[63] But the decree left the Athanasians seething: "They cried out for help, shouting ferociously to the other magistrates and the entire city" that the new bishop was coming solely for the sake of the "Arian heretics."[64] Athanasius noted, disingenuously, given his return from exile by imperial fiat, that the imperial appointment of a bishop had no precedent in the church.[65] In fact, what was really unprecedented was the manner in which the dispute came to intrude into the life of the city: first, a public decree announced the coming of a new bishop; next, the faithful threatened to draw the "magistrates and the entire city" into the fray;[66] then, more conflict and more violence.

Athanasius tells us that immediately after Philagrius's decree the "faithful began to assemble *even more frequently* in the churches."[67] It was Lent—a season for fasting, purification, and incessant vigils, when Christians often spent nights in church, singing, hymning, and praying.[68] At that time of heightened devotion, it did not take much to mobilize and fire up the faithful.[69] In the weeks preceding Gregory's arrival, Athanasius had reached out to his supporters and urged them to resist the new bishop in opposition to the emperor's decree. Monks and virgins responded enthusiastically to his calls, and church crowds swelled even more as the Athanasian clergy doled out alms, oil, and wine to the poor.[70] As the day of Gregory's arrival approached, "enraged by these events and the novelty of the appointment," the faithful "gathered . . . to prevent the Arian impiety from mixing with the faith of the church."[71] The Athanasian clergy then shut the churches to the Arian Christians—a provocative move that Philagrius could not tolerate.[72]

The prefect, pressured to prepare the church for Gregory's arrival, decided to strike and arrest Athanasius with the help of Duke Valacius. During a night vigil at the church of Theonas on March 18,[73] Valacius deployed his troops inside the city and "posted his soldiers in order of battle on every side of the church,"[74] but Athanasius somehow evaded them, fled, and disappeared underground, and from there he continued to lead the resistance to the prefect, guiding his supporters and coordinating their actions.[75] Philagrius now tried to take the church buildings by force. According to Athanasius, he gathered a mob of pagans, Jews, and troublemakers, armed them with swords and clubs, and unleashed them against the faithful crowding the churches.[76] In the church of Theonas, his goons seized the virgins, stripped them naked, and raped a few of them.[77] Some virgins and widows were dragged about and "forced . . . to blaspheme and deny the Lord; those who refused, they trampled underfoot and beat."[78] They also thrashed and beat the monks, killing some of them.[79] Clerics and laymen were arrested, beaten, thrown in jail, and banished.[80] At the end of the raid, Philagrius's men offered sacrifices to the gods in the building, bathed naked in the baptistery, and set the church and the baptistery on fire.[81] Athanasius called these atrocities unprecedented; indeed, the religious riots of the previous generation did not match brutality on this scale, though, had we had a fuller account of the events surrounding Athanasius's or Marcellus's return in 337, we might perhaps find much that was comparable.[82]

This violence escalated further after Gregory's arrival four days later, on March 22, with a military force, "five thousand strong."[83] The deployment of imperial troops on behalf of a bishop conjured ideas and images of authority that projected bishops not only as heads of churches, but also as powerful leaders. The Athanasian Christians, however, refused to receive Gregory and, despite Philagrius's raid on Theonas, held on to the other churches.[84] Athanasius continued to foil the prefect's efforts to arrest him, moving about under the cover of night, showing up unexpectedly in vigils held in parish churches throughout the city, and presenting himself as a victim of persecution, a martyr-like figure not unlike Arius in the early days of the controversy. For his part, Gregory, like Athanasius before him, set out to take over the churches and to impose his authority by force. Philagrius and Valacius stormed every church in the city. Philagrius allowed his men to plunder what remained of Theonas,[85] and then, his men turned their savagery against the Athanasians in the other churches.[86] The cruel, merciless punishment they inflicted on priests, women, and others before the public eye projected episcopal power into new arenas with an aggressiveness not seen in previous years, intended to arouse respect and impose fear on a much larger scale.

The attacks against the Athanasians lasted throughout Lent and beyond.[87] Some of the atrocities could perhaps have been avoided had Athanasius demobilized his followers and delivered the churches to Gregory, but he chose not to—and his priests, virgins, and monks played a leading role in organizing the resistance, gathering the faithful and urging them to fight back. Athanasius finally decided to leave the city; yet waiting until Easter Sunday proved irresistible. What better time than the week before the festival of Christ's rebirth to teach the faithful that the Son was not a creature, not from nothing, but from the essence of the Father?[88] Furthermore, the Easter festival, with its throngs of worshippers and outpouring of devotion, whipped up to new heights in that atmosphere of confrontation, provided Athanasius with an opportunity to stage his leadership and show that he, not Gregory, commanded the power of God's spirit.

When the day of the festival arrived, with the prefect on his heels, Athanasius joined the faithful packing the church where "[he] resided at that time."[89] Singing psalms with his followers, the bishop celebrated the mysteries, ministered baptism to dozens, perhaps hundreds of catechumens, before fleeing the next day to Rome allegedly to attend the council Julius had summoned, but also to seek the ear of Constantius's brothers in the West.[90] His loyal supporters, however, grieving the bishop's departure, rioted and burned the church of Dionysius to the ground, rather than surrender it to Gregory.[91] It was the third church to go up in flames in Alexandria in less than two years, and the second in two weeks![92] This outburst of collective anger—spontaneous, destructive, uncontrollable—was also an extraordinary demonstration of the reach of popular power that was helping to establish the episcopate as a spectacular public force.

With Athanasius gone, Philagrius finally managed to hand all churches over to Gregory and the Arian Christians.[93] Not surprisingly, however, the Athanasians continued to reject Gregory, calling him a heretic.[94] Then, the bishop felt compelled even more aggressively to assert his dominance, filling church and city, in Athanasius's words, with "rapine and death,"[95] though Gregory was probably no more violent than Athanasius had been after his return from exile. Applying the same techniques his rival had honed in previous years, Gregory first surrounded himself with loyal supporters: he promoted clerics previously expelled "because of the Arian heresy" and ordained a new crop of priests and deacons.[96] Relying on their assistance, he demanded, and then constrained, Christians to communicate with him.[97] Those who refused were barred from entering the churches, which he kept under surveillance.[98] In his sermons, Gregory attacked Athanasius and seems to have, in time, convinced at least some Athanasians to join him, though many did so under pressure from the prefect.[99] Many Athanasians, however, like the Arians before them, retreated into private houses, where, together with Athanasius's priests, they prayed and worshipped, "choosing thus to be sick and endanger themselves than to have the hand of the Arians come upon their heads."[100]

But Gregory also sought to break up these domestic assemblies. He and his Eusebian allies convinced Constantius to pass decrees against Athanasius's supporters—cleric and lay.[101] He harassed Athanasian priests and asked Philagrius to disband their clandestine churches.[102] The Athanasian clergy were deprived of their immunities just as the Arians had been by Constantine in 332 or 333.[103] As a result, "uproar and *stasis* spread not only in Alexandria but in all of Egypt ... [as] the Arians convulsed the entire city, ... contaminating with heresy those ... deceived by them."[104]

Gregory also "intercepted the bread of the ministers and virgins" and, like Athanasius before him, withdrew assistance from the poor who rejected him, "for no other reason than to make them join the Arians and receive [him]."[105] And "when the [Athanasian] widows and indigent had received alms, [Gregory] ordered what had been given them to be taken away and the vessels used to carry oil and wine to be broken."[106]

The worst of the violence in Alexandria would have subsided in a few weeks, but Gregory's persecution of Athanasian Christians dragged on at least until 344. Indeed, as we shall see below, after the Council of Serdica, it worsened, deepened, and engaged the civic authorities in some novel ways.[107] In other words, the dispute continued to shape a pattern of behavior marked by increasing brutality as it encouraged church leaders to assert their authority in local communities. This was true even when they practiced charity, from which they now excluded many Christians on account of theological and personal allegiances. The novelty, then, after 337, was not only the scale of the violence, but also its proliferation and persistence, which was reconfiguring the dynamics of power in local communities and making bishops more than just church leaders.

We lack anything close to this detailed narrative for events outside Alexandria in the wake of the synod of 339. We know that in the Egyptian *chora* Gregory demanded that monks and bishops and their congregations communicate with him.[108] Like Athanasius in the late 320s, Gregory and his supporters traveled upcountry, determined to impose his hegemony and prevent clerics from following Athanasius to Rome.[109] The Coptic history of the church of Alexandria notes that George, here a mistake for Gregory, "sent bishops to the cities of Egypt to preach the blasphemy of the pestilential Arians."[110] With the help of Philagrius and Valacius, he forced Egyptian prelates and monks to hold communion with him. "Numerous afflictions and bitter persecutions" followed: bishops, monks, and virgins were terrorized, arrested, scourged, and exiled.[111] Yet not all Egyptian Christians rejected Gregory and the theological views he favored and, later, preached openly; many in fact embraced them. Ephrem was said to have later rescued many monks "contaminated" by Arius's heresy, and as late as the fifth century, Isidore of Pelusium corresponded with "Arian" monks in Egypt.[112]

In other provinces, we know that Marcellus and Asclepas were also expelled from their churches and, like Athanasius, ended up in Rome.[113] Lucius of Adrianople, who had "revealed [his enemies'] impiety," was put in chains and banned for a second time.[114] And "because they hated the heresy," the Thracians Olympius of Aeni and Theodulus of Trajanopolis were falsely accused, deposed, threatened, and forced to flee to save their skin.[115] Diodorus of Tenedos was also banned;[116] and Arius of Palestine and Asterius of Arabia were threatened and bullied.[117] Other prelates from Thrace, Syria, Phoenicia, and Palestine were deposed and banished.[118] Athanasius notes that the Eusebians and their allies traveled as far as the Persian border, filing false charges against all who opposed them, and securing their exile.[119] The correspondence of Julius of Rome gives the impression that a constant stream of exiled and self-exiled clerics left the East after the winter of 339.[120] All of them had terrible tales to tell of violence suffered at the hands of their rivals, whom they must surely have resisted, fighting them back with no less murderous zeal.

The departure of the exiles in 339 did not bring peace to the church. On the contrary, it added more fuel to the dispute. The Eusebians now controlled the three preeminent archbishoprics in the East—the patriarchal sees of Alexandria, Antioch, and Constantinople. Churches in key cities of the East also fell into the hands of their allies and appointees—Heraclea, Adrianople, Nicomedia, Nicaea, Ephesus, Laodicea, Cappadocian and Palestinian Caesarea, Scythopolis, Gaza, Ptolemais, and others.[121] Counting on a sympathetic Constantius, they now felt empowered to reopen the theological debate about the matter of God that resulted in the composition of new creeds of faith in the so-called Dedication Council of Antioch in the summer of 341.[122]

While the Eusebians prepared the ground for that council, the exiles brought the controversy to the Western congregations, implicating in it an ever-larger number of prelates, power brokers, and the Western emperors. Painting a one-sided picture of events in the East, the exiles demanded to be reinstated to office. They insisted their rivals were heretics, and claimed they plotted to introduce heresy into the church. To their supporters in the East and to the Westerners, the publication of creeds at Antioch in 341 would have seemed to confirm those claims, widening the rift that divided Christians in the East and leading to a schism between the Eastern and Western churches. And as the dispute expanded anew and deepened, it challenged church leaders to assert their authority and promote their views on God in ways that created new forms of power in the church and empire. To situate these developments in a larger historical context, let us look at the Eusebians' attempt to rewrite God, and the polarization of the church that resulted from the publication of the creeds of Antioch.

"NOT FROM THE ESSENCE OF THE FATHER": REWRITING GOD

Following Athanasius's departure, Gregory circulated letters against him, charged him before Constantius, and probably that same spring, dispatched an embassy to Julius of Rome and, presumably, to the Western emperors to provide them with his account of events in Alexandria.[123] Basil of Ancyra, Quintianus of Gaza, and other reinstated bishops may also have written to their peers, Constantine II, and Constans along the same lines.

In the meantime, the exiles gradually made their way to Rome. Athanasius arrived in May 339, accompanied by a handful of priests and ascetics. Marcellus came a few months later, probably in summer of that year. Asclepas, Lucius, and others arrived later, but most likely before spring 341.[124]

Athanasius reached out to many powerful people, including, among others, Princess Eutropia, Constantine's half-sister, asking them to intercede on his behalf.[125] The ascetic Isidore, Athanasius's fellow traveler, met with many Christian nobles, bringing Athanasius in contact with senators and the "wives of the great men."[126] Athanasius also sought out Constantine II and informed Constans of events in the East.[127] Then, after Constantine II's death in the spring of 340, together with other exiled bishops, he came to Constans for help.[128]

To counteract the Eusebians' letter-writing campaign, in the summer or early fall of 339, Athanasius published an inflammatory pamphlet in the form of an encyclical letter to bishops in the East and West, giving his version of Gregory's atrocities in Alexandria, naturally omitting his role in the violence. Calling Gregory a puppet of the Eusebians, Athanasius urged the bishops to repudiate him and the Eusebians' letters.[129] Reminding fellow churchmen that the Eusebians had long supported the "Arian heresy," he accused them, as he had already done at Tyre in 335 and Alexandria in 338, of getting rid of him in order to introduce their deadly doctrine.[130] Fashioning himself the victim of a conspiracy, Athanasius called his enemies inveterate heretics and murderers and urged his peers to rise up against "the corruption of the canons of the church and of the faith." "Don't stand in awe of them," he clamored. "Exact revenge, . . . show your outrage" and "nourish a zealous hatred" against them.[131]

These calls were heeded, especially in the West. Julius of Rome refused to hold communion with Gregory and dismissed his emissary.[132] Then, sometime in late summer or early fall 339, probably after Marcellus arrived with more horror stories about his own expulsion from Ancyra, Julius yet again summoned the Eastern bishops to a council at Rome, this time appointing a deadline for the gathering, which I suggest was fall 340.[133] He also wrote to the Eusebians, questioning the charges leveled against Athanasius, complaining they had communicated with "Arians," and casting doubt on the fairness of their synods and appointments.[134] The Roman priests Elpidius and Philoxenus carried Julius's letter and summons to the East and apparently also went around visiting "those who were suffering," that is, bishops and priests sympathetic to the exiles who were now being persecuted.

Not surprisingly, the Eusebians and other Eastern bishops took offense at Julius's letter. The bishop of Rome had arrogated for himself an authority higher than that of his peers.[135] His missive suggested he had prejudged the case in favor of Athanasius—a man with a criminal record who now accused them of heresy.[136] The Eastern bishops were also scandalized to learn Julius had received Marcellus, whom they had twice deposed and anathematized.[137] Julius's letter demanded a strong reply, but one that must come not from the Eusebian circle alone, but from as many Eastern prelates as possible, speaking in one voice against Julius's imputations and Athanasius's calumnies. Thus, instead of coming to Rome for the council, they retained Julius's envoys in the East past the scheduled date and assembled a synod of their own that met in Antioch in December 340 or January 341 to draft a reply to Julius.[138] Elpidius and Philoxenus brought their letter to Rome. Using the Persian war and the shortness of notice as pretexts for not attending the council, the Easterners expressed their frustration with Julius's handling of the affair.[139] Claiming that unanimity and peace prevailed throughout the Eastern churches, they accused the bishop of Rome of sowing discord with his contempt for the decisions of Eastern synods and reception of Athanasius and Marcellus.[140] To restore peace, they demanded that Julius recognize the depositions of these bishops and their replacements, otherwise "they would declare their opposition to him."[141]

By the time Elpidius and Philoxenus returned to Rome with their missive, in February or March 341, the Council of Rome had already met. In late fall 340, some fifty Italian bishops acquitted Athanasius, Marcellus, and others, communicated with them, reinstated them to their sees, and declared their replacements uncanonical and illegitimate.[142] When Julius took up his pen to reply to the Eastern bishops' letter, he invited them once again to come to Rome, but he did not back off from his positions.[143] On the contrary, he defended the Council of Rome's decision to admit Athanasius and Marcellus to communion, condemned yet again the appointment of Gregory and others, and accused the Eastern bishops of becoming the authors of a schism.[144]

We do not know how the Eastern bishops received Julius's letter,[145] but the rift between Rome and the East widened further as the Eusebians proceeded with their plans to revise Nicaea. In summer 341, they assembled again, ninety-plus bishops, at a synod in Antioch, to discuss the doctrine of God and reply to Athanasius's *Epistula encyclica*, which would by now have circulated more widely in the East.[146] Known as the Dedication Council, because the bishops participated in the consecration of the great church began by Constantine in that city, this synod issued three creeds of faith, followed by a fourth, published sometime shortly after the gathering.[147]

Theologians and church historians have dissected these creedal formulas from the moment they were published until the present. I could never do justice here to the wealth of this scholarship, nor am I qualified to discuss their theological intricacies and antecedents.[148] But I do want to mention two features the four creeds had in common. First, all four creeds dropped the *homoousios* and the Nicene phrase "out of the essence (*ousia*) of the Father." Second, despite the anathemas to some of Arius's original teachings,[149] they adopted an ambiguous language that, as S. Parvis noted, could easily accommodate a subordinationist theology that Nicene supporters would later label "Arian" and consider heretic.[150]

In publishing these creeds, the bishops at Antioch did not explicitly reject Nicaea—not formally at least.[151] Drawing on Sabinus, Socrates wrote that the bishops "did not condemn anything in the Nicene creed ... but pursued a policy of assembling frequent synods and proposing formulas of faith so as gradually to establish Arian doctrine."[152] In truth, in 341, a direct attack against Nicaea was probably imprudent and perhaps unnecessary. Imprudent because Constantius, like his father and brothers, was attached to that faith, and respect for Constantine's memory would have discouraged an outright condemnation.[153] Unnecessary because the Antiochene formula provided church leaders with new, "official" doctrinal points of reference that made it possible for prelates to disregard the Nicene conception of the Son in their doxologies, prayers, liturgies, and sermons and avoid the suspicion of heresy. It is also unlikely that the creeds of Antioch (second and fourth) were intended to replace Nicaea as a new "universal" standard of faith.[154] What made these formulas attractive was precisely the fact that they were not being imposed or enforced by imperial decree dictating Christians how to believe and worship. By removing the *homoousian* straitjacket, the new creeds laid out less rigid parameters for defining God, allowing room for a wider spectrum of nuanced theological positions. The relative indeterminacy of these formulas gave church leaders more latitude to define God, offering them the option to dismiss Nicaea or interpret it according to their own belief, as the Eusebians had seemingly been doing for years.[155]

This was a break with the practice established by Constantine after Nicaea and, in a way, a throwback to a time before Arius. At Antioch the bishops seem to have envisioned a church in which orthodoxy was to be continuously shaped through debate and negotiation, an ongoing pious conversation about God. This may in fact have been all the Eusebians wanted or all they could obtain from their peers.

Their project, however, was destined to fail, because, in the wake of Athanasius's and others' calls to "hatred" and "revenge," the publication of these new creeds hardened theological positions and further pulled Christian congregations apart. Athanasius's insistence that the Eusebians were introducing heresy resonated widely with supporters of Nicaea in divided churches throughout the East and in virtually the entirety of the Western church.[156] This polarization drove prelates even more forcefully to prove their ideas represented the truth and to step up their efforts to impart their views to others and extend their authority over large numbers of people. We again see this most clearly in the largest sees—Alexandria, Antioch, Constantinople—where developments set the tone for many smaller sees.

CREATING POWER: BISHOPS, CROWDS, AND POLITICS

Let us begin in Antioch. The publication of the new creeds caused tumult in the city, which apparently quickly subsided.[157] Since Eustathius's deposition in 327, the Antiochene church remained divided.[158] The Eustathians continued to assemble in private houses, but many Nicene Christians still worshipped with the bishop and the pro-Arian congregation, though they apparently did not communicate with each other during the Eucharist.[159] But following the Dedication Council, Nicene Christians reconstituted themselves as a more self-conscious and distinct group. The emergence, in the years after the council, of new, vocal Nicene leaders, like Flavianus and Diodorus,[160] reflected their greater coherence. It is perhaps also in the period after 341 that the Christians of Antioch organized themselves into two groups, each reciting a different doxology: "one giving glory to the Son with the conjunction 'and' [i.e., to Father and Son], while others used the preposition 'through' [to the Father through the Son]."[161] Sozomen also noted that only a fraction of the Antiochene Christians chanted Nicene hymns.[162] The ritual recitation of distinct doxologies and hymns also bespoke a greater theological self-awareness of Christians attached to distinct conceptions of divinity who were still worshipping together in the same churches.

The greater cohesion among Nicene Christians posed new challenges to the anti-Nicene faction in command of the Antiochene church. Yet, whether because during those years Antioch had effectively become the imperial capital or because Constantius had supported the new creeds, the bishops shunned direct confrontation of the kind we have seen in Alexandria, Ancyra, and elsewhere. Instead, careful to avoid being portrayed as agitators, they applied a different kind of pressure on Nicene Christians, especially after Stephen, the pro-Arian priest who succeeded Flacillus, became bishop of Antioch a few months after the Dedication Council, in late 341.

Stephen had lived through the very early years of the Arian controversy, serving continuously as priest since 327. Throughout his episcopate, but especially following his deposition at Serdica in 343 (on which see below),[163] he terrorized the Nicene "involving them in all kinds of calamities"—lawsuits, blackmail, extortion, bribery, and physical violence.[164] Like Athanasius, Gregory, and others, Stephen counted on a posse of henchmen led by a "bully-boy" known as "The Ass" (Ὄναγρος). Unlike the thuggish priests in Alexandria, however, Stephen's gang was made up of lay folk willing to defend the bishop and harm his opponents. The band and its brutal methods became well known in the city, where they operated undisguised, in broad daylight, "with no shame," moving seamlessly between the innermost sanctum of the gilded churches and the city's demimonde of crime and prostitution.[165] Onagros's men used to strut about the agora, threatening people, dragging them away, and beating them. They broke into houses, kidnapping respectable men as well as "women known for their virtuous life."[166] Their conduct reveals how church leaders expanded their repertoire of strategies to gain power and assert dominance in an increasingly polarized environment. They borrowed these strategies from the secular world around them,[167] but they used them primarily to intimidate fellow Christians who thought differently about God. And so here, too, the dispute continued to spawn violence—chronic, grinding, low-level violence—as an instrument of power.

Violence of a different kind also swept Constantinople. The publication of new creeds seems to have galvanized the Nicene, and after Eusebius died in late 341, "the zealous supporters of Nicene doctrine led Paul back into the church."[168] When news that the Nicene had reinstated Paul reached the faithful congregating in the church of Hagia Irene in support of Macedonius's ordination as Eusebius's successor, a riot broke out that escalated into "an intestine war" that continued for weeks "as if," noted a pagan observer, "it would last to eternity."[169] As in Alexandria after Athanasius's return, the city fell into the grip of "continuous seditions . . . and many lives were sacrificed."[170] "Frequent riots," added Sozomen, "erupted all over . . . and as rival crowds came to blows with one another a large number of people perished. The city was filled with disorder."[171] The Eastern bishops at Serdica spoke of "a thousand murders, . . . massacres, and . . . slaughter."[172] Paul obviously counted on many staunch supporters, Christians moved by that "hatred" of the "heresy," now identified with the creeds of Antioch and the followers of Macedonius.

These riots had enormous destructive power, severely disrupting public life,[173] illustrating how the dispute cast bishops at the center of public affairs, transforming them into masters of crowds and altering the traditional dynamics of power in local communities throughout the East. As the turmoil escalated, the authorities at Constantinople were impotent to suppress the unrest. The proconsul himself was wounded in the fray and forced to flee.[174] According to Libanius, who was caught in the violence, the conflict led to a breakdown of law and order, as unruly

Christian and (as often the case) non-Christian gangs armed with clubs and cudgels roamed the streets imposing their own, tough discipline.[175]

The situation so deteriorated that it required military intervention in a way that resembled Constantine's involvement in Antioch after the fall of Eustathius in 327. But the differences between these episodes illustrate how the dispute had expanded bishops' capacities to the point that they would challenge imperial officers and decrees. Notified of the affair, Constantius issued an edict for the eviction of Paul and ordered Hermogenes, master of the horse, at that time on his way to Thrace, to go to Constantinople, expel Paul, and end the disorder.[176] Hermogenes duly came to the city with a detachment of troops and proceeded to enforce Constantius's decree. But "in using force to remove Paul," wrote Socrates, "Hermogenes threw the entire city into confusion, for the people who were determined to defend him straightaway broke out into a riot to prevent his expulsion."[177] In other words, ordinary Christians in Constantinople were ready to stand by their bishop and the idea of God he defended even if it meant opposing the emperor; neither the Eustathians in 327 nor for that matter the Athanasians in 339 resisted the emperor in this manner. But there is more. Hermogenes of course would not be intimidated and, foolishly, ordered his troops to dislodge the bishop by force.[178] Then, "when soldiers tried . . . to carry out their orders," "the crowd went wild."[179] They rose up, attacked the master, broke into his house, set it on fire, and "dragging his body [through the city], they killed him."[180] Ammianus said that "he was torn to pieces by a crowd of people";[181] Paul apparently did nothing to deter them. Later, Macedonius accused Paul's notaries, who lived with him and had much to lose from his deposition, of inciting the crowd to murder the master.[182] Hermogenes' lynching forced Constantius to leave Antioch to come to Constantinople, crossing Anatolia on horseback at the height of winter, to remove the bishop and restore order in person.[183] Paul, however, managed to escape to Trier to seek the help of Constans.[184] Constantius then allowed Macedonius to "congregate the people and preach," but refused to ratify his ordination.[185]

The riots of Constantinople also bespeak the ability of bishops to mobilize expanding crowds to assert themselves. The background to this was church leaders' indefatigable work of preparing the faithful, giving them instruction, stirring their devotions, channeling their loyalties, and so forth. We have discussed this in detail in earlier chapters, but in the 340s, as rival theologies were openly being preached, this work was being carried out on a grander scale and with unmatched vehemence, so that congregations remained restless, turning bishops into power players, dangerously capable of moving crowds, terrorizing rivals, and engineering resistance to imperial power—a development that did not escape the attention of the emperors, who, after the events in Constantinople, sought to intervene more decisively in the dispute, just as their father had once done, by calling another ecumenical council at Serdica in 343.[186]

The Council of Serdica was expected to reexamine the definition of God, address the exiles' claims to have been unjustly deposed, and inquire into the charges of violence committed against the people and clergy in 339.[187] The bishops came to Serdica in late summer 343.[188] Led by Ossius of Cordova, Protogenes of Serdica, and Gaudentius of Naissus, about ninety Western prelates congregated in the city. The Eastern delegation numbered roughly seventy-six bishops, who attended the council more or less coerced by Constantius.[189] Among them were members of the old Eusebian alliance as well as a new crop of prelates who did not always agree on all doctrinal matters but were more or less united in support of the faith of Antioch and in condemning Marcellus and Athanasius. The new leaders of this anti-Nicene alliance included Theodorus of Heraclea, Narcissus of Neronias, Stephen of Antioch, Acacius of Caesarea (who succeeded Eusebius after his death in 339), Menophantus of Ephesus, Ursacius of Singidunum, and Valens of Mursa.[190] The presence of secular officers was now taken for granted: Count Musonianus and the *castrensis* Hesychius accompanied the Eastern bishops, and Philagrius, ex-prefect of Egypt, joined them in Philippopolis, near the Western border of Constantius's territory.[191]

I cannot discuss here the tactical maneuvers and complex deliberations of the two blocks, which never met as single body;[192] the Eastern bishops, at a numerical disadvantage, perhaps never intended to.[193] The latter had convened in synods along the way and, from Philippopolis, forewarned the Westerners they would not join them until Athanasius, Marcellus, Asclepas, and others were excluded from the council.[194] As M. Simonetti has observed, accepting the presence of the exiles in the assembly would have implied an admission that the Western bishops had the right to pass judgment on and interfere in Eastern affairs.[195] The Eastern bishops reiterated their demands at Serdica, but the Westerners did not budge. From their perspective, removing the exiles would have been tantamount to admitting that the Council of Rome had mistakenly acquitted them.[196] Thus, for the duration of the council, the Easterners remained ensconced behind the walls of the imperial palace, where they lodged. Arius of Palestine and Asterius of Arabia managed to "defect" to the Western side,[197] complaining of the threats they received at the hands of their peers, and accusing them of preventing "many of the right faith" from leaving the palace and meeting with the Westerners.[198] The Easterners had other reasons to avoid meeting their peers. Athanasius and Paul, working through a network of loyal clergy and lay folk, managed to mobilize their followers thousands of miles away and arrange for them to travel to Serdica. According to the Eastern bishops, "an immense multitude of all kinds of evildoers and hooligans converged on Serdica, seeping in from Constantinople and Alexandria."[199] This angry crowd demonstrated around the imperial palace and showed how Athanasius and Paul, even from their place of exile, retained the capacity to reach out to loyal followers across the breadth of the empire and use them to intimidate their rivals.[200]

The tense climate at Serdica was not conducive to reconciliation, and after several days of impasse, when news of Constantius's victory over the Persians arrived at Serdica, the Eastern bishops suddenly left the city for Philippopolis, bringing the council to an end.[201] Following the debacle, the two sides convened separately and condemned, deposed, and excommunicated their main opponents.[202] Claiming that Ossius and his friends were trying to "stamp out the Catholic and apostolic faith, introducing the new sect . . . of Marcellus," the Easterners circulated a scathing synodical denouncing the atrocities committed by the exiles, to which they appended a statement of faith, consisting of the fourth creed of Antioch with six new anathemas.[203] The Western bishops, in turn, again acquitted Athanasius, Marcellus, Asclepas, Lucius, Paul, and others of all charges, restored them to their churches, and declared their replacements illegitimate.[204]

Having taken up the cause of Athanasius and other exiles, the Western bishops now also presented themselves as defenders of the truth—that is, the truth of Nicaea. In their synodical, they denounced the "Arians" for persecuting the orthodox and preaching a false doctrine, speaking openly and ominously about the "rise of the Arian heresy,"[205] and urging bishops and their congregations everywhere to take back their "legitimate" pastors and to abstain from communicating with the prelates they had deposed because "those who separate the Word from the Father ought to be separated from the Catholic church."[206] The synodical circulated all over the empire, gathering a large number of signatures in East and West.[207]

In the meantime, the Eastern bishops did not sit quietly. They knew the Westerners would renew their accusations of heresy, and could not predict how Nicene Christians and Constantius would react. As soon as they returned to the East, they convinced Constantius to punish Arius of Palestine and Asterius of Arabia,[208] and to ramp up the persecution of the Athanasians in Alexandria and probably of Nicene supporters elsewhere. Several Athanasian clerics were arrested and banned. Constantius also declared Athanasius a public enemy, issued a warrant for his arrest, and ordered surveillance points set up at the harbors and gates of Eastern cities to prevent the exiles from regaining their sees.[209]

By the end of 343, it was clear that the attempt to bring reconciliation to the church had once again led to naught. After Serdica, Christians were even more divided than before. Nonetheless the exigencies of imperial politics forced them to arrive at an uneasy compromise that would also not last very long.

In early 344, the Western bishops approached Constantius, pleading with him to end the persecution against the "Catholics" and to stop governors from adjudicating ecclesiastical causes and interfering in church affairs "lest they break and vex innocent men with manifold punishments, threats, violence, and acts of terror."[210] They entreated Constantius "to be vigilant" so that all enjoy the "sweetest liberty" and not be forced "to subject themselves unwilling to . . . those who cease not to sow the corrupt seeds of a bastard doctrine."[211] Above all, they asked the emperor to authorize the return of the exiles for the sake of peace: "May your mildness grant to the people to have whom they want ... to teach them and to celebrate the ... divine mysteries."[212]

At about the same time, Constans also wrote to his brother, asking him to restore Athanasius and Paul, take the Western bishops' petitions seriously, and reject the advice of Stephen of Antioch and his circle.[213] Constans sent Vincentius of Capua and Euphratas of Cologne to Constantius, accompanied by Flavius Salia, master of the horse, carrying the Western encyclical, the Western bishops' report on Serdica, and perhaps a letter of his own.[214] This embassy arrived in Constantius's court in spring 344. Then, a change. Stephen of Antioch's plot to frame Euphratas with a prostitute was revealed, and the Eastern bishops were forced grudgingly to depose him, electing the priest Leontius as his successor.[215] The affair compelled Constantius to soften his stance and, to the chagrin of the anti-Nicene, to yield to the Westerners' pleas and his brother's entreaties. By the end of the summer, Constantius recalled the exiled Alexandrian clerics and ordered an end to the persecution of the Athanasians in Alexandria.[216]

Constantius now reached out to his brother, sending Count Thalassius on an embassy to his court at Poetovio. Sensing the tide turn, the Eastern bishops gathered in Antioch in summer 344 to compose yet another formula of faith, a slightly altered version of the fourth creed of Antioch with a series of long glosses explaining in detail their creedal propositions and anathemas in another attempt to dispel suspicions about their orthodoxy and to expose the temerity of their accusers.[217] Perhaps at Constantius's suggestion, they took this creed to the West. However, a violent incident in Constantinople in the summer or early fall 344 delayed these embassies, contributing to their failure, adding to the mounting tension between East and West,[218] and showing not only how bishops were willing openly to disregard imperial law for the sake of preaching their beliefs, but also how deep were the connections they forged with ordinary people.

Slipping through surveillance and in defiance of Constantius's decree, Paul once again returned to Constantinople, with Athanasius abetting him and perhaps escorting him. Constantius at once ordered the praetorian prefect Philip to expel the daring bishop and to make a show of support for Macedonius's ordination.[219] After secretly arresting Paul and shipping him to exile, Philip took Macedonius with him on his chariot through the streets of Constantinople to Hagia Irene. As they approached the church, the restless crowd following the cortege swelled and blocked the prefect's passage. Then, the soldiers, thinking the people were offering resistance, panicked and used force. A massacre ensued. Socrates conjectures that more than three thousand people died, probably an exaggeration, but even if only one-tenth of that number perished, the episode illustrates how ordinary Christians were deeply involved in the dispute and how that involvement made cities dangerously unstable.[220]

With this crisis over, the Eastern embassy finally brought their creed to the Western bishops assembled in Milan in early 345, but when they were told "to condemn the heretical teachings of Arius," the envoys refused, leaving the council *animis iratis*.[221] Yet another mission of reconciliation had failed, but by now, Constans was pressuring the bishops throughout his realm to communicate with Athanasius. In late 344, a few months before the Council of Milan, Ursacius and Valens, whose sees lay in Constans's territory, publicly anathematized Arius and his teachings and declared Athanasius innocent—a remarkable volte-face, which they later attributed to fear of the emperor.[222] Constans also rebuked Constantius's envoy and now demanded that the exiles be restored. Seeing the affair as an opportunity to project his power more widely, he threatened to come to the East in person to reinstate the bishops.[223] Constantius, who had no desire to go to war with his brother, again yielded and, in summer 345, finally authorized the exiles to return, Gregory's death making it easier to justify restoring Athanasius to Alexandria.[224]

Over the next few months, Paul, Lucius, Asclepas, and Marcellus regained their sees.[225] Athanasius delayed his return, leveraging Constans's patronage to demand further assurances and concessions from Constantius, such as the cancellation of the decrees passed against him, the restoration of immunities to his clergy, the transfer of the canon of grain for the poor to his control, and the removal of the anti-Athanasian decrees from the public record as if they had never been issued at all.[226]

The bishop left Rome for Alexandria a year later, on June 26, 346. He interviewed with Constantius in Antioch, who allegedly swore an oath no longer to listen to his enemies' slanders. Mindful of the rioting that attended Athanasius's return in 337 (and perhaps prodded by Athanasius himself), Constantius wrote to the people of Alexandria to receive the bishop peacefully and ordered local magistrates to punish anyone who engaged in sedition and disorder. Yet he also preserved the immunities of Gregory's Arian clergy, perhaps to placate them and reduce the likelihood they would incite Arian Christians against Athanasius.[227]

On his way to Egypt, Athanasius's supporters in Palestine assembled a synod in Jerusalem that confirmed his innocence,[228] because, as Sozomen put it, "he was honored by Constans [and therefore] regarded with greater consideration than before."[229] On October 21, 346, Athanasius entered Alexandria. Many of his supporters, freed of persecution, traveled to the hundredth mile outside the city to greet him and escort him back into the city, among them, magistrates, bishops, monks, and many of the faithful.[230]

The return of the exiles in 345–346 ensured peace between Constantius and Constans, but it did not end the controversy about God. In the East, it led to uncertainty about what orthodoxy was and who possessed it. Constantius did not force Christians to choose between the faiths of Antioch or Nicaea, allowing Nicene and anti-Nicene to worship freely. As suggested above, the emperor may have seen no need to disavow Nicaea. In Christian communities, however, the coexistence of groups of Christians subscribing to discordant notions of God only fueled tensions already on the rise since the Dedication Council. The presence of large numbers of dissenters and in some communities two bishops ministering to separate congregations encouraged fierce competition between bishops eager to settle scores with their rivals. If Constantius was prepared to be tolerant, this was certainly not the case with prelates who found it difficult to coexist with rivals openly teaching a doctrine they considered false and deadly. Already on his way to Alexandria, Athanasius, who at Antioch had communicated only with the Eustathians, urged congregations "in every city" to beware of the "Arians" and to receive only confessors of the Nicene faith[231]—in other words, the bishop, strengthened by Constans's patronage, had no intention of making peace with Christians who rejected Nicaea.

Similarly, the Arian faithful of Alexandria refused to hold communion with Athanasius.[232] Even before his arrival, the Arian clergy seems to have asked Constantius to allow them to retain a church in which they might worship separately. When Constantius asked Athanasius to grant him that wish, the bishop refused, replying he could agree only if the emperor did the same for Christians "in every city" who refused to worship with the Arians. Constantius and his advisers turned down the request, perhaps at the suggestion of Leontius of Antioch, lest the Eustathians, allegedly very numerous, and other Nicene supporters assemble together in opposition to the Antiochene bishop.[233]

In Antioch, too, relations between Nicene and anti-Nicene grew frostier. Led by Flavianus and Diodorus, the Nicene faction became progressively more assertive and less tolerant. Leontius avoided confronting them directly. Keen to please Constantius and mindful of the delicate political circumstances of the mid-340s, the bishop allowed the Nicene to chant their hymns in church, for "fear of an insurrection."[234] But at the same time, he ordained the radical theologian Aetius deacon and allowed him to teach his subordinationist views in the church. Perhaps in response to Aetius's appointment, Flavianus and Diodorus took the Nicene faithful to the streets. They organized choirs to sing antiphons *outside* the church and gathered monks provocatively to recite Nicene doxologies *in public* ("Glory to the Father and the Son and the Holy Spirit").[235] The choirs proved to be so popular that Leontius banned Aetius from the pulpit and invited the Nicene leaders to bring their singers into the church.[236]

In Constantinople and Ancyra, Nicene and anti-Nicene also grew apart. Paul regained the episcopal throne of Constantinople, but Constantius allowed Macedonius to stay in the city and assemble his followers in a separate church.[237] In Ancyra, too, many Christians rejected Marcellus and continued to assemble on their own,[238] an arrangement that inevitably led to confrontation between the two rival bishops and their followers.

Thus, not long after the return of the exiles, both sides were once again engaged in mutual accusations. Athanasius wrote repeatedly against Leontius, Narcissus, Acacius, Theodorus, and others, denouncing them as heretics.[239] The anti-Nicene, in turn, accused Athanasius and the other exiles of promoting false doctrines and fomenting discord between the emperors.[240] By the late 340s, with the political crisis over, the anti-Nicene prelates decided to take action, seeing perhaps that they had more to lose by acquiescing to the status quo forged by the political circumstances of 345 than by attacking their opponents.[241]

The bishops first targeted Paul, deposing him, in 349 in unclear circumstances.[242] In that same year, they assembled a council at Antioch and deposed Athanasius for his "illegal" return and other crimes;[243] the council elected George, another Cappadocian, to replace him, but he could not reach Alexandria for several years. This council probably also deposed Marcellus, Lucius, Maximus of Jerusalem, Flavianus of Antioch, and others.[244] Relying on a more assertive Constantius, the anti-Nicene convinced the emperor to publish various decrees against the deposed bishops and other Nicene leaders,[245] including Athanasius, whom Constantius was about to remove from Alexandria when news of Magnentius's usurpation and Constans's death stopped him. Faced with a new political crisis, the emperor retained Athanasius, but Constans's death ultimately released Constantius from any obligations to Athanasius and other Nicene exiles,[246] so that, when he defeated Magnentius and became sole emperor in 353, he once again turned against them. In the following decade, Constantius sought to end the dispute once and for all by imposing one doctrine of God on the entire church. Then, bishops leading divided congregations throughout the East stepped up their efforts yet again to eliminate opposition, consolidate their authority, and bring all Christians to their side, turning themselves into social and political leaders that increasingly played a role in local and imperial affairs. For examples we can look to Constantinople and Asia Minor.

LEADERS OF THE PEOPLE

Magnentius usurped the imperial throne in January 350, Constans died soon after, and Constantius waged war against the usurper until 353. However, already in September 351, Constantius won a decisive battle in the Balkans.[247] Soon after this victory, a council of Eastern bishops met in Sirmium in the emperor's presence.[248] This council accused and deposed Athanasius yet again; it also reiterated the fourth creed of Antioch, thereafter known as the creed of Sirmium, to which two anathemas were added strongly condemning the use of the term *ousia* to describe the relationship between Father and Son.[249]

Following Magnentius's defeat in 353, Constantius consolidated his control over the West and, determined to unite the church around one faith, forced the Western bishops to subscribe to the creed of Sirmium and to Athanasius's deposition. Prelates who refused were punished with exile.[250] In the East, the new creed now provided a formula of faith that most anti-Nicene could support for most of the 350s. So, the ground was now set for a crackdown on opponents who clung to Nicaea.

During this period, Macedonius ruled the church of Constantinople as sole bishop.[251] Although he had accepted Sirmium, he and other anti-Nicene bishops would eventually join Basil of Ancyra in support of a theology that confessed "Father and Son to be like according to essence," a doctrine labeled *homoiousian*.[252] Determined to crush all opposition to his rule, he persecuted Paul's clergy and the Nicene faithful there and in neighboring churches.[253] Socrates and Sozomen give detailed reports on his methods against the Nicene, including the Novatians: taking over or destroying their churches, forcing communion on the unwilling—seizing them, prying their mouths open with a piece of wood, thrusting the sacred bread into them—torturing others, imprisoning and banishing clerics and lay folk, labeling many people infamous, having them branded on the forehead (!), and stripping them of civic rights. In persecuting his enemies, Macedonius mobilized not only long-standing supporters, and, if necessary, imperial troops,[254] but now also scores of monks and ascetics, whom he incorporated into urban life, creating, together with his enterprising deacon Marathonius, a network of monasteries and convents that proved to be a major source of strength as the monks brazenly confronted the Nicene, helping their bishop evict them from their churches.[255]

Macedonius, however, like Athanasius and others, understood the need to win over Christians by other means than violence. Thus, he combined brutality with an ambitious charitable program and the practice of a new, engaged, urban asceticism, perhaps inspired by Eustathius of Sebaste's (and Arius's?) teachings, that became immensely popular. Sozomen wrote that "the masses paid special attention to their mode of life . . . [as they] carried themselves with gravity and had the discipline of monks. Their speech was simple and meant to persuade."[256] Unlike the asceticism of the desert, this new urban discipline called for being in the world and engaging with the people.[257]

At the heart of Macedonius's charitable program was the care of the poor and the establishment of a network of poorhouses, possibly founded on a model created by Eustathius of Sebaste.[258] These establishments were still something of a novelty in most Eastern cities in the 340s and 350s. Epiphanius notes that they were founded "out of love" for fellow human beings[259]—no doubt, but their proliferation cannot be seen in isolation from the theological conflict and the bitter competition for the hearts and souls of ordinary Christians in Eastern cities. Churchmen embroiled in the conflict and trying to unite divided congregations could not fail to see the advantages of founding hospitals and shelters for the poor and the sick. These institutions put the bishop and his followers in charge of delivering basic services—food and shelter—to a large number of destitute folk with close ties to an even larger group of ordinary people in the community, ranging from the murkier world of city gangs Libanius described to that "middling" group of socially vulnerable townsfolk who, as Peter Brown has shown, lived under perpetual fear of impoverishment.[260] Furthermore, these "houses of God" placed churchmen at the center of an expanding web of relations connecting pious patrons, ascetics, and the poor that was just as valuable to their struggles.[261] Their permanence in the cityscape also enabled church leaders more efficiently to organize their loyal followers and use them against their opponents. Indeed, this engaged charity must be seen as a strategy of self-assertion that not only enhanced a bishop's public image but also made it possible for prelates and monks to step confidently into the lives of ordinary citizens and the exciting world of popular politics. Macedonius's program was highly effective in galvanizing support for the bishop and his idea of God.[262] Sozomen observed that "[Marathonius] . . . and his poorhouses [were] the only reason why the [Arian] heresy was not fully extinguished in Constantinople."[263]

Macedonius's blend of violence and assistance to the poor was also in evidence in several neighboring cities. The deacon Marathonius, ordained bishop of Nicomedia in late 358, brought his expanded charitable work to that city while cracking down on the Nicene.[264] The devastating earthquake that struck Nicomedia that year meant there were plenty of opportunities for the new bishop to display his piety as he cared for the injured, homeless, and poor.[265] Marathonius's assistance to people suffering hardship and his readiness to use force not only helped entrench him in the Christian community, but more than that, like Macedonius in Constantinople, turned him into a powerful figure in the city.

The same was true in Cyzicus, where Macedonius consecrated bishop Eleusis, a former officer in the palace guard and another anti-Nicene from Constantinople. Eleusis was zealous in his faith, but not as "cruel" as Macedonius in persecuting the Nicene.[266] Yet, once in charge of the church of Cyzicus, he seized and destroyed the church of the Novatians.[267] Eleusis started an aggressive evangelization campaign, closing pagan temples and desecrating hallowed areas in a very public manner, "showing contempt" for tradition, mobilizing supporters, advertising his piety, and asserting his faith and authority. And following the example of Macedonius, Marathonius, and others, Eleusis also "established shelters for widows and convents for holy virgins," thereby persuading many pagans to embrace his brand of Christianity.[268] The faithful, whose hearts he won with "simple" sermons, rallied around him and the faith he preached. Like Arius, Athanasius, and Lucius of Adrianople, Eleusis understood the importance of reaching out to organized groups of ordinary people, pagan and Christian. At several critical moments in the years that followed, these groups stood solidly by his side, ready to defend him even when it meant resisting and challenging the emperor.[269]

Another example of a bishop's devotion to service and spread of doctrine in a theologically polarized environment comes from the *Vita Parthenii*, a hagiographical text about the bishop of Lampsacus composed in an anti-Nicene milieu later in the fourth century.[270] Parthenius became bishop in Lampsacus in the late 330s, remaining there at least until 355.[271] Although there is no direct reference to doctrinal rivalry in this largely pagan city, Parthenius clearly belonged to the anti-Nicene faction in charge of the churches of Heraclea, Constantinople, and Cyzicus at that time.[272] The *Vita* dwells at length on how Parthenius spent his time caring for the poor, healing the sick, and converting pagans. Although these themes would become commonplace in later hagiography, they were only just emerging as subjects worthy of attention as that new brand of urban asceticism was spreading in Asia Minor.[273] Like Macedonius, Marathonius, Eleusis, and above all, Eustathius of Sebaste, Parthenius did not renounce the world—he was fully engaged in it and committed to assisting workers and ordinary people.[274]

The work of these prelates reflects the adoption of a new attitude of public assertiveness that brought them respect, power, and recognition in their communities and in the empire. Their behavior strengthened the episcopate and its connection to urban institutions and the plebeian world of the poor, turning bishops into leaders whose authority reached beyond their congregations to the entire community. This attitude was not inherent to Christianity or the church. Rather, it was determined by the atmosphere of conflict in which prelates operated—that is, by the imperative of public assertion and the practical requirements of a complex and persistent struggle to define God, save the faithful, and control the church.

Conclusion

In the summer of 355, following the Council of Milan, Eusebius, bishop of Vercelli, was exiled to Scythopolis with a handful of priests and deacons. Like other Western bishops, Eusebius had resisted Constantius's imposition of the creed of Sirmium and refused to subscribe to Athanasius's deposition.[1] Scythopolis in late antiquity was a large and prosperous city and a major manufacturing center with a substantial pagan population.[2] When Eusebius arrived, the local church remained in the hands of Patrophilus, the venerable anti-Nicene bishop who had occupied the episcopal chair of Scythopolis since the early years of the Arian controversy. According to Epiphanius, by the late 340s and early 350s, the local Christian community was overwhelmingly, albeit not uniformly, "Arian," largely due to Patrophilus's "wealth, harshness, and familiarity and influence with the emperor."[3] Patrophilus had achieved theological hegemony by "terrorizing the rich, threatening them with proscriptions, as well as the poor, since [he] had the power to shut them in prison." Indeed, Eusebius reports he found young (Nicene?) virgins locked up in the public jail;[4] and Epiphanius, speaking of Count Josephus, a Jewish convert to Christianity who owned a house in Scythopolis, noted that "this man was the only orthodox person to remain in the city, all others were Arian.... Had Josephus not been count ... the man would not have been allowed to live there."[5] Over the years, Patrophilus had clearly cracked down on dissent, forcing Christians to communicate with him, subscribe to his faith, and recognize his leadership. Thus, Scythopolis provides yet another example of the pattern of assertive action that we encountered with bishops in other Eastern cities—Antioch under Stephen, Alexandria under Athanasius or Gregory, Constantinople under Macedonius, and so on.

Upon arriving in the city, Eusebius and his companions were placed under the oversight of Patrophilus, whom Eusebius called his "jailer."[6] At first, Patrophilus and his men, who seem to have tried to persuade the exiles to embrace his faith, granted Eusebius and his entourage quite a bit of freedom in the city.[7] Patrophilus even allowed Eusebius to receive visitors and distribute alms to the needy, using the charitable funds he received from the faithful back in Italy.[8] Eusebius started dispensing charity in a very public manner, "every day," with the poor lining up outside his door at the inn where he was lodged or in some other public place to receive his benefactions. To Patrophilus's exasperation, the visitors and the poor massing before Eusebius's door made the exiled bishop look like a patron and benefactor.[9] Not surprisingly, Patrophilus put a stop to Eusebius's activities. The danger was not that Eusebius would set up a rival church in Scythopolis, but rather that his enterprise would "plant the seeds of goodwill toward Eusebius and his [doctrinal] cause."[10] According to Eusebius, Patrophilus forbade the charitable dispensations and separated Eusebius from his companions in the violent "way that he was always used to."[11] In a letter addressed to Patrophilus, but intended as a pamphlet for wide circulation, Eusebius narrates what happened next: "Thugs sprang up to terrorize [us, and] . . . through the violence and ferocity of a throng of men I was not only dragged through the streets, but . . . [was] stripped naked, [and they] carried me on my back." Patrophilus had Eusebius transferred to a different inn where he was shut in one room and denied permission to see his clergy.[12] We have encountered these scenes many times in the course of this study: thugs in action, the public humiliation of fellow clerics, the brutal treatment of rivals, and attempts to monopolize charity.

In response to the violence, Eusebius started a hunger strike, demanding that Patrophilus allow his brethren "who willingly suffered these tribulations with him on account of the faith" to visit him and hand out the provisions stored in the first inn.[13] After four days, Patrophilus relented and returned Eusebius to his original lodging.[14] Reunited with his companions, Eusebius boldly resumed his charitable work. However, as Eusebius himself reported,

> after twenty-five days, [Patrophilus and his men] were hardly able to tolerate it: again they burst forth, and, with the reckless force of a multitude, they came to the inn, cudgels in hand, broke into the building, . . . and the thugs . . . seized us and locked me up with my beloved priest Tegrinus in a harsher place. . . . They arrested and incarcerated our priests and deacons and . . . used their power to banish them to other places. The brethren who honored us with their visit were thrown in jail. . . . [Then], they seized and destroyed all assets and the alms of the poor . . . [and] did not allow my fellow companions to come to me to bring nourishment necessary for the body. . . . In that respect, they revealed the mind-set of a murderer.[15]

The tumult surrounding Eusebius and his followers in Scythopolis, similar to scenes of religious violence in many cities in the Eastern empire, testifies to the phenomenon being investigated in this book—namely, the transformation of the Christian leadership into a powerful social and political force in the first half of the fourth century A.D. During that period, Patrophilus, like many of his contemporaries, came to wield authority over large areas of public life outside the church: he arrested and incarcerated clerics and laypeople, threatened the wealthy with confiscation of property, shamed and humiliated clerics in public, deprived them of food, and used all kinds of violence to assert himself. Like many of his peers, he also exercised his authority openly, publicly, turning displays of strength into public spectacles that helped him project his power and establish himself as a leader in the community and the empire.[16]

In a sense, this expansion of the bishop's role and authority appears inevitable. The imperial patronage of the church and the novelties introduced by Constantine—wealth, status, and privileges—empowered the church and made the "rise" of bishops a matter of course. Yet, our focus in this study has not been the Constantinian revolution and its impact on church institutions but rather the manner in which bishops claimed leadership of communities, and in particular how their engagement in the dispute over the definition of God contributed to the emergence of a new style of church leadership. I have argued that protracted doctrinal conflict in the first half of the fourth century played a central role in the transformation of the leadership of the church. My argument rests on the proposition that the theological dispute generated a pattern of action that pushed bishops to the center of public affairs. As church leaders were repeatedly challenged to prove their orthodoxy and legitimacy, they strove to achieve recognition of their leadership and assumed a new public attitude, a new habitus, a tendency to act in ways that entrenched them in local communities and created new forms of power. This pattern of action first appeared in the fourth century but was in play before Constantine's embrace of the church.

To summarize, the bishops' new pattern of action developed in response to the challenges posed by doctrinal disagreement. These challenges were of a double nature. On the one hand, knowledge of the right, orthodox doctrine was a necessary requisite for the legitimation of leadership in the church: only orthodox prelates possessed the gift of the Spirit, without which their ministrations and claims to hegemony could be contested and invalidated. On the other, orthodoxy itself, founded as it was on theological speculation and interpretation of scripture, was an artificial construct, whose instability engendered frequent disagreement and disputes. Whenever these disputes erupted, they posed a threat to churchmen's claims to orthodoxy and, by extension, to the leadership of church communities.

These challenges were not new to the fourth century. In the early church, however, before the outbreak of the Arian controversy, church leaders responded to them in ways that tended to emphasize compromise and reconciliation. Such a response stemmed in part from the very imprecision of theological concepts, which made it difficult to define universal criteria for orthodoxy, and from a general recognition that the truth was necessarily the product of debate and discussion; but it also derived in part from the cautious manner in which churchmen approached dissent, striving for consensus and the preservation of communion lest the church become divided and its leadership be weakened. Generally speaking, then, in earlier centuries, church leaders carefully cultivated the ties of solidarity that bonded them to one another and to the congregations they led. Despite harsh rhetoric directed against dissent, a concern to keep these ties intact discouraged prelates from taking hard theological positions when controversy arose in their communities.

The Arian controversy broke with this pattern of caution and solidarity. At the beginning of the dispute in Alexandria, two distinct and incompatible views on God emerged and spread. Each reflected a particular way of looking at the relationship between humans and God, and God and creation. Arius's theology drew on certain currents of Christian thought that had been evolving since the late second century. Alexander's reaction to Arius's teaching built on that same tradition but approached it from a different direction. At first, Alexander, Arius, and their respective followers struggled to reach a compromise, but two interrelated factors made that increasingly difficult to attain. First, the theologies fueling the dispute acquired even greater precision, encouraging greater personal investment in them. Secondly, and above all, the progressive involvement of the faithful, who needed to be instructed on the right way to honor and approach God, expanded the dispute, giving it a new public dimension. The second derived from the first: it was churchmen's commitment to saving souls by teaching the people the right way to conceive and worship God that encouraged them to make the people partners in their disputes. Arius in particular did so in some innovative ways, adopting a plebeian stance, mobilizing the faithful, seeking out ascetics, engaging women and the poor, promoting evangelization, transforming his theology into music, and connecting with workers whose occupations helped spread his views. Alexander responded to Arius's challenges by adopting similar strategies and tightening his hold on the church, and as the two sides competed for the hearts and souls of local Christians, they fashioned a new style of church leadership—brash, enterprising, and combative.

Despite the turmoil the dispute caused in Alexandria—and then elsewhere, as it migrated to other sees and churches—in time, the disputants might have hammered out a compromise solution, as had so often happened in the early church. Constantine's involvement, however, made that impossible. This might appear paradoxical, because, after all, after Constantine it was possible, as it had not been before, to impose theological uniformity, bring the secular arm to bear on schism and controversy, and force quarreling clerics to negotiate with one another and settle differences. Moreover, the privileges, immunities, and patronage that Constantine and his successors granted to orthodox churchmen ought to have constituted an incentive to peace and compliance.

However, peace never came. Constantine's demand for doctrinal consensus politicized theological positions as dissenters from Nicene orthodoxy were punished with deposition, exile, disgrace, or worse. At the Council of Nicaea, most prelates indeed accepted the formula that described the Son of God as *homoousios* with the Father, but many retained their original beliefs and, despite nominally subscribing to Nicaea, worked tirelessly to revise its creed, clashing with its proponents and supporters, and perpetuating the dispute under the Constantinian veneer of uniformity. As in Alexandria, what drove these churchmen to engage in this work was their deep-seated concern to save Christian flocks from what they considered to be blasphemy or heresy. After Nicaea, theological rivals appeared no longer interested in extending solidarity to their opponents or in discussing their disagreements collegially. Imperial intervention in the dispute had made it possible for prelates to use other means to validate their views and prove the legitimacy of their positions. During those years, many bishops, challenged by their peers, and faced with the danger of deposition and exile, sought to assert themselves, build strength, and win the support of various constituencies: like-minded peers, congregations, and the imperial officialdom all the way up to the imperial court. In practice, this affirmation of episcopal authority entailed neutralizing and deposing potential rivals, suppressing dissent, and forcing others to recognize one's leadership and orthodoxy.

Under these new circumstances, the old code of behavior faded away. Churchmen consolidated and expanded that new aggressive, bold, and militant pattern of action that had emerged in the pre-Nicene years of the controversy in Alexandria and elsewhere. Instead of minimizing or brushing aside theological differences, prelates actually acted on them, promoting their views on a much broader field and forcibly imposing them on dissenters. Athanasius's early career best illustrates this shift to a new modus operandi: in his struggle to rise to and remain in office, he fashioned the new style of church leadership of the early years of the controversy into an assertive model of episcopal authority.

The new pattern of action brought bishops enormous power, establishing them as formidable public forces after Constantine's death and beyond. Under Constantius, the attacks against Nicaea culminating in the publication of new creeds of faith at Antioch further polarized Christian congregations, deepening and expanding the controversy. Throughout the 340s and 350s, prelates all over the East, particularly in the largest centers, sought to strengthen their relationship with communities, intensifying the efforts to mobilize support inside and outside the church. Their strategies and methods did not differ much from those of Arius, Alexander, or Athanasius in the early years of the controversy, but now they applied themselves to those tasks with new verve and zeal, dramatically expanding their scale of operations and involving many people in their struggles. We saw this, for instance, in the establishment of ambitious assistance programs for the poor in Constantinople, the cities of Asia Minor, and elsewhere, and in the fierce competition to control charitable funds and the distribution of alms in Alexandria and Scythopolis. The concern to provide for the poor is only one example of how prelates increased their efforts to generate loyalty among ordinary Christians and win the support of many people across a broad front. Loyalty made it possible for churchmen to channel popular power in new and dangerous ways, disrupting civic life and transforming bishops into major players in local communities and the empire.

In the 340s and 350s, bishops also strove to eliminate opposition to their views and to rule through the systematic use of violence, dispensed often, openly, and on a new and unprecedented scale. Indeed, the proliferation and routinization of religious violence in various forms was the hallmark of the dispute during Constantius's reign. Fueling the brutality was the unflinching determination of pugnacious prelates to impose and defend their visions of orthodoxy—in other words, the driving force behind the violence remained theological and religious. It was imperative to enlighten Christian souls with the saving truth even against their will. Theology mattered: commitment to an idea of God and the struggle to save souls encouraged bishops to demonstrate their authority, appeal to violence, and adopt a militant attitude of public assertiveness, all of which contributed to establish them as feared and powerful leaders. Yet, as Gregory Nazianzenus noted, religious piety cannot be easily isolated from love of power. Thugs, soldiers, and crowds were pressed into service to secure for feuding prelates positions of leadership that came with substantial rewards for themselves and their followers, including extending their authority over large numbers of people.

Finally, religious violence simultaneously reflected and created power. It bespoke prelates' growing capacity to mobilize the people and the support of the emperor or his officers. But more significantly, churchmen's readiness to use violence, and the willingness of the faithful to join them, also enabled bishops to encroach on imperial sovereignty. We have seen prelates rallying their congregations, occupying churches, conducting clandestine services, and staging or condoning public demonstrations or riots to resist official decrees, oppose imperial commands, and even attack high-ranking officers. These recurrent episodes of defiance removed areas of church life from under imperial authority. In the aggregate, they triggered reconfigurations of power in local communities and the empire, reflected in the emperors' recognition of bishops as leaders or patrons of the people. Thus, in a letter to Alexandria in 356, congratulating its citizens for the acceptance of George as new bishop, Constantius wrote:

> The majority in [Alexandria] are blinded, and a man [i.e., Athanasius] coming from the depths of perdition held power over them, leading those yearning for the truth

into falsehood, ... never providing fruitful words, but corrupting souls with pedantry.... Flatterers shouted and applauded him; astonished at his power, the majority of the simple-minded accepted that as a sign.[17]

"[He] held power over them"; "[people were] astonished at his power." Constantius's words illustrate how Athanasius's hand reached beyond the boundaries of the Christian community, and how the extension of his power was inextricably connected to the promotion of a particular doctrine. Ammianus and Julian offer similar assessments, stressing the bishop's widening reach into affairs outside the church, and the expectation that bishops handle themselves as leaders of the people.[18]

The Arian controversy lasted for several more decades, into the late fourth century; indeed, in some cities and regions anti-Nicene congregations could be found into the early fifth century. The matter of God continued to generate controversy and violence. Under Julian, Jovian, and Valens, the dispute escalated further, and, once again, in many cities, we find bishops battling each other in churches and the streets, mobilizing crowds, persecuting their rivals, occupying and raiding churches, competing for the support of the faithful and the emperor, asserting themselves, and trying to impose their views on others. Indeed, already by the time of Julian's reign, the transformation of bishops into social and political leaders, as traced in this study, was complete and irreversible, as were the changes that transformation entailed.

Appendix

BISHOPS INVESTIGATED OR DEPOSED FOR DOCTRINAL REASONS BEFORE THE ARIAN CONTROVERSY

Listed in chronological order are bishops who came under suspicion of heresy while in communion with the "great church." I excluded bishops of communities constituted outside the "great church" (for instance, Marcionites, Montanists, Manichaeans, some Gnostic groups, and so on). The * preceding the number denotes that a doctrinal reason can be identified with confidence; † indicates that a condemnation and deposition for heresy are certain.

1. The Asian bishops threatened with collective excommunication by Victor of Rome over the date of Easter, "as if . . . they were heterodox."[1] Victor of Rome probably meant the communities of Asian extraction in Rome, not the churches of Asia. In any case, the controversy was more disciplinary than doctrinal and evolved at a time when bishops had only recently begun to assert themselves in Rome.[2]
2. Callistus of Rome, accused of heresy by Hippolytus over his views on the Trinity. In truth, when the dispute over Callistus's teaching began, neither Hippolytus nor Callistus was a bishop, but I have included them here because both later claimed to be so. The affair began in Zephyrinus's episcopate, who made Callistus co-bishop of Rome in 217. According to Hippolytus, in that same year, Zephyrinus died, and Callistus became sole bishop, and changed his mind on the Monarchianist question, which prompted Hippolytus to proclaim himself (schismatic) bishop. Later, Hippolytus apparently reconciled with Pontian, Callistus's second successor.[3]

*3. Beryllus of Bostra, accused of heresy and investigated by fellow prelates. After a debate with Origen in ca. 244, he abandoned his views.[4]

*4. Heracleides, a bishop in Arabia, suspected of heresy. Origen debated with him in ca. 245 and convinced him to change his mind.[5]

†5. Privatus of Lambaesis, whom Cyprian calls *veterus haereticus*.[6] He was condemned by a synod sometime before 248, perhaps during the episcopate of Donatianus, Cyprian's predecessor in Carthage. It is difficult, however, to know whether Cyprian called Privatus a heretic because he proposed or embraced heterodox views or simply because he had been expelled from the church and (perhaps) founded a schismatic community.[7] Cyprian distinguishes between unrepentant *lapsi* (he calls them "apostates") and heretics, classing Privatus among the latter,[8] but Cyprian often called "heretic" anyone who was not in communion with his church.[9] If heresy was the reason for Privatus's condemnation, this case, like that of Paul of Samosata, constitutes a rare example in the early church of a bishop being condemned (and presumably deposed) by a synod of bishops.

6. Felix, bishop of an unknown city. Cyprian calls him a *pseudoepiscopus* "extra ecclesiam in haeresi."[10] It is not clear whether he had been *in* the church and then expelled from it or had always been the bishop of a heretical community. Furthermore, as in Privatus's case above, it is not clear how the term "heresy" is being used here. If we assume Felix had been in communion with the church and then left it, we also cannot tell for sure whether it had been because of his teachings or some other moral or disciplinary reason.

*7. Nepos, "a bishop among those in Egypt," whose views were posthumously refuted by Dionysius of Alexandria.[11]

*8. Dionysius of Alexandria, whose views on the Son of God were censored by Dionysius of Rome and the Italian bishops. He later qualified his opinions and reconciled with the Italians.

*†9. Paul of Samosata (and a few neighboring bishops), who was an exception in being tried and deposed by a large synod for his theological views.[12]

10. Prelates engaged in dispute over Origen's work and exegetical practice (late third and early fourth centuries). In truth, as far as I know, there is no evidence of any specific bishop being deposed for heresy. But the debates were heated, and there were rounds of mutual accusations and much pamphleteering. It is reasonable to expect that bishops would have been accused of holding heterodox views.[13]

COMPROMISE AND SOLIDARITY IN DOCTRINAL CONTROVERSY IN THE EARLY CHURCH

In addition to the examples discussed in chapter 2, see, for instance, the efforts of the Asian bishops urging Victor of Rome to return to peace and unity when he proposed to excommunicate them for "heterodoxy" over the date of Easter, and further, Irenaeus's attempts to conciliate the two sides.[14] Likewise, Polycarp and Anicetus of Rome, who disagreed on this issue, had no desire to quarrel and remained in communion.[15]

We also find a conciliatory mood in the following examples.

1. Serapion of Antioch's dealing with the Christians of Rhossus suspected of heterodoxy. When he learned of their "error," he wrote sympathetically: "I will make every effort to visit you again; so expect me in the near future."[16]
2. Beryllus's affair in Arabia. Two local synods convened to debate Beryllus's proposition that the Son of God did not exist as an independent being before the incarnation. Origen participated in the second synod and settled the dispute.[17]
3. The "Helkesaite" heresy in Arabia. Preachers proposed that the soul died together with one's body. Origen discussed the matter in a synod and persuaded "those who had previously gone astray to change their views."[18]
4. The controversy over the rebaptism of heretics. This was not a doctrinal affair, but what stands out, despite the dispute, are the efforts of Dionysius of Alexandria and others to reconcile the parties involved: several large synods, exchange of correspondence, and calls for tolerance and respect for the traditions of local churches.[19]

THE WORKSHOPS OF ALEXANDRIA

Compared to the abundant information about workshops in the *chora*, we are woefully ill-informed about the city of Alexandria. Gregory Nazianzenus called the city a giant ἐργαστήριον, and the early third century A.D. *Acta Heracliti* mentions the *ergasteria* of sculptors and painters, run by *ergolaboi* (contractors?), and apparently staffed by slaves.[20] Rodziewicz has brought to light several houses-cum-workshops in the Kôm el-Dikka district of Alexandria, where glass, ivory, and bone workshops have been found.[21]

But we would like to know more, especially about the weaving trade. Given the renowned quality of Alexandria's textiles, one would also expect large textile *ergasteria*.[22] Orosius refers to Cleopatra's famous textile workshops.[23] Haas speaks of a concentration of linen weavers in the Rhakotis but does not substantiate his assertion.[24] As elsewhere in the Roman world and Egypt, artisans and weavers most often worked at home, but weaving must also have been carried out in

KOLLUTHUS'S SCHISM AND THE ARIANS

In a difficult passage of *Urk.* 14, Alexander seems to suggest that the Arians left the church only *after* Kolluthus became schismatic, which makes it difficult to explain Kolluthus's subscription to *Urk.* 4b, an encyclical sent out after Arius's excommunication and, in my view, Alexander's first. The passage reads as follows:

> Ἄρειος γοῦν καὶ Ἀχιλλᾶς, συνωμοσίαν ἔναγχος ποιησάμενοι, τὴν Κολλούθου φιλαρχίαν πολὺ χεῖρον ἢ ἐκεῖνος ἐζήλωσαν. ὁ μὲν γὰρ αὐτοῖς τούτοις ἐγκαλῶν τῆς ἑαυτοῦ μοχθηρᾶς προαιρέσεως εὗρε πρόφασιν· οἱ δὲ τὴν ἐκείνου χριστεμπορίαν θεωροῦντες οὐκ ἔτι τῆς ἐκκλησίας ὑποχείριοι μένειν ἐκαρτέρησαν.

How do we reconcile this comment with the evidence in *Urk.* 4b? Let us look more closely at each of Alexander's assertions.

1. "Arius and Achillas have recently formed a conspiracy and, vying with Kolluthus in his love of power, went far beyond that man." Alexander refers to two events in the past—the "conspiracy" of the Arians and Kolluthus's behavior—but the bishop does not establish a precise chronological relationship between them. What connects the "Arians' conspiracy" and Kolluthus is the motivation—namely, the "love of power."
2. "While Kolluthus, in accusing the Arians, found a pretext for his own wretched course of action." I assume that by Kolluthus's "action" Alexander meant his break with the church, but the phrasing does not necessarily imply that the break took place *before* the Arians' excommunication. Kolluthus's willingness to break with Alexander may have gone back to a time when the Arians were first denounced to the bishop. Kolluthus, though willing to break with Alexander from the start of the controversy, remained in the church until after the Arians' excommunication, leaving it after Alexander wrote both *Urk.* 4a and 4b. When exactly? I suggest after Arius had been reinstated by the Palestinian bishops and returned to Alexandria to preach. That would have been the event that led him to break with Alexander. In *Urk.* 14, Alexander did not intend to present events in chronological order, but rather in a way that portrayed the two breakaway priests as sharing the same lust for power.
3. "The Arians, seeing his [Kolluthus's] *christemporia,* could not endure to remain in the church." The sentence also suggests that Kolluthus was *in* the church when the Arians were excommunicated, but when Alexander drafted *Urk.* 14, Kolluthus had already become schismatic. In fact, the odd reference

to Kolluthus in this letter also suggests that his separation from the church had been recent—that is, not long after Arius's excommunication.
4. How do we interpret the statement that the Arians "left" the church "on their own" because of Kolluthus's *christemporia*? If, as suggested above, Alexander wrote *Urk*. 14 after the Arians returned from Palestine with two conciliar decrees reinstating them, Alexander may have wished to convey the impression that they had brought excommunication upon themselves by leaving the church on their own initiative to form a parallel church (hence the emphasis, elsewhere in the letter, on the Arians' "love of power," "avarice," "ambition," and so on). Thus, Alexander portrays the Arians not only as heretics, but also as men driven by sheer ambition. Note that in that same letter, he writes: ἡμεῖς μὲν οὖν ἃ καὶ τῷ βίῳ αὐτῶν καὶ τῇ ἀνοσίῳ ἐπιχειρήσει πρέπει . . . ἐπιστήσαντες, παμψηφὶ τῆς προσκυνούσης Χριστοῦ τὴν θεότητα ἐκκλησίας ἐξηλάσαμεν. The accusation of *christemporia* against Kolluthus would have served only further to denigrate his character.

THE RECALL OF ARIUS AND THE BITHYNIAN BISHOPS

The reconstruction of these events draws on two main pieces of evidence. The first is a letter of "repentance," sent by Eusebius and Theognis (*apud* Socrates and Gelasius), to a synod of bishops, requesting that it take them into communion and intercede with the emperor.[26] The letter is interesting on several counts, not least because Eusebius and Theognis state that they had accepted exile even though they had never been properly tried. Its significance for understanding the sequence of events surrounding Arius's return lies in a reference to Arius's reinstatement. Thus, if the letter is authentic, Arius's recall must have taken place before the return of the Bithynian bishops by at least several weeks.

The other piece of evidence is a letter of Constantine to Arius and Euzoius, dated to November 27 of an unknown year, urging them to come to see him so that, "having experienced his clemency, they might return to their country."[27] Since the letter also asked the exiles why they had hitherto refused his invitation to come to court, Constantine must have been in touch with them before November and most likely, as Socrates suggested, since their banishment. Eager to reunite the church, Constantine had more than once exhorted "[Arius] to change his views, . . . upbraiding his delaying to return to the truth."[28]

According to Socrates, following receipt of that letter, Arius and Euzoius came before the emperor, assented to the faith of Nicaea, and asked to be readmitted into the church. As evidence of their orthodoxy, they offered to the emperor a written profession of faith. The statement made no mention of the controversial *homoousios*, and it did not have to, because it was not intended to replace Nicaea. To the emperor, it was enough that Arius did not seem to oppose the Nicene formula. Delighted that Arius promised to uphold the Nicene faith and put aside all animosity,[29] Constantine received him and Euzoius and sent them to Alexandria after a council of bishops declared them orthodox.[30]

The *terminus post quem* for this sequence of events—the interview with the emperor, the meeting of the council that rehabilitated Arius to the church, and Eusebius's and Theognis's rehabilitation—was November 27, but of what year? Schwartz argued for 327, suggesting that the council that readmitted Arius was the same one Constantine summoned to deal with the Melitian troubles in Egypt. Calling it the "second" Council of Nicaea, Schwartz dated this council to late 327, immediately following Constantine's November letter to Arius. According to Schwartz, soon after this council, having been notified of Arius's rehabilitation, Eusebius and Theognis would have addressed a petition for their own recall and reinstatement to a synod that would have met some time in early 328. This synod would then have rehabilitated the bishops, after which Constantine recalled them from exile in the winter of that same year.[31]

Two additional pieces of evidence are usually adduced to support a date in late 327 or early 328 for the recall of the Bithynian exiles. One is Philostorgius's assertion that Eusebius and Theognis stayed abroad for three whole years, until 328, which reinforces the idea that Arius's recall took place sometime between November 327 and early 328.[32] The second is Athanasius's *ACA* 59.3, a difficult passage, in which Athanasius claims that Alexander of Alexandria died when hardly five months had elapsed since the Council of Nicaea. Since Alexander died on April 17, 328, Athanasius could not have in mind the first but the "second" Council of Nicaea, which Schwartz, as we have seen, identified with the council that restored Arius to communion.

But there are several difficulties with this reconstruction. First, as Simonetti, Barnes, and others have noted, a second council at Nicaea is nowhere mentioned.[33] If the council that readmitted Arius was the same one that dealt with the Melitian troubles, it must have met in Nicomedia, where the emperor resided. Secondly, as Simonetti and Parvis have argued, the council that readmitted Arius and Euzoius was probably a local, provincial synod rather than a large assembly of bishops.[34] Thirdly, we do not really know exactly when Constantine summoned a council to deal with the Melitians, except that this council met before Alexander's death.[35] Fourthly, Athanasius could not have been referring to the Council of Nicaea in 325, even though that was the most obvious antecedent in the preceding phrase.[36] Fifthly, and most important of all, the five-and-a-half-month interval between Constantine's letter to Arius and Euzoius in November of 327 and Alexander's death on April 17, 328, is too short to accommodate the sequence of events following Arius's recall, especially when we consider the narratives of Gelasius and Epiphanius as well as other statements in Athanasius on the complicated dealings between Eusebius and the Melitians *before* Alexander's death.

First, Gelasius. This historian tells us that, after the return of the Bithynian bishops, Constantine was convinced to send Arius to Alexandria, where Alexander refused to receive the priest. Rebuffed by Alexander, Arius sought the help of Eusebius of Nicomedia, who, in turn, convinced the emperor to write a letter rebuking Alexander and Athanasius;[37] I will call this letter *Epistula* 1. Gelasius adds that Athanasius, together with Alexander, wrote to the emperor to explain why they had rejected the Arians. Gelasius's account of these events is not very precise, and we cannot tell with certainty whether Athanasius and Alexander were replying to Constantine's letter or had anticipated the emperor's reaction and taken the initiative to inform him of events in Alexandria. Unfortunately, the letters themselves are not extant,[38] but Gelasius does quote fragments of two other letters of Constantine, one addressed to Athanasius, which I will call *Epistula* 2 (= *ACA* 59.6) and another to Alexander, *Epistula* 3 (= *Urk.* 32). In Gelasius's narrative, both missives appear to have been written in reply to Athanasius's and Alexander's joint letter: "Outraged and moved to anger by those around Eusebius of Nicomedia, [Constantine] wrote a threatening letter to Athanasius . . . and did the same to Alexander."[39]

Gelasius's source for Constantine's *Epistula* 2 is Athanasius's *ACA*, but as we shall see, this letter does not comfortably fit the historical context immediately after Arius's recall. However, *Epistula* 3, sent to Alexander, does, and Gelasius notes that Alexander died shortly after receiving it and presumably before replying to it.[40] Because Gelasius quotes only one letter to Alexander (*Epistula* 3), it is generally assumed that this was in fact the only correspondence the emperor had with the bishop regarding Arius's return. Indeed, given that Gelasius's history is a patchwork stitched together from different sources, many scholars have dismissed his mention of an earlier letter to Alexander (*Epistula* 1). But I see no reason to reject Gelasius's reference to *Epistula* 1, and the importance of this letter will become clear below.

If Gelasius and others were right to suggest that Eusebius helped to convince Constantine to send Arius to Alexandria, Alexander's rebuttal of the priest and Constantine's subsequent letters to the bishop could only have taken place *after* the Bithynians' return from exile. But even if Eusebius played no role in Constantine's decision to send Arius back to Egypt, by the time Alexander refused to receive the priest, Eusebius and Theognis had already been rehabilitated, and Arius was aware of it. So, when did the Bithynians return from exile?

According to Schwartz's chronology, which many scholars have adopted, Arius and Euzoius must have received Constantine's letter in early December 327. They would have come to court in early to mid-December, being readmitted into the church by a council of bishops, at the earliest, in late December or early January. Word of these events traveled to Trier, where Eusebius and Theognis had been exiled. In the winter, this would have taken two to three weeks. Assuming the Bithynians submitted their petition for readmission from Trier, another two to three weeks would have to pass for it to reach a council of Eastern bishops. In the best possible weather conditions, their petition would have reached the council in early to mid-February. Assuming that this council was already in session and that it acted promptly, pleading Eusebius's and Theognis's cause, Constantine may have issued a decree authorizing the Bithynians' return in mid- to late February. By imperial courier the decree would have taken another week or two to reach Trier. At the earliest, then, the Bithynians would have set out on their journey back East in late February to mid-March, arriving in Nicomedia and Nicaea in mid- to late March, taking possession of their sees less than a month *before* Alexander's death. Assuming, too, with Gelasius, that Eusebius played a role in convincing Constantine to send Arius and Euzoius back to Alexandria, we are left with one month to fit the sequence of events following Arius's return to Egypt—namely, the trip itself, Alexander's refusal to receive him, Arius's appeal to Eusebius, Eusebius's appeal to the emperor, the emperor's letter to Alexander (*Epistula* 1), Alexander's reply to the emperor, and the emperor's rejoinder (*Epistula* 3). It is hard to squeeze all these events into one month.

But even if Arius had been sent to Alexandria before Eusebius's and Theognis's return, his appeal to Eusebius and Constantine's subsequent correspondence with Alexander could have taken place only after the Bithynians' return. Here, again, assuming that Arius remained in Egypt, the news of Eusebius's reinstatement must have taken a couple of weeks to reach him in Alexandria, arriving by late March to mid-April. This chronology is still very tight, especially considering the difficulties of travel in winter.

However, if we date Arius's return a year earlier, in late 326, it is possible to offer an alternative to Schwartz's reconstruction. In fact, revising his chronology would seem necessary in light of the evidence in Epiphanius and Athanasius, which has often been ignored.

From Epiphanius, who drew on Melitian sources, we learn that, sometime after Nicaea, a party of Melitians, led by John Arkaph, traveled to court to accuse Alexander of harassing them and to confirm their right to hold church assemblies. As noted in chapter 7, the Melitians were at first unable to secure an audience with the emperor and "for a long time" shuttled back and forth between Nicomedia and Constantinople until Eusebius of Nicomedia arranged an audience with Constantine on the condition that the Melitians receive Arius in Alexandria.[41] In other words, in Epiphanius's account, Eusebius's offer to help the Melitians came *after* Alexander's rejection of the Arians in Alexandria and *after* Eusebius's return from exile, but *before* Alexander's death in April 328, because we also learn from Athanasius that "[the Melitians] accused Alexander even to the emperor himself."[42] It would have made little sense for the Melitians to accuse Alexander if he had already died, so the bishop must have still been alive when Eusebius arranged for the Melitians' interview with the emperor.

If this is correct, according to Schwartz's chronology, the following events would have taken place between November 28, 327, and April 18, 328: Arius's recall from exile; Arius's rehabilitation by a council; Eusebius's and Theognis's recall and reintegration by yet another council; Arius's return to Alexandria; Alexander's refusal to communicate with him; Arius's appeal to Eusebius; Eusebius's complaint to the emperor; Eusebius's meeting with the Melitians; the latter's audience with the emperor; the emperor's letters to Alexander; the emperor's decree allowing the Melitians to assemble. In addition, we would probably also have to place before Alexander's death the council assembled to deal with the troubles in Egypt, which must have taken place while Alexander was alive (the Council of Nicomedia, on which, see discussion below and chapter 7 above), and, depending on how one reads *ACA* 59.3, an additional period of time corresponding to the five-month "Melitian quiet" before Alexander's death. Thus, unless we dismiss the evidence in Gelasius's and Epiphanius's accounts, and I see no compelling reason to do so, I suggest that we push back the date of Constantine's summons of Arius to November 326 and place the recall of Eusebius and Theognis in 327, possibly in the summer. I would propose the following revised chronology:

1. November 27, 326: Constantine's letter to Arius
2. December 326: Arius's interview with Constantine and recall from exile
3. Winter 327: a regional council of bishops readmits Arius and declares him orthodox; Arius's earlier teachings remain condemned
4. Late winter/early spring 327: news of Arius's rehabilitation reaches Trier, prompting Eusebius and Theognis to submit a petition for their own reinstatement to a council of bishops and presumably to the emperor
5. Spring 327: Constantine receives the bishops' petition and agrees to call them back from exile
6. Late spring/early summer 327: Eusebius and Theognis set out from Trier and arrive in Bithynia in the summer of 327;[43] once in Nicomedia, Eusebius may or may not have played a role in persuading Constantine to send Arius to Alexandria;[44] Constantine may well have sent the priest back to Egypt before the Bithynians' arrival as he had promised to do in his letter to Arius
7. Spring/summer 327: Arius in Alexandria; Alexander refuses to receive him
8. Late summer/early fall 327: Arius appeals to Eusebius
9. Fall 327: Eusebius notifies the emperor and persuades him to write to Alexander (*Epistula* 1); Alexander and Athanasius write a letter to justify their rejection of Arius (in reply to *Epistula* 1?); Constantine writes *Epistula* 3 (*Urk.* 32) to Alexander pleading with him to take back Arius, though this letter could also have been written at a later time, in early spring 328, closer to Alexander's death, after the Council of Nicomedia
10. Fall 327: Eusebius strikes a deal with John Arkaph and the Melitians, securing for them an audience with the emperor

Two main objections may be raised to this reconstruction. First, Constantine was in the West continuously from April to December 326.[45] However, this is not really an impediment because, in November 326, the emperor was already en route to Nicomedia through the Balkans, where Arius and Euzoius had been exiled. Constantine seems to have been in Aquileia in November and in Sirmium in December.[46] It is possible that Arius came to see him as he completed the final leg of his journey back East. In his November letter, he invited Arius to come see him in *to stratopedon* (rather than in the *comitatus*). Although *stratopedon* is often translated as "court," it may have been used in the more literal sense of "camp."[47]

The other objection is Philostorgius's claim that Eusebius and Theognis spent "three whole years" in exile, which has led scholars to place their return in 328.[48] But Philostorgius's account is often unreliable, and this information in particular comes from a passage that inspires little credibility. Philostorgius states that Eusebius assembled a synod to overturn the Nicene faith soon after his return. This synod would also have deposed and excommunicated Alexander, because he supported the Nicene creed, though he had previously condemned it.[49] This is of course nonsense. As J. Bidez has noted, Philostorgius (or his sources or compilers) seems to have conflated disparate events narrated in Sozomen, *HE* 1.15.10 and 2.32.7.[50] I would therefore also attribute little weight to his assertion that Eusebius spent three full years in exile.

If we accept the revised chronology proposed above, where do we place the Council of Nicomedia? I would suggest a date in late 327 or the winter of 328.[51]

If, as suggested above, we date the Melitians' audience with the emperor to the fall of 327, it makes sense to date this council, which was summoned specifically to address the persistent troubles in Egypt, to a time when all other measures to reconcile Alexander and the Melitians had failed, for, in calling the council, the emperor was clearly responding to a deepening crisis in the Egyptian church: "The emperor was troubled yet again, . . . [he] summoned [the bishops] a second time, [and] again mediated . . . between the same people."[52] As noted in chapter 7, according to Epiphanius and Sozomen, it was precisely in the weeks or months after Constantine confirmed the Melitians' right to assemble that the dispute in Egypt became even more vicious, so that that council would have been a last-ditch attempt to end, as Eusebius put it, the "split and splinter in the Church."[53] If we allow two or three months for the escalation of the dispute following Constantine's grant authorizing the Melitians to assemble, late fall of 327 or winter of 328 is a plausible date for the council.

The *terminus ante quem* for this council must be May 328, because Constantine, who attended it, left for the West in May only to return in 330. But we can almost be certain of a date before Alexander of Alexandria's death in April. Since this bishop was at the center of the dispute in Egypt, assembling a council without Alexander's participation (or that of a delegate) would have been pointless. A date in December of 327 would suggest itself, given Athanasius's assertion in *ACA* 59.3 that five months had elapsed after the council when Alexander died.

THE ARIAN COMMUNITY OF ALEXANDRIA AFTER NICAEA

Although Athanasius and other Nicene authors had a vested interest in portraying the Arians as a fading minority with little power or influence,[54] the sources suggest that the Arian faithful continued to be not only numerous and strong, but also active, defiant, and supportive of the priest's reinstatement. Indeed, the resilience and vitality of the Arian community constitute the context of Athanasius's efforts to build up his power and impose his authority on the Alexandrian church under Constantine's reign and beyond.

The correspondence Arius exchanged with Constantine in the early 330s provides important evidence for the years immediately after Nicaea. In his letter or letters to the emperor, Arius noted that he "[had] the masses" and "the crowds had joined [him]."[55] Arius of course had reason to exaggerate, but Constantine never questioned those claims, and his reaction to Arius's statements betrays his concern with the extent of support the priest enjoyed from ordinary Christians.

The letter of the synod of Jerusalem to the church of Alexandria in 335 also speaks of a crowd of supporters. In it, the bishops wrote that the Alexandrian Christians would rejoice at the return, "not only those priests around Arius . . . but also the *entire* λαός *and the whole crowd*, which, on account of [Athanasius and his supporters], had for a long time separated from you."[56]

Likewise, a passage in the *Vita Athanasi ex Metaphraste* conveys the impression that the Arians continued not only to enjoy popular support, but also to win followers among ordinary Christians. The author observes that, after Athanasius's exile, "those who shared Arius's views threw the city in turmoil, bringing out Arius's deadly and murderous doctrine, offering it up like a disease to those they had deceived."[57]

Epiphanius also notes that many Christians joined the Arians, "a few having been deceived by them, but many, hypocritically." Epiphanius of course could not bring himself to say that Arius's followers were true believers.[58]

The protests and riots that attended Athanasius's arrival from exile in late 337 and his comment, two years later, that the "ungodly Arians" worked to "overthrow the faith of the simple-minded"[59] bespeak not only the existence of a militant Arian community (under Pistus), but also the Arians' persistent efforts to attract new followers and expand their base of support in Alexandria.

The evidence for the turbulent years under Constantius also suggests that Arian (or at least anti-Nicene) theology remained deeply rooted in the Alexandrian Christian community. Athanasius wrote that, after he left Alexandria in 339, "none of the people of the church were with [the Arians], *only the heretics*."[60] But these "heretics" were among the "many" who, when he returned from his second exile in 346, "came to him and apologized," though obviously not all of them. As noted in chapter 8, Constantius asked Athanasius to allow the Arian Christians to assemble in a separate church.[61]

Even when Athanasius ruled the church from 346 to 356, there are signs that many of the faithful remained loyal to Arian ideas or at least rejected Nicene theology (and its main proponent). In the late 350s, for instance, many virgins, widows, and matrons fiercely opposed Athanasius and attacked Athanasian women in the streets—a sign of strength and, above all, continuity within the Arian Christian community.[62]

ATHANASIUS AND ARSENIUS OF HYPSELE

Since Arsenius does not appear in the list of Melitian clerics Melitius handed to Alexander after Nicaea (*ACA* 71), the Melitians must have ordained him bishop sometime between the drafting of that list (in 325 or 326) and his beating by Plousianos. Because Nicaea had barred the Melitians from making ordinations, Arsenius's elevation to the episcopate constituted a transgression of the Nicene agreement Catholics and Melitians had presumably renewed at the Council of Nicomedia in late 327. Athanasius's election may have been the event that freed the Melitians from their obligations to a bishop they deemed illegitimate.[63] Their disregard for Athanasius's election may have been the reason why the bishop singled out Arsenius for exemplary punishment. Later, when defending himself from the charge of violence, Athanasius accused the Melitians of, among other things, "illegal ordinations,"[64] among which, no doubt, was Arsenius's appointment to the episcopate, which was considered invalid in the eyes of the bishop.

Athanasius may also have held a special grudge against Arsenius.[65] According to Rufinus, who relied on a story concocted to exonerate Athanasius of the charges of battery (and murder), Arsenius had once been a lector in the church of Alexandria. After committing some fault, he fled into hiding, afraid the bishop would discipline him.[66] Omitting the fact that Arsenius was a bishop, Rufinus tells us that the Melitians found him, brought him to a monastery, and bribed him to stay put so they could fabricate the charge of murder against Athanasius. In other words, in this version of the affair, Athanasius had little to do with Arsenius's disappearance. He would have gone into hiding because of his faults and remained hidden because of the Melitians! The Melitians did shelter Arsenius in a monastery and, eventually, fighting back Athanasius, did pretend his death in order to frame the bishop, but that plot was obviously not the reason Arsenius ran away from Hypsele, leaving behind his flock to hide for several years in a monastery. If I am right to place Arsenius's disappearance in 328–329,[67] the Melitians seem to have decided to take advantage of these events to incriminate Athanasius only at a later stage.[68]

Although Rufinus's account inspires little credibility, it is nonetheless possible that Arsenius had indeed been a lector in Alexandria before becoming a Melitian bishop. And if so, he may have left Alexandria to join the Melitians after quarreling with Alexander or Athanasius, possibly after the latter's election. This would help us understand why Athanasius moved against him with such ferocity and why Arsenius chose to hide with the monks.[69]

EVENTS INVOLVING ATHANASIUS FROM SPRING 330 TO WINTER 332

The sequence of events between the Melitian embassy to Constantine in the summer of 330 and the emperor's summons of the bishop in late 331 is difficult to ascertain. Athanasius, our main source, omits John's embassy to court and the charge of violence against the Melitians. Athanasius's narrative jumps from the point where he claimed to have convinced the emperor that Arius could not be readmitted to the church to the plot Eusebius of Nicomedia and the Melitians hatched against him.[70] According to Athanasius, once Eusebius learned the emperor had been persuaded to keep Arius out of the church, he asked the Melitians to find some pretext to incriminate the bishop. When they found nothing, Athanasius continues, "with the advice of the Eusebians," the Melitians invented the charge that Athanasius had imposed a levy of linen tunics on the Egyptians.[71]

Sozomen adds more detail. This historian speaks of the Melitians accusing Athanasius twice. In *HE* 2.22.4, he writes that John Arkaph led an embassy to court with the charges of violence. This embassy appears only in Sozomen, and his source is unknown,[72] but there is no reason to reject it. Then, in 2.22.7–8, now drawing on Athanasius and Socrates, Sozomen speaks of the Melitians accusing Athanasius of imposing a levy of linen tunics and of sending gold to Philomenos.[73] Unfortunately, Sozomen does not reveal what the emperor decided about John's charges against the bishop, as his narrative moves briskly from Constantine "at a loss" regarding John's accusations (2.22.3) to the emperor's letter to Athanasius about Arius's admission (2.22.4–5) to Athanasius's reply convincing the emperor to keep Arius out of the church (2.22.6)—Sozomen's silence conveys the impression that Constantine somehow dismissed the Melitian charges.[74]

In fact, as suggested here, it is more likely that, given the seriousness of the charges brought by John—counteracted by Athanasius's letter accusing the Melitians of mendacity, violence, irregular ordinations, and heresy (2.22.3)—Constantine could not easily make up his mind, and that, as the Melitians added new, even graver charges, the affair dragged on for almost a year. The coming of a second Melitian embassy to the imperial court, whether or not instigated by Eusebius, may in fact have been linked to an ongoing inquiry into Athanasius's violent behavior.

These events must fit an arc of time between Constantine's return to the East in May 330 and Constantine's trial of Athanasius at Psamathia in the winter of 332.[75]

It is plausible to place John's embassy immediately after Constantine's return to the East—so probably in spring or summer 330. Then, enough time must have elapsed between the first and the second embassies to accommodate the sequence of events associated with the set of charges brought by the second Melitian embassy. Since the first charges were likely connected to Athanasius's tour of Egypt in 329/330, and John made no mention of a levy of tunics, the imposition of such a levy (or the threat thereof) would have taken place when that tour was ending, after John had left for court, and perhaps even in reaction to John's embassy; so a date in late 330 or early 331 for the second Melitian embassy appears reasonable, though any time between fall 330 and fall 331 would also do.

We do not know when the emperor summoned Athanasius to court, but the bishop left Alexandria in 331 (*Index* 3) and was in Nicomedia during winter/early spring of 332 (*Festal* 4). Athanasius would have received the summons not too long before the scheduled date for the trial,[76] so it is plausible that he was called to court in late fall 331 or very early 332, in which case, the investigation of the charges brought by John and the other Melitians would have dragged on for much of 331. Constantine may have demanded more evidence or witnesses, and the involvement of powerful courtiers approached by both sides may also have been the reason why it took so long for the emperor to schedule a trial.

FROM ATHANASIUS'S FLIGHT TO THE COUNCILS OF ROME AND ANTIOCH, 339–341

The chronological sequence of events between Athanasius's departure from Alexandria in April 339 and 341, the year of the Dedication Council in Antioch, has been a vexed problem. The appointed date for the Council of Rome, which acquitted Athanasius and Marcellus and admitted them to communion, and even the date when the council met, are uncertain. The difficulty lies partly in reconciling the evidence from Julius's letter to the Eastern bishops quoted by Athanasius in *ACA* 21–36 (which I will call *Epistula* 3)[77] with information about some of the same events provided by Athanasius and Marcellus.

From 339 to 341, three events can be securely dated: Athanasius's departure for Rome in April 339; Constantine II's death in April 340 after invading Constans's territory; and the Dedication Council in Antioch at an uncertain time in 341.[78]

The following details provide us with the elements to reconstruct a chronology of events during the period.

1. In *ACA* 20.1, Athanasius writes: "After we arrived in Rome, Julius . . . wrote to the Eusebians and sent Elpidius and Philoxenus, two of his priests, to them (ἡμῶν τοίνυν ἀνελθόντων εἰς τὴν Ῥώμην ἔγραψεν . . . Ἰούλιος καὶ ἐπὶ τοὺς περὶ Εὐσέβιον ἀποστείλας καὶ δύο πρεσβυτέρους ἑαυτοῦ Ἐλπίδιον καὶ Φιλόξενον.)"[79] This letter, which I shall call *Epistula* 2, is not extant. In

Epistula 3 (*ACA* 21.3), Julius writes that he also sent the priests to those who were suffering in the East. In addition to Julius's letter to the Eusebians, the priests carried to the Eastern bishops his summons for a council in Rome.

2. In his *Epistula* 3 (*ACA* 25.3), Julius says that, in *Epistula* 2, he had appointed a period of time (ἡ προθεσμία) for the Eastern bishops to come to Rome, which they failed to do, alleging that the time frame before the deadline was too short (γράψαντες γὰρ ἐμέμψασθε, ὅτι 'στενὴν τὴν προθεσμίαν τῆς συνόδου' ὡρίσαμεν).

3. In the same letter (*ACA* 25.3), Julius also complains that the Eusebians retained the priests in the East until January (of an unknown year).

4. Athanasius, *HA* 11.2, confirms Julius's statement, adding that the Eusebians retained Elpidius and Philoxenus "until after the assigned period [for the council] had expired" (ὡς τοὺς μὲν πρεσβυτέρους κατασχεῖν καὶ μετὰ τὴν προθεσμίαν).

5. At the opening of his *Epistula* 3 (*ACA* 21.1), Julius tells us that the Eusebians (and other Eastern bishops) replied to his *Epistula* 2 with a quarrelsome letter sent from Antioch. In it, among other things, they upbraided Julius for neglecting the circumstances in the East when summoning the council (25.4: ἀλλ' ἴσως διὰ τὸν καιρὸν οὐκ ἀπήντησαν. τοῦτο γὰρ γράφοντες πάλιν ἐδηλώσατε, ὡς ἄρα ἔδει ἡμᾶς 'σκοπήσαντας τὸν ἐπὶ τῆς Ἑῴας καιρὸν' μὴ προτρέψασθαι ὑμᾶς ἀπαντῆσαι).

6. Seemingly quoting from the Eastern bishops' reply (which has not survived), Athanasius, *HA* 11.2, adds that as a pretext for not showing up, the Eusebians wrote: "We are unable to come now on account of the war begun by the Persians" (πλάσασθαι δὲ πρόφασιν ἀπρεπῆ ὅτι μὴ δυνάμεθα νῦν ἐλθεῖν διὰ τοὺς παρὰ Περσῶν γιγνομένους πολέμους). We find an echo of this statement in *Epistula* 3 (*ACA* 25.4) (item 5 above).

7. In *Epistula* 3 (*ACA* 29.2), Julius notes that Athanasius "remained here [in Rome] for one year and six months waiting for your [the Eusebians'] arrival" (παρέμεινεν ἐνταῦθα ἐνιαυτὸν καὶ ἓξ μῆνας ἐκδεχόμενος τὴν παρουσίαν ὑμῶν . . .).

8. Marcellus, in a statement of faith submitted by letter to Julius, notes that, at the time of his writing, he had been in Rome for one year and three months.[80] In the letter, Marcellus refers to (a) the priests Julius had sent to the East; (b) the fact that the Eastern bishops had no plans to show up (Epiphanius, *Panarion* 72.2.3: ἐπεὶ τοίνυν ἀπαντῆσαι οὐκ ἠβουλήθησαν, ἀποστείλαντός σου πρεσβυτέρους πρὸς αὐτοὺς); and (c) the fact that he was about to leave Rome.[81]

9. Julius, in *Epistula* 3 (*ACA* 26.3), when explaining to the Eastern bishops that the Italians had approved the content of his *Epistula* 2 as well as the opinions he expressed in *Epistula* 3, writes that the bishops had met "at the

appointed time" for the council (ἀμέλει καὶ νῦν τῇ ὁρισθείσῃ προθεσμίᾳ συνῆλθον ἐπίσκοποι).

10. In *ACA* 20.3 and *HA* 15.1, Athanasius writes that more than fifty Italian bishops attended a council in the church of the priest Vito in Rome. The bishops absolved him and communicated with him.

The order of these events hinges on how one interprets Julius's statement in item 7. Although scholars have proposed many different scenarios,[82] I think the most plausible one is that the eighteen months referred to the period from Athanasius's arrival in Rome to the appointed time for the Eastern bishops to come to the city for the council (item 2), as suggested by the phrase "waiting for your arrival." Once the deadline had passed, and no one came, Athanasius would no longer have been "waiting." This helps determine the scheduled date for the Council of Rome.

Athanasius, in *Apol. ad Const.* 4.1, also writes that, after leaving Alexandria, he went straight to Rome. As Barnes noted, there is no reason to doubt that statement.[83] In April, the sea crossing to Rome would have taken up to seventeen days,[84] but if Athanasius took a little longer, he would have arrived in Rome in mid- to late May. Assuming, then, that the eighteen months referred to the interval between Athanasius's arrival and the deadline Julius set for the Eastern bishops to appear in Rome, that deadline would have fallen in November 340. And if we also assume that Marcellus submitted his statement of faith to Julius around the scheduled time for said council, we could deduce that Marcellus arrived in Rome in August 339, three months after Athanasius.

Item 1 tells us that Athanasius was already in Rome when Julius sent Elpidius and Philoxenus to the Eusebians with his *Epistula* 2. Marcellus was also already in the city, having laid his case before Julius when the latter wrote his letter. We infer this from the reference to Julius's reception of Marcellus in the Eastern bishops' reply to Julius's *Epistula* 2 (*ACA* 29, 32, 34) and from the phrasing of Marcellus's letter to Julius (item 8), which suggests he was there when Julius dispatched the envoys. Thus, the *terminus post quem* for Julius's *Epistula* 2 must be August 339.

Schwartz, Simonetti, Barnes, and Parvis have suggested that Julius wrote and sent his letter in the winter or spring of 340, which cannot be completely ruled out.[85] Given the urgency of the matter at hand,[86] however, it is more plausible to think that Julius did not take long to take up the cause of the deposed bishops, especially when, as noted above, other exiled prelates and priests continued to trickle into Rome from the East (*ACA* 33.1). I would therefore suggest a date in fall 339 for Julius's *Epistula* 2.[87] There are two other reasons to place this letter earlier than winter/spring 340. First, Elpidius and Philoxenus were not sent only to the Eusebian party. Julius tells us that, in addition to carrying his *Epistula* 2 to the Eusebians, his emissaries were entrusted with bringing the summons to the council with the stated deadline to other Eastern bishops and with conveying Julius's good wishes to "those who were suffering"[88]—that is, to bishops and priests recently deposed or under persecution. Therefore, if Julius had intended his priests to visit prelates in different places in the East, which meant they needed time to travel about, it would make more sense to place his letter (and Elpidius's and Philoxenus's departure) in the fall of 339, especially when he would have known that his envoys would have to spend the winter abroad. Secondly, in the winter and early spring of 340, the three emperors were preparing for war: in the East, Constantius was about to launch an offensive campaign against Persia; in the West, Constantine II was amassing troops allegedly to assist his Eastern brother, though he ended up instead invading Constans's territory (northern Italy) in April 340. Transportation and communications were likely to have been temporarily disrupted by these conflicts and the preparations that preceded them. Furthermore, these events had important political implications. Constantine II's territory fell into Constans's hands, and the expansion of the latter's power was certainly cause for anxiety if not outright alarm in the East.[89] Constantius, facing a dangerous foe on the Eastern front, a civil war on the Western borders of his territory, and then a brother whose power had suddenly increased substantially, would have been particularly wary of anyone crossing from Constans's territory, especially when the latter had fought a war against the brother who had promised him troop reinforcements for his Persian campaign.[90] It is perhaps significant that Athanasius was unable to send his festal letter that year,[91] which I suspect was due to the disruption of normal channels of communication with the East in winter and early spring. Julius would have been aware of the difficulties of travel while the conflict was brewing and whose outcome was obviously uncertain. Under these unsettled circumstances, no matter how pressing the matter, it is unlikely (and the Eastern bishops would otherwise have pointed this out to him) that he would have dispatched his priests *at that time* on a mission that required extensive travel and that was to lead to the Eastern prelates coming to Rome by the fall of that year. In other words, the nature of Elpidius's and Philoxenus's mission and Julius's expectations for its outcome fit better in fall 339.[92]

On the other hand, the Eastern bishops' complaint that Julius ought to have considered the circumstances in the East (item 5) when calling the synod—most likely a reference to the Persian war, as Athanasius observed (item 6)—would support a date for Julius's embassy in spring 340. The hostilities with the Persians went back to 336, but, as noted above, in 340, Constantius had planned a major campaign, possibly a large-scale invasion of the Persian Empire.[93] Yet, every summer since 337, when the Persians besieged Nisibis, there had been skirmishes and cross-border raids along the Persian frontier.[94] The truce that followed Constantius's restoration of Arsaces to the Armenian throne in 338 did not last long. In 339, Arsaces broke an alliance with Shapur, and hostilities resumed.[95] In that year, too, Shapur stepped up his persecution against the Christians of Persia.[96] It is possible that Constantius had also intended a major offensive for the summer of 339.[97] So the "circumstances of the East" in the Eastern bishops' reply to Julius may have been a vague reference to the ongoing hostilities with Persia since 337 or, more pointedly, to events taking place *in any year* since that time, including 339; a precise date is not easy to establish. That this was so is also suggested by Julius's rejoinder: "If you did not come to the council because the circumstances were such . . . you should have considered them first, and not have become the cause of schism, mourning, and lamentation in the churches"[98]—that is, Julius's retort makes logical sense only if, when the Eastern bishops created a schism (a reference, no doubt, to the appointment of Gregory and others in the winter of 339), the circumstances the Eastern bishops claimed prevented them from coming to Rome were already in place.

As I suggested above, Julius had intended his priests to visit persecuted clerics in the East. Whether or not they did so, we cannot tell for sure. The Eusebians' efforts (mentioned in *Epistula* 3) to prevent persecuted clerics from coming to Rome suggest that the envoys were able to deliver Julius's invitation to many Eastern bishops even in Egypt.[99] But winter would have limited their mobility, and, then, when spring arrived, the war with Persia would have imposed other travel restrictions. Moreover, some Eastern bishops may have been on the road as they prepared to join Constantius's expedition.[100] In any case, Elpidius and Philoxenus must have come to Constantinople and/or Antioch, where they brought Julius's letter to the Eusebian circle, probably in late spring or summer 340, because another reason the Eastern bishops alleged for not coming to Rome was the "short time frame" between their receipt of Julius's letter-cum-summons and the scheduled date for the council (item 2).[101] Upon receipt of Julius's letter, the Eusebians called (a select group of) Eastern bishops to Antioch to draft and sign a common reply to Julius's letter.[102] I argue below that this was not the Dedication Council.

As in item 4, at a certain point in 340, Elpidius and Philoxenus were detained, probably at Antioch, whence they would later depart carrying the Eastern bishops' reply to Julius (item 5). They remained in the East, past the deadline for the Council of Rome (item 4), until January (item 3) of 341 in the timeline being proposed here.[103] The Eusebians may have detained the priests to wait for the Eastern bishops to assemble and agree on a common reply to Julius. It would naturally have taken some time for Eusebius to summon these prelates and assemble them in a synod, especially during a time of war.

January 341 is therefore the *terminus post quem* for Julius's *Epistula* 3, which is generally not disputed. But when did the Council of Rome and the Dedication Council of Antioch meet? And when did Julius write that letter, and what was its relationship to these two councils?

First, the Council of Rome. In *Epistula* 3 Julius notes that the council met "at the appointed time" (item 9). Did he mean that the council met in the fall of 340, which I proposed above as the scheduled date (or assigned deadline) for the council? Scholars are divided on whether the Council of Rome took place before or after the Dedication Council, whose date is also controversial, but excepting Pietri, most agree that the Council of Rome met in the winter or early spring of 341.[104] In doing so, scholars, including Pietri, who dates the council to late 340 or early 341, have either dismissed or overlooked Julius's comment.[105] Yet there is no reason to dismiss Julius's comment or suppose that he assigned a new deadline for his council or called yet another; the evidence in items 4 and 7 strengthens the idea that the Council of Rome met in late fall 340. When declaring that the Italian bishops were of one mind on all matters addressed in his letter, Julius meant that they shared the views already expressed in *Epistula* 2—that is, before the council—and had agreed to receive and communicate with Athanasius and Marcellus at the time of the council.[106]

The relationship between the Council of Rome and Julius's *Epistula* 3 is also not clear-cut. In *ACA* 20.3, immediately after writing about the Council of Rome, Athanasius explains that the Italian prelates, outraged by the Eusebians' letter,[107] asked Julius to write to them. This is important because it would suggest that *Epistula* 3 was prompted by the Italian bishops' request at the Council of Rome and crafted soon after.

However, Athanasius's claim is doubtful. Just as the Eusebians called a synod to express their opinions as the voice of a united Eastern episcopate,[108] Athanasius was later anxious to portray Julius's actions as representing the collective will of the Western (or Italian) church. When we turn to Julius's own words, we find that his comment on the opinion of the Italian bishops (item 9) was made in response to the Eastern bishops' criticism that he alone had written *Epistula* 2.[109] If, as Athanasius claimed, *Epistula* 3 had been prompted by a request from his Italian peers at the council that Julius write to the Eastern bishops, one would have expected Julius to have made a more emphatic statement of that fact. Instead, he is at pains to explain that, even though he alone was writing, everyone agreed with his views. It is in fact odd that the Italian bishops did not subscribe to Julius's *Epistula* 3 and that the Council of Rome did not issue an encyclical.[110] No certainty is possible here, but there is little to suggest that *Epistula* 3 was prompted by the council or written in its immediate aftermath. On the contrary, the evidence we have does not indicate a direct connection between the letter and the Council of Rome, which as I argued above would have met in fall 340.[111]

But there is more. In January 341, Elpidius and Philoxenus were released from Antioch. They would have arrived in Rome in February or March,[112] but Julius did not disclose the Eastern bishops' letter for sometime in hope that, despite their arrogant letter, some Easterners might still come to Rome.[113] They did not; instead, in the months that followed, probably in the spring when the seas were open, more Alexandrian and Egyptian priests arrived in Rome, declaring that many clerics were prevented from coming to the Council of Rome. Julius specifically notes that "even until now"—that is, until the eve of his writing *Epistula* 3—priests kept arriving and denouncing Gregory's atrocities against the Athanasian bishops, including confessors and other venerable prelates.[114] Although Julius does not name these confessors, there is no doubt that this was a reference to the persecution of Sarapammon, Potamon, and others in Egypt.[115] This gives us a clue for the date of *Epistula* 3. In *HA* 12.1, Athanasius writes that Gregory's persecution of these prelates took place *after* the release of Julius's envoys—thus in the winter and early spring of 341.[116] Given the time needed for these events to unfold and become known in Egypt, for the Egyptian priests to travel to Rome and report to Julius, and for Julius to share the contents of the Eastern bishops' letter with "many of those here" (presumably his Italian colleagues),[117] *Epistula* 3 could hardly have been written before the spring of 341, and, most likely, it was composed in the late spring or summer of 341, at least several months after the Council of Rome.

It is much harder to assign a precise date to the Dedication Council. Chronology matters here not only for the sake of establishing a timeline, but also, as often in the Arian controversy, because the order of events affects the way we interpret them; in this particular case, chronology is important for our understanding the motivations behind the doctrinal debates leading to the publication of new creeds at Antioch. For instance, Klein implies that the new creeds were formulated out of a concern of the Eastern bishops to rebut Western imputations that they had embraced a heretic "Arian" doctrine put forth by Athanasius's *Epistula encyclica* and Julius's *Epistula* 3. Klein suggests that Eusebius assembled a council on the occasion of the dedication of the new church in Antioch to reply to those charges.[118] But if the council had been summoned before Julius's *Epistula* 3 arrived in the East the doctrinal debates leading to new creeds need not be seen as a reaction to Western accusations—at least not Julius's. The bishop of Rome probably did send his *Epistula* 3 before the Dedication Council, but the letter does not address issues of theology, and I do not think it was the cause of the council or of the new creeds it published.

The year of the Dedication Council is not in dispute, but the time of year. Schneemelcher, Barnes, Parvis, and others have argued for January 341.[119] These scholars identify this synod as the same that drafted the Eastern bishops' letter replying to Julius's *Epistula* 2, which was brought to Rome by Elpidius and Philoxenus. In this case, Julius's *Epistula* 3 would have been written *after* the Dedication Council. On the other hand, Schwartz, Pietri, Simonetti, Hanson, and Martin date the council in late spring or summer 341.[120] These scholars, relying in part on the evidence from Socrates' and Sozomen's narratives,[121] have proposed two councils in Antioch: one less formal gathering in December 340–January 341 that formulated the reply to Julius; the second, a formal council in the summer of that year (sometime before the end of the consular year in August), probably summoned by Constantius and assembled in his presence, to consecrate the great church and to rewrite orthodoxy.[122] Despite the evidence from the *Liber Calipharum* adduced by Parvis in favor of a date in January 341,[123] I am inclined to side with Schwartz and others and, as argued above, accept two synods at Antioch: the first one in winter 340/341, called by Eusebius and others; the second in the summer of 341, summoned or supported by the emperor to dedicate the great church and discuss doctrinal matters.

One strong reason to place the Dedication Council after the Council of Rome is the conspicuous absence from Julius's *Epistula* 3 of any reference whatsoever to doctrinal innovation or the formulation of new creeds.[124] Had Julius been informed of those developments,[125] it is hard to believe he would have made no comment about the omission of the *homoousios* or the addition of anti-Marcellan anathemas, especially when he was trying to defend himself against the charge of having received and communicated with Marcellus. And given that Athanasius, since his arrival at Rome, had began more insistently to call the Eusebians "Arian" heretics, the promulgation of a new creed, suppressing the *homoousios,* by an imperial council, would have proven an irresistible line of attack. Instead, the thrust of Julius's letter derives from his attempt to defend his decision to communicate with Athanasius and Marcellus, which the Eastern bishops had found unacceptable.[126] Barnes, placing the Dedication Council in January of 341, suggested that the bishops would have withheld the creedal documents from Julius, Athanasius, and Marcellus, while circulating them everywhere in the East.[127] Yet, as Athanasius noted, the bishops swiftly announced their decisions.[128] Furthermore, Elpidius and Philoxenus, detained in Antioch until January 341, would then have attended the council's sessions and would have reported the creedal innovation to Julius. Still, assuming that the Eastern bishops did conceal the council's decisions from the West and that Julius's envoys left Antioch before the council's doctrinal deliberations, Athanasius would surely have been informed of those developments fairly quickly, and before Julius wrote *Epistula* 3, through fresh arrivals from the East and other channels. Finally, probably drawing on the *Vita Pauli*, Socrates, HE 2.8.4, writes that Julius had not sent a representative to the Dedication Council, which would have been untrue had Elpidius and Philoxenus been there.[129]

Admittedly, most of this evidence, though not all of it, was picked up from documents used for polemical ends, whose purpose was often to distort and obscure the truth, not convey it. The accounts of the fifth-century ecclesiastical historians are particularly confusing. Our main source is still Athanasius, who tends to quote only those documents that strengthen his case. Thus, the order of events proposed here must remain tentative, but the same is true for the alternatives.

I would thus reconstruct the chronology of events between April 339 and the summer of 341 as follows.

1. April 16, 339: Athanasius leaves Alexandria.
2. May 339: Athanasius arrives in Rome.
3. August 339: Marcellus arrives in Rome.
4. Summer 339: Athanasius writes the *Epistula encyclica* and sends his own envoys to deliver his pamphlet to bishops in the East.
5. Fall 339: Julius summons the Eastern bishops for a council in Rome scheduled for the fall of 340, writes a letter to the Eusebians (*Epistula* 2), and sends Elpidius and Philoxenus to the East.
6. Late fall 339–spring 340 (?): Elpidius and Philoxenus travel in the East; they deliver Julius's summons to bishops in Constantinople, Antioch, Egypt, and elsewhere but are slowed by winter and preparations for war with Persia; Athanasius's envoys travel in the East but are also delayed by the crisis.
7. Spring/summer 340 (?): Elpidius and Philoxenus are detained in Antioch.
8. Fall 340: The Eastern bishops fail to come to Rome; Marcellus submits a statement of faith to Julius; the Council of Rome assembles and communicates with Athanasius, Marcellus, and others; Marcellus leaves Rome shortly thereafter.
9. December 340/January 341: The Eusebians and other Eastern bishops assemble in Antioch to craft a response to Julius's letter; Elpidius and Philoxenus are released.
10. February/March 341: Elpidius and Philoxenus arrive in Rome and deliver the Eastern bishops' letter to Julius.
11. Spring 341: Julius, scandalized by the letter, does not disclose it for some time, hoping that some Eastern bishops might still show up; as other persecuted clerics arrive from Egypt and elsewhere, Julius decides to share the Eastern bishops' letter with other Italian prelates.
12. Late spring/summer 341: Julius writes *Epistula* 3 to the Eastern bishops.
13. Summer 341: Dedication Council at Antioch.

ABBREVIATIONS

AASS	*Acta sanctorum*
ACO	*Acta conciliorum oecumenicorum,* ed. E. Schwartz (Berlin and Leipzig, 1922–)
Ammianus Marcellinus, *RG*	Ammianus Marcellinus, *Rerum gestarum libri qui supersunt*
ANF	*The Ante-Nicene Fathers* (Grand Rapids, MI, 1950–)
ApPatr	*Apophthegmata patrum* (*The Sayings of the Desert Fathers,* trans. B. Ward, 2nd ed. [London and Oxford, 1981])
Athanasius, *ACA*	Athanasius, *Apologia contra Arianos*
Athanasius, *HA*	Athanasius, *Historia Arianorum*
Barnes, *AC*	T. D. Barnes, *Athanasius and Constantius: Theology and Politics in the Constantinian Empire* (Cambridge, 1993)
Barnes, *CE*	T. D. Barnes, *Constantine and Eusebius* (Cambridge, 1981)
BHG	*Bibliotheca hagiographica graeca*
BHL	*Bibliotheca hagiographica latina*
BHO	*Bibliotheca hagiographica orientalis*
Calderini, *Dizionario*	A. Calderini, *Dizionario dei nomi geografici e topografici dell'Egitto greco-romano* (Cairo, 1935)
CCSG	*Corpus christianorum,* Series Graeca (Turnhout, 1977–)
CCSL	*Corpus christianorum,* Series Latina (Turnhout, 1954–)
CSCO	*Corpus scriptorum christianorum orientalium* (Paris, 1903–)
CSEL	*Corpus scriptorum ecclesiasticorum latinorum* (Vienna, 1866–)
CTh	*Codex Theodosianus* (T. Mommsen, ed., *Theodosiani libri XVI cum constitutionibus Sirmondianis* [Berlin, 1905])

DACL	*Dictionnaire d'archéologie chrétienne et liturgie,* ed. F. Cabrol and H. Leclercq (Paris, 1907–53)
EOMIA	*Ecclesiae occidentalis monumenta iuris antiquissima,* ed. C. H. Turner (Oxford, 1899–1939)
Eusebius, *VC*	Eusebius, *Vita Constantini*
GCS	*Die griechischen christlichen Schriftsteller der ersten drei Jahrhunderte* (Berlin and Leipzig, 1897–1969)
HE	*Historia ecclesiastica*
Hefele, *Histoire*	K. J. Hefele, *Histoire de conciles d'après les documents originaux,* 12 vols. (Paris, 1907)
Hilary, *FH*	Hilary, *Fragmenta historica* (A. L. Feder, ed., *S. Hilarii Pictavensis Opera,* iv: *Tractatus mysteriorum; Collectanea antiariana parisina [fragmenta historica] cum appendice [Liber I ad Constantium]; Liber ad Constantium imperatorem [Liber II ad Constantium]; Hymni; Fragmenta minora; Spuria,* CSEL 65 [Vienna, 1916])
Index	A. Martin, ed., *Histoire "Acéphale" et Index syriaque des lettres festales d'Athanase d'Alexandrie,* SC 317 (Paris, 1985)
Joannou, *Discipline*	P.-P. Joannou, *Discipline génerale antique (IIe-IXe s.)* (Grottaferrata, 1962)
Jones, *LRE*	A. H. M. Jones, *The Later Roman Empire 284–602: A Social, Economic, and Administrative Survey,* 2 vols. (repr., Baltimore, 1990)
Le Quien, *OC*	M. Le Quien, *Oriens christianus,* 3 vols. (Paris, 1740; repr., Graz, 1958)
Maier, *Dossier*	J.-L. Maier, *Le dossier du Donatisme* (Berlin, 1987)
Martin, *Athanase*	A. Martin, *Athanase d'Alexandrie et l'Église d'Égypte au IVe siècle,* Collection de l'École Française de Rome 216 (Rome, 1996)
NHC	*Nag Hammadi Codex* (rev. ed., ed. J. M. Robinson [San Francisco, 1988])
NPNF	*A Select Library of Nicene and Post-Nicene Fathers of the Christian Church,* 2nd series (Grand Rapids, MI)
OCH	S. Elm, E. Rebillard, and A. Romano, eds., *Orthodoxie, christianisme, histoire/Orthodoxy, Christianity, History,* Collection de l'École Française de Rome 270 (Rome, 2000)
Palladius, *HL*	Palladius, *Historia Lausiaca*
PG	*Patrologia graeca* (ed. J.-P. Migne [Paris, 1857–86])
Pietri, *Roma*	C. Pietri, *Roma christiana: Recherches sur l'Eglise de Rome, son organisation, sa politique, son idéologie de Miltiade à Sixte III (311–440),* 2 vols., Bibliothèque des Écoles Françaises d'Athènes et de Rome 224 (Rome, 1976)
PL	*Patrologia latina* (ed. J.-P. Migne [Paris, 1844–64; 2nd ed., 1878–90]

PLRE	*The Prosopography of the Later Roman Empire*, vol. 1, ed. A. H. M. Jones, J. R. Martindale, and J. Morris (Cambridge, 1971); vol. 2, ed. J. R. Martindale (Cambridge, 1980)
PO	*Patrologia orientalis* (ed. R. Graffin et al. [Paris, 1907–])
POxy	*The Oxyrhynchus Papyri* (London, 1898–)
RE	Pauly-Wissowa, *Realencyclopädie der classischen Altertumswissenschaft*
SB	*Sammelbuch griechischer Urkunden aus Ägypten* (ed. F. Preisigke and F. Bilabel [Strassburg, 1915–])
SC	*Sources chrétiennes*
Schwartz, GS	E. Schwartz, *Gesammelte Schriften*, 5 vols. (Berlin, 1959)
Syn.	*Synaxarion*
Urk.	H.-G. Opitz, *Athanasius Werke*, vol. 3.1, *Urkunden zur Geschichte des arianischen Streites* (Berlin, 1934)

NOTES

INTRODUCTION

1. See Eusebius, *VC* 2.71; *Urk.* 17, p. 34, ll. 5–6.
2. Eusebius, *VC* 2.61; Socrates, *HE* 1.6.
3. Scholars have criticized the use of the label "Arian" to describe the theological dispute about the relationship of the Son to the Father not only because the many theologians who rejected Nicaea did not see themselves as intellectual heirs of Arius, but also because doctrinal debates after Nicaea had little to do with Arius's ideas (see L. Ayres, *Nicaea and Its Legacy: An Approach to Fourth-Century Trinitarian Theology* [Oxford, 2004], 13f., with references). However, there is no doubt that Arius's theology was the catalyst of a theological confrontation that had no precedent in the church. In this sense, I think it is useful to retain the term "Arian," especially because this study is less concerned with the theological aspects of the dispute than with the manner in which church leaders responded to theological confrontation.
4. Eusebius, *HE* 4.7; 5.14, 21; Epiphanius, *Panarion* 69.12.25, 73.2.2–3; and E. Wipszycka, *Storia della Chiesa nella tarda antichità*, trans. V. Verdiani (Milan, 2000), 138.
5. Cappadocia was divided partly to provide for an "Arian" bishopric in Tyana. See Basil, *Epp.* 74, 75, 76; and B. Gain, *L'Église de Cappadoce au IVe siècle d'après la correspondance de Basile de Césarée (330–379)* (Rome, 1985), 306–9. War: Socrates, *HE* 2.22.
6. E.g., in Alexandria, where the affair began; then, after Constantine, at the councils of Antioch (early 325), Nicaea, Nicomedia (327/328), Caesarea (334), Serdica, and so on. Cf., for instance, the conciliatory tone of Augustine, *Epp.* 33, 34, 43, and 44, in the Donatist affair with the conduct of such prelates as Eusebius of Nicomedia, Athanasius, Macedonius of Constantinople, George of Alexandria, etc., who did not disguise their mutual hatred and eagerness to quash their opponents. See F. H. Russell, "Persuading the Donatists: Augustine's Coercion by Words," in *The Limits of Ancient Christianity: Essays on Late Antique*

Thought and Culture in Honor of R. A. Markus, ed. W. E. Klingshirn and M. Vessey (Ann Arbor, MI, 1999), 115–24.

7. Athanasius, *ACA* 35 (Julius of Rome to the Eastern bishops); Gregory Nazianzenus, *De vita sua* 460 (ed. C. Jungck); Ammianus Marcellinus, *RG* 21.16.18.

8. M. Simonetti, *La crisi ariana nel IV secolo* (Rome, 1975); T. A. Kopecek, *A History of Neo-Arianism* (Cambridge, 1979); R. P. C. Hanson, *The Search for a Christian Doctrine of God: The Arian Controversy, 318–381* (Edinburgh, 1988); and Ayres, *Nicaea* are important works of historical theology. H. M. Gwatkin's monograph, *Studies of Arianism: Chiefly Referring to the Character and Chronology of the Reaction Which Followed the Council of Nicaea*, 2nd ed. (repr., New York, 1978) remains useful. R. Williams, *Arius: Heresy and Tradition*, rev. ed. (London, 2001) offers sound insights into the early phase of the Arian controversy. See also H.-G. Opitz, "Die Zeitfolge des arianischen Streites von den Anfängen bis zum Jahr 328," *ZNTW* 33 (1934): 131–59; W. Schneemelcher, "Athanasius von Alexandrien als Theologe und als Politiker," *ZNTW* 43 (1950–51): 242–55; E. Schwartz, *Gesammelte Schriften*, vol. 3, *Zur Geschichte des Athanasius* (Berlin, 1959); E. Boularand, *L'hérésie d'Arius et la foi de Nicée* (Paris, 1973); the papers collected in C. Kannengiesser, ed., *Politique et théologie chez Athanase d'Alexandrie, Actes du Colloque de Chantilly, 23–25 septembre 1973*, Théologie Historique 27 (Paris, 1974), 145–56; R. C. Gregg and D. E. Groh, *Early Arianism: A View of Salvation* (London, 1981); C. Kannengiesser, *Athanase d'Alexandrie, évêque et écrivain: Une lecture des traités Contre les Ariens*, Théologie Historique 70 (Paris, 1983); id., "The Athanasian Decade, 1974–84: A Bibliographical Report," *Theological Studies* 46 (1985): 524–41; H. C. Brennecke, *Hilarius von Poitiers und die Bischofsopposition gegen Konstantius*, vol. 2, *Untersuchungen zur dritten phase des arianischen Streites (337–361)*, Patristische Texte und Studien 26 (Berlin and New York, 1984); R. C. Gregg, ed., *Arianism: Historical and Theological Reassessments, Papers from the Ninth International Conference on Patristic Studies*, Patristic Monographs Series 11 (Philadelphia, 1985); J. T. Lienhard, "The 'Arian' Controversy: Some Categories Reconsidered," *Theological Studies* 48 (1987): 415–37; D. Woods, "Three Notes on Aspects of the Arian Controversy c. 354–367 CE," *JTS*, n.s. 44 (1993): 604–19; Barnes, *AC*; the collection of essays entitled *Arianism after Arius*, ed. M. R. Barnes and D. H. Williams (Edinburgh, 1993); D. H. Williams, *Ambrose of Milan and the End of the Nicene-Arian Conflicts* (Oxford, 1995); id., "Defining Orthodoxy in Hilary of Poitiers," *JECS* 9 (2001): 151–71; R. P. Vaggione, *Eunomius of Cyzicus and the Nicene Revolution* (Oxford, 2000); and S. Parvis, *Marcellus of Ancyra and the Lost Years of the Arian Controversy, 325–345* (Oxford, 2006).

9. For instance, Jones, *LRE*. Cf. J.-M. Carrié and A. Rousselle, *L'Empire romain en mutation des Sévères à Constantin 192–337* (Paris, 1999); P. Garnsey and C. Humfress, *The Evolution of the Late Antique World* (Cambridge, 2001); and S. Mitchell, *A History of the Later Roman Empire, AD 284–641* (Malden, MA, 2007).

10. For instance, Schwartz, *GS*, 3:262–64; Barnes, *CE*, 224ff.; O. Norderval, "The Emperor Constantine and Arius: Unity in the Church and Unity in the Empire," *Studia Theologica* 42 (1988): 115f.; P. Brown, *Authority and the Sacred: Aspects of the Christianisation of the Roman World* (Cambridge, 1995), 40f.; and R. Lim, "Christian Triumph and Controversy," in *Interpreting Late Antiquity: Essays on the Postclassical World*, ed. G. W. Bowersock, P. Brown, and O. Grabar (Cambridge, 2001), 201–12.

11. Lactantius, *De mortibus persecutorum* 48.2–12; Eusebius, *HE* 10.5.1–14; Maier, *Dossier*, 143–44. See H. Kraft, *Kaiser Konstantins religiöse Entwicklung* (Tübingen, 1955), 165f. Cf.

Eusebius, *HE* 7.11.7 and 8.17.10 (Galerius's decree), and 9.9.6; and C. Humfress, "Roman Law, Forensic Argument, and the Formation of Christian Orthodoxy (III–VI Centuries)," in *OCH*, 128–42.

12. See Maier, *Dossier*, 157; cf. 195.

13. See R. Lim, *Public Disputation, Power, and Social Order in Late Antiquity* (Berkeley, 1995), 24–29.

14. P. Brown, *Power and Persuasion in Late Antiquity: Towards a Christian Empire* (Madison, WI, 1992), 4, 106–9; Barnes, *AC*, 176–79; and H. A. Drake, *Constantine and the Bishops: The Politics of Intolerance* (Baltimore, 2000), 393ff. So they also grew in their "acquaintance and liberty to speak with [the emperor]"; see Epiphanius, *Panarion* 30.5 (in R. MacMullen, "The Historical Role of the Masses in Late Antiquity," in *Changes in the Roman Empire: Essays in the Ordinary* [Princeton, NJ, 1990], 265). See also R. Lizzi, *Il potere episcopale nell'oriente romano: Rappresentazione ideologica e realtà politica (IV–V sec. d. C.)* (Rome, 1987), 71f.; Brown, *Power*, 106ff.; and Lim, "Christian Triumph," 199ff.

15. Lim, "Christian Triumph," 201, eloquently describes this.

16. Lim, *Public Disputation*, 28–29.

17. See P. Rousseau, *Basil of Caesarea* (Berkeley, 1994), 95.

18. P. Brown, "Response to H. Chadwick's 'The Role of the Christian Bishop in Ancient Society,'" in *The Role of the Christian Bishop in Ancient Society: Protocol of the 35th Colloquy of the Center for Hermeneutical Studies in Hellenistic and Modern Culture, 25 Feb. 1979*, ed. H. Chadwick, E. C. Hobbs, and W. Wuellner (Berkeley, 1980), 19, citing P. Nautin, "L'évolution des ministères au IIe et au IIIe siècles," *Revue de Droit Canonique* 23 (1973): 57; C. A. Bobertz, "Cyprian of Carthage as a Patron: A Social Study of the Role of the Bishop in the Ancient Christian Community" (PhD diss., Yale University, 1988), 2; and E. Hermann, *Ecclesia in re publica* (Frankfurt, 1980), 16ff.

19. Brown, "Response," 16.

20. Athanasius, *HA* 7; cf. id., *ACA* 72. Crowds: Hilary, *Against Valens* 1.3 (trans. Wickham). See also MacMullen, "Historical Role," 260–76; and chapters 7 and 8 below.

21. See, for instance, Williams, *Arius*; Brennecke, *Hilarius*; Barnes, *AC*; Rousseau, *Basil*; J.-R. Pouchet, *Basile le Grand et son univers d'amis après sa correspondance* (Rome, 1992); N. McLynn, *Ambrose of Milan: Church and Court in a Christian Capital* (Berkeley, 1994); Vaggione, *Eunomius*; on Chromatius of Aquileia, see C. Sotinel, *Identité civique et christianisme: Aquilée du IIIe au VIe siècle* (Rome, 2005), 110–69, 180–232; and Parvis, *Marcellus of Ancyra*. On Athanasius, see also D. Brakke, *Athanasius and the Politics of Asceticism* (Oxford, 1995); and Martin, *Athanase*.

22. See Humfress, "Roman Law," 127.

23. Cf. F. E. Sciuto, "Da Nicea a Costantinopoli: Osservazioni sulla prima fase della stabilizzazione teologico-politica cristiana (325–381)," in *La transformazioni della cultura nella tarda antichità*, Atti del Convegno tenuto a Catania Università degli Studi, 27 sett.-2 ott, 1982, ed. C. Giuffrida and M. Mazza (Rome, 1985), 487ff.; K. L. Noethlichs, "Kirche, Recht und Gesellschaft in der Jahrhundertmitte," in *L'Église et l'Empire au IVe siècle*, Entretiens de la Fondation Hardt pour l'Étude de l'Antiquité Classique 36 (Geneva, 1987), 253ff.; and Lizzi, *Potere*, 13ff.

24. Quote: Athanasius, *ACA* 37.2-3 (slightly altered). See, for instance, Gain, *L'Église de Cappadoce*, chaps. 8ff.; Rousseau, *Basil*, 93–158; R. van Dam, "Emperors, Bishops, and

Friends in Late Antique Cappadocia," *JTS*, n.s. 37 (1986): 53–75; id., *Kingdom of Snow: Roman Rule and Greek Culture in Cappadocia* (Philadelphia, 2002); and McLynn, *Ambrose*, 22–31, 220ff. Pietri, *Roma*, 1:398ff., and G. Dagron, *Naissance d'une capitale: Constantinople et ses instituitions de 330 à 451* (Paris, 1974), 367–517, have delineated the rise of the church in the face of the pressures of local and imperial politics. Cf. P. Brown, *Poverty and Leadership in the Later Roman Empire* (Hanover, NH, and London, 2002), 31ff. and 71.

25. P. Bourdieu's concept of *habitus* is helpful here. See P. Bourdieu, *Outline of a Theory of Practice*, trans. R. Nice (Cambridge, 1990), 76–95. *Habitus* is understood as a set of conscious or unconscious dispositions, tendencies, and propensities to act in particular ways.

26. See M. Herzfeld, *A Place in History: Social and Monumental Time in a Cretan Town* (Princeton, NJ, 1991), 168–74.

27. See G. W. Bowersock, "From Emperor to Bishop: The Self-Conscious Transformation of Political Power in the Fourth Century A.D.," *Classical Philology* 81 (1986): 303–7; Barnes, *AC*, 165ff.; Brown, *Power*, 110–13; id., *Poverty*, 71. Cf. M. Humphries, "In nomine patris: Constantine the Great and Constantius II in Christological Polemic," *Historia* 46 (1997): 448–64; and id., "Savage Humour: Christian Anti-Panegyric in Hilary of Poitiers' *Against Constantius*," in *The Propaganda of Power: The Role of Panegyric in Late Antiquity*, ed. M. Whitby (Leiden, 1998), 201–23.

28. G. Dagron, "L'empire romain d'orient au IVe siècle et les traditions politiques de l'Hellénisme: Le témoignage de Thémistios," *Travaux et Mémoires* 3 (1968): 1–242; M. Forlin Patrucco and S. Roda, "Crisi di potere e autodifesa di classe: Aspetti del tradizionalismo delle aristocrazie," in *Società romana e impero tardoantico*, ed. A. Giardina (Rome, 1986), 1:250–60; G. W. Bowersock, *Hellenism in Late Antiquity* (Ann Arbor, MI, 1990), 1–13, 71ff. See also Brown, *Power*, chap. 2; and F. Millar, *A Greek Roman Empire: Power and Belief under Theodosius II (408–450)* (Berkeley, 2006), 1–38.

29. See Brown, *Power*, chaps. 1–2.

30. See A. H. M. Jones, "The Social Background of the Struggle between Paganism and Christianity," in *The Conflict between Paganism and Christianity in the Fourth Century*, ed. A. Momigliano (Oxford, 1963), 26–32; Pietri, *Roma*, 398ff.; M. R. Salzman, *The Making of a Christian Aristocracy: Social and Religious Change in the Western Roman Empire* (Cambridge, 2002), 61ff., 76–80, and 116ff.

31. Rome: Pietri, *Roma*, pp. 405–882; B. Lançon, *La vita quotidiana a Roma nel tardo impero*, trans. M. G. Meriggi (Milan, 1999), 140–43; J. Curran, *Pagan City and Christian Capital* (Oxford, 2000); and C. Hedrick, Jr., *History and Silence: Purge and the Rehabilitation of Memory in Late Antiquity* (Austin, TX, 2000), 37–71. Parnassus: Le Quien, *OC*, vol. 2, col. 415. Hypsius was Nicene; Ecdicius, "Arian."

32. For instance, paganism persisted in the West. Prelates were also called to organize the defense of their communities, paying ransom for prisoners of war, assisting refugees, etc. We also see this in the East (e.g., Synesius of Cyrene), but only on the periphery or after the period under review here.

33. R. Teja, "Auctoritas versus potestas: El liderazgo social de los obispos en la sociedad tardoantigua," in *Vescovi e pastori in epoca teodosiana, XXV Incontro di studiosi dell'antichità cristiana, Roma, 8–11 maggio 1996* (Rome, 1997), 74ff.

PART I. POINTS OF DEPARTURE

1. Arabia: J. Scherer, *Entretien d'Origène avec Héraclide et les évêques ses collègues sur le Père, le Fils et l'âme*, Publications de la Société Fouad I de Papyrologie, Textes et Documents 9 (Cairo, 1949), 13f.; id., *Entretien d'Origéne avec Héraclide*, SC 67 (Paris, 1960), 21; and J. Quasten, *Patrologia*, ed. I. Oñatiba, Biblioteca de Autores Cristianos (Madrid, 1961), 1:362–63; J. Daniélou, *Origène* (Paris, 1948), 37. Palestine: Eusebius, *HE* 6.8.4–5, 6.26; Daniélou, *Origène*, 19, 36–37. Reputation and audience: Eusebius, *HE* 6.3.1–2, 6.3.13, 6.5.1, 6.8.4–5, 6.19.1ff. (philosophers read his work), 6.19.12, 6.19.15 (governor of Arabia), 6.21.3 (Julia Mamaea). See also Daniélou, *Origène*, 34f.; H. Chadwick, *The Early Church* (New York, 1967), 103.
2. Bostra: Eusebius, *HE* 6.33; Daniélou, *Origène*, 37; Quasten, *Patrologia*, 341.
3. Eusebius, *HE* 6.23.4; Daniélou, *Origène*, 36–37.
4. Despite Demetrius's condemnation, Origen became priest in Caesarea, and his massive and influential work continued to be widely read and debated all over the East. See Eusebius, *HE* 6.8.4–5, 6.23.4; Jerome, *Ep.* 33.5; id., *De vir. ill.* 54 (*PL* 23.699); Photius, *Bibliotheca* 118; Daniélou, *Origène*, 37; Quasten, *Patrologia*, 1: 341; C. W. Griggs, *Early Egyptian Christianity: From Its Origins to 451 C.E.* (Leiden and New York, 1993), 62–63; and J. W. Trigg, *Origen* (London and New York, 2002), 15ff.
5. Scherer, *Entretien* (1960), 20f., 24, and 62.
6. Ibid., 62.
7. Ibid., 24; and cf. 62–64; and Origen, *De orat.* 16.1 (*GCS* 3): Τῷ Θεῷ δι' αὐτοῦ λέγοντες πάντες . . . ῍Η οὐχὶ σχιζόμεθα, ἐαν οἱ μὲν τῷ Πατρί, οἱ δὲ τῷ Υἱῷ εὐχώμεθα;
8. Scherer, *Entretien* (1949), 128–29. Monarchianism: B. Studer, *Trinity and Incarnation: The Faith of the Early Church*, trans. M. Westerhoff (Edinburgh, 1993), 65–75.
9. Scherer, *Entretien* (1949), 128–29. Bishops Demetrius and Philip participated in the debate.
10. Scherer, *Entretien* (1949), 128–29.
11. Scherer, *Entretien* (1960), 68.
12. The preface to the debate was not recorded, see Scherer, *Entretien* (1960), 24f. and 52; Quasten, *Patrologia*, 1:363; and Lim, *Public Disputation*, 18–20.
13. Scherer, *Entretien* (1960), 56. On Origen on the "power of God," see M. R. Barnes, *The Power of God: Δύναμις in Gregory of Nyssa's Trinitarian Theology* (Washington, DC, 2000), 103–24, esp. 111ff.; and Ayres, *Nicaea*, 23–24.
14. Scherer, *Entretien* (1960), 56, 58–64.
15. Quote: Scherer, *Entretien* (1960), 22, 68 (reconciliation).
16. Eusebius, *HE* 7.11.26 (deacon).
17. Ibid. 7.32.5.
18. Eusebius, *HE* 7.27–30 is the main source. See also F. Loofs, *Paulus von Samosata* (Leipzig, 1924); G. Bardy, *Paul de Samosate: Étude historique* (Louvain, 1929); H. de Riedmatten, *Les actes du procès de Paul de Samosate: Étude sur la christologie du IIIe au IVe siècle* (Fribourg, 1952); F. Millar, "Paul of Samosata, Zenobia, and Aurelian: The Church, Local Culture, and Political Allegiance in Third-Century Syria," *JRS* 61 (1971): 1–17; Barnes, *CE*, 144–45; and V. Burrus, "Rhetorical Stereotypes in the Portrait of Paul of Samosata," *Vigiliae Christianae* 43 (1989): 215–35.

19. For the first and second (?) synods, see Eusebius, *HE* 7.30.4–5: "Firmilian having twice come... was now about to cross to Antioch." The third synod deposed Paul in 268 (Eusebius, *HE* 7.29–30). A fourth synod, possibly in 271, composed a petition to evict him from the church (ibid. 7.30.19ff.). Emperor Aurelian's decree: ibid. 7.30.19–20; and Bardy, *Paul*, 283ff.

20. If the second synod met in 264 (Millar, "Paul," 11), the first one must have met a few months earlier, because Firmilian went back to Cappadocian Caesarea and returned. At the latest, the first synod would have met in 263, but probably earlier. Since some time would have elapsed from Paul's ordination and the first suspicion of heresy to the first council, a date in the early 260s seems reasonable.

21. Eusebius, *HE* 7.30.16; Barnes, *CE*, 354 n. 161; Studer, *Trinity*, 92–93; and U. M. Lang, "The Christological Controversy at the Synod of Antioch in 268/9," *JTS*, n.s. 51 (2000): 54–80. For Paul's views reworked in the context of later controversies, see Riedmatten, *Actes*, 10; and T. C. Ferguson, *The Past Is Prologue: The Revolution of Nicene Historiography* (Leiden, 2005), 32–35.

22. Eusebius, *HE* 7.30.16–17. The council's letter of 268 accuses him of "tyrannical" and "immoral" behavior (ibid. 7.30.6). Yet the impression we get is that this behavior, if true, had been tolerated, because twice the bishops gave Paul a chance to change his views.

23. Eusebius, *HE* 7.30.4.

24. Ibid. 7.30.1.

25. Ibid. 7.29; Jerome, *De vir. ill.* 71. See also Riedmatten, *Actes*, 157; and Lim, *Public Disputation*, 22–24.

26. Eusebius, *HE* 7.30.18 (Domnus).

27. Bardy, *Paul*, 283–84, referring to Basil, *Supplic. ad Theod.* (Mansi, *ACO* 4.1104). Since Dionysius of Alexandria's letter to the Antiochenes (mentioned in the synodal of 268) was addressed generally to the "Christians," not to the bishop, Bardy, *Paul*, 207–8, suggested that a schism was already in the making before Paul's deposition.

28. Eusebius, *HE* 7.30.19; Bardy, *Paul*, 279.

29. Millar, "Paul."

30. *Conc. Nic.* I, canon 19 (Joannou, *Discipline*, 40).

31. R. A. Markus, "The Problem of Self-Definition: From Sect to Church," in *Jewish and Christian Self-Definition*, ed. E. P. Sanders (London, 1980), 1:8–12.

32. On different components of episcopal authority, see the essays in Chadwick et al., *Role*; and C. Rapp, *Holy Bishops in Late Antiquity: The Nature of Christian Leadership in an Age of Transition* (Berkeley, 2005), 16–18.

33. Lim, "Christian Triumph," 199–201.

1. CHRISTIAN LEADERSHIP AND THE CHALLENGE OF THEOLOGY

1. Scherer, *Entretien* (1960), 54.

2. See B. D. Ehrman, *Lost Christianities: The Battles for Scripture and the Faiths We Never Knew* (Oxford, 2003), 1–8.

3. 1 Romans 12:4; cf. 15:5–6; 1 Cor. 1:10–17, 12:12–26; Col. 3:15; Acts 4:32.

4. See G. G. Stroumsa, "Tertullian on Idolatry and the Limits of Tolerance," in *Tolerance and Intolerance in Early Judaism and Christianity*, ed. G. N. Stanton and G. G. Stroumsa

(Cambridge, 1998), 173–74; and A. Louth, "Unity and Diversity in the Church of the Fourth Century," in *Unity and Diversity in the Church*, ed. R. N. Swanson (Oxford, 1996), 4–5.

5. A. Le Boulluec, *La notion d'hérésie dans la littérature grecque, II-IIIe siècles* (Paris, 1985), 21–36; C. Munier, *Autorité épiscopale et sollicitude pastorale (IIe-VIe siècles)* (Aldershot, UK, 1991), VIII.258–61; and S. G. Wilson, "Dissidents and Defectors: The Limits of Pluralism," in *Fair Play: Diversity and Conflicts in Early Christianity; Essays in Honour of Heikki Räisänen*, ed. I. Dunderberg, C. Tuckett, and K. Syreeni (Leiden, 2002), 442.

6. Cf. 1 Cor. 11:19.

7. On orthodoxy as established tradition, and heresy as "outside" the tradition, see Le Boulluec, *Notion*, 21–36.

8. On the *regula* in second-century theological controversy, see Justin, *Apologia* 1.13.31–35 (*PG* 6.345ff.); Irenaeus, *C. haer.* 1.10.1–12 (*PG* 7.549ff.); Tertullian, *De praescr. haer.* 13 (*PL* 2.26ff.); id., *Adv. Praxean* 2.2 (*PL* 2.356ff.). See also F. Young, *Biblical Exegesis and the Formation of Christian Culture* (Cambridge, 1997), 18–21 (21: "The Rule of Faith ... articulated the essential hermeneutical key without which texts and community would disintegrate in incoherence").

9. See Markus, "Problem," 5ff.; J. T. Burtchaell, *From Synagogue to Church: Public Services and Offices in the Earliest Christian Communities* (repr., Cambridge, 1995), 305ff.; and G. Schöllgen, *Die Anfänge der Professionalisierung des Klerus und das kirchliche Amt in der syrischen Didaskalie*, JAC 26 (Münster, 1998), 57–100.

10. Wilson, "Dissidents," 456.

11. W. Pannenberg, "The Appropriation of the Philosophical Concept of God as a Dogmatic Problem of Early Christian Theology," in *Basic Questions in Theology: Collected Essays*, trans. G. H. Kehm (Philadelphia, 1971), 2:122ff.; Markus, "Problem," 11f.; and J. Rebecca Lyman, *Christology and Cosmology: Models of Divine Activity in Origen, Eusebius, and Athanasius* (Oxford, 1993), 2, 6.

12. Origen, *De principiis*, Preface 2 (*SC* 252): "necessarium uidentur prius ... certam lineam manifestamque regulam ponere, tum deinde etiam de ceteris quaerere." Italics are mine here and elsewhere unless indicated otherwise. On the meaning of the rule: Origen *apud* Scherer, *Entretien* (1960), 76; cf. Origen, *De principiis*, Preface 4–10 (*SC* 252) *and* 4.2.2 (*SC* 268).

13. See, for instance, A. von Harnack, *Manuale di storia del dogma* (Mendrisio, 1913), 3:59 (in Syria and Palestine, interpretation of the rule began to replace the rule itself); H. Lietzmann, *Histoire de l'Église ancienne*, trans. A. Jundt (Paris, 1937), 2:103–22; Chadwick, *Early Church*, 44–45; H. Crouzel and M. Simonetti, eds., *Origène, Traité des principes*, SC 252 (Paris, 1978), 1:47; H. Kraft, "Dalla chiesa ordinaria all'episcopato monarchico," *Rivista di Storia e Letteratura Religiosa* 22 (1986): 428–29; H. Koester, "ΓΝΩΜΑΙ ΔΙΑΦΟΡΟΙ: The Origin and Nature of Diversification in the History of Early Christianity," in *Studies in Early Christianity: A Collection of Scholarly Essays*, ed. E. Ferguson (New York and London, 1993), 197ff.

14. Lietzmann, *Histoire*, 113; cf. Tertullian, *Adv. Praxean* 9.

15. Von Harnack, *Manuale*, 3:6–145, 195–200; J. Pelikan, *The Christian Tradition: A History of the Development of Doctrine*, vol. 1, *The Emergence of the Catholic Tradition (100–600)* (Chicago and London, 1971); Pannenberg, "Appropriation," 119ff.; and Studer, *Trinity*, 44–54. For a more nuanced view, see Lyman, *Christology*, 1ff.; and Ayres, *Nicaea*, 31–40.

16. E. Troeltsch, *The Social Teaching of the Christian Churches*, trans. O. Wyon (London, 1950), 1:94; and Ehrman, *Lost Christianities*, 151. Cf. Tertullian, *Adv. Praxean* 2; Hippolytus, *Philos.* 10.32ff.; and Novatian, *De Trinitate*, passim.

17. On the challenges of Judaism and Gnosticism, see Le Boulluec, *Notion*, 86ff. See also Lim, *Public Disputation*, 29; and E. J. Watts, *City and School in Late Antique Athens and Alexandria* (Berkeley, 2006), 158–68. On the greater penetration of Christianity among the upper classes, see H. Chadwick, "The Church of the Third Century in the West," in *Heresy and Orthodoxy in the Early Church* (Aldershot, UK, 1991), XIV.8–9; and Markus, "Problem," 11–12.

18. Sabellius: Hippolytus, *C. haer. Noet.*, p. 159 (ed. Stevenson). The debate on Origen's thought: Pamphilus, *Apologia pro Origene* (PG 17.544–47); Williams, *Arius*, 132–33; and Ayres, *Nicaea*, 20–30.

19. See Markus, "Problem," 8ff.

20. *Hom. Ezech.* 1.10 *apud* Daniélou, *Origène*, 38.

21. Behind this was the Hellenic idea that the "senses prevent us from seeing the truth." See W. Pannenberg, "What Is Truth?" in *Basic Questions in Theology: Collected Essays*, trans. G. H. Kehm (Philadelphia, 1971), 2:4.

22. Origen, *De principiis* 4.3.14 (SC 268): "Non enim dixit difficile posse scrutari iudicia Dei, sed omnino non posse; nec dixit difficile investigari posse uias eius, sed non posse inuestigari." Cf. Pamphilus, *Apologia pro Origene* (PG 17.544).

23. Cf. Origen, *De principiis*, Preface 8 (SC 252): "Tum deinde quod per spiritum dei scripturae conscriptae sint et sensum habeant non eum solum, qui in manifesto est, sed et alium quendam latentem quam plurimos"; and Trigg, *Origen*, 37.

24. Origen, *De principiis* 4.4.1 (SC 268), 4.2.2, 4.3.14; Chadwick, *Early Church*, 105–6; M. Harl, *Origène, Philocalie 1–20: Sur les Écritures*, SC 302 (Paris, 1983), 133; A. Dihle, *Greek and Latin Literature of the Roman Empire: From Augustus to Justinian*, trans. M. Malzahn (London and New York, 1994), 407–10, 502ff.; and Ayres, *Nicaea*, 32–40.

25. Von Harnack, *Manuale*, 3:200; and Young, *Biblical Exegesis*, 9–10.

26. See Celsus *apud* Origen, *Contra Celsum* 3.12; id., *Fragm. in Ep. ad Titum* (PG 14.1304); cf. id., *De principiis*, Preface 2 (SC 252); and Alexander of Lycopolis, *Contra Manichaeos*, ed. A. Villey (Paris, 1985), 98–100. See also Crouzel and Simonetti, *Origène*, SC 252, p. 47; and Ayres, *Nicaea*, 39.

27. Cf. Tertullian, *De praescr. haer.* 14.

28. See the remarks of Crouzel and Simonetti in the introduction to *De principiis*, SC 252, 1:48.

29. Origen *apud* Pamphilus, *Apologia pro Origene* (PG 17.544–45).

30. Pamphilus, *Apologia pro Origene* (PG 17.543): "Nos tamen perspicimus frequenter ea quae ab eo . . . dicuntur, cum veniam petit pro his quae per nimiam discussionem et per multam scrutationem Scripturarum animo disputantis occurrunt: quae cum exponit, frequente addere solet et profiteri se non haec quasi definitiva pronuntiare sententia, nec statuto dogmate terminare, sed inquirere pro viribus, et sensum discutere Scripturarum." Cf. Origen, *Fragm. in Ep. ad Titum* (PG 14.1303ff.), defining "quid . . . sit haereticus homo" not by reference to the rule, but by listing every possible "error." See also Le Boulluec, *Notion*, 524–37.

31. See Lim, *Public Disputation*, 16–24.

32. For instance, Methodius of Olympus, who saw "wisdom"—knowledge of the truth—arising out of a consensus obtained through debate. See Methodius, *Symposium; On Free Will;* and *On Resurrection*. Cf. Ayres, *Nicaea*, 29.

33. On this paradox and Christianity's embrace of a double notion—Hebrew and Greek—of truth, see Pannenberg, "What Is Truth?" 4–6.

34. So Clement of Alexandria; see H. von Campenhausen, *Ecclesiastical Authority and Spiritual Power*, trans. J. A. Baker (London, 1969), 204f.
35. A. Martin, "Orthodoxie et pouvoirs institutionels," in *OCH*, 344.
36. Cf. Irenaeus, *C. haer.* 5.6.1 (on prophecy and speaking in tongues) and Apollinarius of Hierapolis against the "Montanists" *apud* Eusebius, *HE* 5.16.1–11. See also Studer, *Trinity*, chaps. 4–6.
37. Troeltsch, *Social Teaching*, 94ff.; Lietzmann, *Histoire*, 53; von Campenhausen, *Ecclesiastical Authority*, 181–212, 249–92; and Burtchaell, *Synagogue*, 299–312.
38. *Pace* Cyprian, this was less so in the West. See von Campenhausen, *Ecclesiastical Authority*, 169–77, 241–46, and 272–83 (on Cyprian); and Burtchaell, *Synagogue*, 336–38.
39. A. von Harnack, *The Mission and Expansion of Christianity in the First Three Centuries*, trans. J. Moffatt (New York, 1908), 1:354–62; Lietzmann, *Histoire*, 52–53; Daniélou, *Origène*, 57, 59–63; Chadwick, *Early Church*, 51–53; Kraft, "Dalla 'chiesa,'" 429–33; Burtchaell, *Synagogue*, 299–306 (with references); and Schöllgen, *Anfänge*, 45–50. On the "subordination" of confessors, see V. Saxer, "La mission: L'organisation de l'Église au IIIe siècle," in *Naissance d'une chrétienté (250–430)*, ed. C. Pietri and L. Pietri (Paris, 1995), 58–60; and Burtchaell, *Synagogue*, 305–6.
40. Too much has been written on the authority and charisma of martyrs and confessors vis-à-vis that of bishops and priests to need repetition here. See, for instance, Cyprian, *Epp.* 9, 11, 13, 14, 18, 22, 26, 27; Eusebius, *HE* 6.45 (Dionysius's letter to Novatian); 7.11.1ff.; Lucian, *Peregrinus* 12; W. H. C. Frend, *The Donatist Church: A Movement of Protest in Roman North Africa* (Oxford, 1955), 112–39; F. H. Kettler, "Der melitianische Streit," *ZNTW* 35 (1936): 164f.; B. Kötting, "Die Stellung des Konfessors in der Alten Kirche," *JAC* 19 (1976): 16–22; T. Baumeister, "Ordnungsdenken und charismatiche Geisterfahrung in der Alten Kirche," *Revue de Qumran* 73 (1978): 150ff.; R. Lane Fox, *Pagans and Christians* (New York, 1989), 503–6.
41. Patronage and protection: Chadwick, "Role"; Brown, "Response"; A. Stewart-Sykes, "Ordination Rites and Patronage Systems in Third-Century Africa," *Vigiliae Christianae* 56 (2002): 116. Cf. Bobertz, "Cyprian," p. ii; G. D. Dunn, "Cyprian and His 'Colleague': Patronage and the Episcopal Synod of 252," *JRH* 27 (2003): 1–13; Burtchaell, *Synagogue*, 306–12; and Rapp, *Holy Bishops*, 23–37, on the "pragmatic" aspect of episcopal authority.
42. These writings betrayed the expectation that the episcopal leadership live up to an ideal long ago proposed by Ignatius, who had urged Christians to accept bishops in the "place of God." See W. Bauer, *Orthodoxy and Heresy in Earliest Christianity*, trans. and ed. R. Kraft and G. Krodel (Philadelphia, 1971), 114–20; von Campenhausen, *Ecclesiastical Authority*, 163ff.; and W. H. C. Frend, *The Early Church* (Philadelphia, 1982), 39. See also Irenaeus, *C. haer.* 3.3.2–3, 4.26.2; Hippolytus, *Apostolic Tradition; Apostolic Const.* 2.26, 29, 33–34 (ed. Metzger; p. 14: *Const. Apost.* books 1–6 = *Didascalia* [ed. Connolly]); Cyprian, *De unitate* 10; id., *Epp.* 3.1.1–2.2, 59.2.1–8.2, 64.3, and 67.5.1–2; cf. these testimonies with *Didache* 15. See also E. Pagels, *The Gnostic Gospels* (New York, 1979), 47–48, 54, referring to the *Apocalypse of Peter* and its mockery of the sacralization of episcopal power (p. 48: "Others . . . call themselves bishops and deacons, *as if they received their authority from God*"). Ignatius: see his *Ad Magn.* 6.1. Cf. *Ad Eph.* 4.1; *Ad Trall.* 2.2; *Ad Phil.* Preface; *Ad Smyrn.* 8.1 Ignatius helped to lay the groundwork for the development of church order, but his exhortations did not necessarily represent the conditions of life in most Christian communities at his time. See Lietzmann, *Histoire*, 56–59; R. Gryson, "Les élections ecclésiastiques au IIIe

siècle," *Revue d' Histoire Ecclésiastique* 68 (1973): 356ff.; and R. Markus, *The End of Ancient Christianity* (Cambridge, 1990), 90–92. Further, on canonical-liturgical texts, Saxer, "Mission," 42ff.

43. Hippolytus, *Apostolic Tradition* (SC 11), p. 44. We are unfortunately ill-informed about ordination ceremonies in the third century. After the New Testament, the *Apostolic Tradition* (*AT*) provides the best evidence (Gryson, "Élections"; cf. Rapp, *Holy Bishops*, 57–60), but it is impossible to know whether ordination rituals were ever enacted in the way the *AT* described. Yet, perhaps more important than the ceremony itself is its ritual "prescription," which, by stressing the relationship between bishop and Spirit, reflected a concern to underscore the spiritual basis of episcopal authority.

44. Although it claims to represent ancient church tradition, the *AT* in fact "invented" one and presented it as a model to be emulated (Gryson, "Élections," 378). Following practices steeped in Jewish tradition, ordinations were made through the "laying of hands," which functioned as channels for the Spirit. See Acts 13:3; 1 Tim. 4:14; 2 Tim 1:6; *DACL* s.v. "consécration épiscopale," cols. 2581, 2582, 2588; and Frend, *Early Church*, 40. On the enigmatic Hippolytus, see B. Botte, *La tradition apostolique de Saint Hippolyte: Essai de reconstitution* (Münster, 1963); J. Magne, *Tradition apostolique sur les Charismes et Diataxeis des Saints Apôtres: Identification des documents et analyse du rituel des ordinations* (Paris, 1975); P. Bradshaw, M. E. Johnson, L. E. Phillips, et al., *The Apostolic Tradition: A Commentary* (Minneapolis, 2002). For a survey of the abundant recent scholarship on Hippolytus and the *AT*, see J. F. Baldovin, "Hippolytus and the Apostolic Tradition: Recent Research and Commentary," *Theological Studies* 64 (2003): 520–42.

45. Cyprian, *Ep.* 45.1; and Gryson, "Élections," 384ff. Cf. Eusebius, *HE* 6.29.2–4, on Fabian's election as bishop of Rome. For the practice in mid-third-century Africa, see Stewart-Sykes, "Ordination Rites," 124–26.

46. Cyprian, *Ep.* 58.8.

47. See von Campenhausen, *Ecclesiastical Authority*, 104f. Already in the early second century, Ignatius spoke of himself as *theophoros* (Ignatius, *Ad Eph.* 1, *Ad Trall.* 1, *Ad Magn.* 1, etc.). Cf. P. Brown, *The Making of Late Antiquity* (Cambridge, 1978), 57–58; id., *The Body and Society: Men, Women, and Sexual Renunciation in Early Christianity* (New York, 1988), 144–45; Saxer, "Mission," 44; A. Brent, *The Imperial Cult and the Development of Church Order: Concepts and Images of Authority in Paganism and Christianity before the Age of Cyprian* (Boston, 1999), 310ff.; and Rapp, *Holy Bishops*, 57–66.

48. For Origen's view of episcopal claims, see von Campenhausen, *Ecclesiastical Authority*, 254–55, 257, 260–64; Daniélou, *Origène*, 62–63; Frend, *Early Church*, 81–82; and Trigg, *Origen*, 15 n. 1.

49. Von Campenhausen, *Ecclesiastical Authority*, 225–31 (Tertullian), 251–64 (Origen).

50. Tertullian, *De pudicitia* 21.17: "sed ecclesia spiritus per spiritalem hominem, non ecclesia numerus episcoporum."

51. Daniélou, *Origène*, 201–2, points out that Origen's attitude "sera double. D'une part il adhère à la foi traditionelle; mais, par ailleurs, il 'propose' des opinions qui essaient de l'expliciter." Cf. Irenaeus, *C. haer.* 3.1.

52. Origen, *De principiis*, Preface 2 (SC 252); cf. Preface 4–5, 10.

53. Implied in Origen, *De principiis*, Preface 3 (SC 252). See von Campenhausen, *Ecclesiastical Authority*, 243–54; and Daniélou, *Origène*, 62, 83. Despite his criticism of the eccle-

siastical hierarchy, Origen would have had no difficulty accepting the dictum "Where the bishop is, the church is" (Lietzmann, *Histoire*, 54).

54. Origen, *Hom Jos.* 9.9, *apud* Daniélou, *Origène*, 57. Cf. the Gnostics' arguments *apud* Irenaeus, *C. haer.* 2.1.

55. On Origen on bishops, see von Campenhausen, *Ecclesiastical Authority*, 255ff., who called Origen's critique of the episcopate "pietist," because it had no intention of diminishing the authority of the priesthood (cf. Williams, *Arius*, 83).

56. Origen, *De principiis*, Preface, 10.189-96; ibid., 4.1, 4.2.9 (*SC* 268).

57. See, for instance, his *Fragm. in Ep. ad Titum* (*PG* 14.1305-6). Origen thought that one was capable of judging right from wrong and of deciding for oneself what to believe in: "habendum est autem in ecclesiasticis observationibus, quid neque hominum quis a deo in perditionem traditus est, sed unusquisque pereuntium sua negligentia pereat et culpa, qui habens arbitrii libertatem, eligere quod bonum est et potuit et debuit." Further, Origen, *De principiis*, Preface 5.104-5 (*SC* 252); ibid., 3.1ff. (*SC* 268); von Campenhausen, *Ecclesiastical Authority*, 263; Daniélou, *Origène*, 203; Crouzel and Simonetti, *Origène*, SC 252, p. 49; and Lyman, *Christology*, 62f.

58. Origen, *De principiis* 2.1.2 (*SC* 252).

59. Meaning: Origen, *De principiis*, Preface 3 (*SC* 252); Daniélou, *Origène*, 161-62; Chadwick, *Early Church*, 105; Frend, *Early Church*, 92. Cf. Dionysius of Alexandria's letter to Philemon *apud* Eusebius, *HE* 7.4.7. Accountable to God: Origen, *Fragm. in Ep. ad Titum* (*PG* 14.1303). Origen's attempt to provide a comprehensive interpretation of Christian doctrine (in the *Peri archon*) never intended to be dogmatic. This work was an exercise in theological speculation, where questions were raised and hypotheses formulated γυμναστικῶς. See Crouzel and Simonetti, *Origène*, SC 252, pp. 48f.; Harl, *Origène, Philocalie*, SC 302, 147; Daniélou, *Origène*, 202; and Williams, *Arius*, 136ff., 154-55. Cf. Eusebius, *HE* 5.13, on the debate between Rhodo and Apelles; and Origen's advice to Gregory Thaumaturgos that Christians should not attach themselves to "those whom everyone thought were wise in everything, but to apply [themselves] only to God and His prophets"—that is, to scripture (Gregory Thaumaturgos, *To Origen* 15, SC 148).

60. See Scherer, *Entretien* (1960), 38, 82ff.; von Campenhausen, *Ecclesiastical Authority*, 243-60; and Louth, "Unity," 5.

61. For instance, the Palestinian bishops who asked him to preach in their church, the bishop of Athens, the Arabian bishops involved in the affairs of Beryllus and Heracleides, and Heracleides himself. These clerics recognized Origen's superior authority in theological matters even though he was a layman. Beryllus: Eusebius, *HE* 6.33.1-3; cf. Irenaeus, *C. haer.* 4.3. Independence of judgment: Origen, *Contra Celsum* 3.9-10; id., *Comm. in Joh.* 5 (*PG* 14.196), on the inquisitive souls who came to listen to heretical preachers; Clement, *Strom.* 4.10.76f. (martyrdom against clerical advice); Cyprian, *De lapsis* 8f.; id., *De unitate* 1.17.

62. Cf. von Harnack, *Mission*, 1:439ff.; Nautin, "Évolution," 49; Saxer, "Mission," 43-47; and Burtchaell, *Synagogue*, 337-38.

63. Origen, *Comm. in Joh.* 5 (*PG* 14.196). Seekers: Tertullian, *De praescr. haer.* 1.9-11. Cf. Irenaeus, *C. haer.* 1.1 and 3.2.2 (Gnostics), and 1.13.3 (prophetesses); Clement, *Strom.* 7.15, 7.16 ("those who were eager to learn"). On clerics, see *Apost. Const.* 45 (priests who prayed with heretics) and 65 (who prayed in heretical assemblies) (respectively, Joannou, *Discipline*, 30 and 41).

64. For instance, the Montanist Christians of Phrygia, "elated ... by the Holy Spirit," whose leader, was "raised aloft and taken up to heaven, where he experienced an unnatural ecstasy" (Eusebius, *HE* 5.16.9, 5.16.14). Cf. the Christians who abandoned their properties to follow a prophet in Pontus, in the 260s; or the "credulous" faithful who, in the mid-230s, left the church of Carthage to follow a prophetess. See, respectively, Hippolytus, *Comm. in Danielem* (ed. Bonwetsch, pp. 232ff.) *apud* S. Mitchell, *Anatolia: Land, Men, and Gods in Asia Minor* (Oxford, 1993), 2:60 n. 49; and Cyprian, *Ep.* 75.10ff. Both Cyprian and, later, Peter of Alexandria found themselves rebuking martyrs and confessors for their excessive zeal and for "thinking themselves superior" (Peter, *Ep. Can.* 11 [*PG* 18.496]; cf Cyprian, *Epp.* 9.1, 14.2, 22.3, 26.1; and id., *De unitate* 20).

65. Cyprian, *Epp.* 64.3, 37.2, and 39 passim; and Lane Fox, *Pagans,* 494f. Cf. the heresiological catalogues that emerged at the time (e.g., Irenaeus, *C. haer.*; Hippolytus, *Philos.*); see J. Rebecca Lyman, "A Topography of Heresy: Mapping the Rhetorical Creation of Arianism," in *Arianism after Arius,* ed. M. R. Barnes and D. H. Williams (Edinburgh, 1993), 47.

66. For instance, Troeltsch, *Social Teaching,* 94; Lietzmann, *Histoire,* 57–63; and Chadwick, "Role," 3.

67. Burtchaell, *Synagogue,* 312 ("not the creation of a new office but the political transformation of a primeval one"). See also Gryson, "Élections," 384ff.; and Schöllgen, *Anfänge,* 114–45.

68. Irenaeus, *C. haer.* 4.26 (*ANF* 1): "Those who possess the succession from the apostles have received the gift of truth." The gift of Spirit was necessary for revealing the truth: ibid. 3.24 ("The Spirit is the truth").

69. Hippolytus, *Apostolic Tradition* 2. Cf. Cyprian, *De unitate* 10.

70. Chadwick, *Early Church,* 50; von Campenhausen, *Ecclesiastical Authority,* 124–48, 243f., and 282ff.; and Lane Fox, *Pagans,* 502f.

71. Cyprian, *Ep.* 69.3. Cf. id., *Epp.* 70.3, 71, 75.2; and Athanasius, *Or. contra Arianos* 3.38.

72. *Acts of the VII Council of Carthage* (*ANF* 5:571).

73. Ibid.: Pomponius of Dionysiana: "It is evident that heretics cannot baptize and give remission of sins, seeing that they have not power ... to loose or to bind anything on earth." Quintus of Agiva: "What can heretics give who ... have nothing?" Cf. Eusebius, *HE* 7.9.2, in which a man baptized by heretics wished to receive a second baptism because he thought the first one had been worthless: "He came to me crying ... throwing himself at my feet ... anxious to receive ... cleansing and the gift [of the Spirit]." On boundaries, see J. N. Lieu, *Christian Identity in the Jewish and Greco-Roman World* (Oxford, 2004), 130f.; and F. J. Reine, *The Eucharistic Doctrine and Liturgy of the Mystagogical Catecheses of Theodore of Mopsuestia* (Washington, DC, 1942), 39–40.

74. Cf. Cyprian, *Epp.* 42, 45.2, on Cornelius of Rome, who lost many faithful to Novatian; and Cyprian himself, who was challenged by Felicissimus (ibid. 37.1 and 39) and the confessors of Carthage (ibid. 9.1, 14.2, 22.3, 26.1).

2. "NOT IN THE SPIRIT OF CONTROVERSY"

1. See Origen, *Comm. in Joh.* 5 (*PG* 14.196); Irenaeus, *C. haer.* 3.2.1; *The Second Treatise of the Great Seth* (*NHC* VII.2), 59.20–28, 59.30–35; *Apocalypse of Peter* (*NHC* VII.3) 73.24ff., 74.16ff.; Lactantius, *Div. inst.* 4.30; Eusebius, *HE* 7.7.4; see also "Bishops Investigated or

Deposed for Doctrinal Reasons before the Arian Controversy" in the appendix to this study; and chapter 3 below (Alexander of Alexandria's excommunication of Arius). Cf. the attitude of bishops accused of "betrayal" during the persecutions (e.g., Cyprian, Cornelius of Rome, Dionysius of Alexandria, Peter of Alexandria).

2. Origen, *Contra Celsum* 3.9–10; cf. Alexander of Lycopolis, *Contra Manichaeos* 1.
3. Titus 2:15.
4. Cyprian, *Ep.* 54.2.2.
5. Eusebius, *HE* 7.30.12.
6. Cyprian, *Ep.* 54.5.1; cf. Tertullian, *De praescr. haer.* 41–42; Origen, *Fragm. in Ep. ad Titum* (PG 14.1304); and Alexander of Lycopolis, *Contra Manichaeos* 1.
7. See the appendix ("Bishops Investigated or Deposed") and the discussion below.
8. See, for instance, Eusebius, *HE* 5.13.5 and 7.7.5.
9. J. de Roulet, *Tolérance dans l'Église? Une réponse du deuxième siécle: D'Irénée à Arius* (Geneva, 1998), 64–67.
10. Scherer, *Entretien* (1960), 22; and chapter 1.
11. Eusebius, *HE* 7.30.4.
12. Cyprian, *Ep.* 59.10.1; and the appendix ("Bishops Investigated or Deposed").
13. Hippolytus, *Philos.* 9.6–7 (a contorted affair). Whether the Hippolytan Sabellius was the same Libyan Sabellius is unclear. On (the Libyan) Sabellius's views, see Eusebius, *HE* 7.6; and Athanasius, *De sent.* 4–5 and 10ff.
14. Sabellius's followers were apparently very successful "so that the Son of God was scarcely preached in the churches" of Libya (Athanasius, *De sent.* 5). Epiphanius, *Panarion* 62: Sabellius's teachings spread as far as Rome and Mesopotamia. Cf. Eusebius, *HE* 7.24.5 and below on the spread of Nepos's doctrine in Egypt even after it had been condemned.
15. Eusebius, *HE* 7.6.1; Athanasius, *De sent.* 5.
16. Eusebius, *HE* 7.6.1; Athanasius, *De sent.* 10–12, 13–16.
17. Athanasius, *De sent.* 13; H.-I. Marrou, "L'arianisme comme phénomène alexandrin," *CRAI* (1933): 538.
18. Athanasius, *De sent.* 14.1.
19. See R. Lane Fox, "Literacy and Power in Early Christianity," in *Literacy and Power in the Ancient World*, ed. A. K. Bowman and G. Woolf (Cambridge, 1994), 134–37.
20. For instance, Cyprian, *Epp.* 37.2, 39.3, 42, and 45.2.
21. Cyprian, *Ep.* 30.5 (*ANF* 5); cf. *Ep.* 27.
22. Cyprian, *Ep.* 51.6 (*ANF* 5).
23. Cyprian, *Ep.* 54.16 (*ANF* 5). On Felicissimus, see also *Epp.* 37 and 39.
24. The appendix ("Compromise and Solidarity in Doctrinal Controversy in the Early Church") lists other examples of prelates who spared no effort to bring about compromise and to be tolerant of opponents, even when a great deal of bad blood remained.
25. 2 Tim. 2:23–26.
26. Titus 3:10–11. See also Roulet, *Tolérance*, 63–66.
27. Cyprian, *Ep.* 39.5 (*ANF* 5); cf. *Ep.* 54.8–9.
28. For instance, *Epp.* 59.10.2 (calling *pseudoepiscopi* those who did not submit to a council's verdict) and 59.11.1, 14.1–2.
29. For instance, Cyprian, *Epp.* 55.21.2 and 54.1–2; cf. id., *De unitate* 10 and *Ep.* 15.2; and Dunn, "Cyprian," 1–13.

30. E. Gibbon, *The History of the Decline and Fall of the Roman Empire*, ed. D. Womersley (repr., London, 2005), 1:487.

31. Cyprian, *Ep.* 55.21.2: "manente concordiae vinculo et perseverante catholicae ecclesiae individuo sacramento, actuum suum disponit et dirigit unusquisque episcopus, rationem propositi sui Domino redditurus." See Frend, *Donatist Church*, 128–39.

32. See the remarks of G. Clemente, "Cristianesimo e classi dirigenti prima e dopo di Costantino," in *Mondo antico e cristianesimo* (Atti del Convegno su "Mondo greco-romano e cristianesimo") (Rome, 1982), 54–55.

33. Eusebius, *HE* 7.7.5 (quoting Deut. 19:14).

34. Threat of dispersal or schism: Eusebius, *HE* 6.41–42, 7.11, and 6.45; Origen, *Comm. in Joh.* 5 (*PG* 14.196). Cf. Eusebius, *HE* 6.2.14 (crowds attended "heretic" assemblies); Cyprian, *Ep.* 59.8.1 (those who left the church on *our* account); id., *Epp.* 51.13, 54.8, 45.2, and 59.10.3; and Kettler, "Der melitianische Streit," 161–63. Impoverishment: Cyprian, *De lapsis* 6; id., *Epp.* 52.1.2; 67.6.1–2 (poor bishops: Martialis became a member of a pagan college), 74.8.4 (importance of wealthy patrons); cf. 51.1.1. Even in the fourth century small churches found it hard to fund themselves: *Vie de sainte Mélanie* 21, ed. and trans. D. Gorce, SC 90 (Paris, 1962): church of Thagaste was πενιχρά. Cf. Ammianus Marcellinus, *RG* 27.3.14–15; Jones, *LRE*, 2:905; E. Wipszycka, *Les ressources et les activités économiques de l'église en Égypte du 4e au 8e siècle* (Brussels, 1972), passim (esp. 154–73); and R. Bagnall, *Egypt in Late Antiquity* (Princeton, NJ, 1993), 292. In general (but drawing mostly on Western evidence), see C. Sotinel, "Le personnel épiscopal: Enquête sur la puissance de l'évêque dans la cité," in *L'évêque dans la cité du IVe au Ve siècle: Image et autorité, Actes de la table ronde organisée par l'Istituto patristico Augustinianum et l'École française de Rome (Rome, 1er et 2 dec. 1995)*, ed. E. Rebillard and C. Sotinel (Rome, 1998), 122–26. Disengagement: *The Testimony of Truth* (NHC IX.3), 69.34ff. ("Some of them fall away [to the worship of] idols"); Lucian, *Peregrinus* 16; Origen, *Hom. Gen.* 10.1 (*apud* Daniélou, *Origène*, 54); id., *Hom. Ezech.* 14.3 (*apud* Daniélou, *Origène*, 55: "We have urged the youth to study the scripture, vainly. . . . We have wasted our time").

35. Cf. Repostus of Sutunurca, in North Africa: after being condemned for lapsing, he continued to serve as local bishop, because "maximam partem plebis suae sacrilega persuasione dejecit" (Cyprian, *Ep.* 59.10.3). See also Lietzmann, *Histoire*, 62–63.

36. Saxer, "Mission," 63–68.

37. For instance, Origen (see above) or Dionysius of Alexandria (see below). See also Eusebius, *HE* 5.16.4 (Apollinarius of Hierapolis) and 7.7.24ff.

38. Markus, "Problem," 9ff. (on the growth of the "great church" in the third century).

39. R. MacMullen, *Corruption and the Decline of Rome* (New Haven, CT, 1988), 65–69, esp. 67; and id., *Voting about God in Early Church Councils* (New Haven, CT, 2006), 16f. See also Hermann, *Ecclesia*, 47f. and 290ff.; Roulet, *Tolérance*, 13–53.

40. See discussion above. Cf. Eusebius, *VC* 1.51; and H. C. Brennecke, "Bischofsversammlung und Reichssynode: Das Synodalwesen im Umbruch der konstantinischen Zeit," in *Einheit der Kirche in vorkonstantinischer Zeit*, ed. F. v. Lilienfeld and A. M. Ritter (Erlangen, 1989), 36–37.

41. Itinerant preachers: Ignatius, *Ad Eph.* 9.1; *Ad Trall.* 9.1; *Ad Smyr.* 4.1. Laypersons, prophets, and teachers: for instance, Marcion, charged with immorality and excommunicated; Valentinian, accused of breaking with the church because he failed to attain the episcopate (Tertullian, *Adv. Valent.* 4); Marcellina, a Gnostic missionary (Irenaeus, *C. haer.*

1.25.6); Bardaisanes, teacher and philosopher (Eusebius, *HE* 4.30); the Montanist leaders and prophets (ibid. 5.14–20); Blastus and Florinus of Rome, who founded a separate (Montanist) community (ibid. 5.15.1 and 5.20.1); Theodotus, the shoemaker, excommunicated by Victor of Rome (ibid. 5.28.6 and 9); Sabellius (see above; and an anonymous prophetess in Carthage (Cyprian, *Ep.* 75.10ff.). Bishops: see the appendix ("Bishops Investigated or Deposed").

42. Eusebius, *HE* 7.24.1ff.; and Lim, *Public Disputation*, 20–22.

43. Eusebius, *HE* 7.24.

44. Although Dionysius noted that Nepos's views had spread in the Fayum for a long time (Eusebius, *HE* 7.24.6), we cannot be sure whether he had been informed about them in advance of his trip to Arsinoë (at 7.24.7, he expresses surprise at the book the priests brought to argue with him, and at 7.24.8 admits to having been "lost" in their argument). The second of the two pamphlets Dionysius wrote refuting Nepos's teachings was composed after his visit to Arsinoë, but it may be that the first one was, too (7.24.1–5).

45. Eusebius, *HE* 7.24.6–8.

46. Ibid. 7.24.4.

47. Note, too, Dionysius's remarks about the love and admiration he felt for Nepos; see Eusebius, *HE* 7.24.4.

48. See the appendix ("Bishops Investigated or Deposed").

PART II. GOD IN DISPUTE

1. Licinius's defeat: September 18, 324, at Chrysopolis (Barnes, *CE*, 77).

2. The traditional date for the beginning of the controversy is 318; see Hanson, *Search*, 3.

3. Williams, *Arius*, 131–57; Studer, *Trinity*, 89–98; Lyman, *Christology*, 39–81; Lim, *Public Disputation*, 16ff.; P. Widdicombe, *The Fatherhood of God from Origen to Athanasius* (Oxford, 1994), 122–44; Ayres, *Nicaea*, 20–30; and chapter 1 above.

4. See P. Gavrilyuk, *The Suffering of the Impassible God: The Dialectics of Patristic Thought* (Oxford, 2004), 31–36, 105.

5. *Urk.* 6, p. 12, l. 19, and p. 13, ll. 19–20; and chapter 3 below.

6. Proverbs 8:22–23. New English Bible: "The Lord created me the beginning of his works, before all else that he made, long ago. Alone, I was fashioned in times long past, at the beginning, long before earth itself." See also Williams, *Arius*, 98.

7. *Urk.* 14, pp. 22–23, 26, l. 30–p. 27, ll. 1ff.: γεννηθέντα οὐκ τοῦ μὴ ὄντος, ἀλλὰ ἐκ τοῦ ὄντος πατρός. See also chapter 3 below.

8. Ayres, *Nicaea*, 2, has proposed that Arius's ideas be situated in a "wider theological trajectory" that did not originate with him. Nonetheless, Arius was able to articulate his theology in a much more forceful and precise way than before. As Williams, *Arius*, 176, noted, "With Arius' arrival on the scene, several strands of theological argument intertwine." See also the remarks of Gregg and Groh, *Early Arianism*, 193: "The outbreak of the Arian controversy heralded a new era in the history of Christianity . . . [demonstrating] the new place held by Christian controversy on the center stage of late antiquity. . . . With . . . the controversy, competing notions of salvation . . . were offered for consideration . . . to a vast Eastern constituency." Further, Studer, *Trinity*, 102f.; Widdicombe, *Fatherhood*, 122–44; and Parvis, *Marcellus*, 38.

3. PRECISION, DEVOTION, AND CONTROVERSY IN ALEXANDRIA

1. C. Kannengiesser, "Current Theology: Arius and the Arians," *Theological Studies* 44 (1983): 456–57.

2. Eusebius, *VC*; id., *Chronici Canones*, on which see R. W. Burgess, *Studies in Eusebian and Post-Eusebian Chronography*, Historia Einzelschriften 135 (Stuttgart, 1999), 63–64; for the dossier of documents called "Collection d'Alexandre," used by Socrates: see P. van Nuffelen, *Un héritage de paix et de piéte: Étude sur les histoires ecclésiastiques de Socrate et de Sozomène* (Leuven, 2004), 318–19. The *Continuatio Antiochensis Eusebi* (ed. Burgess), used by Jerome, Socrates, the anonymous author of the *Chronicon Paschale*, Theophanes, and several Syriac chroniclers and epitomators, begins in 325 (Burgess, *Studies*, 123–29).

3. See Kannengiesser, "Current Theology," 459–60; and Ferguson, *Past*, arguing that fourth-century ecclesiastical histories functioned as narratives of community origins and "theological statement[s]" (11). For Socrates' and Sozomen's sources, see Barnes, *AC*, 205–8; and Van Nuffelen, *Héritage*, chap. 5 and app. 5. Used by Socrates and Sozomen, the nonextant anti-Nicene *Synagoge* of Sabinus of Heraclea did not treat the pre-Nicene phase of the controversy. Neither did the so-called Arian chronicler of the fourth century—a source for the anonymous author of the *Chronicon Paschale* and others. On this chronicler, see M. Whitby and M. Whitby, trans., *Chronicon Paschale, 284–628 AD*, Translated Texts for Historians 7 (Liverpool, 1989), xv–xx; Ferguson, *Past*, 63–65, 78–79; and Burgess, *Studies*, 124–27.

4. For instance, the "Collection d'Alexandre"; and the dossier of documents in Van Nuffelen, *Héritage*, 321, called "Collection Alexandrine," compiled in the late fourth century and preserved in part in the *Codex Veronensis* LX together with a copy of the *Historia Acephala*. Sozomen used both.

5. See works cited in the introduction, note 8, above; E. Stein, *Histoire du Bas-Empire*, trans. J.-R. Palanque (Amsterdam, 1968), 2:464 n. <156>38, discussing much earlier bibliography; and U. Loose, "Zur Chronologie des arianischen Streites," *Zeitschrift für Kirchengeschichte* 101 (1990): 88–92.

6. Malalas contains little information; the *Chronicon Paschale* and Theophanes, drawing on the *Continuatio Antiochensis* and the Arian chronicler, and Jerome and the *Chronica minora* also tell us little about the early controversy. Michel the Syrian and the *Chronicle of 724* draw on a Syriac translation of Eusebius, *Chronici canones*, and the *Continuatio Antiochensis*. Other Syriac chronicles (i.e., *Chronicle of Edessa*, *Chronicle of Seert*, etc.) rely on Syriac epitomes of the latter. See Burgess, *Studies*, 126–29; and Whitby and Whitby, *Chronicon*, xx.

7. See E. Clark, "Rewriting the History of Early Christianity," in *The Past Before Us: The Challenge of Historiographies of Late Antiquity*, Smith Studies in History Series 54, Bibliothèque de l'Antiquité Tardive 6, ed. C. Straw and R. Lim (Turnhout, 2004), 65–68.

8. It is amusing to follow this in the literature on the Arian controversy, as one scholar after another claims to have the best reconstruction.

9. Sozomen, *HE* 1.15.3, followed by Theodoret, Gelasius of Cyzicus, Agapius, several Syrian chroniclers (via Theodoret), Nicetas, and Nicephorus.

10. Epiphanius, *Panarion* 69.2. Pride: *Urk.* 14, p. 26, l. 15. Foreign: Gelasius, *HE* 2.2.1–2. Quotes: *Urk.* 6, p. 13, ll. 8–12; *Urk.* 1, p. 3, ll. 2–4; and *Urk.* 6, p. 12, l. 9. Father preexisted the Son: not exactly Arius's words, but an idea he approved (*Urk.* 1, p. 2, l. 6). "Creature, but not as one of the creatures": Athanasius, *Or. contra Arianos* 2.19. Cf. Sozomen, *HE* 1.15.3; Simonetti, *Crisi,* 27–30, 46–55; Williams, *Arius,* 95–115; and Hanson, *Search,* 3–18, 99–128.

11. *Urk.* 6, p. 12, ll. 3–4.

12. Simonetti, *Crisi,* 47–51; Hanson, *Search,* 3–18; Williams, *Arius,* 95–116; and Arius's statement of faith, discussed below.

13. See *Urk.* 6, p. 12, ll. 12f.; *Urk.* 14, p. 27, ll. 4–7 (Alexander's effort to justify his views as non-Sabellian); and Simonetti, *Crisi,* 28–29.

14. Socrates, *HE* 1.5. Cf. Arius's reaction to Alexander's teaching: *Urk.* 6, p. 12, ll. 11–13; Nicephorus, *HE* 8.5.

15. Ignatius of Selymbria, *Vita Constantini* (*BHG* 362), ed. T. Ioannou, *Mnemeia hagiologica* (Venice, 1884), 164–229 (reprint: ed. J. Dummer [Leipzig, 1973]; henceforth *VC*), together with P. Heseler, "Hagiographica II: Zur Vita Constantini et matris Helenae des Ignatius von Selymbria (*BHG* 362)," *Byzantinisch-neugriechische Jahrbücher* 9 (1930): 320–37. Heseler (337) suggests that Gelasius of Caesarea was one of the sources for Ignatius's account. On Gelasius of Caesarea as a Nicene continuator of Eusebius, see T. D. Barnes, "Emperor and Bishops, A.D. 324–344: Some Problems," *American Journal of Ancient History* 3 (1978): 53.

16. *Urk.* 17, p. 33, ll. 1ff. See Simonetti, *Crisi,* 52–60; and Williams, *Arius,* 108–9.

17. Opitz, "Zeitfolge," 146. Sozomen provides the more detailed account (see note 3 above on his sources). Epiphanius used a Melitian source; see Martin, *Athanase,* 284–85.

18. Epiphanius, *Panarion* 69.1. Not necessarily situated in the eastern suburbs by assimilation of Baukalis to "Boucolia" and Τὰ Βουκόλου, as A. Martin, "Les églises d'Alexandrie aux 3e et 4e siècles," *Revue des Études Augustiniennes* 30 (1984): 216–17, suggested, followed by T. Vivian, *Saint Peter of Alexandria, Bishop and Martyr* (Philadelphia, 1988), 25 n. 85; C. Haas, "The Arians of Alexandria," *Vigiliae Christianae* 47 (1993): 235; and id., *Alexandria in Late Antiquity: Topography and Social Conflict* (Baltimore, 1997), 269–70. Boucolia was an eastern suburb of Alexandria where the shrine of St. Mark stood, on which see Epiphanius, *Panarion* 23.116.14–16; *Acta Petri* (*BHG* 1502), ed. J. Viteau, *Passions de saints Écaterine et Pierre d'Alexandrie . . .* (1897), 77; A. Bernard, *Alexandrie la Grande* (Paris, 1966), 85; and Calderini, *Dizionario,* 72. Recently, Martin, *Athanase,* 148, suggested that the church may have been located in one of the alleys of Alexandria's *emporion,* which is plausible. Near the gymnasium: Nicetas, *Thesauri* 1; near the agora: Haas, *Alexandria,* 31; at the eastern end of the Dromos: Calderini, *Dizionario,* p. 107, *pace* Strabo.

19. Epiphanius, *Panarion* 68.4, 69.1–2; Sozomen, *HE* 1.15.12; Marrou, "Arianisme," 535; Williams, *Arius,* 42; and W. Telfer, "Episcopal Succession in Egypt," *Journal of Ecclesiastical History* 3 (1952): 1–13.

20. Epiphanius, *Panarion* 69.1–2; Sozomen, *HE* 1.15.12; Marrou, "Arianisme"; and Williams, *Arius,* 41–47.

21. Epiphanius, *Panarion* 69.1–3; Williams, *Arius,* 44–46; and Haas, *Alexandria,* 270.

22. Achillas: Williams, *Arius*, 45. Kolluthos: *Urk.* 14, pp. 19–20, ll. 11ff. The story of the priest nicknamed "Baukalis" who accused Arius to Alexander is apocryphal; see Philostorgius, *HE* 1.4; and Nicephorus, *HE* 8.5 (*PG* 146.25: "another Alexander, nicknamed Baukalis").

23. Epiphanius, *Panarion* 69.3; Sozomen, *HE* 1.15.4; and Nicephorus, *HE* 8.5. Epiphanius makes the schismatic Melitius report Arius to the bishop. Martin, *Athanase*, 275–85, suggests that this was an attempt on the part of later Melitians to rehabilitate Melitius's memory (and, by extension, their own). Regardless of the veracity of these events, there may be a kernel of truth in the idea of a priest denouncing Arius to the bishop. See Barnes, *CE*, 204.

24. *Urk.* 14, p. 20, ll. 1–2.

25. Socrates, *HE* 1.6.

26. Sozomen, *HE* 1.15.4–6 (1.15.5: Ἀμφηρίστου ... Ἀλέξανδρος); Theodoret, *HE* 1.1; Gelasius, *HE* 2.2.3.

27. Sozomen, *HE* 1.15.2 (Ἀλέξανδρος ἐν τιμῇ εἶχεν αὐτὸν); Gelasius, *HE* 2.2.1–2; Nicephorus, *HE* 8.5 (*PG* 146.25); Ignatius of Selymbria, *VC* 34 (ed. Ioannou, p. 198). Cf. Philostorgius, *HE* 1.4; and Simonetti, *Crisi*, 28.

28. Nicephorus, *HE* 8.5 (*PG* 146.24): Alexander entrusted him with τὴν τῶν Γραφῶν ἑρμενείαν. Cf. Sozomen, *HE* 1.15.2; Williams, *Arius*, 38–41. Alexander's hesitation: *Urk.* 14, p. 20, l. 18f.; cf. Epiphanius, *Panarion* 69.3.3; and Socrates, *HE* 1.6.

29. Alexander did not immediately refute Arius's propositions and took time to formulate a clear alternative to them; see P. Nautin, "Deux interpolations orthodoxes dans une lettre d'Arius," *Anal. Boll.* 67 (1949): 132–33; Kopecek, *History*, 11–15; and discussion below.

30. *Urk.* 4b, p. 7, ll. 2–3.

31. Simonetti, *Crisi*, 28ff. Melitian schism: Kettler, "Der melitianische Streit"; H. I. Bell, *Jews and Christians in Egypt: The Jewish Troubles in Alexandria and the Athanasian Controversy* (London, 1924), 38ff.; Vivian, *Saint Peter*, 26ff.; H. Hauben, "La première année du schisme mélitien (305/306)," *Ancient Society* 20 (1989): 267–80; Martin, *Athanase*, esp. 217–98 and 303–12.

32. Epiphanius, *Panarion* 67.1ff. Hieracas had been in the minds of the Alexandrian clergy. A letter written by Eustathius of Beroea, later of Antioch, addressed to Alexander, seems to have been a reply to a question raised by Alexander on the subject of Melchisedech, whom the Hierakites identified with the Holy Spirit. See Eustathius of Antioch, Fragment 113 (*CCSG* 51). Both Alexander and Arius considered Hieracas's views heretical (see *Urk.* 6, p. 13, ll. 1–2). See also S. Elm, *Virgins of God: The Making of Asceticism in Late Antiquity* (Oxford, 1994), 339–42.

33. Implied in Alexander's account of Kolluthus's behavior (*Urk.* 14, p. 19, l. 11–p. 20, ll. 1–2), on which see the appendix ("Kolluthus's Schism and the Arians"). See also Epiphanius, *Panarion* 68.4 and 69.3; Sozomen, *HE* 1.15.4; *Chronicle of Seert* 9 (*PO* 4.246–47); Agapius, *HU* (*PO* 7.544); and Nicephorus, *HE* 8.5.

34. Williams, *Arius*, 19, 82–91; Brakke, *Athanasius*, 59–75. Cf. Simonetti, *Crisi*, 22.

35. Dionysius by Germanus (Eusebius, *HE* 7.11.1ff.) and Peter by Melitius (Vivian, *Saint Peter*, 26ff.).

36. Epiphanius, *Panarion* 69.3; Sozomen, *HE* 1.15.4.

37. Arius on Alexander: *Urk.* 6, p. 12, ll. 3–6 and p. 13, ll. 13–14. He never called Alexander a heretic, as he did other bishops (*Urk.* 1, p. 2, ll. 5ff.). See also J. N. D. Kelly, *Early Christian Doctrines* (New York, 1978), 230.

38. Sozomen, *HE* 1.15.5.

39. Debates and disputations: Sozomen, *HE* 1.15.5. Cf. *Urk.* 4b, p. 8, ll. 7–10; ibid., p. 9, ll. 20ff.; *Urk.* 14, p. 21, ll. 15ff.; Athanasius, *Or. contra Arianos* 2.19 (the Arians' reply to Alexander). Hints of the exchange of letters between the two parties and of local synods: *Urk.* 4a, p. 6, ll. 1–5; Sozomen, *HE* 1.16.1; Nicephorus, *HE* 8.11.

40. Sozomen, *HE* 1.15.5–6, emphasizing first Alexander's reluctance, and then his sudden change of heart, once he understood Arius's propositions: Ἀμφηρίστου ... Ἀλέξανδρος ... Τελευτῶν δὲ τοῖς ὁμοούσιον καὶ συναΐδιον εἶναι τὸν υἱὸν ἀποφαινομένοις ἔθετο. Note that Ἀμφηρίστου and Τελευτῶν come first in the sentence for added emphasis. Alexander himself admitted surprise and outrage when he heard the Arians profess the idea of Christ's mutability (see below), conveying the impression that he formed his opinion as Arius's ideas became clearer. Arius's bafflement at the bishop's reception of his teachings also supports this view. Cf., however, Socrates, *HE* 1.6, who gives a different account.

41. On the evolution of and alleged contradictions in Arius's thought, see Gwatkin, *Studies*, 23 n. 2 and 26 n. 3; Gregg and Groh, *Early Arianism*, 8–30, 48f.; and R. Williams, "The Quest of the Historical Thalia," in *Arianism: Historical and Theological Reassessments (Papers from the Ninth International Conference on Patristic Studies, Oxford, September 5–10, 1983)* (Philadelphia, 1985), 9–16. Williams notes the difficulty in isolating Arius's thought from that of other Arian thinkers and, above all, from "Arianism" as created by Alexander and Athanasius, who underscored Arius's supposed inconsistencies.

42. Many priests and deacons sided with Arius (Sozomen, *HE* 1.15.6), perhaps more than the usual list of those deposed by the bishop (Athanasius, *HA* 71). Some, like Pistus, supported Arius *after* his deposition (*Urk.* 4a, p. 6, ll. 8ff.), implying early hesitation. Alexander's initial hesitation to condemn Arius, and then insistence on having his clergy express support for his position (ibid., ll. 1–8) also suggest uncertainty about the orthodox position.

43. To judge from the number of priests who later signed Arius's deposition: seventeen (*Urk.* 4b, p. 10).

44. Sozomen, *HE* 1.15.6; Theodoret, *HE* 1.1 (*NPNF*, 3:34). Even after deposing and excommunicating Arius, Alexander seems to have tried to persuade the priest to reject his views: *Urk.* 4a, p. 6, ll. 3–7.

45. Gregg and Groh, *Early Arianism*, 1–30, 43–58 (cf. M. Simonetti, "Review of R.C. Gregg and D.E. Groh, *Early Arianism: A View of Salvation*," *RSLR* 18 [1981]: 304–6); Williams, *Arius*, 18–20, 82–91; id., "Quest," 15; and Brakke, *Athanasius*, 69.

46. *Urk.* 4b, p. 8, ll. 7–10. G.C. Stead, "Athanasius' Earliest Written Work," *JTS*, n.s., 39 (1988): 76–91, and Barnes, *AC*, 16, have argued that *Urk.* 4b (*Henos somatos*) was the work of the young Athanasius. But Athanasius's views would have been very close to those of the bishop.

47. *Urk.* 14, p. 21, ll. 11–14.

48. As Brakke, *Athanasius*, 69, observed, "Whether or not Arian Christians actually held [Arius's] soteriology [i.e., based on spiritual progress], their opponents saw it as a clear implication of their Christology."

49. *Urk.* 14, p. 20, ll. 5–10.

50. Ibid., p. 24, ll. 6ff.

51. See Gregg and Groh, *Early Arianism*, 29, 50–70, 152–53; and cf. Williams, *Arius*, 114–16.

52. Peter, *Ep. Can.* 11 (*PG* 18.496).

53. Christians like the Hermopolite Paese, who came to Alexandria to visit a friend during the Diocletianic persecution. Making the rounds of the prisons to console and feed the confessors, he came to the theater where a young Christian named Victor was being tortured. Then, "straightaway [his] eyes were opened and he saw the angel of the Lord standing by [Victor] . . . and when he saw the great miracles which the holy . . . Victor was performing, the Holy Spirit descended upon him." See the "Passion of SS Paese and Thecla," in *Four Martyrdoms from the Pierpont Morgan Coptic Codices*, ed. E. A. E. Reymond and J. W. B. Barns (Oxford, 1973), 151–84 (157: quote). This *Passio* never once mentions a cleric; it is entirely about lay piety evolving outside the framework of the church.

54. *Urk.* 14, p. 24, ll. 11–12.

55. Gregg and Groh, *Early Arianism*, 47, 58–59.

56. *Urk.* 14, p. 20, ll. 10–11; p. 24, ll. 3ff.; p. 25, ll. 19–21; p. 26, ll. 25ff.; and p. 27, l. 31–p. 28, l. 7. On Alexander's and Athanasius's perception of the "Arian" Son and their reaction to it, see Simonetti, *Crisi*, 56–59; and Gregg and Groh, *Early Arianism*, 47–70.

57. Also in *Urk.* 4b, p. 9, ll. 22–25, and *Urk.* 14, *passim*. Cf. Constantine on the outbreak of the controversy, who also suggests that the bishop abruptly changed his mind about Arius (*Urk.* 17, p. 33, ll. 1ff.).

58. *Urk.* 1, p. 3, l. 3, and *Urk.* 6, p. 12, l. 9.

59. Simonetti, *Crisi*, 50–51; Gregg and Groh, *Early Arianism*, 29, 67–69; Williams, "Quest," 10–11; and id., *Arius*, 161.

60. But see *Urk.* 14, p. 21, ll. 16ff. Williams, "Quest," 10, conjectures that Arius's associates may have not conveyed those fine distinctions in the debates, and that Alexander would thus have clumped Arius together with them for polemical purposes. See Simonetti, *Crisi*, 50–51; and id., "Review," 306.

61. See the faith of the Council of Antioch (*Urk.* 18, p. 39, ll. 4f.) or the creed of Nicaea; cf. Athanasius, *Or. contra Arianos* 1.5–7. See also Gregg and Groh, *Early Arianism*, 19–30, 50–70; Williams, *Arius*, 103–5; and Brakke, *Athanasius*, pp. 68ff.

62. *Urk.* 14, p. 25, ll. 2–5.

63. See Brakke, *Athanasius*, 64–72.

64. See Marrou, "Arianisme," 535, 537–38; and Simonetti, *Crisi*, 28–29.

65. *Urk.* 4a, p. 6, ll. 3–5, and *Urk.* 14, p. 20, ll. 2–3. Cf. Didymus of Alexandria (ed. Gronewald, p. 104), who later reported that καὶ Ἄρειος ὅτε ἤμελλεν τοῦ σχίσματος τούτου ἀπὸ τοῦ φρονήματος ἄρχεσθαι . . . ἔτι ἔσω ὢν ἐν τῇ ἐκκλησίᾳ.

66. Theodoret, *HE* 1.1.

67. See Gelasius, *HE* 2.2.3; Nicephorus, *HE* 8.5; Nicetas, *Thesauri* 3. Kolluthus: *Urk.* 14, p. 20, ll. 1–2; and the appendix ("Kolluthus's Schism and the Arians").

68. Cyprian, *Ep.* 54.2.2.

69. See Simonetti, *Crisi*, 51ff.; Hanson, *Search*, 138–45.

70. See Arius's complaints in *Urk.* 6, p. 13, ll. 2ff.; Simonetti, *Crisi*, 15–22, 58–59 ("Alessandro reduce di molto il subordinazionismo tradizionale nella teologia alessandrina"); Kopecek, *History*, 8, 11–15; Hanson, *Search*, 143–44; Williams, *Arius*, 154–56, 170; and Ayres, *Nicaea*, 44.

71. Socrates, *HE* 1.5, making this preaching the reason that Arius proposed his views in the first place (cf. chapter 6 on Constantine's comments on the outbreak of the controversy). Attributes: *Urk.* 14, p. 27, ll. 1–2, 13, 14–15; and *Urk.* 4b, p. 8, ll. 4–5 and p. 9, ll. 13–14. See also Simonetti, *Crisi*, 55ff.; Hanson, *Search*, 140–42.

72. Sozomen, *HE* 1.15.6 (co-eternal and co-substantial). In his letters, Alexander does not use these terms, but the ideas underlying them are implied (see *Urk.* 4b, p. 9, l. 3, and *Urk.* 1, p. 2, ll. 1–3, where Arius paraphrases him). It has often been objected that these terms could not have been used at this stage in the controversy (e.g., Simonetti, *Crisi*, 29 n. 8; and Hanson, *Search*, 139–40), but *homoousios* and other *ousia* terms had been used in Alexandria before, not least by Arius himself (*Urk.* 6, p. 12, l. 11), even if they did not have the full technical meaning they acquired later; see Kelly, *Doctrines*, 132–36; Williams, "Quest," 3; Sciuto, "Da Nicea," 482; M. J. Edwards, "Did Origen Apply the Word *Homoousios* to the Son?" *JTS* 49 (1998): 658–70; and Ayres, *Nicaea*, 24–25. On the changing meaning of *ousia* and similar terms, see Simonetti, *Crisi*, 58; and R. P. C. Hanson, "The Achievement of Orthodoxy in the Fourth Century AD," in *The Making of Orthodoxy: Essays in Honour of Henry Chadwick*, ed. R. Williams (Cambridge, 1989), 144.

73. Hanson, *Search*, 142.

74. See discussion below and chapter 5.

75. Simonetti, *Crisi*, 59: "Manca ad Alessandro una formulazione tecnica dell'unione del Padre e del Figlio."

76. *Urk.* 14, p. 24, ll. 8ff. and l. 25. Cf. ibid., pp. 27ff.

77. *Urk.* 14, p. 22, ll. 23–24, and p. 23, ll. 4–5.

78. See chapter 1 above.

79. Cf. Cyprian, *De unitate* 5; and Arius's remarks in *Urk.* 6, p. 13, ll. 3–4.

80. *Urk.* 1, p. 1, l. 8–p. 2, ll. 1–3: δημοσίᾳ λέγοντι, ἀεὶ θεὸς ἀεὶ υἱός, ἅμα πατὴρ ἅμα υἱός, συνυπάρχει ὁ υἱὸς ἀγεννήτως τῷ θεῷ, ἀειγεννής, ἀγεννητογενής. See also Kelly, *Doctrines*, 228; Kopecek, *History*, 15–16 (cf. 8–9); Hanson, *Search*, 139; Widdicombe, *Fatherhood*, 133–35; and Ayres, *Nicaea*, 45.

81. See Nautin, "Deux interpolations," 132–33; and Kopecek, *History*, 15–16. Cf. Arius's "timeless" begetting (*Urk.* 6, p. 13, ll. 8–9). On Origen's "eternal generation" and its posterity, see Kelly, *Doctrines*, 128; Williams, *Arius*, 167ff.; Widdicombe, *Fatherhood*, chap. 3; and Ayres, *Nicaea*, 29.

82. Hanson, *Search*, 139–40. See also, e.g., *Urk.* 14, p. 26, ll. 20–29. The bishop, however, may have seen no contradiction at all. By placing the generation of the Son before the creation of time, by removing it from the realm of human experience, he could speak of the Son in the language of paradox—"ingeneratedly generated"—in the same way that quantum physicists today describe subatomic particles simultaneously as particle and wave.

83. Kopecek, *History*, 15, and Hanson, *Search*, 140ff., suggest that he refined his arguments later.

84. *Urk.* 1, p. 2, ll. 8–9 (καὶ τούτων τῶν ἀσεβειῶν οὐδὲ ἀκοῦσαι δυνάμεθα . . .).

85. *Urk.* 6, p. 12, ll. 11–12, and p. 13, ll. 18–20 (quote). Even if Alexander never used the term, it could easily be used to qualify his ideas. See also Williams, *Arius*, 271.

86. Socrates, *HE* 1.5; Nicephorus, *HE* 8.5. Alexander felt the need to defend himself from that imputation (*Urk.* 14, p. 27, l. 6).

87. *Urk.* 14, p. 26, ll. 22–27 (l. 25: ἀγέννητα . . . δύο); *Urk.* 6, p. 13, l. 12; and *Urk.* 1, p. 2, l. 7.

88. Epiphanius, *Panarion* 69.3; Nicephorus, *HE* 8.5.

89. Sozomen, *HE* 1.15.7 (note: ἀκρίτως). Cf. *Urk.* 1, passim.

90. Hostility: *Urk.* 1, p. 1, ll. 7–8, and p. 3, ll. 4ff. Cf. Libanius, *Autobiography* 19–21 (rivalry between teachers in Athens), 25, and 31ff. Preaching: *Urk.* 1, p. 1, l. 8–p. 2, l. 9; Nicephorus, *HE* 8.5; and Ignatius of Selymbria, *VC* 34 (ed. Ioannou, p. 198).

91. Boularand, *L'hérésie*, 1:48.

92. Manifesto: *Urk.* 6, p. 12, l. 1, and p. 13, l. 21. Epiphanius, *Panarion* 69.3.3, suggests the Libyans became involved even before Alexander had learned of the controversy, but it is difficult to determine when that happened. Williams, *Arius*, 58, dates Alexander's deposition and excommunication of the Libyan bishops to the winter of 324/325 in the council Ossius assembled in Alexandria (below, chapter 6). It is unlikely, however, that the Libyans became involved only at such a late date, practically on the eve of Nicaea, whose creed they would refuse to sign and then suffer exile for it. Arius called on the support of bishops all over the East; why not begin with those in his native country, where the heretic "Sabellians" had won over so many? The Libyans were among the priest's staunchest supporters and probably so from the earliest stages of the controversy.

93. See *Urk.* 1, p. 2, ll. 4–5; *Urk.* 14, p. 20, ll. 23ff. Cf. *Urk.* 14, p. 29, ll. 13ff.; *Urk.* 4a, p. 6, ll. 1–7.

94. *Urk.* 6, pp. 12–13. Most scholars date this statement after Arius's deposition. Schwartz, *GS*, 3:120–21, 126, and Opitz, "Zeitfolge," 148, place its composition in Nicomedia, after Arius left Alexandria. But the tone of the letter, though firm, is still too deferential for someone who would likely have been ill disposed toward the bishop (cf. *Urk.* 1).

95. *Urk.* 6, p. 12, ll. 3–4 and p. 13, ll. 13–14.See also Williams, *Arius*, 270–71.

96. *Urk.* 6, pp. 12–13. Note the language: Μακαρίῳ πάπᾳ καὶ ἐπισκόπῳ ἡμῶν (l. 1). Phrases implying respect and recognition of the bishop's authority also occur in ll. 3, 21. The emphasis on having learned about God *from* the bishop appears on p. 13, ll. 2–4, 14. Yet the fact that Arius staked out his position in writing suggests that, at that point, he had little hope that the bishop would change.

97. Williams, *Arius*, 271.

98. *Urk.* 6, p. 13, ll.1ff.

99. *Urk.* 4b, p. 8, ll. 11ff.; ibid., p. 9, ll. 25f.; and Socrates, *HE* 1.6. Cf. Epiphanius, *Panarion* 69.3.6–7. Cabal: *Urk.* 14, p. 19, ll. 2–3.

100. Sozomen, *HE* 1.15.7; Epiphanius, *Panarion* 69.3.6–7 (ἀνέτασις . . . ἀνάκρισις).

4. MAKING THE PEOPLE A PARTNER TO THE DISPUTE

1. On popular participation in ecclesiastical disputes, see MacMullen, "Historical Role," 265–75. For an attempt to refute the church-historical parts of MacMullen's exposition, see N. McLynn, "Christian Controversy and Violence in the Fourth Century," *Kodai* 3 (1992): 15–44. MacMullen has convincingly restated his case in his "Cultural and Political Changes in the Fourth and Fifth Centuries," *Historia* 52 (2003): 478–95. See also E. Gregory, *Vox populi: Popular Opinion and Violence in the Religious Controversies of the Fifth Century* (Columbus, 1979); R. Lizzi, "Discordia *in urbe*: Pagani e cristiani in rivolta," in *Pagani e cristiani da Giuliano l'Apostata al sacco di Roma*, ed. F.E. Consolino (Soveria Mannelli, 1995), 116ff.; J.H.W.G. Liebeschuetz, *Decline and Fall of the Roman City* (Oxford, 2001), 257–69; T.J. Hahn, *Gewalt und religiöser Konflikt: Studien zu den Auseinandersetzungen zwischen Christen, Heiden und Juden im Osten des Römischen Reiches (von Konstantin bis*

Theodosius II), Klio Beihefte 8 (Berlin, 2004), questioning (wrongly in my view) the role religion played in popular violence; C. R. Galvao-Sobrinho, "Embodied Theologies: Christian Identity and Violence in Alexandria in the Early Arian Controversy," in *Violence in Late Antiquity: Perceptions and Practices,* ed. H. D. Drake (Aldershot, UK, 2006), 321–31; T. Sizgorich, *Violence and Belief in Late Antiquity: Militant Devotion in Christianity and Islam* (Philadelphia, 2009); B. D. Shaw, *Sacred Violence: African Christians and Sectarian Hatred in the Age of Augustine* (Cambridge and New York, 2011), 168–259; and especially J. C. O. Magalhães, *Potestas populi: Participation populaire et action collective dans les villes de l'Afrique romaine tardive (vers 300–430 apr. J.-C.),* Bibliothèque de l'Antiquité Tardive 24 (Paris, 2012). On the debate over the use of violence in religious disputes, see M. Gaddis, *There Is No Crime for Those Who Have Christ: Religious Violence in the Christian Roman Empire* (Berkeley, 2006).

2. On the church-going public and their concerns, see Augustine, *De catechizandis rudibus* 3.5, 13.18; *Sermo* 9.3–5, 252.4; etc. Cf. R. MacMullen, "The Preacher's Audience (A.D. 350–400)," *JTS* 40 (1989): 503–11; and id., *The Second Church: Popular Christianity, A.D. 200–400* (Atlanta, 2009), 12–15, 101–3, 111, whose findings of limited attendance in church are not relevant to Alexandria in the 320s. Cf. P. Rousseau, "The Preacher's Audience: A More Optimistic View," in *Ancient History in a Modern University, Festschrift for Edwin Judge,* ed. T. W. Hillard, R. A. Kearsley, C. E. V. Nixon, et al. (Grand Rapids, MI, and Cambridge, 1998), 391–400; and A. Stewart-Sykes, "Hermas the Prophet and Hippolytus the Preacher: The Roman Homily and Its Social Context," in *Preacher and Audience: Studies in Early Christian and Byzantine Homiletics,* ed. M. B. Cunningham and P. Allen (Leiden, 1998), 33–62.

3. Eusebius, *HE* 6.2.12ff.

4. Ibid. 7.30.9.

5. *Urk.* 1, p. 2, l. 1: δημοσίᾳ; *Urk.* 17, p. 33, ll. 10–21; Socrates, *HE* 1.5.

6. Ignatius of Selymbria, *VC* 34 (ed. Ioannou, p. 198).

7. *De anima et corpore* (*PG* 18.603–4).

8. Anastasius *apud* Telfer, "St. Peter," 130; Epiphanius, *Panarion* 69.1; and Sozomen, *HE* 1.15.12. Cf. Eusebius, *VC* 2.69; Socrates, *HE* 1.5; Theodoret, *HE* 1.2; Nicephorus, *HE* 8.5. In the Syriac tradition: *Chronicle of Seert* (*PO* 4.246); Agapius, *HU* (*PO* 7.544); Barhadbasabba Arbaia, *Historia* (*PO* 23.201): at first Arius did not teach publicly but secretly tried "to pervert the whole city." Exegesis: Socrates, *HE* 5.22.43–46 *apud* Marrou, "Arianisme." Fasting: Peter of Alexandria, *Ep. can.* 15 (*PG* 18.508).

9. *Urk.* 6, p. 13, ll. 2–4.

10. The sources distinguish between "private" assemblies (Epiphanius, *Panarion* 69.1: κατ' ἰδίαν; Sozomen, *HE* 1.15.12: ἰδίᾳ) and, more vaguely, the general meetings of the church. The former seem to refer to gatherings in churches held by individual priests (perhaps also house-churches, on which see discussion below). Public meetings were seemingly open to believers (and nonbelievers) from different congregations. Zonaras, *Annals* 13.4 (*PG* 134.1113), blames the ferociousness of the controversy on its "publicization." Cf. Eusebius, *VC* 2.69 (Τοῦτο εἰς ἀκοὰς ἐμπεσὸν τοῦ λαοῦ, ταραχὴν ἐγείρει μεγίστην); Ignatius, *VC* 35 (ed. Ioannou, p. 198); Agapius, *HU* (*PO* 7.544), on the progressively expanding reach of Arius's preaching; and Barhadbasabba Arbaia, *Historia* (*PO* 23.201). See also Galvao-Sobrinho, "Embodied Theologies," 326f.

11. *Urk.* 17, p. 33, ll. 4–5, 12–13 (δημοσίας συνόδους ἐκφέρειν . . . ταῖς τῶν δήμων ἀκοαῖς). Cf. *Urk.* 14, p. 20, ll. 1ff.

12. Theodoret, *HE* 1.1: οὐ μόνον ἐν ἐκκλησίᾳ διετέλει λέγων, ἀλλὰ κἀν τοῖς ἔξω συλλόγοις καὶ συνεδρίοις.

13. Anastasius, *Epilogue* (*apud* Telfer, "St. Peter," 130). Telfer, "St. Peter," 118, 123ff., argues that Anastasius used not only the *Historia tripartita* (the Latin translation of Socrates, Sozomen, and Theodoret), but also another source known to Sozomen, possibly a dossier of documents containing the *Historia acephala* and other material. Van Nuffelen, *Héritage*, 321, suggests this source was the "Collection Alexandrine" or another incorporating material from it.

14. Ignatius of Selymbria, *VC* 34–35 (ed. Ioannou, pp. 198–99).

15. Zonaras, *Annals* 13.4 (*PG* 134.1113).

16. Agapius, *HU* (*PO* 7.544f.).

17. Sozomen, *HE* 1.15.11 (Arius, though excommunicated, asked permission to preach); and Theodoret, *HE* 1.2, 1.19. Proper worship: Origen, *De orat.* 2.1; J. Rebecca Lyman, "Lex orandi: Heresy, Orthodoxy, and Popular Religion," in *The Making and Remaking of Christian Doctrine: Essays in Honour of Maurice Wiles*, ed. S. Coakley and D. Pailin (Oxford, 1993), 136ff.; and Widdicombe, *Fatherhood*, 106–8.

18. Origen, *De orat.* 15.1 and 16.1.

19. *Urk.* 14, p. 28, ll. 1ff. Arius noted Alexander preached these views in public (*Urk* 1, pp. 1–2, ll. 8ff.).

20. Athanasius, *De synodis* 15, paraphrasing the *Thalia*. Cf. id., *Or. contra Arianos* 1.5–6 (translated by Williams, *Arius*, 101): "The Word is not true God.... It is only by participating in grace . . . that He too is . . . God." Cf. *Chronicle of Seert* 10 (*PO* 4.244) ("taught the people not to say Glory to Father, Son, and Holy Spirit."). On the *Thalia*, see Williams, *Arius*, 63–66, 85–87, 98–116.

21. God was summoned as Holy Spirit (in Cyril of Jerusalem's liturgy) or as Christ himself—see G. Dix, *The Shape of the Liturgy* (Westminster, 1945), 280–81. On the ritual, see Theodoret of Mopsuestia, *Catecheses* 5 and 6 (*apud* Dix, *Shape*, 282–84).

22. See M. Johnson, *The Prayers of Sarapion of Thmuis: A Literary, Liturgical, and Theological Analysis* (Rome, 1995), 34f., 114ff, 47ff. Cf. also Pseudo-Athanasius, *Fragm. ad baptizandos* 7 (*PG* 26.1325); Cyril of Jerusalem, *Catech. Mystag.* 5.7; John Chrysostom, *In Coemet. appelat.* 3 (*PG* 49.397–98); and Theodoret of Mopsuestia, *Catech. Mystag.* (*apud* Reine, *Eucharistic Doctrine*, 116). See also Dix, *Shape*, 167–70, 191, 198–99, 238ff., and 276–77; and V. Saxer, "La messe au IVe s. et sa réforme," in *Les transformations dans la societé chrétienne au IVe. siècle, Congrès de Varsovie, 25 juin-1er juillet 1978*, Miscellanea Historiae Ecclesiasticae 6 (Brussels, 1983), 208ff., esp. 210, and 214.

23. Johnson, *Prayers*, 47ff. Cf. Eusebius, *HE* 6.44.2–6; Dix, *Shape*, 169, 254–55; and Reine, *Eucharistic Doctrine*, 35–39.

24. C. W. Bynum, *Holy Feast and Holy Fast: The Religious Significance of Food to Medieval Women* (Berkeley, 1987), 3 (quote), 31–34.

25. Theodoret of Mopsuestia, *Commentary on the Lord's Prayer, apud* Reine, *Eucharistic Doctrine*, 36. See also Irenaeus, *C. haer.* 4.18.5; Serapion of Thmuis *apud* Johnson, *Prayers*, 49; and Dix, *Shape*, 137.

26. On the importance of expressing proper rank in the liturgy, see Serapion of Thmuis *apud* Johnson, *Prayers*, 47ff.; *Pap. Strassbourg* 254, in M. Andrieu and P. Collomp,

"Fragments sur papyrus de l'Anaphora de saint Marc," *Revue des Sciences Religieuses* 8 (1928): 489–515; and *Ostraka Tait-Petrie* 415, in J. van Haelst, "Une ancienne prière d'intercession de la liturgie de saint Marc (O. Tait-Petrie 415)," *Ancient Society* 1 (1970): 95–114 (late fourth century?). See also Basil of Caesarea, *De Spiritu Sancto* 26.63; Cyril of Jerusalem, *Catech. Mystag.* 5.6; *Apostolic Constitutions* 8; and Theodore of Mopsuestia, *Catech. Mystag.* (apud Reine, *Eucharistic Doctrine*, 106ff.). Cf. Origen, *De orat.* 15–16; Scherer, *Entretien* (1960), 24f.; Fragment 10, *Scripta Arriana latina* (*CCSL* 87, p. 235) (post-380s); Epiphanius, *Panarion* 73.34, 38, and 78.24; Sozomen, *HE* 4.28; Socrates, *HE* 2.43; and in Vandal North Africa, Fulgentius, *Sermo* 4.10, and *Ep.* 14.37.

27. *Urk.* 17, p. 33, ll. 20–21.

28. *Urk.* 4b, p. 9, ll. 26ff.

29. Agapius, *HU* (*PO* 7.545).

30. Alexander: Socrates, *HE* 1.5; Arius: Anastasius *apud* Telfer, "St. Peter," 130.

31. *Urk.* 14, p. 20, ll. 4–5. Cf. Basil, *Ep.* 207; and E. Wipszycka, "Les confréries dans la vie religieuse de l'Egypte chrétienne," *Proceedings of the 12th International Congress of Papyrology*, ed. D. H. Samuel (Toronto, 1970), 514, on the *philoponoi*, who attended the church "jour et nuit."

32. *Urk.* 34, p. 71, ll. 11 and 19 (addressing Arius after Nicaea).

33. Epiphanius, *Panarion* 69.3. Cf. Alexander's comment in *Urk.* 14, p. 21, ll. 1–2 ("seductive and deceptive sermons"); Athanasius, *Letter to the Virgins* 1.43 apud Brakke, *Athanasius*, 288 (quoting Alexander: "deceitful person who is stealing the truth . . . to deceive the simple folk"); Nicephorus, *HE* 8.5, 6.

34. Epiphanius, *Panarion* 69.1–2. Martin, *Athanase*, 252–53, notes these portraits were given by anti-Arian authors, but that does not mean we have to reject them. Cf. Jerome, *De vir. ill.* 76, on Pierius, who pursued ascesis and poverty.

35. Williams, *Arius*, 32.

36. Rapp, *Holy Bishops*, 17.

37. *Urk.* 14, p. 28, ll. 22–23: ὑπερ ὧν καὶ ἀποθνῄσκομεν. Cf. Gaddis, *No Crime*, 69ff.

38. *Urk.* 4b, p. 10, ll. 15f.

39. *Urk.* 14, p. 26, ll. 7–9; *Urk.* 17, p. 33, ll. 5–16 (Constantine on competition for public support). Both sides expressed concern about their opponents' public preaching; see *Urk.* 1, p. 1, l. 8–p. 2, l. 1. Cf. Eusebius, *VC* 2.61; and Ignatius of Selymbria, *VC* 35 (ed. Ioannou, pp. 199–200).

40. *Urk.* 4b, p. 7, l. 1; and *Urk.* 14, p. 29, ll. 18ff.

41. *Urk.* 4a, p. 6 (referring to letters sent previously).

42. *Urk.* 4a, p. 6.

43. Alexander *apud* Athanasius, *First Letter to the Virgins* 37–43, apud Brakke, *Athanasius*, 286–88. Cf. Elm, *Virgins*, 353; Brown, *Body*, 259ff.; Brakke, *Athanasius*, 18–31; Martin, *Athanase*, 198; and cf. McLynn, *Ambrose*, 60–68.

44. On the Alexandrian virgins and their charitable activities, see Brakke, *Athanasius*, 23–30. But not all virgins were rich—Constantine gave assistance to at least some of them; see Sozomen, *HE* 5.5; and E. Wipszycka's reservations in "La sovvenzione costantiniana in favore del clero," *Rend. Mor. Acc. Lincei*, s. 9, 8 (1997): 483–98 (esp. 488); Palladius, *HL* 1 and 29. See also Elm, *Virgins*, 321–24; and Brown, *Body*, 147–50.

45. Athanasius, *First Letter to the Virgins* 36, apud Brakke, *Athanasius*, 286: Alexander "[brought] them to love for the Word and zeal for virginity."

46. Letters: Epiphanius, *Panarion* 69.4 (in one round, at least seventy letters were sent); and MacMullen, *Voting*, 35. After Arius's excommunication: Sozomen, *HE* 1.15.8; Socrates, *HE* 1.6; and Opitz, "Zeitfolge," 146f.

47. Alexander mentions the *Tomos* in the *He philarchos* (*Urk.* 14). At the time that this letter was written many bishops had already signed the *Tomos* and returned it to Alexander (see *Urk.* 14, p. 29, ll. 14–15). But the *Tomos* probably circulated after *Urk.* 4b, the *Henos somatos*, the first of Alexander's encyclicals, sent to bishops everywhere, informing them of the affair.

48. See chapter 5.

49. *Urk.* 14, p. 29, ll. 19–21.

50. Dossier: Socrates, *HE* 1.6; cf. Theodoret, *HE* 1.5. Handed out to clergy: *Urk.* 14, p. 29, ll. 15–18. Sharing: implied in *Urk.* 4a, p. 6, where he keeps his clergy informed of recent events; cf. Cyprian, *Epp.* 37.2 (listing those who had been excommunicated), 38, 39, 42, and 44.3.

51. Circulated: cf. MacMullen, *Voting*, 36–37. Subscribers: *Urk.* 15, p. 30, l. 1, only Philogonius name is extant, but see p. 31, ll. 3–8, for the list of "provinces" (not Roman administrative units; see Jones, *LRE*, 1456–61).

52. Schwartz, *GS*, 3:118. The Arians did the same: *Urk.* 14, p. 20, ll. 22–25. Cf. Cyprian, *Epp.* 31 and 37.2.

53. Were these names inscribed in the diptychs of the "book of life"—a practice that seems to have become widespread later? Then, those entries would have been used as evidence of orthodoxy; see *DACL*, s.v. "Diptyques" (cols. 1051–57).

54. *Urk.* 15, p. 31, ll. 9–12; and Schwartz, *GS*, 3:129.

55. John Chrysostom, *De beato Philogonio* (*PG* 48.751); and *Syn. Arabe Jacobite*, Dec. 20 (*PO* 3.517).

56. *Urk.* 1, p. 2, l. 7.

57. For instance, during the Novatianist schism: Cyprian, *Epp.* 28.4, 31, 37.2 (cf. 38 and 39), 44.3, 45.1, 51.2; and Eusebius, *HE* 6.43.1ff., 6.45.1, and 6.46.1–4.

58. *Urk.* 4b, p. 7, ll. 1–2.

59. *Urk.* 1, p. 1, l. 8.

60. *Urk.* 4b, p. 10, l. 14.

61. *Urk.* 14, p. 29, ll. 13–14. See also *Urk.* 4a, p. 6, ll. 5 and 11; *Urk.* 14, p. 28, ll. 20–23, and p. 29, ll. 19–22 (unity to help restore the "deceived" faithful).

62. See his exhortation to the virgins *apud* Athanasius, *First Letter to the Virgins* 37–43, *apud* Brakke, *Athanasius*, 286–88.

63. Such groups were also found in other Alexandrian parishes; see Epiphanius, *Panarion* 69.2: e.g., the "Areianoi," "Kolluthianoi," etc. Did they function as claques or factions? Cf. Haas, *Alexandria*, 270; Martin, *Athanase*, 182–83; and Libanius, *Autobiography* 44.

64. See MacMullen, "Historical Role," 272–74; id., "Cultural and Political Changes," 490; and id., *Voting*, 38–39. For a later period, see Gregory, *Vox*, 211–14; and McLynn, *Ambrose*, 200–201, 225–26. On the "use" of the *Thalia*, see Williams, *Arius*, 64–65, 84–86; and Brakke, *Athanasius*, 64–65. On the legacy of Arius's hymns, see *DACL*, s.v. "Ariens"; and K. Mitsakis, "The Hymnography of the Greek Church in the Early Christian Centuries," *Jahrbuch der Österreichischen Byzantinistik* 20 (1971): 37ff.

65. *De synodis* 15 and *Or. contra Arianos* 1.5–6. According to Athanasius, Arius wrote the *Thalia* in Nicomedia. But if he did, it is hard to imagine, as Williams, *Arius*, 64, suggests,

that this work was a statement of belief intended "to clarify the ground on which the theological battle would be fought"—that is, a theological treatise intended only for ecclesiastical circles. The *Thalia*, whose mock title is Athanasian, was probably composed, like Arius's other songs, to be sung by congregations and taught to the λαός. Meter: M. L. West, "The Metre of Arius' *Thalia*," *JTS* 33 (1982): 98–106; and G. C. Stead, "Arius in Modern Research," *JTS*, n.s., 45 (1994), 27f.

66. MacMullen, "Cultural and Political Changes," 490; Barnes, *AC*, 55.

67. West, "Metre," 105.

68. Arius was not the first to write Christian hymns. See Pliny, *Ep.* 10.96.7; Eusebius, *HE* 7.30.10 (Paul of Samosata's hymns), 7.24.4 (Nepos's hymns); Methodius, *Symposium* 11.2–12; and below.

69. Earlier Christian hymns also contained ideas of God as revealed truth presented in proclamatory or self-proclamatory style—that is, God himself spoke, and when believers sang the hymn, they reaffirmed that truth. For instance, the "Hymn to Christ" in the *Acts of John;* the "Odes of Solomon" (if truly Christian); and Melito of Sardis, *Paschal Homily (apud* Mitsakis, "Hymnography," 34–35). See J. H. Charlesworth, *The Odes of Solomon* (Oxford, 1973); K. Schäferdiek, "The Acts of John," in *New Testament Apocrypha*, ed. W. Schneemelcher, trans. J. Clarke (Louisville, 1992), 152–212; and D. Liderbach, *Christ in the Early Christian Hymns* (New York, 1998), 38ff. See also Socrates, *HE* 6.8; and Pseudo-Lucian, *Philopatris* 26, 27.

70. Athanasius, *Or. contra Arianos* 1.5. See West, "Metre," 102ff.; and Williams, *Arius*, 102–3.

71. Cf. *P. Amherst* 1.2 *apud* B. P. Grenfell and A. S. Hunt, *The Amherst Papyri* (London, 1900), 23–28 (early fourth century).

72. *Urk.* 14, p. 26, ll. 24–26: οἱ ἀπαίδευτοι . . . ἀγνοοῦντες οἱ ἀνάσκητοι.

73. See chapter 3 above; and Gregg and Groh, *Early Arianism,* 163f. On advancement by virtue and obedience, ibid., 19–30, 43–70.

74. See Von Campenhausen, *Ecclesiastical Authority,* 249–64; Williams, *Arius,* 85–90, 257–58; Brakke, *Athanasius,* 62–72; and chapter 3.

75. See chapter 1.

76. Athanasius, *Or. contra Arianos* 1.22. Athanasius may well have been right to say that the poem was "danced to," probably accompanied by the "shaking of hands" or the "tapping of feet" to the meter, which, by the fifth century, but more likely earlier, had become an established custom in the Alexandrian church (see Misakis, "Hymnography," 41). Arius would later say to Constantine: "I am full of joy and I leap and I jump with grace and I soar" (*Urk.* 34, p. 74, ll. 5–6). Singing and dancing heightened sensory experience of the divine and created a sense of belonging together. Music, noted Augustine, reminiscing about the tears he had shed at the sound of the church choirs in Milan, stirred emotions and brought to life, as W. James, put it, a "sense of divine presence"; see W. James, *The Varieties of Religious Experience* (London, 1961), 337. In Alexandria, the Arians would have used music "to conjure," in Augustine's words, "piety and devotion in the weaker souls," to unite and energize the faithful, to inject in them a zeal for the truth, and to engage them in teaching one another. Subsequently, Athanasius and others did not hesitate to use similar tactics to achieve these results. See Augustine, *Confessions* 10.33; and R. MacMullen, *Feelings in History, Ancient and Modern* (Claremont, 2003),

113–21. Cf. Athanasius, *Ep. ad Marcell.* (*PG* 27.40–41); Basil, *Ep.* 207; and Pseudo-Lucian, *Philopatris* 26.

77. Athenaeus, *Deipnosophists* 14.618d-619. Cf. Aelian, *Varia historia* 7.4.

78. On the workshops of Alexandria, see the appendix ("The Workshops of Alexandria"). Looms in Roman Egypt: E. Wipszycka, *L'industrie textile dans l'Égypte romaine* (Wroclaw, 1965), 49–51. A bakery in Alexandria: *BGU* 4.1117.

79. Philostorgius, *HE* 2.2. Post-Nicaea? But Arius's target audience must have been Alexandrian.

80. Philostorgius, *HE* 2.2a.

81. See Haas, *Alexandria*, 42–43, 57–59, and 382 n. 33.

82. In Lucian, *Toxaris* 31, Demetrius "hired himself out to the merchants in the harbor from early morning until about midday."

83. Liturgist-sailors assisting with the shipping of grain: *POxy* 3912; *Pap. Sakaon.* 29, 35 (ed. Parássoglou); and N. Lewis, *The Compulsory Public Services of Roman Egypt* (Florence, 1997), 37, 112–13. Liturgists nominated to accompany grain from the *chora* to Alexandria: *POxy* 4078 (A.D. 327), 4609 (A.D. 363), 4610, etc. (cf. *POxy* 4063 and 4065). Migrants or refugees as sailors in Alexandria: *P. Giss.* 40.2, *apud* A. Lukaszewicz, "Activités commerciales et artisanales dans Alexandrie romaine," in *Commerce et artisanat dans l'Alexandrie hellénistique et romaine, Actes du Colloque d'Athènes, 11–12 décembre 1988,* ed. J.-Y. Empereur (Paris, 1998), 113.

84. Philo, *Legatio* 3.15; and G. Rickman, *The Corn Supply of Ancient Rome* (Oxford, 1980), 15, citing Vegetius 4.39; and *CTh* 13.9.3.

85. Migrants or refugees from the *chora*: Dio 78.23.2; *P. Giss.* 40.2; *POxy* 1643 (A.D. 298); and Haas, *Alexandria,* 35.

86. Athanasius, *HA* 55; and Haas, *Alexandria*, 61.

87. Athanasius (Athanasius, *HA* 81), Gregory (Athanasius, *Ep. enc.* 5; and chapter 8 below), and Theophilus (Socrates, *HE* 6.15) also courted the *naukleroi*, i.e., shipmasters or owners. See R. MacMullen, *Enemies of the Roman Order: Treason, Unrest, and Alienation in the Empire* (Cambridge, 1966), 343–44; id., "Cultural and Political Changes," 488 n. 59; and Haas, *Alexandria*, 57–60. Arius, however, may have been more interested in poor sailors and stevedores.

88. Many sailors also worked for enterprising shipmasters and shipowners, many of whom possessed curial or equestrian status. See *CTh* 13.5.7, 13.5.5, 13.5.16; and *SB* 15618 and 15620 on wealthy *nautai*. See also J. Schwartz, "Le Nil et le ravitaillement de Rome," *BIFAO* 47 (1948): 187–88; and B. Sirks, *Food for Rome: The Legal Structure of the Transportation and Processing of Food Supplies for the Imperial Distributions in Rome and Constantinople* (Amsterdam, 1991), 128–145.

89. Dio Chrysostom, *Or.* 32.9.

90. *Acta Petri* (*BHG* 1502), ed. Viteau, *Passions,* 83; and the Coptic Acts (*BHO* 932), ed. H. Hyvernat, *Les Actes des Martyrs de l'Égypte* (New York, 1977), 279–80. Temples: Ammianus Marcellinus, *RG* 22.16.12.

91. Palladius, *HL* 26.4; *Syn. Arabe Jacobite,* Nov. 6 (*PO* 3.271–72): Apa Markya, who "habitait dans les bains à Alexandrie."

92. See Viteau, *Passions,* 69, 83; and Eusebius, *HE* 7.21.2ff.

93. Achilles Tatius, *Leuc.* 4.18.3.

94. Strabo 17.1.17.

95. See D. Roques, "Alexandrie tardive et protobyzantine (Ive–VIIe s.): Témoignages d'auteurs," in *Alexandrie: Une mégapole cosmopolite, Actes du 9ème colloque de la Villa Kérylos à Beaulieu-sur-Mer, 2–3 octobre 1998*, ed. J. Leclant (Paris, 1999), 206–7.

96. *POxy* 1383 (late third century A.D.): Ῥοδίοις ἀνέμοις; and *POxy* 425 (second or third century A.D.), incipit Ναυται βυθοκυα (sic). See West, "Metre," 105f.

97. Millers in Egyptian cities: Bagnall, *Egypt*, 79. Milling and baking together: *BGU* 4.1117 (13 B.C.); Wipszycka, *Les ressources*, 59; and *CTh* 14.3.7. Elsewhere: Apuleius, *Metamorphoses* 9.10; R. Laurence, *Roman Pompeii: Space and Society* (London and New York, 1994), 55–57; and *The Mill-Bakeries of Ostia: Description and Interpretation*, ed. J. T. Bakker (Amsterdam, 1999).

98. On the civic bread, see Procopius, *Anecdota* 26.40–44; Calderini, *Dizionario*, 185; and J. Durliat, *De la ville antique à la ville byzantine: Le problème des subsistances*, Collection de l'École Française de Rome 136 (Rome, 1990), 324–34. For the third century, see J. Rea, "Public Documents: The Corn Dole in Oxyrhynchus and Kindred Documents," *The Oxyrhynchus Papyri* 40 (1972): 1f.

99. See T. Reil, *Beiträge zur Kenntnis des Gewerbes im hellenistischen Ägypten* (New York, 1979; repr., 1913), 152. Cf. *POxy* 3625 (A.D. 359); *CTh* 14.3.1ff., on breadmakers in Rome; and *P. Sakaon* 25 (ed. Parássoglou) (A.D. 327).

100. Basil, *Ep.* 204. Cf. Apuleius, *Metamorphoses* 9.15ff. Singing: Plutarch, *Moralia* 157DE. See also the Talmudic references to women at the mill in G. Clark, *Women in Late Antiquity: Pagan and Christian Lifestyles* (Oxford, 1994), 94–95.

101. See Schwartz, "Le Nil," 190–92; and Sirks, *Food*, 194. Cf. *POxy* 1748; and D. Rathbone, *Economic Rationalism and Rural Society in Third-Century Egypt: The Heroninos Archive and the Appianus Estate* (Cambridge, 1991), 106, 266ff.

102. See Roques, "Alexandrie," 206–7; *POxy* 4063 (A.D. 182), 4609–13 (A.D. 363–364), and 4078 (A.D. 327).

103. Donkeys of Alexandria: *POxy* 1905. Traveling to the *chora*: *Pap. Lond.* 3.1170 (date unknown); and *P. Sakaon* 19 (ed. Parássoglou) (A.D. 315–316): a caravan.

104. Associations of *onelatai*: Reil, *Beiträge*, 184. Public *onelatai*: Schwartz, "Le Nil," 191; *Pap. Lond.* 2.258. Donkeys in the imperial post (mostly from the West): *CTh* 8.5.10, 14, 31, 58; cf. 14.3.9–10. Prefect of the annona in Alexandria: *POxy* 4369 (A.D. 345).

105. Not all millers, donkey drivers, and other workers were Christian, but reaching out to ordinary Christians may have also helped to attract new converts. See Athanasius's later remark on pagans joining the Arians in *Or. contra Arianos* 1.3.

106. See Roulet, *Tolérance*, 119: by condemning Arius, the Council of Nicaea (on which, see below) "a ... exclu de l'Eglise une certaine forme de vie chrétienne, enthousiaste, charismatique."

107. *Urk.* 4b, p. 7, l. 1; *Urk.* 14, p. 20, ll. 3–4 and 6–7.

108. *Urk.* 14, p. 20, ll. 23–25.

109. *Urk.* 14, p. 20, ll. 6–10 (ll. 7f.: τὴν θεότητα τοῦ σωτῆρος ἡμῶν ἀρνούμενοι καὶ τοῖς πᾶσιν ἴσον εἶναι κηρύττοντες); p. 25, ll. 17–21 (l. 16: ταπεινώσεως ... αὐτοῦ πτωχείας); p. 26, ll. 11–13; and Athanasius, *Letter to the Virgins* 1.43 *apud* Brakke, *Athanasius*, 288 (quoting Alexander).

110. Although many well-educated Christians supported Arius (Didymus of Alexandria 249.5 [ed. Gronewald, p. 104]: καὶ ὅσους ἐὰν ἐνηνόχεις τελείους ἄνδρας, ἔλεγ[εν ἀ]εί), there

is nothing to suggest that his followers were mostly upper class (cf. Simonetti, *Crisi,* 29–30 n. 9). See Constantine's remarks in *Urk.* 17, p. 33, ll. 12–21, doubting that the "slow-witted" would understand the subtlety of the arguments. Likewise, one should take with a grain of salt the view that the "orthodox" had the majority just because Athanasius said so; see W. H. C. Frend, "Athanasius as an Egyptian Christian Leader in the Fourth Century," in *Religion Popular and Unpopular in the Early Christian Centuries* (Aldershot, UK, 1976), XVI.20–37; and C. Kannengiesser, "Athanasius of Alexandria vs. Arius: The Alexandrian Crisis," in *The Roots of Egyptian Christianity,* ed. B. A. Pearson and J. E. Goehring (Philadelphia, 1985), 215.

111. Cf. Methodius, *Hom. on the Passion of Christ* 2: not about Christ's suffering, but an attempt to explain why he died an ignonimious death, the point of the homily was to exalt Christ's divinity.

112. W. L. Countryman, *The Rich Christian in the Church of the Early Empire: Contradictions and Accommodations* (New York, 1980); S. Holman, *The Hungry Are Dying: Beggars and Bishops in Roman Cappadocia* (Oxford, 2001), 10–21; and Brown, *Poverty,* 26–44. One wonders whether the interest in portraying the woes of the poor in fourth-century homiletics owed something to the success of Arian preaching with its new emphasis on the suffering and poverty of Christ.

113. Bourdieu, *Outline,* 170–71.

114. Arius's ideas about the Son and his apparent insistence on Christ's mutability forced contemporaries to think deep and hard about Christ's emotions, particularly his experience on the cross, which in the fourth century attracted enormous interest. See Asterius: *Homilies* 11, 12.5, 22.6 (M. Richard, *Asterii Sophistae commentariorum in Psalmos quae supersunt,* Symbolae Osloenses, suppl. 16 [Oslo, 1956]), with Hanson, *Search,* 38–39, and Gavrilyuk, *Suffering,* 121–34 (questioning Asterius's authorship); and a homily attributed to Athanasius of Anazarbus on the Passion of Christ (Hanson, *Search,* 43). See also Hanson, *Search,* 109–22; Parvis, *Marcellus,* 59.

115. *Urk.* 14, p. 20, ll. 3–4 (clandestine meetings); ibid., ll. 6–7 (*ergasteria*). The term is used metaphorically, but the choice of metaphor and the emphasis placed on Arius's "corruption" of the common people may suggest that he held meetings close to or in working places. On working-class houses, see M. Rodziewicz, *Alexandrie, III: Les habitations romaines tardives d'Alexandrie à la lumière des fouilles polonaises à Kôm el-Dikka* (Warsaw, 1984), 249, 331 ("ergasteria" and "popular houses"); and R. Alston, *The City in Roman and Byzantine Egypt* (London and New York, 2002), 115.

116. Theodoret, *HE* 1.1. Visitations: Theodosius, *Ep. ad Melitium* 1.6 and 2.5 *apud* Kettler, "Der melitianische Streit," 160–62; Peter of Alexandria, *Ep. ad Alexandrinos* 3.15; Eusebius, *HE* 7.11.24 (Dionysius of Alexandria); and the "Passion of SS Paese and Thecla," in Reymond and Barns, *Four Martyrdoms,* 152, 155, and 170.

117. Origen, *Contra Celsum* 3.44, 55, 59; *Syn. Arabe Jacobite,* Dec. 28 (*PO* 11.514): "Les fidèles, jusqu'au temps de Théonas, priaient et célébraient les saints mystères dans les maisons"; J. van Haelst, "Les sources papyrologiques concernant l'Église en Egypte à l'époque de Constantin," in *Proceedings of the 12th International Congress of Papyrology,* ed. D. H. Samuel (Toronto, 1970), 498; R. MacMullen, *Christianizing the Roman Empire* (New Haven, CT, 1984), 40; L. M. White, *Building God's House in the Roman World: Architectural Adaptation among Pagans, Jews, and Christians* (Baltimore, 1990), 102–23; and

E. Wipszycka, "Les papyrus documentaires concernant l'Église d'avant le tournant constantinien," *Atti del XXII Congresso Internazionale di Papirologia* (Florence, 2001), 2:1308f. Further, Epiphanius, *Panarion* 69.2: the names of the churches of Pierios, Serapion, Persaia, and Dizya suggest their origin in private houses or pious donations; they were still being used in the early fourth century. Photius notes that devout Christians of Alexandria built νεὼς καὶ οἶκοι (Calderini, *Dizionario*, s.v. *Pieriou*). See also Martin, "Églises," 214ff.; Williams, *Arius*, 42–43; Haas, *Alexandria*, 199ff.; and K. Bowes, *Private Worship, Public Values, and Religious Change in Late Antiquity* (Cambridge, 2008), esp. chap. 2 (on Rome and Constantinople).

118. H. O. Maier, "Religious Dissent, Heresy, and Households in Late Antiquity," *Vigiliae Christianae* 49 (1995): 49–63, esp. 50–53.

119. As suggested in a fragmented fourth-century Coptic papyrus from Oxyrhynchus quoted by Reymond and Barns, *Four Martyrdoms*, 16.

120. For instance, in Alexandria, under Gregory, the Athanasians met in private houses (Athanasius, *Ep. enc.* 5); and chapter 8 below.

121. As Haas justly noted in *Alexandria*, 274.

122. Athanasius, *Or. contra Arianos* 1.22.

123. Ibid. Cf. Elm, *Virgins*, 353.

124. Athanasius, *Letter to the Virgins* 1.42 apud Brakke, *Athanasius*, 288 (quoting Alexander). On clerics visiting virgins, see also Palladius, *HL* 6.

125. *Urk.* 14, p. 20, ll. 10–11.

126. Optiz, *Urk.* 14, p. 20, ll. 15–16 (rendering πᾶσαν ἀγυιὰν as "collection of streets" or every street). On Alexander's comment, see Elm, *Virgins*, 350–53. Independent virgins in early fourth-century Alexandria and Egypt: Brakke, *Athanasius*, 19f., 26–68. Evangelization: also suggested by H. Juliussen-Stevenson, "Performing Christian Female Identity in Roman Alexandria" (master's thesis, University of Maryland, College Park, 2008), 54, 58.

127. Little is certain about the topography of Roman Alexandria, but the Rhakotis seems to have been a sprawling popular district in the southwestern part of the city, ranging south from the Dromos to the vicinity of the Serapeum Magnum. In Ptolemaic times, it may have been inhabited by "Egyptians," but it is unlikely to have retained an "ethnic" character into late antiquity. Given its proximity to the Serapeum, many of its inhabitants may have been pagan (see Haas, *Alexandria*, 148, 160ff., and 165). *Laures* as quarters in the city's periphery: Athanasius, *HA* 58.4; Epiphanius, *Panarion* 69.1.2; A. Martin, "Topographie et liturgie: Le problème des 'paroisses' d'Alexandrie," in *Actes du XIe Congrès international d'archéologie chrétienne* (Rome, 1989), 2:1133ff. Moharrem Bey: B. Tkaczow, *The Topography of Ancient Alexandria (An Archaeological Map)* (Warsaw, 1993), 167.

128. For lower-class dwellings in the Roman period, see MacMullen, *Enemies*, 166–67. On the Rhakotis, see Haas, *Alexandria*, 49. Kôm el-Dikka and Moharrem Bey: Tkaczow, *Topography*, 167; and Rodziewicz, *Alexandrie*, 249, 331.

129. On the involvement of wealthy women (not all virgins) in the Christian community of Alexandria, see, for instance, Palladius, *HL* 1 and 6 (rich virgin), 66.2 ("When a famine raged ... [their charity] helped bring heretics back to orthodoxy"), 67.2, and 69.3; Elm, *Virgins*, 357f.; and Brakke, *Athanasius*, 23–29, 41. On the attendants of wealthy ascetic women, see Clark, *Women*, 102–3.

130. Epiphanius, *Panarion* 69.3. See also Elm, *Virgins,* 352ff. (quote: 352 n. 54).

131. Brakke, *Athanasius,* 19–31, 41. More generally, Elm, *Virgins,* 12–18.

132. See Elm, *Virgins,* 351–53, 362; Brakke, *Athanasius,* 63–79; and Martin, *Athanase,* 198–99.

133. Although it was not uncommon for priests and ascetic males to offer ascetic women spiritual guidance, shelter, and assistance, in the early fourth century most virgins lived on their own, alone, with their kin, in discrete groups, and sometimes with male ascetics. See, for instance, Epiphanius, *Panarion* 63.2; *Conc. Anc.* 29; *Conc. Nic.* I, canon 3 (Joannou, *Discipline,* 25 and 70); Brakke, *Athanasius,* 21, 25–28, 33–34, and 299–300 (Athanasius, *Letter to the Virgins* 2.20ff.). Clerics and ascetics as spiritual mentors: Arius, Hieracas (Elm, *Virgins,* 340; Brakke, *Athanasius,* 20, 44ff.), Alexander (Athanasius, *Letter to the Virgins* 1.36 *apud* Brakke, *Athanasius,* 286), and Athanasius himself. Cf. Eusebius, *HE* 7.30.12 (Paul of Samosata's "spiritual brides"). On the importance of virgins to the Arian "movement": Juliussen-Stevenson, "Performing," 59–61. Athanasius's efforts to win over virgins: Elm, *Virgins,* 354ff.; and Brakke, *Athanasius,* 21ff.

134. Sozomen, *HE* 1.15.2ff., drawing on the "Collection Alexandrine." See Williams, *Arius,* 32–41; Martin, *Athanase,* 253–98, esp. 286ff. Cf. Bell, *Jews,* 41f., and Van Nuffelen, *Héritage,* 322 n. 39.

135. Socrates, *HE* 1.6. Melitius may not have sided with Arius, but the passage, whose source is unclear (Van Nuffelen, *Héritage,* 456), is important because it refers to division among the Melitians even before Nicaea. See also chapter 7.

136. *Urk.* 4a, p. 6, ll. 8–10.

137. Epiphanius, *Panarion* 69.3, 68.4 (ἅμα αὐτῷ πλῆθος πολύ); Sozomen, *HE* 1.15.7 (τοῦ λαοῦ οὐκ ὀλίγη μοῖρα); Zonaras, *Annals* 13.4 (*PG* 134.1113); and Nicephorus, *HE* 8.5.

138. Sozomen, *HE* 1.15.7.

139. Constantine: *Urk.* 34, p. 69, l. 27–p. 70, l. 1. Commitment: Alexander's remarks in *Urk.* 14, pp. 20ff.; and Arius's in *Urk.* 1, p. 2, l. 9; Eusebius, *VC* 2.61, 2.73; Socrates, *HE* 1.6; Theodoret, *HE* 1.5; Nicephorus, *HE* 8.8, 8.11; and chapters 7 and 8 below.

140. *Urk.* 14, p. 20, l. 13.

141. *Urk.* 1, p. 1, l. 7. Cf. Libanius, *Autobiography* 19–21, 44 (Bemarchius organized a gang to get rid of Libanius); id., *Or.* 19; and Eunapius, *Vitae philos.* 477, 483, 487.

142. *Urk.* 14, p. 20, l. 14, and p. 29, l. 10. Cf. appeals to the emperor in the dispute with Paul of Samosata; the Donatists' appeal to Anulinus (Maier, *Dossier,* 144–48); etc.

143. *Urk.* 17, p. 33 passim; Theodoret, *HE* 1.5.

144. Eusebius, *VC* 3.4; Theodoret, *HE* 1.6.9.

145. *Urk.* 17, p. 33, ll. 6–7.

146. Nicephorus, *HE* 8.11, drawing on Theodoret, *HE* 1.6.9, and Eusebius, *VC* 2.61 and 3.4, but with details not found in these authors. See G. Gentz, *Die Kirchengeschichte des Nicephorus Callistus Xanthopulus und ihre Quellen* (Berlin, 1966), 79–82.

147. For instance, rioting over the choice of a site to bury Peter's body; see *Acta Petri* (*PG* 18.464), with Telfer, "St. Peter," 124ff.

148. Martyrs' festivals: *Acta Petri* (*PG* 18.455–56); Sozomen, *HE* 2.17.6 (Alexander's celebration of Peter's martyrdom); and *Vita S. Athanasii* (Metaphrastes) (*PG* 25.ccxxiv). Conflicts during festivals: Agapius, *HU* (*PO* 7.544); Ignatius of Selymbria, *VC* 34 (ed. Ioannou, p. 198); *Vita S. Athanasii* (*PG* 25.cciii); and chapters 7 and 8 below (during Easter).

149. Theodoret, *HE* 1.5. See also MacMullen, "Cultural and Political Changes," 484–85; and Galvao-Sobrinho, "Embodied Theologies," 330f.

150. Eusebius, *VC* 3.4, in unclear circumstances. See also Haas, *Alexandria*, 70, on imperial statues in the city.

151. Complaining of persecution (*Urk.* 1), for Palestine and perhaps Nicomedia: Epiphanius, *Panarion* 69.4; and Athanasius, *De synodis* 15. Cf. Libanius, *Autobiography* 48.

152. MacMullen, "Cultural and Political Changes," 483: "It was the church elite who gave birth to [popular] power by appealing to the people, ... awakening a different, ordinarily dormant force."

5. "FOR THE SAKE OF THE LOGOS"

1. *Urk.* 1, p. 2, ll. 1–3; Sozomen, *HE* 1.15.8; and Socrates, *HE* 1.5 (Arius thought Alexander taught Sabellian views).

2. Sozomen, *HE* 1.15.8; and Opitz, "Zeitfolge," 146. Cf. Socrates, *HE* 1.6 (contacted other bishops after his excommunication); and Williams, *Arius*, 56: the synod that excommunicated the Arians had considered the letters of Syrian and Palestinian bishops.

3. Epiphanius, *Panarion* 69.4; Opitz, "Zeitfolge," 147; Simonetti, *Crisi*, 31; Williams, *Arius*, 56; and Loose, "Chronologie," 91.

4. Epiphanius, *Panarion* 69.4. Alexander's first encyclical (*Urk.* 4b) also says nothing about Arius's trip to other provinces. The letter was written *after* the involvement of the Palestinian bishops named in Arius's letter to Eusebius (*Urk.* 1), and thus probably *before* Arius left Alexandria for Palestine. In his second encyclical (*Urk.* 14), Alexander refers several times to the Arians journeying to other cities, which, with Opitz, I place after *Urk.* 4b (contra Williams, *Arius*, 56–61; and Parvis, *Marcellus*, 69–72), though, admittedly, we cannot tell whether Alexander meant Arius himself or his envoys.

5. Sozomen, *HE* 1.15.8, speaks of "embassies," but he places them after Arius's excommunication. On Arius's envoys, see, e.g., *Urk.* 1, p. 1, l. 4.

6. Sozomen, *HE* 1.15.9. Eusebius: Barnes, *CE*, 128ff. Paulinus: Eusebius, *Contra Marcellum* 1.4.19; cf. id., *HE* 10.4. See also *DCB*, vol. 4, 231–2. Theodotus: Eusebius, *HE* 7.32; and Le Quien, *OC*, vol. 3, col. 792.

7. Sozomen, *HE* 1.15.8; cf. *Urk.* 1. Statement of faith: *Urk.* 6, quoted by Eusebius in *Urk.* 7, p. 14, ll. 7ff. (and n. *ad loc.*). See chapter 4 above.

8. Sozomen, *HE* 1.15.8; and Nicephorus, *HE* 8.7.

9. Socrates, *HE* 1.6.

10. Sozomen, *HE* 1.15.9.

11. Inferred from *Urk.* 1, p. 2, ll. 4–8.

12. Paulinus: *Urk.* 9 (cf. *Urk.* 7, p. 15, l. 7; and Socrates, *HE* 1.6). Theodotus and Athanasius: *Urk.* 11, p. 18; Optiz dates this letter to a later phase of the controversy, but it would also fit here (cf. Schwartz, *GS*, 3:125); D. De Bruyne, "Deux lettres inconnues de Theognius l'évêque arien de Nicée," *ZNTW* 27 (1928): 110 (Fragment 4, [*CCSL* 87, p. 235]); Kopecek, *History*, 41–42; and Hanson, *Search*, 41–43. Aetius: *Urk.* 1, p. 2, ll. 4–5. Opposition to the Arians: *Urk.* 1, p. 2, ll. 6–8; cf. Theodoret, *HE* 1.4.

13. *Urk.* 1, p. 2, ll. 4–5; Sozomen, *HE* 1.15.8. Eusebius of Caesarea: *Urk.* 1, p. 2, l. 4; *Urk.* 7; and Williams, *Arius*, 56. Paulinus of Tyre: *Urk.* 8, p. 15. Athanasius: De Bruyne, "Deux

lettres," 109–10. *Urk.* 9 (from Paulinus) and *Urk.* 11 (from Athanasius) seem to date later, together with *Urk.* 12 and 13. Eustathius of Beroea to Alexander: Theodoret, *HE* 1.3. See also Schwartz, *GS*, 3:121–23; Simonetti, *Crisi*, 39, 73–76; Kopecek, *History*, 41–42, 47–48; Hanson, *Search*, 42–45; and Parvis, *Marcellus*, 57–59.

14. *Urk.* 1, p. 2, ll. 7–8; *Urk.* 3, p. 4, l. 9 (Eusebius of Caesarea); *Urk.* 9, p. 18, l. 5 (Paulinus of Tyre). See also Simonetti, *Crisi*, 75–76.

15. Eusebius of Caesarea, Athanasius of Anazarbus, and Paulinus of Tyre formulated their opinions on the subject in broad agreement with the priest. Their letters circulated widely in the East. Paulinus: *Urk.* 9 (cited by Marcellus of Ancyra; defended by Asterius). Athanasius: De Bruyne, "Deux lettres," 109–10. Cf. Schwartz, *GS*, 3:122; and Kopecek, *History*, 47f.

16. *Urk.* 3, p. 4, ll. 4–6. See also Simonetti, *Crisi*, 60–66; Hanson, *Search*, 46–59; Williams, *Arius*, 261; and Ayres, *Nicaea*, 57–61.

17. Possibly before Nicaea: see Parvis, *Marcellus*, 57; and chapter 7.

18. *Urk.* 1, p. 2, ll. 4–7. At the Council of Antioch in 325 (*Urk.* 18, p. 36, ll. 4–10), Aetius of Lydda and Gregory of Berytus changed their minds (see Schwartz, *GS*, 3:152–53; and chapter 6 below).

19. Sozomen, *HE* 1.15.9.

20. *Urk.* 1, p. 3, l. 7; and Williams, *Arius*, 30–31. Lucian's disciple: G. Bardy, *Recherches sur Saint Lucien d'Antioche et son école* (Paris, 1936), v–vi.

21. *Urk.* 1, p. 1, ll. 1–3. Contra Opitz, "Zeitfolge," 147, I suggest Arius sent this letter while he was still in Alexandria.

22. *Urk.* 1, p. 2, ll. 9–10, and p. 3, ll. 4–6, rendering λοιπὸν as "hereafter," "from this point to the future," and not "the rest," which would have implied previous communication with Eusebius.

23. *Urk.* 2, p. 3, l. 2. See also Hanson, *Search*, 29–32.

24. *Urk.* 8, p. 15, ll. 5–10.

25. Sozomen, *HE* 1.15.10. Take back the Arians: implied in *Urk.* 4b; and Socrates, *HE* 1.6 (placing this after Alexander wrote his *Henos somatos* [*Urk.* 4b]).

26. *Urk.* 8, p. 17, l. 9, and p. 15, ll. 2 and 6. See also *Urk.* 9.

27. Epiphanius, *Panarion* 69.4. Cf. Opitz, "Zeitfolge," 147.

28. Epiphanius, *Panarion*, 69.4; Ignatius of Selymbria, *VC* 35 (ed. Ioannou, p. 199) (εἰς τὴν Ἀσίαν διαβαίνει, καὶ μέχρι Νικομηδείας τε καὶ Ξαλκηδόνος χωρεῖ); Opitz, "Zeitfolge," 147; and Williams, *Arius*, 56–57.

29. Epiphanius, *Panarion* 69.4.

30. *Urk.* 10, p. 18, ll. 3–4; *Urk.* 14, p. 25, ll. 16–17. See also Epiphanius, *Panarion* 30.5; and Hanson, *Search*, 135, 507–8.

31. Philostorgius, *HE* 1.8a. Cf. Parvis, *Marcellus*, 43–44.

32. A< . . . >, bishop of Hierapolis (?), Philoxenus's predecessor. He must have died (or have been removed before the Council of Antioch); see Agapius, *HU* (*PO* 7.545).

33. Epiphanius, *Panarion*, 69.5; Athanasius, *De synodis* 17. See also Hanson, *Search*, 599f.; and Vaggione, *Eunomius*, 22–23. Later, Leontius became bishop of Antioch and teacher of Aetius and Eunomius.

34. George resided in Antioch: Athanasius, *De synodis* 17; and *Urk.* 12 and 13. On the others, see Parvis, *Marcellus*, 78 n. 179; and chapter 7. Eustathius may have been a priest there.

35. Jerome, *De vir. ill.* 94 (*PL* 23.734–35); Simonetti, *Crisi*, 31, 65; Kopecek, *History*, 28–34; Hanson, *Search*, 32–41; and discussion below. Asterius's works: fragments of the *Syntagmation* in Bardy, *Recherches*, 341–53; and Richard, *Asterii* (homilies).

36. Narcissus: *Urk.* 18, p. 40, l. 5; *Urk.* 19, p. 41; Philostorgius, *HE* 1.8a; Theodoret, *HE* 1.6; and Hanson, *Search*, 45 and 146. Amphion of Epiphaneia and Tarcondimantus of Aegeai: Philostorgius, *HE* 1.8 (sided with Arius at Nicaea). For Tarcondimantus's theological preferences, see Le Quien, *OC*, vol. 3, col. 895; and Parvis, *Marcellus*, 43f.

37. Theodorus of Tarsus, younger brother of the confessor Auxentius, later became bishop of Mopsuestia. Macedonius was later a member of so-called Mareotic commission to investigate Athanasius (Le Quien, *OC*, vol. 3, cols. 889–90). Both subscribed to Nicaea, which does not necessarily imply support for the creed.

38. They were said to share Arius's views at Nicaea (Philostorgius, *HE* 1.8 and 1.8a). However, the list is problematic. Basil of Amasea died a martyr under Licinius, but this does not rule out the possibility that he had supported the priest—Philostorgius may have converted the memory of that support into a defense of the priest at Nicaea. According to Gelasius (*apud* Le Quien, *OC*, vol. 3, col. 370), Leontius of Caesarea strongly supported Nicaea, which makes it less likely, albeit not impossible, that he embraced Arius's theology. The *Martyrologium Romanum* (January 13) mentions Leontius's struggles against the Arians, presumably after Nicaea, but the *Martyrologium* is not a reliable source, as it often appropriated Arian sympathizers for the cause of Nicene orthodoxy. See also Barnes, *CE*, 72; and Parvis, *Marcellus*, 44ff.

39. Basil, *Ep.* 263.

40. See chapter 7 below.

41. Menophantus and Theognis pleaded for Arius at Nicaea (Theodoret, *HE* 1.6). Philostorgius, *HE* 1.9 and 1.8a, adds Maris of Chalcedon. See Hanson, *Search*, 43–44 (on Theognis); and Williams, *Arius*, 57–58.

42. The phrases "party of Eusebius" and "the Eusebians," attacked in recent scholarship as Athanasian "constructs," are used throughout this study to refer to a diverse group of churchmen allied with or acting in concert with Eusebius of Nicomedia and Theognis of Nicaea in support of the latter's quest to revise the creed of Nicaea. The terms are not meant to signify a party in the sense of a group of prelates sharing the same theological view (other than a dislike for Nicaea) or as a stable, institutionalized entity. I refer to "the Eusebians" here in the same way that, below, I use the term "Athanasians," which is how, incidentally, the Eusebians referred to Athanasius's supporters, as in Athanasius, *ACA* 27: ἔγραψαν οἱ περὶ Εὐσέβιον πρότερον κατὰ τῶν περὶ Ἀθανάσιον ... See D. M. Gwynn, *The Eusebians: The Polemic of Athanasius of Alexandria and the Construction of the "Arian Controversy"* (Oxford, 2006), esp. chaps. 2 and 5, but cf. Parvis, *Marcellus*, 96.

43. Marcellus's support of Alexander: Parvis, *Marcellus*, 50. Anti-Arian writings: Jerome, *De vir. ill.* 86.

44. *Urk.* 4b.

45. Ammianus Marcellinus, *RG* 22.9.4; Simonetti, *Crisi*, 32; Barnes, *CE*, 70; and Hanson, *Search*, 28.

46. Sozomen, *HE* 1.15.9; Socrates, *HE* 1.6; Epiphanius, *Panarion* 69.4.

47. Barnes, *AC*, 16.

48. *Urk.* 4b, p. 7, ll. 7–8.

49. Ibid., p. 7, ll. 5, 11, and p. 10, ll. 12–13, 15–16. See also Epiphanius, *Panarion,* 69.4; and Sozomen, *HE* 1.15.9.

50. *HE* 1.15.10.

51. Socrates, *HE* 1.6. Cf. Sozomen, *HE* 1.15.10.

52. Epiphanius, *Panarion* 69.4.

53. *Urk.* 7, p. 14, ll. 5–6, 14–15, and p. 15, ll. 1–6.

54. Ibid., p. 15, ll. 2–3.

55. *Urk.* 11, p. 18 (Athanasius of Anazarbus's reply to Alexander's encyclical [*Urk.* 4b]?); *Urk.* 12 and 13, p. 19. See also De Bruyne, "Deux lettres," 110; Fragment 4, *CCSL* 87, p. 235; Hanson, *Search,* 43f. Cf. *Urk.* 6.

56. Sozomen, *HE* 1.15.10; Nicetas, *Thesauri* 4.

57. *Urk.* 5; Sozomen, *HE* 1.15.10.

58. Socrates, *HE* 1.6.

59. *Urk.* 10, p. 18. Simonetti, *Crisi,* 34–35.

60. See chapter 4 above.

61. *Urk.* 14, p. 19, l. 11–p. 20, l. 3; Athanasius, *ACA* 12; and the appendix ("Kolluthus's Schism and the Arians"). See also Opitz, "Zeitfolge," 149; Marrou, "Arianisme," 537; Simonetti, *Crisi,* 37 n. 21; Williams, *Arius,* 46f.; and Loose, "Chronologie," 89.

62. *Urk.* 15 and 14. Cf. Opitz, "Zeitfolge," 149, and Hanson, *Search,* 136, on the chronology. Although *Urk.* 14 omits Eusebius of Nicomedia, this does not mean that it should be dated before *Urk.* 4b (Williams, *Arius,* 56–61). The omission may have been intentional to avoid references to the Bithynian synod that proclaimed Arius orthodox. Cf. the letter from the Council of Antioch in 325, which, likewise, does not mention Eusebius of Nicomedia or any of the Asian bishops.

63. For instance, Melitius of Sebastopolis, to whom the extant Syriac fragment of the *Tomos* was seemingly addressed (*Urk.* 15, p. 30, l. 4). At the Council of Antioch in 325, many bishops who had first supported Arius migrated to Alexander's camp (see *Urk.* 18).

64. *Urk.* 18, p. 37, ll. 14–15; Eusebius, *VC* 1.51.1–2 and 2.47.1–3; Opitz, "Zeitfolge," 145 (dating the ban to 322); Barnes, *CE,* 88 (to 323); and Williams, *Arius,* 49.

65. Eusebius, *VC* 2.61 (cf. 2.73 and 3.4); Socrates, *HE* 1.6; Nicephorus, *HE* 8.11; Ignatius of Selymbria, *VC* 35 (ed. Ioannou, pp. 198–99).

66. Theodoret, *HE* 1.5.

67. Partly because of Licinius's ban on synods, which made it difficult to elect bishops properly.

68. On episcopal succession at Antioch, see Burgess, *Studies,* 184–91, who has convincingly shown that Philogonius died in 323 (December 20, *pace* John Chrysostom) and was succeeded by Paulinus of Tyre.

69. Sometime in 324 after Paulinus's (not Philogonius's) death. Theodoret, *HE* 1.6, speaks of Eustathius being dragged "unwillingly" from Beroea to Antioch "by the bishops and priests of the province together with the people of the Lord" (cf. Nicetas, *Thesauri* 5.4), but the circumstances of his appointment are obscure, though it seems that, after Paulinus's death, the pro-Alexander faction managed to get the upper hand. The prelates of Coele Syria, where, with the exception of Theodotus and the anonymous bishop of Hierapolis,

Arius found little support, may have played a role—all of them signed the letter of the Council of Antioch denouncing Arius's theology. The choice of Eustathius, however, was repeatedly contested by those with Arian sympathies; see chapter 7 below.

70. John Chrysostom, *In sanctum Eustathium* 3 (*PG* 48.602); and *Urk.* 18, p. 38, ll. 9–11.

71. John Chrysostom, *In sanctum Eustathium* 3 (*PG* 48.602). Eustathius may have launched his campaign in late 324 or early 325, which coincided with his *translatio* from Beroea to Antioch, or even earlier and then continuously.

72. *Urk.* 18, . 38, ll. 1–3. See also Schwartz, *GS*, 3:147.

73. *Urk.* 18, p. 37, ll. 2ff. See also Barnes, *CE*, 213, but the reason for the troubles was theology, not electoral rivalry. See also chapter 6 below. Schwartz's suggestion (*GS*, 3:147) that the synod met in response to the Arians' attempts to place one of their own on the throne of Antioch is not convincing.

74. Athanasius, *De synodis* 18–20 (*PG* 26.713–16). Did this happen before Nicaea? Athanasius wrote: διὰ ταῦτα μάχονται πρὸς τὴν ἀρχαίαν σύνοδον· ὅτι μὴ τὰ ὅμοια αὐτῶν ἔγραψαν οἱ συνελθόντες ἐν αὐτῇ, ἀλλὰ μᾶλλον ἀνεθεμάτισαν τὴν Ἀρειανὴν αἵρεσιν, ἣν ἐσπούδαζον οὗτοι συστῆσαι. Διὰ τοῦτο καῖ Ἀστέριον . . . προὐβάλλοντο. If the phrase Διὰ τοῦτο refers to its immediate antecedent, Asterius's activities could be situated before Nicaea, though they continued after. Cf. Socrates, *HE* 1.36; Sozomen, *HE* 2.33.4; Bardy, *Recherches*, 320–25; and chapter 7 below.

75. For instance, *Homily* 12.4 (ed. Richard, p. 83). See also Hanson, *Search*, 37–39; and Gavrilyuk, *Suffering*, 121–34 on the authorship. Adjusting sermons to the audience: Rousseau, "Preacher's Audience," 395–400.

76. Jerusalem: According to the *Chronicle of Seert* (*PO* 4.275), bishop Macarius, whom Arius had called a heretic, addressed Helena, saying that it was useless to build so much in the region when "heresiarchs . . . have, in large number, driven away so many faithful. If one neglects . . . to disperse their assemblies, . . . to refute their doctrines, they will prevail in this country . . . and make many faithful . . . [who] have embraced their error, by force or voluntarily, perish" (slightly altered). Cf. Maruta of Maipherqat; see A. Vööbus, ed., *The Canons Ascribed to Maruta of Maipherqat and Related Sources*, CSCO 440 (Louvain, 1982), 104. Despite the fictitious nature of these accounts, they seem to echo a memory of a church divided over theology, and Maruta's reference to Alexander of Alexandria would also suggest that "heresy" meant Arius's teachings. Elsewhere: Eusebius, *VC* 2.61; cf. 2.73 and 3.4.

77. Sozomen, *HE* 1.15.8. Cf. Socrates, *HE* 1.6; Gelasius of Cyzicus, *HE* 2.2.4–5; and Nicephorus *HE* 8.7.

78. *Urk.* 10, p. 18, ll. 9–10. Cf. Nicephorus, *HE* 8.11. See also Simonetti, *Crisi*, 35 n. 16.

6. "TO PLEASE THE OVERSEER OF ALL"

1. Nicetas, *Thesauri* 4. Cf. *Urk.* 17, p. 35, ll. 23–27; and Eusebius, *VC* 3.12.3. Donatists: Maier, *Dossier*, 144–46, 153–58.

2. Eusebius, *VC* 2.61 (pagans mocked bickering Christians); Socrates, *HE* 1.6; Theodoret, *HE* 1.3, 6; and Ignatius of Selymbria, *VC* 36 (ed. Ioannou, p. 200), quoting Constantine's letter to Arius and Alexander whose wording differs from *Urk.* 17 (= Eusebius, *VC* 2.63ff.).

3. *Urk.* 14, p. 20, l. 14; and chapter 4 above.

4. Tour: *Urk.* 17, p. 35, ll. 21ff.; and *Urk.* 25, p. 54, ll. 6–7. Africa: *Urk.* 17, p. 32, ll. 11–23. On Constantine's possible trip to Antioch, see Barnes, "Emperor," 55f.; Burgess, *Studies,* p. 191 n. 43; Lane Fox, *Pagans,* 638f.; and C. M. Odahl, *Constantine and the Christian Empire* (New York, 2004), 192f.

5. *Urk.* 17, p. 32, l. 27, and p. 33, ll. 1ff. Constantine also attributed the controversy to Licinius's ban on synods (ibid., p. 32, ll. 14–16), which must have been information passed on to him by clerics.

6. *Urk.* 17, p. 32, ll. 25–26.

7. Agent of God: Eusebius, *VC* 2.28–29, 31, 55; 3.8; and 4.24. Cf. Barnes, *CE,* 43. Danger: Eusebius, *VC* 2.42 and 3.12; *Urk.* 17, p. 35, ll. 1–15; and *Urk.* 26, p. 54, l. 1–p. 55, l. 9. Cf. *Urk.* 17, p. 32, ll. 8–9; and Maier, *Dossier,* 143–44 and 149. See also H. A. Drake, *In Praise of Constantine: A Historical Study and New Translation of Eusebius' Tricennial Orations* (Berkeley, 1975), 24; id., *Constantine,* 240–45; and MacMullen, *Voting,* 27.

8. Cf. Maier, *Dossier,* 170–71, on Constantine on the Donatists.

9. Maier, *Dossier,* 193.

10. *Urk.* 17, p. 32, ll. 27ff.; ibid., p. 34, ll. 5–6

11. Ibid., p. 34, ll. 3ff., 22–24.

12. Ibid., p. 34, ll. 3–4.

13. Plans: Eusebius, *VC* 2.48, 49ff., 55f. (on pagans), 65, 71; 4.29; and Norderval, "Emperor," 120f.

14. Eusebius, *VC* 2.51. See also *Urk.* 17, p. 34, ll. 2–8.

15. Eusebius, *VC* 2.56.

16. *Urk.* 17, pp. 34–35 passim. Cf. Drake, *Praise,* 64; id., *Constantine,* 240–41; G. Gottlieb, "Les évêques et les empereurs dans les affaires ecclésiastiques du 4e siècle," *Museum Helveticum* 33 (1976): 38; and Norderval, "Emperor," 119.

17. Ayres, *Nicaea,* 88–92; and chapters 7 and 8 below.

18. Eusebius, *VC* 2.63, 73. Marianos: B. H. Warmington, "The Source of Some Constantinian Documents in Eusebius' *Ecclesiastical History* and *Life of Constantine,*" in *Studia Patristica,* vol. 18, ed. E. A. Livingstone, Papers of the Ninth International Conference on Patristic Studies, Oxford 1983 (Kalamazoo, MI, 1985), 95–97; and Parvis, *Marcellus,* 77.

19. *Urk.* 17, p. 35, ll. 2–6.

20. Ibid., p. 34, ll. 22ff. and 35.

21. Synod: Athanasius, *ACA* 76. Kolluthians: Eusebius, *VC* 2.73, 3.4, and 3.6; and Simonetti, *Crisi,* 37.

22. Eusebius, *VC* 2.73 and 3.4.

23. Ibid. 3.4; the context suggests Alexandria. See also chapter 4 above.

24. In late fall 324, because, by early 325, Ossius and other bishops had been notified that a large council was to meet at Ancyra (*Urk.* 18, p. 40, l. 17).

25. *Urk.* 18, p. 37, ll. 17–18, and p. 30, ll. 1–4.

26. Some ancient authors (see Hanson, *Search,* 154) and modern scholars (Barnes, *CE,* 213) have suggested that Ossius or Alexander proposed the idea of a large council (cf. Drake, *Constantine,* 250; Lane Fox, *Pagans,* 641; and Odahl, *Constantine,* 193), but Constantine had previously called synods to deal with the Donatist affair. Given his concern with church unity, he would have been involved in the decision.

27. Eusebius, *VC* 3.5.3.
28. Ibid., 3.6 with 3.15–16 and 4.47; Socrates, *HE* 1.8.
29. Eusebius, *VC* 3.6 and 4.47. See also Norderval, "Emperor," 123.
30. *Urk.* 20, pp. 41–42 (sent in early 325). Alastair Logan has argued that Marcellus suggested Ancyra as the site for the synod; see Logan, "Marcellus of Ancyra and the Councils of AD 325: Antioch, Ancyra, and Nicaea," *JTS*, n.s., 43 (1992): 434, 438.
31. From Syria, Cilicia, Palestine, Phoenicia, Arabia, and Cappadocia. See Schwartz, *GS*, 3:147ff.; Opitz, "Zeitfolge," 151ff.; and H. Chadwick, "Ossius of Corduba and the Presidency of the Council of Antioch, 325," *JTS*, n.s., 9 (1958): 292–304.
32. *Urk.* 18, p. 37, ll. 2–6 and ll. 10–14; and chapter 5 above.
33. *Urk.* 18, p. 37, l. 12 (and ll. 2ff.).
34. Ibid., p. 38, l. 6, and p. 37, ll. 5–6.
35. The need to confirm Eustathius's election is the usual justification given for the synod of Antioch (Schwartz, *GS*, 3:147; Simonetti, *Crisi*, 39; Barnes, *CE*, 213; Hanson, *Search*, 149; but see Chadwick, "Ossius," 301), on the assumption that the See of Antioch had been vacant since the death of Paulinus. However, the synodical letter mentions neither the death of a bishop nor the appointment of another. Eustathius signed the letter after Ossius's name, suggesting that he was already in charge of the local church and probably presiding over the synod with Ossius (*Urk.* 18, p. 36, l. 4). See also chapter 5 above. Syrian bishops: seventeen out of eighteen signed the letter (Schwartz, *GS*, 3:150–51), and the same seventeen also subscribed to Nicaea, suggesting, as noted above, that Eustathius, like Philogonius, enjoyed the support of a good number of Syrian prelates.
36. Twelve bishops from Palestine and four from Arabia—provinces outside the jurisdiction of the diocese of Antioch and thus not needed for his election. Cf. *Conc. Anc.*, canon 18; and *Conc. Nic.* I, canon 4. Schwartz, *GS*, 3:183, suggests that the synod was called by "einige Heisssporne in Syrien," but to whose advantage?
37. *Urk.* 18, p. 38, ll. 7–8; and *Urk.* 19.
38. Scholars who accept that Constantine visited Antioch in late 324 argue that he simply accompanied the emperor. Then, having witnessed the turmoil in the church, he would have called the council, helped elect Eustathius, and left for Alexandria (Logan, "Marcellus," 434; Odahl, *Constantine*, 193). Others suggest that Ossius stopped there on his way back to Nicomedia from Alexandria (Opitz, "Zeitfolge," 151; Barnes, *CE*, 213; id., *AC*, 16; and cf. Hanson, *Search*, 148), but why not go straight to Asia by sea? Lane Fox, *Pagans*, 642, suggested that Ossius was sent "to prepare [Constantine's] path in the East." Upon arriving in Antioch, he would have summoned a synod to deal with the turmoil, then left for Alexandria. It is also possible that Constantine dispatched Ossius to Alexandria *and* to "those in the East who disputed the date of Easter" (cf. Eusebius, *VC* 3.5): Antioch would have been the ideal place for a meeting to discuss the matter when Ancyra/Nicaea had not yet been announced; on which, see Nicetas, *Thesauri* 5; and Nicephorus, *HE* 12 (drawing on Theodoret of Mopsuestia?). Yet, as V. C. de Clerq noted (*apud* Chadwick, "Ossius," 304), there is nothing about Easter in the synodical letter of the Council of Antioch. I suggest that Ossius called the synod, but with full knowledge of the emperor and *after* his visit to Alexandria, to try to reconcile the bickering parties.
39. The synod excommunicated bishops who refused to sign its statement of faith. See *Urk.* 18, p. 40, ll. 5ff.; and below.

40. J. N. D. Kelly, *Early Christian Creeds* (Oxford, 1960), 205; P. Smulders, "Some Riddles in the Apostles' Creed," in *Studies in Early Christianity: A Collection of Scholarly Essays*, ed. E. Ferguson (New York and London, 1993), 148.

41. *Urk.* 18, p. 40, ll. 5–13, and p. 39, ll. 16ff. (quote); and *Urk.* 19, p. 41. The synodical portrayed Arius as a priest who blasphemed "against the Savior" and had been rightly expelled from the church (*Urk.* 18, p. 38, ll. 1–3).

42. Hanson, *Search*, 150; cf. Parvis, *Marcellus*, 78–80. The bishops also drafted a series of canons dealing with questions of church discipline, perhaps already with a view to the meeting at Ancyra; see Schwartz, *GS*, 3:143–45.

43. Chadwick, "Ossius," 300ff. Cf. Schwartz, *GS*, 3:183; Hanson, *Search*, 148; and Burgess, *Studies*, 190f.

44. See Chadwick, "Ossius," 301; and chapter 5 above.

45. *Urk.* 18, p. 40, ll. 5–6, 16–17.

46. Schwartz, *GS*, 3:183. Lane Fox, *Pagans*, 643–54, suggested that Constantine delivered his *Oration to the Saints* to the bishops in Antioch, in which case he would have known firsthand of the synod's outcome. On the controversy surrounding this *Oration*, see Barnes, *CE*, 73–76; Hall, *Documents*, 96; Drake, *Constantine*, 292–305; and Odahl, *Constantine*, 269 and 368 n. 4.

47. Agapius, *HU* (*PO* 7.546–47).

48. Ibid. (*PO* 7.546): وقل بز الجمع الاقل اجتموا باقورا مدينة انطاكية. I am grateful to Ellen Amster and Abbas Hamdani who have kindly translated the Arabic text for me.

49. *Urk.* 20, pp. 41–42.

50. The synodical is extant in another Syriac manuscript; see Chadwick, "Ossius," 297–98.

51. Vasiliev suggested an emendation of the Arabic text ("Il faut lire غالاطية" [Galatia] for انطاكية [Antioch]), rendering it as follows: "Le premier synode avait été déjà réuni à Ancyre, ville de Galatie." Vasiliev identified this synod as that of Ancyra in 314 (*PO* 7.546, n. 1). Note also the possible confusion between أَنْقَرَة (Ancyra) and باقورا (contentiously). Vasiliev's translation of the second part of Agapius's *Historia*, was published in 1911. Schwartz published the synodical letter of the Council of Antioch, the only evidence for this synod, in 1905 (Opitz, *Urk.* 18, p. 36). But Vasiliev was apparently unaware of the existence of this document and of Constantine's letter transferring the synod from Ancyra to Nicaea published by Schwartz in 1908 (*Urk.* 20).

52. Constantine's letter in Agapius does not mention the council scheduled to meet at Ancyra and, therefore, the transfer to Nicaea (see *Urk* 20), but the letter may have been only one among many sent out from the imperial court to bishops in the East. The document provides important evidence for the maneuverings of Constantine and other parties in the months leading up to Nicaea. The letter deserves to be fully analyzed and discussed in the context of Agapius's work. The language of sections of the letter matches that of *Urk.* 20—at least as far as I could ascertain from Schwartz's Greek translation—which suggests that the document is legitimate.

53. Eusebius may have corresponded with members of Constantine's court even before 324; see Warmington, "Source," 94–96.

54. *Urk.* 27, p. 61, ll. 9–13. The request may have had more to do with Eusebius's alleged support of Licinius than his doctrinal views. See Drake, *Constantine*, 251.

55. Philostorgius, *HE* 1.7a; Simonetti, *Crisi*, 37.

56. Maier, *Dossier*, 160–71, 192f., 194–98, and 198ff. (the *Passio Donati Abioccalensis* under Constantine). See also Lane Fox, *Pagans*, 641, 655.

57. *Urk.* 25, p. 53, ll. 2-4. See also Schwartz, *GS*, 3:183-84; and Drake, *Constantine*, 250ff.

58. See Simonetti, *Crisi*, 41 n. 29; Lane Fox, *Pagans*, 654; Logan, "Marcellus," 440; and Drake, *Constantine*, 251. Cf. Chadwick, "Ossius," 302f.; and Barnes, *CE*, 214.

59. On Marcellus's possible contact with Constantine, see M. J. Edwards, "The Arian Heresy and the *Oration to the Saints*," *Vigiliae Christianae* 49 (1995): 383.

60. *Urk.* 20, p. 42, ll. 7-8. Cf. Agapius, *HU* (*PO* 7.546). See also Barnes, *CE*, 214; and Hanson, *Search*, 152-53.

61. *Urk.* 25, p. 53, ll. 1-2.

62. Sciuto, "Da Nicea," 481 n. 9; Lane Fox, *Pagans*, 654-55; Hanson, *Search*, 153; Logan, "Marcellus," 440; and Drake, *Constantine*, 252ff.

63. Photius, *Bibliotheca* 471b, claims that, following the council, Ossius brought the acts of the council to the West, but see Hanson, *Search*, 152-56; and Lim, *Public Disputation*, 184-85.

64. Eusebius, *VC* 3.7-16; and *Urk.* 22, pp. 42ff. Theodoret, *HE* 1.7 (quoting Eustathius). Socrates, *HE* 1.14.2, and Sozomen, *HE* 1.16.3 (Eusebius of Nicomedia) (= *Urk.* 31, pp. 65ff.). Athanasius, *De decretis*; and id., *Ep. ad Afros*. See also Hanson, *Search*, 158ff.

65. See also Hefele, *Histoire*, 270-71; and Hanson, *Search*, 162.

66. Rufinus, *HE* 10.2-5; and Sozomen, *HE* 1.19.1. Cf. Socrates, *HE* 1.8.

67. Rufinus, *HE* 10.2.

68. Uproar: Theodoret, *HE* 1.6-7 (Eustathius's remarks), though this may also have taken place later. See Barnes, *CE*, 216; Hanson, *Search*, 160; Drake, *Constantine*, 254; and Ayres, *Nicaea*, 101, suggesting that the document read in the council was Eusebius of Nicomedia's letter to Paulinus of Tyre (*Urk.* 8). Defending Arius: Rufinus, *HE* 10.2; Theodoret, *HE* 1.6; and Philostorgius, *HE* 1.8a.

69. Athanasius, *De decretis* 16ff.; id., *Ep. ad Afros* 5-9. Cf. Theodoret, *HE* 1.6-7 (drawing on Athanasius); and Sozomen, *HE* 1.17.

70. Hefele, *Histoire*, 278-81; O. Skarsaume, "A Neglected Detail in the Creed of Nicaea," *Vigiliae Christianae* 41 (1987): 34-54; Hanson, *Search*, 162; Barnes, *AC*, 16-17; and Drake, *Constantine*, 255.

71. Athanasius, *De decretis* 20.

72. *Urk.* 6, p. 12, l. 11. See also Kelly, *Creeds*, 252f.; Barnes, *CE*, 215; Skarsaume, "Neglected Detail," 50; Hanson, *Search*, 16; and Ayres, *Nicaea*, 90-91.

73. Socrates, *HE* 1.8 (*NPNF*, vol. 2, p. 10; italics in the original), referring to the arguments of Eusebius of Nicomedia, Theognis of Nicaea, Maris of Chalcedon, and Secundus and Theonas. Socrates places this after the drafting of the creed, but Arius and his supporters would have advanced these arguments earlier (cf. Rufinus, *HE* 10.5) and communicated their views to Constantine (below). On Socrates' source, see Van Nuffelen, *Héritage*, 456-57. Ambrose later wrote that the Fathers chose *homoousios* because the term offended Eusebius of Nicomedia and his allies; see *Urk.* 21, p. 42.

74. Sozomen, *HE* 1.17.6 (unknown source; see Van Nuffelen, *Héritage*, 457); and chapter 7 below.

75. Philostorgius, *HE* 1.7 and 1.7a. See also Kelly, *Creeds*, 251f. (drawing on Athanasius); and Simonetti, *Crisi*, 37.

76. *Urk.* 22, pp. 45ff. See also Sciuto, "Da Nicea," 481 n. 9; Skarsaune, "Neglected Detail," 39; Barnes, *AC*, 16-17; and Drake, *Constantine*, 254-56.

77. Eusebius, *VC* 3.10-13.

78. Ibid. 3.10; Barnes, *CE*, 215f.; and Drake, *Constantine*, 252f.

79. Rufinus, *HE* 10.2; Socrates, *HE* 1.8; Sozomen, *HE* 1.17.3; and Theodoret, *HE* 1.10. See also Hefele, *Histoire*, 274–75; Barnes, *CE*, 215; and Parvis, *Marcellus*, 82. When exactly this happened is unclear.

80. Sozomen, *HE* 1.17.4. Whether or not Constantine made this speech, the public destruction of the *libelli* is credible. Cf. Eusebius, *VC* 3.13–14.

81. Eusebius, *VC* 3.13.

82. Ibid. See also Drake, *Constantine*, 255.

83. Parvis, *Marcellus*, 85, suggests that Eusebius composed a simple creed to appeal to Constantine and the majority of bishops.

84. *Urk.* 22, p. 44, ll. 1–9.

85. Support for Alexander: implied in the *Tomos*, the outcome of the Council of Antioch, and the preliminary debates at Nicaea. Cf. the anti-Nicene Sabinus of Heraclea on the "ignorance" of the bishops assembled at Nicaea (Socrates, *HE* 1.8.25 and 1.9.28). Constantine's concerns: Kelly, *Creeds*, 253f.

86. Eusebius, *VC* 3.60 and 4.34–36; cf. Hanson, *Search*, 165–66, 170; and Ayres, *Nicaea*, 89–90.

87. Colossus (Rome): built by Maxentius, but retrofitted with Constantine's image. Icons: Eusebius, *VC* 4.15. See also Drake, *Constantine*, 255; and Barnes, *CE*, 216.

88. *Urk.* 22, p. 44, ll. 8–9. See Hanson, *Search*, 163–64; and Logan, "Marcellus," 438f.

89. Logan, "Marcellus," 441–46, contends that Marcellus, working closely with Alexander and Ossius, contributed to shaping the final creed and suggested the *ousia* language. Parvis, *Marcellus*, 85ff., argues that Eusebius's creed provided the model for the Nicene formula. Whatever the case, Alexander would have felt vindicated with the insertion of the *homoousios* and the anti-Arian anathemas.

90. Philostorgius, *HE* 1.9a; cf. Kelly, *Creeds*, 252; and Skarsaume, "Neglected Detail," 50.

91. Philostorgius, *HE* 1.9a.

92. *Urk.* 22, 45–46: *homoousios* understood in a spiritual sense; the phrase "of the *ousia*" implying that the Son did not subsist as part of the Father, etc. See also Hanson, *Search*, 165–66; Ayres, *Nicaea*, 90–91; and chapter 7 below for the aftermath of Nicaea.

93. *Urk.* 22, p. 45, l. 13.

94. *Urk.* 31, p. 65, ll. 5f.

95. Theodoret, *HE* 1.7. See also chapter 7 below.

96. *Urk.* 23, p. 48, ll. 1ff.; Socrates, *HE* 1.8; and Sozomen, *HE* 1.21.3.

97. Philostorgius, *HE* 1.9a; and Rufinus, *HE* 10.5.

98. Philostorgius, *HE* 1.9a. See K. Girardet, *Kaisergericht und Bischofsgericht: Studien zu den Anfängen des Donatistenstreites (313–315) und zum Prozess Athanasius von Alexandrien (328–346)* (Bonn, 1975), 58f.; Barnes, *AC*, 21 (*magister officiorum*); Martin, *Athanase*, 349 (*magister officiorum* or *scriniorum*).

99. *Urk.* 23, p. 48, ll. 1ff.; Socrates, *HE* 1.8; Sozomen, *HE* 1.21.3; Theodoret, *HE* 1.7; Philostorgius, *HE* 1.9c; and H. Chadwick, "Faith and Order at the Council of Nicaea: A Note on the Background of the Sixth Canon," *Harvard Theological Review* 53 (1960): 176–78.

100. *Urk.* 23, p. 50, l. 12, and p. 51, ll. 4–6.

101. See Chadwick, "Faith," 175 n. 11; and chapter 7 below.

102. Eusebius, *VC* 4.35. Cf. Kelly, *Creeds*, 250.

103. *Urk.* 17, p. 34, ll. 10–11.
104. Ibid., ll. 3–5.
105. Ibid., ll. 10–11.
106. Ibid., p. 35, ll. 3–6. As Kelly, *Creeds*, 262, put it, "The emperor left it to [churchmen] to read their own meaning into the formula, provided they were ready to attach their names to it." See also Drake, *Constantine*, 298–305, for Constantine's message of religious tolerance.
107. *Urk.* 26, p. 55, ll. 7–9.
108. *Urk.* 30, p. 64.
109. Ayres, *Nicaea*, 84–88, suggests Constantine saw the creed only as a formula designed to put an end to division in the church, but cf. Lim, *Public Disputation*, 185f.; and chapter 7 below.
110. See Hanson, *Search*, 164–65, 172.
111. Rufinus, *HE* 10.5; Sozomen, *HE* 1.21.3–4; Philostorgius, *HE* 1.9–10; and Gelasius, *HE* 1.27.10–12.
112. Letters: *Urk.* 25, 52–54. See Socrates' comment in *HE* 1.9. Cf. *Urk.* 26, 54–57 (on the date of Easter). Force of law: Sozomen, *HE* 1.21.4: νομοθετῶν. See also Eusebius, *VC* 3.23; and Barnes, *CE*, 215 and n. 78.
113. *Urk.* 25, p. 52, ll. 1–6, and p. 53, ll. 9–14.
114. Eusebius, *VC* 3.63–65: Constantine banned "heretical and schismatic" churches. Later, he confirmed immunity from taxation and public service only for clerics of the "Catholic law," excluding "heretics and schismatics"; see *CTh* 16.5.1 and 16.2.10 (emending Constantius and Constans to Constantine). Cf. *CTh* 16.2.7; Rufinus, *HE* 10.5; and Ammianus Marcellinus, *RG* 15.13.2.
115. Jones, *LRE*, 2:934; and Lane Fox, *Pagans*, 624ff.
116. At the end of the council, Constantine spoke as "archbishop": Eusebius, *VC* 3.21. Cf. A.H.M. Jones, *Constantine and the Conversion of Europe* (Toronto, 1978), 103.
117. Bishops: Secundus and Theonas; Eusebius of Caesarea, Narcissus of Neronias, and Theodotus of Laodicea (at Antioch); Eusebius of Nicomedia, Theognis of Nicaea, and, Philostorgius (*HE* 2.1a and 2.1b) adds, Maris of Chalcedon.
118. Kelly, *Creeds*, 250, stresses the "ambiguity" of the *homoousios*, which admitted many different interpretations (on which, see chapter 7 below), but only within a well-defined framework. See also Simonetti, *Crisi*, 89ff.; Hanson, *Search*, chap. 5; Ayres, *Nicaea*, 92–104.
119. See chapter 7 below.
120. Eusebius, *VC* 3.15–16 and 22.
121. Ibid. 3.10 and 3.14; Philostorgius, *HE* 2.1; and Barnes, *CE*, 219.

PART III. DEFINING GOD

1. Rufinus, *HE* 10.5; Photius, *Biblioteca* 256.471b (ed. Henry); Philostorgius, *HE* 1.9 and 2.1b. See also Sciuto, "Da Nicea," 481; and Kelly, *Creeds*, 254.
2. Socrates, *HE* 1.23; Hanson, *Search*, 274f.; Smulders, "Some Riddles," 148; Roulet, *Tolérance*, 120–22. Kelly, *Creeds*, 250, 254; and Ayres, *Nicaea*, 84–88.
3. See Parvis, *Marcellus*, 54; and Gavrilyuk, *Suffering*, 113–34.
4. See *CTh* 16.5.15, 16.7.4.

5. *Urk.* 25, p. 54, l. 4; cf. Sozomen, *HE* 1.25.4.

6. See E. A. Judge, "Christian Innovation and Its Contemporary Observers," in *History and Historians in Late Antiquity,* ed. B. Croke and A. M. Emmett (Sydney, 1983), 28: "The struggle over orthodoxy . . . itself [shifted] the centre of power in the community out of the hands of civil rulers." Cf. F. Paschoud, "L'Église dans l'empire romain: Tendences dans l'église contre et pour l'empire," in *Actes du Congrès de la Federation Internationale des Associations d'Études Classiques* (Budapest, 1984), 2:206.

7. CLAIMING TRUTH, PROJECTING POWER

1. Kelly, *Creeds,* p. 255f., suggested that the Nicene formula was "a definition of orthodox faith for bishops . . . a conciliar . . . creed," not intended to be taught to the faithful, but this seems unlikely. The creed would have informed the way congregations approached God in prayers, rituals, etc. (cf. chapter 4 above). See Athanasius, *De synodis* 30.8 (bishops speaking against *"ousia"* language in 357: τὸ δὲ ὄνομα τῆς οὐσίας . . . ἀγνοούμενον δὲ τοῖς λαοῖς σκάνδαλον ἔφερε, διότι μηδὲ αἱ γραφαὶ τοῦτο περιέχουσιν . . .); Eusebius was forced to explain his subscription to his flock (below), and Gelasius, *HE* 2.26.4, tells us explicitly that one of the reasons for writing a creed was to make it easier for "the simple" to learn the truth about God. See also Severus ibn-al-Moqaffa, *Refutations of Eutychius* (PO 3.162–63); id., *Histoire des conciles* (PO 6.508); and *Syn. Arabe Jacobite,* Nov. 5 (PO 3.270).

2. *Urk.* 22, p. 45, l. 13–p. 46, l. 3. Cf. Hilary, *De synodis* 87–89. See also Hanson, *Search,* 58f.; Chadwick, "Faith," 173; and Ayres, *Nicaea,* 90ff. Criticism of Eusebius: Theodoret, *HE* 4.7 (*NPNF,* vol. 3, p. 112).

3. *Urk.* 27, p. 62, l. 4.

4. Faction: George (of Alexandria), Stephen, Eudoxius, Eustathius the Armenian, joined by the eunuch Leontius (see chapter 5). Eustathius's reaction: Athanasius, *HA* 4, 28; id., *Ep. ad episc. Aeg.* 7; and id., *De fuga* 26.

5. *Urk.* 27, p. 59, ll. 20–21; and Sozomen, *HE* 2.21.6.

6. Maris: Philostorgius, *HE* 2.1b; Agapius, *HU* (PO 7.550). Theodotus: *Urk.* 28.

7. Support for Arius's views: *Urk.* 27, 60–61; and discussion below. Unrest: *Urk.* 27, p. 61, l. 2 (Constantine's testimony); and Sozomen, *HE* 2.21.6 (Bithynia and the Hellespont).

8. Sozomen, *HE* 2.21.7; cf. Philostorgius, *HE* 2.1a and 2.1b.

9. *Urk.* 27, p. 62, ll. 5–6.

10. Ibid., ll. 1–6.

11. *Urk.* 28.

12. Kopecek, *History,* 68 n. 2, with reference to Aetius's and other Arians' displeasure with Arius and his allies, who dissembled their views to achieve reconciliation. See also Theodoret, *HE* 2.19 (on Leontius's dissimulation); and discussion below.

13. Constantine's movements: T. D. Barnes, *The New Empire of Diocletian and Constantine* (Cambridge, 1982), 77.

14. See Simonetti, *Crisi,* 100ff.; Hanson, *Search,* chap. 7; and Ayres, *Nicaea,* 92–165. Mutual accusations: Socrates, *HE* 1.23.

15. Socrates, *HE* 1.23. Cf. Sozomen, *HE* 2.18.3–4, 2.19.1; Simonetti, *Crisi,* 101–5; Barnes, *CE,* 227; and Parvis, *Marcellus,* 97–101.

16. *De anima contra ariomanitas* (= Fragment 6 [*CCSG* 51, p. 67]); *On Proverbs* 8.22 (= Fragments 18–32, ed. M. Spanneut, *Recherches sur les écrits d'Eustathe d'Antioche avec une édition nouvelle des fragments dogmatiques et exégétiques* [Lille, 1948], 69f., [dated 327–328]); the *Orations against the Arians*, Fragments 39–58; and *On Faith against the Arians* (= Fragments 59–63, ed. Spanneut, pp. 71–75).

17. Theodoret, *HE* 1.7 (Eustathius, Fragment 32, ed. Spanneut).

18. Eusebius, *Contra Marcellum* 1.4.42, quotes Marcellus saying that ἐξ ἀκοῆς μεμαθηκέναι τὸν Εὐσέβιον ὡμιληκέναι τινὰ ἐν Λαοδικείᾳ (probably post-Nicaea). Support for Eusebius: Sozomen, *HE* 2.19.1. See also Simonetti, *Crisi*, 104 n. 15.

19. Socrates, *HE* 1.23; Sozomen, *HE* 2.18.4 and 2.19.1 (quote).

20. Sozomen, *HE* 2.20.3.

21. Division: chapter 5 above. Succession: Sozomen, *HE* 2.20.1–3. Holy Sepulcher: Eusebius, *VC* 3.30–32.

22. Sozomen, *HE* 2.18.4.

23. Ibid. Eustathius took the *homoousios* to signify "one divine reality" (*hypostasis*), implying full equality between Son and Father (Hanson, *Search*, 214–16; Ayres, *Nicaea*, 69; and Parvis, *Marcellus*, 57–60).

24. The date of this council is a vexed question. Eustathius would have been deposed before Asclepas (Athanasius, *HA* 5.1), and the letter of the Eastern bishops at Serdica in 343 states that Asclepas was deposed "seventeen years" earlier—that is, in 327/328, counting inclusively. H. Chadwick, "The Fall of Eustathius of Antioch," *JTS* 49 (1948): 27–35, suggests 326, but he misdates Serdica. Schwartz, *GS*, 3:216; Simonetti, *Crisi*, 107, and Parvis, *Marcellus*, 100–107, prefer 327, and I think they are right. Cf. Barnes, *CE*, 228; id., *AC*, 17; Martin, *Athanase*, 341 n. 2; and Burgess, *Studies*, 194–96.

25. The main addressees of Constantine's letter to the synod were pro-Arian; see Eusebius, *VC* 3.62.1; and cf. *EOMIA* 2.2, p. 231. Charges: other charges were added; see Simonetti, *Crisi*, 106; Parvis, *Marcellus*, 101. Quote: Sozomen, *HE* 2.19.1.

26. Eulalius: Theodoret, *HE* 1.21; and Gelasius, *HE* 3.16.21, even though the local clergy and faithful asked for Eusebius's transfer to Antioch (Sozomen, *HE* 2.19.3; Burgess, *Studies*, 195; and below). Eulalius's death: three months later (Burgess, *Studies*, 195), in the winter of 328, assuming Eustathius was removed in the fall of 327. Parvis, *Marcellus*, 107–8, suggests that Paulinus of Tyre was recognized as bishop for six months before Eulalius was elected, but see chapter 5 above. Because Eustathius resisted deposition and his accusers tried to have Constantine endorse it (Theodoret, *HE* 1.20), the council may have remained in session for several weeks waiting for the emperor's approval (cf. Sozomen, *HE* 2.19.3). Perhaps the same council elected Euphronius in early 328. Euphronius: Eusebius, *VC* 3.62.1–3; Sozomen, *HE* 2.29.6; and Simonetti, *Crisi*, 108.

27. Theodoret, *HE* 1.20; Sozomen, *HE* 2.19.2. John Chrysostom, *In sanctum Eustathium* 4 (*PG* 48.604).

28. Socrates, *HE* 1.24.6.

29. Eusebius, *VC* 3.59.1–2. Cf. Socrates, *HE* 1.24; and Sozomen, *HE* 2.19.2. Non-Christians may have rioted, too. Canon 2 of the Council of Antioch of 328 (*EOMIA* 2.2, pp. 238–40) speaks of those who came to church to listen to readings but did not pray—were they pagan?

30. Agapius, *HU* (*PO* 7.552).

31. Sozomen, *HE* 2.19.2; cf. Eusebius, *VC* 3.59.2.

32. Eusebius, *VC* 3.59.3: "[Constantine] himself listened to the author of the sedition." Cf. Sozomen, *HE* 2.19.2; and Theodoret, *HE* 1.20. See also Athanasius, *HA* 4 (quote); Jerome, *De vir. ill.* 85; and Philostorgius, *HE* 3.18.

33. Theodoret, *HE* 1.21; Gelasius, *HE* 3.16.23, but Sozomen, *HE* 2.32.1 and Theodoret, *Ep.* 112.10 (*SC* 11), suggest that, in Antioch, "Eustathian" and "Arian" celebrated communion together until the time of Euzoius, though, *pace* Philostorgius, *HE* 3.14, not the Eucharist. Private house: Sozomen, *HE* 3.20; *Chronica minora* 3, p. 216 ("Arians" obtained all churches, except for a "tiny one," which the priest Paulinus held on to). Paulinus managed to escape the purge and later became the "Eustathian" bishop of Antioch (Jerome, *Chronicle* [*PL* 27.503–4]).

34. Eusebius, *VC* 3.60.1–9 (quote: 3.60.5); Socrates, *HE* 1.24; and Sozomen, *HE* 2.19.3–6. For Constantine's involvement, see also Eusebius, *VC* 3.62.1–3; Sozomen, *HE* 2.19.6; Theodoret, *HE* 1.21; Gelasius, *HE* 3.16.21–23. Socrates leaves it unclear whether this took place immediately after Eustathius's deposition or, later, following Eulalius's death.

35. *Conc. Nic.* I, canon 6 (Joannou, *Discipline*, 28–29).

36. Athanasius, *HA* 4; and id., *Ep. ad episc. Aeg.* 7, referring to Leontius (ordained priest) and Stephen (reinstated to the priesthood). See also Philostorgius, *HE* 3.15.

37. That the signatories of the canons (*EOMIA* 2.2, pp. 231 and 313) match the addressees of Constantine's letter to the council electing Euphronius (Eusebius, *VC* 3.62.1) suggests that the synod issuing the canons and the council electing Euphronius were the same; the exceptions to that list are Eusebius of Caesarea (on which, see below) and Aetherius (only in *EOMIA*), which according to Parvis, *Marcellus*, 109, 257, is perhaps a *corruptella* for Aetius (in *VC*). Strengthening prelates: canons 9, 11, 14, and 19 (*EOMIA* 2.2, pp. 256, 266, etc.); Schwartz, *GS*, 3:216–30; and Parvis, *Marcellus*, 109. Eustathians and private assemblies: canons 2 and 5 (*EOMIA* 2.2, pp. 240–42 and 248–50).

38. This is borne out by the figures Parvis presented in *Marcellus*, 220–21.

39. Above, chapter 5.

40. On Patricius and Theodosius, see *EOMIA* 2.2, pp. 231, 313 (Latin lists); Athanasius, *HA* 4; id., *De fuga* 3; Le Quien, *OC*, vol. 3, col. 799; Schwartz, *GS*, 3:221; and Parvis, *Marcellus*, 257.

41. In early 328. The letter of the Western bishops at Serdica in 343 notes that Asclepas "brought forth the Acts redacted at Antioch in the presence of his enemies and Eusebius of Caesarea and proved that he was innocent by the sentence of the bishops who judged him" (Athanasius, *ACA* 47; Hilary, *FH B* 2.1.6 [*CSEL* 65, p. 118]). This passage suggests that Asclepas was charged—with heresy, *pace* Theodoret, *HE* 1.27, or for overturning an altar in Sozomen, *HE* 3.8—and defended himself at a synod probably assembled at Antioch. The council electing Euphronius in early 328 provides the best possible context for these events, because Asclepas's "enemies"—that is, those who charged him—would have been present, including Eusebius of Caesarea. Banned: Athanasius, *De fuga* 3.

42. Socrates, *HE* 1.24; Athanasius, *HA* 5; and id., *De fuga* 3.

43. Eustathius, *De Engastromytho* (*apud* Le Quien, *OC*, vol. 1, col. 1171); Parvis, *Marcellus*, 57; Eusebius's critic: Athanasius, *HA* 5. Date: ante-332, given Basilina's role in his deposition. Domnus of Sirmium: Athanasius, *HA* 5; Hanson, *Search*, 156.

44. Athanasius, *HA* 4. George had replaced Theodotus as bishop of Laodicea by the time of Tyre (Athanasius, *ACA* 8.3). See also M. DelCogliano, "George of Laodicea:

A Historical Reassessment," *JEH* 62 (2011): 667–92. Eudoxius was bishop at the Dedication Council in 341 but was probably appointed not long after Eustathius's deposition, given that his predecessor would have been of advanced age (see Le Quien, *OC,* vol. 2, col. 939).

45. Eustathius: Athanasius, *HA* 4. Arius's disciple: Basil, *Epp.* 263 and 244 (cf. Sozomen, *HE* 4.24; and Socrates, *HE* 2.43). Eustathius's ordination: during Hermogenes of Caesarea's episcopate, possibly before 335 and certainly by 341, when Dianius appears as bishop of Caesarea (Le Quien, *OC,* vol. 2, col. 372). Eusebius, *VC* 4.43.4, mentions "the leading Cappadocians" as participants of the councils of Tyre and Jerusalem, a compliment more likely to be paid to the Eusebian-friendly Dianius than to the Nicene Hermogenes. Eustathius's asceticism: Socrates, *HE* 2.43; Elm, *Virgins,* 106–13, 121–33; P. M. Beagon, "The Cappadocian Fathers, Women, and Ecclesiastical Politics," *Vigiliae Christianae* 49 (1995): 168–70, 165–79; and D. F. Stramara, Jr., "Double Monasticism in the Greek East, Fourth through Eighth Centuries," *Journal of Early Christian Studies* 6 (1998): 278–80. Theodorus: Athanasius, *Ep. ad episc. Aeg.* 7 (before 335; attended Tyre in 335; see Parvis, *Marcellus,* 258); Athanasius, *HA* 17; Jerome, *De vir. ill.* 90; and chapter 8 below.

46. Cizycus: Le Quien, *OC,* vol. 1, col. 749. Date: *sub Constantino,* see the *Vita S. Parthenii (AASS,* February 7), with P. Batiffol, "Étude d'hagiographie arienne: Parthénius de Lampsaque," *Römische Quartalschrifte für die christliche Altertumskunde und Kirchengeschichte* 6 (1892): 38–51. On the date, see Batiffol, 42f.: Ascholius ordained Parthenius, who approached "Constantine" (Batiffol would emend this to Constantius, but that does not seem necessary). See also P. Batiffol, "Saint Parthénius et les nouveaux Bollandistes," *Römische Quartalschrifte für die christliche Altertumskunde und Kirchengeschichte* 7 (1893): 298–301.

47. Athanasius, *HA* 5; id., *De fuga* 3.

48. Constantine's letters to Eusebius and to the bishops at Antioch show admiration and respect for Eusebius (*VC* 3.61–62). See also chapter 6 on Constantine's treatment of Eusebius at Nicaea; cf. his letters praising Eusebius's scholarship and recruiting him to lead the project of making copies of scripture (ibid. 4.35–36). See also Barnes, *CE,* 267, with Cameron, *Eusebius,* 327. Women: Athanasius, *HA* 6.

49. Athanasius, *HA* 5–6. Constantia may also have embraced Arian doctrine, taught by Eusebius of Nicomedia or pro-Arian priests in the capital (see Rufinus, *HE* 10.12). Letters: Mansi, *ACO* 13.313.

50. Chronology: see the appendix ("The Recall of Arius and the Bithynian Bishops"); and Theodoret, *HE* 1.20 (Eusebius's possible role in Eustathius's deposition).

51. Eusebius, *Contra Marcellum* 1.4.38; Socrates, *HE* 1.36 and 2.23; and Sozomen, *HE* 2.33.4. *Ep. Or. Sardic.* 9 (*CSEL* 65, p. 55): riots when Marcellus was restored in 337.

52. Asterius's treatise is cited in Marcellus's own *Against Asterius, apud* Eusebius, *Contra Marcellum.* Parvis, *Marcellus,* 100–116, suggests Asterius published it just after Eusebius's return from exile. On Marcellus, *Against Asterius:* Parvis, *Marcellus,* 99, 113, and 116–23 (quote on p. 122), dating it to 329–330.

53. Jerome, *De vir. ill.* 86 (Asterius), 89 (Basil). Eusebius's *Contra Marcellum* was written for the emperor (Parvis, *Marcellus,* 129–31).

54. Parvis, *Marcellus,* 99 (date) and 116 (quote: Fragment Re 59 Kl 65 S/V 1 P1).

55. See the appendix ("The Recall of Arius and the Bithynian Bishops").

56. See Simonetti, *Crisi,* 32–33, 123; Sciuto, "Da Nicea," 487; Drake, *Constantine,* 259f. Cf. Rufinus, *HE* 10.12 (on Constantia's role in the recall); Socrates, *HE* 1.25; Sozomen, *HE*

2.27.1-6 (placing it in 335); Theodoret, *HE* 2.2; Gelasius, *HE* 3.12.1-10; Jerome, *Ep.* 133.4.18-19. See also Ferguson, *Past*, 96-97; and M. Amerise, *Il battesimo di Costantino il Grande: Storia di una scomoda eredità*, Hermes Einzelschriften 95 (Stuttgart, 2005), 50-63.

57. *Urk.* 29.

58. Barnes, *New Empire*, 77.

59. *Urk.* 30. Cf. Socrates, *HE* 2.35; and Sozomen, *HE* 4.12. Simonetti, *Crisi*, 116-18, suggests that Arius distinguished generation before time from generation *ab aeterno*, but Arius may have made adjustments to his theology. See also Barnes, *CE*, 229; Williams, *Arius*, 278f.; Drake, *Constantine*, 259f.; and Parvis, *Marcellus*, 116, 171. Place and date: see the appendix ("The Recall of Arius and the Bithynian Bishops").

60. Rehabilitated by a provincial council? See Rufinus, *HE* 10.12; and Parvis, *Marcellus*, 107. Cf. Simonetti, *Crisi*, 119-20; Hanson, *Search*, 177f.; and Martin, *Athanase*, 348 and 387-89 (only at the Council of Jerusalem in 335). Sent to Alexandria: Socrates, *HE* 1.14, and Sozomen, *HE* 2.16.1, deny it, perhaps to whitewash Constantine's image as a restorer of heretics. Cf. Gelasius, *HE* 3.13.15-19; and the "Vita Metrophanis et Alexandri" (*BHG* 1279) (ed. Winkelmann).

61. *Urk.* 31; and the interesting evidence from the ninth-century George Hamartolus, *Chronicon* 412 (*PG* 110.621). See Simonetti, *Crisi*, 119-23, revising Schwartz's chronology. Barnes, *CE*, 229, and Parvis, *Marcellus*, 100-107, place the recall of Arius and the Bithynians after Eustathius's fall, but see the appendix ("The Recall of Arius and the Bithynian Bishops").

62. Socrates, *HE* 1.14; Sozomen, *HE* 2.16.1-7; and Gelasius, *HE* 3.13.6-9. See also Kelly, *Creeds*, 262; Simonetti, *Crisi*, 119-23; Barnes, *CE*, 229; id., *AC*, 17-18; Hanson, *Search*, 175-78; and the appendix ("The Recall of Arius and the Bithynian Bishops").

63. On Egypt post-Nicaea, see Schwartz, *GS*, 3:212-15; discussion below; and the appendix ("The Arian Community of Alexandria after Nicaea").

64. *Urk.* 23, p. 48, l. 14-p. 50; Sozomen, *HE* 1.24.1-3; H. Hauben, "La réordination du clergé mélitien imposée par le Concile de Nicée," *Ancient Society* 18 (1987): 203-7; A. Martin, "Les conditions de la réadmission du clérge mélitien par le Concile de Nicée," *Ancient Society* 20 (1989): 281-90; and id., *Athanase*, 313-17.

65. After the council, Melitius made peace with Alexander; see Athanasius, *ACA* 71-72. See also ibid. 11, 59; Sozomen, *HE* 2.21.1; Martin, *Athanase*, 260, 312-15; D. W.-H. Arnold, *The Early Episcopal Career of Athanasius of Alexandria* (Notre Dame, IN, 1991), 56-60 (and others cited in n. 239); and H. Hauben, "Heraiscus as a Melitian Bishop of Heracleopolis Magna and the Alexandrian See," *Journal of Juristic Papyrology* 34 (2004): 65.

66. Sozomen, *HE* 2.21.2-3; and Martin, *Athanase*, 260, 313-15, 347 (Melitians deprived of autonomy).

67. Epiphanius, *Panarion* 68.4.1; Martin, *Athanase*, 315-17. See also Sozomen, *HE* 2.21.2, and Epiphanius, *Panarion* 68.5.3, on the appointment of John Arkaph as Melitius's successor, apparently without Alexander's approval. Date of Melitius's death: John Arkaph was in Constantinople in the spring and summer of 327; see the appendix ("The Recall of Arius and the Bithynian Bishops").

68. Epiphanius, *Panarion* 68.5.1 (after Melitius's death).

69. Sozomen, *HE* 2.21.3-4.

70. Martin, *Athanase*, 347.

71. Sozomen, *HE* 2.21.5. Cf. Athanasius, *HA* 78 (the Melitians' "ignorance" made it easy for them to accept Arian views.). Notice that, later, Gregory and George of Alexandria were interchangeably called Melitian and Arian (Epiphanius, *Panarion* 69.2 and 76.1).

72. Epiphanius, *Panarion* 68.6.6; Sozomen, *HE* 2.21.4–5.

73. Theodoret, *HE* 1.13; Gelasius, *HE* 3.13.19 (quote); Photius, *Bibliotheca* 472a. Cf. Rufinus, *HE* 10.12 (combining events of 327 and 335?).

74. Gelasius, *HE* 3.13.21, is the only source to report that Alexander (and Athanasius) wrote to Constantine to explain his refusal to receive the priest. However, Gelasius seems to conflate different moments in an exchange of correspondence between the emperor and Alexander/Athanasius. See the appendix ("The Recall of Arius and the Bithynian Bishops").

75. Gelasius, *HE* 3.13.20; and the appendix ("The Recall of Arius and the Bithynian Bishops"). Theodoret, *HE* 1.13, and Photius, *Bibliotheca* 473a (drawing on *Vita Metrophanis et Alexandri*, which in turn drew on Gelasius of Caesarea), claim that Arius raised a commotion and disseminated his heresy. It is unlikely, however, that Arius would have been interested in causing a disturbance now, immediately after his first return, when he counted on the support of a sympathetic emperor and several Melitians. Cf. Epiphanius, *Panarion* 69.12; and Socrates, *HE* 1.27 (unrest during Athanasius's episcopate).

76. Esteemed Arius: *Urk.* 31, p. 65, ll. 7–10.

77. Gelasius, *HE* 3.14.1 (= Athanasius, *ACA* 59) and 3.15.1–5 (= *Urk.* 32). Socrates, *HE* 1.27, rightly places the letter to Athanasius after Alexander's death. See the appendix ("The Recall of Arius and the Bithynian Bishops").

78. *Urk.* 32. Severus ibn-al-Moqaffa, *Histoire des conciles* (*PO* 6.499), reports the same story, substituting Constantius for Constantine.

79. Melitians' reputation: Epiphanius, *Panarion* 68.6; Martin, *Athanase*, 347.

80. Athanasius, *ACA* 11; Epiphanius, *Panarion* 68.5–66.6.1–6; Socrates, *HE* 1.27 (Socrates leaves out the Melitians' accusations against Alexander); and Martin, *Athanase*, 314–15, 344 (quote). Barnes, *AC*, 20f., places these events in the summer of 330, ignoring that the Melitians first accused Alexander to the emperor. See also the appendix ("The Recall of Arius and the Bithynian Bishops").

81. Epiphanius, *Panarion* 68.6, noting that the Melitians accepted Eusebius's offer, because "Arius had recanted . . . though falsely."

82. Epiphanius, *Panarion* 68.5–6; Martin, *Athanase*, 317.

83. Epiphanius, *Panarion* 68.6, and Sozomen, *HE* 2.21.5, report that many (but not all) Melitians received Arius and his followers. Quote: Photius, *Bibliotheca* 473a. Chronology: see the appendix ("The Recall of Arius and the Bithynian Bishops").

84. To judge from Athanasius's (later) complaints: Sozomen, *HE* 2.22.3; and discussion below.

85. Eusebius, *VC* 3.23 (ed. Cameron, p. 131).

86. Implied in Theodoret, *HE* 1.13, and possibly in Rufinus, *HE* 10.12. Cf. Gelasius, *HE* 3.13.19 (μύσος), and Photius, *Bibliotheca* 473a, drawing on Gelasius of Caesarea and/or the *Vita Metrophanis et Alexandri* (*BHG* 1279). Cf. Mohammad al-Birouni, *Les fêtes des Melchites* (*PO* 10.300): an echo of the struggle between Alexander and the Arians over churches?

87. Cf. Eutychius, *Annals* 11.9 (ed. Pirone, pp. 194f.), on Alexander's seizure of the temple of Saturn.

88. See, for instance, MacMullen, *Second Church*, 22–29, 65–67, and 104–8. Churches were also places where bishops held court audiences; see N. Lenski, "Evidence for the *Audientia episcopalis* in the New Letters of Augustine," in *Law, Society, and Authority in Late Antiquity*, ed. R. W. Mathisen (Oxford, 2001), 83–97.

89. Eusebius, *VC* 2.46.

90. Control of church buildings was perceived as evidence of orthodoxy; see Athanasius, *Ep. enc.* 6.2–3.

91. Eusebius, *VC* 3.23. Nicomedia: Barnes, *AC*, 17f.; and Philostorgius, *HE* 2.7 and 2.7a (if this was the same council mentioned in Eusebius). Chronology: the appendix ("The Recall of Arius and the Bithynian Bishops").

92. Eusebius, *VC* 3.23.

93. Ibid.; and Barnes, *AC*, 18.

94. The silence of our sources on this synod suggests an unfavorable outcome for the bishop. If Athanasius's comment that "the Melitians were quiet for five months, during which time Alexander died" (*ACA* 59.2–3) refers to a time after this council, the "quiet" would also suggest that Alexander and the Melitians agreed on a truce. The joint effort of Catholics and Melitians to find a successor to Alexander after his death, and a reference to an oath jointly sworn by the two parties not to ordain a bishop until they had addressed their mutual grievances, also suggest a compromise (Sozomen, *HE* 2.17.4 and 2.25.6).

95. Cf. Schwartz, *GS*, 3:207f.; and Barnes, *AC*, 18. Athanasius's trip to court in late winter or early spring of 328 (Epiphanius, *Panarion* 68.7.2–3 and 69.11.4), if not to attend the synod, may have been connected to Alexander's refusal to receive Arius, perhaps, as Barnes speculated, to explain to the emperor why he continued to reject the priest.

96. At a certain point, Arius moved to Libya (*Urk.* 34, p. 71, l. 28–p. 72, ll. 1f.), but Constantine's testimony in *Urk.* 34,, dated to 333, suggests that until close to that date Arius had remained in Alexandria; see below. Cf. Theodoret, *HE* 1.13; Schwartz, *GS*, 3:240–42; and Barnes, *AC*, 21.

97. By assuming a human form, the Logos had sanctified human flesh and saved humanity. To Athanasius, by depriving the Son of the Father's divine attributes and making him foreign to the essence of the Father, the Arians threatened to annul the cosmic effects of Christ's incarnation. See *Or. contra Arianos* 2.20.56; Gregg and Groh, *Early Arianism*, 48–70.

98. Epiphanius's reports on the election of a Melitian Theonas or of two rival bishops, Theonas and Achillas (*Panarion*, 68.7 and 69.11, respectively), are not very credible, though perhaps indicative of how disputed the election was; see Hauben, "Heraiscus," 54–58; and Martin, *Athanase*, 323–31.

99. Two "Arianizing" accounts of Athanasius's election survive, one in Sozomen, *HE* 2.17.4 and 2.25.6 (already circulating in the 330s, see Athanasius, *ACA* 6); the other in Philostorgius, *HE* 2.11 (cf. *ApPatr* 78 [*PG* 65.341b]; and the *Letter of Ammon* 13 [ed. Goehring]). Athanasius, *ACA* 6, preserves the pro-Athanasian version, composed ten years later to counter charges of an irregular election (on these charges, see Sozomen, *HE* 2.25.7). All three accounts present the election as the work of Athanasian partisans or thugs (or both). Cf. Gregory Nazianzenus's attempt "to sanitize" Athanasius's record: "[Athanasius] was elected by the vote of all the faithful, not . . . by means of *bloodshed* and *tyranny*" (*Or.* 21.8). See also Hanson, *Search*, 247–49; Arnold, *Early Episcopal Career*, 24–63; Barnes, *AC*, 18; and Martin, *Athanase*, 321–39 and 348–89.

100. In Coptic, Arabic, and Ethiopian sources, possibly drawing on the archives of the church of Alexandria: Eutychius, *Annals* 8 (*PO* 1.411); *Storia della chiesa di Alessandria: Da Pietro ad Atanasio*, ed. T. Orlandi, Testi e Documenti per lo studio dell'antichità 17 (Milan, 1967), 58; *Le livre du Synaxaire*, August 25 (*PO* 9.351: "Abba Athanase a renouvelé la proclamation d'excommunication d'Arius"). See A. Camplani, "L'autorappresentazione del'episcopato alessandrino tra IV e V secolo: Questioni di metodo," *Annali della Storia dell'Esegesi* 21 (2004): 150f.

101. Inferred from Constantine's letter to Athanasius in *ACA* 59.6. See also *Urk.* 34, p. 70, ll. 10f. (Arius's later complaints to Constantine); and Sozomen, *HE* 2.18.2 and 2.22.4.

102. On Arian Christians in Alexandria, see discussion below and the appendix ("The Arian Community of Alexandria after Nicaea"). Quote: Athanasius, *Or. contra Arianos* 1.10.36, dated to 340? (Barnes, *AC*, 53f.), but the sentiments would have been the same earlier.

103. Sozomen, *HE* 2.22.1; Theodoret, *HE* 1.13. Cf. Athanasius, *ACA* 59.6 (Constantine's letter to Athanasius).

104. Athanasius's election pushed many Melitians back into schism—for instance, Callinicos of Pelusium had reconciled with Alexander but became one of Athanasius's fiercest critics—see Sozomen, *HE* 2.25.4; Martin, *Athanase*, 317 n. 33; and Girardet, *Kaisergericht*, 54f. Athanasius (*ACA* 63, 72, and 77) claims that the Melitians were never active in the Mareotis, but see Epiphanius, *Panarion* 68.7.5–6 and 69.11. To judge from the activities of Ischyras, who "was trying to lead the villagers astray," the Melitians were probably doing the same (*ACA* 12, 76; cf. *ACA* 11). In fact, Ischyras may have communicated with the Melitians, who, later, recognized him as priest, made him bishop, and used him to charge Athanasius (*ACA* 16, 63, 74, 85). The idea that Ischyras was ordained by Kolluthus may well have been contrived to justify Athanasius's closure of his church.

105. Epiphanius, *Panarion* 68.7.5–6; Gelasius, *HE* 3.15.18 (Ἀθανάσιος ... καταλαβὼν τὸν Μαρεώτην, τὰς ἐκεῖσε ἐκκλησίας ἐπεσκέπτετο), independent of Socrates, Theodoret, or Sozomen; and Athanasius, *ACA* 85.

106. Before Nicaea, there were at least nineteen (Catholic) priests in the Mareotis (*Urk.* 4b, p. 11, ll. 13–24), each one, I suppose, in charge of a parish church. Athanasius (or Alexander after Nicaea) reduced their number to ten, concentrating priestly power and strengthening loyal priests (*ACA* 85, 63). See also, Martin, *Athanase*, 113 n. 267.

107. Athanasius, *ACA* 74.6. Cf. *ACA* 17: "*All* [of them] accompany him in his visitations [to the district]"; and Epiphanius, *Panarion* 68.7.

108. Epiphanius, *Panarion* 68.7, from a partisan source, but credible.

109. Prelates were often suspicious of Christians assembling outside their purview, but in a divided church, these gatherings appeared even more dangerous as potential breeding grounds for dissent and opposition. On the tension between public and private worship, see Bowes, *Private Worship*, 48–60, 189–200.

110. Athanasius, *ACA* 85 (see also Martin, *Athanase*, 350 n. 330). We know of at least one other private church-cum-*xenodochium* in the Mareotis in the early fourth century, owned by a wealthy Christian family; see "Passion of S. Shenoufe and His Brethren," in Reymond and Barns, *Four Martyrdoms*, 189 (rendering "Empaiat" as Mareotis).

111. Barnes, *AC*, 21.

112. Athanasius, *ACA* 63–64; cf. 37, 83; and Socrates, *HE* 1.27.

113. Athanasius, *ACA* 11–12, 28, 74, 83. In some versions, Athanasius himself was accused of these deeds: ibid. 68 ("lawless violence," "heinous crime"). We owe these accounts to Athanasius's reporting on what his enemies said, so the account is not strictly speaking Ischyras's version.

114. Book burning: *ACA* 37, 83. Church demolished: *Ep. Or. Sardic.* 6 (*CSEL* 65, p. 53). Athanasius and his followers later accused the Melitians and Eusebius of fabricating the story to incriminate him.

115. Date: *Index* 2. Barnes, *AC*, 21, suggests that he retired to chill out in the Thebaid, but the trip was probably prompted by Melitian advances in Egypt and perhaps new "uncanonical" ordinations such as those of Arsenius and, possibly, Heraiscus of Heracleopolis. See *Vita Pachomii* 30 (ed. Athanassakis, p. 41); Brakke, *Athanasius*, 117–20; and Martin's comments in *Histoire*, 282 n. 9.

116. Sozomen, *HE* 2.22.2.

117. Epiphanius, *Panarion* 69.11 and 68.7. Cf. Griggs, *Early Egyptian Christianity*, 140: "The first years of Athanasius' episcopacy seem relatively calm" (!).

118. Athanasius, *ACA* 63, calls Arsenius "some bishop." Arsenius described himself as ἐπίσκοπος [τῶν ποτε ὑπὸ Μελίτιον] (*ACA* 69), but the phrase may have been interpolated (see Martin, *Athanase*, 354 n. 51). Schwartz, *GS*, 3:197f., suggests Arsenius did not reconcile with Alexander after Nicaea, but it is also possible that he had recently been ordained, probably after Athanasius's election. See the appendix ("Athanasius and Arsenius of Hypsele").

119. Sozomen, *HE* 2.25.12; and Martin, *Athanase*, 36–40, 50, 305, and, for lists and maps of Melitian bishoprics, 308–11.

120. Sozomen, *HE* 2.25.12. That the Melitians used Arsenius's "disappearance" to charge Athanasius with murder does not mean he did not suffer violence (see below). See Martin, *Athanase*, 353; and the appendix ("Athanasius and Arsenius of Hypsele").

121. Athanasius, *ACA* 14.3, though this may refer to a later time.

122. Local and imperial authorities generally did not interfere in "intracommunal" quarrels, but charges would presumably have been pressed against Athanasius and his bishops, and the clashes between Catholics and Melitians would have disrupted peace; cf. Libanius, *Autobiography* 25. Intracommunal quarrels: Acts 18:13–17. Authorities "turning a blind eye" to corruption: Libanius, *Or.* 47.6 (ὁρώντων καὶ οὐχ ὁρώντων). Collusion: MacMullen, *Corruption*, 146–48; and C. Kelly, "Empire Building," in *Late Antiquity: A Guide to the Postclassical World*, ed. G. W. Bowersock, P. Brown, and O. Grabar (Cambridge, 1999), 176–77.

123. As in, for example, Athanasius, *HA* 58–60.

124. Athanasius, *ACA* 59; Socrates, *HE* 1.23 and 1.27; Sozomen, *HE* 2.18.2. Eusebius wrote to Athanasius as soon as it became clear that he would not admit Arius—late 328 and 329?

125. Date: Barnes, *New Empire*, 78.

126. Athanasius, *ACA* 59.6; Socrates, *HE* 1.27; Sozomen, *HE* 2.22.4–5; and the appendix ("The Recall of Arius and the Bithynian Bishops"). Martin, *Athanase*, 346, referring to the Melitians, but this is unlikely, given Athanasius's reply to the emperor.

127. Athanasius, *ACA* 60.1; cf. Sozomen, *HE* 2.22.6.

128. Athanasius, *ACA* 60.1 (γράφων ἔπειθον). Socrates, *HE* 1.27, follows Athanasius but does not say the emperor was convinced, and Athanasius does not provide evidence of that either, which we would have expected, given the apologetic nature of his narrative and the

care he took to cite imperial letters that portrayed him as a victim of his enemies' machinations. Investigating Arius: Constantine's correspondence with Arius, debating theological questions, may have conceivably begun here, in mid- to late 330; see discussion below.

129. Generally, on Eusebians and Melitians: Athanasius, *ACA* 59–60; Socrates, *HE* 1.27, telescoping events; and Sozomen, *HE* 2.22.6–7, providing more details.

130. John's embassy: only in Sozomen, *HE* 2.22.2; see the appendix ("Events Involving Athanasius from Spring 330 to Winter 332").

131. Sozomen, *HE* 2.22.3; and the appendix ("Events Involving Athanasius from Spring 330 to Winter 332"). Athanasius may have sent Apis and Macarius on the heels of John to carry his letter accusing the Melitians; see Sozomen, *HE* 2.22.7; and Athanasius, *ACA* 60.3.

132. The Melitians accused Athanasius of imposing a levy of linen tunics, committing crimes in the Thebaid, and rising to the episcopate by means of perjury and before attaining the canonical age of thirty. See Athanasius, *ACA* 60; id., *Festal* 4 (ed. Parker); *Index* 3; Socrates, *HE* 1.27; Sozomen, *HE* 2.22.6–7; Gelasius, *HE* 3.15.17; Hanson, *Search*, 255–59; Arnold, *Early Episcopal Career*, 104–12; Barnes, *AC*, 21; Martin, *Athanase*, 348ff.; and cf. Girardet, *Kaisergericht*, 60f. Athanasius, *ACA* 60.3, writes that his priests convinced Constantine to dismiss all charges, which is unlikely, given the summons.

133. Chronology: see the appendix ("Events Involving Athanasius from Spring 330 to Winter 332").

134. Sacrilege, for breaking the sacred chalice in Ischyras's church, and treason, for allegedly sending gold to Philomenos, probably the master of offices recently accused of plotting against the emperor. See Athanasius, *ACA* 60.4; Socrates, *HE* 1.27; Sozomen, *HE* 2.22.8; Theodoret, *HE* 1.25; and Barnes, *AC*, 21. Philomenos: see chapter 6; and H. G. Opitz, *Athanasius Werke*, vol. 2.1 (Berlin, 1940), p. 141 n. ad loc. Eusebius of Nicomedia had also been suspected of treason in 325; see *Urk.* 27, p. 60, ll. 8–13.

135. Athanasius must have sought the help of Ablabius, praetorian prefect of the East, because he arranged for the delivery of the bishop's paschal letter from Nicomedia to Egypt. See Athanasius, *Festal* 4 (ed. Parker); *PLRE* 1.3; and Barnes, *CE*, 252. Did Athanasius also approach Philomenos before he fell from grace? Cf. Girardet, *Kaisergericht*, 58f.; Barnes, *CE*, 59; and id., *AC*, 247 n. 4 (Philomenos may have been a *suffragator* for Donatus in 317). Barhadbesabba Arbaia, *Historia* (*PO* 23.212), remarked that Eusebius owed his influence in court "to the gold he [and his allies also] gave to the powerful."

136. Athanasius, *ACA* 60–61; id., *Festal* 4 (ed. Parker); Barnes, *AC*, 2. Cf. Ammianus Marcellinus, *RG* 15.5.13: a prefect, condemned by the emperor for complicity in a case of forgery incriminating Silvanus, "absolutus est enixa conspiratione multorum."

137. Athanasius, *ACA* 61–62, 65; *Index* 3; Socrates, *HE* 1.27; Sozomen, *HE* 2.22.8; Barnes, *CE*, 232; and Martin, *Athanase*, 351.

138. Athanasius, *ACA* 62.2.

139. Athanasius, *Festal* 4 (ed. Parker).

140. Bell, *Jews*, 56.

141. See text below.

142. *Ep. Or. Sardic.* 6 (*CSEL* 65, p. 53). These events must be placed between Athanasius's acquittal at Psamathia in 332 and the spring of 334 when he set out to look for Arsenius in anticipation of the Council of Caesarea. Easter 334 is an unlikely date, given that Athanasius had already received the summons to appear before Dalmatius's court (Bell, *Jews*, 48; *PLond.*

1913: in March 334, the Melitians were preparing for the council). Easter of 332 or 333 is possible, but I would favor 332 in order to fit the sequence of events connected with Arius's activities during the rest of that year and in early 333 (see below).

143. *Ep. Or. Sardic.* 6 (*CSEL* 65, p. 53: "tyrannico more terreret"). Athanasius's abusive priests and deacons would not have hesitated to harass the people into communion. Like Macarius in the Mareotis, the bishop's loyal subordinates would have been eager to prove themselves, show their loyalty, and earn kudos or a promotion from the bishop. Nor would Athanasius have discouraged their actions, which may have been justified as necessary and noble in the war against God's enemies.

144. *Urk.* 34, p. 69, l. 22: δόλῳ, [Arius] φησίν, ἢ δεινότητι πανουργίας.

145. Constantine complained that he σιγὴν πλάττεσθαι. τῇ μὲν τοῦ σχήματος τέχνῃ τιθασσὸν σεαυτὸν καὶ χειροήθη σύ γε παρέχεις, κακῶν δὲ μυρίων καὶ ἐπιβουλῶν ἔνδον γέμων τοὺς πολλοὺς λέληθας (*Urk.* 34, p. 70, ll. 24–27). Cf. Socrates, *HE* 2.35; and Sozomen, *HE* 4.12.

146. Perhaps since Athanasius accused him of being a heretic; see above.

147. *Urk.* 34, p. 69, ll. 12–13. Constantine echoes Arius's *parrhesia* in ibid., p. 70, ll. 24–26.

148. Ibid., p. 70, ll. 27–28, and p. 72, ll. 27–28, addressing God!

149. Ibid., p. 72, ll. 9f. (λόγοις) and 13.

150. Exegesis: Epiphanius, *Panarion* 69.12, referring to a time after Athanasius's election, but impossible to be precise. Singing ... pleasing: *Urk.* 34, p. 71, ll. 10–12 (p. 72, l. 12: "wretched"). Hope and salvation: ibid., p. 72, ll. 10–13.

151. *Urk.* 34, p. 70, ll. 29–30.

152. Ibid., p. 69, ll. 4–7. Constantine's letter, dated to the winter or early spring 333 (ibid., p. 75, ll. 6–7 with *Festal* 5; see also Barnes, *CE*, 233), is a rambling diatribe against Arius and his followers, but it is our best evidence for events in the previous months and year. It also appears to be the only letter to have survived of what seems to have been an extended correspondence between the two (see *Urk.* 34, p. 70, l. 20–p. 71, l. 18, with Arius seemingly proposing "to modify [the creed] [with the phrase] a 'foreign hypostasis'" [p. 71, ll. 3–4], and suggesting an extended debate, perhaps since 330).

153. *Urk.* 34, p. 73, ll. 7–9 and ll. 18–19.

154. Ibid., p. 70, l. 7.

155. For Constantine's comments, see *Urk.* 34, p. 72, ll. 14–15. Cf. ibid., p. 69, ll. 18f. and 24; p. 70, l. 1; p. 72, ll. 20f. (concern to expose Arius's "meanness" *to the demos*); and p. 74, ll. 19f.

156. Many left Alexandria with Arius; see *Urk.* 34, p. 74, l. 16; and text below.

157. Ibid., p. 69, ll. 18f., and p. 71, ll. 16f.

158. Ibid., p. 70, l. 10: ἀπελαυνόμεθα. See also *Le livre du Synaxaire,* August 25 (*PO* 9.351): "Athanase ... l'a expulse [Arius] ainsi que tous ses partisans, de la ville d'Alexandrie."

159. See Athanasius, *Or. contra Arianos* 2.18.32, 43 (*NPNF* 4), dated to 339, but similar arguments would have been advanced earlier.

160. The *terminus post quem* is Athanasius's return from Psamathia (March/April 332); the *terminus ante quem* is Arius's letter to Constantine, apparently sent from Libya (*Urk.* 34, p. 72, ll. 1–2), probably in late 332 (see above). Since *Urk.* 34 is dated to early 333, summer or fall 332 is a good bet. Multitude: ibid., p. 74, l. 16; cf. Dionysius of Alexandria's exile at Kephro under Valerian, noting that τῶν μὲν ἀπὸ τῆς πόλεως ἀδελφῶν ἑπομένων

(Eusebius, *HE* 7.11.12). Well-to-do: given the fines Constantine imposed on them (see text below).

161. Popular in Libya (and Alexandria): *Urk.* 34, p. 72, ll. 2 and 26f.; p. 69, l. 24; and p. 71, ll.16f. The Libyans Secundus and Theonas would also have opened their arms to Arius. They seem to have returned from exile probably in the same year Arius and the Bithynian bishops were recalled; see Philostorgius, *HE* 2.1; Chadwick, "Faith," 192; and Barnes, *CE*, 386 n. 73. Arnold's assertion (*Early Episcopal Career*, 121) that "on balance, the evidence would tend to support the conclusion that Secundus and Theonas had not yet been restored to their sees at the time of Athanasius' journey through the Pentapolis" (in 332; see text below) makes little sense, given the evidence he discusses.

162. In 332: *Index* 4; Barnes, *CE*, 232; id., *AC*, 21. Arnold, *Early Episcopal Career*, 121, acknowledges the visit but notes oddly that "the evidence . . . does not suggest that . . . any . . . single issue impelled Athanasius to engage upon this course of visitations."

163. *Urk.* 34, p. 70, ll. 9–10.

164. Quote: *Urk.* 34, p. 72, l. 2. Anti-Nicene sentiments: Chadwick, "Faith," 177–78, 193–95, citing Synesius, *Ep.* 67.70–75 and 165.

165. *Urk.* 34, p. 70, ll. 12–14: "We ask that, if the bishop of Alexandria remains of the same opinion, hereafter permission may be given to us, according to the provisions of the law, to celebrate the lawful and indispensable services to God." Barnes, *CE*, 232: an ultimatum.

166. *Urk.* 34, p. 74, ll. 19–20, and p. 69, ll. 25f. Constantine's reaction: p. 70, ll. 14ff. (immediately after quoting Arius's petition). Decrees: *Urk.* 33, p. 66, l. 1, and 67–68 for the Latin and Syriac translations; and *Urk.* 34, p. 74, ll. 17–29 (see below on the penalties imposed on the Arians).

167. *Urk.* 34, p. 71, ll. 15f., and p. 74, ll. 18–20.

168. Approaching 24,000 drachmas (*POxy* 3789), but the rates for Alexandria would have been higher. On the controversy over whether urban dwellers were subject to a *capitatio* tax, see *POxy* 3789 (contradicting *CTh* 13.10.2); J. R. Rea, ed., *The Oxyrhynchus Papyri*, vol. 55, p. 43; Jones, *LRE*, 63; Carrié and Rousselle, *L'Empire*, 601; and Bagnall, *Egypt*, 154.

169. *Urk.* 34, p. 74, l. 19.

170. See *Urk.* 34, p. 74, ll. 27–29 and ad loc. Quote: ibid., p. 74, ll. 29–30.

171. *Urk.* 33, p. 68, ll. 1–6.

172. *Urk.* 34, p. 75, l. 7; date: see above. The letter called Arius "an evil interpreter and image of the Devil" (ibid., p. 69, l. 2). Athanasius would have shared it with the faithful in church assemblies. Note that, later, Constantine himself asked Athanasius to organize public readings of his letters, so that there would be no doubt about the bishop's innocence (Athanasius, *ACA* 68.6).

173. As his opponents would later do; cf. Athanasius, *HA* 59 and 63.

174. Lists: implied in the reference to soldiers expelling one's kin from their houses in *HA* 63, where Athanasius is speaking of his opponents, but he may have done the same at an earlier time. See also Sozomen, *HE* 3.21, who notes that Constantius ordered the names of Athanasius's supporters erased from the public registers. The practice of entering names into public lists would not have been new, and it is likely that Athanasius and the imperial authorities in Egypt, following the decrees of 333, drafted lists of their own, entering the names of Arians and other opponents of the bishop into their registers. Liturgies:

J. Lallemand, *L'administration civile de l'Égypte de l'avènement de Dioclétien à la création du diocèse (284–382)*, Mémoires de l'Academie Royale de Belgique, Cl. des Lettres 57.2 (Brussels, 1962), 85f., 145. The *katholikos* Theodorus (later promoted to prefect of Egypt) would have collaborated with Athanasius in this persecution. See Athanasius, *ACA* 14.2, 75, 77, 78. Theodorus: id., *ACA* 5; Martin, *Histoire acéphale* (SC 317), 286 n. 27; *PLRE* 1.900.

175. See discussion below.

176. The Melitians also became victims of Athanasius's wrath after Psamathia: "Athanasius accused [Ischyras]" of pelting the statues of the emperor, "working to have him thrown into prison" (Sozomen, *HE* 2.25.3; cf. *Ep. Or. Sardic.* 6 [*CSEL* 65, p. 53]). Probably with the collusion of secular authorities, Athanasius "deposed Callinicos [of Pelusium], . . . delivered him to a military garrison, and subjected him to insults and the law courts." Callinicos was "tied up with iron chains . . . [and Athanasius] did not cease to abuse him," replacing him with a certain Mark (Sozomen, *HE* 2.25.4; Philostorgius, *HE* 2.11). Throughout 332 and 333, Melitian leaders from the Thebaid to the Delta were assaulted, beaten, and detained (Sozomen, *HE* 2.25.5–6; Martin, *Athanase*, 363, 365). These campaigns paid off. Ischyras confessed in writing that he had falsely accused him and Macarius (Athanasius, *ACA* 63–64, 74)—a confession likely obtained under duress, because, later, Ischyras accused Athanasius again (Athanasius, *ACA* 27; Sozomen, *HE* 2.25.3).

177. Athanasius, *ACA* 63, 65–66, 70 (implied in John's later letter of repentance); Sozomen, *HE* 2.23.2–3; cf. Epiphanius, *Panarion* 68.7.9. Sacrilege: Athanasius, *ACA* 17, 68; Bell, *Jews*, 46f.

178. Council of Caesarea: *Index* 6; Bell, *Jews*, 48 (*PLond*. 1913, ll. 4–7, with quote); *Ep. Or. Sardic.* 7 (*CSEL* 65, p. 54); Sozomen, *HE* 2.25.1, 2.25.17; Theodoret, *HE* 1.26; and Barnes, *CE*, 234. Dalmatius: Athanasius, *ACA* 65; Socrates, *HE* 1.27; Epiphanius, *Panarion* 68.8.1–2 (mixing up Caesarea with Tyre); Barnes, *AC*, 21; and Martin, *Athanase*, 353 (n. 45), 358.

179. Searching Arsenius: Athanasius, *ACA* 65; Socrates, *HE* 1.27; Sozomen, *HE* 2.23.4; and Martin, *Athanase*, 353. Duke: Athanasius, *ACA* 67; Sozomen, *HE* 2.23.5. Monastery: Athanasius, *ACA* 67; Sozomen, *HE* 2.23.4. When the Athanasians arrived at the monastery, Arsenius had already left, but they had some Melitians arrested and brought before the duke, to whom they confessed that Arsenius was alive (Athanasius, *ACA* 67; and Sozomen, *HE* 2.23.5).

180. Athanasius's men were probably the dreaded priests Archelaus and Athanasius, the son of Capito, whom, earlier in 334, Athanasius had sent to Palestine and Syria, perhaps to spy on John Arkaph or to canvass support for the bishop in Dalmatius's court; see Athanasius, *ACA* 65; Theodoret, *HE* 1.28; Socrates, *HE* 1.27, 29; cf. Rufinus, *HE* 10.17 (on an otherwise unattested Archelaus serving as governor of Phoenicia); and *PLond*. 1914, ll. 36f. Flight to Tyre: Martin, *Athanase*, 356 n. 56: to find protection with the Eusebians. John at Antioch (to depose against Athanasius?): Athanasius, *ACA* 66.

181. Athanasius, *ACA* 65; cf. Rufinus, *HE* 10.17, and Socrates, *HE* 1.29.

182. Athanasius, *ACA* 65, 68; and Sozomen, *HE* 2.23.6–7. John Arkaph then sought to communicate with Athanasius (Athanasius, *ACA* 70.2). Arsenius and his clergy also acknowledged Athanasius as the head of the church, renounced their association with Melitians, and begged to be received into communion, which Athanasius refused. See the appendix ("Athanasius and Arsenius of Hypsele").

183. Athanasius, *ACA* 71.1.

184. Troubles in Egypt: Eusebius, *VC* 4.41.1 and 4.42.1-5 (Constantine's letter to the bishops at Tyre; in 4.42.5: τὴν τῆς εἰρήνης χάριν τοῖς νῦν στασιαζομένοις ἀποδόντες); Sozomen, *HE* 2.25.7-8 (on the grievances against Athanasius at Tyre: "Unexpected accusers sprang forth even among those who were thought to be friends"); and Barnes, *AC*, 22. One reason for the disturbances may have been the continued application of the anti-Arian decrees in Alexandria and Libya and the persecution of Melitians in Egypt; Athanasius's trip to the Delta in 334 may also have been connected with these troubles (*Index* 6). Persuaded Constantine: Athanasius, *ACA* 71 (cf. ibid. 10, 17), perhaps working closely with John Arkaph and the Melitians, as in *ACA* 17, 70 (John traveled to court in late 334?); and *PLond.* 1914, l. 34 (John in Antioch in early 335). Athanasius claimed that it was all a plot to readmit Arius. On the emperor's push for consensus: Kelly, *Creeds*, 261f.; Drake, *Constantine*, 263-68; and Martin, *Athanase*, 359.

185. Eusebius, *VC* 4.42.1-5.

186. Ibid. 4.41.3; and Sozomen, *HE* 2.26.2.

187. If Athanasius rejected John's request to be admitted to communion, John's trip to court in late 334 may have had the purpose of complaining to Constantine, who would certainly have frowned at Athanasius's arrogance (cf. the tone of the emperor's letter to John, in *ACA* 70, praising John for his decision to make peace with Athanasius, and his exasperation with the hubris of a few who threatened to destroy harmony; see Eusebius, *VC* 4.42.1; and cf. Theodoret, *HE* 1.26). That the Council of Tyre communicated with John and readmitted him suggests that Athanasius never communicated with him; see Sozomen, *HE* 2.25.15 and 2.31.4.

188. Eusebius, *VC* 4.42.1 and 4.42.5.

189. Ibid. 4.41.2 and 4.42.1-5, but perhaps the reexamination of the Arians was also on the agenda, as suggested in Constantine's exhortation that the bishops τοὺς ἀδελφοὺς ἰάσασθαι κινδυνεύοντας (ibid. 4.42.10). Tyre: Athanasius, *ACA* 71.1-3.

190. George Hamartolus, *Chronicon* 412 (*PG* 110.621): "The emperor ordered the bishop of Constantinople [sc. Eusebius of Nicomedia] to proceed to Aelia and assemble a synod ... and inaugurate the holy sites."

191. Eusebius, *VC* 4.41.2-3, 4.42.1-5; *Ep. Or. Sardic.* 7 (*CSEL* 65, p. 54: "imperatoris iussone constricti"); Athanasius, *ACA* 71 ("I was obliged to go"), 10, 17, 77, 78; Epiphanius, *Panarion* 68.8; Socrates, *HE* 1.27; Sozomen, *HE* 2.26.2; and Simonetti, *Crisi*, 124f.

192. *Index* 6.

193. *PLond.* 1914, l. 30; Athanasius, *ACA* 71; and Socrates, *HE* 1.28 (from Alexandria, probably incorrect). Athanasius may have sent Macarius to court after John Arkaph or following his receipt of the summons to plead with the powerful on his behalf.

194. *PLond.* 1914, ll. 32-34; Athanasius, *ACA* 40 (Archelaus, Athanasius, son of Capito, Aphthonius, Plutio, and Paul).

195. *PLond.* 1914, ll. 35-36: arrested because they carried letters slandering the Melitian Heraiscus, bishop of Heracleopolis Magna, but the charges would have been more serious because Athanasius, son of Capito, was exiled "by the Eusebians," before Tyre (Athanasius, *ACA* 40 and 17, for reasons that Athanasius naturally omits).

196. *PLond.* 1914, l. 38: πάνυ ἀθυμεῖ. Mobilizing supporters: Athanasius, *ACA* 17, 77, 78, implied in 8; Epiphanius, *Panarion* 68.8; and Sozomen, *HE* 2.25.18. Obstructing opponents: see text below.

197. *PLond.* 1914 *apud* Bell, *Jews,* 53-71. According to the letter, several Melitians arrived in Alexandria in early May of 335. One party lodged at an inn in the eastern suburbs of the city. Another group stayed with a Melitian monk in Parembole, next to the Roman military camp, where the Melitians seem to have led a thriving Christian congregation. Bell cautions that this was an *ex-parte* account, but so were all of Athanasius's writings. See also Arnold, *Early Episcopal Career,* 71-89; and Barnes, *AC,* 32. Parembole: *PLond.* 1914, ll. 3-8; and evidence of a Melitian congregation in Athanasius, *ACA* 71 (Melitius listed Macarius as priest there); "Passion of S. Shenoufe and His Brethren" (Reymond and Barns, *Four Martyrdoms,* 189) (a Melitian bishopric?); and B. Kramer and J.C. Shelton, eds., *Das Archiv des Nepheros und verwandte Texte* (Mainz, 1987), 45-48 (letters 4, 5, and 8) (Horion in Parembole paid the monastery of Hathor's agents in Alexandria).

198. *Commentariensis:* Jones, *LRE,* 587. *PLond.* 1914, ll. 3-5. Cf. Athanasius, *Apol. ad Const.* 29.3.

199. *PLond.* 1914, ll. 8-12. Bell, *Jews,* 62, 64, rendered ἐν ταῖς κέλλαις as "in the storehouses," but the phrase may have been a reference to monastic dwellings.

200. *PLond.* 1914, ll. 13-23.

201. Ibid., ll. 19-21, 24-26, 44-48.

202. Ibid., ll. 47ff. Letters: see discussion above on the banishment of bishops in Syria and Palestine.

203. *PLond.* 1914, ll. 38-42; Athanasius, *ACA* 77. Departure: *Index* 8; Athanasius, *ACA,* 77, 78; Sozomen, *HE* 2.25.18; and Martin, *Athanase,* 362.

204. Sozomen, *HE* 2.25.13 and 18; cf. Philostorgius, *HE* 2.11.

205. Epiphanius, *Panarion* 68.8.

206. Eusebius, *VC* 4.42.3; Athanasius, *ACA* 72 (soldiers), 8 (jailor; bishops dragged about), 9 (threats of violence). Recalcitrant: Sozomen, *HE* 2.25.18; Philostorgius, *HE* 2.11.

207. Charges: Sozomen, *HE* 2.25.2-12, drawing on the lost acts of the council (2.25.11). Rufinus, *HE* 10.18, and Philostorgius, *HE* 2.11, add a few extra details. Acquittal: Socrates, *HE* 1.32 (of murder); Sozomen, *HE* 2.25.8.

208. Athanasius, *ACA* 72; cf. 13, 27, 77 and 78. Council unconvinced: Sozomen, *HE* 2.25.13; Socrates, *HE* 1.131 (Athanasius's objections not allowed; council asked for more evidence). Mareotic commission: Athanasius, *ACA* 72 (quote), 80, and 81.

209. Athanasius, *ACA* 72-73, 75-76, 13; Socrates, *HE* 1.31; Barnes, *AC,* 22. On the first three, see chapter 5. According to Athanasius, the Pannonians had received instruction from Arius himself during his exile in the Balkans.

210. Athanasius accused the Eusebians and their allies of being the patrons of heretics; see Athanasius, *ACA* 72. He approached the count, "shouting, ... 'I've been wronged ... I've been framed,'" (ibid. 81; cf. ibid. 13, 27, 31, 83; and Socrates, *HE* 1.31). The Catholic Egyptian bishops and others also warned the count and the council that a plot was being hatched "for the sake of Arius's madness" (Athanasius, *ACA* 16, 77-80; quote: ibid. 77.3). Cf. ibid. 75.3-4 (quoting the Mareotic clergy: the committee was "under the patronage of the Ariomaniacs"); and Gwynn, *Eusebians,* 82. Dionysius himself expressed his disapproval of the proceedings and concern about the turmoil in Egypt (Athanasius, *ACA* 81). The Eastern bishops at Serdica, however, insisted that the council had selected the delegates "suo de concilio" (*Ep. Or. Sardic.* 7 [*CSEL* 65, p. 54]). Date of delegates' departure: to allow sufficient time for

the committee to come to Egypt, carry out the investigations, return to Tyre, report to the council, and travel to Jerusalem in early September.

211. Melitians: Athanasius, *ACA* 77.4; cf. 78 and 80. Athanasians: monks and virgins were present in large numbers in the Mareotis (Athanasius, *ACA* 15; cf. Palladius, *HL* 7, on the number of suburban monks in Alexandria in the 380s). Prodded by Athanasius's priests, a rowdy crowd of Athanasians—"all of the faithful of the church"—rallied in the Mareotic villages, occupied churches, and staged demonstrations and protests (Athanasius, *ACA* 72.6; quote: ibid. 14.2). Collectively, the Athanasian clergy wrote letters to several officials protesting the committee (ibid. 73, 74-75, and 76). See also Sozomen, *HE* 2.31.2; and text below.

212. *PLRE* 1.694; and Martin, *Histoire*, 282f. n. 17. Philagrius's appointment in the summer of 335: Paterius is attested as prefect until December 334, but since Philagrius was consistently hostile to Athanasius, it is unlikely that the bishop would have had a free hand against the Melitians in the spring of 335 if Philagrius had already been in power. Friendly to Arians and the committee: Philagrius provided the committee with a military escort, clamped down on the Athanasians, beat monks and virgins, and prevented Athanasius's priests from intimidating witnesses and blocking the inquiries; see Athanasius, *ACA* 14, 73-75, 83; cf. id., *HA* 7, 10, 12, 18, etc. Eusebius's patronage: id., *Ep. enc.* 3.

213. Athanasius, *ACA* 86, is vague, but in the *Apol. ad Const.* 1, he notes that no evidence was brought against Macarius and that, after he left (below), the council managed as it pleased. Cf. Socrates, *HE* 1.32; Sozomen, *HE* 2.25.15-16; Philostorgius, *HE* 2.11.

214. Sozomen, *HE* 2.27.1, 4; cf. Socrates, *HE* 1.26 and 1.3, with Van Nuffelen, *Héritage*, 458. The circumstances of Arius's readmission are obscure. Socrates and Sozomen conflate the events of 327 and 335. Rufinus, *HE* 10.12, and Sozomen, *HE* 2.27-2-4, place here the story of Constantia's intervention in Arius's recall. If there is any truth to that story, this was probably the right context for it, though Sozomen, *HE* 2.27.6-10, wrongly places here the statement of faith Arius presented to the emperor in late 326.

215. Sozomen, *HE* 4.12. Parvis, *Marcellus*, 172, suggests that this statement was the first creed of the Dedication Council of 341; the anti-Marcellan clauses would have been added later. The bishops also communicated with John Arkaph, Arsenius of Hypsele, and other Melitians (Sozomen, *HE* 2.25.15, 2.31.4; Socrates, *HE* 1.32), and ordained Ischyras bishop of Peace of Secontaturus (Athanasius, *ACA* 85).

216. Athanasius, *De synodis* 21 (21.3: quote); id., *ACA* 84. See also Williams, *Arius*, 79.

217. Eusebius, *VC* 4.47.

218. Athanasius, *HA* 50; id., *Ep. enc.* 6 (bishop "of the Arians"); id., *ACA* 19 and 24. Athanasius's replacement was appointed "ex iudicio concilii," in *Ep. Or. Sardic.* 8 (*CSEL* 65, p. 55), so this would have been the most likely occasion. Contra: Simonetti, *Crisi*, 139; R. Klein, *Constantius II. und die christliche Kirche* (Darmstadt, 1977), 70; Martin, *Athanase*, 405. Barnes, *AC*, 23, suggests the Melitian Heraiscus, but this is unlikely; see Hauben, "Heraiscus." Ineffective: Kopecek, *History*, 79; and Hanson, *Search*, 263-64. Cf. Klein, *Constantius*, 70f.

219. Athanasius, *ACA* 82, 87; *Index* 8 (Constantinople; cf. *ACA* 9 and 86); *Ep. Or. Sardic.* 7 (*CSEL* 65, p. 54: "fled" to the emperor after his deposition); Epiphanius, *Panarion* 68.9.4; Socrates, *HE* 1.31; Sozomen, *HE* 2.25.13-14 (Constantinople, because his life was in danger). See also Arnold, *Early Episcopal Career*, 163-67; Barnes, *AC*, 23.

220. Athanasius arrived in Constantinople on October 29/30: *Index* 8. Cf. Athanasius, *ACA* 86; Socrates, *HE* 1.33-34; Simonetti, *Crisi*, 129; Barnes, "Emperor," 63; and id., *AC*, 23-24.

221. Athanasius, *ACA* 9 and 86; Socrates, *HE* 1.34; and Sozomen, *HE* 2.28.1-2. Constantine's letter suggests that he did not know what had transpired at Tyre.

222. On the (disputed) sequence of events from the consecration of the Holy Sepulcher (September 13-20: Sozomen, *HE* 2.26.3; and Cameron, *Eusebius*, 329) to Athanasius's first exile (November 7), see Athanasius, *ACA* 87; Socrates, *HE* 1.34-35; Sozomen, *HE* 2.28.13; Barnes, *AC*, 23; and Parvis, *Marcellus*, 126f.

223. Sozomen, *HE* 2.28.13-14; cf. Socrates, *HE* 1.35; source: Athanasius, *ACA* 87 (Van Nuffelen, *Héritage*, 458). Athanasius later suggested that the Eusebians blocked a new inquiry into the charges filed at Tyre, adding new charges (*ACA* 9). In *ACA* 9, 87f., he claimed the emperor condemned the "injustice" done against him and exiled him to spare him from his enemies (!) (see chapter 8 below); and in *HA* 50, he notes that Constantine would not agree to send to Alexandria the man the Eusebians chose to replace him. Yet, in letters to Alexandria and Antony, Constantine confirmed that Athanasius had been condemned by an ecclesiastical sentence that could not be overthrown—that is, he upheld the decisions of Tyre (Sozomen, *HE* 2.31.2-3). Cf. Martin, *Athanase*, 383-85.

224. Exile: *Index* 8; Athanasius, *ACA* 87; Epiphanius, *Panarion* 68.9.5-6; Socrates, *HE* 1.35; Barnes, *AC*, 24. Reasons for exile: Sozomen, *HE* 2.31.2-3; *Ep. Or. Sardic.* 7 (*CSEL* 65, p. 54): "ob meritum facinorum suorom." The Eusebians also turned against Marcellus of Ancyra, who had angered the bishops by dissenting from the council's condemnation of Athanasius and refusing to communicate with Arius. The Eusebians accused him of heresy and demanded that he recant and destroy his writings, which, for now, Marcellus, to save his skin, promised to do (see Sozomen, *HE* 2.33.2; Socrates, *HE* 1.36; Simonetti, *Crisi*, 132; Hanson, *Search*, 217; Barnes, *CE*, 240f.; and Parvis, *Marcellus*, 116f., 126).

225. Sozomen, *HE* 2.29.1, 2.31.2-4; Socrates, *HE* 1.37; Barnes, *CE*, 242; Williams, *Arius*, 79. Arius and his associates would have returned to Alexandria in late 335 or early 336.

226. Sozomen, *HE* 2.31.2.

227. Ibid.

228. Ibid. 2.31.3, 5.

229. Arius: Socrates, *HE* 1.37; Barnes, *CE*, 242 (to examine Arius's orthodoxy? But if he had been admitted in Jerusalem, that seemed unnecessary, as Williams, *Arius*, 79, noted); and Parvis, *Marcellus*, 132 (for the tricennalia?). John Arkaph was banned in unclear circumstances: Sozomen, *HE* 2.31.4, to help restore order to the Alexandrian and Egyptian church.

230. Barnes, *CE*, 241; id., *AC*, 56; and Parvis, *Marcellus*, 127.

231. Epiphanius, *Panarion* 73.2; Sozomen, *HE* 2.33.1-2; Socrates, *HE* 1.36 (abbreviating events); *Ep. Or. Sardic.* 3 (*CSEL* 65, p. 51, to Illyrium); Barnes, *CE*, 241; id., "Emperor," 64f.; and esp. Parvis, *Marcellus*, 127-32, noting that the Eusebians handpicked the bishops attending the council.

232. Arius's death and the events preceding it: Athanasius, *Ep. ad episc. Aeg.* 18-19; id., *Ep. ad Serap.* 2ff.; Epiphanius, *Panarion* 68.6.7; Sozomen, *HE* 2.29.1-5 (confusing Alexander

of Constantinople with Alexander of Alexandria); Williams, *Arius*, 81; Martin, *Athanase*, 388; and Parvis, *Marcellus*, 132f.

233. Sozomen, *HE* 2.32.8 (not in Socrates).

8. THE CHALLENGE OF THEOLOGY AND POWER IN ACTION

1. Eusebius, *VC* 4.56; Barnes, *CE*, 259–63.

2. Barnes, *CE*, 251, 261–62. Cf. M. Di Maio and W. H. Arnold, "*Per vim, per caedem, per bellum*: A Study of Murder and Ecclesiastical Politics in the Year 337 A.D.," *Byzantion* 62 (1992): 158–66.

3. Socrates, *HE* 2.2; Sozomen, *HE* 3.1.

4. Eusebius, *VC* 4.61.3. Philostorgius, *HE* 2.16, reports that Constantine, thinking he had been poisoned, wrote a will ordering whichever of his sons arrived first to avenge his death. He then entrusted the will to Eusebius, who dutifully handed it over to a grateful Constantius (cf. Di Maio and Arnold, "*Per vim*," 169 n. 82). Rufinus's account omits Constantine's poisoning and replaces Eusebius with that "Arianizing" priest dear to Constantia. The priest would not only have turned the will over to Constantius but also suppressed news of the emperor's death until Constantius's arrival, thus preventing a plot against Constantine's sons from coming to fruition. See Rufinus, *HE* 10.11, with Ferguson, *Past*, 97–100; and Amerise, *Battesimo*, 55f. Socrates, *HE* 2.2, and Sozomen, *HE* 3.1, add that the priest charmed the court eunuchs, Constantius's wife, and Constantius himself (cf. Theodoret, *HE* 2.2). As Amerise noted, these stories do not inspire much credibility, but there is no question that Eusebius of Nicomedia won Constantius's trust and access to the emperor by offering loyalty—an asset in that dangerous and fluid world of imperial politics, especially at such a delicate time.

5. Athanasius, *ACA* 27; id., *HA* 8; Socrates, *HE* 2.2; Sozomen, *HE* 3.2; Simonetti, *Crisi*, 138.

6. Athanasius, *ACA* 87; id., *HA* 8.1 and 50.2; cf. Epiphanius, *Panarion* 68.10; Simonetti, *Crisi*, 137; Barnes, *AC*, 34; and Parvis, *Marcellus*, 137. The precedent was set in the recall of Eusebius of Nicomedia and Theognis of Nicaea. Constantine exiled them, pardoned and restored them, and their replacements peacefully stepped aside. But Constantine recalled those bishops only after a council had rehabilitated them, which was not the case with Athanasius.

7. Philostorgius, *HE* 2.18. Athanasius (*HA* 8) claimed that he was restored to his see by the three emperors (by the time he wrote the *HA*, he took care not to mention Dalmatius), but the only document quoted in support of this statement is Constantine II's letter, dated to June 337. Yet, as Parvis, *Marcellus*, 137–38, noted, it is unlikely that Athanasius and other bishops were allowed to return without Constantius's permission. This emperor must have acquiesced to his brother's (or brothers') wishes or yielded to the intervention of powerful courtiers (see Barnes, *AC*, 34–36, 56; Parvis, *Marcellus*, 138, 140). Simonetti, *Crisi*, 138, suggests that Constantine II broke with his father's policy in allowing the other bishops to return. Marcellus: Parvis, *Marcellus*, 132, 142.

8. Gregory Nazianzenus, *De vita sua* (ed. C. Jungck) 460: ψυχαὶ πρόφασις, τὸ δ' ἔστιν ἡ φιλαρχία.

9. I borrow from S. J. Tambiah, *Leveling Crowds: Ethnonationalist Conflicts and Collective Violence in South Asia* (Berkeley, 1996), 221–24.

10. Athanasius's restoration by an imperial decree was therefore at odds with the traditions of the church; see Socrates, *HE* 2.8; Sozomen, *HE* 3.5. Cf. Philostorgius, *HE* 2.18.

11. Athanasius, *ACA* 5; Barnes, *CE*, 213; Parvis, *Marcellus*, 139–42.

12. In Viminacium, Moesia; see Barnes, *AC*, 41.

13. *Ep. Or. Sardic.* 8 (*CSEL* 65, pp. 54f.). Cf. Theodoret, *HE* 2.2; Barnes, *AC*, 35; Parvis, *Marcellus*, 139f.

14. Simonetti, *Crisi*, 138f.

15. *Index* 10; Barnes, *AC*, 36.

16. Athanasius, *ACA* 7: "crowds ... wishing to see him ... rejoicings in the church ... thanksgivings offered to the Lord." Cf. id., *Ep. enc.* 2: all at peace until Gregory's arrival.

17. Athanasius, *ACA* 5, 7.

18. Sozomen, *HE* 3.5, drawing on Socrates, *HE* 2.8, who in turn drew on Sabinus (Van Nuffelen, *Héritage*, 459). Forced communion: *Ep. Or. Sardic.* 22 (*CSEL* 65, p. 62: "adversus nos machinabantur ... ex scriptis imperatorum terrere putabant, ut invitos ad suam communionem traherent"). On efforts to convince monks and virgins, see Brakke, *Athanasius*, 98, 109; and discussion below.

19. Socrates, *HE* 2.3, drawing on Athanasius, *ACA* 7.4, and Sabinus of Heraclea (Van Nuffelen, *Héritage*, 459); Sozomen, *HE* 3.2.

20. Athanasius, *ACA* 19.2 (letter of the Egyptian bishops in 338, which Athanasius probably authored).

21. Julius of Rome, quoted in Athanasius, *ACA* 24, complained that the Eusebians urged him to communicate with Pistus while Athanasius was in the city.

22. *Ep. Or. Sardic.* 8 (*CSEL* 65, p. 55). Cf. Gregory Nazianzenus, *Or.* 21.31 (*NPNF*, vol. 7, p. 278: "[Athanasius] cleansed the temple of those who made merchandise of God"). Prefect Theodorus, who as *katholikos* had persecuted Arians in 333 and 334 (see chapter 7), again assisted Athanasius. He arrested, sentenced, and banned several people, including many Arian clerics. Athanasius never denied these events, only his involvement in them (Athanasius, *ACA* 5.4). See also Simonetti, *Crisi*, 144; Barnes, *AC*, 45, 49 (it is unclear why Barnes says it is not necessary to believe Athanasius's enemies, but believe Athanasius?); Parvis, *Marcellus*, 139.

23. Athanasius, *ACA* 18.

24. Athanasius may have given or sold grain to the mill-bakeries of Alexandria to process into bread, which the church then bought back and distributed to the poor. This would allow recipients to bypass the millers and their fees. It is noteworthy that, in the following year, when Gregory sought to control Christian charity, Athanasius no longer speaks of grain (σῖτος), but of "bread" (ἄρτοι; ἄρτους; see below).

25. Brown, *Power*, 77–103 (p. 97: charity "carried a clear ceremonial message that was closely watched by contemporaries"). Cf. id., *Poverty*, 26–44.

26. Socrates, *HE* 2.23.42 (referring to events after Serdica), suggests broad popular support for Basil in Ancyra.

27. *Ep. Or. Sardic.* 9 (*CSEL* 65, p. 55).

28. We do not know the immediate fate of Basil. To judge from events in Antioch and elsewhere, it is possible that he and his followers formed a parallel church.

29. *Ep. Or. Sardic.* 9 (*CSEL* 65, p. 55). Cf. Parvis, *Marcellus*, 143–45, downplaying, however, the gravity of these events and Marcellus's involvement in them. Cf. Libanius, *Or.* 1.228

(Loeb ed.) (bakers of Antioch, paraded with backs bared); id., *Or.* 32.8 and 33.20. Agora: C. Humfress, *Orthodoxy and the Courts in Late Antiquity* (Oxford, 2007), 47.

30. This was new. Alexander of Alexandria had portrayed Arius's virgins as disreputable women, but he never violated their *pudicitia* or treated them like wrongdoers.

31. *Ep. Or. Sardic.* 9 (*CSEL* 65, p. 55). On the *fabricenses*' support of Lucius, see Athanasius, *HA* 18; Barnes, *AC*, 82–86. Cf. Ammianus Marcellinus, *RG* 31.6.2, on arming the *fabricenses* of Adrianople to resist the Goths.

32. See Julian, *Ep.* 111 (ed. Bidez), in reply to a petition of the Alexandrian people to allow Athanasius to return from his fifth exile. Julian calls Athanasius unworthy to προστατεύειν δήμου.

33. *Ep. Or. Sardic.* 25 (*CSEL* 65, p. 64: "primatus ecclesiae contra fas appetentes").

34. *Ep. Or. Sardic.* 24 (*CSEL* 65, p. 64).

35. As George Hamartolus, *Chronicon* 412 (*PG* 110.621), nicely put it, κατέσχε τὸν θρόνον τῆς βασιλευούσης πόλεως ὁ Εὐσέβιος. Ἐπιλαβόμενος δὲ τῆς μείζονος ἐξουσίας τοὺς σύμφρονας αὐτοῦ κατέστησε ταῖς οἰκείαις παροικίαις, ἐξεώσας τοὺς χειροτονηθέντας ἀντ' αὐτῶν. Cf. Athanasius, *ACA* 47.4 (= *Ep. Oc. Sardic.* 7 [*CSEL* 65, p. 119]: "ut impiam doctrinam dilatare ac disseminare possent").

36. Alexander of Byzantium's death in the summer of 337 and the need to elect a new bishop led the Christian of Constantinople to coalesce around rival candidates representing divergent theological views (Socrates, *HE* 2.6–7; Sozomen, *HE* 3.4). Dagron, *Naissance*, 422–23, suggests that Socrates projected the theological conflict retrospectively onto the contest for the Constantinopolitan see, but there is no reason to doubt that the faithful were divided (see Socrates, *HE* 1.37, 2.2). On the chronology of succession to the Constantinopolitan church: Barnes, *AC*, 36, 212f.; contra, Schwartz, *GS*, 3:273. On Paul's deposition, subsequent exile, and Eusebius's appointment, see Athanasius, *HA* 7; Philostorgius, *HE* 2.10; Theodoret, *HE* 2.4; Cedrenus, *Compendium* (ed. Bekker); and Dagron, *Naissance*, 423–24.

37. Eusebius transferred the relics of the martyrs Pamphilus of Caesarea and his companions from Antioch to Constantinople, in a move that perhaps helped him unite a divided congregation and strengthen his hand; see Cedrenus, *Compendium* (ed. Bekker); *Syn. Arménien de Ter Israël*, Feb. 16 (*PO* 21.56); Dagron, *Naissance*, 398. Cf. *Chronicon Paschale* 357 (ed. Whitby and Whitby): the relics of Saints Andrew and Luke were received in Constantinople in 357 "with zeal and piety, amid psalmody and hymnody"; and Jerome, *Chronicle* (*PL* 27.503f.): "with great enthusiasm." See P. Brown's remarks in his *The Cult of the Saints: Its Rise and Function in Latin Christianity* (Chicago, 1981), 92.

38. Athanasius, *ACA* 3 (among the recipients, many Egyptian bishops), 19 (new round with Melitian subscriptions); id., *ACA* 45.3 (= *Ep. Oc. Sardic.* 3 [*CSEL* 65, p. 111]: Theognis of Nicaea's letters to the emperors against Athanasius, Marcellus, and Asclepas). Cf. id., *Ep. Serap.*, apud Barnes, *AC*, 44; Athanasius, *HA* 9 (including Julius of Rome); *Ep. Sardic. ad Const.* 5 (*CSEL* 65, p. 184): letters sent by the two Eusebii and their successors perhaps at this time (but before Serdica). Against Marcellus et al.: Athanasius, *ACA* 27 (Julius's letter to Eastern bishops).

39. Athanasius, *ACA* 3–4 and 5 (charges), 18 (grain). Cf. Sozomen, *HE* 3.5. Simonetti, *Crisi*, 139, and Barnes, *AC*, 36–37, postulate a synod at Antioch in the winter of 338, which also elected Pistus, but there is no evidence for it. See chapter 7, where I suggest Pistus

was appointed at Tyre or soon after. Cf. Hanson, *Search*, 263–64; and Parvis, *Marcellus*, 148, 153–55.

40. Athanasius, *ACA* 18; Barnes, *AC*, 41.

41. Athanasius, *HA* 9, 51; *Index* 11 (with Martin, *Histoire*, 287 n. 33). Petition and popularity: Gregory Nazianzenus, *Or.* 21.28–29; see also *PLRE* 1.694. Arrival in Alexandria: in *Festal* 10 (ed. Parker), dated to the winter of 338 (Barnes, *AC*, 43, 189–90, convincingly), Athanasius already knew of Philagrius's appointment. Since Theodorus served as prefect into 338, the most likely date for Philagrius's arrival was spring 338.

42. Athanasius, *ACA* 19. They probably did the same with Basil of Ancyra, Quintianus of Gaza, and other displaced bishops.

43. Athanasius, *ACA* 19.2. Cf. Socrates, *HE* 2.2.11 (drawing, *pace* Van Nuffelen, *Héritage*, 459, on an unknown source).

44. Athanasius, *ACA* 22, 24. The reason for approaching Julius now, and urging him to communicate with Pistus, was Athanasius's return to the city. Athanasius, *ACA* 20, notes the Eusebians wrote to Julius asking him to call a council and adjudicate, but Julius tells it differently (below). Date: the decision to send an embassy may have been made earlier, but the envoys would plausibly have waited until the spring to leave for Rome. See Parvis, *Marcellus*, 147.

45. Athanasius, *ACA* 23 (Julius of Rome's letter).

46. Constantine II and Constans: Athanasius, *HA* 9 (date: winter or spring 338). In *Apol. ad Const.* 4.2, he notes that he wrote to Constans when he was still in Alexandria and was compelled to defend himself against the Eusebians—hence spring 338. Cf. Barnes, *AC*, 39, 67. To Julius: Athanasius, *ACA* 22, 24 (possibly carrying the encyclical of the Council of Alexandria).

47. Athanasius, *Festal* 10 (ed. Parker).

48. The synodical is reproduced in Athanasius, *ACA* 3–19 (sent to the emperors: Barnes, *AC*, 52). Quote: Athanasius, *ACA* 17 (τὴν ἀσέβειαν ἐγκαταπήξωσι καὶ τοὺς Ἀρειανοὺς εἰσαγάγωσι τῇ ἐκκλησίᾳ). The synod probably also anathematized and excommunicated Pistus (Athanasius, *Ep. enc.* 6).

49. Barnes, *AC*, 41–46, and Parvis, *Marcellus*, 155, claim that Athanasius defended himself successfully before Constantius, but we do not know. Parvis also does not explain why, after accepting Athanasius's apology in Caesarea (or, as above, postponing the judgment of Athanasius), Constantius "had had enough of Athanasius" and decided to expel him. Cf. Simonetti, *Crisi*, 142f.; and Hanson, *Search*, 268. The Eusebians, with Constantius's approval (or even at his urging), seem to have planned a council for Antioch for the winter of 338/339 to debate the charges against Athanasius and the troubles of the church. It is also possible that Pistus died during that year, which would explain their readiness to appoint a successor to Pistus/Athanasius at that council, to which Athanasius of course was not invited.

50. *Ep. Or. Sardic.* 10 (*CSEL* 65, pp. 55–56); Barnes, *AC*, 42–43. If a council was to decide his fate in the winter of 339, it would have been to his advantage to have as many clerics as possible to vote for him; see MacMullen, *Voting*, 20–23. After his return to Egypt, Athanasius also arranged for the monk Antony to come to Alexandria as the competition between Arians and Athanasians for the support of ascetics (Athanasius, *Life of Antony* 68–69) and the faithful (Athanasius, *Festal* 11 [ed. Parker]) rose to a new pitch. See esp. Athanasius, *Life*

of Antony 69–71; Schwartz, *GS*, 3:286–87; and Barnes, *AC*, 45. Date of the visit: end of July/early August (*Index* 10).

51. The debate must have centered on the question, Who was the legitimate bishop of Alexandria? Macarius had come to Rome to ask Julius to communicate with Pistus, and, in his third letter to the Eusebians, after referring to the debate, Julius wrote that it was impossible to consider Pistus's ordination valid (Athanasius, *ACA* 24). If Pistus had died, this would not yet have been known in Rome.

52. Athanasius, *ACA* 21, with id., *HA* 9 (quote). The *terminus post quem* for Julius's letter is the debate between Athanasius's envoys and Macarius et al.; the *terminus ante quem* is Gregory's appointment in the winter of 339. Cf. Athanasius, *Ep. enc.* 7.2, where he notes that the brethren at Rome wrote letters to call a council "last year, before these things [Gregory's appointment in the winter of 339 and events in the subsequent months] happened."

53. Constantius may have called this synod. He was at Antioch in the winter of 339 (Barnes, *AC*, 219).

54. Socrates, *HE* 2.8 and 10, and Sozomen, *HE* 3.5–6, conflate the synods of 339 and 341; Simonetti, *Crisi*, 143; Barnes, *AC*, 45f., 201 (on evidence from Socrates); Parvis, *Marcellus*, 148, 150.

55. Socrates, *HE* 2.9–10; Sozomen, *HE* 3.8; Parvis, *Marcellus*, 115.

56. Athanasius, *ACA* 33.

57. Constantius could not count on his brothers in a conflict with Persia: Julian, *Or*. 1.14; R. C. Blockley, "Constantius II and Persia," in *Studies in Latin Literature and Roman History*, Collection Latomus 206 (Brussels, 1989), 471–73; id., *East Roman Foreign Policy: Formation and Conduct from Diocletian to Anastasius* (Leeds, 1992), 13f. See also the appendix ("From Athanasius's Flight to the Councils of Rome and Antioch, 339–341").

58. He may also have issued an order for the arrest of Athanasius (and others, below), given that criminal charges had been brought against him.

59. Sozomen, *HE* 3.5 and 3.6.9; Athanasius, *ACA* 29–30.

60. Athanasius, *Ep. enc.* 2.1–2; Barnes, *AC*, 47–50 (Barnes notes that the allegation that Gregory came from court "does not . . . lack plausibility," but Athanasius wanted to give the impression that he had been appointed by the emperor).

61. Gregory Nazianzenus, *Or*. 21.15 (*SC* 270); Simonetti, *Crisi*, 143.

62. Their first choice, Eusebius of Emesa, a well-bred *rhetor* who knew how to inflame a crowd, had also studied in Alexandria. See Jerome, *De vir. ill.* 91 (*PL* 23.734); and Simonetti, *Crisi*, 143. Socrates, *HE* 2.9, and Sozomen, *HE* 3.6, write that he declined the appointment because of Athanasius's popularity, which is only partly true.

63. Athanasius, *Ep. enc.* 2 (μόνους δὲ Ἀρειανοὺς . . . σὺν αὐτῷ [Gregory]); Sozomen, *HE* 3.6.9. Widows recipients of imperial grain: Athanasius, *ACA* 18; and text above.

64. Athanasius, *Ep. enc.* 2.3: οἱ λαοὶ . . . κατεβόων μαρτυρόμενοι τοὺς ἄλλους δικαστὰς καὶ πᾶσαν τὴν πόλιν.

65. Athanasius, *Ep. enc.* 2.2.

66. Athanasius, *Ep. enc.* 2.3. Cf., later, Gregory Nazianzenus, *De vita sua* (ed. C. Jungck), ll. 540–42, recommending that bishops appoint someone as head of the church who had not yet taken some church "by public proclamation."

67. Athanasius, *Ep. enc.* 2.3.

68. Athanasius, *Festal* 11 (ed. Parker): "We begin the fast of forty days . . . having served the Lord with abstinence, and first purified ourselves" (Barnes, *AC,* 188: February/March 339); Sozomen, *HE* 3.6.

69. Sermons: to judge from the content of *Festal* 11. In 352 or 353, during Lent, crowds of worshippers nearly crushed one another in the churches: Athanasius, *Apol. ad Const.* 14–15.

70. To judge from events when Gregory arrived; Athanasius, *HA* 13.3.

71. Athanasius, *Ep. enc.* 3.2 (τῶν . . . λαῶν δυσανασχετούντων).

72. Athanasius knew Philagrius would react, but he may have welcomed the showdown so he could pin the blame for the ensuing troubles on the Arians and pose as victim.

73. *Index* 11; Barnes, *AC,* 46 (March 16); Martin, *Athanase,* 406 n. 59.

74. Socrates, *HE* 2.11.3; Martin, *Athanase,* 406 n. 58; *PLRE* 1.929 (Valacius).

75. Socrates, *HE* 2.11.3–4, and Sozomen, *HE* 3.6, conflate the two "flights" of Athanasius, in 339 and 356 (see Athanasius, *De fuga* 24). Simonetti, *Crisi,* 144.

76. Athanasius, *Ep. enc.* 3; Barnes, *AC,* 47–48; Martin, *Athanase,* 405f. Gwynn, *Eusebians,* 53, sees these episodes of violence as rhetorical constructions, but, as Martin noted (406 n. 57, arguing against Opitz), despite the polemical nature of the evidence, acts of violence were not rhetorical *topoi*. See text below for official documents confirming governors' use of violence in ecclesiastical matters. That, in this episode, Athanasius omits the direct participation of the Arians (Philagrius may have been trying to avoid Arian involvement) and gives specific details about different episodes of violence makes them even more credible.

77. Theonas is more likely than the church of Dionysius, because the former was larger, recently renovated, and had the adjacent baptistery. See Martin, *Athanase,* 405 n. 54. Rape: Athanasius, *Ep. enc.* 3.4 (ἔπασχον ἃ μὴ θέμις). Cf. Athanasius, *Ep. enc.* 7; and id., *ACA* 30.

78. Athanasius, *Ep. enc.* 3.4, 6.

79. Ibid. 3.2.

80. Athanasius, *ACA* 28, 30; and id., *HA* 10, 12 (before and after Gregory's arrival and Athanasius's flight).

81. Athanasius, *Ep. enc.* 3.

82. Unprecedented: Athanasius, *Ep. enc.* 3.3. Athanasius's violence: see discussion above.

83. *Index* 11; Athanasius, *HA* 10 and 14 ("sent from court . . . as one entrusted with secular power"); Barnes, *AC,* 46, 48; Martin, *Athanase,* 406. Number: Socrates, *HE* 2.11.1 (cf. Athanasius, *De fuga* 24); cf. Sozomen, *HE* 3.6.

84. Resistance: Barnes, *AC,* 49. Services held simultaneously in different parishes: Athanasius, *Apol. ad Const.* 16.3.

85. Athanasius, *Ep. enc.* 4. Athanasius claims Gregory acted out of sheer wickedness, but the burning and dismantling of the building may have been intended to purify a church profaned by a sacrilegious bishop. Cf. Athanasius's burning of a church upon his return from exile; see above.

86. See Athanasius, *Ep. enc.* 4.3–5.1: raiding churches; beating priests; stripping, flogging, and jailing virgins, matrons, and men of high birth. On public floggings (including flogged *bouletai*), cf. Libanius, *Or.* 33.20; Jerome, *Ep.* 1; Humfress, *Orthodoxy,* 47.

87. Athanasius, *Ep. enc.* 5.1: Τούτων γενομένων οὐχ ἡσύχαζον οὐδὲ εἰς τὰ ἑξῆς. See also Athanasius, *HA* 10.2, misleadingly placed after his flight for Rome.

88. See Athanasius, *Festal* 11 (February/early March 339).

NOTES TO PAGES 134–135   253

89. Athanasius, *Ep. enc.* 5.1, but of course he was not living there since Gregory's arrival. Probably the church of Dionysius: Calderini, *Dizionario,* 167; Martin, *Athanase,* 407 n. 63; id., *Histoire,* 146–47, 163 (with n. 139): in 356 he was attacked in the church of Dionysius, and in 366 was searched for in the same church. Was Gregory assembling the Arians in another church? Easter: *Index* 11; Martin, *Athanase,* 407 n. 65; Barnes, *AC,* 46, 49, but suggesting other churches.

90. Easter celebration: *Index* 11. Departure for Rome: Athanasius, *ACA* 28; id., *Ep. enc.* 5.2; id., *HA* 11.1 (claiming he had done so to prevent more murders and suffering); Barnes, *AC,* 52ff.

91. Socrates, *HE* 2.11.3, as Martin, *Athanase,* 408 n. 68, points out, is the only source to mention it (followed by Sozomen, *HE* 3.6, and Photius, *Bibliotheca* 475a and 481b). The church would have been rebuilt in the late 340s/early 350s. Simonetti, *Crisi,* 144, suggests that the Eastern bishops were referring to this event when they spoke of Athanasius setting fire to a church in *Ep. Or. Sardic.* 8 (see text above), but that does not fit the subject of that passage, which dealt with events at the time of Athanasius's return from exile or when was still in the city.

92. That in the early 350s space for worship in the Alexandrian churches had become too small to accommodate the faithful may have been due not only to the number of converts, but also to the damage so many churches suffered during this time. See Athanasius, *Apol. ad Const.* 16.

93. Athanasius, *Ep. enc.* 5.4 and 6.2.

94. Ibid. 5.8: οἱ λαοὶ καταγινώσκοντες τῆς ἀσεβείας τῶν αἱρετικῶν Ἀρειανῶν.

95. Athanasius, *Ep. enc.* 4.2: ὅλως ἁρπαγὴ καὶ θάνατος ἦν ἐν τῇ ἐκκλησίᾳ. Cf. Theodoret, *HE* 2.3.

96. Promotions: Athanasius, *ACA* 47; id., *Ep. enc.* 7 (Amon, Arius's friend from the early days of the controversy, became his secretary). Ordinations: id., *HA* 17 (declared invalid at Serdica). Hilary, *Contra Auxentium* 8: Auxentius, future bishop of Milan, was probably first ordained priest by Gregory.

97. Athanasius, *HA* 13; id., *ACA* 33, 39.3 ("Epistula of Western bishops at Serdica to Alexandria").

98. Athanasius, *Ep. enc.* 5.4 (ὁ δὲ τοῦ θεοῦ λαὸς καὶ οἱ κληρικοὶ τῆς καθολικῆς ἐκκλησίας βιάζονται ἢ κοινωνεῖν τῇ ἀσεβείᾳ τῶν αἱρετικῶν Ἀρειανῶν ἢ μὴ εἰσέρχεσθαι εἰς τὰς ἐκκλησίας).

99. Denouncing Athanasius: Athanasius, *Ep. enc.* 5.6–7. Joining Gregory: ibid. 6.3 (only "heretics" and those forced to); id., *HA* 27; and id., *ACA* 39.3 ("Epistula of Western bishops at Serdica to Alexandria"). Cf. Epiphanius, *Panarion* 69.12; and chapter 7 above, on Arians forced to join Athanasius after Psamathia.

100. Athanasius, *Ep. enc.* 5.7–8.

101. Athanasius, *HA* 21 (decree reversing the persecution of the Athanasian clergy and faithful in 344; see discusion below).

102. Athanasius, *Ep. enc.* 5.8, 7.3. Cf. *Index* 13.

103. These decrees were abrogated, and the immunities restored in 346: see text below.

104. *Vita S. Athanasii ex Metaphraste* (*PG* 25.ccxxix), partisan but believable.

105. Intercept: Athanasius, *Ep. enc.* 4.3; cf. id., *HA* 31.2. Join the Arians: id., *HA* 10.2.

106. Gregory and his supporters also managed to confiscate the property of (recalcitrant) Athanasian virgins (Athanasius, *HA* 10.2; id., *Ep. enc.* 4.3), which may have been used to fund his charitable schemes and boost his position in the community.

107. Athanasius, *HA* 19; id., *De fuga* 3; and text below.

108. Athanasius, *HA* 13 ("to establish the heresy").

109. Athanasius, *ACA* 33; cf. 42.

110. *Storia*, p. 61 (ed. Orlandi), adding that "the people did not communicate with him; they congregated in private houses with priests ordered by Athanasius or his Father, Alexander." The *Storia* places George before Gregory. The two are often conflated in later sources, but the reference to domestic congregations (mirroring events in Alexandria) and priests ordained by Alexander suggests Gregory's rather than George's episcopate.

111. Athanasius, *Festal* 13 (ed. Parker) (dated 341, sent from Rome), on Egypt under Gregory: "For heretics ... rising against the truth, violently persecute the Church; of the brethren some are scourged, and others torn asunder by the rack; and ... the ill-treatment reaches even to the Bishops." Athanasius, *HA* 12–13: Potamon of Heraclea was beaten and perished of his injuries; Bishop Sarapammon was banned from Egypt. Cf. id., *ACA* 38.5, 39.1 ("Epistula of Western bishops at Serdica to Alexandria"). See also Martin, *Athanase*, 409, 414f. Cf. Athanasius, *Ep.* 53 (*PG* 26.1185), warning monks to stay away from Arians going about the monasteries—more plausible in 339 than in the late 350s, when Athanasius was hiding with the monks.

112. B. Outtier, ed., *Textes Arméniens relatifs à S. Éphrem*, CSCO 474 (Louvain, 1985), 1.24 (p. 13); Isidore of Pelusium, *Ep.* 1.109 (*PG* 78.256).

113. Athanasius, *ACA* 32–33 (evicted amid atrocities); id., *HA* 6; *Ep. Or. Sardic.* 4, 11 (*CSEL* 65, pp. 52, 56); Epiphanius, *Panarion* 72.2.3; Sozomen, *HE* 3.8; Barnes, *AC*, 57; and Parvis, *Marcellus*, 148.

114. Athanasius, *De fuga* 3; id., *HA* 19 (quote); Socrates, *HE* 2.15; Sozomen, *HE* 3.8. Barnes, *AC*, 84, places the quote in *HA* after Serdica, but *ACA* 45.1 (= *Ep. Oc. Sardic.* 3 [*CSEL* 65, p. 109]) suggests a pre-Serdican date.

115. Athanasius, *HA* 19. The Eusebians secured a warrant for their arrest and hunted them down; sometime before Serdica, but not necessarily immediately before the council (Barnes, *AC*, 84). Olympus of Aeni managed to escape to the West, but Theodulus of Trajanopolis died during his flight; see Athanasius, *De fuga* 3, with id., *ACA* 45, and id., *HA* 19. Olympus made it to Serdica (Barnes, *AC*, 85).

116. Athanasius, *HA* 19; Barnes, *AC*, 84 (before Serdica).

117. Athanasius, *ACA* 48 (before Serdica). Asterius: Le Quien, *OC*, vol. 3, col. 723. After Serdica, they were exiled to Libya (Athanasius, *HA* 18).

118. Athanasius, *ACA* 33, 45 (= *Ep. Oc. Sardic.* 3 [*CSEL* 65, pp. 109–12]); id., *ACA* 37.2 ("Epistula of Western bishops at Serdica to Alexandria"); *Ep. Sardic. ad Iulum* 3 (*CSEL* 65, p. 128).

119. Athanasius, *HA* 11.

120. Athanasius, *ACA* 30, 33; *Ep. Or. Sardic.* 11 (*CSEL* 65, p. 56); Martin, *Athanase*, 410f.

121. Sozomen, *HE* 3.7.1–2.

122. See the appendix ("From Athanasius's Flight to the Councils of Rome and Antioch, 339–341").

123. Letters: Athanasius, *Ep. enc.* 5–7. Carpones' embassy: id., *ACA* 24.

124. See the appendix ("From Athanasius's Flight to the Councils of Rome and Antioch, 339-341").

125. Athanasius, *Apol. ad Const.* 4, claimed he devoted his time in Rome to prayer and worship. Eutropia: ibid. 6.5. Cf. Barnes, *AC,* 53; and Klein, *Constantius,* 39 n. 91.

126. Palladius, *HL* 1.4

127. Barnes, *AC,* 52; cf. Athanasius, *HA* 9 (in 338).

128. Constantine II's death: Barnes, *AC,* 218. Later, accused of treason, Athanasius denied having contacted Constans at this stage (Athanasius, *Apol. ad Const.* 2-5). According to Theodoret, *HE* 2.3, after Constantine II's death, Athanasius complained to Constans about the plots against his life and the true faith. Cf. Philostorgius, *HE* 3.3 and 12 (after Serdica).

129. Athanasius, *Ep. enc.* 5-7. See also Barnes, *AC,* 48-51 (on the date and purpose). Barnes suggests the letter was addressed to prelates who did not take part in Athanasius's deposition, but not necessarily.

130. Athanasius, *Ep. enc.* 2, 7 ("Arian heresy"), and 2, 6, 7. Tyre: chapter 7 above; and Athanasius, *ACA* 5, 8. On the "invention" of Arianism as a "full-blown ... heresy" while Athanasius was in Rome, see Parvis, *Marcellus,* 180f. Cf. Lyman, "Topography," 53-58; and Barnes, *AC,* 53. But as Gwynn, *Eusebians,* 82f., noted, this was not the first time Athanasius had denounced a heretical conspiracy.

131. Athanasius, *Ep. enc.* 6.4, 7.1.

132. Athanasius, *ACA* 24.

133. See the appendix ("From Athanasius's Flight to the Councils of Rome and Antioch, 339-341").

134. Athanasius, *ACA* 25-26. Chronology of Julius's letters: see the appendix ("From Athanasius's Flight to the Councils of Rome and Antioch, 339-341"). "Invalid" synods (i.e., Tyre, Jerusalem, Constantinople, and Antioch) to appoint Gregory (Athanasius, *ACA* 22).

135. Athanasius, *ACA* 22, 29. Cf. id., *HA* 11; Sozomen, *HE* 3.8. See also Pietri, *Roma,* 204-7; Hanson, *Search,* 271-72; Martin, *Athanase,* 412-13; and Parvis, *Marcellus,* 165.

136. Athanasius, *ACA* 32, 34. Klein, *Constantius,* 39f., suspects Athanasius's authorship.

137. Athanasius, *ACA* 32 (Julius had not officially communicated with Marcellus but apparently saw nothing wrong with his teaching).

138. Athanasius, *ACA* 21.1 Chronology: see the appendix ("From Athanasius's Flight to the Councils of Rome and Antioch, 339-341"). Eusebians' reply: reconstructed from Julius's reply and Sozomen's narrative; see Schwartz, *GS,* 3:297-300; Klein, *Constantius,* 40 n. 92; H. C. Brennecke, U. Heil, A. Stockhausen, et al., eds., *Bis zur Ekthesis Makrostichos,* Dokumente zur Geschichte des arianischen Streites 3.1.3 (Berlin, 2007), 150-52.

139. See the appendix ("From Athanasius's Flight to the Councils of Rome and Antioch, 339-341").

140. Peace in Egypt: Athanasius, *ACA* 30, 34; Socrates, *HE* 2.15. Contempt: Athanasius, *ACA* 22, 25; Sozomen, *HE* 3.8.5-6. Reception: Athanasius, *ACA* 29, 32, 34; Sozomen, *HE* 3.8.6.

141. Sozomen, *HE* 3.8.7.

142. Athanasius, *ACA* 20; id., *HA* 15; Socrates, *HE* 2.15; Sozomen, *HE* 3.8.4; and see the appendix ("From Athanasius's Flight to the Councils of Rome and Antioch, 339-341"). See also Martin, *Athanase,* 416-17.

143. Athanasius, *ACA* 34.4f.–35.1.

144. Defense of the council: Athanasius, *ACA* 27 (revisiting the affairs of the chalice, Arsenius's murder, and the Council of Tyre), 32 (Marcellus's orthodoxy), 25 (schism), 30, and 35 (Gregory).

145. Barnes, *AC*, 61. Schwartz, *GS*, 2:310; Klein, *Constantius*, 40f.; and Ayres, *Nicaea*, 117, who place the Council of Rome and Julius's letter before the Dedication Council, assume the Eusebians received the letter and proceeded with the latter council to draft a reply to Rome to show Marcellus was a heretic. Barnes, *AC*, 57, and Parvis, *Marcellus*, 160–62, dating the Dedication Council before the Council of Rome, suggest that the former would have dealt with Julius's second letter (not extant). See the appendix ("From Athanasius's Flight to the Councils of Rome and Antioch, 339–341").

146. Athanasius, *De synodis* 22, 25.1; Sozomen, *HE* 3.8. Plans for this synod may have been under way for a while (cf. Jerusalem, 335). The Eusebians would have waited as long as possible to assemble a synod large enough to deliver a strong reply to Athanasius's accusations, implicating in it as many Eastern bishops as possible.

147. Athanasius, *De synodis* 25. The first creed was probably a statement of faith imbedded in a synodical in reply to Athanasius's *Epistula encyclica* (Klein, *Constantius*, 42; Ayres, *Nicaea*, 117–18). The second may have been the official creed of the council. In its opening sentence, between "We believe" and "in one God," the bishops inserted the phrase "following the evangelical and apostolic tradition" (Athanasius, *De synodis* 23.2), thus claiming that, in contrast to Nicaea with its unscriptural *homoousios*, the new formula distilled the true, pure, unadulterated faith. On the third and fourth creeds, see Athanasius, *De synodis* 24–25; Hilary, *De synodis* 29; Kelly, *Creeds*, 271–73; Hanson, *Search*, 291–92; Ayres, *Nicaea*, 121–22; and Parvis, *Marcellus*, 207.

148. See Schwartz, *GS*, 3:311–18; Kelly, *Creeds*, 263–74; Simonetti, *Crisi*, 154–57; Hanson, *Search*, 284–92 (287 n. 39: with reference to scholars' view of them as Arian vs. anti-Arian); Parvis, *Marcellus*, 113–16, 170–77; Ayres, *Nicaea*, 117–22. These authors variously discuss the creeds' putative Lucianic, Asterian, Arian, Eusebian (of Caesarea), etc. theological influences and their Origenist, anti-Marcellan, anti-Sabellian, etc. tendencies but have not reached a consensus.

149. The Eusebians had supported the reintegration of Arius into the church but did not necessarily subscribe to all of Arius's original views as Athanasius portrayed them and all who rejected Nicaea. See Socrates, *HE* 2.10; M. Wiles, "Attitudes to Arius in the Arian Controversy," in *Arianism after Arius*, ed. M. R. Barnes and D. H. Williams (Edinburgh, 1993), 31–43; Lienhard, "'Arian' Controversy," 417–19; Drake, *Constantine*, 261; Gwynn, *Eusebians*, 101–244.

150. Parvis, *Marcellus*, 171–73, 208. Some scholars refer to (1) Hilary's later reception of these creeds as orthodox (*De synodis* 32, 34; Hanson, *Search*, 287 n. 39) and (2) Sozomen, *HE* 3.5, as evidence of their anti-Arian drift, but Hilary adopted a softer stance in the late 350s when the Nicene were seeking an alliance with the *homoiousians* against the *anomoians*. The fourth creed not only excluded the *homoousios* but also avoided any reference to the essence (*ousia*) of God; see Hanson, *Search*, 292; and cf. Ayres, *Nicaea*, 122. Contra: Kelly, *Creeds*, 273.

151. Sozomen, *HE* 3.5, drawing on Sabinus. Kelly, *Creeds*, 286; Ayres, *Nicaea*, 137–38 (it would take sixteen years for the *homoousios* to be officially banned). Contra: Hanson, *Search*, 290.

152. Socrates, *HE* 2.10.1–2; Van Nuffelen, *Héritage,* 459.
153. Sozomen, *HE* 3.18.1 (independent of Socrates).
154. Ayres, *Nicaea,* 120: unclear; Hanson, *Search,* 290: replaced; Kelly, *Creeds,* 274: did not replace.
155. So Sozomen, *HE* 3.5, noting the similarity of the second creed to Nicaea; Socrates, *HE* 2.22 (no rupture with the Nicene); and Hilary, *De synodis* 87–89. Gwynn, *Eusebians,* 224–27: "broad theological position, within which considerable individual divergences could and did exist."
156. Sozomen, *HE* 3.13; and *Ep. Or. Sardic.* 25 (*CSEL* 65, p. 64).
157. *Chronica minora* 3, p. 301.
158. Philostorgius, *HE* 3.15: heated disputations (Aetius victorious when Leontius was priest); Kopecek, *History,* 73; Vaggione, *Eunomius,* 22–23.
159. Eustathians: Sozomen, *HE* 3.20. Division: Philostorgius, *HE* 3.14; Kopecek, *History,* 97. Cf. Theodoret, *Ep.* 112.10 (*SC* 111, p. 48).
160. By 344, Flavianus and Diodorus were at the head of Nicene opposition, but probably since 341. See Philostorgius, *HE* 3.13, 18; Theodoret, *HE* 2.19; id., *Historia religiosa* 2.16 (*SC* 234, p. 230): in the 360s, Flavianus and Diodorus brought monks from the desert into the city "to assist thousands of people lost to salvation by the [Arian] deception."
161. Theodoret, *HE* 2.19. See also Sozomen, *HE* 3.20; Philostorgius, *HE* 3.13, with Kopecek, *History,* 100–101.
162. Sozomen, *HE* 3.20, with Van Nuffelen, *Héritage,* 482, drawing on an Antiochene source.
163. Athanasius, *ACA* 49 (= *Ep. Oc. Sardic.* 8 [*CSEL* 65, p. 124]). The Eastern bishops did not recognize this deposition, and Stephen remained in charge until 344.
164. Theodoret, *HE* 2.7: τὰ κατὰ τῶν ἀστῶν ὑπ' ἐκείνου παρανόμως πραχθέντα. ... ἕνα γὰρ τῶν οἰκετῶν ... χρήμασιν ἐπεπείκει.
165. Theodoret, *HE* 2.7: τινα χαμαιτύπην παραγενόμενος.
166. Theodoret, *HE* 2.7. Cf. Athanasius, *HA* 20.
167. R. MacMullen, "Personal Power in the Roman Empire," *AJP* 107 (1986): 512–24.
168. Sozomen, *HE* 3.7.4, with Van Nuffelen, *Héritage,* 480. Paul unexpectedly returned to the city. Though "restored," he was unable to take the main church; see Socrates, *HE* 2.12; and Barnes, *AC,* 68, 213.
169. Socrates, *HE* 2.12; Sozomen, *HE* 3.7.4–5: the faithful were congregating with the Eusebian bishops. Riots: Libanius, *Autobiography* 44 (Loeb ed.); Socrates, *HE* 2.12.6.
170. Socrates, *HE* 2.12 (*NPNF,* vol. 2, p. 41). *Ep. Or. Sardic.* 9 (*CSEL* 65, p. 55: "de Paulo ... post reditum exilii sui, si quis audierit, perhorrescet").
171. Sozomen, *HE* 3.7.5, with Van Nuffelen, *Héritage,* 480.
172. *Ep. Or. Sardic.* 20 (*CSEL* 65, p. 61).
173. For an alternative interpretation of these events, see McLynn, "Christian Controversy," 23ff.
174. Libanius, *Autobiography* 44–45. Pronconsul Alexander: *PLRE* 1.40 (3).
175. Libanius, *Autobiography* 44: on Bemarchius's gang.
176. *PLRE* 1.422f.
177. Socrates, *HE* 2.13.2.
178. Ibid. 2.13.3.

179. Sozomen, *HE* 3.7.6; and Socrates, *HE* 2.13.3.

180. Socrates, *HE* 2.13.3. Sozomen, *HE* 3.7.6 (independent of Socrates: Hermogenes murdered, then "a rope attached to his body dragged it through the city"). Cf. *Historia acephala* 1.6 (Martin, *Histoire*, 140–41).

181. *RG* 14.10.2.

182. Sozomen, *HE* 4.3.

183. Socrates, *HE* 2.13; Sozomen, *HE* 2.7. As punishment for the violence, Constantius halved the free supply of grain of Constantinople.

184. Dagron, *Naissance*, 430; Barnes, *AC*, 214.

185. Socrates, *HE* 2.13.7.

186. Athanasius, *ACA* 36; id., *HA* 15; id., *Apol. ad Const.* 4.5. After Paul arrived in Trier in spring 342 (Barnes, *AC*, 67–69), Constans demanded an account of his and Athanasius's deposition (Socrates, *HE* 2.18.1; Sozomen, *HE* 3.10, drawing on Athanasius, *De synodis* 25). Constantius sent an embassy of bishops, which the Western prelates refused to receive (Athanasius, *De synodis* 25; *Ep. Or. Sardic.* 27 [*CSEL* 65, p. 67]; Parvis, *Marcellus*, 210). The latter then convinced Constans to call a council together with his brother (*Ep. Or. Sardic.* 14 [*CSEL* 65, p. 5]; Athanasius, *Apol. ad Const.* 4.4; Barnes, *AC*, 67–69; Martin, *Athanase*, 422).

187. At the top of the agenda was theology: *Ep. Oc. Sardic.* 1 (*CSEL* 65, pp. 103–4) (= Athanasius, ACA 44): "ut . . . iniqua doctrina penitus expulsa"); id., ACA 37 (= "Epistula of Western bishops at Serdica to Alexandria"); *Ep. Sardic. ad Iulum* 3 (*CSEL* 65, p. 128); "Epistula of Western bishops at Serdica to Constantius" 3 (*CSEL* 65, p. 183); Barnes, *AC*, 71; Martin, *Athanase*, 423; and Parvis, *Marcellus*, 229, 236. Debate the faith: *Ep. Sardic. ad Iulum* 3 (*CSEL* 65, p. 128). Other items: *Ep. Sardic. ad Iulum* 3 (*CSEL* 65, p. 128).

188. Hanson, *Search*, 293; Barnes, *AC*, 71; Parvis, *Marcellus*, 210–17.

189. Athanasius, *HA* 15; *Ep. Or. Sardic.* 27 (*CSEL* 65, p. 66). See also Simonetti, *Crisi*, 169; Barnes, *AC*, 72f.; Parvis, *Marcellus*, 218, 226.

190. *Ep. Oc. Sardic.* 7 (*CSEL* 65, p. 119) (= Athanasius, *ACA* 48). Cf. Athanasius, *ACA* 36; and id., *HA* 17. Together with Gregory of Alexandria, Basil of Ancyra, and Quintianus of Gaza, the leaders of the anti-Nicene faction were deposed and excommunicated by their Western peers: *Ep. Oc. Sardic.* 8 (*CSEL* 65, p. 123) (= Athanasius, *ACA* 49). George of Laodicea was also deposed. Valens and Ursacius were technically Westerners, but bilingual and closely associated with the Eusebian circle. See also Hefele, *Histoire*, 544 (on Patrophilus of Scythopolis); Simonetti, *Crisi*, 169; Barnes, *AC*, 72; Parvis, *Marcellus*, 221–22. Maris of Chalcedon, Macedonius of Mopsuestia, Eudoxius of Germanicia, and Dianius of Caesarea were spared.

191. Athanasius, *ACA* 36; id., *HA* 15, 18; and *Index* 15.

192. This council has generated a large volume of scholarship; see L. W. Barnard, *The Council of Serdica, 343 A.D.* (Sofia, 1983); Hefele, *Histoire*, 525ff.; and Hanson, *Search*, 293–306.

193. *Ep. Oc. Sardic.* 7 (*CSEL* 65, p. 120) (= Athanasius, *ACA* 48). Following, perhaps, Philagrius's tactical advice? See Barnes, *AC*, 72.

194. *Ep. Or. Sardic.* 14–17 (*CSEL* 65, pp. 58–59).

195. Simonetti, *Crisi*, 170.

196. Demands: *Ep. Or. Sardic.* 15 (*CSEL* 65, p. 58); Athanasius, *HA* 16. Mistake: Simonetti, *Crisi*, 170; Barnes, *AC*, 73. Both sides rejected offers to compromise: Athanasius, *HA* 44; *Ep. Or. Sardic.* 18 (*CSEL* 65, p. 60).

197. Athanasius, *ACA* 48; id., *HA* 18; Simonetti, *Crisi*, 170; Barnes, *AC*, 72.
198. *Ep. Oc. Sardic.* 7 (*CSEL* 65, p. 121) (= Athanasius, *ACA* 48); Parvis, *Marcellus*, 232f.
199. *Ep. Or. Sardic.* 19 (*CSEL* 65, p. 60). Cf. *Ep. Oc. Sardic.* 3 (*CSEL* 65, pp. 109–12) (= Athanasius, *ACA* 45).
200. *Ep. Oc. Sardic.* 3 (*CSEL* 65, p. 110) (= Athanasius, *ACA* 45).
201. Athanasius, *HA* 16; Simonetti, *Crisi*, 172; Barnes, *AC*, 73; Ayres, *Nicaea*, 124; Parvis, *Marcellus*, 233 n. 247 (on the problematic sources).
202. Athanasius, *HA* 17.
203. *Ep. Or. Sardic.* 28 (*CSEL* 65, pp. 67ff.).
204. Paul: Socrates, *HE* 2.20 (a garbled chapter); Barnes, *AC*, 77 (convincing); Parvis, *Marcellus*, 228f. Lucius: Sozomen, *HE* 3.12.
205. *Ep. Oc. Sardic.* 1 and 8 (*CSEL* 65, pp. 104, 122) (= Athanasius, *ACA* 44, 49). Cf. Athanasius, *ACA* 37 ("Epistula of Western bishops at Serdica to Alexandria"); id., *HA* 20; *Ep. Sardic. ad Const.* 5 (*CSEL* 65, p. 184); Simonetti, *Crisi*, 181; and Barnes, *AC*, 81.
206. *Ep. Oc. Sardic.* 8 (*CSEL* 65, p. 124) (= Athanasius, *ACA* 49). See also Athanasius, *ACA* 36–43 (letters addressed to specific church communities); Sozomen, *HE* 3.12. For other matters transacted by the Westerners, see Hefele, *Histoire*, 547–604; Simonetti, *Crisi*, 175f.; Barnes, *AC*, 78–80.
207. Athanasius, *HA* 50. The Westerners also issued reports to the emperors: Athanasius, *ACA* 39, with Barnes, *AC*, 80.
208. Athanasius, *HA* 18, with id., *ACA* 50 (Arius's subscription to the Western encyclical).
209. Athanasius, *De fuga* 3; and id., *HA* 19.
210. *Ep. Sardic. ad Const.* (*CSEL* 65, pp. 182–84); Barnes, *AC*, 80.
211. *Ep. Sardic. ad Const.* (*CSEL* 65, pp. 182–84).
212. Ibid., p. 183; Barnes, *AC*, 80.
213. Athanasius, *HA* 20; Socrates, *HE* 2.20; Sozomen, *HE* 3.20; and Theodoret, *HE* 2.6 (reject Stephen). Barnes, *AC*, 89, discusses this evidence in great detail.
214. Athanasius, *HA* 20; Theodoret, *HE* 2.6–7; Simonetti, *Crisi*, 188; Barnes, *AC*, 87 (April 344).
215. Theodoret, *HE* 2.3, 6–7; Athanasius, *HA* 20.
216. Athanasius, *HA* 21.2; Barnes, *AC*, 88. Cf. Hanson, *Search*, 307. Constantius may have reinstated Arius and Asterius here (or in the summer of 345) because Arius subscribed to the synod of Jerusalem that confirmed Athanasius's return in 346 (Athanasius, *ACA* 57).
217. Poetovio: Athanasius, *Apol. ad Const.* 3, with Barnes, *AC*, 90. Meeting at Antioch: Athanasius, *De synodis* 26; Socrates, *HE* 2.19. *Macrostichos* creed: Kelly, *Creeds*, 279f.; Hanson, *Search*, 312; Barnes, *AC*, 88; and Ayres, *Nicaea*, 127–29, have seen this creed, with its attribution to the Son of likeness "to the Father in all things," a phrase acceptable to Athanasius, and avoidance of *ousia* and *hypostasis* language, as an attempt to appease the Westerners. If it was that, it was not because Leontius had a "tolerant disposition" (Hanson, *Search*, 312), but because reconciliation had become a political imperative. See *Ep. Liberi ad Const.* 4 (*CSEL* 65, p. 91).
218. Barnes, *AC*, 88.
219. On this episode, see Socrates, *HE* 2.16; Sozomen, *HE* 3.9; Dagron, *Naissance*, 431f. (on the "legend" of Paul in Socrates and Sozomen); Barnes, *AC*, 86, 214.

220. Socrates, *HE* 2.16; Photius, *Bibliotheca* 475b (*Vita Pauli*). Cf. Sozomen, *HE* 3.9.3f.

221. Barnes, *AC*, 88f.; Parvis, *Marcellus*, 248. Quote: *Ep. Liberi ad Const.* 4 (*CSEL* 65, 91). Cf. Photius, *Bibliotheca* 476a (*Vita Pauli*).

222. Volte-face: *HA* 26, 29. See Hilary, *FH B* 2.19 (*CSEL* 65, pp. 142 and 144; also in Athanasius, *ACA* 58, and id., *HA* 26): the Pannonians' *libellum* anathematizing Arianism before the Council of Milan, and their plea with Julius to be readmitted to communion in early 345.

223. Barnes, *AC*, 89f. Threats: Rufinus, *HE* 10.20; Socrates, *HE* 2.22; Sozomen, *HE* 3.20; Philostorgius, *HE* 3.12; Theodoret, *HE* 2.8 (suggesting, wrongly, that Vicentius and Euphratas had carried the letter).

224. Socrates, *HE* 2.23; Sozomen, *HE* 3.24; Barnes, *AC*, 91: authorizing Paul, Marcellus, Asclepas, and Lucius. Constantius writes to Athanasius and Constans: Athanasius, *ACA* 51.1.3–6; and id. *HA* 21. Gregory's death: Athanasius, *HA* 21; *Index* 18.

225. Barnes, *AC*, 92f., and Parvis, *Marcellus*, 250f., question whether Marcellus ever returned to Ancyra before Julian, but there is no reason to doubt Socrates, who mentions (in 2.26) a second expulsion in the early 350s after Constans's death (below). Basil of Ancyra's continued attacks against Marcellus suggest that Marcellus had not only returned but also become the "other" bishop of Ancyra. Below, on communities with two ministering bishops after the mid-340s.

226. Athanasius, *ACA* 54–56; id., *HA* 23, 31.

227. Date: *Index* 18. Meeting with Constantius: Athanasius, *HA* 22; id., *ACA* 54; Socrates, *HE* 2.23; Barnes, *AC*, 91. Constantius's letters: Athanasius, *ACA* 54–56; id., *HA* 23. Immunities to Arian clergy: implied in id., *ACA* 56.3. Cf. Constantius's letters to other churches: Socrates, *HE* 2.23; Sozomen, *HE* 3.24.

228. Socrates, *HE* 2.24, 26; Barnes, *AC*, 92. Athanasius, *HA* 25, claimed that all bishops in Palestine but two or three received him. If they had previously written against him, they declared now they had done so under compulsion.

229. Sozomen, *HE* 3.21.5 (*NPNF*, vol. 2, p. 299); cf. Philostorgius, *HE* 3.12.

230. *Index* 18; *Historia acephala* 1 (Martin, *Histoire*, 139); Athanasius, *HA* 25; Martin, *Athanase*, 446–47 n. 263.

231. Socrates, *HE* 2.24; Philostorgius, *HE* 3.12.

232. Rufinus, *HE* 10.20; Socrates, *HE* 2.23; Sozomen, *HE* 3.20.

233. Constans's patronage: Barnes, *AC*, 97. Athanasius's refusal: Rufinus, *HE* 10.20; Socrates, *HE* 2.23 (καθ'ἑκάστην πόλιν τοῖς διακρινομένοις πρὸς τὴν τῶν ἀρειανιζόντων κοινωνίαν); Sozomen, *HE* 3.20. Rufinus, *HE* 11.22, notes that Constantius did give a church to the Arians in Alexandria—was it at this time or after 350, when he became sole emperor?

234. Sozomen, *HE* 3.20; Theodoret, *HE* 2.19 (while the faithful uttered two different doxologies, Leontius offered his own praises to Father and Son in silence).

235. Aetius's ordination: Philostorgius, *HE* 3.17; Kopecek, *History*, 96 (in 346); and Vaggione, *Eunomius*, 26–27. Split between Aetius's followers and the Nicene: Philostorgius, *HE* 3.14; Theodoret, *HE* 2.19, 23; and Kopecek, *History*, 98, 102. Choirs and monks: Theodoret, *HE* 2.19 (antiphons); and Philostorgius, *HE* 3.13 (the novelty here was not the doxologies, but the public gathering of monks to recite them).

236. Theodoret, *HE* 2.19, 23; Kopecek, *History*, 103–4; Vaggione, *Eunomius*, 27. Cf. Philostorgius, *HE* 3.17. Aetius left Antioch for Alexandria to preach to the Arian Christian community under Athanasius.

237. Socrates, *HE* 2.23; Dagron, *Naissance*, 432.
238. Socrates, *HE* 2.23. On Marcellus, see note 225 above.
239. Athanasius, *HA* 30.
240. Sozomen, *HE* 4.8.3-4 (partly from Sabinus of Heraclea; see Van Nuffelen, *Héritage*, 483).
241. Athanasius, *HA* 28-29.
242. Barnes, *AC*, 215-17. On Paul's deposition, arrest, exile, and execution, possibly for treasonable dealings with the usurper Magnentius, see *Historia acephala* 1.2-3 (Martin, *Histoire*, 139); Athanasius, *De fuga* 3; id., *HA* 7; Socrates, *HE* 2.26 (cf. ibid. 5.9); and Sozomen, *HE* 4.2. Martin, *Histoire*, 175 n. 13, follows Dagron, *Naissance*, 432-33, in doubting treason. But as Barnes, *AC*, 215, rightly noted, Magnentius wrote to Athanasius, so there is no reason why he should not have written to Paul.
243. Athanasius, *HA* 30; Sozomen, *HE* 4.8, with Barnes, *AC*, 98f.
244. Sozomen, *HE* 4.8.4 (George). Marcellus and Lucius ("loaded with chains"): Socrates, *HE* 2.26; and Sozomen, *HE* 4.2. Maximus of Jerusalem: Socrates, *HE* 2.38.1; Sozomen, *HE* 4.20.1; Jerome, *Chronicle ad ann.* 353 (*PL* 27.501-2); Barnes, *AC*, 107. Flavianus (and Paulinus or Diodorus?): Philostorgius, *HE* 3.18; Kopecek, *History*, 104, probably deposed or excommunicated in the Council of Antioch.
245. Socrates, *HE* 2.27 (the Nicene were expelled from cities) and 2.38; Sozomen, *HE* 4.2.
246. Athanasius, *Apol. ad Const.* 10, 23; id., *HA* 51; John of Antioch, *Fragm.* 175, *FHG* 4, p. 604 (ed. Müller).
247. Barnes, *AC*, 106.
248. Hanson, *Search*, 325; Ayres, *Nicaea*, 134.
249. Athanasius, *Apol. ad Const.* 1-2, 6, 18; Socrates, *HE* 2.26. Creed: Barnes, *AC*, 109; Ayres, *Nicaea*, 134-38.
250. For Constantius's efforts to unite the church in West and East through persuasion and force from 351 to 356, and the conciliar activity that resulted from it (Sirmium, 351; Arles, 353; Milan, 355), see Barnes, *AC*, 101-19; Hanson, *Search*, 325-41; Kelly, *Creeds*, 281-87. This represented a change from Constantius's willingness to tolerate rival creeds after the Dedication Council.
251. Socrates, *HE* 2.27, 38; Sozomen, *HE* 4.2; Dagron, *Naissance*, 437.
252. Ayres, *Nicaea*, 150-53 (quote on 151). See also Hanson, *Search*, 349-53; and Socrates, *HE* 4.4 (spread of *homoiousian* doctrine in the Hellespont, with the work of Macedonius, Marathonius, Eleusis, Basil of Ancyra, and others).
253. On what follows: Socrates, *HE* 2.27, 38; Sozomen, *HE* 4.2-3; Photius, *Bibliotheca* 476b (*Vita Pauli*).
254. Socrates, *HE* 38.29-31, reports that Macedonius, after hearing that a larger number of Novatian Christians lived in Paphlagonia, who on account of their number could not be handled by ecclesiastical men alone, convinced the emperor to send troops to terrify them into accepting the "Arian" doctrine, but in the town of Mantineion, the Novatians, animated by a fervor for their Nicene faith, armed themselves with "sickles and hatchets" and gave battle, resulting in great mortality. Cf. Sozomen, *HE* 4.21.
255. Monasteries: Sozomen, *HE* 4.20; Socrates, *HE* 2.38. Monks in action: Sozomen, *HE* 4.2.

256. Sozomen, *HE* 4.27.3; Elm, *Virgins*, 112.

257. Ascetic teachings emphasized a rejection of ownership of property and minimized distinctions of gender and social status. See *Vita S. Parthenii* 13, 15, 17 (note the deaconess, 40), etc.; and Elm, *Virgins*, 125. One wonders whether Arius's ideas of Christ's humanity and divinity, via Eustathius of Sebaste, influenced these churchmen, shaping their ascetic practices and strong commitment to the care of the poor. Cf. Brown, *Poverty*, 36–38; and A. Sterk, *Renouncing the World yet Leading the Church: The Monk-Bishop in Late Antiquity* (Cambridge, MA, 2004), 36 n. 5.

258. Epiphanius, *Panarion* 75.1, observed that Eustathius had entrusted to the presbyter and ascetic Aërius the ξενοδοχεῖον . . . ὅπερ ἐν τῷ Πόντῳ καλεῖται πτωχοτροφεῖον. See also Brown, *Poverty*, 36–38.

259. Epiphanius, *Panarion* 75.1.

260. Libanius, *Autobiography* 44; Brown, *Poverty*, 46–57; Liebeschuetz, *Decline*, 141–42.

261. Sozomen, *HE* 4.27.4; Brown, *Poverty*, 42–43. *Chronicon Paschale* 360 (ed. Whitby and Whitby): Constantius's gift to the hospices, beggars, virgins, widows, orphans, and prisoners of Constantinople.

262. Marathonius, "overseer of the poor and the monastic houses" of Constantinople (Sozomen, *HE* 4.20.2), "contributed so much enthusiasm and so much of his own money to support this heresy that the followers of Macedonius were called 'Marathonians.'" (ibid. 4.27.4). Cf. *Chronicon Paschale* 350 (ed. Whitby and Whitby): Leontius of Antioch appointed men "devout in their concern for [the hospices of the poor]." See also Elm, *Virgins*, 111f.; and A. T. Crislip, *From Monastery to Hospital: Christian Monasticism and the Transformation of Health Care in Late Antiquity* (Ann Arbor, MI, 2005), 130–32.

263. Sozomen, *HE* 4.27.5; cf. ibid. 4.27.2: "[Macedonius's] teaching was embraced . . . by no small part of the faithful of Constantinople, Bithynia, Thrace, the Hellespont, and the regions roundabout." Cf. Palladius, *HL* 66.

264. Socrates, *HE* 2.38; Sozomen, *HE* 4.20.

265. Marathonius's predecessor died in the earthquake; see Socrates, *HE* 2.39; Sozomen, *HE* 4.16. Cf. Libanius, *Autobiography* 78.

266. Socrates, *HE* 2.27, 38; Sozomen, *HE* 4.20; Photius, *Bibliotheca* 476b (*Vita Pauli*).

267. Socrates, *HE* 38.27; Sozomen, *HE* 4.21.

268. Sozomen, *HE* 5.15.5 (unknown source; see Van Nuffelen, *Héritage*, 486).

269. Eleusis reached out to the wool-weavers and the workers of the imperial mint (Sozomen, *HE* 5.15.7). The Cyzicenes rose up to defend him (or threatened to do so) whenever Eleusis's control of the church was in jeopardy; see Socrates, *HE* 2.42, 4.6–7.10; Sozomen, *HE* 5.15.6–7, 6.8; and Philostorgius, *HE* 5.3 and 9.13.

270. *Vita S. Parthenii*, *AASS*, February 7, with Batiffol, *Étude*, and id., "Saint Parthénius."

271. The *terminus ante quem* for his ordination is the Council of Serdica, because Macedonius was bishop of Cyzicus there, and Parthenius was ordained by his predecessor, Ascholius (see chapter 7 above). The *terminus post quem* is 355, because that was when Hypatianus became bishop of Heraclea, in which capacity he attended Parthenius's funeral; see Le Quien, *OC*, vol. 1, col. 1104.

272. Parthenius was close to Theodorus of Heraclea and Eleusis of Cyzicus, and Hypatianus, Theodorus's successor in Heraclea, attended his funeral; see *Vita S. Parthenii* 27 (p. 42); and Batiffol, *Étude*, 46.

273. Antony, the prototypical fourth-century ascetic, also healed the sick and cast away demons, but he spent most of his life isolated, outside the world. Cf. the *Life of Gregory Thaumaturgos,* which is a roughly contemporary text, but unlike Gregory, Parthenius was of humble origins. The *Vita Parthenii* also lacks reference to the institutionalized asceticism common in the *vitae* of many later monk-bishops (see, for instance, Rapp, *Holy Bishops,* 160–64).

274. He made himself accessible not only to townsfolk, but also to poor villagers in the surrounding countryside (*Vita S. Parthenii* 9, 10–15 [pp. 39–40]; cf. *Syn. Arménien de Ter Israël,* Feb. 8 [*PO* 21.8]). He approached the workers in the imperial dye factory and the sailors and fishermen, who spread his fame as a holy man and, no doubt, his brand of doctrine (*Vita S. Parthenii* 8, 18–19 [pp. 39–41]).

CONCLUSION

1. Athanasius, *Apol. ad Const.* 27; id., *HA* 33; Sulpicius Severus, *Chronicon* 2.39.3–6; Jerome, *De vir. ill.* 96; Barnes, *AC,* 117; D. A. Washburn, "Tormenting the Tormentors: A Reinterpretation of Eusebius of Vercelli's Letter from Scythopolis," *Church History* 78 (2009): 732f.

2. Manufacture: J. Price, "Glass Working and Glassworkers in Cities and Towns," in *Roman Working Lives and Urban Living,* ed. A. MacMahon and J. Price (Oxford, 2005), 167–190; D. Sperber, *The City in Roman Palestine* (Oxford, 1998), 161, 171; Washburn, "Tormenting," 733. Pagan presence: Washburn (735f.) suggests that the city was mostly pagan, based on the desecration of Patrophilus's tomb by pagans under Julian, but that alone does not necessarily imply most Scythopolitans were heathen.

3. Epiphanius, *Panarion* 30.5; Washburn, "Tormenting," 735f., 748.

4. Eusebius, *Ep.* 2.8.1 (*CCSL* 9).

5. Epiphanius, *Panarion* 30.5.

6. Eusebius lodged in a *hospitium* (*Ep.* 2.4.1–2; 2.6.1). As Washburn, "Tormenting," 743, noted, the word has many meanings, including "inn or lodge."

7. Eusebius, *Ep.* 3.1.

8. Eusebius, *Ep.* 2.6; Washburn, "Tormenting," 739–43, 754.

9. Eusebius, *Ep.* 2.6; Washburn, "Tormenting," p. 754.

10. Washburn, "Tormenting," 743. And indeed, Eusebius did win the sympathy of many city dwellers: later, he recorded that, when he was being transferred to another inn, the people expressed their joy and "hanged lanterns around our [building]." See *Ep.* 2. 6.1.

11. Eusebius, *Ep.* 2.3.1.

12. Quote: Eusebius, *Ep.* 2.4.1; cf. ibid. 3.4, 4.2; Washburn, "Tormenting," 744, suggests a less sensationalist reading of "nudatum," but given what we have seen elsewhere and learn from Libanius, "naked" or nearly so, appears right.

13. Eusebius, *Ep.* 2.3.4, 4.2; Washburn, "Tormenting," 755.

14. Eusebius, *Ep.* 2.6.1.

15. Ibid. 2.6.2–5.

16. Cf. Socrates, *HE* 2.43, on Basil of Ancyra accused of imprisoning an individual, loading him with chains, and subjecting him to torture.

17. Athanasius, *Apol. ad Const.* 30.3.

18. On events of the 350s, see Ammianus Marcellinus, *RG* 15.7.7 (Athanasius "ultra professionem altius se efferentem, scitarique conatum externa"); Julian, *Epp.* 110 (ed. Bidez) (Ἀθανάσιον ... τὸν τολμηρότατον, ὑπὸ τοῦ συνήθους ἐπαρθέντα θράσου); 111 (πολυπράγμων ἀνήρ). Cf. Socrates, *HE* 2.20, 43, for Eudoxius in Antioch and Constantinople, etc.

APPENDIX

1. Eusebius, *HE* 5.24, and 5.24.9.6.
2. A. Brent, "Was Hippolytus a Schismatic?" *Vigiliae Christianae* 49 (1995): 200ff.
3. Hippolytus, *Philos.* 9.12.1-2, 4-6; Chadwick, *Early Church*, 88-89; and Brent, "Hippolytus," 215-44.
4. Eusebius, *HE* 6.33, with Brent, "Hippolytus," 221f.
5. Scherer, *Entretien* (1960); and chapter 1 above.
6. Cyprian, *Ep.* 59.10.1, 36.4.1.
7. Cyprian, *Ep.* 59.10.1.
8. Ibid.
9. Cf. Cyprian, *Ep.* 40.2ff.
10. Cyprian, *Ep.* 59.10.2.
11. Eusebius, *HE* 7.24.1ff.; and chapter 2 above.
12. Eusebius, *HE* 7.27ff.; and chapter 1 above.
13. Pamphilus, *Apologia* (*PG* 17.542ff.); Methodius of Olympus, *On Ressurrection* 1.2. See also Eusebius, *HE* 8.1.1-9; Alexander of Lycopolis, *Contra Manichaeos* (ed. Villey), 98-100; Simonetti, *Crisi,* 20-21; Barnes, *CE,* 196ff.; and Lyman, *Christology,* 39-81.
14. Eusebius, *HE* 5.24.18ff.
15. Ibid., 5.24.16-17.
16. Ibid., 6.12.4, trans. G. A. Williamson, Penguin ed. (1989).
17. Eusebius, *HE* 6.33.2-3.
18. Ibid., 6.37, trans. G. A. Williamson, Penguin ed. (1989).
19. Eusebius, *HE* 7.5.5 and 7.7.5.
20. *Or.* 7.6 apud Calderini, *Dizionario,* 112; cf. *Descriptio totius orbis* 35. H. A. Musurillo, ed., *The Acts of the Pagan Martyrs* (New York, 1979), 77f., with P. Benoit and J. Schwartz, "Caracalla et les troubles d'Alexandrie en 215 après J.-C.," *Études de papyrologie* 7 (1948): 22-23.
21. Rodziewicz, *Alexandrie,* 249ff., 331-38. See also Haas, *Alexandria,* 34-35 (Alexandrian crafts in general), 50 (glassworkers on the Kôm el-Dikka), and 192ff. (commercial and manufacturing activities in the same area). Cf. further *BGU* 4.1115; and the bone-carving workshops studied by E. Rodziewicz, "Archaeological Evidence of Bone and Ivory Carvings in Alexandria," in *Commerce,* 155-58. On glass, see also Reil, *Beiträge,* 48-49.
22. Reil, *Beiträge,* 114 (*tarsika alexandrina* in the *Edict of Prices* and other sources); E. Wipszycka, *Industrie,* 77; the evidence of *PGissen;* and F. Ippolito, "I tessitori del Fayyum in epoca greca e romana: Le testimonianze papiracee," in *Atti del XXII Congresso internazionale di papirologia, Firenze, 23-29 agosto 1998,* ed. I. Andorlini et al. (Florence, 2001), 2:705, 710f.
23. Orosius, *Contra paganos* 6.19.20.

24. *Alexandria*, 50.
25. Wipscyzka, *Industrie*, 47, 55–57, and, for the large workshops, 67f., 81ff. See also M. Bergamasco, "Le διδασκαλικαί nella ricerca attuale," *Aegyptus* 75 (1995): 154ff., on a shift from domestic to large-scale textile production in the third century and beyond.
26. See chapter 7 above.
27. *Urk.* 29.
28. Socrates, *HE* 1.25.
29. *Urk.* 32, p. 66, ll. 17–21. Cf. Sozomen, *HE* 2.27.12, on Constantine's satisfaction, but mixing up the first recall of Arius and his later reintegration at the Council of Jerusalem in 335. See chapter 7 above.
30. Chapter 7 above.
31. Schwartz, *GS*, 3:206–8.
32. Philostorgius, *HE* 2.7 and 2.7a; Parvis, *Marcellus*, 104.
33. Simonetti, *Crisi*, 120–21; Barnes, *AC*, 246–47 n. 75.
34. Simonetti, *Crisi*, 119–20; Parvis, *Marcellus*, 107.
35. On the Council of Nicomedia, see chapter 7 above.
36. The reference may have been to some other council or perhaps Alexander's reception of the Melitians.
37. On these events, see chapter 7 above.
38. Though Gelasius, *HE* 3.13.21, seems to paraphrase from Athanasius's and Alexander's joint letter (or another source), writing: "It was impossible to readmit into the church those who had once been judged, anathematized, and expelled from the church by such a holy synod and by the emperor's god-loving piety."
39. Gelasius, *HE* 3.14.22.
40. Ibid. 3.15.7.
41. See chapter 7 above.
42. *ACA* 11: Ἀλεξάνδρου κατηγορήσαντες μέχρις αὐτοῦ τοῦ βασιλέως, referring to a time after Nicaea. Barnes, *CE*, 231, 386 n. 64, dismissed Epiphanius's account, because it would have been impossible for the Melitians to accuse Alexander, but the evidence in Athanasius, which Barnes did not consider, corroborates Epiphanius's narrative.
43. By land, roughly 1,800 (via Aquileia and the Balkans) to 2,100 (south to Italy and Greece) miles separate Trier from Nicomedia. Assuming the bishops covered 25–35 miles/day, the average day's travel over land, it would have taken them 52–72 days (shortest route) and up to 60–84 days (longest route). See L. Casson, *Travel in the Ancient World* (London, 1974), 185, 188–90. The trip would have been shorter if the bishops sailed from a Western port (e.g., Aquileia or Rome) or traveled with the imperial post (perhaps 30–40 days or so).
44. Gelasius, *HE* 3.13.17.
45. Barnes, *New Empire*, 77.
46. Ibid.
47. Cf. *ACA* 70.2, in 334, while campaigning in the Balkans (Barnes, *New Empire*, 79), but simply "court" in *ACA* 86?
48. Simonetti, *Crisi*, 119; Parvis, *Marcellus*, 100, 104.
49. Philostorgius, *HE* 2.7 and 2.7a.
50. Bidez, 18: "eine willkürliche Contamination dieser Philostorgiusstelle mit Sozomen."

51. Cf. Barnes, *AC*, 17f.
52. Eusebius, *VC* 3.23 (trans. Cameron).
53. Ibid.
54. And so many modern scholars: Williams, "Quest," 25, speaks of Arius's (intellectual) isolation; Haas, *Alexandria*, 273-77, admits that the "Arian 'community' possessed enough of a self-identity" (276), but postulates that, in the 340s at least, allegiance to Arian leaders rested on patronage and outside pressure rather than theology; Martin, *Athanase*, 348, 386, and 388, denies that Arius ever returned to Alexandria.
55. See chapter 7 above.
56. Chapter 7 above; cf. Athanasius, *ACA* 84.
57. *PG* 25.ccxxix. Cf. Athanasius, *Or. contra Arianos* 1.22 (see chapter 4 above).
58. Epiphanius, *Panarion* 69.12.
59. See chapter 8 above. Quote: Athanasius, *Festal* 11 (ed. Parker).
60. Athanasius, *Ep. enc.* 6.3.
61. Quote: Athanasius, *HA* 27.2. Church: chapter 8 above.
62. Athanasius, *HA* 59.3: "They allowed the women of their party freedom to insult whomever they wished. And when the respectable and faithful women moved aside and gave them the road, they surrounded them like maenads and furies and thought it a misfortune if they did not find a way to injure them."
63. It is unlikely that Arsenius was elected before Athanasius's election for the following reasons: (1) the Melitians hoped to win the emperor's sympathy in their struggle against Alexander; hence it would have been imprudent to disrespect the provisions of Nicaea; (2) hostile sources would likely have mentioned that; (3) after Nicomedia Alexander and the Melitians seem to have agreed to a truce (see chapter 7 above); and (4) Arsenius may have served in the church of Alexandria and left it after quarreling with Athanasius.
64. Sozomen, *HE* 2.22.3.
65. Athanasius never received him back even after he regretted accusing the bishop; see Athanasius, *ACA* 69; and ibid. 8.4f.: in 338, Athanasius wrote: "[Arsenius] wishes to communicate with us."
66. Rufinus, *HE* 10.18; Sozomen, *HE* 2.23.1-3. Epiphanius, *Panarion* 68.7.9, calls him a priest in the Mareotis. Cf. *Vita Pachomii* 94 (ed. Athanassakis, pp. 134-35) on Abba Theodore, Pachomius's successor, who was a lector in Alexandria.
67. Counting inclusively, based on Athanasius's comment in 334 that he had not seen Arsenius for five or six years (*ACA* 65).
68. Neither John nor the second Melitian embassy to Constantine brought charges of murder against Athanasius in 330-331 (see chapter 7 above). In other words, the plot must have been hatched later.
69. Even in Rufinus's pro-Athanasian story, fear of punishment is what drove Arsenius into hiding.
70. Athanasius, *ACA* 59.
71. Ibid. 60.
72. Van Nuffelen, *Héritage*, 460, suggests Socrates and Athanasius, but this is not the case.
73. This was the embassy led by Ision, Eudaemon, Callinicos, and Eulogius (Athanasius, *ACA* 60; Socrates, *HE* 1.27).

74. Sozomen places Constantine's letter ordering Athanasius to receive Arius after John's embassy, which is possible, but see chapter 7 above for an alternative reconstruction.

75. Athanasius, *ACA* 60; id., *Festal* 4 (ed. Parker).

76. But long enough for the fateful events in the Mareotis involving Macarius breaking the sacred chalice in Ischyras's church to take place; see chapter 7 above.

77. To distinguish it from *Epistulae* 1 and 2—the first being the letter Julius sent to the Eastern bishops in 338 inviting them to a council in Rome, and the second the letter addressed to the Eusebians together with a formal summons for a synod at Rome with a scheduled date (on which, see below). There may of course have been more letters than these three, as Parvis, *Marcellus*, 157–60, suggests, but there is no evidence of them.

78. Athanasius's flight: chapter 8 above. Constantine II: Barnes, *AC*, 218; W. Schneemelcher, "Die Kirchweihsynode von Antiochen 341," in *Bonner Festgabe Johannes Straub zum 65. Geburtstag am 18. Oktober 1977* (Bonn, 1977), 330; and R. Lane Fox, "The Itinerary of Alexander: Constantius to Julian," *Classical Quarterly* 47 (1997): 243f. Dedication Council: Athanasius, *De synodis* 25 (consular date).

79. Also in Athanasius, *HA* 11.2.

80. In *ACA* 32.1, Julius says he asked Marcellus to provide that statement.

81. Epiphanius, *Panarion* 72.2.3: "Since ... they did not plan to come (for the council), though you had sent your priests to them, and since I had spent one year and three months in Rome, as I was about to leave the city, I thought it necessary to give to you in writing an account of my faith." See also Brennecke et al., *Ekthesis*, 153ff.

82. Schwartz, *GS*, 3:291–92, 301 (assuming, wrongly, that Athanasius arrived in Rome in the fall of 339), followed by Simonetti, *Crisi*, 144, and Schneemelcher, "Kirchweihsynode," 322, 324–30. Barnes, *AC*, 50, suggests that the eighteen-month period must have ended in January 341, which is the date he assigns to Julius's composition of *Epistula* 3, so he backdates Athanasius's arrival in Rome to June/July 339 to fit his timeline. Parvis, *Marcellus*, 158f., considering the possibility that the eighteen-month sojourn began when Julius sent *Epistula* 2, rather than from Athanasius's arrival, postulates that Julius wrote many letters. Julius might have had in mind the period from Athanasius's arrival to the moment when he was writing *Epistula* 3 to the Eastern bishops, but, as will become clear below, this is unlikely.

83. Schwartz, followed by others, suggested that the travels and turmoil of which Athanasius was accused by the Eastern bishops at Serdica took place between Athanasius's departure from Alexandria and arrival in Rome; hence they have placed his Rome arrival in late fall 339. But as Barnes, *AC*, 42f., has convincingly shown, those activities belong in 338, so there is no reason to doubt (as Schneemelcher, "Kirchweihsynode," 322, does) that Athanasius was not being straightforward about his whereabouts after leaving Alexandria. Parvis, *Marcellus*, 159, conjectures that Athanasius arrived in September 339, because he "would have taken a circuitous route to avoid imperial apprehension," but there is no evidence for this.

84. Alexandria–Rome by sea in April: 17 days (http://orbis.stanford.edu).

85. Schwartz, *GS*, 3:295; Schneemelcher, "Kirchweihsynode," 324; Simonetti, *Crisi*, 144; Hanson, *Search*, 269; Barnes, *AC*, 57 (placing Marcellus's arrival in Rome in the spring of 340, hence implying Julius wrote to the Eusebians around that time); Brennecke et al., *Ekthesis*, 137; and Parvis, *Marcellus*, 148, 158f. (first half of 340). Except for Barnes, these scholars postulate that Athanasius arrived in Rome in the fall of 339 or later.

86. So Julius wrote in *Epistula* 3 (*ACA* 21.3) that he had summoned a council ἵνα πάντα θᾶττον λύσιν λαβόντα διορθωθῆναι δυνηθῇ.

87. So does Pietri, *Roma,* 1:199 n. 3, suggesting an even earlier date, soon after Athanasius's arrival.

88. *ACA* 21.3: συμπαθεῖν τοῖς πάσχουσι.

89. Schwartz, *GS,* 3:296; Klein, *Constantius,* 161; Blockley, "Constantius," 471f.; id., *East Roman Foreign Policy,* 14. See also J.-P. Callu, "La préface à *l'Itinéraire* d'Alexandre," in *De Tertullien aux Mozarabes* (Paris, 1992), 1:435 n. 26.

90. Zosimus 2.41 *apud* Lane Fox, "Itinerary," 244–46; Blockley, "Constantius," 470–74; id., *East Roman Foreign Policy,* 12–15.

91. *Index* 12 (contra Schwartz *apud* Barnes, *AC,* 188), though the *Index* notes Athanasius sent a memo to the Alexandrian priests (cf. *Festal* 17 and 18). In his commentary, Martin, *Histoire,* 289 n. 40, first suggested the memo was the *Ep. Serap.*, but see Barnes, *AC,* 191. Athanasius had no problem sending the *Festal* for 341 from Rome (on which, see below).

92. Julius might have sent his priests in late spring 340, once the hostilities in the West were over, but why would he have waited so long after Athanasius's arrival? And then why send his men out when the East was preparing for war?

93. T. D. Barnes, "Constantine and the Christians of Persia," *JRS* 75 (1985): 135; id., *AC,* 51–52, 219, relying on the evidence of the *Itinerarium Alexandri,* but see also *Chronicle of Seert* (*PO* 4.306: "In the year when Constantine II attacked Constans, Shapur took advantage and invaded Roman territory").

94. Zonaras, *Annals* 13.5; Schwartz, *GS,* 3:295; Barnes, *AC,* 35; Blockley, "Constantius," 469–74; B. Dignas and E. Winter, *Rome and Persia in Late Antiquity: Neighbors and Rivals* (Cambridge, 2007), 33, 88–90.

95. Blockley, "Constantius," 470–74; P. Peeters, "Le début de la persécution de Sapor d'après Faustus de Byzance," *Revue des Études Arméniennes* 1 (1920–21): 15–18, 27–31.

96. Peeters, "Début," 26, 29ff.; Klein, *Constantius,* 232. But see Burgess, *Studies,* 264, 268f. (higher taxation of Christians since 337, placing Shapur's edict ordering destruction of churches in 340).

97. The evidence of the *Itinerarium Alexandri* suggests this much. Callu, "Préface," 429–32, Barnes, *AC,* 51–52, and Lane Fox, "Itinerary," 246, have dated the *Itinerary* to 340 and so, based on "Preface" 1, Constantius's preparations for an invasion of Persia. One difficulty with this date is that, in "Preface" 4, the author of the *Itinerary* praises Constantine II, whose memory, after his invasion of Constans's territory in 340, had been abolished. Barnes, "Constantine," 135, first argued that the author of this piece was ill informed about imperial propaganda. Lane Fox, "Itinerary," 244ff., making the case for the *Itinerary*'s authorship by Flavius Polemius, cos. 338, and thus someone close to the imperial court, argued that, immediately after Constantine II's death, there was no consistent policy on his memory. Subsequently, Barnes, *AC,* 51f., adopted the position that that emperor's memory was not abolished at once. However, there is no reason to rule out preparations for a campaign in 339, when it would have been admissible to praise Constantine II. During that year, Shapur broke the truce established in 338 after Arsaces' perjury (Blockley, "Constantius," 474) and continued to oppress the Christians of Persia (Peeters, "Début," 26; Burgess, *Studies,* 268f.). Another argument for dating the *Itinerary* (and Constantius's planned invasion) to 340 is, *pace* Barnes, "Constantine," 135, the mention that Constantius was the same age as Alexan-

der ("Preface" 8). Yet, if the flattering comparison was not only for rhetorical effect, there is also controversy about the year of Constantius's birth and the Roman way of reckoning years: Alexander was twenty-two when he invaded Persian territory. If Constantius were born in 318, he would have been twenty-two or twenty-three (counting inclusively) in 340; if born in 317, he would have been twenty-two or twenty-three in 339. See Callu, "Préface," 441.

98. ACA 25.4: εἰ μὲν οὖν διὰ τὸ τοιοῦτον εἶναι τὸν καιρὸν οὐκ ἀπηντήσατε, ὥς φατε, ἔδει προτέρους ὑμᾶς τὸν καιρὸν τοῦτον σκοπήσαντας μὴ αἰτίους σχίσματος μηδὲ ὀλολυγῆς καὶ θρήνων ἐν ταῖς ἐκκλησίαις γενέσθαι.

99. In *ACA* 33.2, Julius mentions letters recently brought by priests from Alexandria, complaining that clerics "wishing to come to the synod were prevented from doing so." It is of course possible that these clerics were informed by letters not carried by Julius's priests or they had intended to come after having received Julius's first summons (*Epistula* 1), but the phrasing in *ACA* 21.3 again suggests they also received the summons brought by Julius's envoys.

100. Athanasius, *HA* 11.3, asks rhetorically: "What do bishops have to do with war?" A lot—at least since Constantine, as Eusebius, *VC* 4.56, noted. In 337, Constantine not only discussed the Persian campaign with bishops but also arranged for some of them to come with him "for divine worship." Constantius took Eusebius of Emesa to the front with him (Sozomen, *HE* 3.6).

101. Julius did not concede the Easterners had a point, as Parvis, *Marcellus*, 159, suggests.

102. Combining different synods: Socrates, *HE* 2.15 (cf. 2.8); and Sozomen, *HE* 3.8 (cf. 3.5). See also Brennecke et al., *Ekthesis*, 138ff.; and below on the Dedication Council. Eusebius of Nicomedia (with his close associates) was the letter's likely author, with the other bishops adding their names (*ACA* 21.1 on the assembled bishops = addressees of Julius's *Epistula* 3; Schwartz, *GS*, 3:297; and Parvis, *Marcellus*, 163).

103. Schwartz, *GS*, 3:296 n. 1: not 342.

104. Schwartz, *GS*, 3:301 (notes that the deadline had passed, but does not take issue with item 9); Simonetti, *Crisi*, 146; Klein, *Constantius*, 40; Hanson, *Search*, 270; Barnes, *AC*, 50, 59 (contending that Julius composed *Epistula* 3 in January 341 and took it to the Council of Rome, whose participants endorsed it); Martin, *Athanase*, 415; and Parvis, *Marcellus*, 161–62 (failing to consider the possibility that the Eastern bishops' letter, though sent from Antioch, was not necessarily sent by the bishops attending the Dedication Council).

105. Pietri, *Roma*, 1:200f.

106. *ACA* 26.3.

107. But not necessarily because of their reply letter to Julius, which, if they met in late 340, as I argue here, the Italians could not have yet seen it.

108. In *ACA* 26.1, they complained that Julius wrote only to the Eusebians, as if only the latter had deposed Athanasius, Marcellus, and others.

109. *ACA* 26.2.

110. See Pietri, *Roma*, 1:201–7.

111. Of course, Julius did share the Eastern bishops' letter sent from Antioch with the Italians (*ACA* 21.4), who expressed the same sentiments as Julius (26.3), but this need not have happened in a council. Note that Julius had also insisted that he and the Italians were

of one mind when he wrote *Epistula* 2 to the Eusebians, and no council was needed for that agreement to emerge.

112. http://orbis.stanford.edu: as fast as 22 days by fastest sea route, traveling on open sea; 61 days (Antioch-Constantinople by coastal sea; Constantinople-coast of Epirus on land; coast of Epirus-Rome, crossing the Adriatic to Brundisium); 83 days (taking the land route from Antioch to Constantinople).

113. *ACA* 21.4: νομίζων ὅμως ἥξειν τινὰς.

114. *ACA* 33.2: μέχρι γὰρ νῦν.

115. Athanasius, *HA* 12–13.

116. *Festal* 13 (ed. Parker), composed in Rome, alludes to persecution in Alexandria and Egypt, but Athanasius only vaguely mentions bishops. In 341, Easter fell on April 19 *(Index* 13), and Athanasius calls for fasting to begin on March 9. If the letter was written in time to arrive in Egypt before March 9, Athanasius, and therefore Julius, would have been informed of events in Egypt at the latest by early February. However, the passing comment on the "ill treatment" of bishops, without mentioning their names and confessor status, suggests that, when Athanasius wrote the letter, he (and Julius) was not yet fully informed of the extent of Gregory's persecution in the *chora*, later so vividly described in *HA*. So it is possible that *Festal* 13 was composed before the arrival of fresh news of persecution brought by the exiled or refugee Egyptian priests in spring 341, as suggested here.

117. *ACA* 21.4.

118. Klein, *Constantius*, 40–43; cf. Kelly, *Creeds*, 264. On the imputations of heresy in Julius's *Epistula* 3, see below.

119. Schneemelcher, "Kirchweihsynode," 328–30; Barnes, *AC*, 57–59; Parvis, *Marcellus*, 160–62 (and n. 128). Brennecke et al., *Ekthesis*, 148, are also inclined to date this synod before the Council of Rome.

120. Schwartz, *GS*, 3:310; Pietri, *Roma*, 1:200 n. 2; Simonetti, *Crisi*, 154 (fall 341); Hanson, *Search*, 284; Martin, *Athanase*, 415 n. 117, 419. Cf. Klein, *Constantius*, 40f., and Ayres, *Nicaea*, 109, 117: later in 341, in response to the Council of Rome.

121. Socrates, *HE* 2.8 and 15; Sozomen, *HE* 3.5 and 8.

122. Athanasius, *De synodis* 25 (given Constantius's presence). Brennecke et al., *Ekthesis*, 138, 144.

123. Parvis, *Marcellus*, 161–62.

124. One would have expected it especially at *ACA* 23, 25 (when accusing the Eastern bishops of having subverted Nicaea by communicating with the Arians and transferring bishops for one city to another, Julius makes no comment on the publication of new creeds), and 32 (when he writes that he was reminding the bishops of Marcellus's opposition to the Arians at Nicaea: ἵνα μηδεὶς τὴν τοιαύτην αἵρεσιν ἀποδέχηται, ἀλλὰ βδελύττηται ὡς ἀλλοτρίαν τῆς ὑγιαινούσης διδασκαλίας; it's hard to understand this mild warning if Julius already knew the Eastern bishops had published new creeds omitting the *homoousios* and appending to them anti-Marcellan anathemas). Sozomen, *HE* 3.8.8, seems puzzled and finds it necessary to explain that the Eastern bishops did not touch on their "deeds against the decrees of Nicaea" in their reply to Julius. But the phrase τῶν πεπραγμένων παρὰ τὰ δόξαντα τοῖς ἐν Νικαίᾳ does not necessarily refer to doctrinal innovation, because when Julius, in his *Epistula* 2, alluded to the Eusebians' disregard for Nicaea, he complained of their receipt of the Arians in communion and repeated transfers of bishops from one see to

another (Athanasius, *ACA* 23, 25; cf. Sozomen, *HE* 3.8.3; Julius complained that the Eusebians τὰς ἐκκλησίας ταράττουσι τῷ μὴ ἐμμένειν τοῖς ἐν Νικαίᾳ δόξασιν—this refers to events in the past, not to recent doctrinal developments).

125. Brennecke et al., *Ekthesis,* 148, suggests that the first creed of Antioch (formulated at the Dedication Council) was sent with the envoys to Rome.

126. *ACA* 32, 34, etc.; *Ep. Or. Sardic.* 10, 23 (*CSEL* 65, pp. 56, 63).

127. Barnes, *AC,* 58. Constantius would in fact have been interested in disseminating the new creeds. The emperor would have been told that the revised faith would end the controversy and bring much desired peace and stability to the church.

128. Athanasius, *De synodis* 22: τὴν προαίρεσιν ἑαυτῶν ταχέως ἐξήγγειλαν.

129. Van Nuffelen, *Héritage,* 459, does not mention Socrates' source, which in this case was probably not Sabinus of Heraclea. Socrates did use the *Vita Pauli* as a source, and this information is mentioned in Photius's version of the *Vita;* see Photius, *Bibliotheca* 474b.

BIBLIOGRAPHY

Alston, R. *The City in Roman and Byzantine Egypt*. London and New York, 2002.
Amerise, M. *Il battesimo di Costantino il Grande: Storia di una scomoda eredità*. Hermes Einzelschriften 95. Stuttgart, 2005.
Andrieu, M., and P. Collomp. "Fragments sur papyrus de l'Anaphora de saint Marc." *Revue des Sciences Religieuses* 8 (1928): 489–515.
Arnold, D. W.H. *The Early Episcopal Career of Athanasius of Alexandria*. Notre Dame, IN, 1991.
Athanassakis, A. N. *The Life of Pachomius (Vita Prima Graeca)*. Society of Biblical Literature Texts and Translations 7. Early Christian Literature Series 2. Missoula, MT, 1975.
Ayres, L. *Nicaea and Its Legacy: An Approach to Fourth-Century Trinitarian Theology*. Oxford, 2004.
Bagnall, R. S. *Egypt in Late Antiquity*. Princeton, NJ, 1993.
Bakker, J. T., ed. *The Mill-Bakeries of Ostia: Description and Interpretation*. Amsterdam, 1999.
Bakker, J. T., and B. Meijlink, Introduction to *The Mill-Bakeries of Ostia: Description and Interpretation*, ed. J. T. Bakker, 1–15. Amsterdam, 1999.
Baldovin, J. F. "Hippolytus and the Apostolic Tradition: Recent Research and Commentary." *Theological Studies* 64 (2003): 520–42.
Bardy, G. *Paul de Samosate: Étude historique*. Louvain, 1929.
———. *Recherches sur Saint Lucien d'Antioche et son école*. Paris, 1936.
Barnard, L. W. "Athanase et les empereurs Constantin et Constance." In *Politique et théologie chez Athanase d'Alexandrie, Actes du Colloque de Chantilly 23–25 septembre 1973*, ed. C. Kannengiesser, 127–44. Théologie Historique 27. Paris, 1974.
———. *The Council of Serdica, 343 A.D.* Sofia, 1983.
Barnes, M. R. *The Power of God: Δύναμις in Gregory of Nyssa's Trinitarian Theology*. Washington, DC, 2000.

Barnes, T. D. *Athanasius and Constantius: Theology and Politics in the Constantinian Empire.* Cambridge, MA, 1993.
———. "Constantine and the Christians of Persia." *Journal of Roman Studies* 75 (1985): 126–36.
———. *Constantine and Eusebius.* Cambridge, MA, 1981.
———. "Emperors and Bishops, A.D. 324–344: Some Problems." *American Journal of Ancient History* 3 (1978): 53–75.
———. *The New Empire of Diocletian and Constantine.* Cambridge, MA, 1982.
Batiffol, P. "Étude d'hagiographie arienne: Parthénius de Lampsaque." *Römische Quartalschrifte für die christliche Altertumskunde und Kirchengeschichte* 6 (1892): 38–51.
———. "Le Περὶ Παρθενίας du pseudo-Athanase." *Römische Quartalschrifte für die christliche Altertumskunde und Kirchengeschichte* 7 (1893): 275–86.
———. "Saint Parthénius et lex nouveaux Bollandistes." *Römische Quartalschrifte für die christliche Altertumskunde und Kirchengeschichte* 7 (1893): 298–301.
Bauer, W. *Orthodoxy and Heresy in Earliest Christianity.* Ed. R. Kraft and G. Krodel. Philadelphia, 1971.
Baumeister, T. "Ordnungsdenken und charismatiche Geisterfahrung in der alten Kirche." *Revue de Qumran* 73 (1978): 150–71.
Beagon, P. M. "The Cappadocian Fathers, Women, and Ecclesiastical Politics." *Vigiliae Christianae* 49 (1995): 165–79.
Bell, H. I., ed. *Jews and Christians in Egypt: The Jewish Troubles in Alexandria and the Athanasian Controversy, Illustrated by Texts from the Greek Papyri in the British Museum.* Oxford, 1924.
Benoit, P., and J. Schwartz. "Caracalla et les troubles d'Alexandrie en 215 après J.-C." *Études de Papyrologie* 7 (1948): 17–33.
Bergamasco, M. "Le διδασκαλικαί nella ricerca attuale." *Aegyptus* 75 (1995): 95–167.
Bernard, A. *Alexandrie la Grande.* Paris, 1966.
Blockley, R. C. "Constantius II and Persia." In *Studies in Latin Literature and Roman History* 5, ed. C. Deroux, 465–90. Collection Latomus 206. Brussels, 1989.
———. *East Roman Foreign Policy: Formation and Conduct from Diocletian to Anastasius.* Leeds, 1992.
Bobertz, C. A. "Cyprian of Carthage as a Patron: A Social Study of the Role of the Bishop in the Ancient Christian Community." PhD diss., Yale University, 1988.
Botte, B. *La tradition apostolique de Saint Hippolyte: Essai de reconstitution.* Münster, 1963.
Boularand, E. *L'hérésie d'Arius et la foi de Nicée.* 2 vols. Paris, 1972–73.
Bourdieu, P. *Outline of a Theory of Practice.* Trans. R. Nice. Cambridge Studies in Social Anthropology 16. Cambridge, 1990.
Bowersock, G. W. "From Emperor to Bishop: The Self-Conscious Transformation of Political Power in the Fourth Century A.D." *Classical Philology* 81 (1986): 298–307.
———. *Hellenism in Late Antiquity.* Ann Arbor, MI, 1990.
Bowes, K. *Private Worship, Public Values, and Religious Change in Late Antiquity.* Cambridge, 2008.
Bradshaw, P., M. E. Johnson, L. E. Phillips, et al. *The Apostolic Tradition: A Commentary.* Minneapolis, 2002.
Brakke, D. *Athanasius and the Politics of Asceticism.* Oxford, 1995.

Brennecke, H. C. "Bischofsversammlung und Reichssynode: Das Synodalwesen im Umbruch der konstantinischen Zeit." In *Einheit der Kirche in vorkonstantinischer Zeit*, ed. F. v. Lilienfeld and A. M. Ritter, 35–53. Erlangen, 1989.

———. *Hilarius von Poitiers und die Bischofsopposition gegen Konstantius II: Untersuchungen zur dritten Phase des arianischen Streites (337–361)*. Patristische Texte und Studien 26. Berlin and New York, 1984.

Brennecke, H. C., U. Heil, A. Stockhausen, et al., eds. *Bis zur Ekthesis Makrostichos*. Dokumente zur Geschichte des arianischen Streites 3.1.3. Berlin, 2007.

Brent, A. *The Imperial Cult and the Development of Church Order: Concepts and Images of Authority in Paganism and Christianity before the Age of Cyprian*. Boston, 1999.

———. "Was Hippolytus a Schismatic?" *Vigiliae Christianae* 49 (1995): 379–87.

Brown, P. *Authority and the Sacred: Aspects of the Christianisation of the Roman World*. Cambridge, 1995.

———. *The Body and Society: Men, Women, and Sexual Renunciation in Early Christianity*. New York, 1988.

———. *The Cult of the Saints: Its Rise and Function in Latin Christianity*. Chicago, 1981.

———. *The Making of Late Antiquity*. Cambridge, MA, 1978.

———. *Poverty and Leadership in the Later Roman Empire*. Hanover, NH, 2002.

———. *Power and Persuasion in Late Antiquity: Towards a Christian Empire*. Madison, WI, 1992.

———. "Response to H. Chadwick, 'The Role of the Christian Bishop in Ancient Society.'" In *The Role of the Christian Bishop in Ancient Society, Protocol of the 35th Colloquy, Center for Hermeneutical Studies*, ed. H. Chadwick, E. C. Hobbs and W. Wuellner, 15–22. Berkeley, 1980.

Burgess, R. W. *Studies in Eusebian and Post-Eusebian Chronography*. Historia Einzelschriften 135. Stuttgart, 1999.

Burrus, V. "'In the Theater of This Life': The Performance of Orthodoxy in Late Antiquity." In *The Limits of Ancient Christianity: Essays on Late Antique Thought and Culture in the Honor of R. A. Markus*, ed. W. E. Klingshirn and M. Vessey, 80–96. Ann Arbor, MI, 1999.

———. "Rhetorical Stereotypes in the Portrait of Paul of Samosata." *Vigiliae Christianae* 43 (1989): 215–35.

Burtchaell, J. T. *From Synagogue to Church: Public Services and Offices in the Earliest Christian Communities*. Cambridge, 1992.

Bynum, C. W. *Holy Feast and Holy Fast: The Religious Significance of Food to Medieval Women*. Berkeley, 1987.

Cabrol, F., and H. Leclercq, eds. *Dictionnaire d'archéologie chrétienne et liturgie*. Paris, 1907–53.

Calderini, A. *Dizionario dei nomi geografici e topografici dell'Egitto greco-romano*. Cairo, 1935.

Callu, J.-P. "La préface à l'Itinéraire d'Alexandre." In *De Tertullien aux Mozarabes*, ed. L. Holtz, J.-C. Fredouille, M.-H. Jullien, et al., 1:428–44. Paris, 1992.

Cameron, A., and S. Hall, eds. *Eusebius, The Life of Constantine*. Oxford, 1999.

Camplani, A. "L' autorappresentazione dell' episcopato alessandrino tra IV e V secolo: Questioni di metodo." *Annali della Storia dell'Esegesi* 21 (2004): 147–85.

Carrié, J. M., and A. Rousselle. *L'Empire romain en mutation des Sévères à Constantin 192–337*. Paris, 1999.

Casson, L. *Travel in the Ancient World*. London, 1974.

Chadwick, H. "The Church of the Third Century in the West." In *Heresy and Orthodoxy in the Early Church*, XIV.5–13. Aldershot, UK, 1991.

———. *The Early Church*. New York, 1967.

———. "Faith and Order at the Council of Nicaea." *Harvard Theological Review* 53 (1960): 171–95.

———. "The Fall of Eustathius of Antioch." *Journal of Theological Studies* 49 (1948): 27–35.

———. "Ossius of Cordova and the Presidency of the Council of Antioch, 325." *Journal of Theological Studies* 9 (1958): 292–304.

———. "The Role of the Christian Bishop in Ancient Society." In *The Role of the Christian Bishop in Ancient Society, Protocol of the 35th Colloquy, Center for Hermeneutical Studies*, ed. H. Chadwick, E. C. Hobbs, and W. Wuellner, 1–14. Berkeley, 1980.

Charlesworth, J. H. *The Odes of Solomon*. Oxford, 1973.

Clark, E. A. "Rewriting the History of Early Christianity." In *The Past Before Us: The Challenge of Historiographies of Late Antiquity*, ed. C. Straw and R. Lim, pp. 61–68. Smith Studies in History Series 54. Bibliothèque de l'Antiquité Tardive 6. Turnhout, 2004.

Clark, G. *Women in Late Antiquity: Pagan and Christian Lifestyles*. Oxford, 1994.

Clemente, G. "Cristianesimo e classi dirigenti prima e dopo di Costantino." In *Mondo antico e cristianesimo, Atti del Convegno su "Mondo greco-romano e cristianesimo,"* 51–64. Rome, 1982.

Colantuono, G. "L'ordinamento della Chiesa nelle codificazioni tardoantiche." *Vetera Christianorum* 41 (2004): 355–67.

Countryman, W. L. *The Rich Christian in the Church of the Early Empire: Contradictions and Accommodations*. New York, 1980.

Crislip, A. T. *From Monastery to Hospital: Christian Monasticism and the Transformation of Health Care in Late Antiquity*. Ann Arbor, MI, 2005.

Curran, J. *Pagan City and Christian Capital*. Oxford, 2000.

Dagron, G. "L'empire romain d'orient au IVe siècle et les traditions politiques de l'Hellénisme: Le témoignage de Thémistios." *Travaux et Mémoires* 3 (1968): 1–242.

———. *Naissance d'une capitale: Constantinople et ses instituitions de 330 à 451*. Paris, 1974.

Daniélou, J. *Origène*. Paris, 1948.

De Bruyne, D. "Deux lettres inconnues de Theognius l'évêque arien de Nicée." *Zeitschrift für die Neutestamentliche Wissenschaft* 27 (1928): 106–10.

DelCogliano, M. "George of Laodicea: A Historical Reassessment." *Journal of Ecclesiastical History* 62 (2011): 667–92.

Dignas, B., and E. Winter, *Rome and Persia in Late Antiquity: Neighbors and Rivals*. Cambridge, 2007.

Dihle, A. *Greek and Latin Literature of the Roman Empire, from Augustus to Justinian*. Trans. M. Malzahn. London and New York, 1994.

Di Maio, M., and F. Arnold, "*Per vim, per caedem, per bellum*: A Study of Murder and Ecclesiastical Politics in the Year 337 A.D." *Byzantion* 62 (1992): 158–211.

Dix, G. *The Shape of the Liturgy*. Westminster, 1945.

Drake, H. A. *Constantine and the Bishops: The Politics of Intolerance.* Baltimore, 2000.
———. *In Praise of Constantine: A Historical Study and New Translation of Eusebius' Tricennial Orations.* Berkeley, 1976.
Dunn, G. D. "Cyprian and His 'Colleague': Patronage and the Episcopal Synod of 252." *Journal of Religious History* 27 (2003): 1–13.
Durliat, J. *De la ville antique à la ville byzantine: Les problèmes des subsistences.* Collection de l'École Française de Rome 136. Rome, 1990.
Edwards, M. J. "The Arian Heresy and the Oration to the Saints." *Vigiliae Christianae* 49 (1995): 379–87.
———. "Did Origen Apply the Word *Homoousios* to the Son?" *Journal of Theological Studies* 49 (1998): 658–70.
Elm, S. *Virgins of God: The Making of Asceticism in Late Antiquity.* Oxford, 1994.
Empereur, J.-Y., and M. Picon. "Les ateliers d'amphores du Lac Mariout." In *Commerce et artisanat dans l'Alexandrie hellénistique et romaine, Actes du Colloque d'Athènes, 11–12 décembre 1988*, ed. J.-Y. Empereur, 75–91. Paris, 1998.
Ferguson, T. C. *The Past Is Prologue: The Revolution of Nicene Historiography.* Leiden, 2005.
Forlin Patrucco, M., and S. Roda. "Crisi di potere e autodifesa di classe: Aspetti del tradizionalismo delle aristocrazie." In *Società romana e impero tardoantico*, ed. A. Giardina, 1:245–72. Rome, 1986.
Frend, W. H. C. "Athanasius as an Egyptian Christian Leader in the Fourth Century." In *Religion Popular and Unpopular in the Early Christian Centuries*, XVI.20–37. Aldershot, UK, 1976.
———. "The Church in the Reign of Constantius II (337–361): Mission—Monasticism—Worship." In *L'Église et l'Empire au IVe siècle*, ed. F. Vittinghoff and A. Dihle, 73–111. Entretiens de la Fondation Hardt pour l'Étude de l'Antiquité Classique 36. Geneva, 1989.
———. *The Donatist Church: A Movement of Protest in Roman North Africa.* Oxford, 1955.
———. *The Early Church.* Philadelphia, 1982.
Gaddis, J. M. *There Is No Crime for Those Who Have Christ: Religious Violence in the Christian Roman Empire.* Berkeley, 2006.
Gain, B. *L'Église de Cappadoce au IVe siècle d'après la correspondence de Basile de Césarée (330–379).* Rome, 1985.
Galvão-Sobrinho, C. R. "Embodied Theologies: Christian Identity and Violence in Alexandria in the Early Arian Controversy." In *Violence in Late Antiquity: Perceptions and Practices*, ed. H. D. Drake, 321–31. Aldershot, UK, 2006.
Garnsey, P., and C. Humfress. *The Evolution of the Late Antique World.* Cambridge, 2001.
Gavrilyuk, P. *The Suffering of the Impassible God: The Dialectics of Patristic Thought.* Oxford Early Christian Studies. Oxford, 2004.
Gentz, G. *Die Kirchengeschichte des Nicephorus Callistus Xanthopulus und ihre Quellen.* Berlin, 1966.
Gibbon, E. *The History of the Decline and Fall of the Roman Empire.* Ed. D. Womersley. Vol. 1. Reprint, London, 2005.
Girardet, K. M. *Kaisergericht und Bischofsgericht: Studien zu den Anfängen des Donatistenstreites (313–315) und zum Prozess Athanasius von Alexandrien (328–346).* Antiquitas 1.21. Bonn, 1975.

Goehring, J. E. *The Letter of Ammon and Pachomian Monasticism*. Berlin and New York, 1986.
Gottlieb, G. "Les évêques et les empereurs dans les affaires ecclésiastiques du 4e siècle." *Museum Helveticum* 33 (1976): 38–50.
Gregg, R. C., ed. *Arianism: Historical and Theological Reassessments; Papers from the Ninth International Conference on Patristic Studies, Oxford, September 5–10, 1983*. Patristic Monographs Series 11. Philadelphia, 1985.
———, trans. *The Life of Antony and the Letter to Marcellinus*. New York, 1980.
Gregg, R. C., and D. E. Groh. *Early Arianism: A View of Salvation*. London, 1981.
Gregory, T. E. *Vox populi: Popular Opinion and Violence in the Religious Controversies of the Fifth Century A.D.* Columbus, 1979.
Grenfell, B. P., and A. S. Hunt. *The Amherst Papyri*. London, 1900.
Griggs, C. W. *Early Egyptian Christianity from Its Origins to 451 C.E.* 3rd ed. Leiden, 1993.
Gryson, R. "Les élections épiscopales en Orient au IVe siècle." *Revue d'Histoire de l'Église* 74 (1979): 302–45.
Gwatkin, H. M. *Studies of Arianism: Chiefly Referring to the Character and Chronology of the Reaction Which Followed the Council of Nicaea*. 2nd ed. Reprint, New York, 1978.
Gwynn, D. M. *The Eusebians: The Polemic of Athanasius of Alexandria and the Construction of the "Arian Controversy."* Oxford, 2006.
Haas, C. J. *Alexandria in Late Antiquity: Topography and Social Conflict*. Baltimore, 1997.
———. "The Arians of Alexandria." *Vigiliae Christianae* 47 (1993): 234–45.
Hahn, J. *Gewalt und religiöser Konflikt: Studien zu den Auseinandersetzungen zwischen Christen, Heiden und Juden im Osten des Römischen Reiches (von Konstantin bis Theodosius II)*. Klio Beihefte 8. Berlin, 2004.
Hall, S. "Some Constantinian Documents in the *Vita Constantini*." In *Constantine: History, Historiography, and Legend*, ed. S. N. C. Lieu and D. Montserrat, 86–103. London and New York, 1998.
Hansen, T. B. *Wages of Violence: Naming and Identity in Postcolonial Bombay*. Princeton, NJ, 2001.
Hanson, R. P. C. "The Achievement of Orthodoxy in the Fourth Century AD." In *The Making of Orthodoxy: Essays in Honour of Henry Chadwick*, ed. R. Williams, 142–56. Cambridge, 1989.
———. *The Search for a Christian Doctrine of God: The Arian Controversy, 318–381*. Edinburgh, 1988.
Hauben, H. "Heraiscus as a Melitian Bishop of Heracleopolis Magna and the Alexandrian See." *Journal of Juristic Papyrology* 34 (2004): 51–70.
———. "La première année du schisme mélitien (305/306)." *Ancient Society* 20 (1989): 266–79.
———. "La réordination du clergé mélitien imposée par le Concile de Nicée." *Ancient Society* 18 (1987): 203–7.
Hedrick, C., Jr. *History and Silence: Purge and the Rehabilitation of Memory in Late Antiquity*. Austin, TX, 2000.
Hermann, E. *Ecclesia in re publica*. Frankfurt, 1980.
Hefele, K. J. *Histoire de conciles d'après les documents originaux*. 12 vols. Paris, 1907.
Herzfeld, M. *A Place in History: Social and Monumental Time in a Cretan Town*. Princeton, NJ, 1991.

Heseler, P. "Hagiographica II: Zur Vita Constantini et matris Helenae des Ignatius von Selymbria (*BHG* 362)." *Byzantinisch-neugriechische Jahrbücher* 9 (1930): 320–37.
Holman, S. *The Hungry Are Dying: Beggars and Bishops in Roman Cappadocia*. Oxford, 2001.
Humfress, C. *Orthodoxy and the Courts in Late Antiquity*. Oxford, 2007.
———. "Roman Law, Forensic Argument and the Formation of Christian Orthodoxy (III-VI Centuries)." In *Orthodoxie, christianisme, histoire/Orthodoxy, Christianity, History*, ed. S. Elm, E. Rebillard, and A. Romano, 125–47. Collection de l'École Française de Rome 270. Rome, 2000.
Humphries, M. "In nomine patris: Constantine the Great and Constantius II in Christological Polemic." *Historia* 46 (1997): 448–64.
———. "Savage Humour: Christian Anti-Panegyric in Hilary of Poitiers' Against Constantius." In *The Propaganda of Power: The Role of Panegyric in Late Antiquity*, ed. M. Whitby, 201–23. Leiden, 1998.
Hyvernat, H. *Les Actes des Martyrs de l'Égypte*. New York, 1977.
Ippolito, F. "I tessitori del Fayyum in epoca greca e romana: Le testimonianze papiracee." In *Atti del XXII Congresso internazionale di papirologia, Firenze, 23–29 agosto 1998*, ed. I. Andorlini et al., 2:701–15. Florence, 2001.
James, W. *The Varieties of Religious Experience*. London, 1961.
Joannou, P.-P. *Discipline générale antique (IIe–IXe s.)*. 3 vols. Grottaferrata, 1962–1964.
———. *La legislation impériale et la christianisation de l'empire romain (311–476)*. Orientalia Christiana Analecta 192. Rome, 1972.
Jones, A. H. M. *Constantine and the Conversion of Europe*. Medieval Academy Reprints for Teaching, Medieval Academy of America. Toronto, 1978.
———. *The Later Roman Empire 284–602: A Social, Economic, and Administrative Survey*. 2 vols. Reprint, Baltimore, 1990.
———. "The Social Background of the Struggle between Paganism and Christianity." In *The Conflict between Paganism and Christianity in the Fourth Century*, ed. Arnaldo Momigliano, 15–37. Oxford, 1963.
Judge, E. A. "Christian Innovation and Its Contemporary Observers." In *History and Historians in Late Antiquity*, ed. B. Croke and A. M. Emmett, pp. 13–29. Sydney, 1983.
Juliussen-Stevenson, H. "Performing Christian Female Identity in Roman Alexandria." Master's thesis, University of Maryland, College Park, 2008.
Kannengiesser, C. *Athanase d'Alexandrie, évêque et écrivain: Une lecture des traités Contre les Ariens*. Théologie Historique 70. Paris, 1983.
———. "The Athanasian Decade 1974–84: A Bibliographical Report." *Theological Studies* 46 (1985): 524–41.
———. "Athanasius of Alexandria vs. Arius: The Alexandrian Crisis." In *The Roots of Egyptian Christianity*, ed. B. A. Pearson and J. E. Goehring, 204–15. Philadelphia, 1985.
———. "The Blasphemies of Arius: Athanasius of Alexandria *De synodis* 15." In *Arianism: Historical and Theological Reassessments; Papers from the Ninth International Conference on Patristic Studies*, ed. R. C. Gregg, 69–75. Cambridge, MA, 1985.
———. "Current Theology: Arius and the Arians." *Theological Studies* 44 (1983): 456–75.
———, ed. *Politique et théologie chez Athanase d'Alexandrie, Actes du Colloque de Chantilly 23–25 septembre 1973*. Théologie Historique 27. Paris, 1974.

Kelly, C. "Empire Building." In *Late Antiquity: A Guide to the Postclassical World*, ed. G. W. Bowersock, P. Brown, and O. Grabar, 170–95. Cambridge, MA, 1999.
Kelly, J. N. D. *Early Christian Creeds*. 2nd ed. Oxford, 1960.
———. *Early Christian Doctrines*. Rev. ed. New York, 1978.
Kettler, F. H. "Der melitianische Streit in Ägypten." *Zeitschrift für die Neutestamentliche Wissenschaft* 35 (1936): 155–93.
Klein, R. *Constantius II. und die christliche Kirche*. Impulse der Forschung 26. Darmstadt, 1977.
Koester, H. "ΓΝΩΜΑΙ ΔΙΑΦΟΡΟΙ: The Origin and Nature of Diversification in the History of Early Christianity." In *Studies in Early Christianity: A Collection of Scholarly Essays*, ed. E. Ferguson, 4:197–236. New York and London, 1993.
Kopecek, T. A. *A History of Neo-Arianism*. 2 vols. Patristic Monograph Series 8. Cambridge, MA, 1979.
Kötting, B. "Die Stellung des Konfessors in der Alten Kirche." *Jahrbuch für Antike und Christentum* 19 (1976): 16–22.
Kraft, H. "Dalla chiesa ordinaria all'episcopato monarchico." *Rivista di Storia e Letteratura Religiosa* 22 (1986): 411–38.
———. *Kaiser Konstantins religiöse Entwicklung*. Tübingen, 1955.
Kramer, B., and J. C. Shelton, eds. *Das Archiv des Nepheros und verwandte Texte*. Aegyptiaca Treverensia 4. Mainz, 1987.
Lallemand, J. *L'administration civile de l'Égypte de l'avènement de Dioclétien à la création du diocèse (284–382)*. Mémoires de l'Academie Royale de Belgique, Cl. des Lettres 57.2. Brussels, 1962.
Lançon, B. *La vita quotidiana a Roma nel tardo impero*. Trans. M. G. Meriggi. Milan, 1999.
Lane Fox, R. "The Itinerary of Alexander: Constantius to Julian." *Classical Quarterly* 47 (1997): 239–52.
———. "Literacy and Power in Early Christianity." In *Literacy and Power in the Ancient World*, ed. A. K. Bowman and G. Woolf, 126–48. Cambridge, 1994.
———. *Pagans and Christians*. New York, 1989.
Lang, U. M. "The Christological Controversy at the Synod of Antioch in 268/9." *Journal of Theological Studies*, n.s., 51 (2000): 54–80.
Laurence, R. *Roman Pompeii: Space and Society*. London and New York, 1994.
Le Boulluec, A. *La notion d'hérésie dans la littérature grecque, II-IIIe siècles*. Paris, 1985.
Lenski, N. "Evidence for the *Audientia episcopalis* in the New Letters of Augustine." In *Law, Society, and Authority in Late Antiquity*, ed. R. W. Mathisen, 83–97. Oxford, 2001.
Lewis, N. *The Compulsory Public Services of Roman Egypt*. 2nd ed. Florence, 1997.
Liderbach, D. *Christ in the Early Christian Hymns*. New York, 1998.
Liebeschuetz, J. H. W. G. *Decline and Fall of the Roman City*. Oxford, 2001.
Lienhard, J. T. "The 'Arian' Controversy: Some Categories Reconsidered." *Theological Studies* 48 (1987): 415–37.
Lietzmann, H. *Histoire de l'Église ancienne*. Trans. A. Jundt. Paris, 1937.
Lieu, J. N. *Christian Identity in the Jewish and Greco-Roman World*. Oxford, 2004.
Lim, R. "Christian Triumph and Controversy." In *Interpreting Late Antiquity: Essays on the Postclassical World*, ed. G. W. Bowersock, P. Brown, and O. Grabar, 196–218. Cambridge, MA, 2001.
———. *Public Disputation, Power, and Social Order in Late Antiquity*. Berkeley, 1995.

Lizzi, R. "Discordia *in urbe*: Pagani e cristiani in rivolta." In *Pagani e cristiani da Giuliano l'Apostata al sacco di Roma*, ed. F. E. Consolino, 115–40. Soveria Mannelli, 1995.

———. *Il potere episcopale nell'oriente romano: Rappresentazione ideologica e realtà politica (IV-V sec. d. C.)*. Rome, 1987.

Logan, A. H. B. "Marcellus of Ancyra and the Councils of AD 325: Antioch, Ancyra, and Nicaea." *Journal of Theological Studies*, n.s., 43 (1992): 428–46.

Loofs, F. *Paulus von Samosata*. Texte und Untersuchungen zur Geschichte der altchristlichen Literatur 44.5. Leipzig, 1924.

Loose, U. "Zur Chronologie des arianischen Streites." *Zeitschrift für Kirchengeschichte* 101 (1990): 88–92.

Louth, A. "Unity and Diversity in the Church of the Fourth Century." In *Unity and Diversity in the Church*, ed. R. N. Swanson, 1–18. Oxford, 1996.

Lukaszewicz, A. "Activités commerciales et artisanales dans Alexandrie romaine." In *Commerce et artisanat dans l'Alexandrie hellénistique et romaine, Actes du Colloque d'Athènes, 11–12 décembre 1988*, ed. J.-Y. Empereur, 107–13. Paris, 1998.

Lyman, J. R. *Christology and Cosmology: Models of Divine Activity in Origen, Eusebius, and Athanasius*. Oxford, 1993.

———. "*Lex orandi*: Heresy, Orthodoxy, and Popular Religion." In *The Making and Remaking of Christian Doctrine: Essays in Honour of Maurice Wiles*, ed. S. Coakley and D. Pailin, 131–42. Oxford, 1993.

———. "A Topography of Heresy: Mapping the Rhetorical Creation of Arianism." In *Arianism after Arius*, ed. M. R. Barnes and D. H. Williams, 45–80. Edinburgh, 1993.

MacMullen, R. *Christianizing the Roman Empire*. New Haven, CT, 1984.

———. *Corruption and the Decline of Rome*. New Haven, CT, 1988.

———. "Cultural and Political Changes in the Fourth and Fifth Centuries." *Historia* 52 (2003): 465–95.

———. *Enemies of the Roman Order: Treason, Unrest, and Alienation in the Empire*. Cambridge, MA, 1966.

———. *Feelings in History, Ancient and Modern*. Claremont, CA, 2003.

———. "The Historical Role of the Masses in Late Antiquity." In *Changes in the Roman Empire: Essays in the Ordinary*, 250–76. Princeton, NJ, 1990.

———. "Personal Power in the Roman Empire." *American Journal of Philology* 107 (1986): 512–24.

———. "The Preacher's Audience (A.D. 350–400)." *Journal of Theological Studies* 40 (1989): 503–11.

———. "Response to H. Chadwick, 'The Role of the Christian Bishop in Ancient Society.'" In *Protocol of the 35th Colloquy, Center for Hermeneutical Studies*, ed. E. C. Hobbs and W. Wuellner, 25–29. Berkeley, 1980.

———. *The Second Church: Popular Christianity, A.D. 200–400*. Atlanta, 2009.

———. *Voting about God in Early Church Councils*. New Haven, CT, 2006.

Magalhães, J. C. O. *Potestas populi: Participation populaire et action collective dans les villes de l'Afrique romaine tardive (vers 300-430 apr. J.-C.)*. Bibliothèque de l'Antiquité Tardive 24. Paris, 2012.

Magne, J. *Tradition apostolique sur les charismes et diataxeis des saints apôtres: Identification des documents et analyse du rituel des ordinations*. Paris, 1975.

Maier, H. O. "Religious Dissent, Heresy, and Households in Late Antiquity." *Vigiliae Christianae* 49 (1995): 49–63.
Maier, J.-L. *Le dossier du Donatisme*. Berlin, 1987.
Majcherek, G. "Kom El-Dikka: Excavations and Preservation Work, 2002/2003." *Polish Archaeology in the Mediterranean* 15 (2004): 25–38.
Mango, C. *Le dévelopment urbain de Constantinople (IVe-VIIe siècles)*. Travaux et Mémoires du Centre de Recherche d'Histoire et Civilisation de Byzance. Collège de France, Monographies 2. Paris, 1985.
Markus, R. A. *The End of Ancient Christianity*. Cambridge, 1990.
———. "The Problem of Self-Definition: From Sect to Church." In *Jewish and Christian Self-Definition*, ed. E. P. Sanders, 1:1–15. London, 1980.
Marrou, H.-I. "L'arianisme comme phénomène alexandrin." *Académie des Inscriptions et Belles Lettres, Comptes Rendus* (1973): 533–42.
Martin, A. "Alexandrie: L'investissement chrétien de la ville." In *Les chrétiens dans la ville*, ed. J.-O. Boudon and F. Thelamon, 47–63. Rouen, 2006.
———. *Athanase d'Alexandrie et l'église d'Égypte au IVe siècle*. Collection de l'École Française de Rome 216. Rome, 1996.
———. "Athanase et les Méletiens (325–335)." In *Politique et théologie chez Athanase d'Alexandrie, Actes du Colloque de Chantilly 23–25 septembre 1973*, ed. C. Kannengiesser, 31–62. Théologie Historique 27. Paris, 1974.
———, ed. *Histoire "Acéphale" et Index syriaque des lettres festales d'Athanase d'Alexandrie*. SC 317. Paris, 1985.
———. "Les conditions de la réadmission du clérge mélitien par le Concile de Nicée." *Ancient Society* 20 (1989): 281–90.
———. "Les églises d'Alexandrie aux 3e et 4e siècles." *Revue des Études Augustiniennes* 30 (1984): 211–25.
———. "Orthodoxie et pouvoirs institutionels." In *Orthodoxie, christianisme, histoire/ Orthodoxy, Christianity, History*, ed. S. Elm, E. Rebillard, and A. Romano, 343–52. Collection de l'École Française de Rome 270. Rome, 2000.
———. "Topographie et liturgie: Le problème des 'paroisses' d'Alexandrie." In *Actes du XIe congrès international d'archéologie chrétienne*, ed. N. Duval, F. Baritel, and P. Pergola, 2:1133–44. 3 vols. Collection de l'École Française de Rome 123. Rome, 1989.
McLynn, N. *Ambrose of Milan: Church and Court in a Christian Capital*. Berkeley, 1994.
———. "Christian Controversy and Violence in the Fourth Century." *Kodai (Journal of Ancient History, Japan)* 3 (1992): 15–44.
Millar, F. *A Greek Roman Empire: Power and Belief under Theodosius II (408–450)*. Berkeley, 2006.
———. "Paul of Samosata, Zenobia, and Aurelian: The Church, Local Culture, and Political Allegiance in Third-Century Syria." *Journal of Roman Studies* 61 (1971): 1–17.
Mitchell, S. *Anatolia: Land, Men, and Gods in Asia Minor*. 2 vols. Oxford, 1993.
———. *A History of the Later Roman Empire, AD 284–641*. Malden, MA, 2007.
Mitsakis, K. "The Hymnography of the Greek Church in the Early Christian Centuries." *Jahrbuch der österreichischen Byzantinistik* 20 (1971): 31–49.
Mommsen, T., ed. *Theodosiani libri XVI cum constitutionibus Sirmondianis*. Berlin, 1905.
Munier, C. *Autorité épiscopale et sollicitude pastorale (IIe-VIe siècles)*. Aldershot, UK, 1991.

Nautin, P. "Deux interpolations orthodoxes dans une lettre d'Arius." *Analecta Bollandiana* 67 (1949): 132–41.

———. "L'évolution des ministères au IIe et au IIIe siècles." *Revue du Droit Canonique* 23 (1973): 47–58.

Noethlichs, K. L. "Kirche, Recht und Gesellschaft in der Jahrhundertmitte." In *L'Église et l'Empire au IVe siècle*, ed. F. Vittinghoff and A. Dihle, 251–94. Entretiens de la Fondation Hardt pour l'Étude de l'Antiquité Classique 36. Geneva, 1989.

Norderval, O. "The Emperor Constantine and Arius: Unity in the Church and Unity in the Empire." *Studia Theologica* 42 (1988): 113–50.

Odahl, C. M. *Constantine and the Christian Empire*. New York, 2004.

Opitz, H.-G. *Athanasius Werke*. 8 fasc. Berlin and Leipzig, 1934–40.

———. "Die Zeitfolge des arianischen Streites von den Anfängen bis zum Jahr 328." *Zeitschrift für die Neutestamentliche Wissenschaft* 33 (1934): 131–59.

Orlandi, T. *Storia della chiesa di Alessandria: Da Pietro ad Atanasio*. Testi e documenti per lo studio dell' antichità 17. Milan, 1967.

Outtier, B., ed. *Textes arméniens relatifs à S. Éphrem*. CSCO 474. Louvain, 1985.

Pagels, E. *The Gnostic Gospels*. New York, 1979.

Pannenberg, W. "The Appropriation of the Philosophical Concept of God as a Dogmatic Problem of Early Christian Theology." In *Basic Questions in Theology*, trans. G. H. Kehm, 2:119–83. Reprint, Philadelphia, 1983.

Parássoglou, G. M., ed. *The Archive of Aurelius Sakaon: Papers of an Egyptian Farmer in the Last Century of Theadelphia*. Bonn, 1978.

Parker, J. H. ed. *The Festal Epistles of S. Athanasius*. Oxford, 1854.

Parvis, S. *Marcellus of Ancyra and the Lost Years of the Arian Controversy, 325–345*. Oxford, 2006.

Paschoud, F. "L'Église dans l'empire romain: Tendences dans l'église contre et pour l'empire." *Actes du Congrès de la Federation Internationale des Associations d'Études Classiques*, 2:197–207. Budapest, 1984.

Peeters, P. "Le début de la persécution de Sapor d'après Faustus de Byzance." *Revue des Études Armeniennes* 1 (1920–21): 15–33.

Pelikan, J. *The Christian Tradition: A History of the Development of Doctrine*. Vol. 1, *The Emergence of the Catholic Tradition*. Chicago and London, 1971.

Pietri, C. *Roma christiana: Recherches sur l'Eglise de Rome, son organisation, sa politique, son idéologie de Miltiade à Sixte III (311–440)*. 2 vols. Bibliothèque des Écoles Françaises d'Athènes et de Rome 224. Rome, 1976.

Pietri, C., and L. Pietri, eds. *Naissance d'une chretienté (250–430)*. Vol. 2 of *Histoire du christianisme des origines à nous jours*. Paris, 1995.

Pouchet, J.-R. *Basile le Grand et son univers d'amis après sa correspondence*. Rome, 1992.

Price, J. "Glass Working and Glassworkers in Cities and Towns." In *Roman Working Lives and Urban Living*, ed. A. Mac Mahon and J. Price, 167–90. Oxford, 2005.

Quasten, J. *Patrologia*. Ed. I. Oñatiba. Biblioteca de Autores Cristianos. Madrid, 1961.

Rapp, C. *Holy Bishops in Late Antiquity: The Nature of Christian Leadership in an Age of Transition*. Berkeley, 2005.

Rathbone, D. *Economic Rationalism and Rural Society in Third-Century Egypt: The Heroninos Archive and the Appianus Estate*. Cambridge, 1991.

Reil, T. *Beiträge zur Kenntnis des Gewerbes im hellenistischen Ägypten*. Reprint, New York, 1979.
Reine, F. J. *The Eucharistic Doctrine and Liturgy of the Mystagogical Catecheses of Theodore of Mopsuestia*. Washington, DC, 1942.
Reymond, E. A. E., and J. W. B. Barns. *Four Martyrdoms from the Pierpont Morgan Coptic Codices*. Oxford, 1973.
Richard, M. *Asterii Sophistae commentariorum in Psalmos quae supersunt*. Symbolae Osloenses 16. Oslo, 1956.
Rickman, G. *The Corn Supply of Ancient Rome*. Oxford, 1980.
Riedmatten, H. de. *Les actes du procès de Paul de Samosate: Étude sur la christologie du IIIe au IVe siècle*. Fribourg, 1952.
Rodziewicz, E. "Archaeological Evidence of Bone and Ivory Carvings in Alexandria." In *Commerce et artisanat dans l'Alexandrie hellénistique et romaine, Actes du Colloque d'Athènes, 11–12 décembre 1988*, ed. J.-Y. Empereur, 135–58. Paris, 1998.
Rodziewicz, M. *Alexandrie, III: Les habitations romaines tardives d'Alexandrie à la lumière des fouilles polonaises à Kôm el-Dikha*. Warsaw, 1984.
Roques, D. "Alexandrie tardive et protobyzantine (IVe-VIIe s.): Témoignages d'auteurs." In *Alexandrie: Une mégapole cosmopolite; Actes du 9ème colloque de la Villa Kérylos à Beaulieu-sur-Mer, 2–3 octobre 1998*, ed. J. Leclant, 203–35. Paris, 1999.
Roulet, J. de. *Tolerance dans l'Église? Une réponse du deuxième siécle: D'Irénée à Arius*. Geneva, 1998.
Rousseau, P. *Basil of Caesarea*. Berkeley, 1994.
———. "The Preacher's Audience: A More Optimistic View." In *Ancient History in a Modern University: Festschrift for Edwin Judge*, ed. T. W. Hillard, R. A. Kearsley, C. E. V. Nixon, et al., 391–400. New South Wales, Australia, and Grand Rapids, MI, and Cambridge, 1998.
Russell, F. H. "Persuading the Donatists: Augustine's Coercion by Words." In *The Limits of Ancient Christianity: Essays on Late Antique Thought and Culture in Honor of R. A. Markus*, ed. W. E. Klingshirn and M. Vessey, 115–38. Ann Arbor, MI, 1999.
Salzman, M. R. *The Making of a Christian Aristocracy: Social and Religious Change in the Western Roman Empire*. Cambridge, MA, 2002.
Saxer, V. "La messe au IVe s. et sa réforme." In *Les transformations dans la société chrétienne au IVe. siècle, Congrès de Varsovie, 25 juin-1er juillet 1978*, 202–15. Miscellanea Historiae Ecclesiasticae 6. Brussels, 1983.
———. "La Mission: L'organisation de l'Église au IIIe siècle." In *Naissance d'une chrétienté (250-430)*, vol. 2 of *Histoire du christianisme des origines à nous jours*, ed. C. Pietri and L. Pietri, 41–75. Paris, 1995.
Schäferdiek, K. "The Acts of John." In *New Testament Apocrypha*, ed. W. Schneemelcher, trans. J. Clarke, 152–212. Louisville, 1992.
Scherer, J. *Entretien d'Origène avec Héraclide et les évêques ses collègues sur le Père, le Fils et l'âme*. Publications de la Societé Fouad I de Papyrologie. Textes et Documents 9. Cairo, 1949.
———. *Entretien d'Origéne avec Héraclide*. SC 67. Paris, 1960.
Schneemelcher, W. "Die Kirchweihsynode von Antiochen 341." *Bonner Festgabe Johannes Straub zum 65. Geburtstag am 18. Oktober 1977*, 319–46. Bonn, 1977.
———. "Zur Chronologie des arianischen Streites." *Theologische Literaturzeitung* 79 (1954): 393–400.

Schöllgen, G. *Die Anfänge der Professionalisierung des Klerus und das kirchliche Amt in der syrischen Didaskalie*. Jahrbuch für Antike und Christentum 26. Münster, 1998.
Schwartz, E. *Gesammelte Schriften*. 5 vols. Berlin, 1959.
Schwartz, J. "Le Nil et le ravitaillement de Rome." *Bulletin de l'Institut Français d'Archéologie Orientale* 47 (1948): 179–200.
Sciuto, F. E. "Da Nicea a Costantinopoli: Osservazioni sulla prima fase della stabilizzazione teologico-politica cristiana (325–381)." In *La transformazioni della cultura nella tarda antichità, Atti del Convegno tenuto a Catania Università degli Studi, 27 sett.-2 ott, 1982*, ed. C. Giuffrida and M. Mazza, 479–90. Rome, 1985.
Shaw, B. D. *Sacred Violence: African Christians and Sectarian Hatred in the Age of Augustine*. Cambridge and New York, 2011.
Simonetti, M. *La crisi ariana nel IV secolo*. Studia Ephemeridis "Augustinianum" 11. Rome, 1975.
———. "Review of R. C. Gregg and D. E. Groh, *Early Arianism: A View of Salvation*, London, 1981." *Rivista di Storia e Letteratura Religiosa* 18 (1981): 304–6.
Sirks, B. *Food for Rome: The Legal Structure of the Transportation and Processing of Food Supplies for the Imperial Distributions in Rome and Constantinople*. Amsterdam, 1991.
Sizgorich, T. *Violence and Belief in Late Antiquity: Militant Devotion in Christianity and Islam*. Philadelphia, 2009.
Skarsaume, O. "A Neglected Detail in the Creed of Nicaea." *Vigiliae Christianae* 41 (1987): 34–54.
Smulders, P. "Some Riddles in the Apostles' Creed." In *Studies in Early Christianity: A Collection of Scholarly Essays*, ed. E. Ferguson, 146–96. New York and London, 1993.
Sotinel, C. *Identité civique et christianisme: Aquilée du IIIe au VIe siècle*. Bibliothèque des Écoles Françaises d'Athènes et de Rome 324. Rome, 2005.
———. "Le personnel épiscopal: Enquête sur la puissance de l'évêque dans la cité." In *L'évêque dans la cité du IVe au Ve siècle: Image et autorité; Actes de la table ronde organisée par l'Istituto patristico Augustinianum et l'École française de Rome (Rome, 1er et 2 dec. 1995)*, ed. E. Rebillard and C. Sotinel, 105–26. Rome, 1998.
Spanneut, M. *Recherches sur les écrits d'Eustathe d'Antioche avec une édition nouvelle des fragments dogmatiques et exégétiques*. Lille, 1948.
Sperber, D. *The City in Roman Palestine*. Oxford, 1998.
Stead, G. C. "Arius in Modern Research." *Journal of Theological Studies*, n.s., 45 (1994): 24–36.
———. "Athanasius' Earliest Written Work." *Journal of Theological Studies*, n.s., 39 (1988): 76–91.
Sterk, A. *Renouncing the World yet Leading the Church: The Monk-Bishop in Late Antiquity*. Cambridge, MA, 2004.
Stewart-Stykes, A. "Hermas the Prophet and Hippolytus the Preacher: The Roman Homily and Its Social Context." In *Preacher and Audience: Studies in Early Christian and Byzantine Homiletics*, ed. M. B. Cunningham and P. Allen, 33–62. Leiden, 1998.
———. "Ordination Rites and Patronage Systems in Third-Century Africa." *Vigiliae Christianae* 56 (2002): 115–30.
Stramara, D. F., Jr. "Double Monasticism in the Greek East, Fourth through Eighth Centuries." *Journal of Early Christian Studies* 6 (1998): 269–312.

Stroumsa, G. G. "Tertullian on Idolatry and the Limits of Tolerance." In *Tolerance and Intolerance in Early Judaism and Christianity*, ed. G. N. Stanton and G. G. Stroumsa, 173–84. Cambridge, 1998.
Studer, B. *Trinity and Incarnation: The Faith of the Early Church*. Trans. M. Westerhoff. Edinburgh, 1993.
Tambiah, S. J. *Leveling Crowds: Ethnonationalist Conflicts and Collective Violence in South Asia*. Berkeley, 1996.
Teja, R. "*Auctoritas versus potestas*: El liderazgo social de los obispos en la sociedad tardoantigua." In *Vescovi e pastori in epoca teodosiana: XXV Incontro di studiosi dell'antichità cristiana, Roma, 8–11 maggio 1996*, 73–82. Rome, 1997.
Telfer, W. R. "Episcopal Succession in Egypt." *Journal of Ecclesiastical History* 3 (1952): 1–13.
Tkaczow, B. *The Topography of Ancient Alexandria (An Archaeological Map)*. Warsaw, 1993.
Trigg, J. W. *Origen*. London and New York, 2002.
Troeltsch, E. *The Social Teaching of the Christian Churches*. Trans. O. Wyon. London, 1950.
Turner, C. H., ed. *Ecclesiae occidentalis monumenta iuris antiquissima*. 2 vols. Oxford, 1899–1939.
Vaggione, R. P. *Eunomius of Cyzicus and the Nicene Revolution*. Oxford, 2000.
Van Dam, R. "Emperors, Bishops, and Friends in Late Antique Cappadocia." *Journal of Theological Studies*, n.s., 37 (1986): 53–75.
Van Haelst, J. "Une ancienne prière d'intercession de la liturgie de saint Marc (O. Tait- Petrie 415)." *Ancient Society* 1 (1970): 95–114.
———. "Les sources papyrologiques concernant l'Église en Egypte à l'époque de Constantin." In *Proceedings of the 12th International Congress of Papyrology*, ed. D. H. Samuel, 497–505. Toronto, 1970.
Van Nuffelen, P. *Un héritage de paix et de piéte: Étude sur les histoires ecclésiastiques de Socrate et de Sozomène*. Leuven, 2004.
Viteau, J., ed. *Passions de saints Écaterine et Pierre d'Alexandrie, Barbara et Anysia: Publiées d'après les manuscrits grecs de Paris et de Rome avec un choix de variantes et une traduction latine*. Paris, 1897.
Vivian, T. *Saint Peter of Alexandria, Bishop and Martyr*. Philadelphia, 1988.
Von Campenhausen, H. *Ecclesiastical Authority and Spiritual Power in the Church of the First Three Centuries*. Trans. J. A. Baker. London, 1969.
Von Harnack, A. *Manuale di storia del dogma*. Mendrisio, 1913.
———. *The Mission and Expansion of Christianity in the First Three Centuries*. Trans. J. Moffatt. 2 vols. New York, 1908.
Vööbus, A., ed. *The Canons Ascribed to Maruta of Maipherqat and Related Sources*. CSCO 440. Louvain, 1982.
Warmington, B. H. "Did Constantine Have 'Religious Advisers'?" *Studia Patristica* 19 (1987): 117–30.
———. "The Source of Some Constantinian Documents in Eusebius' *Ecclesiastical History* and *Life of Constantine*." In *Studia Patristica* 18, ed. E. A. Livingstone, 93–97. Papers of the Ninth International Conference on Patristic Studies, Oxford 1983. Kalamazoo, MI, 1985.
Washburn, D. A. "Tormenting the Tormentors: A Reinterpretation of Eusebius of Vercelli's Letter from Scythopolis." *Church History* 78 (2009): 731–755.
Watts, E. J. *City and School in Late Antique Athens and Alexandria*. Berkeley, 2006.

West, M. L. "The Metre of Arius' *Thalia*." *Journal of Theological Studies* 33 (1982): 98–106.
Whitby, M., and M. Whitby, trans. and comm. *Chronicon Paschale, 284–628 AD*. TTH 7. Liverpool, 1989.
White, L. M. *Building God's House in the Roman World: Architectural Adaptation among Pagans, Jews, and Christians*. Baltimore, 1990.
Wickham, L. R., ed. and trans. *Hilary of Poitiers: Conflicts of Conscience and Law in the Fourth-Century Church*. TTH 25. Liverpool, 1997.
Widdicombe, P. *The Fatherhood of God from Origen to Athanasius*. Oxford, 1994.
Wiles, M. "Attitudes to Arius in the Arian Controversy." In *Arianism after Arius*, ed. M. R. Barnes and D. H. Williams, 31–43. Edinburgh, 1993.
Williams, D. H. *Ambrose of Milan and the End of the Nicene-Arian Conflicts*. Oxford, 1995.
———. "Defining Orthodoxy in Hilary of Poitiers' *Commentarium in Matthaeum*." *Journal of Early Christian Studies* 9 (2001): 151–71.
Williams, R. D. *Arius: Heresy and Tradition*. London, 1987.
———, ed. *The Making of Orthodoxy: Essays in Honour of Henry Chadwick*. Cambridge, 1989.
———. "The Quest of the Historical Thalia." In *Arianism: Historical and Theological Reassessments, Papers from the Ninth International Conference on Patristic Studies, Oxford, September 5–10, 1983*, 1–36. Philadelphia, 1985.
Wilson, S. G. "Dissidents and Defectors: The Limits of Pluralism." In *Fair Play: Diversity and Conflicts in Early Christianity; Essays in Honour of Heikki Räisänen*, ed. I. Dunderberg, C. Tuckett, and K. Syreeni, 441–56. Leiden, 2002.
Winkelmann, F. "Vita Metrophanis et Alexandri, *BHG* 1279." *Analecta Bollandiana* 100 (1982): 147–83.
Wipszycka, E. "L'attività caritativa dei vescovi egiziani." In *L'évêque dans la cité du IVe au Ve siècle: Image et autorité; Actes de la table ronde organisée par l'Istituto patristico Augustinianum et l'École française de Rome (Rome, 1er et 2 dec. 1995)*, ed. E. Rebillard and C. Sotinel, 71–80. Rome, 1998.
———. "Les confréries dans la vie religieuse de l'Egypte chrétienne." In *Proceedings of the 12th International Congress of Papyrology*, ed. D. H. Samuel, 511–26. Toronto, 1970.
———. *L'industrie textile dans l'Egypte romaine*. Wroclaw, 1965.
———. "Les papyrus documentaires concernant l'Église d'avant le tournant constantinien." In *Atti del XXII Congresso Internazionale di Papirologia*, 2:1307–30. Florence, 2001.
———. *Les ressources et les activités économiques de l'église en Égypte du 4e au 8e siècle*. Brussels, 1972.
———. "La sovvenzione costantiniana in favore del clero." *Rend. Mor. Acc. Lincei*, s. 9, 8 (1997): 483–98.
———. *Storia della Chiesa nella tarda antichità*. Trans. V. Verdiani. Milan, 2000.
Woods, D. "Three Notes on Aspects of the Arian Controversy c. 354–367 CE." *Journal of Theological Studies*, n.s., 44 (1993): 604–19.
Young, F. *Biblical Exegesis and the Formation of Christian Culture*. Cambridge, 1997.

INDEX

Ablabius (praetorian prefect), 114, 239n135
Acacius (bishop of Caesarea), 143, 148
Adrianople, 103; violence in, 129, 136; weapons factory in, 129, 249n31
Aërius (ascetic), 262n258
Aetius (bishop of Lydda), 68, 82, 219n12, 220n18
Aetius (theologian): preaching in Antioch, 147; 220n33, 230n12, 257n158, 260n235; preaching in Alexandria, 260n236
Agapius (bishop of Menbidj), 102; *Historia universalis*, 83, 226nn51–52
Alexander (bishop of Constantinople), 123, 246n232, 249n36
Alexander (patriarch of Alexandria): anathema of peers, 68–69, 76; on Arian violence, 63, 74; on Arius's Christology, 39–40, 55, 59, 74, 205n40, 206n56, 215n109; attack on Eusebius of Nicomedia, 71–72, 76; authority of, 37, 38, 41, 42, 46, 53–54, 64, 69, 156; challenges to authority of, 37, 41, 42, 45, 52, 62, 64, 69, 73, 107; challenges to orthodoxy of, 42, 66, 73, 107; Christology of, 32, 40, 41, 42, 43, 49, 73, 85, 110, 203n13, 207nn72,82,85, 228n89; claim to truth, 42, 50, 54, 63, 71, 76, 77, 108; conflict with Arius, 32, 37–46, 50–65, 68–70, 73–74, 76, 107–9, 115, 156, 167, 169, 204nn29,37, 205nn39,40,44, 236n95; conflict with Melitians, 37, 106–7, 108, 110, 168, 169, 170, 234n65, 235n80, 236nn36,42,94, 265nn36,42, 266n63; conflict with peers, 68–69, 71–72, 74, 107, 109; confrontational tactics of, 51–54, 63, 72, 106, 108, 156; Constantine's correspondence with, 79, 107, 167, 168, 169, 223n2, 235n74; and Council of Alexandria (324), 80; at Council of Nicaea, 85, 86, 87–88, 89–90; and Council of Nicomedia, 110, 169, 170; creation of Arianism, 205n41, 206n60; cultivation of public opinion, 52–54; death of, 110, 166, 168, 236n94; debates on Arius, 37–38, 39, 205n39, 206n60; defections from, 62; Eustathius' correspondence with, 204n32, 220n13; excommunication of Arius, 45–46, 72, 205nn43,44; excommunication of Arius's supporters, 52, 60, 62, 208n92, 219n2; exhortation to virgins, 52, 211n45, 212n62; first encyclical (*Henos somatos*), 71, 205n46, 219n4, 220n25; hesitation against Arius, 37, 38, 204nn27,28–29, 205n40; imputations of Sabellianism against, 36, 43, 203n13, 207n86, 219n1; on knowledge of God, 43; and Kolluthus, 37, 41, 73, 80, 164–65, 204n33; legitimacy of, 42, 66, 107; on Melchisedech, 204n32; Melitian support of, 62, 218n135; militancy of, 51, 71; mobilization of supporters, 51, 52, 53, 54, 64, 107, 108; monarchical episcopate of, 108–9, 156; Ossius's support of 80, 81, 82, 86, 88, 228n89; petitioning of peers, 52–53; portrayal of Arians, 50, 52, 53, 54, 55, 59, 71,

289

Alexander (*continued*)
73, 74, 165; preaching by, 42, 47, 48, 50, 51, 206n71, 210n19; rallying of clergy, 52, 54, 64, 108, 156; reaction against pro-Arians, 68–69, 71–73; relationship with Melitius, 106, 172, 204n23, 234n65; rhetoric of, 51, 54, 71; role in drafting Nicene creed, 85, 86, 88, 228n89; rule of faith of, 42; second encyclical (*He philarchos*), 73–74, 212n47, 219n4; seizure of church buildings, 108–9, 235nn86–87; self-portrayal of, 50–51; supporters at Council of Nicaea, 88, 95, 228n85; supporters at synod of Antioch, 82, 84, 222n63; synod of Alexandria (on Arius), 45, 66; *Tomoi* of, 52–53, 73, 74, 80, 212nn47,50, 222n63, 228n85; use of violence, 53, 63, 64, 75, 78, 106; on women supporters of Arius, 61, 217n126, 249n30

Alexandria: Antony's visit to, 250n50; attacks against Arians in, 63, 69, 115–16, 117, 118, 128, 129, 240n158; attacks against Athanasians in, 133–35, 144, 172, 270n116; attacks against Melitians in, 120–21; civic bread of, 58, 215n98; Constantine's envoys to, 80–81; donkey drivers of, 58–59; grain economy of, 57, 58, 214n83; harbors of, 57, 61, 107, 214n82; holy sites of, 63; Jews of, 61, 133; laborers of, 56–60, 156, 163, 164, 215nn97,105, 216n115; lower-class dwellings of, 61, 163, 217n128; millers of, 58; onset of Arian controversy in, 5, 6, 31, 187n6; pagans of, 61, 128, 133; popular preaching in, 36–37, 42, 46–47, 48, 50, 51, 61, 73, 116, 117, 158–59, 206n71, 210n19; popular unrest in, 63, 64, 69, 75, 78, 80, 99, 111, 115, 117, 120–21, 122–23, 128, 129, 133–36, 156, 171, 172; Rhakotis district, 61, 163; sailors in, 57–58, 214nn83,87; secular authorities of, 63, 78, 132; social networks of, 57, 58, 215n105; suburban monks of, 245n211; topography of, 36, 217n127; urban crowd of, 57, 61, 62, 74, 117, 171, 248n16, 252n69; wealthy women residents, 61, 62, 164, 217n129; workshops of, 56–57, 60, 163–64, 214n78, 216n115, 264n21. *See also* Arian controversy; church, Alexandrian

Alexandria, Council of (on Arius, early 320s), 45–46
Alexandria, Council of (324), 80
Alexandria, Council of (338), 131
Amerise, M., 247n4
Ammianus Marcellinus: on Athanasius, 159, 264n18; on riots in Constantinople, 142
Amon (friend of Arius), 253n96

Amphion (bishop of Epiphaneia), 221n36; pro-Arianism of, 70
Amphion (bishop of Sidon), 70
Anastasius (papal librarian): on Arius's preaching, 50; on preaching, 48; sources for Arius, 210n13
Ancyra: planned assembly at, 82, 226n51; rival orthodoxies in, 147; violence in, 128–29, 130 *anomoians*, 256n150
Antioch: Constantine's visit to, 224n4, 225n38; hospices for poor in, 262n262; riots in, 102–3; travel to Rome from, 270n112; unrest in, 140, 232n33; violence in, 141. *See also* church, Antiochene
Antioch, Council of (264), 13, 192nn19–20
Antioch, Council of (268), 13, 192nn21–22,27
Antioch, Council of (325), 75, 81–84, 187n6, 220n18; Alexander's supporters at, 82, 222n63; anti-Arian findings of, 82–83, 223n69; on church discipline, 226n42; Constantine at, 226n46; Constantine's reaction to, 83; excommunication of bishops, 82–83, 87, 225n39; portrayal of Arius, 226n41; reasons for, 81–82, 225nn35,38; sources for, 83, 226nn50–52; statements of faith at, 82; synodical letter of, 222n62, 225n38. *See also* church, Antiochene
Antioch, Council of (327/8), 101–2, 103, 231n24, 232n41; canons of, 231n29, 232n37; Constantine's letter to, 231n25
Antioch, Council of (339), 132, 251nn53–54
Antioch, Council of (340/1), 138, 178, 180–81, 182
Antioch, Council of (341): on Arian controversy, 139; chronology of, 174, 179, 180–82; consensus-building at, 139; Eusebians at, 256n145; on *homoousios*, 139, 181; plans for, 256n146; tensions following, 147. *See also* creeds of Antioch
Antioch, Council of (344), 145
Antioch, Council of (349), 148
Antony (monk), 123, 246n223, 250n50, 263n273
Apelles, debate with Rhodo, 11, 197n59
Apollinarius of Hierapolis, 195n36, 200n37
Arabia, bishops of, 197n61
Areianoi. *See* Arians
Arian chronicler (fourth century), 202nn3,6
Arian controversy: Alexandrian church in early phase of, 32–33, 35–46; challenges to episcopal authority, 5–7, 14, 30, 41, 91, 96, 126, 136, 157; chronology of, 35; Constantine's information concerning onset of, 64, 78, 81; Constantine's intervention in early phase

of, 7, 65, 67, 77, 78–93, 156, 157; Council of Antioch (325) on, 81–84; Council of Antioch (341) on, 139; Council of Nicaea (325) on, 84–91, 187n6; devotion to God and intensity of, 7, 32, 36, 44, 45, 50, 61, 62, 64, 76, 92, 116–17, 156, 158; effect on church leadership, 1, 5–7, 9, 61, 63, 64, 69, 76, 96, 104–5, 108–9, 113, 124, 126–27, 129–30, 135, 141, 151, 153, 155–56, 157–59; escalation of, 4, 5, 6, 32, 42, 46, 63, 68, 76, 105–9; following Arius's excommunication to Eusebius of Nicomedia's involvement, 46–71; following Constantine's death 125–59; following Council of Nicaea to Constantine's death, 99–111, 113–20, 121–23; following Eusebius of Nicomedia's involvement to Council of Nicaea, 71–84; intensity of, 32; label "Arian," 187n3; in late fourth century, 159; Libyan involvement in early phase, 44, 66, 208n92; and Melitian schism, 62, 106–8, 235nn71,75,83; obstacles to resolution of, 74; onset of, 6, 31–33, 36, 201n2; from onset to Arius's excommunication, 36–46; perception of evil in, 1–2, 36, 54, 91; precision/imprecision in, 6, 33, 76, 155–56; politicization of, 78–93, 96, 157; "publicization" of, 48, 49, 65, 209n10; reconciliation attempts in, 2, 32, 36, 44, 52, 67, 68, 76, 80, 107–13, 143–45, 156, 187n6; rival notions of authority/community in, 39, 41, 56, 74, 76, 110; role of state in, 2–3, 91; rupture of church history, 6, 63–64, 156–57; scholarship on, 2–3, 35; scriptural exegesis in, 32, 36, 37, 60, 72; sectarian narratives of, 35, 36; sociopolitical aspects of, 2, 4, 187n3; sources for early phase of, 35–36, 38, 40, 202nn3–4,6; spread of, 7, 64, 66–77; Syrian chronicles of, 35, 202n6; theological aspects of, 2, 4, 32–33, 187n3. *See also* Alexander; Arius; Athanasius; church, Alexandrian; church leadership; violence, religious

Arians: Alexandrian, from Arius's excommunication to Council of Nicaea, 60; Alexandrian, from Constantine's anti-Arian decrees to Constantine's death, 118–22, 171; Alexandrian, from Constantine's death, 128, 131–32, 135, 144, 147, 171–72, 232n233; Alexandrian, from Council of Nicaea to Constantine's anti-Arian decrees, 99–100, 106, 110, 113–17; access to Alexandrian holy sites, 63; allegiance to, reasons for, 117, 172, 266n54; Antiochene, 74–75, 99, 101, 223n69, 230n4; appeal to virgins, 52; appeal to women, 61; Ariomaniacs, 100, 121, 128, 131, 244n210; arrest of Alexandrian preachers, 100; assistance to the poor, 61, 128, 132, 262n257; Athanasius's conflict with, 61, 111, 113, 115–18, 128–29, 131, 132, 139, 147, 171–72, 252n72; capitation taxes for, 117–18; Constantine's decrees against, 117–18, 243n184; Constantine's punishment of, 91, 100, 241n160; control of Antiochene church, 102–3; at Council of Nicaea, 84, 85, 86, 89; departure from Alexandria, 70, 117, 240nn156,158; embassies to bishops, 66; Eustathius's conflict with, 75, 81, 99, 101, 102, 103, 223nn69,71, 230n4; excommunication of, 52, 62, 92, 99, 208n92, 219n2, 230n4; exegesis, topics for, 59–60; instruction through music, 55–56; investment in belief, 44, 45, 50, 62, 96, 117, 171–72; Kollouthian schism and, 164–65; of Libya, 117, 241n161; militancy of, 50, 61, 63, 128, 171; mobilization of public support, 59, 63, 75, 99, 116, 128, 171; opposition to Nicene creed, 99, 105; proselytizing zeal, 60–61, 75; public lists of, 118, 241n174; public preaching, 48, 49–51, 60, 75, 99, 117, 171; relationship with Melitians, 106–8, 235nn71,83; spatial practices of, 60–61; on suffering of Christ, 59, 60, 74, 75, 107, 216n122; support from virgins, 61, 132, 172, 249n30; at synod of Antioch (325), 82–83. *See also* bishops, pro-Arian; Eusebians; preachers, Arian

Arius: accusers of, 36–37; on Alexander's Christology, 43–44, 45, 204n37; Alexander's condemnation of, 38–42, 44, 45, 69, 74, 107; Alexander's synod on, 45; anathematizing of, 89, 90, 107, 139, 146, 228n89, 260n222, 265n38; appeal to Alexandrian laborers, 56–60, 214nn79,83,87, 216n115; appeal to Alexandrians, 46, 51–52, 54, 56–60; appeal to civic authorities, 63; appeal to Eusebius of Nicomedia, 69–70, 107, 113, 168, 169; appeal to Libyans, 44, 66; versus Arianism, 205n41; asceticism of, 50, 62; Athanasius's conflict with, 56, 107, 109, 110, 111, 113, 114, 115–16, 117, 118, 123, 169; in Balkans, 105, 170, 244n209; at Baukalis, 36–37, 48; bishops rejecting, 68, 70, 71, 101, 123; bishops supporting, 44, 59, 66–69, 70–71, 72–73, 74, 76, 101, 221nn38,41; charisma of, 50, 116; Christology of, 32, 38–40, 43–44, 45, 49, 59, 203n10, 206n56, 216n114, 234n59; chronology of recall (326), 165–70; conflict with Alexander, 32, 37–46, 50–65, 68–70, 73–74, 76, 107–9, 115, 156, 167, 169, 204nn29,37, 205nn39,40,44, 236n95; Constantine's correspondence with, 79, 105,

Arius (*continued*)
116–17, 165–66, 167, 169, 171, 223n2, 239n128, 240nn152,160; contradictions in thought of, 205n41; correspondence with Eusebius of Nicomedia, 40, 69–70, 107, 113, 167, 168, 169, 219n4; correspondence with overseas bishops, 66, 67; costume of, 50; at Council of Nicaea, 84, 85, 87, 89; death of, 123, 246n232; defiance of Constantine, 116; departures from Alexandria, 63, 70, 117, 122; desire for reconciliation, 44, 52, 67, 68, 80, 107, 111, 115; dissembling of views, 91, 115, 122, 230n12; educated supporters of, 215n110; Eusebius of Nicomedia's esteem for, 107; excommunication of, 45–46, 72, 89, 205nn43–44; as exegete, 31, 32, 60; exile of, 89, 91, 244n209; following Constantine's anti-Arian decrees, 118; following Council of Nicomedia, 110; instruction through music, 54–57, 58–60, 107, 116, 118, 156, 212n64; integration of marginal groups, 59–60; intellectual isolation of, 266n54; and Kolluthus, 37, 41, 73, 164–65; Libyan supporters of, 44, 66, 208nn92,94, 241n161; mobilization of popular support, 50, 51–65, 74, 116–17, 156, 171; model of church community, 39, 41, 56, 80–81, 110; in Nicomedia, 70; opposition to Nicene creed, 85–86, 89, 115–16, 119; as orator, 33, 50, 116; *parrhesia* of, 116, 240n147; petition to Constantine, 117, 241nn165–66; and popular power, 63, 64; popularity of, 54, 60, 62, 64, 68–69, 74, 80, 106, 107, 116–17, 241n161; preaching by, 36–37, 48, 50, 51, 73, 116–17, 210n17; prestige in Alexandria, 68; priests supporting, 62, 99, 117, 205n42; readmission to communion, 72, 105, 122, 165, 169, 234n61, 245n214; recall from exile, 105, 165–70; relationship with Melitians, 62, 106, 107, 168, 218n135, 235nn75,83; return to Alexandria, 73, 76, 105, 107, 110, 122, 168, 169, 234n61, 235n75, 246n225; soteriology of, 205n48; statements of faith, 44–45, 67, 82, 91, 105, 208nn94,96, 245n214; strengthening public support, 51–52, 54, 56, 59, 60, 64; on suffering and poverty of Christ, 59, 60, 74; synod of Bithynia on, 72, 222n62; synod of Palestine on, 73; *Thalia*, 54–57, 58, 210n20, 212nn64–65, 213n76; theological milieu of, 201n8; travels, 219nn4–5; travels in Asia Minor 70; travels in Libya, 117, 236n96, 241n161; travels in Palestine, 66, 70, 219n4; women followers of, 62

Arius (bishop of Palestine), 136, 143–44, 259n216

Armenia, Arians of, 71
Arnold, D.W.-H., 241nn161,162
Arsaces (monarch of Armenia), 177
Arsenius (bishop of Hypsele), 256n144; conflict with Athanasius, 119, 121, 172–73, 239n142, 242n179; disappearance of, 172, 238n120; election of, 172, 238n115, 266n63; as *episkopos*, 238n118; renunciation of Melitians, 242n182; violence against, 112
Arsinoë, synod of, 28
asceticism: Arius's, 50, 62; contact with Holy Spirit through, 39, 50; Eustathius of Sebaste's, 104, 149, 233n45; institutionalization of, 263n273; urban, 149–51
ascetics: Arius and, 50, 156; Athanasius and, 121–22, 137; female, 62, 218n33; Hieracas and, 37, 204n32; Macedonius of Constantinople and, 149; Marathonius and, 149; ownership of property, 262n257; rivals for support of, 250n50, 254n111; spiritual authority of, 50, 218n133; violence of, 121–22, 149. *See also* monks; virgins, Christian
Ascholius (bishop of Cyzicus), 104; ordination of Parthenius, 233n46
Asclepas (bishop of Gaza), 103; acquittal of, 144, 232n41; charges of heresy against, 232n41; deposition of, 231n24; exile of, 136, 137; reinstatement of, 126, 129, 146; use of violence, 129, 130
Asia Minor: anti-Arians of, 71; charitable programs of, 158; opposition to Nicaea in, 99–100, 103–4; support for Arius in, 71, 107
assemblies, popular, 47; Arian preaching at, 47–48, 49–51, 60, 117; heretical, 200n34, 223n76; Licinius's ban on, 61, 74, 222n67, 224n5; rivals' disruption of, 53. *See also* preaching; public assemblies, private, 209n10; Athanasius's suppression of, 111–13, 117; of Eustathians', 102–3, 140; Gregory's suppression of, 135; in Ancyra, 248n28; in homes, 60, 217nn117,120; of the Mareotis, 111–12, 237n110; tension with public worship, 237n109
Asterius (bishop of Arabia), 136, 143–44, 259n216
Asterius (sophist), 75, 104, 223n74; *Against Marcellus*, 104; defense of Eusebius of Nicomedia, 233n52; *Homilies*, 216n114; pro-Arianism of, 70
Athanasians: 221n42; attacks against, 133–34, 245n212, 252n86; clashes with Arians, 111, 117, 134; clergy, 123, 131–35, 245n211; erasure from records, 241n174; Gregory of Cappadocia's persecution of, 135, 144, 253nn101–3, 270n116;

monks, 133, 134, 146; violence against Athanasian women, 133–35, 172, 266n62; virgins, 123, 133–34, 245n211–12; 254n106

Athanasius (patriarch of Alexandria): abusive subordinates of, 111, 112, 120, 121–22, 240n143, 242n180, 243n195; acquittal at Alexandria, 131; acquittal in Jerusalem (346), 146; acquittal in Milan, 146; acquittal at Psamathia, 114, 115, 118, 173, 239nn135,142; acquittal at Rome, 138, 174, 175, 182; acquittal at Serdica, 144; on Alexander's death, 166; Antony's support of, 123, 250n50; appeal to Constantine, 122; appeal to Constantine II, 125–26, 137; on Arian preaching (in Alexandria), 61; on Arians, 111, 128, 136, 171; on Arians as Ariomaniacs, 121, 128, 131, 244n210; on Arius, 110, 114, 115, 205n46; and assertion of episcopal power, 105, 109, 111–13, 115, 118, 126, 130, 134, 153, 157, 158–59, 171, 237n105; assistance to the poor 128, 130, 133, 135, 146, 248n24; on Asterius, 75, 223n74; burning of church, 128, 252n85, 253n91; calls for revenge, 137, 140; and chalice desecration incident, 112, 121, 122, 123, 238nn113–14, 239n134; charge of murder against, 119, 122; charge of retaining grain fleet against, 123; charge of stealing grain against, 130; charges (violence, sacrilege, treason, imposition of levy of tunics) against, 112, 113, 114, 121, 130, 173, 174, 239nn128,132,134; Christology of, 110, 236n97; collusion with secular authorities, 112–13, 115, 118, 120, 128, 129, 238n122, 239nn135–36; condemnation for sacrilege and violence, 122–23; conflict with anti-Nicene, 143–48; conflict with Arians, 61, 111, 113, 115–18, 128–29, 131, 132, 139, 147, 171–72, 252n72; conflict with Arius, 56, 107, 109, 110, 111, 113, 114, 115–16, 117, 118, 123, 169; conflict with Arsenius, 112, 119, 121, 172–73, 238nn118,120, 239n142, 242nn179,182, 266nn65,67; conflict with Eusebians, 107, 113–14, 118, 120, 121–23, 127–28, 130–31, 136, 137–40, 173, 181, 238nn114,124, 248n18; conflict with Gregory, 132–36, 137, 171, 180, 252nn85,86, 253nn89,90,94, 254nn106,110,111; conflict with Melitians, 111, 112, 113–15, 119, 120–22, 172, 173, 237n104, 238nn114,122, 239nn131–32, 242nn176,182; conflict with Pistus, 128, 131, 246n223; confrontation of opponents, 109; Constantine's commands to, 107, 113–14, 119–20, 123, 167, 174, 267n74; Constantine's dismissal of charges, 119; in Constantinople, 122–23, 236n95, 246n220; Constantius' decrees against, 144, 146, 148; control of church buildings, 111, 113, 128; control of grain subsidies, 128, 132, 146, 248n24; control of Mareotic church, 111–12; correspondence with Constantine, 107, 113–14, 167, 173, 237n101, 238n128; and Council of Alexandria (338), 131, 248n20; on Council of Antioch (341), 181; and Council of Caesarea, 119, 239n142; at Council of Nicaea, 84, 85; and Council of Rome, 132, 134, 138, 174, 175, 179, 181, 182; and Council of Serdica, 143–44; Council of Tyre on, 120–22, 243nn184,187, 244nn208,210, 246n223; creation of Arianism, 40, 139, 140, 205n41; as deacon, 71, 110; demonstrations against, 128, 171; demonstrations for, 122–23, 134–35, 143, 245n211, 251n64; deposition of, 122, 123, 148–49, 245n219; deposition of Callinicos, 242n176; divisiveness of, 119; election of, 110, 236nn98–99, 237n104, 266n63; embassy to Julius, 131–32, 174, 175, 176, 251n51; encyclical against Eusebians (*Epistula encyclica*), 137, 139, 180, 182; establishing churches outside Egypt, 127, 131; exiles of, 123, 134, 174, 176, 176, 249n32; *Festal* (341), 177, 268n91, 270n116; flight from Philagrius, 133–34, 174, 176, 182, 252n75, 253n90, 267n82; following acquittal at Psamathia, 115–18, 239n142, 240nn142–43; hiding with monks, 254n111; as leader of the people, 130; letter to Egyptian Christians, 114; and Mareotic committee, 121–21, 244n210; mobilization of supporters, 111, 117, 121–22, 123, 128, 132–35, 143, 146, 243n196, 245n211, 254n110, 261n64; ordinations outside Egypt, 127, 128, 131; and orthodoxy of Alexandrian Christians, 216n110; Palestinian supporters of, 143, 144, 146, 260n228; patronage of imperial officers, 113, 114, 137, 173, 239n135, 243n193, 248n22; public enemy, 144; public image of, 130; received by Julius, 136, 143; relationship with Constans, 137, 145, 146, 250n46, 255n128; relationship with Constantius, 131, 144, 146, 147, 148, 158–59, 172, 250n49, 251n58, 260n224; restorations of, 127–28, 146–47, 247n7, 248n10; return from Psamathia, 115, 240n160; returns from exile, 127, 132, 146, 171, 248n16, 250n44, 253n91; in Rome, 134, 137–38, 174, 175, 176, 181, 182, 255n125, 267nn82–83,85; support of Western bishops, 137, 138, 10, 143, 144, 145, 146, 149, 153, 175, 179, 181; suppression of dissent, 113–24; suppression of private assemblies,

294   INDEX

Athanasius (*continued*)
111–13, 117; on *Thalia*, 56, 213n76; travel to Caesarea, Cappadocia, 131; travels in Egypt, 112–13, 120, 174, 238n115, 243n184; travel to Libya, 117, 241n62; travel to Nicomedia, 236n95; use of violence, 109, 110–13, 115, 117–18, 120–21, 122, 126, 127–28, 129, 130, 236n99, 238n113, 240n143, 252n76; violence against Arians, 111, 113, 115, 117–18, 119, 128, 129, 243n184, 248n22; violence against Melitians, 111, 112, 120–21, 129, 238n122, 242n176, 243n184; women opponents of, 172; women supporters of, 122, 123, 133–35, 254n106. *See also* Arian controversy; church, Alexandrian

Athanasius (son of Capito), 242n180, 243nn194–95

Athanasius of Anazarbus, 216n114; pro-Arianism of, 68, 70, 220n15; response to Alexander, 72

Augustine, Saint: conciliatory efforts of, 187n6; on music, 213n76

authority, episcopal: Arius's challenges to, 30, 39, 41, 62–64, 73, 107; assertiveness of, 23, 33, 54, 96, 107, 109, 111, 130, 134–35, 150, 151, 153, 155–57, 158; challenges to, 5, 13, 14, 18, 23, 26–30, 91, 96, 126, 157; charity and, 109, 128, 146, 154, 248n25, 254n106; components of, 192n32; consolidation of, 18, 105; Cyprian on, 23; effect of Arian controversy on, 4, 5–6, 37, 53, 92, 96, 105, 127, 135–37, 140, 148, 157–58, 171; impact of theological dispute on, 4–6, 14, 22; legitimacy of, 4, 22, 126, 155; Origen on, 17, 19–20, 37, 196nn48,53, 197n55; orthodoxy of, 22; rivalry for, 26; and spiritual authority, 6, 18–19, 21–26, 37, 195n42, 196n43. *See also* Arian controversy; bishops; church leadership; episcopate; power, episcopal

authority, spiritual: alternative sources of, 20; of ascetics, 50, 218n133; bishops' claims to, 18–19, 196n47; and episcopal authority, 6, 18–19, 21–22, 26, 37, 195n42, 196n43; hierarchical view of, 89; of laity, 20–21, 39, 41, 55–56, 81; of martyrs, 195n40; Origen on, 37, 196n51; through inspiration, 19, 40

Ayres, L., 201n8, 229n109

Bardaisanes (teacher), 201n41
Barnes, T.D., 112, 205n46, 236n95, 238n115, 245n218, 249n39, 250n49, 251n60, 255n129, 259n213, 260n225, 265n42; on Athanasius's second exile, 176, 267nn82,83; on Council of Antioch (341), 181; on Council of Rome, 256n145; on second Council of Nicaea, 166

Basil (bishop of Amasea), 71, 221n38

Basil (bishop of Ancyra): *Against Marcellus*, 104; conflict with Marcellus, 128–29, 260n225; excommunication of, 258n190; *homoiousian* doctrine of, 149; popular support for, 248n26; reinstatement of, 132; use of violence, 263n16

Basil, Saint: on rumor, 58

Basilina (mother of Julian), and Eutropius's deposition, 104, 232n43

Baukalis (Alexandria): Arius's preaching at, 36–37, 48; Arius's support in, 54; location of, 203n18

Baukalis (apocryphal priest), 204n22

Bell, H.I., 120, 244n197

Bemarchius, 257n175; gang violence by, 218n141

Beryllus (bishop of Bostra), 11, 163, 197n61; heresy investigation against, 162

Bidez, J., 170, 265n50

bishops: access to emperors, 82, 104, 125, 131, 189n14, 247n4; Arabian, 197n61; as arbiters of divine truth, 20, 97, 147, 158; assistance to the poor, 128, 149–51, 154, 262n262; challenges to imperial power, 3, 8, 96, 97, 122, 127, 142, 144–45, 153, 158–59; charitable programs of, 149–51; checking of spiritual free will, 21–22; claims to spiritual authority, 18, 19, 196n47; collegiality among, 27; compromise by, 6–7, 25–36, 155–56, 163; consensus-building by, 22, 26, 27–30, 76, 139, 155–56, 199n24; control of scriptural exegesis, 21; deposition of, 27, 28, 92, 103, 110, 132, 136, 144, 148, 162, 254nn115,117; disciplining of dissenters, 7, 23, 26, 29, 91–92, 96–97, 111, 113–18, 126, 147, 153, 157; distancing from laity, 26; embodiment of God's spirit, 19, 20; excommunication for heresy, 23, 161–62; fear of insubordination, 74; imperial patronage of, 3, 6, 156; impoverished, 200n34; Italian, 138, 162, 175–76, 179, 269nn107,111; legitimacy struggles of, 5–6; Libyan, 25, 44, 46, 89, 91, 208n92, 241n161; military escorts for, 133; mobilization of community support, 104–5, 129, 145, 158; mobilization of crowds, 51, 74, 102, 108, 111, 120, 123, 127, 128, 133–34, 141, 142, 143, 150, 231n29, 236n99, 245n211; ordination by, 19; Palestinian, 76, 197n61, 219n4; patronage from, 18, 20, 154, 158; pre-Constantinian, 27, 29; privileges of, 3, 117–18, 135, 146, 155–56, 229n114, 253n103, 260n223; public assertiveness of, 5, 23, 33, 54, 57, 96, 107, 108, 109, 111–15, 117–19, 122, 127–30, 134–36, 141, 142, 150, 151, 153, 155–57, 158; relationship to Holy Spirit, 4, 6, 14, 18, 22, 26, 29, 40, 129, 130, 134, 155, 196nn43,47, 198nn68,73; resolution of disputes, 2, 24–30, 76; responses to Alexander's encyclical, 72–73; responses to Arius, 67–68; role in salvation, 40, 74, 89; spiritual power of, 18, 21, 26, 40; strategies of power, 8, 30, 64, 109, 141, 156–57; suspicion of heresy regarding, 14, 25, 46, 66, 91, 139, 161–62; vulnerability to dissent, 21–22, 24, 29. *See also* authority, episcopal; church leadership; episcopate; power, episcopal

bishops, anti-Arian, 53, 68, 71, 74–75, 82, 101; Constans's patronage of, 145–47; Constantine II's amnesty for, 126; deposition of, 148–49, 254nn115,117; exile of, 102–4, 123, 125, 132, 136; return from exile, 127–29, 146–47

bishops, pro-Arian, 44, 66–69, 70–71, 73, 82, 101–2; anti-Nicene preaching, 99–100; election of, 103–4; excommunication of, 89, 208n92, 225n39; exile of, 91; following Council of Nicomedia, 110; imperial patronage of, 104, 135–36, 144, 147–48; recall of, 105. *See also* Eusebians

bishops, Western: at Council of Serdica, 143–44, 232n41, 259nn206–7; denunciation of Arians, 144; embassy to Constantius, 144–45

Bithynia: exiled bishops of, 166–68, 169; synod of, 72–73, 222n62

Blastus (Montanist), 201n41

books: banning of Arius's, 118; burning of sacred, 112, 238n114

Bourdieu, P., 60; on *habitus*, 126, 190n25

bread, holy, 49; desecration of, 128–29; forced communion with, 149

Brennecke, H.C., 271n125

Brown, Peter, 3, 150; on distribution of church wealth, 128; on charity and episcopal power, 248n25

Burgess, R.W., 74–75

Bynum, Caroline, 49

Caesarea (Cappadocia), 131, 250n49

Caesarea (Palestine), Council of (334), 119, 187n6, 239n142, 242n178; Melitians at, 240n142

Callinicos (bishop of Pelusium), 237n104, 266n73; deposition of, 242n176

Callistus (bishop of Rome), 24; heresy accusations against, 161

capitation taxes, for Arians, 117–18

Cappadocia: 8; Arians of, 71, 102, 132, 148; division of, 187n5

Carterius (bishop of Antaradus), 103

Catholic Church: and Melitians, 106, 172, 236n94, 238n122; rule of faith in, 15–16

Celsus, on church leadership, 23

Chadwick, H., 231n24

chalice, sacred: desecration of, 112, 121, 123, 238n113, 239n134, 256n144, 267n76

charisma: Arius's, 50, 116; in church leadership, 18, 198n64; cultivation of, 51; of martyrs, 195n40

charity, Christian: bishops and, 128, 149–51, 154, 262nn258,262; competition for popular support and, 128, 135, 150, 154, 158; episcopal authority and, 109, 128, 146, 154, 248n25, 254n106; and imperial subventions 128, 211n44. *See also* authority, episcopal; communities; virgins, Christian

chora, Egyptian: Arius's appeal to, 57, 58, 59; Athanasius's activities in, 112–13, 119, 238n115, 239n132, 242n176; grain shipments from, 58, 214n83; Gregory's persecution in, 135, 180, 254n111, 270n116; Melitians in, 106, 112, 129; migrants from, 214n85

Christ: emotions of, 216n114; as generated being, 32, 36, 40, 42, 45, 59, 61, 68, 95, 105, 110, 163, 234n59; *homoiousios*, 149; *homoousios*, 42, 43, 85–91, 95, 99, 115, 116, 157, 207n72; humanity of, 56, 59, 74, 89, 262n257; kinship with humans, 40, 60; mutability of, 39, 40, 44–45, 80, 85, 90, 205n40, 216n114; perfect nature of, 40; poverty of, 59, 60, 74, 75, 216n112; relationship to God the Father, 11–12, 13, 31–32, 36, 38–39, 40, 42, 43, 45, 49, 55, 67, 74, 85–91, 95, 110, 116, 134, 140, 147, 148, 207n35, 228n92, 231n23, 236n97, 259n217; suffering of, 59, 75, 116, 216nn111–12. *See also* God; Logos

Christianity, early: challenges to, 194n17; intellectual responsibility of, 16. *See also* church, early

Chronicle of 724, 202n6

Chronicon Paschale, 202nn3,6

church, Alexandrian: Alexander's supporters in, 52, 53, 63, 108; anti-Nicene theology in, 171–72; Arius's opponents in, 36–37, 41, 73; Arius's supporters in, 41, 44, 62, 73, 89, 91, 99, 105–6, 116, 118, 171; autonomy of parishes in, 36, 37, 108; celebration of Lent, 133, 252nn68–69; disputes on Arius, 37–39;

church, Alexandrian (*continued*)
  in early Arian controversy, 32–33, 35–46, 51–54; Eusebius of Caesarea on, 108; following Council of Nicaea, 99; hierarchy of, 52; idea of God in, 49; letter from the Council of Nicaea to, 89–90; letter from synod of Jerusalem to, 171; Melitian schism in, 37; music in, 54–56, 213n76; organizational structure of, 36, 111; polarization in, 47, 54, 147, 260n233; sources for history of (pre-Constantine), 35; pursuit of precision, 33; rival preaching in, 42, 47–48, 49–51, 210n19. *See also* Alexander; Arian controversy; Arius; Athanasius
church, Antiochene: differing doxologies of, 140, 260n234; disputes of, 13; in early Arian controversy, 74–75, 81; episcopal succession in, 74–75, 102–3, 222nn68–69; Nicene choirs of, 147, 260n235; polarization in, 75, 140–41, 147; pro-Arians of, 70, 75, 102–3; rival factions in, 100–101, 140–41; rival orthodoxies in, 147; rival preaching in, 75, 81. *See also* Eustathius
church, Constantinopolitan: Eusebius of Nicomedia's control of, 130; rival orthodoxies in, 147; succession in, 130, 249n36
church, early: academic model of, 40–41, 56; compromise in, 6–7, 25–26, 32, 36, 76, 84, 86–88, 90, 144, 155–56, 163; Constantine's letters to, 91; control of hierarchy in, 108, 111; expanding resources of, 126; imperial intervention in, 3, 83, 86–88, 91, 142, 143, 145, 146, 148–49, 155; institutional unity for, 2–3; internal structures of, 3; personal religiosity in, 40–41; popular assemblies of, 47; . *See also* authority, episcopal; authority, spiritual; bishops; great church
church, Jerusalem, 101, 223n76
church, Libyan, 25, 199n14; Arians of, 44, 117, 208nn92,94, 241n161
church, Palestinian: Arius's supporters in, 68, 73, 76, 101–3, 107, 223n76; bishops of, 68, 73, 76, 101–3, 164, 197n61, 219n2, 225n36; conflict over *homoousios*, 100; depositions in, 103, 110; support for Athanasius, 146, 260n228
church, post-Nicene: East-West division in, 138, 144, 145, 146; polarization of, 137–38, 147–48, 157; wealth of, 7, 96, 128, 155
church, Syrian: Arius's supporters in, 68, 107; bishops of, 81, 219n2, 225n35; conflict over *homoousios*, 100; depositions in, 103, 110; public preaching in, 75
church buildings: Alexander's seizure of, 108–9, 235nn86–87; Athanasius's control of, 111, 128, 133; barring of Arians from, 111, 133; barring of Athanasians from, 135; bishops' audiences at, 236n88; burning of, 114, 128, 133, 134, 252n85, 253n91; community activities at, 109; conflict for control of, 13, 102–3, 111, 128–29, 133–35; control of, 149, 236n90; lack of space in, 253n92
church leadership: aggressive, 5, 96, 105, 107, 118, 130, 132, 134, 140, 157; assertion through violence, 53, 109, 110, 112, 115, 117, 118, 120, 126, 128–30, 133–36, 141, 150, 154, 155, 158, 248n18, 253n99; challenge of controversies to, 3, 5–6, 13, 14, 18, 22, 23, 24–25, 26–30, 33, 91, 96, 126, 155, 157, 161–62; changes in style of, 5, 33, 51, 61, 96, 105, 109, 151, 153, 157, 158; charismatic, 18, 198n64; creation of power, 4–5, 96–97, 140–48, 155, 158; displays of strength, 63, 64, 111, 127, 155; dynamic model of, 6; effect of Arian controversy on, 1, 5–7, 9, 61, 63, 64, 69, 76, 96, 104–5, 108–9, 113, 124, 126–27, 129–30, 135, 141, 151, 153, 155–56, 157–59; Ignatius on, 195n42; interpretation of Nicene creed, 95; performative style of, 61, 96, 127; polarization of, 47, 52, 72, 130, 137, 140, 141, 147–48, 157; of Roman West, 8; theological challenges to, 6, 13, 14, 16, 17–18, 21–22, 24–25, 28, 29, 33, 91. *See also* authority, episcopal; bishops; episcopate; power, episcopal
Church of Dionysius (Alexandria), 252n77, 253n89; burning of, 134; rebuilding of, 253n91
Church of Dizya, 217n117
Church of the Holy Sepulcher: building of, 101, 231n21; consecration of, 119, 120, 246n222
Church of Pierios, 217n117
Church of Serapion, 217n117
Church of Theonas (Alexandria), 252n77; violence at, 133, 134
cities, Roman eastern: dynamism of, 8
Cleopatra, workshops of, 163
clergy: consensus-building among, 29–30, 37–38; cultivation of public opinion, 49–65; Mareotic, 52, 111, 129, 237n106, 244n210; Melitian, 106, 112, 114, 120–21, 129, 237n104; rise in Christian communities, 26. *See also* bishops; church, early; Melitians; preachers
clergy, Arian (in Alexandria): Constantine's decrees on, 117; excommunication of, 62, 92, 99, 128, 134, 171; immunities of, 146, 260n227; persecution of, 128, 248n22. *See also* Arians
clergy, Athanasian, 120, 123, 135, 245n211; immunities for, 135, 253n103; persecution of, 133, 135, 144, 145, 253n101. *See also* Athanasians

INDEX   297

"Collection Alexandrine" (fourth century), 202n4
communities, Christian: Arius's model of, 39, 41, 56, 80–81, 110; charitable programs for, 128, 135, 149–50, 211n44, 254n106, 262nn257,258,262; competing orthodoxies in, 129, 136, 144, 147–48, 260n225; control of membership in, 21, 46; diversity of thought in pre-Nicene, 15, 16, 26; creeds in, 82; episcopal leadership of, 5–6, 9, 14, 18, 20, 23, 29, 33, 42, 53, 64, 107, 108, 112, 126, 129, 135, 148–51, 155, 157, 158; of great church, 15, 26; ideological coherence in pre-Nicene, 15; intellectual makeup of early 16; outside great church, 27, 161; reception of Nicene creed in, 95–96, 99–100; rise of clergy in early, 18, 22, 26, 41; rise of monarchical bishops in, 14, 18, 22, 23; spiritual knowledge within, 56, 81; spiritual power in, 18, 20–21, 41, 55–56, 81 theological disagreement in early, 22, 27, 29, 156, 161–63. *See also* authority, episcopal; authority, spiritual; church leadership; controversies, theological
compromise: in Arian controversy, 32, 36, 76, 84, 86–88, 90, 144; in early church, 6–7, 25–26, 29, 155–56, 163
confessors, rebukes to, 198n64
consensus: among bishops, 22, 24, 26, 27–30, 38, 76, 139, 155–56, 199n24; under Constantine, 87, 88, 90; at Council of Antioch (325), 81, 83; at Council of Antioch (341), 139; obtained through debate, 22, 32, 194n32; in theological controversies, 6–7, 12, 14, 22, 29, 38
Constans, Emperor, 125, 137, 142, 148; conflict with Constantine II, 174, 177, 268nn93,97; reinstatement of bishops, 146; relationship with Athanasius, 145, 146–47, 250n46, 255n128, 260n233; relationship with Constantius, 146, 177, 258n186, 260n224
Constantia (sister of Constantine), 104, 233nn49,53, 245n214, 247n4
Constantine, Emperor: absence from East, 100; acquittal of Athanasius, 114, 115, 118, 239n142; as agent of consensus, 81, 84, 87, 88, 90; as agent of God, 78, 79; anti-Arian decrees of, 117–18, 243n184; on Arius, 48, 50, 91, 107, 116, 240nn145,152, 241n172; Arius's defiance of, 116; on Arius's followers, 62, 117–18; Arius's petition to, 117, 241nn165–66; assistance to Christian virgins, 211n44; on Athanasius, 114, 119, 123, 246n223; Athanasius's appeal to, 122; Balkans campaign of, 170, 265n47; on ban on synods, 224n5; banning of heretical churches, 229n114; burning of *libelli*, 86, 88; censuring of Eustathius, 102, 232n32; colossus of, 88, 228n87; commands to Athanasius, 107, 113–14, 119–20, 123, 167, 174, 267n74; convocation of Council of Nicaea, 81, 83–84; convocation of synods, 109, 119, 120, 224n26; correspondence with Arius, 79, 105, 116–17, 165–66, 167, 169, 171, 223n2, 239n128, 240nn152,160; correspondence with Alexander, 79, 107, 167, 168, 169, 223n2, 235n74; and Council of Caesarea, 119; at Council of Nicaea, 78, 84, 86–89, 229n116; and Council of Tyre, 120, 122, 243n189, 246n221; cultivation of Arians, 100; death of, 96, 124, 125, 247n4; defeat of Licinius, 31, 201n1; demand for church unity, 79, 83, 85, 87, 90, 91, 92, 100, 105, 107, 109–10, 119–20, 156–57, 243n184; and Donatist schism, 78, 83–84, 224n26; on early Arian dispute, 78–79; envoys to Alexandria, 80–81; episcopal privileges under, 117–18, 154, 156; on episcopal rivalries, 86–87, 120; Eusebius of Nicomedia's influence with, 113, 119, 125, 167, 168, 169, 247n4; exile of Athanasius, 123, 126, 246n223; exile of Marcellus, 123; exile of Nicene clerics, 104; on *homoousios*, 87, 88, 96, 99; information concerning early Arian controversy, 64, 78, 81; intervention in Antiochene riots, 102; intervention in Arian controversy, 7, 65, 67, 77, 78–93, 104, 156, 157; letter to Alexandrians (335), 123, 246n223; letter to Antony, 123, 246n223; letters to churches, 91; letter to synod of Antioch (327/8), 231n25; Melitians' embassy to, 108, 114, 168, 170, 173, 174, 266nn68,73; *Oration to the Saints*, 226n46; on outbreak of Arian controversy, 78–79, 206n57; Persian campaign of, 125, 269n100; on prayer, 50; promotion of Nicene creed, 79, 95, 96, 100, 125, 229nn106,109; punishment of Arians, 91, 100, 117–18, 241n160, 243n184; recall of Arius, 105, 165–68, 169; recall of bishops, 105, 168, 169, 247n6; relations with Melitians, 108, 110, 114, 119, 166, 168, 169, 170; respect for Eusebius of Caesarea, 83, 87, 88, 89, 233n48; as restorer of heretics, 234n60; return to East (330), 114; on standard for orthodoxy, 90; summoning of Arius, 123; at synod of Antioch (325), 226n46; on synod of Antioch (325), 83; *tricennalia* of, 119, 123; *vicennalia* of, 81; visit to Antioch (324), 225n38; Western sojourns of, 105, 170; will of, 247n4

Constantine II, Emperor, 125; amnesty under, 126, 247n7; Athanasius's appeal to, 125–26, 137; conflict with Constans, 174, 177, 268nn93,97; death of, 137, 174, 255n128, 267n78, 268n97; exiles' petitions to, 125–26
Constantinople: charitable programs of, 150, 158; gangs of, 142, 150; grain supply for, 123, 258n183; poor of, 149–50, 262n261–62; violence in, 141–42, 145. *See also* church, Constantinopolitan
Constantinople, synod of (336), 123–24; bishops attending, 246n231
Constantius, Emperor: birth date of, 269n97; charitable programs of, 262n261; conflict with Paul of Constantinople, 130, 142, 145, 249n36; and Council of Serdica, 142–43; creed of Sirmium under, 149, 153; and creeds of Antioch, 140, 271n127; defeat of Magnentius, 148; dissenting bishops under, 97; embassy to Western bishops, 258n186; imposition of doctrinal uniformity, 97, 148, 149, 153, 261n250; laity's opposition to, 142, 158; Nicene faith of, 139; Persian campaign of, 131, 132, 144, 177–78, 251n57, 268n97, 269n100; patronage of pro-Arian bishops, 104, 135–36, 144, 147–48; reducing of Constantinople grain supply, 258n183; reinstatement of exiled bishops, 145, 146, 259n216; relations with Eusebians, 125, 130, 131, 132, 135, 136, 247n4, 251n53; relationship with Athanasius, 127, 131, 144, 146, 147, 148, 149, 158–59, 172, 241n174, 247n7, 250n49, 251n58, 260n224; relations with Constans, 145–46, 177, 251n57, 258n186, 260n224; religious tolerance under, 146–47, 172, 260nn227,233; Roman East under, 125; Western bishops' embassy to, 144–45
Continuatio Antiochensis Eusebi, 202nn2,6
controversies, theological, 2, 3, 7, 14; challenges to church leaders, 3, 6, 13, 14, 22, 24–25, 29, 33, 155, 161–62; consensus-building in, 6–7, 12, 14, 24, 26–27, 32–33; effect on church communities, 1, 12, 13; episcopal authority in, 4, 14, 24–25, 33; and episcopal power, 4, 5, 6, 14, 22; Origen's arbitration of, 11–13, 109; over prayer, 12; over scriptural exegesis, 2; over the subject of God, 11–12, 13, 17, 31; popular participation in, 47, 208n1; precision/imprecision in, 6, 12, 14, 18, 24, 29, 30, 76, 155–56; regional, 1; use of music in, 54–57, 147, 156. *See also* Arian controversy; Alexander; Arius; Christ; dissent, theological; exegesis, scriptural; God; heresy; laity; music; orthodoxy; theology, Christian; truth, divine
convents: in Alexandria, 122; in Constantinople, 149; in Cyzicus, 150
Cornelius of Rome, 198n74
creed of Sirmium, 148–49, 153
creeds of Antioch, 136–37, 138–39, 180, 245n215, 256nn147,150; ; Constantius and, 140, 271n125; divisiveness of, 140–41, 157; first, 271n125; fourth, 144, 145, 148, 259n217; identification with heresy, 141; indeterminacy of, 139, 256n148; second, 257n155. *See also* Antioch, Council of (341)
Cymatius (bishop of Gabala), 103
Cymatius (bishop of Paltus), 103
Cyprian of Carthage, 19; on bishops, 26, 38, 200n31; on collective deliberation, 25; on episcopal authority, 23; on heresy, 26, 162; on Holy Spirit, 21; on Privatus, 162; rebuke to martyrs, 198n64
Cyrus (bishop of Beroea), 103
Cyzicus, charitable programs of, 150

Dalmatius (brother of Constantine), 119, 242n178
Dalmatius (nephew of Constantine), 125, 247n7
Damasus (bishop of Rome), 8
De Clerq, V.C., 225n38
Dedication Council. *See* Antioch, Council of (341)
Demetrius (bishop of Alexandria), 11, 191n4
Demetrius (bishop in Arabia), 191n9
Dianius (bishop of Caesarea, Cappadocia), 233n45, 258n190
Didascalia, 19
Didymus of Alexandria, 206n65, 215n110
Diodorus (bishop of Tenedos), 136
Diodorus (Nicene leader), 140, 147, 257n160, 261n244
Dionysius (bishop of Alexandria): arbitration of disputes, 109; challenged by Germanus, 204n35; censorship of, 162; on collegiality, 27; exile of, 240n160; letter to Antiochenes, 192n27; in Nepos's controversy, 28–29, 162, 201nn44,47; on rebaptism of heretics, 163; in Sabellian controversy, 25, 162
Dionysius (bishop of Rome), 25
Dionysius, Count: at Council of Tyre, 121, 244n210
dissent, theological: Athanasius's suppression of, 111, 113–24; bishops' management of, 26, 27, 28, 30, 156; bishops' vulnerability to, 25, 29, 79; challenges to church leadership, 5–6, 13–14, 23, 26, 79; collective punishment of,

26; criminalization of, 7, 91–93, 157; disciplining of, 23; discourse of, 60; episcopal power and suppression of, 113–24, 127, 129, 147, 150, 157; following Council of Nicaea, 91–93, 99–100; frequency of, 21, 24; irreconcilable, 26; Patrophilus's suppression of, 153; threat to public order, 2, 100, 132, 142. *See also* Arian controversy; controversies, theological; heresy; orthodoxy; theology, Christian; truth, divine; violence, religious

Domnus (bishop of Sirmium), 103

Donatist schism, 1, 8, 78, 187n6; Constantine and, 83–84, 218n142, 224nn8,26

donkey drivers, Alexandrian, 58, 215nn103–4; songs of, 57; spread of doctrine, 58–59

East, Roman: Arian controversy in, 8; civil war threats in, 2, 146; Constantine's absence from, 100, 170; under Constantius, 125; political culture of, 8; secular assemblies of, 27; sociocultural uniformity of, 8

Eleusis (bishop of Cyzicus): charitable programs of, 150; *homoiousian* faith, 261n252; persecution of Nicene, 150; reaching out to laborers, 262n269

Elm, S., 62

Elpidius (priest), envoy from Julius, 138, 174–77, 178–80, 182, 268n92

emperors, Christian: bishops' access to, 189n14; legitimacy of, 8; patronage of bishops, 3, 6, 156; theological uniformity under, 97. *See also* bishops, anti-Arian; bishops, pro-Arian

Ephrem, Saint, 136

Epiphanius: on Alexander's encyclical, 71–72; on Arius, 50, 66; on charitable programs, 149; on churches of Alexandria, 217n117; on early Arian controversy, 35, 36–37, 62, 71, 171, 208n92; on Marcellus of Ancyra, 175, 267n81; on Melitian compromise with Arians, 106; on Melitians, 106, 111, 112, 166, 168, 170, 204n23, 234n67, 235nn81,83, 265n42; Melitian sources of, 203n17; on Scythopolis, 153

episcopate: apostolic origins of, 18–19; militant, 109, 126, 127, 157; monarchical, 18, 19–20, 23, 26, 108; politicization of, 96, 118; as public force, 111, 134; as sociopolitical force, 126–27, 129, 133–35, 141, 148, 151, 155, 158–59; strengthening of, 109. *See also* bishops; church leadership

Eucharist: communion during, 140, 232n33; Holy Spirit during, 49–50; instruction concerning, 49

Eudoxius (bishop of Germanicia), 70, 103, 230n4, 233n44, 258n190, 264n18

Eulalius (bishop of Antioch), 102; death of, 231n26; reinstatement of priests, 103

Euphratas (bishop of Cologne), embassy to Constantius, 145, 260n223

Euphration (bishop of Balanea), 68; deposition of, 103

Euphronius (bishop of Antioch), 102, 231n26; appointment of pro-Arian bishops, 103; election of, 232nn37,41

Eusebians, 71; as an Athanasian construct, 221n42; conflict with Athanasius, 113, 118–19, 122–23, 127–28, 130–31, 136, 137–38, 140, 173, 181, 243n195, 250nn46,49; conflict with Marcellus of Ancyra, 123, 246nn224,231; conflict with Nicene, 130, 136, 137, 254n115; at Council of Antioch (341), 138–39, 256n145; at Council of Serdica, 143; at Council of Tyre, 121–22, 244n210, 246n223; disregard for Nicaea, 270n124; correspondence with Julius of Rome, 131–32, 138, 174–76, 178–81, 182, 248n21, 250n44, 251n51, 267nn77,85, 268n86, 269n108; opposition to Nicene creed, 99, 100, 114, 123, 125, 138–39, 227n73; reply to Julius of Rome, 138, 175, 178, 182, 255n138, 256n145, 269nn102,111; rewriting of God, 137–40; support of Arians, 100, 101, 113, 119, 131, 137, 138, 248n21, 256n149; support of Arius, 123, 256n148; synod at Antioch (340–1), 138, 178–79, 180, 182, 256n146. *See also* bishops, pro-Arian; Constantius; Eusebius (bishop of Nicomedia and Constantinople)

Eusebius (bishop of Caesarea), 66; on Alexandrian church, 108; on Alexandria unrest, 80; anathematized, 68, 76; on Antioch unrest, 102; appointment of pro-Arian bishops, 110; Christology of, 68, 87, 99; on church assemblies, 47; conflict with Nicene, 101–4, 110; Constantine's respect for, 83, 87, 88, 89, 233n48; at Constantinople (335), 122; *Contra Marcellum*, 104, 231n18; correspondence with Constantia, 104; correspondence with Constantine, 233n48; correspondence with court, 226n53; at Council of Antioch (325), 81–82; on Council of Jerusalem (335), 122; and Council of Nicaea, 84, 86, 87, 88–89, 103, 228n83, 229n117; on Council of Nicomedia, 109–10, 170; death of, 143; deposition of Eustathius's supporters, 103; deposition of Marcellus of Ancyra, 123; dislike of Nicene creed, 87, 89, 90, 99, 101, 230n1; on early

300 INDEX

Eusebius (*continued*)
  Arian controversy, 36; Eustathius's attacks on, 101, 102; excommunication of, 82, 83, 87, 229n117; Macarius of Jerusalem's attacks on, 101; Marcellus of Ancyra's attacks on, 104; statement of faith, 87, 88, 228n83; support for Arius, 66, 68, 70, 72, 73, 88, 101, 220n15; support for Nicene formula, 89, 101; at synod of Antioch (327/8), 101, 103, 232n41; at synod of Constantinople (336), 123; transfer to Antioch (failed), 104; travels in Syria, 101, 231n18
Eusebius (bishop of Nicomedia and Constantinople): Alexander's attack on, 71–72, 76; Arius's correspondence with, 40, 69–70, 107, 113, 167, 168, 169, 219n4; arrival in Bithynia, 105, 169; Asterius's defense of, 104; as bishop of Constantinople, 130, 249n37; conflict with Athanasius, 110, 113–14, 118–20, 121–22, 173; Constantine's cultivation of, 100; and Constantine's will, 247n4; at Constantinople (335), 122; at Council of Antioch (340/341), 180, 181; at Council of Jerusalem (335), 243n190; and Council of Nicaea, 84, 227nn68,73; at Council of Tyre, 121; death of, 141; deposition of, 229n117; deposition of Marcellus of Ancyra, 123; disregard for Nicaea, 270n124; esteem for Arius, 107; exile of, 91, 100, 101, 154, 166–67, 170, 247n6; imperial court, connections with, 104, 120, 239n135; imperial family, ties with, 71; influence with Constantine, 113, 119, 125, 167, 168, 169, 247n4; influence with Constantius, 131, 247n4; intervention in early Arian controversy, 69–70; and John Arkaph, 114, 169; letter of repentance, 165, 169; letter to Paulinus of Tyre, 227n68; and Licinius, 226n54; Marcellus of Ancyra's attacks on, 104; mediation attempts by, 70, 107; and Melitians, 107–8, 113–14, 119, 166, 168–69, 173, 238n114; opposition to Nicene creed, 99–100, 105, 123; patronage of Philagrius, 122; pro-Arianism of, 71–72, 83, 85, 100, 101, 118; return from exile, 104, 105, 127, 166, 167, 169, 170, 247n6, 265n43; and revision of Nicene creed, 105, 107, 114, 123, 221n42; rise in imperial capital, 110; support of Arius, 69, 70, 85, 107, 113, 115, 122, 167, 169, 227n73; support for Nicene formula, 89, 105; at synod of Constantinople, 123; transfer of relics, 249n37; treason, suspicion of, 239n134. *See also* Eusebians
Eusebius (bishop of Vercelli): charitable work of, 154; exile of, 153–54, 263nn6,10

Eusebius (deacon), in controversy over Paul of Samosata, 13
Eusebius of Emesa (rhetor), 251n62, 269n100
Eustathians, 102, 103, 142, 147; private assemblies of, 140, 232n33
Eustathius (bishop of Sebaste): asceticism of, 149, 151, 262n257; charitable program of, 149, 262n258; ordination of, 233n45; priest in Antioch, 70, 220n34; pro-Arianism of, 70, 71, 104, 230n4
Eustathius of Beroea (bishop of Antioch), 75, 84, 104, 105; anti-Arianism of, 68, 75, 99, 100–101, 223n71; Antiochene opponents of, 75, 101, 102, 223n69, 230n4; on Ariomaniacs, 101; *Commentary on Proverbs*, 101; Constantine's censuring of, 102, 232n32; on Council of Nicaea, 84, 89, 227n64; deposition of, 101–2, 103, 231n24; deposition of pro-Arian clerics, 99; election of, 75, 81, 222n69, 225nn35–36,38; on *homoousios*, 101, 231n23; John Chrysostom on, 75; mobilization of supporters, 102, 108; ordination of, 233n45; support of Alexander, 84; at synod of Antioch, 81–82, 225n35
Eutropius (bishop of Adrianople), 103; banishment of, 104, 232n43
Euzoius (Alexandrian priest): bishop of Antioch, 232n33; exile of, 170; recall from exile, 105, 107, 165–68
exegesis, scriptural: in Alexandria, 48, 116, 209n8, 240n150; Arian's choices in, 59–60; controversies over, 2, 17, 21; episcopal control of, 21; and orthodoxy, 24; parameters for, 18; rationality in, 20. *See also* controversies, theological

Fabian (bishop of Rome), ordination of, 196n45
factories, imperial: dye (Lampsacus), 263n274; textile (Cyzicus), 262n269; weapons (Adrianople), 129, 249n31
Felicissimus: challenge to Cyprian, 198n74; expulsion from church, 25
Felix (bishop), accusations of heresy against, 162
Flavianus (Nicene leader), 140, 147, 148, 257n160, 261n244
Flavius Polemius, 268n97
Florinus of Rome, 201n41
Fox, Lane, 225n38, 226n46, 268n97
free will, spiritual, 20, 21

Gaudentius (bishop of Naissus), 143
Gaza, violence in, 129, 130
Gelasius of Caesarea, 36, 203n15, 235nn75,86

Gelasius of Cyzicus: on Alexander's correspondence with Constantine 235nn74,77, 265n38; on Leontius of Caesarea, 221n38; on Nicene creed, 230n1; on recall of Bithynian bishops, 165, 166–68
George Hamartolus, 234n61, 243n190, 249n35
George of Cappadocia (bishop of Alexandria), 135, 148, 158, 187n6, 235n71, 254n110, 261n244
George of Laodicea: deposition of, 258n190; election as bishop, 103, 232n44; pro-Arianism of, 70, 72, 230n4; residence in Antioch, 220n34; response to Alexander, 72
Gibbon, Edward: on bishops, 26
Gnosticism, challenge to Christianity, 194n17
God: Alexander's view of, 43, 49, 52, 207n82; Arius's views of, 36, 39, 43, 44–45, 49, 55, 61, 72, 110, 116; Eusebians' rewriting of, 137–40; human understanding of, 17, 43; nature of, 31–33; orthodox definition of, 1, 2, 4, 5, 6, 7, 12, 16–17, 79, 85, 91, 96, 139, 155; *ousia* of, 85, 89, 95, 139, 148, 207n72, 228nn89,92, 230n1, 256n150, 259n217; Platonic, 31–32; power of, 12, 191n13; proper relations with, 15, 49, 51, 76, 156. *See also* Christ, relationship to God the Father
great church, 14, 15, 19, 25, 46, 200n38; communities outside of, 64, 161; heresy in, 161. *See also* church, early
Gregg, R.C., 201n8
Gregory (bishop of Berytus), 68, 82, 220n18
Gregory Nazianzenus: on Arian controversy, 31, 63, 126; on Athanasius, 236n99, 248n22; on episcopal appointments, 251n66; on bishops' love of power, 158, 248n8; on workshops of Alexandria, 163
Gregory of Cappadocia (bishop of Alexandria): Arians' support of, 135, 137, 251n63, 253n99; arrival in Alexandria, 133, 248n16, 251n60; assistance to the poor, 135, 248n24, 254n106; called Melitian, 235n71; confiscations of property, 254n106; conflict with Athanasius, 132–36, 137, 252nn85–87, 253n89, 254nn106,111; death of, 146, 260n224; excommunication and deposition, 258n190; ordination of, 132, 178, 251n52; ordination of Arian clerics, 135, 253n96; persecution in *chora*, 135–36, 180, 254n111, 270n116; Julius's opposition to, 137–38; military protection for, 133; persecution of Athanasians, 135, 144, 145, 180, 252n86, 254nn106,111, 270n116; Philagrius's aid to, 133, 136; seizure of church buildings, 134, 252nn85–86; suppression of private assemblies, 135; theological views of, 136; use of violence, 134–36, 180, 252nn85–86, 254n111
Gregory Thaumaturgos, 197n59, 263n273
Griggs, C.W., 238n117
Groh, D.E., 201n8
habitus, 126, 155, 190n25

Hanson, R.P.C., 42, 43
Hegesippus, 18
Helkesaite heresy, 163
Hellanicus (bishop of Tripoli), 103
Heracleides (Arabian bishop), 11, 14, 16, 23, 162, 197n61; debates with Origen, 11–13, 15; disputes with, 191nn9,12; suspected of heresy, 12, 14, 20, 21–22, 162; loss of legitimacy, 21–22; peers' debates over, 24
Heraclius (*commentariensis*), 120
Heraiscus (bishop of Heracleopolis Magna), 243n195
heresy: bishops investigated for, 11, 13, 14, 23, 24, 28, 161–62; catalogues of, 198n65; conciliatory treatment of, 24, 26, 27, 163; Cyprian on, 23, 26, 162; excommunication for, 23, 162–63; Helkesaite, 163; loss of Spirit in, 14, 21, 129, 198n73; loss of legitimacy in, 14, 21–2, 91, 155; versus orthodoxy, 42, 43, 193n17; rebaptism following, 163; rhetoric against, 24. *See also* controversies, theological; dissent, theological; orthodoxy
Hermogenes (bishop of Caesarea), 233n45
Hermogenes (master of horse), 142; murder of, 258n180
Hesychius (*castrensis*), 143
Hesychius (deacon), 131
Hieracas of Leontopolis, 37, 204n32, 218n133
Hilary, on creeds of Antioch, 256n150
Hippolytus: accusations against Callistus, 161; *Apostolic Tradition*, 196nn43–44 on idea of God, 16; on ordination rituals, 19, 196nn43–44; on Sabellius, 24; on spiritual authority, 21
Holy Spirit: bishops' relationship to, 4, 6, 14, 18, 22, 26, 29, 40, 129, 130, 134, 155, 196nn43,47, 198nn68,73; during Eucharist, 49–50; loss of gift, 14, 21, 129; lay contact with, 18, 39, 206n53; prelates' control of, 22
homoiousians, 149; alliance of Nicenes with, 256n150; of Hellespont, 261n252
homoousios (epithet): Alexander on, 85, 227n73, 228n89; ambiguity of, 229n118; applied to Christ, 42, 43, 85–91, 95, 157, 207n72, 228n92; Arians' condemnation of, 99; Arius on, 43 85, 91, 105, 115, 116, 165; banning of, 256n151;

302 INDEX

homoousios (continued)
   and creeds of Antioch, 139, 181, 256n150, 270n124; Constantine on, 87–88, 96 Eusebius of Nicomedia's rejection of, 105; Eustathius of Antioch on, 101, 231n23; interpretations of, 99, 100, 101, 228n92; in Nicene creed, 86, 89, 92, 228n89, 256n147; post-Nicene conflict over, 99–101, 157, 270n124. *See also* Nicene creed
hospitals, 149, 262n261
hymns, Christian, 213nn68–69; Arian, 107, 116, 212n64; Nicene, 140, 147. *See also* music
"Hymn to Christ," 213n69
Hymn to the Rhodian Winds, 58
hypostasis, 43, 45, 231n23, 240n152, 259n217

Ignatius of Antioch, Saint: on episcopal leadership, 195n42, 196n47
Ignatius of Selymbria, 36; on Alexander's preaching, 48; on Arius's teaching, 48; sources of, 36, 203n15
intellect, human: deficiencies of, 17, 43
Irenaeus, 18, 163
Ischyras, 237n104, 239n134; bishop of Peace of Secontaturus, 245n215, 267n73; violence against, 112, 242n176
Isidore of Pelusium, 136
Ision, house-church of, 111–12
Itinerarium Alexandri, 268nn93,97

James, W.: *The Varieties of Religious Experience,* 213n76
Jerome, Saint: on Pierius, 211n34
Jerusalem, synod of (335), 122; Cappadocians at, 233n45; letter to Alexandria, 171; reintegration of Arius, 122, 265n29
Jerusalem, synod of (346), 146
Jews, 61, 133, 153
John Arkaph: at Antioch, 119, 120, 242n180, 243n182; Athanasius's surveillance of, 242n180; banning of, 246n229; embassy to court, 114, 168, 173–74, 243nn184,187,193; and Eusebius of Nicomedia, 169, 243n184; leadership of Melitians, 114; readmission of, 243n187; recognition of Athanasius, 242n182, 243n187; sheltering of Arsenius, 119; succession to Melitius, 234n67
John Chrysostom, panegyric to Eustathius, 75
Jones, A.H.M., 8
Josephus, Count, 153
Jovian, Emperor: Arian controversy under, 159
Judaism, challenge to Christianity, 194n17

Judge, E.A., 230n6
Julian, Emperor: Arian controversy under, 159; on Athanasius, 159, 249n32
Julius (bishop of Rome), 95; Athanasius's embassy to, 131–32, 251n51; correspondence with Eastern bishops, 138, 174–76, 178–81, 182, 188n7, 267nn77,85, 268n86, 269nn101,108, 270nn118,124; and Council of Rome, 138, 175, 176, 178–79, 256n145; Eastern bishops' reply to, 138, 175, 178, 179, 180, 182, 255n138, 269nn102,111; Eusebians' embassy to, 131–32, 250n44, 251n51; on exiles, 136, 180, 269n99; Gregory's embassy to, 137; and Italian bishops, 179, 269n111; and Marcellus of Ancyra, 255n137, 267n80; opposition to Gregory, 137–38; readmission of Athanasius and Marcellus of Ancyra, 138

Kelly, J.N.D., 229nn106,118, 230n1
Klein, R., 180, 255n136
knowledge, divine, 4, 15, 18, 43, 48, 90; laity's attainment of, 55–56
Kolluthian schism, 80; Arians and, 164–65
Kolluthus (priest), 37, 41, 73; Alexander on, 164–65, 204n33; and Ischyras, 237n104; readmission to communion, 80

laborers: Adrianople, 129, 249n31; Ancyra, 128; Cyzicus, 262n269; Lampsacus, 151, 263n274; Scythopolis, 263n2
laborers, Alexandrian, 57, 163–64, 214nn82–83, 215nn97,105, 264n21; Arius's' appeal to, 56–60, 156, 216n115; music of, 56, 58–59
laity: Alexander's appeal to, 51, 52–53, 68, 74, 107, 108, 212n61; Arius's appeal to, 48, 50, 51–64, 73,80, 116–17, 156, 171, 212n62, 215n105; attainment of divine knowledge, 18, 19, 39, 55–56, 81; bishops' distancing from, 26; charisma of, 18; competition for support of, 36, 46, 50–54, 60, 63–64, 68, 75, 76, 93, 96, 106, 111, 149, 158, 159, 250n50; concerns of, 209n2; in episcopal ordinations, 19; excommunication of, 27, 28, 62, 99; involvement with early Arian controversy, 33, 36, 38, 46, 47–65, 74–76, 78, 80; involvement with post-Nicene Arian controversy, 92, 99, 102, 107–8, 111, 116–17, 123, 126–29, 132, 133–35, 141, 142, 145, 147, 150, 156, 158, 172, 230n1, 231n26, 241n172, 249n36, 257n169, 260n234, 262n263, 266n62; involvement with theological controversy, 12, 18, 20–21, 25, 36, 64; mobilization for violence, 63, 102, 111, 128, 133, 134, 141, 158; mobilization

of, 4, 7, 74, 76, 102–3, 107–8, 129, 142, 147, 150, 156, 213n76; opposition to Constantius, 142, 158; piety of, 198nn64,74, 206n53; participation in synods, 35, 28; spiritual authority of, 20–21, 41, 55–56, 81; teaching through music, 54–57, 59, 213n76; violence against, 126, 128–29, 133–35, 141, 142, 149, 253n101, 257n169, 266n62. *See also* bishops, mobilization of community support; bishops, mobilization of crowds; power, popular; violence, religious

Lake Mareotis, 61; laborers of, 57

Leontius (bishop of Antioch), 145, 147, 148, 220n33, 232n36, 257n158, 259n217, 260n234; charitable programs of, 262n262; support for Arius, 70

Leontius of Caesarea, 71, 221n38

Libanius, 150; on violence in Constantinople, 141; gang violence against, 218n141

Libya: Arius's travels in, 117, 236n96, 240n160, 241n161; exiled bishops in, 254n117; support for Arius in, 66, 117

Licinius: ban on Christian meetings, 61, 74, 77, 222n67, 224n5; defeat of, 31, 201n1

Lietzmann, H., 16

Life of Constantine (anonymous text): on Arius's music, 57; on Council of Nicaea, 89

liturgy: bishops' names in, 53, 212n53; expression of rank in, 210n26. *See also* Eucharist

Logan, Alastair, 225n30; on Marcellus, 228n89

Logos: 32, 48, 70, 76, 89, Alexander on, 42, 73; Athanasius on, 236n97; immutability of, 39. *See also* Christ

Lucian (martyr): and creeds of Antioch, 256n148; disciples of, 69, 70, 71

Lucius (bishop of Adrianople): deposition of, 148; exile of, 137; *fabricenses*' support of, 129, 249n31; imprisonment of, 136, 261n244; readmission of, 144; return from exile, 146, 260n224; use of violence, 129

Macarius (Athanasian priest), 242n176, 239n131, 240n143, 243n193; arrest of, 120; at Council of Tyre, 245n213; violence by, 112, 267n76

Macarius (bishop of Jerusalem): address to Helena, 223n76; anti-Arianism of, 101

Macarius (Eusebian priest), 131, 251nn51,52

Macarius (Melitian priest), 244n197

Macedonius (bishop of Constantinople), 141, 142, 145, 147, 153, 187n6, 262n263; charitable program of, 149–50, 262n262; conflict with Novatians, 261n254; conflict with Paul, 130, 147; homoiousian doctrine of, 149; persecution of Nicene, 149; use of violence, 149, 150

Macedonius (bishop of Cyzicus), 262n271

Macedonius (bishop of Mopsuestia), 82, 221n37, 258n190; at Council of Tyre, 121; Mareotic committee, 121; pro-Arianism of, 70–71

MacMullen, R., 208n1, 219n152

Magnentius, 261n242; Constantius's defeat of, 148

Maier, H., 60

Malchion (priest), 45; debate with Paul of Samosata, 13

Marathonius (bishop of Nicomedia), 149, charitable program of, 150, 262n262; homoiousian doctrine of, 261n252

Marcellus (bishop of Ancyra): acquittal at Rome, 134, 138, 182, 256n144; acquittal at Serdica, 144; anti-Arianism of, 71, 84, 221n143; charge of heresy against, 104, 123, 144, 246n224; conflict with Basil, 128–29, 147, 260n225; conflict with Eastern bishops, 143, 144, 267n81; conflict with Eusebians, 104–5, 129, 131, 137–38, 246n224, 249n38, 256n145; contact with Constantine, 227n59; *Contra Asterium*, 104, 123, 233n52; at Council of Nicaea, 270n124; and Council of Rome, 138, 182; depositions of, 104, 123, 125, 138, 148, 261n244; exile of, 123, 136, 137, 138, 175, 176, 182, 267n85; humiliation of opponents, 130; and Julius, 138, 255n137, 267n80; reinstatement of, 126, 128, 133, 146, 260nn224,225; role in Nicene creed, 228n89; statement of faith, 175, 176, 182, 267nn80,81; use of violence, 128–29, 133, 233n51, 248n29

Marcion (preacher), charges against, 200n41

Mareotic committee, 121, 122, 131, 221n37, 244nn208,210

the Mareotis: Catholic clergy of, 52, 111, 129, 237n106, 244n210; chalice incident in, 112, 121, 123, 238n113, 256n144, 267n76; Melitians in, 111, 121, 237n104; monks of, 122, 245n211; private churches of, 111–12, 237n110; violence in, 112, 121, 122, 129, 240n143, 245n211; virgins in, 122, 245n211. *See also* Lake Mareotis; Mareotic committee

Marianos (*notarius*), embassy to Alexandria, 80

Maris (bishop of Chalcedon): at Council of Tyre, 121; exile of, 229n117; Mareotic committee, 121; opposition to Nicene creed, 99, 230n6; support for Arius 71, 227n41, 227n73

Markus, R.A., 14

Marrou, H.-I., 48

Martin, A., 18, 203n18, 204n23, 211n34, 238n126, 245n218, 252n76, 253n91, 266n54

304   INDEX

Martyrologium Romanum, 221n38
martyrs, 20, 51; Arians as, 117; Arius as, 73; Athanasius as, 134; charisma of, 195n40; contact with Holy Spirit, 39; festivals of, 63, 218n148; rebukes to, 197n61, 198n64; relics of (Pamphilus and companions), 249n37
Melchisedech, 204n32
Melitians: Alexander's conflict with, 37, 106–7, 108, 110, 168, 169, 170, 234n65, 235n80, 236nn36,42,94, 265nn36,42, 266n63; and Alexander's succession, 236nn94,98; Alexandrian congregations of, 37, 106, 244n197; arrest of, 120–21; Arsenius's renunciation of, 242n182; Athanasius's conflict with, 110, 111, 112, 113–15, 119, 120–22, 129, 172, 173, 237n104, 238n122, 239nn131–32, 242nn176,179, 243nn184,195, 266n68; charged with corrupt faith, 108, 114; charged with irregular ordinations, 114, 172, 173, 234n67, 238n115; in *chora*, 112, 238n119, 242n176; "Church of Martyrs," 61; and Council of Caesarea, 120–21, 240n142; and Council of Nicaea, 106, 172; at Council of Nicomedia, 110, 166, 170; at Council of Tyre, 121, 245n215; embassy to Constantine, 108, 114, 168, 170, 173, 174, 266nn68,73; and Eusebians, 107–8, 113–14, 119, 166, 168–69, 173, 238n114; levy of tunics against, 173, 174, 231n132; in the Mareotis, 111, 121, 237n104; ordination of Arsenius, 172, 266n63; relationship with Arians, 106–8, 235nn71,83; relationship with Arius, 62, 106, 107, 168, 218n135, 235nn75,83; relationship with Catholics, 106, 172, 236n94, 238n122; relations with Constantine, 114, 119, 166, 169, 170
Melitian schism, 37, 64, 80, 106, 237n104; Alexandrians' involvement in, 65; Arian entanglement in, 106–8, 235nn71,83
Melitius (schismatic), 204nn23,35; accord with Alexander, 234n65, 236n94; death of, 106, 234n67; relationship with Arius, 62, 218n135
Melitius of Sebastopolis, 222n63; pro-Arianism of, 71
Melito of Sardis, 213n69
Menophantus (bishop of Ephesus), 71, 143, 221n41
Methodius (bishop of Olympus), 194n32, 216n111
Michel the Syrian, 202n6
Milan, Council of (345), 146, 260n222
Milan, Council of (355), 153, 261n250
millers, Alexandrian, 57–58, 215nn97,105; songs of, 58; spread of doctrine, 58

mint, imperial, 262n269
Monarchianism, 12, 24, 161
monasteries, 122, 149, 248n24, 254n111; Melitian, 119, 172, 242n179, 244n197
monks: in Alexandria, 57, 245n211; anti-Nicene, 149; "Arian," 136; Athanasian, 121–22, 133, 134, 146, 245n211; Flavianus's mobilization of, 147, 257n160, 260n235; Macedonius's mobilization of, 149, 261n255; of the Mareotis, 245n211; Melitian, 244n197; violence against, 133, 135–36, 245n212; violence of, 134, 149, 261n255. *See also* ascetics; monasteries
Montanist controversy, 195n36, 201n41; in Phrygia, 198n64
muleteers, spread of doctrine, 58. *See also* donkey drivers
music: antiphons, 147; Arius's, 54–57, 58–59, 107, 116, 156, 212n64; in church, 213n76; Constantine's banning of Arius's, 118; early Christian, 54–55, 213n68–69; everyday importance of, 56; laborers', 58–59; use in doctrinal disputes, 54–57, 147, 213n65. *See also* hymns; theology, Christian
Musonianus, Count, 143

Narcissus (bishop of Neronias), 143, 148; at Council of Antioch (325), 81; excommunication of, 82, 229n117; Marcellus of Ancyra's attacks on, 104; pro-Arianism of, 70
naukleroi (shipmasters), 214n87
Nautin, Pierre, 3
Nepos (bishop), 28, 162, 201n47; posthumous condemnation of, 29
Nepos controversy, 28–29, 201n44; Egyptian churches in, 28
Nicaea, Council of (325), 84–91, 187n6; adjournment of, 92; Alexander at, 85, 86, 87–88, 89–90; Arian controversy following, 91, 92, 95, 96, 99–105, 124–25, 234n63; Arians at, 84, 85, 88, 89; Arian preachers of Alexandria following, 99, 100, 105, 171–72; Arius following, 91, 115–16, 165; communication to West, 227n63; condemnation of Arius, 89, 215n106; Constantine at, 78, 81, 84, 86–90, 229n116; criminalization of dissent following, 7, 91–93, 100; Eusebians' disregard to, 270n124; Eusebius of Caesarea at, 87, 88; failure of unity following, 86, 92, 95; and *homoousios*, 85–88, 157, 256n147; letter to churches, 89–90; Marcellus of Ancyra at, 131, 228n89; on Melitian schism, 106, 172; motivations of, 81, 83; objectives of, 85; opening of, 84; participants in, 84;

preliminary debates at, 84, 228n85; rejection of doctrines, 84–86, 187n3; sources for, 84; statements of faith at, 84–85; summoning of, 81, 83; support for Arius at, 84, 85, 89, 221nn36,38,41. *See also* Nicene creed

Nicaea, Council of (327), 166

Nicene creed, 79; Arius's rejection of, 89, 115–16, 119, 165; Constantine's promotion of, 79, 95, 96, 100, 125, 229nn106,109; Constantine's understanding of, 90–91; and Constantius, 139, 146–47; as criterion of orthodoxy, 96; defense of, 144; as definition of God, 89, 95, 96; discontent with, 89, 91, 92, 95, 96, 99, 100, 101, 104, 108, 124, 138–39; as divine truth, 91, 96; drafting of, 86–89; Eusebians' opposition to, 89, 99, 104, 125, 170, 270n124; Eusebius of Caesarea's opposition to 89; Eusebius of Caesarea's subscription to, 89, 230n1; Eusebius of Nicomedia's subscription to, 89; following Constantine's death, 96–97, 125; *homoousios* in, 86, 88–89, 92, 228n89; interpretation of, 95, 99, 124, 229n106; justification to congregations, 99; Marcellus of Ancyra's role in drafting, 228n89; Novatians' support of, 261n254; opposition to, 79, 95, 99, 101, 104, 108, 110, 112, 124, 125, 147, 157, 170; preaching against, 99–100; purpose of, 230n1; reception in Christian communities, 95–96, 99–100; revision attempts, 96, 103, 114, 123–24, 125, 138–39, 157, 221n42

Nicephorus: on Alexander, 204n28; on Arius, 37; on riots in Alexandria, 63, 64

Nicetas Choniates: on Baukalis, 36, 203n18; on Constantine's knowledge of Arian controversy, 78; on synod of Bithynia, 72

Nicomedia: Constantine's death in, 125; earthquake (358), 150, 262n265; persecution of Nicene in, 150

Nicomedia, Council of (327/8), 109–10, 169, 172, 187n6, 236n91, 265n35; chronology of, 170–71

Novatianist schism, 212n57, 261n254

Novatians, Eleusis's conflict with, 150; Macedonius's persecution of, 149, 261n254; support of Nicene creed, 261n254

"Odes of Solomon," 213n69

Olympius (bishop of Aeni), 136, 254n115

Onagros (thug), 141

Optiz, H.-G., 36, 208n94, 219n12

ordination: ceremonies of, 19, 196n43; Jewish tradition of, 196n44

Origen: arbitration of disputes, 11–13, 27, 109, 162; authority of, 197n61; in Beryllus affair, 162–63; controversy over, 162, 191n4, 194n18; on divine truth, 17, 20; on episcopal authority, 20, 37, 196n48, 197nn53,55; on exegesis, 20, 194n23; on free will, 20, 197n57; in Helkesaite heresy, 163; in Heracleides' affair, 11–13, 15, 28, 162; on knowledge of God, 43, 194n22; on lay piety, 20; on monarchical episcopate, 19–20; ordination of, 11, 191n4; on power of God, 12, 191n13; on prayer, 49, 191n7; on priesthood, 20, 197n55; on rule of faith, 16, 193n12; on the Son's eternal generation, 207n81; speculative theology of, 197n59; on spiritual authority, 19–20, 37, 196n51; on theological controversies, 67; on worship, 210n17

orthodoxy: competing choices in, 32, 76, 146–48, 158, 230n6; Constantine on, 90, 100, 117; as established tradition, 193n7; fluidity of, 7, 15, 18, 24, 28, 79; imprecision of, 24, 29, 30, 92, 146, 155; and legitimation of episcopal authority, 5, 21, 22, 29, 33, 42, 64, 66, 96, 102, 129, 155, 157; litmus tests for, 82, 96; Nicene, 7, 79, 100, 101, 117, 157; politicization of, 79, 90, 96, 157; and power, 4, 230n6; problems of definition for, 15–18, 24, 124, 139, 146; and rule of faith, 16; setting of boundaries for, 42, 43, 82, 95, 96; and spiritual authority, 21, 22, 26, 33, 42; universal criteria for, 90, 156. *See also* controversies, theological; dissent, theological; heresy; theology, Christian; truth, divine

Ossius (bishop of Corduba), 224nn24,26; authority of, 82; as Constantine's ambassador, 80–81, 82, 83, 224n24, 225n38; and Council of Alexandria (324), 80, 83, 208n96; at Council of Nicaea, 86, 88, 224n26, 227n63; at Council of Serdica, 143; Eastern bishops' attacks on, 144; on *homoousios*, 86; and Nicene creed, 88, 228n89; support for Alexander, 80, 88; at synod of Antioch, 75, 81–82, 225n35; visit to Antioch, 82, 225n38

ousia: in Christological debates, 95, 139, 148, 207n72, 228nn89,92, 230n1, 256n150, 259n217; of God, 85, 89, 139. *See also homoousios* (epithet); God

Paese (Hermopolite), 206n53

pagans, 79, 127, 141; in Alexandria, 61, 128, 133, 217n127; in Cyzicus, 150; in Lampsacus, 151; in Scythopolis, 153, 263n2; in West, 8, 190n32

Palestine, Arius's travels in, 66, 70, 165, 219n151; support for Arius in, 68, 70, 73 *See also* church, Palestinian

Pannonians. See Ursacius of Singidunum; Valens of Mursa
Parthenius (bishop of Lampsacus), 151, 233n46; anti-Nicene program of, 151; associates of, 262n272; charitable program of, 151, 263n274; ordination of, 233n46, 262n271; origins of, 263n273
Parvis, S., 104, 139, 228nn83,89, 231n26, 232nn37,38, 245n215, 246n231, 247n7, 248n29, 250n49, 260n225, 267nn77,82,83; on Council of Rome, 256n145; on synod of Antioch, 181
Paterius (prefect of Egypt), 245n212
Patrophilus (bishop of Scythopolis), 153; at Constantinople (335), 122; confiscation of alms, 154; deposition of Eustathius's supporters, 103; desecration of tomb, 263n2; Eustathius's attacks on, 101, 102; Macarius of Jerusalem's attacks on, 101; pro-Arianism of, 70, 73, 102, 153; at synod of Antioch (327/8), 101, 103; use of violence, 153, 155
Paul (bishop of Constantinople): Athanasius's support of, 145; conflict with Constantius, 145, 147, 260n224; conflict with Macedonius, 130, 147; and Constans, 145, 258n186; and Council of Serdica, 143–44; depositions of, 130, 142, 148, 249n36, 258n186, 261n242; election of, 130; escape to Trier, 142, 258n186; execution of, 261n242; exile of, 145, 249n36, 259n219, 261n242; mobilization of crowds, 142, 143; Nicene supporters of, 130, 141, 142; reinstatement of, 141, 144, 146–47, 257n168; return to Constantinople, 145, 146, 257n168; use of violence, 141; 257n170
Paul, Saint, 15, 23; on tolerance, 25–26
Paul of Antioch (preacher), 47
Paul of Samosata (bishop of Antioch), 42; charges of heresy against, 13, 20–21, 23, 37, 66, 162; debates with Malchion, 13, 45; deposition of, 13, 23, 28, 162, 192nn19–20; excommunication of, 23; following his deposition, 13, 23, 102, 200n35; hymns of, 213n68; loss of legitimacy, 21–22; ordination of, 192n20; peers' debates over, 24, 28, 32, 42; preaching style of, 47; priests under, 23; schism following deposition, 1, 13, 23, 27, 192n27; spiritual brides of, 218n133; synods over, 13, 28, 42, 67, 192nn19,20
Paulinus (bishop of Tyre), 66–67; correspondence with Eusebius of Nicomedia, 227n68; death of, 222n69, 225n35; election as bishop of Antioch, 74–75, 222n68, 231n26; Eustathius's attacks on, 102; Marcellus of Ancyra's attacks on, 104; support for Arius, 67, 68, 73, 220nn13,15

Paulinus (Eustathian priest), 232n33, 261n244
Peace of Secontarurus (village), 112, 245n215
Pentapolis: Athanasius's travels in 241n161; Sabellian controversy in, 25. See also Libya
Persia: conflict with Rome, 125, 131, 132, 138, 144, 175, 177, 178, 182, 251n57, 268nn63,97, 269n100; Christians of, 178, 268n97
Peter (patriarch of Alexandria), 39; burial of, 218n147; celebration of his martyrdom, 218n148; challenged by Melitius, 204n35; Passio of, 48; rebuke to zealots, 198n64
Philagrius (prefect of Egypt): aid to Gregory, 134–36; appointment of, 122, 131, 245n212, 250n41; and Arians, 122, 245n212, 252n77; conflict with Athanasius, 133–35,252nn72,76; decree on Gregory, 132, 133; and Eastern bishops, 143, 258n193; and Mareotic committee, 122, 131, 245n212
Philip (bishop in Arabia), in Heracleides dispute, 191n9
Philip (praetorian prefect), 145
Philippopolis, Eastern bishops at, 143
Philogonius (bishop of Antioch), 53, 70; Antiochene supporters of, 75; on Arius, 57; death of, 222nn68,69; support of Alexander, 53, 212n51; Syrian support for, 225n35
Philomenos (master of offices): accused of treason, 173, 239n134; Athanasius's dealings with, 239n135; at Council of Nicaea, 89
Philostorgius: on Aetius, 257n158, 260nn235–36; on Arius's appeal to workers, 57; on Athanasius's election, 236n99; on Council of Nicaea, 84, 86, 221n38; on Eusebius of Nicomedia's exile, 166, 170; on Nicene creed, 88; reliability of, 170, 265n50; on support for Arius, 71
Philoxenus (priest), envoy from Julius, 138, 174–77, 178, 180, 182, 268n92
Photius, *Bibliotheca*, 217n117, 227n63, 235n75, 271n129
Phrygia, Montanists of, 198n64
Pierius, ascesis of, 211n34
Pietri, C., 179, 268n87
Pistus (bishop of Alexandria): 122, 171, 249n39, 251n51; conflict with Athanasius, 128, 131, 250n48; death of, 250n49; election of, 249n39; Eusebian support for, 131, 248n21, 250n44; support for Arius, 62, 205n42
Platonism, in Christian theology, 31–32
Plousianos (bishop of Lykopolis), 112, 172
Pomponius of Dionysiana, 198n73

INDEX   307

Pontian (bishop of Rome), 161
Potamon (bishop of Heraclea), 180; violence against, 254n111
poverty, sermons on, 59–60, 216n112. *See also* hospitals; *xenodochia*
power, episcopal, 4–5, 6, 21, 26, 46, 96–97, 108, 111, 115, 118, 126, 128, 134, 150–51, 153–55, 171, 248n25; creation of, 96–97, 140–48, 155, 158; sociopolitical, 126–28, 129, 134–35, 137, 141, 148, 150–51, 153–55, 157–59; strategies of, 8, 30, 64, 109, 141, 156–57; through violence, 109, 110, 115, 126, 129, 141, 150, 155, 158, 248n18. *See also* authority, episcopal; church leadership; violence, religious
power, popular, 51, 64, 134, 158, 219n152. *See also* bishops, mobilization of crowds; laity; violence, religious
power, spiritual: bishops' claim to, 18, 19, 21, 26, 40, 89, 134; in Christian communities, 18, 20–21, 40–41, 55–56, 81; personal communion with, 20, 39; signs of, 50. *See also* authority, spiritual; Holy Spirit
prayer: disputes over, 12; instruction in, 49, 50, 99; Origen on, 49
preachers: abandoning the church, 64; heretical, 28, 197n61; itinerant, 200n41
preachers, Arian: arrest of, 100, 105; condemnation of *homoousios*, 99; conflict with rivals, 47, 75, 81, 101; deposition of, 62; at popular assemblies, 48, 49–51, 60, 75, 99, 117, 171; proselytizing by, 60–61, 75; public visibility of, 61, 75; sermons to women, 61, 62; spatial practices of, 61
preaching, public, 48, 60–61, 64, 75, 210n19, 211n39; anti-Nicene, 99–101; Arius's, 36, 48, 50, 73, 85, 116, 210n17, 211n33; in early Arian controversy, 42, 44, 47–48, 49–51, 60–61, 64, 75, 81, 209n10; motives for, 49, 51; popular, 46, 50, 51, 60–61, 64, 75, 99, 102; on poverty, 59–60, 216n112; in response to Arian controversy, 51; rivalry in, 42, 44, 47, 50, 51, 64, 75, 81, 102, 206n71. *See also* Alexander; Arius; assemblies, popular
Privatus (bishop of Lambaesis), 24; deposition of, 28, 162
prophets, 18, 20; condemned for heresy, 22, 28, 201n41
Protogenes (bishop of Serdica), 143
Psamathia (Nicomedia): Athanasius's acquittal at, 114, 115, 118, 173, 239n142; Athanasius's return from, 240n160
pseudobishops, 26, 199n28

public opinion, clerics' cultivation of, 49–65, 68, 130

Quintianus (bishop of Gaza), 129, 132, 137, 250n42, 258n190

Rapp, Claudia, 50
regula fidei. *See* rule of faith
revelation, contact with Holy Spirit through, 39
Rhakotis district (Alexandria), 61, 217nn127–28; weavers of, 163
Rhodo, debate with Apelles, 197n59
Rodziewicz, E., 163
Rome: aristocracy of, 8, 137; Athanasius's flight to, 134, 174, 175, 176, 181, 182, 267nn82–83,85; exiled clerics in, 136, 137, 176, 179, 180, 182, 267nn81,85, 270n114; pagans in, 8; travel from Antioch to, 270n112
Rome, Council of (341), 132, 138, 143, 174–75, 176, 256n145, 268n86; chronology of, 178–79, 180, 181, 182; clerics barred from, 135, 178, 269n99; Italian bishops at, 179, 269n111; relationship to the Council of Antioch (341), 178–82, 256n145
Rufinus: on Arius's recall, 245n214; on Arsenius, 172, 173; on Constantine's death, 247n4; on Council of Nicaea, 84
rule of faith, 7, 15–16, 24, 193nn8,12; Alexander's, 42; interpretation of, 193n13; limitations of, 16, 194n30

Sabellian controversy, 24–25
Sabellian heresy: 95, 104, 203n13, 208n92; Alexander and, 36, 207n86, 219n1; in Libya, 208n92
Sabellius of Libya, 24, 199n13; followers of, 199n14
Sabinus of Heraclea: on Council of Antioch (341), 139; on Council of Nicaea, 228n85; as source for Arian controversy, 202n3
sailors: Alexandrian, 57, 58, 214nn83,88; of Lampsacus, 263n274
Sailors of the Deep Waters (song), 58
salvation: Alexander's theology and, 40, 44; Arius's theology and, 39, 40, 41, 74, 89, 116, 205n48, 240n150; Arians on, 46, 104; Athanasius on, 110; and Eucharist, 49, 129; paternalistic view of, 89; rival views on, 39–40, 73, 74, 89, 110, 201n8; role of bishops in 21, 40, 89; and truth, divine, 44, 49–50, 64, 70, 76, 79, 110, 126, 130, 158, 257n160
Sarapammon (bishop), 180; exile of, 254n111

308 INDEX

Schwartz, E., 53, 83, 223n73, 225n36, 226n51, 238n118; on Athanasius's flight to Rome, 267nn82,83; on Julius's correspondence, 176; on recall of Arius, 166, 167, 168

Scythopolis: Eusebius of Vercelli at, 153–54; pagans of, 153, 263n2

secular authorities, Roman: 78, 128, 135, 142, 145, 239n135; collusion with Athanasius, 112–13, 118, 120, 238n122, 241n174, 242n176; shift of power from, 230n6. See also Dionysius, Count; Hermogenes (master of horse); Philagrius; Philomenos; Theodorus (prefect of Egypt)

Secundus (bishop of Ptolemais): at Council of Nicaea, 89, 227n73; deposition of, 229n117; exile of, 89, 91; support of Arius, 44, 241n161

Serapion (bishop of Antioch), 163

Serdica, Council of (343), 141–44, 187n6, 258n186; agenda of, 143, 258n187; anti-Nicene bishops at, 143, 258n190; compromise efforts at, 258n196; East-West division at, 143, 144; persecution of Athanasians following, 135, 144; scholarship on, 258n192; Western bishops at, 143, 259nn206–7

Shapur (ruler of Persia), 177–78, 268n97; persecution of Christians, 268n96

Simonetti, M., 143, 247n7, 249n99, 253n91; on Alexander's theology, 206n70, 207n75; on Arius's theology, 234n59; on second Council of Nicaea, 166

Sirmium, Council of (351), 148, 261n250; creed of, 149, 153

Socrates: on Alexander, 42, 52; on anti-Nicene violence, 149; on Athanasius, 238n128, 260n233; on Basil of Ancyra, 263n16; on Council of Antioch (341), 139; on Council of Nicaea, 227n73; on early Arian controversy, 36, 71, 72; on Eusebius of Emesa, 251n62; on exegesis in Alexandria, 48; on Macedonius, 149, 261n254; on Melitians' support of Arius, 62; on (post-Nicene) Arian controversy, 100; on readmission of Arius, 165, 234n60, 245n214; on riots at Antioch, 102; on riots in Constantinople, 142, 145, 257n169; sources of, 202n3; use of *Vita Pauli,* 271n129

Sozomen, 203n17; on Alexander, 37, 38, 204n27, 205n40; on anti-Nicene violence, 149; on Antiochene church, 140; on Arian entanglement in Melitian schism, 106; on Arius, 66, 204n27, 210n17, 219n5; on Athanasius, 123, 241n174; on Athanasius's use of violence, 242n176; on creeds of Antioch, 257n155; on Council of Nicaea, 84; on Council of Jerusalem (346), 146; on early Arian controversy, 36–37, 38, 66, 71, 72, 76; on Eusebians' attacks on Athanasius, 122; on Eusebians' opposition to Nicene creed, 123–24; on Eusebius of Emesa, 251n62; on Eusebius of Nicomedia, 100; on Eustathius, 102; on Hermogenes's death, 258n180; on Julius's correspondence, 270n124; on Macarius of Jerusalem, 101; on Macedonius, 149, 262n263; on Marathonius's charitable programs, 150, 262n262; on Melitians, 106, 114, 170, 173; on Melitius' relationship with Arius, 62; on readmission of Arius, 234n60, 245n214; on riots in Constantinople, 141, sources of, 202n3

space, sacred: control of, 108–9, 111, 128. See also church buildings

state, Roman: control of dissent, 2, 91, 100, 157; episcopal defiance of, 3, 8, 79, 97, 158; relationship with church, 58, 91; role in Arian controversy, 2–3, 91. See also authority, episcopal; bishops, challenges to imperial power; Constantine; Constans; Constantius; dissent, theological; power, episcopal

Stead, G.C., 205n46

Stephen (bishop of Antioch): and anti-Nicene faction, 143, 145; deposition of, 141, 145, 257nn163,164; election of, 140; episcopate of 141, 153; plot against Euphratas of Cologne, 145; pro-Arianism of, 70, 232n4; reinstatement to priesthood, 232n36; use of violence, 141

Storia della chiesa di Alessandria, 254n110

synods: and theological controversies, 27–28, 32, 42; Licinius's ban on, 77, 222n67, 224n5

Syria: anti-Arians of 68, 75, 81, 225n35; Asterius preaching in churches of, 75; Eusebius of Caesarea travels in, 101; opposition to Nicene creed in, 99–101; pro-Arian bishops of, 103–4; support for Arius in, 68, 70, 75. See also church, Antiochene; church, Syrian

Tarcondimantos (bishop of Aegeai), 82, 221n36; pro-Arianism of, 70

teachers (early church), 18, 22, 28, 40, 41, 55–56, 62, 200n41

Telfer, W., 210n13

Tertullian: on idea of the church, 19, 196n50; on idea of God, 16;

Thalia (Arius), 54–57, 210n20, 212n64; composition of, 212n65; doctrinal ideas in, 54; encouragement of believers' authority, 56;

INDEX   309

meter of, 55, 58; performance of, 56, 57, 58, 213nn65,76
Theodoret of Cyrrhus: on Antiochene church, 232n33; on Arius's pastoral activities, 60; on Arius's public preaching, 48, 210n11; on early Arian controversy, 74; on Stephen of Antioch, 257n164
Theodoret of Mopsuestia, on Eucharist, 50
Theodorus (bishop of Heraclea), 43, 148, 262n272; pro-Arianism of, 104
Theodorus (bishop of Tarsus), 221n37; pro-Arianism of, 70
Theodorus (*katholikos* and prefect of Egypt), 128, 131, 242n174, 250n41; persecution of Arians, 248n22, 242n174
Theodotus (bishop of Laodicea): Constantine's warning to, 100; death of, 103; excommunication of, 82–83, 229n117; opposition to Nicene creed, 99; support for Arius, 67, 68
Theodotus (shoemaker), 201n41
Theodulus (bishop of Trajanopolis), 136, 254n115
Theognis (bishop of Nicaea), 84, 122, 221n41; arrival in Bithynia, 169; Constantine's cultivation of, 100; at Council of Nicaea, 221n41, 227n73; at Council of Tyre, 121; deposition of, 229n117; disregard for Nicaea, 270n124; and Eusebians, 221n42; exile of, 91, 100, 101, 165, 166, 170, 247n6; letter of repentance, 165; letters to emperors, 249n38; and Mareotic committee, 121; opposition to Nicene creed, 99–100, 170; return from exile, 105, 127, 166, 167, 168, 169, 247n6; response to Alexander, 72; revision of Nicene creed, 105, 123; support for Arius, 71–72, 221n41; support for Nicene formula, 89, 105. *See also* Eusebians
theology, Christian: challenges to church leaders, 6, 13, 14, 16, 17–18, 21–22, 24–25, 28, 29, 33, 91; and church boundaries, 14; diversity in, 2, 15–16, 26; and music, 54–56, 147, 156, 213n65; politicization of, 79, 91–92, 96, 100–101, 148–49, 157; official, 91, 96; Platonism in, 31–32; spread by laborers, 56–60; uniformity in, 14, 17. *See also* Arian controversy; controversies, theological; dissent, theological; heresy; Nicene creed; orthodoxy; rule of faith; truth, divine
Theonas (bishop of Marmarica): at Council of Nicaea, 89, 227n73; deposition of, 229n117; exile of, 89, 91; support of Arius, 44, 241n161
Tomoi: Alexander's, 52–53, 73, 74, 80, 212nn47,50, 222n63, 228n85
Troeltsch, E., 16

truth: double idea of, 194n33; Hellenic idea of, 194n21
truth, divine: Alexander's claim to, 42, 50, 54, 63, 71, 76, 77, 108; Arius's claim to, 38, 51–52, 68, 76, 77; Arians' claims to 44, 45, 55, 56, 61, 122; Constantine on, 79, 84, 90; definition of, 1, 4, 7, 17, 24, 96; episcopal arbiters of, 20, 97; episcopal claims to, 4, 7, 14, 20, 22, 33, 93, 110, 130, 140, 144; fluidity of, 4, 21, 22, 38, 41; God's spirit and, 4, 14, 21, 22, 29, 198n68; human understanding of, 17, 42–43, 56; laity and, 20, 55, 158; lay teaching of, 56, 58, 213n76; Nicene creed as, 90, 91, 96, 115, 125, 230n1; Origen on, 17, 20; orthodoxy and, 18; politicization of, 96; product of debate and rational argumentation, 17, 18, 20, 156; and rule of faith, 16; salvation and, 44, 49–50, 64, 70, 76, 79, 110, 126, 130, 158, 217n160; sources of, 17, 19, 20; violence and, 110, 129. *See also* Arian controversy; authority, episcopal, and spiritual authority; controversies, theological; dissent, theological; God; heresy; orthodoxy; theology, Christian
Tyre, Council of (335), 120; Athanasius at, 121–22, 137, 243n184, 244nn208,210, 246n223; attendees, 121; Cappadocians at, 233n45; condemnation of Athanasius, 122; Constantine's knowledge of, 122, 246n221; lost acts of, 244n207; Macarius (priest) at, 245n213; and Mareotic committee, 121–22, 245n210; readmission of John Arkaph, 243n187

Ursacius (bishop of Singidunum), 122, 143; anathematization of Arius and Arianism, 146, 260n222; association with Eusebians, 258n190; and Mareotic committee, 121; taught by Arius, 244n209

Valacius, Duke, 133, 134, 136
Valens (bishop of Mursa), 122, 143; anathematization of Arius and Arianism, 146, 260n222; association with Eusebians, 258n190; and Mareotic committee, 121; taught by Arius, 244n209
Valens, Emperor: Arian controversy under, 159
Valentinian (preacher), charges against, 200n41
Van Nuffelen, P., 210n13, 271n129
Vasiliev, Alexandre, 83, 226n51
Victor (bishop of Rome), 163, 201n41; excommunication threats from, 161
Victor (martyr), 206n53

Vincentius (bishop of Capua), embassy to Constantius, 145

violence, religious, 209n1; in Adrianople, 129; in Ancyra, 128–29, 130; anti-Athanasian, 133–36, 245n212, 252n86; in Antioch, 102, 141; against Athanasian women, 172, 266n62; Athanasius's use of, 109, 110–13, 115, 117, 118, 120–21, 122, 123, 127–28, 129, 134, 238nn113,122, 240n143, 245n211, 252n76; Basil of Ancyra's use of, 263n16; challenges to imperial authority, 127, 142; against church buildings, 128, 133, 134, 149, 150, 252n85; in Constantinople, 141–42, 145, 258n183; during festivals, 63, 218n148; in early Arian controversy, 2, 3, 53, 62, 63, 64, 70; in Gaza, 129, 130; Gregory of Cappadocia's use of, 134–36, 180, 252n85; in Hellespont, 149, 150; Macedonius's use of, 149, 150; Marcellus of Ancyra's use of, 128–30, 248n29; military intervention in, 102, 142; Patrophilus's use of, 154, 155; at Peter of Alexandria's burial, 218n147; in post-Nicene Arian controversy, 95, 126, 127, 129, 132–36, 141, 143, 158, 159, 209n1; power through, 115, 127, 141, 158, 159; as rhetorical construct, 252n76; routinization of, 126, 132–37, 141; ; against virgins, 128, 129–30, 133, 135, 136, 153, 245n312, 252n86. *See also* church leadership

virgins, Christian, 217nn124,126; Alexander's exhortation to, 52, 211n45, 212n62; Arian, 61, 132, 172, 249n30; assistance to, 211n44, 262n261; Athanasian, 123, 133–35, 245n212, 254n106; charitable activities of, 52, 61, 211n44, 217n129; competition for support of, 52, 61, 62, 211n45, 218n33, 248n18; confiscation of property from, 254n106; deprivation of grain, 132, 135; followers of Arius, 61, 62, 74, 218n33; followers of Basil of Ancyra, 128; of the Mareotis, 245n211; opposition to Athanasius, 172; rape of, 133; of Scythopolis, 153; shelters for 150; as symbols of virtue, 52; violence against, 128, 129–30, 133, 135, 136, 153, 245n312, 252n8; violence of, 134, 172; wealth of, 211n44, 217n129. *See also* ascetics; convents; women

Vita Athanasi ex Metaphraste, on Arians, 171
Vita Parthenii (hagiography), 150–51, 233n46, 263n273

West, M.L., 55

West, Roman: bishops of, 137, 143–45, 148, 153, 179, 180, 232n41, 258nn186,190, 259nn206–7, 217; bishops of at Council of Serdica, 143; church leadership of, 8; civil war in, 148, 177, 268nn93,97; communication of Council of Nicaea to, 227n63; Constantine in, 105, 170; under Constans, 137, 146; under Constantine II, 125, 137; Constantius's control of, 148, 261n250; Magnentius's usurpation in, 148–49; pagans of, 8, 190n32; spread of Arian controversy to, 136–40

Williams, R., 43, 45, 50, 201n8, 205n41, 206n60, 266n54; on Arius's *Thalia,* 212n65

women: Arians' preaching to, 52, 61, 62; ascetic, 62, 122, 217n129, 218n133; charitable activities of, 61, 217n129; deprivation of grain, 132, 135; followers of Arius, 61, 62, 74; imperial, 104; mobilization of, 156; proselytizing, 61, 217n126; violence against Athanasian, 133, 134, 141, 172, 266n62; wealthy, 61, 217n129; workers, 58, 164. *See also* virgins, Christian

xenodochia, 237n110, 262n258. *See also* hospitals

Zephyrinus (bishop of Rome), 161

www.ingramcontent.com/pod-product-compliance
Lightning Source LLC
Chambersburg PA
CBHW021648230426
43668CB00008B/554